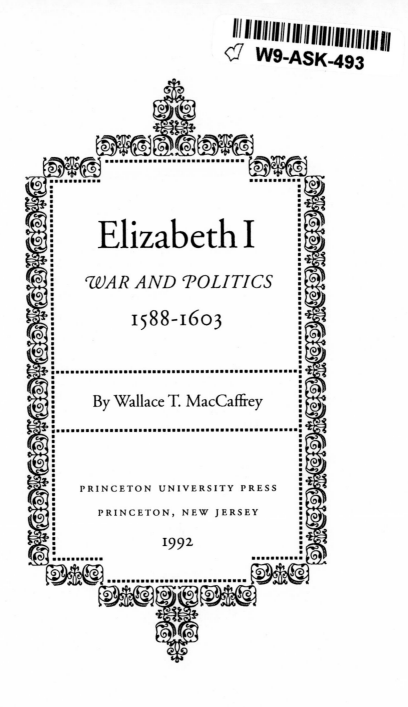

Elizabeth I

WAR AND POLITICS

1588-1603

By Wallace T. MacCaffrey

PRINCETON UNIVERSITY PRESS

PRINCETON, NEW JERSEY

1992

Copyright © 1992 by Princeton University Press
Published by Princeton University Press, 41 William Street,
Princeton, New Jersey 08540
In the United Kingdom: Princeton University Press, Chichester, West Sussex

Library of Congress-in-Publication Data
MacCaffrey, Wallace T.
Elizabeth I : war and politics, 1588–1603 / Wallace T. MacCaffrey
p. cm.
Includes bibliographical references (p.) and index.
ISBN 0-691-03188-6
ISBN 0-691-03651-9 (paperback)
1. Great Britain—Politics and government—1558–1603. 2. Great
Britain—History, Military—Tudors, 1485–1603. 3. Great Britain—
History—Elizabeth, 1558–1603. 4. Elizabeth I, Queen of England,
1533-1603. I. Title.
DA355.M25   1992
942.05'5—dc20   91-33656

Publication of this book was made possible by a grant
from the Publications Program of the National Endowment for the
Humanities, an independent Federal agency.

This book has been composed in Linotron Granjon

Princeton University Press books are printed on acid-free paper
and meet the guidelines for permanence and durability of the
Committee on Production Guidelines for Book Longevity of the
Council on Library Resources

First Princeton Paperback printing, 1994

Printed in the United States of America
3   5   7   9   10   8   6   4   2

TO BERNARD BAILYN
AND JOHN CLIVE
IN LONG FRIENDSHIP

CONTENTS

CONTENTS

FIGURES AND MAPS

PREFACE

THIS THIRD VOLUME shares many of the characteristics of its two predecessors. Like them, it is intended not as a general history of England, but as a study of selected themes. These are themes that, I have argued, preoccupied the rulers of England during these decades. They are also short-term in nature and consequently vary markedly across the forty-five years of Elizabeth's reign. The first volume focused on the problems of establishing a new political regime and of restoring political order after a period of turbulence. The second volume dealt with the issues that arose in the wake of the religious settlement of 1559, as differing conceptions of a reformed church polity became acute. That volume also had much to say about the growing pressures from the outside world that relentlessly drew England into the network of Continental politics. The regime had established itself by the early 1570's; the pressures engendered by religious dissent had somewhat abated by the end of the 1580's. The first phase of Puritan agitation had been contained; the Catholic menace was dwindling into manageable proportions. The uncertain years of diplomatic maneuvering had ended with the coming of war.

This final volume necessarily deals with another set of short-term issues: those associated with the waging of a war that effectively ended with the death of the Queen. As in the earlier studies, I have sought to limit the horizons of the work to those of Elizabeth and her contemporaries. Their decisions were made on the basis of limited information, particularly in waging the war against Spain. Intelligence sources were scanty and poorly organized; many decisions were made in a mist of uncertainty and ignorance. Consequently, this is not a general history of the war. Such a study would have to include the perspectives of Madrid, Brussels, the Hague, and Paris. This work is limited to those of London. It is an effort to explore the ways in which the English leaders went about the task of waging war—of defining their goals and of finding ways to realize them. Faced with demands from two allies and the threat of renewed attack from Spain, how were they to allocate scarce resources? What strategies would best serve their purposes?

It is also a study of a new problem—or, rather, an old problem that had become acute, a once low-grade infection that was now a raging fever. Ireland, long a low priority on the royal agenda, now required the commitment of men and money on a scale unprecedented in the reign.

Final, these years also mark a new epoch in domestic politics. The passing of a generation of councillors on whom the Queen had depended for decades past and the mortality of the aging monarch, whose departure from the scene loomed up—a certainty in everything but its timing—were in themselves unsettling factors. They were compounded by the sudden rise of a new favorite who, by his presence and even more by his ambitions, revived the specter of faction that had haunted the early years of the reign. The denouement of that episode would preoccupy the English political world until the very last phase of the Queen's life.

I HAVE MANY acknowledgments to make. The Guggenheim Foundation provided a second fellowship, which made possible a year of research; Harvard University's research funds added substantial support for my needs. The staff of Harvard College Library were unfailingly helpful, especially Miss Carolyn Fawcett, whose intelligent and ready helpfulness made many tasks measurably easier. The staff of the Cambridge University Library were similarly helpful. I owe particular thanks to Dr. Steven Ellis of University College, Galway, for the generosity with which he shared his deep knowledge of Irish historical matters and for his time and patience in giving a critical reading to my draft manuscript. I am similarly indebted to Dr. Hiram Morgan of the Queen's University, Belfast, for advice and counsel in using the Irish materials. Professor William Tighe of Muhlenberg College gave me his expert assistance in searching the Patent Rolls. Professor John Guy of the University of Rochester and Professor Richard McCoy of the City University of New York were helpful with important references. Dr. Richard W. Stewart kindly provided me with a copy of his unpublished Yale University dissertation. Dr. Ian Archer kindly allowed me to read his unpublished manuscript on London taxation. Participation in the seminars conducted by Professor Sir Geoffrey Elton provided an opportunity for tying out new ideas for fruitful discussion of old ones. I owe much to the skill and intelligence of Mrs. Madeline Rowse Gleason, who piloted the manuscript through the final editorial stages. Last but not least I have a major debt of gratitude to David Steiner, whose generosity with his time and patience with an inept learner initiated me into the mysteries of the word processor.

ABBREVIATIONS

APC	*Act of the Privy Council*
BL	British Library
CSPD	*Calendar of State Papers, Domestic*
CSPF	*Calendar of State Papers, Foreign*
CSPI	*Calendar of State Papers Relating to Ireland*
CSPSc	*Calendar of State Papers Relating to Scotland*
CSPSp	*Calendar of State Papers Spanish (Simancas)*
CSPVen	*Calendar of State Papers Venetian*
DNB	*Dictionary of National Biography*
HMC	Historical Manuscripts Commission
L&A	*List and Analysis*
PRO	Public Record Office

ELIZABETH I

INTRODUCTION

ON 24 NOVEMBER 1588 Queen Elizabeth went in state to give thanks for her people's deliverance of the past summer. It was indeed an occasion for thankfulness; had not God Himself—so the commemorative medal asserted—fought on their side? He had blown upon the waters and dispersed the Queen's enemies. A more secular account might have explained the English success in terms of their navy's seamanship, Spanish ineptitude, and, above all, the play of winds and waters in the North Atlantic. Whatever the successes of the past season, the Queen and her court, assembled in St. Paul's, were nevertheless acutely aware that they were rendering thanks for victory in a single battle, not for a triumphal conclusion to a successful war. They well knew—and events would confirm—that the King of Spain could launch more such fleets. Unsubdued, he would return to the assault. The war had yet to be fought.

The coming of the Armada was the definitive turning point of the Queen's reign. After nearly thirty years of struggle in which she had striven with all her might to preserve England in peace, events too mighty to be mastered forced her hand and drove her reluctantly to war. When conflict had erupted on the Continent she had used all her skills in a hard-fought struggle to maintain English neutrality and to avert the ultimate catastrophe of war. The revolt of the Low Countries against their Spanish masters and the French religious wars had proved dangerously powerful magnets that inexorably drew the English into their field of attraction. After the events of 1576, which temporarily overturned Spanish control in the seventeen provinces, Elizabeth had assumed a more active role and launched a vigorous diplomatic offensive designed, by means of alliance with France, to bring pressure on the King of Spain for a settlement and, if an Anglo-French marital link were to be forged, a similar stabilization of the French struggle. Her goal was to mobilize French cooperation in a diplomatic offensive that would persuade Philip II to restore the status quo of his father's time in the Low Countries. In such a regime the Spanish presence would be too weak to allow the use of the provinces as a base for aggression across the North Sea, but strong enough to check French ambitions in that direction.

Her efforts, however, had not prospered, and between 1581 and

3

1585 England and Spain drifted towards war as Philip's suspicions deepened into a resolve to act. His distrust of English activity in the Low Countries was augmented by the experience of English exploits in the Spanish Indies, above all Drake's voyage of 1577–1580. In the early 1580's the rebels seemed destined to succumb to the inexorable advance of Parma's armies. When, after the assassination of William of Orange in 1584, they turned for succor first vainly to France and then to England, the Queen was left with little choice. To abandon the provinces to their fate now would mean sacrificing the central goal of English policy: to prevent the establishment of a dangerous neighbor across the North Sea. More immediately it would leave England naked to attack from an aggrieved, suspicious, and militantly Catholic Spain. However reluctantly, the Queen had to accede to alliance with the States General.

Yet even after Elizabeth had dispatched Leicester with an expeditionary force to the Netherlands in the winter of 1585–1586, she remained persistently hopeful of an accommodation through the mediation of the Spanish viceroy in the Netherlands, the Duke of Parma. Her continued negotiations with the Duke, culminating in the Bourbourg conference of summer 1588, angered and frightened her Dutch allies and undercut the position of her lieutenant, Leicester. It took the thunder of guns in the Channel finally to shock the Queen out of her illusory hopes of compromise.

The arrival of an invasion fleet manifestly intended not just to harass but also to subdue England meant that the character of the war altogether changed. From a somewhat peripheral encounter with Spanish arms, as auxiliaries to the Dutch rebels, the English now moved to face-to-face confrontation with the whole power of the Spanish monarchy, although the enemy's first assault in the summer of 1588 had been repulsed. Philip's will to continue the war was not quelled nor his capacity to wage it more than temporarily diminished. For Elizabeth this meant the painful abandonment of all that she had stood for—and fought for—since her accession. Her policy of peace reflected deeply held personal convictions as well as temperamental biases; it was also the basis for her immense popularity. Thirty years of internal and external peace when half the Continent was in flames, relatively light taxation through long stretches of years, and growth in wealth and population were the solid underpinning of experience on which the Elizabethan myth had been built. That mythology was replete with the symbols of peace and plenty. The English Astraea had led her people out of the mid-century epoch of iron into the glow of a golden age. The supreme literary celebration of the reign, Spenser's *Faery Queen*, restated this program. But now, at the end of her sixth decade, the Queen reluctantly found herself cast in the Amazonian role that she had so long sought to avoid.

Her feelings at this unhappy juncture of her career were shaped not only by the shock of actual invasion but even more by her anger at Spanish betrayal. For Parma to have kept her in play at Bourbourg, solemnly disclaiming the existence of the Armada when it was actually under sail, had shaken the Queen's fundamental policy assumptions. From a persistent conviction that Philip could be brought to reason she swung around to an ineradicable distrust of the Spanish monarch and his councillors, which never abated, even after his death. And the actual appearance of his fleet off her coasts had filled her with a haunting fear of its reappearance that would permeate all her judgments about the conduct of the war for the next decade.

Elizabeth's perception of Spanish intentions (shared largely by her ministers) was consequently shaped by the assumption that Spain aimed at nothing less than the destruction of the regime and the enslavement of the country. In retrospect, and with our superior knowledge of Spanish intentions, we can see that Philip's ultimate goals were defensive rather than aggressive: the recovery of power in the Low Countries and the security of his unwieldy empire. He would in the final resort have been satisfied to settle for the withdrawal of England from Continental affairs, coupled with toleration for the English Catholics. But in English eyes his ambitions seemed to aim at nothing less than universal hegemony, entailing the destruction of the Elizabethan regime and the subordination of the realm to Spanish domination. In 1590, when the Emperor was seeking to mediate between the States and Philip, Burghley's vigorous protest mirrored his conviction that Spain's goals were limitless—"to be lord and commander of all Christendom, jointly with the Pope and with no other associate." The Spaniards had been "a tyrannous nation" in every part of Christendom where they sought to rule; they had struck down Netherlands liberties, while in France they had murdered Henry III in their determination to control that kingdom's destiny. And in the English case they had faith-

lessly negotiated with the Queen even while their Armada was setting sail.[1] With Spanish intervention in France from 1589 it was
difficult to see how Philip could be effectively checked in these far-
reaching aims. Was he not the patron and ally of the Guises in their
struggle to deny the throne to Henry IV? Surely a Guisan France
would be, if not the client, at least the closely linked ally and dependent of Madrid.

All these circumstances left England with few choices. For the
best part of half a century the Queen and her councillors had
counted on a balance of power on the Continent in which Franco-
Spanish rivalry would be an effective check against the intervention
of either country in English affairs. In 1559–1560 Spain's interest in
the preservation of English independence had provided useful support against French ambitions in Scotland. In the next decade,
when England and Spain were sparring uneasily with one another,
the obvious English ploy had been a lurch towards France, in the
Treaty of Blois of 1572. Later, in her efforts to resolve the Low
Countries conundrum, Elizabeth had made a determined effort to
energize the French monarchy into alliance against Spain, failing
to realize how far paralysis had spread through the French body
politic as the disease of religious faction grew apace. Now, with
France about to be absorbed into the Habsburg sphere of influence,
no effective combination of anti-Spanish interests seemed remotely
possible. England was left to fight for her life with two weak and
beleaguered allies: the provinces of Holland and Zealand, clamorous suppliants for English support to preserve their independent
existence, heavy liabilities rather than helpful assets. England was,
as Essex put it a few years later, "little in territory, not extraordinarily rich and defended only by itself."[2]

This was a painfully novel experience for Englishmen. Almost
all their past wars within historical memory—above all the Hundred Years' War with France—had been struggles in which they
retained the advantage of being the aggressors and only at rare moments the defenders. But in the aftermath of Henry VIII's bumbling intervention in Scotland they found themselves facing the ter-
rifying presence of an invader within the island. In 1559–1560
Cecil's resolution prodded Elizabeth into intervening against the
French in Scotland. By great good luck that intervention coincided

---

[1] BL, Lansdowne Ms. 103/63/182–86. [2] *CSPD* 4 (1595–1597): 232.

with the first stirring of civil war in France and so forced the invader's withdrawal. No such happy conjunction obtained when, thirty years later, they faced an even mightier invader. England would have to soldier on as best she could, hoping for ultimate deliverance, but in early 1589 there was no more light in the tunnel than there would be for Churchill in 1940.

In July 1589 the assassination of Henry III and the accession of Henry of Navarre brought about the first alteration in this grim scenario. But the appearance of a new ally created as many liabilities as assets. Henry IV's desperate condition and his insatiable need for help with money and men made him an importunate suitor. His entrance into the struggle meant that English resources, already stretched to meet the demands of the Dutch allies and the need to counter possible Spanish designs on England and Ireland, had now to be further strained to provide for the French king.

Yet superficially England's position in the 1590's seemed comparable with that a century later—in the wake of the Glorious Revolution. In both eras she was part of a grand alliance that, in the 1590's as in the 1690's, aimed at checking the overweening ambitions of one great power and focused on a succession crisis. The maritime powers, England and the United Provinces, were partners, and England's enemies would seek to strike at her soft underbelly, Ireland. However, the analogy cannot be pressed further. The alliance of the 1690's was guided by the directing intelligence and the authority of William III. Elizabeth's England was little more than an auxiliary to her clamant partners. In the United Provinces Count Maurice of Nassau, as general, and Oldenbarnevelt, the Advocate of Holland, as civil leader, were, with rapidly growing self-confidence, hewing out their highly successful strategy of counteroffensive. The initiative was theirs; the English were called on to assist in carrying out Dutch campaign plans. In France Henry IV went his own way, turning to his English ally when he needed some fresh infusion of English men or gold for the next move in his desperate struggle for survival. Threatened by Spanish invasion from the Low Countries, he sought English auxiliaries to strengthen his polyglot forces of Germans, French, and Swiss. How he would use them was a matter entirely at his discretion. When the threat diminished, Henry was free to turn to his main objective, the essentially political task of weaning his rebel subjects from their Guisan loyalties to acceptance of his uncontested kingship. In this undertaking England had but a small role to play.

Nevertheless, the dispatch of English forces to France or Holland could not be refused; the fate of England was bound up with the survival of the States General and the Bourbon King. Yet necessarily these campaigns diverted English resources needed to defend the homeland itself. The return of a Spanish Armada was an ever-besetting fear, and in the first season after the Armada the English sought to wipe out the still-formidable remnants of the enemy's war fleet. They launched a counterattack as large in scale as the Spanish effort of the previous year. It failed in its goals, and no more major naval expeditions were mounted against Spain until 1595, although season after season the English lived in anxious expectation of another invasion attempt. A stream of uncertain information about naval flotillas gathering at Lisbon or on the Biscay coast kept London in a state of nervous alert and led more than once to a mobilization of English resources against a threat existing only in their imagination. Defense and, if possible, preventive offense were essential to the safety of the realm. If the end was certain, the means were not.

How difficult it was to provide adequate protection of the English coasts and at the same time use the Queen's naval power to scotch Spanish preparation in the Spanish ports was highlighted in the events of the Armada year, when a combination of two tactics had been essayed. One squadron cruised in the Narrow Seas, ready to intercept an approaching enemy; the other, based in Plymouth, boldly set out to meet him, perhaps to check him in his own seas. Had it not been for the chance of the winds, Drake at sea might have passed unseen the very Armada that he sought to encounter. That fleet might have been unimpeded in its descent on the southern coasts of England. The most tempting lesson to be drawn from this experience—and one thereafter drawn consistently by the Queen—was that her ships were best kept at home in readiness for any approaching invader.

The disadvantage of such a wholly defensive policy was that it left the initiative entirely with the enemy and offered no hope of bringing him to terms. Even the cautious Queen could be brought to see the need for offensive action. What strategies of direct offense were then possible against an enemy separated from England by a great waste of stormy water? Two at least had been tried out before

8

the Armada came: to strike at the Spanish Indies, as in 1585, or to "singe the King of Spain's beard," as in 1587. The latter tactic aimed at shattering his invasion fleets before they could set sail. The former sought to disrupt the flow of Spanish treasure from South America. A variant on this strategy, already suggested before 1588 by the veteran seaman John Hawkins, was an interception of the treasure on its way across the Atlantic. All these strategies would be tested in the 1590's, with varying degrees of success; each would exhibit its special difficulties.

Any attempt to deal directly with the Spanish menace by attack on the enemy's home soil (in Europe or beyond the seas) required a formidable concentration of resources. Here the pinch came in the competing claims of other theaters of action. Although in the 1590's the Dutch enjoyed a steady series of successes in reclaiming territory from Spain, their own resources were small and hard to mobilize. Almost every major campaign required an appeal to the English for additional soldiers. And even though the fortunes of the Dutch were improving, their position was still fragile enough so that at times they were overtaken by crises that required prompt English support.

The French, of course, were even more exigent in their demands. Henry was living from hand to mouth in the early years of his reign, lurching from one crisis of survival to the next as Parma's armies surged over his frontiers. Every few months saw the arrival of yet another French mission urgently clamoring for instant succor in men and money, insisting that the very survival of their master depended on its being granted. Elizabeth grumbled and balked, but in the end usually could not refuse. Such unpredictable intrusions of French and Dutch demands tended to throw the English leadership off balance, leaving them in a constant state of uncertainty and frustrating any attempt to plan their strategies.

It was not until the middle of the 1590's that the Continental scenario changed radically, in ways that relieved the pressure on the English and opened up the possibility of independent initiatives against Spanish power. In the Netherlands Dutch military success drove the Spanish back over the Rhine and threw them on to the defensive. In France Henry's suppleness enabled him to disarm his domestic foes and to exclude the Spanish from his borders. These changes were obviously much to England's advantage, although her contribution to their accomplishment had been modest, to say the least. In France successive infusions of English men and money had had little effect in shifting power to the new king; in the Low Countries English contingents, by providing a substantial addition to the limited forces of the States General, had played an important supportive role.

The lessening of pressure on the Continent was all the more important, for there now loomed in Ireland a threat that had to be met solely by England and that directly endangered her vital interests. Disorder and open violence were hardly new in the smaller island, where peace was always a relative term. A garrison of some size had always to be maintained there to contain all-too-frequent outbreaks of local insurrection. At the turn of the 1590's the country was more or less quiescent, after a terrible bout of violence in the preceding decade. But in the next half-dozen years civil relations with the two great northern Gaelic princes, O'Neill and O'Donnell, deteriorated into open civil war, which showed every sign of spreading throughout the island. This crisis, great enough in itself, was brought to fever pitch when Spain began to lend her countenance to the rebels. Money and arms arrived and an expeditionary force was more than half promised. Ireland might well become for England the Achilles heel that the Low Countries were for Spain.

Indeed, from 1595 onward the dimensions of the whole war altered drastically as the fulcrum of English action shifted from the continent to Ireland and to the high seas. Fear of a Spanish invasion of the smaller island, fed by intelligence reports, prodded Elizabeth into approving three major naval expeditions against Spain in the years 1595–1597. Only one of them enjoyed any measure of success. On the high seas, as in France, Elizabethan military initiatives ended in frustration and disappointment.

In Ireland a series of disasters seemed to threaten failure in this theater also. Only when Elizabeth was brought, at long last and much against her will, to a full-scale, all-out effort to crush the Irish rebellion was success laboriously achieved. The destruction of Tyrone entailed, almost as a by-product, a larger accomplishment—the final conquest of all Ireland. This immense and sustained undertaking, which would require the services of half the men drafted for service between 1585 and 1603, reoriented the whole direction of English efforts. Action in France ceased altogether; the forces in the Netherlands became mere mercenaries in the Dutch service, while the naval effort came to an abrupt halt after the bitter disappointments of the 1597 expedition. Ireland now became the grand theater of war that absorbed English men, money, and supplies on an ever-growing scale. It was here that the last great engagement with Spanish arms was to take place, at Kinsale in 1601–1602, and indeed the making of peace would pivot on the outcome of the Irish struggle. Nor were English domestic affairs unaffected by events in the smaller island. Political life at the English court had been dominated by the rise of the Earl of Essex and the ensuing rivalry with the house of Cecil. The penultimate act in that drama would be played out on Irish soil.

Thus, what follows in the course of this work naturally falls into three major parts. The first is an account of war waged on the Continent and the high seas, a war marked in large part by an almost unbroken series of English failures. Only in Holland did the English—as auxiliaries—share in the satisfactions of sustained victory against the enemy. Yet paradoxically England saw her principal war aims realized, one by one. A war in which almost every independent military initiative had been a failure ended in a peace that, if not triumphal, nevertheless realized the principal goals for which England had gone to war almost twenty years earlier.

In the second part the focus of the book necessarily turns from the larger European scene to the smaller theater of Ireland. Although from 1595 on events there merge, at least in part, with those of the international struggle, they can be understood only in the context of Irish developments, dating back at the very least to the reign of Henry VIII. With Tyrone's bid for Spanish assistance the long-term English aim of subduing the island to English rule was to become inextricably linked with the larger conflict. Success in Ireland would be added to the already existing list of war aims. It would become as necessary a condition for the conclusion of a general peace as the re-establishment of the French monarchy or the independence of the United Provinces.

The third section of the book turns away from the foreign scene to England itself. The political history of England in the final decade and a half of Elizabeth's reign is by no means summed up wholly in the events of the war. The year of the Armada was the thirtieth of the Queen's reign and the fifty-fifth of her life. She had already exceeded the life span of her grandfather and almost reached that of her father. Physically vigorous and seldom troubled by serious illness, she was nevertheless approaching what contemporaries saw as old age. Increasingly Englishmen were to look uncertainly to a future in which she would no longer be their ruler. The Queen's resolute refusal to face that contingency left the succession question an open one. Her tacit acquiescence in the claims of James of Scotland made that sovereign certainly the leading and virtually the only plausible contender, even though the Queen was disturbed by the erratic and often provocative antics of a young man restive under the leading strings of an elderly cousin who mercilessly bullied him and clearly regarded him as a blundering and not very promising amateur at the royal game. Elizabeth's refusal to allow any resolution of the succession question left her subjects in troubled unease about an event both inevitable and unpredictable.

Not only the Queen was growing old. In the month after the Armada fled northwards the Earl of Leicester—the Queen's favorite and a fixture on the English scene for thirty years—suddenly died. For the last twenty he had been one of a team of four sturdy workhorses who drew the coach of state. Along with his rival, the Treasurer Burghley, the second favorite, Lord Chancellor Hatton, and Secretary Walsingham, he had formed the inner circle of confidants to whom the Queen had given her fullest trust. Leicester had stood for an interest: at home the advancement of evangelical Protestantism, abroad the championship of international Protestantism against the Papist enemy. In the last years of his life he had finally realized his ambition to lead an army overseas in defense of the Protestant Dutch. His record had not been distinguished and the Queen had not veiled her displeasure with his conduct, yet in the summer of 1588 she appointed him Lieutenant General of the English armies. To the last his favored position in the royal esteem endured.

His disappearance must have been greeted with relief in at least one quarter; his longtime rival, Cecil, could only have been pleased to see the end of a career of which he had always disapproved, on both private and public grounds. But Burghley himself was now almost seventy and his collaborators on the Council, Hatton and Walsingham, both in fragile health. The latter was to die in April 1590, and the former followed him to the grave some eighteen months later. In short, the central coalition of ministers who under the firm hand of the ruler had done the principal business of the English state for two decades was about to dissolve. Their cooperation, although enforced by the Queen's will, had given steadiness and consistency not only to policy but also to politics. The abiding loyalty of the Queen to her ministers had given assurance and guidance to the political classes in a time of great insecurity. Now that this familiar political landscape was fading away the Queen was driven to find new counsellors to replace the trusted intimates of half a lifetime. For a woman of fixed likes and dislikes—*semper eadem* in her attachments public and private—this was an acutely painful task. As the decade of the 1590's unfolded, it became clear that a reconstruction of the Privy Council—and thereby of the whole upper reaches of the English political world—was in process.

That process, necessarily difficult and full of uncertainties, was made yet more difficult by the emergence of a new favorite within the world of high politics when Elizabeth's eye fell upon the handsome face of Robert, Earl of Essex. In a few short years he rose to a place of prominence comparable with that of his late father-in-law Leicester, the Queen's "dear Robin." The emergence of this young man into high politics altered the whole court scene. Most ominously it revived the rage of faction, an evil that had not afflicted English politics since the far-off days of the 1560's. It would darken the political skies until the very last years of the reign and cast its shadow on the succession issue. Nor was it solely a matter of domestic politics, for Essex's far-ranging ambitions for military glory meant that with his appearance domestic faction and war policy would soon become inextricably intertwined.

PART I

THE ENGLISH MONARCHY

AT WAR

FIGURE 1. *William Cecil, first Baron Burghley* (National Portrait Gallery, London)

CHAPTER 1

THE MACHINERY OF WAR:

THE COUNCIL

THE INTRODUCTION has set forth the circumstances of English affairs in the aftermath of the Armada and glanced ahead at the developments that would follow in the next decade. But before proceeding to an exploration of these developments, it is necessary to pause in order to examine the capacity of the English monarchy for making war. How were the shaping of strategy and the issuing of commands organized? What resources—military, bureaucratic, fiscal— were at the monarchy's disposal? What was the machinery for executing the government's commands and deploying its military and naval might?

When the struggle with Spain began, obliquely in 1585 and then head-on in 1588, England's capacity to wage war stood in striking contrast to that of her mighty adversary, owing not only to the wide variance in population and wealth but also to the differing nature of the two state structures. A brief excursus, with glances at Continental developments in the sixteenth century, may serve to illuminate the differences between the two warring monarchies.

New and powerful momentums speeded up the process of historical change in sixteenth-century Europe. Some of them, like the Reformation, were highly visible to contemporaries and compel our attention. Others were less apparent but no less powerful. In varying ways they were all part of the long, drawn-out process that was metamorphosing the Western European political world as the dynastic feudal monarchies moved into the first phases of becoming modern, impersonal, and bureaucratic states. Seen in very long view this process seems to have a programmed linearity, almost an inevitability. Yet, viewed closely and locally, without the meandering curves smoothed out, it is seen to be spasmodic, accidental, and halting; sometimes there is even regression. Obviously bureaucracy was not invented by the Renaissance princes; their medieval predecessors had built sophisticated structures that they passed on to their successors. Yet it is clear that a quantum leap did take place in the governmental structures of Western Europe between the fifteenth and seventeenth centuries, although it certainly did not come in one sudden transformation. Old and new often blended in uncertain juxtapositions, and the rhythm of change was irregular, but by the late sixteenth century at least one regime, that of Philip II, embodied all the leading characteristics of a new political order in which the personal, dynastic structure of the past was overlaid by a vast new structure of civil and military bureaucracy.

Many factors influenced this change. The emergence of an unprecedently large political entity, the dynastic empire of Charles V, and the long-term struggle with the French monarchy of the Valois altered the scale of European political and military competition. Armies were proportionately inflated in size to unprecedented dimensions. More important, the standing army (and navy) became a fixed part of the state structure, a new and permanent charge on the state's finances. At the same time radical changes in military technology, the exploitation of firearms in all their forms from siege cannon to pistols, and the concomitant revolutions in siege warfare and in naval combat left the competitors in the power game no choice but to adopt the new technology, at whatever cost.

The consequences for the domestic economies were all too obvious. Arms cost money; old sources of revenue had to be expanded and new ones invented. The taxing powers of the monarchs were ruthlessly extended and new levies piled on old. A European-wide money market developed in response to the omniverous appetite of the Habsburgs, and new bureaucracies sprang into being to administer the collection and expenditure of these monies.

These changes in the intensity and scale of international conflict not only affected the armies, navies, and bureaucracies of the monarchies but also had far-reaching consequences for their internal political order. They wrought a fundamental alteration in the very raison d'être of European monarchy. Quantitative increases in war-making capacity begot qualitative change in the very nature of the power structure. Slowly but surely the ancient rivalry of dynasties was being replaced by the competition of states. Medieval kings were active soldiers—some, like the fourteenth-century Plantagenets, by choice; others, like their Valois opponents, by force of circumstance. But in each case their goals were the advancement of dynastic, of family, interests. It was the struggle of Percy and Neville writ large.

By the late sixteenth century the scenario was a very different one. Philip II, presiding over his vast array of scattered dominions from his study in the Escorial, is the most obvious example of a new order. The palace itself is a striking symbol of the change. Here, away from the publicity of a capital, the sovereign and his government were permanently fixed, in sharp contrast to the era of Philip's peripatetic father. The king, no longer an active leader in the field or a visible presence in his various realms, delegated military and naval command to his captains, the governance of Italy or the Low Countries to his viceroys. The making of decisions, large and small, was the exclusive business of the ruler, but the decisions were made largely on the basis of a voluminous correspondence between the sovereign and a host of functionaries scattered from Brussels to Lima. Royal power, exercised indirectly by written orders and through the mediation of bureaucrats in the Escorial and in the provinces, was increasingly a remote and impersonal presence. The Duke of Parma in the Low Countries or the Duke of Medina-Sidonia on the flagship of the Armada was carrying out the commands of an invisible sovereign in a distant palace. Clearly such a system required, at the lower levels, the services of a multitude of officials who formed part of a vast professional corps, civil and military. At the top it demanded managerial and policy-making skills of a high order, lower down a staff of specialized functionaries. There was a further consequence. These developments marked the gradual emergence of an impersonal state of which the monarch was the symbol and the head but no longer necessarily the immediate active force of government. Increasingly the private persona of the sovereign was drifting apart from the public persona of the state.

What has been argued so far is wholly concerned with continental monarchy and particularly with the Spanish state of Philip II. What is the relevance of this to the English scene? How far do these

propositions apply to the island case? The easy answer is to emphasize the wide differences that distinguished the Tudor regime from
that of the Habsburgs or the Valois. If one laid out a spectrum of
European political development in the sixteenth century, England
and Spain would lie at opposite ends, England an example of an
"underdeveloped" polity, Spain the exemplar of maturity. The
comparison clearly has some validity; the absence of a standing
army or a developed bureaucracy and the limited taxing power of
the English crown are obvious examples. One need only contrast
the tercios of Philip with Elizabeth's trained bands, or the multiple
councils and secretaries of the Escorial with the all-purpose Privy
Council and single principal secretary of state, which sufficed to
transact the business of the English kingdom. These differences
were accentuated by the factor of size. A small compact island
realm, blessed with excellent internal communications and long
united in a single legal and political community, differed sharply
from the sprawling territories of the Continental rulers. It was altogether a more intimate society, in which the direct impact of a
royal personality, particularly of Henry VIII or his daughter,
counted for much. It was a small political community, in which
greater and lesser aristocrats were linked together by myriad social
and familial relations and which lacked the deep-rooted provincial
identities that made of Spain or France federal rather than national
societies.

Yet England was by no means untouched by the processes of
adaptation that were altering all Western European societies. From
Yorkist times onward there had been a slow but continuing process
of "modernization." The land revenue of the Crown had been reorganized so as to improve yields; accounting methods had been
rationalized; old sources of income such as wardship had been revived and systematized. Wolsey had obtained larger and more flexible Parliamentary levies by his institution of the subsidy, and his
successors had succeeded in making it a regular, although not annually recurrent, source of income. Cromwell had effectively asserted royal authority in the peripheries of the Welsh and Scottish
borders and made the first moves to extend it effectively to all Ireland. In the wake of his fall a new form of Council had appeared.
The Privy Council of the 1540's, slimmed down, with a carefully
defined membership (including a large infusion of lay meritocrats)
and equipped with records and a secretariat, was a far more profes-

sional instrument of executive power than hitherto, a focus for administration, politics, and policy-making.[1] There had been no attempt to build up the kind of permanent army that was appearing on the Continent (except for a brief experiment with mercenaries), but the Scottish crisis of the mid-century had left some residue in the office of the lord lieutenant. In each county he presided over a reformed militia, the trained bands, which possessed at least the rudiments of martial skills. More important, the instrument of military power more vital to England, the navy, had been transformed by the construction of a new breed of ships designed uniquely for war, armed for the first time with a whole battery of artillery. Here England was at least abreast if not ahead of modern developments.

In one important respect it may be argued that the English monarchy had achieved a "modernity" of view denied to its continental partners. This was in the underlying perceptions, the ethos, that governed the conduct of external policy. The change was the result of an all-important shift in the nature of England's foreign relations, which had taken place during the middle years of the century. Henry VIII had been a free agent who was able to indulge his personal and dynastic ambitions in bouts of aggression against his neighbors without running serious risks of retaliation. His aspirations are not unfairly symbolized by the wrestling match with Francis I at the Field of Cloth of Gold. Throughout his reign the announced goals of his wars were echoes of his Plantagenet predecessors' ambitions for dominion on the Continent or in Scotland.

This pattern, in which the English king aggressed upon neighbors without serious intent of major conquest and without serious risk to English security, continued into the last years of Henry's reign. A casual player, he dealt in and out of the game according to his pleasure. To the other players he was sometimes a nuisance and sometimes a useful ally, but England for them remained outside the ambit of their ambitions and of their fears.

This favored situation came to an end in the wake of a series of events, separate in origin but linked in consequence. The earliest of these arose from the fortuitous circumstances of Scottish politics in the 1540's, when the death of James V and the accession of his

[1] For this argument, see G. R. Elton, *The Tudor Revolution in Government* (Cambridge, 1953), and his subsequent work, summarized in *Reform and Reformation: England, 1509–1558* (Cambridge, Mass., 1978). See also C. Coleman et al., eds., *Revolution Reassessed* (Oxford, 1986).

week-old daughter opened up the glittering possibility of annexing the smaller British kingdom to the larger. The policy of Henry and of his successor Somerset, alternating brutal assault with honey-tongued persuasion, only succeeded in driving the Scots into the arms of the French. France, which had long treated Scotland merely as a useful pawn to distract the English enemy, now embarked on a serious effort to annex the Scottish crown to the French, and England, in a sudden reversal of roles, found herself no longer the aggressor but the defender, engaged in a desperate effort to prevent a permanent French lodgment in the island. After more than a decade the French were expelled—as much by good fotrune as by good management. But for yet another decade the English remained anxiously apprehensive of further French intervention in the north.

The second event that signally shifted England's relative strategic advantage for the worse was Elizabeth's decision in 1559 to opt for Protestantism. Necessarily this move aligned England with the Continental Protestants and set her in potential enmity with Catholic Spain. However reluctant the Queen might have been to assume an ideological stance, the polarization of European politics made a genuine neutrality impossible. Moreover, ideological differences interlocked with strategic considerations. The centralization of Philip's inheritance into a Spanish empire meant that England was now flanked across the North Sea not by the relatively weak Burgundian confederation but by the most powerful state in Europe—a state, moreover, that was militantly Catholic. The experience of Mary's reign had convinced many English statesmen that domination of England might well be a goal of Habsburg Spain.

The consequences for England of these changes in the international power structure were profound. The accustomed freedom of action that her relative isolation had provided was now badly eroded. England, an irresponsible aggressor for the past half-century, was now very much on the defensive. Both of the great continental powers had an active interest in British affairs. In Elizabeth's first years the French were the more feared, but from 1572 on they seemed the lesser menace, as the rapprochement of that year suggested; but this condition held only so long as the Guisan faction were kept from control of the monarchy. With the coming of civil war England was inevitably drawn into involvement. Similarly, with the rising at Brill, English fears, equally divided between dread of Spanish militancy and suspicion of French expansionism, led to English intervention in the Low Countries. England was being pulled irresistibly into a dangerous role in the international power struggle.

As the possibility of war drew nearer, the divergence between English and Continental development became more apparent. Although the development of the English state was proceeding along lines familiar among its Continental neighbors (albeit at a slower pace and on a narrower scope), there remained a fundamental difference. Spain and France were monarchies in which, for the best part of a century, the making of war had been the main business of state and the state machinery had developed accordingly. The apparatus of power had been used deliberately and almost exclusively to advance personal, dynastic, and ultimately national aims by foreign war. In England the development of what contemporaries were beginning to call the "state" had taken place along quite divergent lines.

The main thrust of English government since the close of the Wars of the Roses, and particularly under Elizabeth, had been irenic, aimed at the establishment and the maintenance of domestic harmony. While France and Spain invested more and more of their states' resources in the making of war, the English government had settled down to the humdrum arts of peace. In England, as on the Continent, royal power and the functions of central government had increased measurably, but in the island kingdom this growth had been designed primarily to cope with the problems of settling a new dynasty, and then of governing a people whose numbers were growing dismayingly fast, spawning poverty and unemployment and adding to the endemic problem of disorder in a society in which violence was never far below the surface.

The problem of maintaining domestic order was, of course, one with which the rulers of England had wrestled since the early Middle Ages. Kings had striven for generations with their unruly and recalcitrant subjects; in the end a kind of bargain had been struck. Subjects would respect monarchs who could provide a viable system of courts in which justice was administered with reasonable impartiality. To achieve these ends the whole sprawling array of overlapping courts of law had been built. Under the Tudors the ancient common-law courts had been augmented by an expanding Chancery, by the Court of Requests, and by the newly minted Star

Chamber, while at the local level the JP's had been laden with a vast increase of business. But even this expanded array of judicial institutions failed to contain the ever-growing flood of litigation, and the overflow continued to be dealt with at the highest level— in the Privy Council, which remained, even after the creation of the Star Chamber, as much an arbitral body as an administrative one. All these courts shared in the traditional tasks of the judicial branch of government—the prevention of violence by the settlement of disputes among property holders and the punishment of those wrongdoers who had in fact resorted to violence. For Elizabeth's subjects, as for their ancestors, it was in these judicial institutions that the state—to use a term just coming into use—impinged upon their lives.

The Tudors and their ministers had been intelligent enough to perceive that something more than the restraints of arbitral judgments or punitive measures was needed to deal with the unrest of sixteenth-century society. The all-too-obvious pressures of a growing population, with its concomitants of hungry mouths and idle hands, had stimulated men like Thomas Cromwell and his successors to bold new thinking and bold new measures.[2] Dimly they perceived the possibility of using the state's power to ameliorate and even to alter socioeconomic institutions to the benefit of the subject. The most sustained—and the most successful—of their efforts had been the creation, over some decades, of a safety net for the poor and helpless. Successive acts of Parliament had shaped a system of nationwide poor relief, statutorily imposed but locally administered. The same large concept of public responsibility had led to a long list of regulatory and supervisory statutes, such as Artificers, that sought to remedy economic dislocation by treating what contemporaries believed to be the underlying structural defects. English government had considerably broadened its functions in order to serve the cause of domestic tranquility and to promote domestic prosperity rather than to wage war.

These developments had necessarily brought about changes in the instruments through which the Crown governed England. Little novelty had been introduced; in large part old institutions had been remodelled to serve the new purposes. The linchpins of Tudor government were the Privy Council, a body that in one form or

[2] See G. R. Elton, *Reform and Renewal* (Cambridge, 1972).

24

another was as old as the monarchy, and that medieval invention, the commission of the peace. It was the JP's who became the work-horses of this busy government, at once policemen, examining mag-istrates, judges, welfare officers, district engineers, and intelligence agents within their neighborhoods. On each of them fell the respon-sibility for administering the multiplying regulatory statutes of the Tudor parliaments as well as carrying out older "law and order" functions. With far wider duties than his late medieval predecessor, the JP was a general agent of government, representing all its facets and doing business of every kind.

This meant that, though Tudor England was a much-governed country, the business of government was carried out largely at the local level with minimal interference from above. The courts of law and equity were autonomous bodies with their own largely self-made rules. Royal intervention in their business or royal manipu-lation of their personnel was rare under the Tudor princes. Simi-larly the JP's, although their duties were laid down by acts of Parliament, were left in their respective counties to do their own work, loosely supervised by a council that contented itself with the issuance of general orders, intervening only when there was a mal-function at the local level.

That Council was, of course, the other fulcrum of Tudor govern-ment. It too had been reshaped to serve the wider purposes of six-teenth-century government. The office of Privy Councillor had been more precisely identified; the number of councillors had been pared down and, more important, limited largely to those who were continuously present and active. The Council was no longer an amorphous collection, mingling notables and bureaucrats, but a compact committee of politicians and administrators. Its business had been routinized, a secretariat established, its record-keeping regularized. Under Elizabeth, Secretary Cecil honed it down to a tightly organized administrative board that monopolized all rou-tine government business, large and small, and included within its ranks all top-level political figures of the court.[3]

This was the body, shaped to handle the work of peacetime gov-ernment, that from 1585 had to shoulder the unfamiliar tasks of organizing and sustaining a major war effort. It is worth glancing

[3] For the transformation of the Privy Council, see Elton, *Tudor Revolution*, chap. 5; C. Coleman et al., chap. 3.

at the Council as it was on the eve of war before examining its role in that conflict. First of all, what was its composition? It was pre-eminently a hybrid body. Unlike a modern cabinet, it included only two members who presided over departments of public business, the lord treasurer and the lord admiral. The lord chancellor was a judge, and the primate the leading officer of the national church. The secretary was the most truly professional bureaucrat among them; over his desk flowed all the correspondence of the government, and he played a large role in shaping its agenda. A jack-of-all-trades, he found himself involved in every piece of business, large or small, that touched the public weal. The rest of the Council included a clutch of nobles of ancient descent, such as Derby, Shrewsbury, Cobham—or, later, Worcester. Of these only Cobham was a regular attender at meetings of Council. There was also a handful of courtiers, officers of the household, and three lords of Elizabeth's creation—Leicester, Buckhurst, and Hunsdon (Lord Chamberlain)—all of whom were frequently at the Council board.

In the year from February 1586 to March 1587 the highest number of recorded appearances for any member was about 150. Among those attending more than one hundred times were eight workhorses: Lord Treasurer Burghley, Lord Admiral Howard, Secretary Walsingham, Buckhurst, Hunsdon, Cobham, Hatton (then Captain of the Guard), and Comptroller Crofts. (These appearances do not necessarily coincide with actual full Council meetings.) Where it is possible to make this distinction, in the 1590's, for the ten months from October 1597 to July 1598, seventy-one sessions were recorded, roughly one every four days. In the next nine months the number of meetings was identical with that during the previous ten, while in eleven months of 1600 there were sixty-seven sessions.[4]

What did these men do when they came together at the Council board? It was, of course, the organ through which instructions flowed from the Crown to its subordinate officers, civil or military. In its very style it bore the imprint of majesty—the "Lords of Her Majesty's Most Honorable Privy Council"—and in the range and extent of its commands it was omnicompetent. In the conduct of "national" business the Council filled center stage, although as the executor not the formulator of decisions. It was effectively the dis-

---

[4] See attendance lists in APC 1586–87, 1597–98, 1599–1600.

bursing agent for national expenditures. The decision to spend (large or small) was always the Queen's, but the actual business of paying out, whether to individual creditors or to fiscal agents such as the treasurers at war in the Low Countries and Ireland, was the Council's responsibility. Quite frequently (although not always), instructions to military commanders abroad, to ambassadors, or to the Lord Deputy in Dublin went out under the Council's signature. In addition, the Council exercised a general supervision over the local authorities, county and municipal. Orders to hold musters (followed by the filing of muster returns) or other details of militia management were recurring entries in its agenda. Emergency measures, such as restriction of grain movements in times of dearth, were conciliar business, as were inquiries into the behavior of suspect persons or the prevalence of recusancy. There was of course continuing Council interest in the implementation of statutory obligations, for which the local governors were responsible. Nevertheless, in its relations with these men, who carried out the quotidian functions of government, the Council held very loose and light reins. It was not a centralized bureaucracy exercising minute regulation and close control of every function, but a loosely supervisory body that left the locals free to get on with their business, intervening only when emergencies arose or when disputes among the justices threatened local disruption. It was then the Council's task to tidy up and to repair machinery that for one reason or another was failing to operate efficiently.[5]

Nevertheless, important as the Council's executive functions were, an examination of its records makes clear that they were only a part of its business, that in fact this body was akin as much to its medieval predecessors as to its modern successors. Council had always been the place of final resort for all suitors, whether for favors from the Crown or for redress of grievances for which no remedy had been found elsewhere. It is this quasi-judicial business that fills the pages of its act books. In spite of the development of the Star Chamber and the Court of Requests and the broadening of the Chancery's role, the Privy Council still found itself flooded with petitions, most of which were of a purely private nature. In 1589, in

[5] See Michael B. Pulman, *The Elizabethan Privy Council in the Fifteen-Seventies* (Berkeley and Los Angeles, 1971), chap. 6; Penry H. Williams, *The Tudor Regime* (Oxford, 1979), chaps. 1, 3; A. Hassell Smith, *County and Court: Government and Politics in Norfolk, 1558–1603* (Oxford, 1974).

sheer desperation, the Council declared that it was unable to do its business because of the excess of private suits and laid down regulations for referring them to the ordinary courts. Two years later, facing the same problem, it made another desperate, and unavailing, effort to stem the flow of petitions.[6] In the preceding year, in the six months from March to September, the modern index lists forty-seven such petitions. This meant that the Council spent a great deal of its time in mediating or arbitrating among the Queen's subjects. Sometimes it acted as a court, issuing definitive judicial decrees intended to settle a suit; more often, after discussion and even hearing, there was reference back to a municipal court, to one of the provincial councils, to the justices of a particular county, or to a specially nominated committee of arbitration.

Having said all this, one has immediately to enter an emphatic caveat. Certainly what has been described depicts the face that the Council showed to the Queen's subjects. But, Janus-like, it had a second countenance, which turned towards the Queen herself. These men were her chosen counsellors, to whom she gave her confidence and with whom she shared the business of state. About this second role it is more difficult for the historian to give a full account. Here the formal records fail us or at best cast an uncertain light. In part this is because of the protean characteristics of the Council. It remained as plastic an object in the Queen's hands as it had been in those of her remote predecessors. She was under no obligation to consult the body collectively, although she might do so—as for instance at the time of the Darnley marriage or when she was wooing the Duke of Anjou. But "consultation" usually meant the collection of individual opinions rather than the solicitation of a collective judgment. And in the conduct of foreign affairs, the surviving correspondence suggests yet another variation.

Four men stand out as members of an inner elite—Burghley, Leicester, Walsingham, and Hatton. They all shared in a knowledge of ambassadorial reports from the English agents abroad, interviewed foreign ambassadors in London, and discussed with the Queen the making of decisions. In the late 1580's the lion's share of actual business probably fell to the lord treasurer and the secretary; Hatton was from 1587 preoccupied with his great judicial post, and Leicester was abroad in the Low Countries a good deal of the time

[6] *APC* 1589–90: 181, and 1595–96: 240.

before he died in September 1588. The successive deaths of Secretary Walsingham in April 1590 and of Lord Chancellor Hatton in November 1591 broke up this quartet and forced on the reluctant Queen a readjustment of her inner circle of confidants. This problem preoccupied her for nearly a decade, and its consequences reverberated through the political world. Discussion of these events is reserved for Chapter 23.

If the Council was indeed the arena of high politics, of the struggles for place around the Crown and for the shaping of grand policy, it was also the forum for day-to-day direction of the war. We need now to turn to those more mundane concerns. How did the Council deal with the waging of war? The difficulties of transforming a peacetime institution, quasi-judicial in character with only sketchy executive functions, are obvious. Its staff was minimal: a handful of clerks and messengers to write its letters and deliver them. There was little or nothing in the way of bureaucratic routines to link it with the agents who were to do its bidding in London, the counties, or the towns. There was only a rudimentary chain of command, no well-developed system for regular feedback on performance, and few fixed routines for the carrying out of specific procedures. On the other hand it was a body with established work habits, meeting regularly and frequently. Its members were used to working together, and collectively they wielded an authority that commanded obedience throughout the realm. In part this rested on the august nature of their authority and their proximity to the ruler, but it was also built on their own personal eminence, both national and local. Burghley was Lord Lieutenant of Essex and Lincolnshire, Cobham of Kent, Buckhurst of Sussex, Hunsdon of Norfolk, Knollys of Berkshire, Warwick of Warwickshire. In most cases they were considerable landowners in their respective counties. And, of course, the deputy lieutenants, to whom the Council would now turn for execution of its orders, came from the same pool of gentry who sat on the Commission of the Peace or other local government bodies and who were linked by family, social, and political ties to the great men at the Council board. The unpopular tasks that the logistics of war would impose on them were formidable—conscripting and equipping soldiers for foreign service from which they might never return, raising the necessary funds by local taxation, and moving men and supplies to distant ports of embarkation. The tasks were not unfamiliar, the scale and the burdens of the operation quite unprecedented.

The last mobilization of English forces for action on land had been during the 1569 rebellion. Ireland had for some decades required frequent infusions of English conscripts to bolster the garrison there in carrying out duties that were a cross between police action and guerrilla warfare.[7] The procedure for obtaining them was simple: orders were sent from the Council to a lord lieutenant (or his deputies) in a particular county to conscript a given number—anywhere from 50 to 300—in his shire. The orders were passed on from the deputy lieutenants to JP's not of their number, down to the constables of hundreds, and thence to the churchwardens in each parish.[8] The local officials were to see that the conscripts were clothed, equipped with appropriate arms, fed, and paid until a locally appointed conductor turned them over to a captain of the Irish garrison at Chester, Bristol, or elsewhere. The costs of mobilization were borne by the county out of funds raised by a local rate, some of which were refunded by Exchequer order.[9] In such an operation the role of the Council was simply to issue the order. Execution was entirely in the hands of the local authorities; the process of conscription, procurement, and transport was largely left to them with only occasional general directives from the Privy Council. Shortcomings in their performance, however, as reported by the army commanders, brought down prompt and angry rebukes from the Council.

The growing threat of war during the 1570's and 1580's had stimulated the Council into adopting measures of military preparedness. The loosely organized militia, nominally composed of all able-bodied men between sixteen and sixty, was reorganized to provide a defense force trained and ready for rapid mobilization in case of invasion or rebellion. In each county, out of the mass of eligibles available, a select group was chosen—the "trained bands"—who were mustered, drilled and instructed in the use of

---

[7] In 1579, for instance, something like 1,000 men had been levied for Irish service. In the following year some 2,000 had been readied for dispatch and at least half, probably more, sent over to Ireland (*APC* 1578–80).

[8] John McGurk, "The Recruitment and Transportation of Elizabethan Troops and Their Service in Ireland, 1594–1603" (unpublished Ph.D. dissertation, University of Liverpool, 1983), 63.

[9] *Ibid.*, 154, 334, 147–48, 275, 421, for examples of these transactions.

their weapons. An armory of weapons and munitions was maintained in a central store. In this process the Council had been active, not only in laying down detailed regulations but also in requiring regular reports from the counties as to the state of their preparations. The lord lieutenant was now firmly established as the official responsible for all these matters, although in cases in which, as a Privy Councillor, he was an absentee, the real work was done by his deputies.[10]

These were the defense arrangements for the land forces. Those for the navy were more complex, more centralized, and far more professional. Since Henry VIII's time there had been a permanent squadron of specially designed warships, serviced by dockyards on the Thames and Medway and at Portsmouth. They were virtually the first generation of a new navy, composed of ships carrying a full complement of heavy artillery and designed to assail their enemies with firepower rather than by boarding. An elementary administrative board, dominated by Sir John Hawkins as treasurer of the navy, was responsible for shipbuilding, maintenance, and repairs. He and his fellow board members, the comptroller and the surveyor, were men of professional knowledge and experience. In 1585, and again in 1587 under Drake's command, this navy, augmented by armed merchantmen, had carried out with striking success what were effectively the first overseas naval offensives to employ the new naval technology.[11]

The first real test of these preparations, on land and on sea, came in 1588, when the country had to face an attack aimed at nothing less than destroying the Queen's navy, landing an invasion force, and overthrowing her government. It would be hard to find as serious a precedent for such a threat from a foreign foe later in date than 1066. On the sea the English took the initiative and sought to catch the Spaniards in their own waters, or at least before they approached English shores. But the winds, and the Queen's not unreasonable fears for her unprotected coasts, prevented them from following through with this strategy, and they had to fight a defensive battle off their own coast. On land they could do nothing but

---

[10] Lindsay Boynton, *The Elizabethan Militia* (London, 1967).
[11] See Michael Oppenheim, *History of the Administration of the Royal Navy* (London, 1896), 140–44, 144–49.

make defensive preparations, hoping to check the enemy wherever he might come ashore.

The Council's role in 1588 became an active and rapidly expanding one at the point when it was necessary to take extraordinary measures to insure active preparedness.[12] As early as March it issued a general detaining order for all vessels on the south and east coasts,[13] and a few days later set in motion an ancient procedure that harked back to an earlier age but had since then been little used. The Queen possessed a fleet of some thirty specially built warships, but they would not be enough to meet the formidable array being prepared in Spain and Portugal. Hence, as in earlier times, the Crown called on the port towns to arm merchant vessels. This procedure was employed once more in 1589, 1595, 1596, and 1597. Hence, at the beginning of April the Council sent out a general order to the ports of the south and east coasts to provide some fifty armed ships (and twenty pinnaces) to join the royal ships.[14] Each maritime community was to meet the charge of arming, manning, and victualling for several months. Individual ports and their dependent creeks were locally assessed for this service and the tax locally collected, but questions immediately sprang up as to how far the burden should be spread outside the immediate coastal areas. In most cases the whole county in which the port lay was expected to contribute, but the disputes about liability and the efforts to avoid the tax were numerous, and the Council was to spend a good deal of time in the next months adjudicating such disputes and lending its authority to insure that those who were liable did in fact pay up.

Naval requirements would take up less Council time than those of the land forces, but here too it was soon intervening in matters of detail. Export of cables and cordage was embargoed; the Master of Ordnance was ordered to send powder to Drake; money for naval pay (£6,000) was dispatched to Plymouth in May (but it was not

[12] See for instance the Council meeting of 15 February 1588, which gave orders for the disposition of the eastern and western naval squadrons: Julian S. Corbett, ed., *Papers Relating to the Navy during the Spanish War, 1585–1587*. Navy Record Society 11 (vols., London, 1898) 2: 137–38, citing BL, Cotton Mss., Vespasian C viii, fol. 12.

[13] *APC* 1588: 7.

[14] *Ibid.*, 9. According to Oppenheim, as many as 163 ships were commandeered in 1588 (p. 163).

to be paid until the end of service).[15] Lord Henry Seymour was in command of the Straits squadron, cruising between Dover and the Flemish coast. In a series of letters spread across the summer, the Council directed him how to dispose his ships: at one time to protect the east coast, at another to blockade Parma, again to convoy the Merchant Adventurers fleet to Middleburgh. During the summer the Council was also busy with orders for revictualling the fleet.[16]

On land, the Council's tasks were larger since it had to create from scratch a whole army by mobilizing the militia. In February lists of foot to be provided from the counties of England and Wales were already at hand. As early as April the Council was urgently asking for reports from county commanders, already overdue, and sending two veteran captains, John Norris and Thomas Leighton, to survey the situation on the south and east coasts.[17] Surrey, well ahead in its preparations, was asking for instructions on where to send its forces once the beacons signalled the enemy's arrival. They were told to send their men to the Hampshire borders and await further instructions from the Council.[18]

From that time forward the Council was busy with reports from the counties as to their various stages of preparation. On 16 June the lord lieutenants were warned that the Armada was at sea, and on the next day the Council was occupied with details of defense, at home at the Thames mouth and overseas in Ireland, and with the dispatch of powder to the counties. All noblemen were to attend on the Queen's person with their retainers.[19] Again on 27 June there is a glimpse of the Council with a full agenda of defense matters, while on this same day the lord lieutenants were ordered to move to a general muster of the army of defense.[20] On 22 July the Council took order for setting up the camp at Tilbury and providing a staff, and the next day, aware that the Spanish fleet was on the high seas,

---

[15] *Ibid.*, 19, 25, 57–58.

[16] *Ibid.*, 104–5, 166, 180, 182, 189, 213, 219. For the revictualling orders, see *ibid.*, 132, 165, 171, 183; *CSPD* 2 (1581–90): ccxii, 42, and ccxi, 52.

[17] *APC* 1588: 16, 20; *CSPD* 2 (1581–90): ccviii, 60.

[18] *APC* 1588: 30–31.

[19] For county reports, see *CSPD* 2 (1581–90): ccxi, 71–94. For the news of the Armada, see *APC* 1588: 126, and for the noblemen, 144; also *CSPD* 2 (1581–90): ccxi, 34.

[20] *CSPD* 2 (1581–90): ccxi, 61; *APC* 1588: 137.

ordered the county forces to rendezvous at Brentwood in Essex.[21] Sir Thomas Heneage, treasurer of the chamber, was appointed treasurer at war. As events would speedily demonstrate, this imposing array would not be called into action, and, as the Armada faded into the northern sea, the Council ordered its demobilization and later that of the ships.[22]

The record displays in much more abundant detail than is cited here the central directive role of the Council in this moment of expected invasion. Clearly that role was entirely pragmatic in character; problems were dealt with as they arose, with reliance on the large and indeterminate authority of the Council. Sometimes it acted as a body, just as often through the secretary or the lord treasurer. As the intelligence center of the government—receiving the flow of reports from merchant captains, travellers, reconnaissance pinnaces, or foreign embassies—the Council could dispose the national forces accordingly. Its traditional oversight of the militia, supervisory and monitory in the past, now became active, as the Council transformed itself into something resembling a war office in full control of logistics. Orders flowed down to the counties, reports streamed back; a sizable army was brought into being for the defense of the Queen and of London. Reaching out beyond these functions, the Council assumed the role of a general staff in its instructions to Seymour and his squadron in the Narrow Seas. However, one uses these formal, modern terms anachronistically; the actions of the Council were entirely informal, *ad hoc* responses to a particular problem. Knowledgeable about Parma's intentions, they intervened directly at Dover; in the Channel the Lord Admiral and Drake were left entirely on their own and indeed the instructions to Seymour had a caveat, giving priority to any command from the lord admiral.

On balance the government could congratulate itself on its performance. The Council on short notice had been able to meet the demands of the situation quite efficiently. The necessary logistical support for the navy had been maintained (except in the one vital instance of gunpowder), and on land an army had been brought into being. The ready-made machinery put together in peacetime had been tested; it had turned over satisfactorily. The cadres of the

[21] *CSPD* 2 (1581–90): ccxiii, 4, 21; *APC* 1588: 169, 195, 196.
[22] *CSPD* 2 (1581–90): ccxiii, 26; *APC* 1588: 179, 221, 265.

shires and the towns had shifted gear and met the requirements of the emergency. Yet the circumstances had in fact been favorable and the test a very imperfect one. The visible threat to the kingdom—symbolized by the blazing beacons reaching from Cornwall to Cumberland and made all too real by the sight of Spanish sails off the coasts of Dorset or Hampshire—had insured an ardent outpouring of patriotic effort. The emergency needed neither explanation nor justification. Moreover, the crisis proved to be of short duration; the problem of feeding thousands of men under arms for an extended time was not posed. And, most important, the fighting qualities of the armed yeomanry were not put to the proof.

The Council had been able to function at top efficiency because the action was largely on its own doorstep, where communication was easy. Many of the councillors, as we have seen, doubled as lord lieutenants themselves. Two of their members, Leicester and Howard, assumed high command. And, while the financial burdens were not light, they were passed on in large part to the country. Coat and conduct money for this mobilization was not reimbursable to the counties[23] since the militia were being called out for home defense. Hence, the expense of land mobilization fell directly on the local ratepayer. Similarly, much of the cost of naval mobilization was borne by the maritime counties through the ships that they supplied to the royal navy. The Council, characteristically, was called on to intervene in the constant squabbling among the local authorities as to the sharing of the tax burden.

The flight of the Armada and its ruinous voyage home left England with a breathing space. But, grievous as the damage was, the Spanish fleet was by no means destroyed; the English leaders had no doubt that the effort at invasion would be renewed; a pre-emptive strike was imperative. The strategy chosen for the strike and the consequent action are discussed in Chapter 4.

The administrative tasks the Lisbon expedition imposed were different from those of 1588. The first proposals for retaliative action were made as early as September, but evidence of preparations for the voyage surfaces in the Council records only in late December. Troops were to be withdrawn from the Low Countries to provide a stiffening of veterans among the soldiery involved in the enterprise. This initiated a pattern, which was followed repeatedly in

[23] *Ibid.*, 191, letter to Chandos.

successive years, of drawing on the body of men hardened by service in the Low Countries, who constituted a more or less professional fighting force. Arrangements had to be made for quartering these troops in England during the preparatory period. Here again was a novelty that would soon become familiar. Lacking any other accommodations, these men had to be lodged and fed by the villagers of the southeastern counties.[24]

Additional forces had to be conscripted in England and the usual orders for levies and equipment went out to twenty English counties and to Wales on 30 December. Simultaneously privy seals were sent out for a forced loan to provide ready cash. The Council would be busy with the details of mobilization for weeks to come (the fleet sailed about 17–18 April). The numbers summoned were not so large as in the previous year, but this time the men were to go overseas. No such invasion force had been launched from England since Henry VIII's time, and his armies had had only to cross the Narrow Seas to the secure base of Calais. However, the machinery worked with commendable efficiency; men, victuals, and ships were assembled at Plymouth. All told, between 15,000 and 20,000 soldiers and sailors, sailing in 83 ships and accompanied by 60 Dutch flyboats, set off for the Spanish coasts.[25]

These men were not going to camp in the fields of Essex. With the disappearance of Drake's sails over the southwestern horizon the fleet vanished from the Council's ken for many weeks. An effort was made to revictual it, and the Plymouth officials were rebuked for their backwardness in assembling supplies, but the problem was not easy when the destination and timing were so uncertain. A supply of victuals was still on hand at the fleet's return. Some attempt at maintaining communications was made, but the Council seems to have known little of what was happening beyond seas. One unavailing effort to direct operations was made when letters were sent off after the fleet in late May ordering the com-

[24] Ibid., 423; 1588–89: 11, 15, 268; 1590: 188.
[25] See Sir William Monson, The Naval Tracts of Sir William Monson, ed. M. Oppenheim. Navy Record Society, 22, 23, 43, 45, 47 (5 vols., London, 1902–1914) 1: 186; Anthony Wingfield, "A True Discourse (as is Thought) by Colonel Antonie Winkfield Employed in the Voiage to Spain and Portugal, 1589," etc., in Richard Hakluyt, The Principal Navigations, Voyages, Traffiques of Discoveries of the English Nation, etc., ed. Walter Raleigh (10 vols. London and New York, 1927) 4: 306–354; CSPD 2 (1581–90): ccxxiii, 69, 75.

manders to intercept, if possible, a fleet of sixty Eastland grain ships bound for Spain. Again when they were on their way home they were urged to catch eighteen hulks laden with grain at Torbay.[26]

If the Council had little to do while the fleet was away, the consequences of its return left them with a mare's nest of loose ends. The expedition had been in large part privately financed as a giant privateering speculation. Much of the cost had to be charged to the putative profits, i.e., the booty, which in this instance consisted solely of some sixty Baltic grain ships seized off the Tagus (presumably the same as those mentioned in the Council's letter). Immediately upon return the Council took measures to handle the prize grain and to pay the debts charged against it. A commission set up for this purpose found its task onerous. Creditors were numerous and clamorous, and the booty not a very salable item. There was far too much of it to be absorbed locally, and licenses to export had to be granted. The most demanding creditors were the unpaid soldiers and seamen. In July there was a riot at the Royal Exchange; in August claimants were still hanging about the capital, and there was another riot, involving a hundred or so desperate men.[27]

Other creditors included the unlucky victuallers of Canterbury, who had supplied the soldiers quartered there for six weeks while they were waiting to sail. Here the Council had to intervene to protect the local merchants from their own angry creditors. In the same county companies of veterans, scheduled for return to the Low Countries, were living off the local inhabitants; money had to be found from the prize funds to pay their bills. In the following March payments were still being made to Essex, Kent, and Middlesex for quartering expenses from spring 1589, and as late as 1591 Feversham was owed for victuals for the Lisbon voyage, the Council apologetically admitting "by reasons of some impediments happened the general accounts of that voyage have hitherto remained imperfect." Debtors were not to be sued; payment was promised— in the future.[28]

Of course, the adventurers who had financed the voyage had a claim; the expenses of cleaning and refitting the ships were also to be met from the same source. In the meantime much of the grain

[26] *APC* 1588–89: 152, 192, 200, 352, 384, 389.
[27] *APC* 1588–89: 358–60, 381, 398, 403–4, 416, 453; 1589–90: 3, 14, 46–47.
[28] *APC* 1588–89: 268; 1589–90: 391; 1591: 18.

was disappearing into private hands. Frantic orders were sent down by the Council to recover such goods; worse still was the discovery of fraud in the sale of the goods, perpetrated by members of the prize commission themselves. Scenes of this kind would recur in the future when prizes brought in by royally sponsored expeditions arrived in English ports. The best efforts of the Council to gain administrative control over the disposal of prize goods would prove to be inadequate. The greed of the returning combatants and of the port communities was too much for the fragile administrative machinery available. Here local interests quickly outbid national ones.[29]

The Lisbon expedition revealed with glaring clarity the limitations of the English government's military machinery. The united efforts of the local authorities, private merchant adventurers, and the military commanders, coordinated by the Council, had mobilized an array of armed might comparable to that of the Spanish Armada and probably unprecedented in English experience. Nevertheless, it failed to achieve any of the stated ends of the enterprise, highlighting vividly the structural defects of the English military machine when it turned to offensive effort. The immediate cause for failure is probably to be found in the confusion of goals that was implicit in the instructions to the commanders (see Chapter 4 for a discussion of this matter). The government could mobilize potential military and naval might, but it could not formulate effective strategic plans, much less provide the chain of command, effective communication, reliable intelligence, or adequate supply. Lack of money precluded the existence of a corps of military professionals or a supporting bureaucracy and forced resort to private entrepreneurial assistance. These problems, acute enough when the theater of action was on the Continent, became quite unmanageable when naval action carried the Queen's forces outside English waters. The Queen's bitter disappointment in the Lisbon expedition foreclosed another attempt to attack the enemy in his homeland for some years to come, and it also meant that nothing was done to remedy the defects revealed by the experience of 1589.

Even as the demobilized soldiers rioted for their pay for the Lisbon expedition, a new burst of events was about to add another dimension to the war. Henry III of France was assassinated on 31

[29] *APC* 1589: 360, 381, 398–401, 403–4, 407–10; 1589–90: 3, 81.

July and the new king, Henry of Navarre, struggling to establish his power in France, turned to Elizabeth for help. Within a month of his accession he had appealed for the urgent dispatch of an English force, and by early September Council orders for levying 4,000 foot were being sent out and Lord Willoughby was summoned from the Low Countries command to assume charge of the new expedition. The Council registers for September were filled with orders to the county officials to conscript men, clothe and arm them, and move them to the ports of embarkation. Officers were appointed, a chaplain found, and shipping ordered. The burden fell on the three southeastern coastal counties closest to France—Kent, Sussex, and Hampshire—plus London. They could provide the speediest succor for the beleaguered king in Normandy. Consequently this was very much a regional effort. Each county contributed a thousand men, under a single commander and divided into companies of men coming from the same locality. They sailed from Southampton, Portsmouth, Dover, and Rye and would at the end of their three months' service return to their respective ports. It must have given some sense of identity to these ready-made companies of men, summoned so hastily from their fields and farms to the alien countryside of France, that they were a band of neighbors. (At the same time the southwestern counties along with the Welsh Borders and Wales provided 1,500 men for Ireland.)[30]

This expedition was, of course, different again from either that of 1588 or the Lisbon voyage. The English role was little more than a recruiting and financing one. England was to provide the men, transport them to France, and find a month's pay; the money itself would come out of a loan to Henry IV. Tactical disposition of the troops was entirely in the hands of the king, and for three months they accompanied him in his sweep through Normandy and Maine, living off the land as they moved. During these months communications between Willoughby and the Council were almost nonexistent and the latter's role virtually nil. It was only when the French king had finished with the troops' services that the Council once more had to busy itself, now at finding the means for their return. Sadly depleted in numbers, they limped home at the end of the year.[31] They might have been mercenaries, hired out for a campaign (except that it was the seller, not the buyer, who footed the bill).

[30] *APC* 1589–90: 86–146.   [31] *APC* 1589–90: 291–344.

The next intervention in France—at Rouen in 1591—cast the English Council in a different and difficult role. It had of course the usual responsibilities for organizing the expedition, which did not cease, however, with the departure of the ships and men for Normandy. This time, in contrast to 1589, the strategic goal, the capture of Rouen, was designated by mutual agreement. Local tactical control would be in French hands, but the English expected to share in vital decisions and to be involved in the development of the campaign. These hopeful expectations went rapidly astray; the king, distracted by Parma's looming threat, failed to appear at Rouen, and the siege was only perfunctorily pursued. These circumstances aroused the Queen's bitter anger and the Council found itself caught up in the acrimonious wrangling that ensued among Elizabeth, Henry, and Essex. This was a scenario to be played out again and again with variations, in the Breton expedition and the other, smaller English interventions in France. Nominal agreement between the allies as to general strategic purposes would be frustrated by French failure to live up to their side of the contract. Royalist armies were hopelessly inadequate, their leadership feeble and strategy erratic or nonexistent; neither money nor supplies were made available; English lives were wasted in futile skirmishing or debilitating inactivity. Under these circumstances it was impossible for the Queen or her ministers to pursue any consistent strategy or indeed to control events at all.

Although it was the Queen who made final decisions, correspondence from the field commanders flowed both to the sovereign and to the Council, and the latter clearly shared in responsibility for shaping action. As a consequence, the Council frequently found itself an uncomfortable middleman, caught between the fulminations of the frustrated Queen, whose angry impulse at every check was almost always to withdraw, and the obstinacy of field commanders, who took advantage of their inaccessibility to make independent decisions and to drag their feet in sullen protest against royal commands. Much of the Council's effort was expended in mediating between the Crown and its errant generals or in dissuading the ruler from peremptory withdrawal from France. Under these circumstances any kind of sustained direction of policy was out of the question; all the Council could do was to make *ad hoc* responses to constantly recurring crises, a series of stop-and-start directives that were often irrelevant by the time they reached the commander abroad. The best they could do was to moderate the bouts of royal frustration while seeking to give some guidance and support to the generals in the field until events themselves resolved the situation. Not surprisingly, France was a theater of action from which the Queen and her advisors withdrew at the earliest moment consistent with English security.

In the other theater of war, where the English cooperated with an ally, conditions were radically different. The preoccupation of both England and Spain with the Armada had given the Dutch leadership a breathing space in which they moved rapidly to an assertion of independence and of sovereignty. A barely disguised protectorate was transformed into an alliance between equals in which the initiatives of action lay with the Dutch. The English forces in the Low Countries were integrated into the States' military operations; its rapidly developing professional skills were assimilated by the English officer corps while the English rank and file were becoming seasoned and knowledgeable veterans. Strategic and tactical decisions were largely made by the States' leaders, Count Maurice and Oldenbarnevelt. Under these conditions the role of the Council was necessarily a mixed one. As relations with The Hague became those of two sovereign powers, the Council's role was the accustomed one of advisor and consultant to the Queen, but it still retained administrative concerns of some importance. The disbursement of the annual subsidy to the States provided for by the Treaty of Nonsuch posed major problems for English financial management, as did the payment of the garrisons in the cautionary towns.

The archaic fiscal practice by which large dollops of cash were sent at somewhat irregular intervals to the treasurer at war for distribution to the officers in the field led to large leakages. Council supervision and intervention was frequent but of limited effect; at least three of the seven treasurers at war in the Low Countries and Ireland served the Council badly. In two cases, those of Sir Thomas Sherley and Sir George Carey,[32] there was embezzlement on a large scale. This was a problem on which the Council expended time and energy, but to little effect, for no resolution was found in Elizabethan times. In the Low Countries the success of their allies allowed

---

[32] C. G. Cruickshank, *Elizabeth's Army*, 2nd ed. (Oxford, 1966), 148–50; Hubert Hall, *Society in the Elizabethan Age* (London, 1888), 128–32.

the English to reduce their commitment of money, particularly after the renegotiations of 1598. Moreover, monetary waste was substantially offset by solid advantages. The reservoir of trained men that was created by the Dutch service was invaluable to English operations in Ireland or overseas, while Count Maurice's victories diminished the threat of Spanish power. The alliance with the States, unlike that with France, yielded benefits both substantial and immediate.

The urgencies of war in those theaters in which the English, acting by themselves, bore sole responsibility made quite different demands on the Privy Council. In the naval enterprises the brute facts of geography effectively left the commanders free of control once they were under sail. Ireland on the other hand was quite another case. Here the Council was to find itself very deeply involved indeed. Irish business was already conspicuous on its agenda at the end of the 1580's. A survey of the Privy Council acts for 1587 reveals the Council appointing a storekeeper and seneschal for Clandeboy, approving Tyrone's elevation to an earldom, receiving a rebel into grace, appointing a new deputy, and recommending undertakers for the Munster plantation. Just as this omnicompetent body at different times played the role of war minister or foreign secretary, so it was also called upon to be colonial secretary, managing the affairs of England's first colony. As disorder escalated into organized warfare, its responsibilities steadily grew. Grand strategy, immediate tactical moves, finance, victualling, personnel, and the tangled complexity of Irish politics would consume the whole energies and much of the time of the English Council until the very end of the reign. The direction of the Irish war looms large in the business of the English state from the mid-1590's onward, but before examining that experience it may be useful to stand aside from particular episodes and attempt a general overview of English war administration.

The first and greatest commodity in demand was soldiers. Since the English government lacked the funds to hire mercenaries, it had to draft men from the general population. This brings us to the first question, that of numbers. How many in absolute figures and what percentage of the able-bodied males did Elizabeth's armed forces represent? The best estimates of totals for the land forces conscripted by the Crown between 1585 and 1602 give a figure of

75,000 to 76,000, of whom half, about 37,000, served in Ireland.[33] This does not include mariners serving the naval expeditions abroad; one would need to add roughly another 16,500 to 17,500, thus yielding a total of at least 91,000.[34]

How was the burden of service spread? Geographically it was quite evenly distributed. The Privy Council took some pains to even out the incidence of levies. Not surprisingly it was the inland counties of the west Midlands and the western maritime shires that bore a heavier share of the Irish levies while London and the southeast provided the larger share of those destined for the Continent.[35]

In social terms the burden was less equally distributed. The squirearchy and the nobility of course provided the volunteer officer cadre; some 475 captains of companies served in Ireland (each company usually consisted of 100 men). The conscripted enlisted men came largely from the opposite end of the social pyramid. Although the Privy Council instructed the commissioners for musters to enroll the younger sons of freeholders in preference to laborers, they in fact drew on the lowest strata of the population. In the towns this often meant the masterless vagrant. Indeed, in London a government demand for another draft of soldiers was the occasion for ridding the city of the homeless and unemployed. In 1600 the Council roundly rebuked the Lord Mayor, "to say the troth Your Lordship made no levy of men at all but only used an ordinary search to rid the city of rogues and loose people." On another occasion an official source admitted that the city had so many idle men that each levy could be made up without touching artificers or men's necessary servants.[36]

In the rural districts the pattern of recruitment was immortalized by Shakespeare in the person of Mr. Justice Shallow. Farmers of

---

[33] Cruickshank, app. 1, 290; McGurk, 100: table 1.

[34] Monson 1: 125, gives combined land and sea forces of 2,300 in 1585, allowing 1,600 seamen; *ibid.*, 138, gives an overall total of 2,658 in 1587, including 800 to 1,000 foot companies, i.e., 1,600–1,800 mariners. Monson cites contemporary accounts for 1589 varying between 2,500 and 3,200 mariners (1: 186) and lists 4,832 for 1596 (1:358–60). None of these totals includes seamen who served in the routine guard duties of the Queen's ships or the larger number who were members of the privateering crews, another couple of hundred ships.

[35] McGurk, 101.

[36] *Ibid.*, 503; *APC* 1587–88: 99–100; 1599–1600: 620; Ian Archer, citing City of London Record Office Journal 25, fol. 346. I am grateful to Dr. Archer for permission to read and quote from an unpublished paper.

middling rank had either the influence or the cash to avoid conscription. Freeholders were ready to pay £20, £30, or even £50 for exemption, and the hapless laborers were left to bear the burden. The sons of well-to-do farmers often found a safe haven in the trained bands that were not normally available for overseas service. A proposal to use them set a hornet's nest of protest buzzing. "What a charge and discontentment that would breed here you can well conceive," the magistrates of one county warned Robert Cecil.[37]

Nevertheless there were times when urgency overrode custom. Lancashire, Kent, and Northamptonshire all provide instances of trained band service in the war. In 1602 a kind of bribe was offered; in return for the service of the Kentish trained bands the Queen agreed to pay for arms and apparel, charges normally borne locally. In 1599 Lancashire was given special exemption from other burdens in return for the use of its trained bands, but in 1601 and 1602 it was required to raid their ranks to fill up decayed bands in Ireland. Gloucestershire trained bands were summoned in 1594, 1596, and 1599. Those of London were called up on six occasions during the war years.[38]

[37] HMC, *Calendar of the Manuscripts of the . . . Marquis of Salisbury . . . Preserved at Hatfield House, Hertfordshire* (24 vols., London, 1883–1976) 9: 430 [hereafter cited as HMC, *Hatfield*].

[38] McGurk, 175, 245, 246, 257; Archer, 22.

CHAPTER 2

THE MACHINERY AT WORK:

AT HOME AND ABROAD

ONCE A MAN was unlucky enough to have been drafted into the Queen's service, what were his chances of returning home? There was of course no time limit for his services. The men drafted for Normandy in 1589 were home in a few months (those who survived), but dispatch to Brittany in 1591 could have entailed at least three years' service (and some of those unfortunate men were dispatched directly to Ireland after their victory at Crozon). Participants in the naval expeditions saw relatively brief service, although the casualty rate was very high. Those sent to service in the Low Countries or Ireland could anticipate no particular date of release; some may conceivably have served a decade or more. What about the chances of actual survival? We know, of course, that mortality rates were high in any sixteenth-century army. Disease and the hardships of camp life were even more deadly than battle wounds. Naval expeditions were particularly dangerous because of the infections that bred so readily on shipboard. As to exact figures, however, or even percentages, we can say little. Muster figures are abundant but untrustworthy since the fiscal practices of the government encouraged the inflation of the reported figures and it was difficult to check them effectively. And, in the opposite direction, commanders like Norris or Essex might overestimate their losses when seeking reinforcements from home.

Nevertheless, there are pointers that give us a rough guide. Out of 475 captains serving in Ireland after 1585, 65 (14 percent) died in action.[1] Of the roughly 20,000 who sailed for Portugal in 1589, some 8,000 were reported dead before the fleet returned. Both Essex and Norris claimed the loss of half their original forces in France. Irish casualty figures were always high, inflated by the ease with which deserters could procure passage home. But at Lough Foyle, where isolation made desertion virtually impossible, the original force of 4,000 was reduced to 1,500 after a year's service.[2] Essex crossed to Ireland with 16,000 in the spring of 1599; when he left in the fall the number had fallen to 11,250.

The fatality rate was always likely to be high among recruits in the first months of service. Untrained and quite unprepared, they were taken directly from plough or shop and decanted into the bogs of Ireland or the hedgerows of Brittany. Those who survived their initiation seemed to have developed some sort of immunity; they were, no doubt, the toughest of their lot. On the other hand, commanders abroad frequently returned figures not only for the sick and dead but also for those men whom repeated sickness and sustained hardship had made quite useless for further service. All in all there can be little question that the prospects facing a new recruit to the Elizabethan armies were grim. And even those who survived to return to civilian life were often cripples or invalids who had to rely on the licenses to beg issued by the government to keep body and soul together.

What percentage of the able-bodied male population saw military service in the war years 1585–1602? The best modern estimate for England's population in 1600 is about 4,000,000. Taking an average of the estimates for 1586, 1591, 1596, and 1601 gives a figure of 3,955,000. To this must be added an estimate of 250,000 for Wales.[3] If we suppose a sex ratio of 1:1 this gives a male population of 2,102,500. Modern historical demography suggests that in 1600 the proportion of population aged fifteen to sixty (the age group liable to military service) was about 58.8 percent of the whole.[4] If

[1] McGurk, 503.   [2] Ibid., 500.
[3] For England, see E. A. Wrigley and R. S. Schofield, *The Population History of England, 1541–1871: A Reconstruction* (Cambridge, Mass., 1981), 207–8, table 7–8; for Wales, see L. Owen, "The Population of Wales in the Sixteenth and Seventeenth Centuries," *Transactions of the Honourable Society of Cymmrodorion* (London) (1959): 99–113. I am indebted to Professor E. A. Wrigley for checking my calculations.
[4] Wrigley and Schofield, 444 (fig. 10.13) and 528 (table A3.1).

there were 91,000 soldiers and sailors, the percentage of men serving would have been about 7 percent. But if, more realistically, we were to limit the pool to those sixteen to thirty-nine (37.5%), the result would be a participation rate of between 11 and 12 percent of the young adult pool. These estimates are, of course, speculative, and there is the further complication that the actual pool from which the recruits were drawn was smaller still since the trained bandsmen were usually exempt. This could push the percentage of men drafted from the limited pool of the untrained considerably higher.

There can be little doubt that the great majority of the soldiers came from the most helpless and least able of the population. The evidence bears out the accuracy of Shakespeare's representation in the Justice Shallow scenes. Complaints about their quality were endemic. The local officers responsible for embarkation and the commanders in Ireland were loud in their outcries of indignation, and the Privy Council persistent in its rebukes to the county commissioners. A letter from the muster commissioners at Bristol in 1602 can serve as one example out of almost innumerable representations of the same kind through the past decade. The levies of eight hundred men from twelve counties had arrived. "There was never man beheld such strange creatures brought to any muster. They are most of them either old, lame, diseased, boys or common rogues." Weak in body, without proper clothing, they had been "taken up in fairs, markets and highways to supply the place of better men kept at home."[5]

By the middle of the 1590's the destination of most of these conscripts was Ireland, and it is there, where the English, fighting alone, had to sustain the "nine years' war," that we can obtain our fullest view of the English government at war. The direct military responsibilities of the Council were numerous. First of all, it was at its behest that each decision to reinforce the army in Ireland was made. Orders went out under its signature to the lords lieutenant of each county for their particular quota. Delinquencies in performance led to rebuke; occasionally there were letters of thanks for work well done. Among the routine operations were instructions as to equipping and clothing the men, appointing officers, allocating funds, and reimbursing the counties for coat and conduct money.

[5] HMC, *Hatfield* 12: 169–70.

Many lesser matters demanded the Council's attention—the appointment of the keeper of a storehouse in Clandeboy, permission to Waterford to trade with Spain (and its revocation), appointment of a commander for Dungannon fort, specifying the size of his garrison, assigning guards for the grain warehouse in Dublin.[6]

Apart from such multifarious detail, the Council was also the medium through which all major policy decisions were filtered. Campaign plans, negotiations with the Gaelic lords Tyrone and O'Donnell, the treatment of lesser chieftains, the quarrels between Bingham (commissioner in Connaught) and the Dublin council or between general Norris and Deputy Russell were the staple of Council letters to Dublin. In most matters of any importance (and many of less) the councillors were the mouthpiece of the Queen, transmitting her decisions to Ireland. They were also in the opposite direction the channel through which requests from the Deputy and Council reached the royal ear. It is, of course, impossible to sort out individual responsibility in each decision. What is clear is the ever-increasing role of Robert Cecil, who from 1598 on became the correspondent of everyone of any consequence in Ireland. Information flowed from many sources into his hands, and it is hard to imagine that any decision, large or small, was made without his voice being heard. Both the Deputy Mountjoy and Carew, President of Munster, did all their business with London through the Secretary. When in 1599 the Queen finally opened her purse to allow that a resolute effort be made to end the conflict, Cecil's influence was determinative. For him the end of the Irish war was a necessary prelude to peace with Spain.

Behind Cecil, of course, there stood the formidable figure of the Queen. However much distaste she felt for the endlessly troubled affairs of her lesser kingdom, she kept the closest watch on every move made by her servants or her rebels. No deputy took any action without reference back to the Queen; it was she who had to approve every major move on the military chessboard and whose consent guided every turn of negotiation with the Irish leaders. Often critical of the Dublin government when it acted, and reproachful when it hesitated to act, endlessly demanding information and justification, she was in a state of permanent irritation with the unfortunate

[6] *APC* 1587–88: 87; 1590–91: 163; 1596: 467; 1598–99: 179–80; 1599–1600: 596; *Cabala sive Scrinia Sacra*, ed. Dudley Digges (London, 1654), 42: F. Bacon to Essex.

Englishmen whom she set to govern this intractable realm. Most often, faced by a proposal for firm action or simply pressed by the urgency of circumstance, the royal reaction was to back away, seeking the least decisive (and cheapest) option. The result was the worst of both worlds. Every move had to have royal approval, but the Queen's reluctance to give Ireland first priority in her considerations—until events forced her hand—led to the hesitations, the contradictions and the fatal lack of direction in English policy towards the other island.

These top-level decisions, made at court and transmitted to Dublin, had to be turned into reality by the labors of a whole host of officials, civil and military, scattered across England and Ireland. The initial responsibility fell on the shoulders of the local authorities in the counties where the peacetime machinery was now adapted to the needs of war. Having issued the orders for a particular draft of men, the Council left the entire responsibility for finding the men, clothing and arming them, and conducting them to the port of embarkation in the hands of the lord lieutenant of each county, or, more usually, his deputies (or, in counties without a lieutenant the commissioners for musters). Virtually everything that had to be done to ready the soldier for active service was the business of the local authorities; their responsibility ended only when the troops actually set sail for Ireland.

In actual practice, as noted in Chapter 1, this meant that, on receipt of a letter by the lord lieutenant, orders were passed down through the deputy lieutenants and those JP's who were not also on the martial commission to the constables of hundreds and thence to the parish officers. Each county was assigned a quota, usually in multiples of fifty or a hundred. The required number had to be made up (not more than two or three from one parish) by conscription from the whole county. The footmen, once chosen and paid the royal shilling, had to be fully clothed with coat and cap, shoes and stockings, hose and doublet, and armed with musket, caliver, or pike. They then had to be taken by a locally appointed conductor to Chester, Bristol, Southampton, Portsmouth or wherever they were to embark. Only when the conductor turned them over to the captain of their company (or the mayor of the port town) was the county freed of responsibility and cost.[7]

[7] McGurk, 252, 155.

The charges for this operation had to be funded locally, i.e., by a local rate, usually based on the subsidy rolls. In 1594 the Kentish rate was 3d. in the pound on land, 2d. on goods; in 1596, 8d. and 5d., respectively.[8] The financial burden was not a light one. In 1596 in Shropshire a levy of 1,500 men cost the county £462, of which £300 went to armor (which they optimistically hoped to recover after use). The cost of readying a foot soldier in 1598 was roughly £3 a head for clothing and arms.[9] A levy of 100 men in Kent in 1600 (even after a 10 percent reduction for dead pays) cost £379.[10] In Northamptonshire in 1595 a levy of 150 cost £246, but a year later 96 conscripts cost £319.[11] The Kentish levy for Kinsale (2,000 men) cost £400 for apparel and £207 for arms. (Armor for pikemen and muskeeers cost 30s. a head; for those bearing calivers, 20s.)[12] A Kentish account totals the cost for conscription for Continental and Irish service between 1596 and 1602 at £10,911.[13] In Lancashire military rates ran to nearly £2,500 in a nine-year period, while a recent estimate suggests a total cost in local military taxes in London (including the ships of 1588, 1596, and 1599) of no less than £82,571, of which £27,083 went for troops. Parliamentary taxation in the same years cost Londoners £110,400.[14] Some of these costs was reimbursed by the Exchequer, including the daily 8d. per head allowed for conduct money during the journey from home to the port of embarkation.[15] The Crown also made a uniform reimbursement of 4s. for each coat provided for the men, although the Council admitted in a 1591 letter that the cost per coat was then 14s. and might rise as high as 20s.[16]

On occasion, as a sweetener, the Crown would make concessions. In 1602, a year of record levies, the Queen offered to reimburse

---

[8] *Ibid.*, 171; *APC* 1598–99: 336.

[9] *Ibid.*, 328–29; see also McGurk, 252, for a Lancashire estimate of £3.10.

[10] McGurk, 155; Edmund Lodge, *Illustrations of British History*, etc., 2nd ed. (3 vols., London, 1838) 3: 74–76.

[11] McGurk, 195.   [12] *Ibid.*, 171.

[13] *Ibid.*, 151, citing BL, Additional Ms. 34,128, fol. 87.

[14] McGurk, 266, and Archer, 44, 47. In 1596 the city provided twelve ships and twelve pinnaces, paid for out of taxation. See HMC, *Report on the Manuscripts of Lord De L'Isle and Dudley Preserved at Penshurst Place*, Vol. 2 (London, 1934): 203 [hereafter cited as HMC, *De L'Isle and Dudley*].

[15] *APC* 1590–91: 58; 1599–1600: 119, 449–51; McGurk, 208, citing SP 12/262/159.

[16] *APC* 1591: 306–7; 1598–99: 76–78. McGurk cites costs of 16s. for cap and coat (p. 252), and 15s. in 1595 (p. 195).

Kent for the arms and apparel of one hundred men, but on condition that they be drawn from the trained bands, a move that triggered loud objections.[17] But later in the same year, for a draft of fifty men there was to be no reimbursement for either coat or conduct money. Similarly, in Northamptonshire in 1600 the Crown paid not only coat and conduct money but also money for arms. On occasion the government bought the coats wholesale in London for delivery at the port;[18] the county was then required to pay cash to the Exchequer. Clearly, in most cases the costs of mobilization were borne by the ratepayer, a charge over and above the subsidy payments that in the 1590s were an annual demand. Between 1595 and 1602 levies were even more frequent—twelve in Derbyshire, and fifteen in Northamptonshire.[19]

We have seen that the responsibility for choice of recruits fell solely on the local justices. So too, usually, did the nomination of a conductor to convoy the men to the port. Sometimes the conductor was also the prospective commander of the company and would continue with them to Ireland. The conductors were paid a modest sum for the service they rendered, but the temptation to corruption was great. They took advantage of the reluctance of their unhappy charges and encouraged desertion en route by taking bribes, pocketing the proceeds, and hiring stand-ins for the muster at the port. The problem of desertion en route from home, at the port, and in Ireland was endemic. The Council made unavailing efforts to check it in England by requiring an indenture for each soldier, to include personal appearance and equipment as well as the name of his parish. The Council also, against local wishes, began to choose professional captains as conductors.[20]

At the port, responsibility was shifted from the county officers to the mayor of Chester, Bristol, or other ports. It was his responsibility to muster the forces, feed them at the port, stay sufficient shipping for transport overseas, arrange for the payment of the shipmaster, embark the troops and see them off. A task burdensome enough in itself, it was made worse by the vagaries of the winds that often delayed shipping for weeks on end. Successive mayors of Chester had to supervise fifteen embarkations in eight years, a total

[17] McGurk, 175.
[18] *CPSD* 5 (1598–1601): 151; *APC* 1591: 307; McGurk, 147–48, 161, 215. See *APC* 1599–1600: 650–51 for counties delinquent in payments for apparel.
[19] McGurk, 226.   [20] *Ibid.*, 72, 147–48, 276–77; *APC* 1599–1600: 192–93.

of some 18,000 men. (Bristol handled 10,000.) Delay could of course arouse unrest and lead to mutiny, as at Chester in 1600 or at Bristol in 1601. The ringleaders at Chester were sent to Newgate by Council order; at Bristol a local trial and mock execution quelled the disturbance.[21]

What is apparent in all these arrangements is the minimal presence of any central bureaucracy, any vestige of a war office to handle the complex problems of mobilization and transportation. Training too (such as it was) was the obligation of the local authorities, but since drafts on the trained bands were controversial and spasmodic, many of the soldiers arriving overseas hardly knew one end of the musket from the other. They passed from the amateur management of the civilian county authorities directly to that of the garrison or battlefield commander.

Once the soldiers passed beyond the Irish Sea they became the responsibility of the Irish authorities. The Irish establishment was under much closer supervision by the Privy Council than was the decentralized regime of the county magistracies. Its officers were feed servants of the Crown, executing its orders under detailed and continuous direction. The large funds they expended were provided by the Council, to whom they were accountable. That body itself had a much greater direct involvement than in the mobilization process, for the forces in Ireland had to be paid, fed, clothed, and armed almost entirely from England. It was the responsibility of the Council to find the money and provide the necessary supplies. On paper at least the measures necessary to acomplish these tasks were well organized. Budgets were drawn up for each department in the Irish government and army—the central organs at Dublin, the provincial presidencies, and the individual garrisons, allocating their expenditures for the year.[22] The local commanders were expected to keep within these allocations. There was to be strict "treasury control." No extraordinary payments were to be made except with Privy Council authorization, with the sole exception of £6,000 allowed to the Deputy for contingency costs. Contracts were let in

[21] *Ibid.*, 155, 156, 163–65; McGurk, 342.
[22] See, for instance, the budgeted costs of Essex's expedition: McGurk, 405; Fynes Moryson, *Itinerary Written by Fynes Moryson* (4 vols., Glasgow, 1907–8) 2: 222–24, 229; *Calendar of the Carew Manuscripts Preserved in the Archiepiscopal Library at Lambeth, 1515–1624,* ed. J. S. Brewer and William Bullen (6 vols., London, 1867–73) 3: 288–89.

London for the bulk supply of food and clothing for the soldiers.[23] Provision was made for two outfits annually for each soldier, a summer and a winter uniform.[24] For his food bread, butter, cheese, oatmeal, fish, and, of course, beer were shipped over to Ireland.[25] Prepayment was made on clothing contracts; acquittances were given on delivery in Ireland. For victuals, half the money was paid in advance, the other half upon presentation of receipts for delivery.[26] There was thus a clear-cut chain of responsibility from the Council through the treasurer at war in Ireland, the auditing officials under his control, and ultimately the officers in the garrisons or in the field. But, however well designed in intention, the system was in operation riddled by corruption and inefficiency.

The key figure in this chain was the company captain, the workhorse of the army. He was not only the field commander but also quartermaster and finance officer, through whose hands flowed the funds for pay, food, clothing, and munitions. He was also the weak link in the chain. Many of the captains were semi-professional, some with service in the Low Countries, dating back as far as the 1570s, but appointment to their post was often influenced more by patronage considerations than by military efficiency. Nominally the deputy had the power of appointment, although sometimes it was delegated to regional officials such as Carew.[27] The great difficulty, however, arose at court. Instances of direct appointment by the Queen were numerous enough to cause friction. While acknowledging that choice of captains should be the deputy's, the Privy Council rather apologetically admitted that when "gentlemen and ancient servitors have access to Her Majesty" and win the royal promise, it could do nothing but obey. In similar vein they wrote in 1601 that "it standeth not with the reputation of a Council of State here at home to forbear to confer some employment upon such as do plead merit to the Queen ... for it is fit that they be so retained in hope as not to abandon their place by despairing of preferment." Mountjoy must perceive how many occasions arise when such persons must be employed. Even more candidly the councillors had written in 1600 "that in our remembrance the court did never swarm with so many suitors." He should remember that "as a dep-

[23] See APC 1599–1600: 194 and 724, for examples of victualling contracts.
[24] See CSPD 5 (1598–1601): cclxvii, 43, for such a contract.
[25] CSPD 2 (1581–90): clxii, 107; clxiii, 107; McGurk, 413, 414.
[26] APC 1599–1600: 194–95, 724.   [27] See Carew 3 (1589–1600): 353–55.

53

uty would be glad to send men away contented" yet he must consider "that it is as fit that Her Majesty be not driven to discontent them."[28]

These somewhat shamefaced admissions of the Privy Council highlighted the problems facing the Irish command in maintaining military efficiency when patronage considerations outweighed the needs of the service. Many of these captains viewed their commission in a straightforwardly mercenary light and sought to avoid active service while eagerly exploiting its pecuniary advantages to the utmost. Their value was illustrated by the experience of Robert Sidney. In 1596 he was offered, but refused, £300 for a company at Flushing. In 1600 he proposed to enlarge his companies by fifty men each, for which he would receive £100 per company. If on the other hand he created new companies he would have £300 to £400 for each new unit.[29] Civil servants of the Crown similarly regarded their posts as opportunities for increasing their income beyond the modest official fee they received. But among them established custom and the prospects of a lifetime income kept peculation within certain bounds. Service in the army was a more precarious occupation. Cuts in the size of forces and ultimately the coming of peace gave only short-term advantages that needed to be exploited vigorously and promptly. The results were wholesale cheating of the Crown and an alarming frequency of absenteeism. Service in Ireland was toilsome, painfully uncomfortable, and not without considerable risk. Captains took as many opportunities as possible to escape home. In the opinion of observers at the fateful battle of Clontibret, the defeat of the English owed something to the absenteeism of many captains.[30]

The disposition of English captains to view their commissions as licenses for augmenting their income beyond the modest allowance of £60 to £100 a year paid by the crown were facilitated by the administrative practices of the government and by its own half-conscious impulses to evade its direct responsibilities in the actual management of the war. Arrangements for paying the troops were

---

[28] *APC* 1599–1600: 354, 455; 1601–4: 188, 270–71.

[29] HMC, *De L'Isle and Dudley*, 227–28, 485.

[30] *Calendar of State Papers Relating to Ireland, of the Reign of Elizabeth* (11 vols., 1974) 7: 43, 72; 8: 192, 193, 212, for instances of absenteeism. For Clontibret, see L. O'Mearain, "The English Army of Clontibret," *Irish Sword* 2 (1954–56): 368–71.

based on practices inherited from an earlier age when the commander was a military contractor, providing a force for the government and paying the soldiers as his employees. The Elizabethan captain was both commander and finance officer. He received a weekly "lending" or "imprest," which was an advance against the officially budgeted sum, the "full pay" due at the end of each half-year. This was an all-purpose sum, basically a subsistence allowance to cover the cost of the soldiers' food, clothing, gunpowder and other necessities. Any surplus left at the end of the six-month period constituted his net reward. This system meant that the captain had full control of the wage fund without having to account for its use for a long period of time. The clerk whose business it was to keep track of disbursements for the individual soldier was the captain's employee. On paper the Privy Council had set up an adequate system of audit, but in practice it failed almost completely. The poorly paid officials who were supposed to monitor the system were all too easily bribed into collaboration with the peculating captains.

Abuses abounded. Companies soon shrank from their nominal strength one hundred to a mere fraction of the total. Captains continued to report full strength and draw funds accordingly. Irishmen were recruited to fill the ranks on muster day or at some emergency when men were needed, but they supported themselves by living off the country. Musters were held several times a year at some point distant from the garrison station. En route the soldiers forced the country people to supply both food and money, while the captain charged the costs of the journey to the Crown and pocketed the sum. These and other practices enabled dishonest captains to build up fraudulent claims against the Crown amounting to £1,500 or £2,000. Honest commanders, left without funds for long intervals, ran up bills on their own credit and then, in desperation, sold their claims against the Crown at heavy discount to their fellows who had access to court or council. The victims were, of course, the ordinary soldiers. It was said "they had as lief go to the gallows as to the Irish wars."[31]

Exhortation and rebuke from the Council or the Queen herself had little or no effect in the bogs and woods of distant Ireland or the garrison towns of Holland, especially as the superior officers, the treasurers at war, were themselves peculators on a grand scale.

[31] CSPI 7 (1598–99): 205–10; Carew 3 (1589–1600): 353–55.

The scandal of Sir Thomas Sherley (treasurer in the Low Countries) was the most spectacular, but he may have profited less than Sir George Carey (treasurer in Ireland), whose frauds came to light only after his death.[32]

The consequences of this general corruption were obvious to contemporaries. Their indignation filled the posts; the mayors of Chester and Bristol bombarded the Council with complaints about the deficiencies in both number and quality of the men arriving at the ports. The Irish commanders were equally vociferous in denouncing the inadequacy of the forces they received. The Council was insistent in its reproaches to the county authorities and to the local commanders in Ireland, but quite in vain. Friends in high places, the determined resistance of the captains to every proposed reform, and the circumstances of war waged far from home all contributed to the failure of all reform efforts.

The difficulties of achieving any systematic accounting for these monies were compounded by the government's own fiscal practices. Although detailed and quite precise projections of military and civil costs were drawn up—effectively a budget—there was no serious effort to match income with outgo in fiscal operations or to keep effective supervision of expenditure. Virtually all the expenses of Irish government had to be met out of English revenues. Money came across the seas in irregular and unpredictable dollops, often delayed by adverse winds or storms in the Irish Sea. The payments' irregularity also reflected corresponding hiccoughs in the government's own revenue. In any case, in the interims of financial drought the Dublin administration had to borrow in Dublin (or sometimes in London), and when money arrived the supply was immediately exhausted in the repayment of loans.[33] This hand-to-mouth system often meant that money for pay was held up; lacking the means to buy food, the troops had to live off the country. Clothes were worn out but could not be replaced; men went barefoot and half-clad in the sodden damp of Ireland, driven to sell their equipment to keep body and soul together. It was a system that enriched the officers, victimized the soldiers, and seriously hindered the Queen's service.

How can one account for the failure of the Elizabethan Council

[32] See Cruickshank, chap. 9; for Cary, see Hall, 122–32.
[33] *CSPI* 7 (1598–99): 205–10.

to check the gross corruption and the wasteful inefficiency of this system? How could administrators of the caliber of the Cecils put up with such a shameless squandering of the Queen's all-too-scarce revenues? The answer lies in several directions. Most fundamental was the mind-set of the Elizabethan government, evident in so many different areas. It insisted on treating the war as a temporary phenomenon that made it unnecessary to alter the established routines of peacetime life. Scratch armies were tacked together by using the traditional machinery of local government and dispatched overseas. In Holland they could be turned over to the care of a government that was methodically building a professional military establishment. In France their efforts were largely wasted, but once the French ship of state righted itself, they could be withdrawn. But in Ireland there were responsibilities that could not be delegated or ignored. A mode of war-time administration designed for the needs of a few short campaign seasons was grievously inadequate for a very different kind of task. Reluctantly the English leadership came to the realization that what was required was an all-out drive, aimed at the final extinction of Gaelic autonomy. This was bound to be a slogging, time-consuming effort, requiring the services of a substantial army. Mountjoy's combination of energy and patience, sustained by Cecil's steady support, finally won the day, but it was not matched by a corresponding adaptation of administrative practice.

The instrument at Mountjoy's disposal was a very imperfect one, for the men with whom he had to work regarded the war as an enterprise in which greed rather than patriotism took first place. There were, of course, men such as Philip Sidney or Robert Devereux, who were deeply moved by a chivalric ideal of martial prowess. There were also the battle-scarred veterans like Sir John Norris, for whom war had truly become a profession. And last but not least there were the responsible, hard-working servants of the Crown, the Mountjoys or the Carews, who labored mightily at a task they loathed. But for a large mass of officers, military command provided a livelihood rather than a calling. Like their sea-going counterparts, the privateers, these men saw war as a golden opportunity to line their pockets. We shall see how this mentality affected naval expeditions. *Mutatis mutandis*, it influenced the behavior of Elizabeth's soldier servants, particularly in the largest theater of war, Ireland.

There the picture was colored even more darkly by another factor, the mingled contempt and disgust with which the enemy was regarded. The Spaniard, however hated, was seen as a worthy opponent, and the war as one of high purpose. None of these considerations obtained in a struggle that foreshadowed, all too unhappily, future warfare in the forests of North America. The restraints, flimsy as they were, that checked the worst excesses of military violence elsewhere were altogether lacking here. Against these dispositions the Privy Council struggled in vain. There was neither time nor will to transform this ramshackle force by creating the esprit de corps of a trained army, imbued with habits of obedience and controlled by a rigorous discipline. Nor was there time or will to establish the trained and costly bureaucracy that, by managing the smooth flow of supplies and money, could control expenditure and check abuses.

Yet, having painted this grim picture of corruption and inefficiency, one has to record the successful conclusion of the war. It was not a triumphal victory, but one that did realize the goals that the Elizabethan government had set before itself. Against the shortcomings of the Elizabethan war effort one has to set the record of its enemies. The characteristics of military administration that have been sketched above were by no means peculiar to the English; Continental armies were more professional in their organization, but wracked by most of the same problems. In addition, those events on the Continent that decisively shifted the balance in England's favor did not depend primarily on English effort; they were the results of Dutch and French achievement. In the one theater where the English had to bear the sole burden, the enemy was an intrinsically weaker foe in men, money, supplies, and organization; they were strategically isolated and uncertain as to their goals. Once the full energies of the English state were brought to bear (and the inadequate Spanish intervention crushed), English superiority was bound to make itself felt. In short, it was a war in which the margin of safety provided by circumstance and by the enemy's weaknesses was large enough to contain the shortcomings of the English effort and allow the realization of their limited war aims.

CHAPTER 3

PAYING FOR

THE WAR

THE COMBINED efforts of the Council, the local magistracies, and the military commanders carried the war to its successful conclusion. All these efforts required money, however, and in large quantities. How was this war paid for? The new techniques and the new professionalism that transformed the face of Continental warfare in the sixteenth century could not have succeeded without corresponding alterations in the fiscal operations of the European monarchies. Large new sources of funds had to be tapped to pay for these great wars, and on the Continent a vastly increased burden of taxation of the subject went hand in hand with the growth of an international money market and long-term government borrowing. While England lagged behind in these developments, as in others, there were important changes that substantially increased the revenue at the disposal of the English crown.

What was the fiscal position of the English crown when Elizabeth ascended the throne? She inherited a patchwork system that reflected late medieval financial and constitutional practice as well as the innovations that her father's councillors had devised to pay for his extravagances. His wars had made huge demands on the English economy just at the moment when the great inflation of the sixteenth century began to bite. To increase royal tax revenue his ministers had been able to break the convention that limited parliamentary provision to the old tenth-and-fifteenth of the fourteenth century with its fixed and hopelessly inadequate yields. The invention of the subsidy, a tax based on new and realistic assessment and open-ended in its yield, raised the scale of parliamentary contribution to royal needs; firmly in place by the 1520's, it would subsist largely unchanged until the Civil War. It was, of course, still seen as a supplement to the sovereign's "ordinary" resources.

The revenues that made up Elizabeth's ordinary, recurrent income were essentially those of her medieval predecessors, the royal lands and the customs duties. Together they provided roughly two-thirds of annual receipts. The rest consisted of small items, in which clerical tenths and the receipts of wardship and of the Duchy of Lancaster were the largest components. At the beginning of her reign these revenues were more than enough to cover the calculable annually recurring expenses of the Crown and leave a comfortable surplus.[1]

Yet this reserve was, for several reasons, an illusory sum. First, Elizabeth was burdened with an inherited debt equal to a single year's income, half of which was owed abroad.[2] Second, the events of the next decade—the Scottish expedition of 1559–1560, the French of 1562–1563, the suppression of O'Neill in Ulster, the rising in the north—forced on the Queen a series of unanticipated and unpredictable expenditures. The Queen and her ministers were resolute in their determination to balance the budget, but that goal was forever receding as repayments of old debt were offset by the accumulation of new liabilities.[3]

In fact, the ancient dictum that the Crown should live off its own in times of peace, resorting to taxation only for the extraordinary costs of war, was already becoming a fiction. In the 1530's Henry VIII had asked for and obtained two grants from Parliament when the country was at peace. The preambles of the subsidy statutes of 1534 and 1541 skillfully blended general reference to the king's services to his subjects with a specific list of quasi-military costs, such as coastal forts, the suppression of the Pilgrimage of Grace, and

---

[1] For detailed studies of Elizabethan finances, see William R. Scott, *The Constitution and Finance of English, Scottish, and Irish Joint Stock Companies to 1720* (3 vols., London, 1912) 3: 510; R. B. Outhwaite, "Studies in Elizabethan Government and Finance: Royal Borrowing and the Sale of Crown Lands, 1572–1603" (unpublished Ph.D. dissertation, University of Nottingham, 1964).

[2] Scott 3: 510–11.

[3] See HMC, *Hatfield* 15: 2; *CSPD* 6 (1601–3): cclxxxvii, 59.

Irish expenditures.[4] This subtle shift, which implied the responsibility of the subject to pay for the general benefits of good government, was masked by the events of the next decade, when the country was caught up in the extravaganza of Henry's last fling in France and Scotland and its baneful aftermath in his son's reign. These enterprises were paid for by selling the monastic lands, debasing the coinage, and borrowing lavishly abroad. Henry also made three arbitrary levies (one initially a loan, its repayment later remitted by Parliament). It looked for a moment as if a breach had been made in the very principle of consent, but any such development was choked off by the king's death. The fumbling leadership of his successors precluded further experimentation. Both Edward and Mary had to seek peacetime subsidies in order to pay off the accumulated debts of war. Elizabeth at the opening of her reign faced the same situation, and what had been an irregular and presumably terminable need arising from past commitments became, imperceptibly, a steadily recurring demand for dealing with new enterprises; the temporary was becoming permanent. The old distinction between ordinary and extraordinary expenses was fast blurring.

The empty treasury and the mounting debt that faced the Queen on her accession left an indelible impression. To the end of her days she was obsessed with a sense of her poverty and a horror of accumulated debt. The result was a fiscal policy, based on stringent economy in expenditure, that often verged on parsimony. This was matched by an irenic foreign policy, but until the 1570's events were too much for her. Expenditure ran steadily ahead of income and resort to parliamentary assistance was inevitable. In the high tensions of late-sixteenth-century Europe the distinctions of war and peace were increasingly blurred into the gray mist of cold war. England was not officially at war in the early Elizabethan decades, yet she mounted two military expeditions in Scotland and one in France, as well as suppressing major rebellions in England and Ireland. Warships and coastal forts had to be kept in constant readiness. The moral of these circumstances was clear. The day-to-day conduct of international relations in this world of unremitting fric-

[4] G. R. Elton, "Taxation for War and Peace in Early Tudor England," in his *Studies in Tudor and Stuart Politics and Government* (3 vols., Cambridge, 1938) 3: 216–33.

tion and persistent insecurity made unprecedented demands on Crown expenditure, which could be met only by regular infusions of parliamentary taxation at each successive meeting of that body. In thirteen of the first twenty-five years of the reign subjects had to bear the burden of a parliamentary subsidy. The assumption that each new parliament would grant a subsidy was now firmly rooted.

In the more favorable circumstances of the 1570's the government was at last able, with the income from recurring subsidies, to realize its goal of a balanced budget, and indeed to achieve a surplus on ordinary account. In 1572 the new lord treasurer could congratulate himself on a surplus of £74,000. In the last years of the reign this had risen to £100,000, but in an era of rapid inflation the Crown's fiscal position had in fact barely changed. Ordinary revenue was down by 7.6 percent, expenditures by 6.8 percent, but the value of the surplus in real terms had fallen by 9.9 percent.[5] What is more notable than the maintenance of a surplus on ordinary account is the absence of any measures to make large-scale increases in ordinary revenue. Customs yields rose substantially, but the improvement was probably owing to shifts in the composition of goods, certainly not to any attempt to raise the rate of charge, as had been done in Mary's time. Land income remained stagnant as no effort was made to increase rents proportionately to inflation.[6] Income from renewal fines during the war years was less than that in the preceding fifteen.[7]

Such a resolutely conservative, not to say unimaginative, approach meant that all expenses beyond the bare minimum of the peacetime establishment had to be met from taxation, but once the debt was paid off and the budget brought into balance the justification for another subsidy ended. This the government readily acknowledged.[8] In the Parliament of 1576, however, Mildmay took a new and important tack in his approach to the Commons. Admitting that there was no present need to seek more money from them, he went on to an unprecedented burst of confidence. Painting a broad but detailed picture of the international scene, he warned

[5] Outhwaite, "Studies," 16–18.

[6] *Ibid.*, 27–28, citing H. J. Habbabuk (*Economic History Review*, ser. 2, 10 [1957–58]: 362–80).

[7] Outhwaite, "Studies," 29.

[8] T. E. Hartley, ed., *Proceedings of the Parliaments of Elizabeth I*, Vol. 1: *1558–81* (Leicester, 1981): 440–44.

them of the contingent dangers that it contained, pointing his finger directly at Rome and its ally, Spain. He went on to ask them for money that would give the Queen the means to deal with whatever contingency might arise from these threatening circumstances. They were being asked to pay for the costs not of past or present wars but of putative future conflict. He won their approval and repeated his performance in the next parliament of 1581.

Mildmay's successes in these parliaments reflected a new kind of partnership between Crown and Parliament in which the latter accepted the need for regular infusions of income to cover the continuing year-to-year costs of government in peace as in war. Parliament would not reject a royal request for funds but it needed to be persuaded, to have at least a statement of the case. The traditional rhetoric of persuasion in the earlier Tudor reigns had continued to echo that of the late Plantagenet kings, of the Hundred Years' War. The repeated theme of every request for parliamentary aid was the recovery of the king's ancient rights in France—or in the 1540's in Scotland. The last time this note was sounded had been in 1548. From that time on the rhetoric swiftly changed. There was an interim in the 1550's when the Crown's plea was for aid to clear away the debts incurred by the errors of the past. Under Elizabeth an entirely new theme was developed. Over and over again her spokesmen in Parliament insisted on the Queen's entirely peaceful intentions towards all her neighbors. She sought only to live in harmony with them, coveting no single fragment of their territories. At the same time she made great play of her own frugality at home. She built no palaces, wasted no money in vain show or in the indulgence of her own pleasures. The contrast with her predecessors was pointed up. Eschewing all personal or dynastic ambitions, she asserted her royal role as one of protectress of her people's rights, properties, and religion. The royal will was to be subordinated entirely to the needs of her subjects. The image of a national ruler was to supplant that of a dynastic lord. The growth of the foreign threat served to confirm and strengthen the validity of this new formulation of royal policy.

This change in rhetoric was certainly much more than a mere shift of tactics. It mirrored Elizabeth's own conceptions of her royal office as well as those of the councillors in whom she placed most trust. And it was reflected in the actual course of policy (the one plausible exception would be the New Haven adventure). It won the confidence of her subjects, as their willingness to bear peacetime taxation in the later 1570's showed. It also laid the psychological groundwork for the coming of war. By 1585 the ruling elites had come fully to accept the reality of the Spanish threat and to rally to the support of a government whose responsible fiscal behavior and defensive foreign policy they thoroughly trusted.

With the actual coming of war in 1585 government expenditures necessarily soared. There was a nest egg of some £324,000 in the Exchequer in 1584, but this would not last long. By the Treaty of Nonsuch the English had committed themselves to an annual outlay of £126,000; the Armada would cost £161,000; and after 1589 several hundred thousand more had to be found for the support of Henry IV. Roughly speaking, annual expenditure would increase fivefold during the war years.[9] Total costs are difficult, probably impossible, to state with precision, but contemporary figures give us at least their magnitude. An estimate, made at the very beginning of James's reign, sets a figure of approximately £3,982,000; one modern historian suggests £4,555,000, another £4,636,000.[10] Probably a round figure of £4,500,000 would be a fair estimate. This of course does not include the sums levied locally in the counties for coat and conduct money or the fitting out of ships. The indications given by preliminary research, cited above, suggest that an estimate of some 50 percent more would be conservative.

How was it paid for? The rather startling answer to that question is that the war was paid for almost entirely out of current resources. Counting the arrears still due on the last subsidy grant of the reign, the costs of the war were entirely met in 1603, although the balance in the Exchequer was not adequate for the immediate expenses of the new reign. The strong sense of fiscal responsibility displayed by the government in peacetime had not deserted it in the war years. As in peacetime taxation had to provide a substantial share. The total yield from lay subsidies (including tenths-and-fifteenths) from 1585 to 1603 inclusive was about £1,632,000; there was an additional £300,000 still to be collected on the 1601 subsidy after the death of the Queen. Clerical subsidies brought in somewhere between £240,000 and £270,000 in the same years. Land was

---

[9] Outhwaite, "Studies," 21.

[10] HMC, *Hatfield* 15: 2; see also *CSPD* 6 (1601–3): cclxxxvii, 59; Outhwaite, "Studies," 19; Scott 3: 503–9, 516–27. For Irish costs, see BL, Lansdowne Ms. 156, fol. 258.

sold by the Crown to the value of least £500,000 (possibly £600,000). Taken together this totals roughly £2,700,000. (If we were to increase clerical subsidies to £400,000, as shown in the 1603 calculation, this would increase to £2,850,000.) At the death of the Queen there was a debt of some £364,000 (with about £60,000 in Exchequer hands), covered by the remaining installments of subsidy. On paper at least the books balanced; income covered outlay. In fact the last loans of the Queen's reign were never repaid.[11] In other words, a little under half of the war expenses was paid out of taxes and a little over 10 percent from the sale of lands. The balance was found out of the surpluses on ordinary account, which in the final years of the reign were running at about £100,000 annually. The Crown had financed the war from the same sources that had paid the bills in peacetime. War finance, like war administration, had been a continuation of peacetime practice.

The government, in making this choice, had in fact few options. Borrowing abroad was impossible; borrowing at home was limited to short-term loans from the London merchant community and from a small elite of the wealthiest taxpayers. In 1588 about £73,000 was raised on Privy Seals, which were repaid by 1592; in 1590, £84,000, repaid in 1595; and in 1597, £98,000, which was owing at the Queen's death and which James's government failed to repay. In the first instance some 2,400 prospective lenders were addressed; in the second and third, 5,932 and 4,957, respectively.[12] It is interesting that in each case the targeted figure was considerably larger than the sum received; in 1590, £146,000, and in 1597, £145,000. The actual process of extracting money from the prospective borrower was left to local JP's with power to exempt those with reasonable excuses. In Norfolk in 1590, out of 114 on the original Council list,

[11] F. C. Dietz, *English Public Finance, 1558–1641* (New York, 1932), 392–93; see also R. Schofield, "Taxation and the Political Limits of the Tudor State," in *Law and Government under the Tudors*, ed. C. Cross et al. (Cambridge, 1988), 232. Clerical subsidies are listed as £400,000 in HMC, *Hatfield* 15: 2, but Dietz, 395, gives an annual income of £8,000 to £9,000 for 1586–88, £9,000 to £10,000 for 1589–93, and £17,000 to £19,000 for the remaining years of the reign. Land sales in the years 1591–1603 are given in Dietz, 298, quoting SP 14/47/99–102; Dietz adds £63,000 worth sold in 1589. The debt owing in 1603 is found in University of Kansas Mss. Q12:39, a reference I owe to the kindness of Dr. John Guy; see also BL, Add. Ms. 36,970, fol. 17.

[12] Outhwaite, "Studies," 140–46, 162–63.

only 34 were adjudged able to lend.[13] This kid-glove treatment of the lenders, and the anxiety to repay them as soon as possible, are all signals of the caution, not to say timidity, with which the government approached its subjects when seeking their financial aid.

Alternative modes of raising money, such as excises or long-term loans, widely used on the Continent, were apparently not even thought of. The faintly disguised prerogative taxation to which Henry VIII had resorted in the 1540's was resolutely eschewed; so was his debasement of the coinage (except in Ireland). It is a measure of the changed climate of opinion that these alternatives were not, so far as we know, ever considered in the 1590's. The Queen refused the special benevolence that was proposed by the expansionists in 1586 and resisted the proposal to label the fourth subsidy of 1601 a benevolence. She was determined to drive home the lesson that the difference between her customary revenues and the total costs of government was to be borne, in war as in peace, by her subjects. The logic of this was plain enough, since it was a war being fought solely for the defense of their interests.

If there was strong insistence on the subjects' obligations to pay for the services rendered them by the state, there was also a sense that those obligations were not unlimited. The government recognized that the whole shortfall could not be met by the taxpayer. The Crown was prepared to sell off its own assets, its land, to meet part of the bill. Wherever possible, particularly in the overseas naval expeditions, there was an effort to "privatize" costs by luring private investment in the hope of returns from prizes or booty. At the same time, as a tactical move, the burden of taxation was to some extent disguised by dispersing it onto the local communities, in coat and conduct money or in the levies of ships. A judicious distribution of these local levies from year to year shifted the pressure from one area to another and afforded at least temporary relief to individual localities.

Above all, care had to be taken in the management of Parliament. We have seen how this had been done in prewar years by a carefully measured rhetoric designed to engage the fullest possible commitment of the taxpaying community. This policy was of course continued in wartime. In 1589, in the wake of the Armada, the government had a strong case; nevertheless, precautions were

[13] *Ibid.*, 145–46, 162.

taken to ensure Commons' agreement to an unprecedented double subsidy. A special committee with representation from every shire was used to push the measure through, and a special proviso that this should not be a precedent was written into the measure.[14] In 1593 the increase to a triple subsidy required elaborate stage management. When the Lower House showed no willingness to go beyond the limit of two, heavy artillery was brought in from the Lords. The message, conveyed by Burghley himself, cited hard figures to show the Queen's financial plight. Some scattered murmurs of doubt were heard in the Commons, and Bacon made the ill-timed speech in which he prophesied that gentlemen would have to sell their plate and yeomen their brass to meet this charge, but the bill passed without a division, albeit with another disclaimer that it should not be a precedent.[15]

In 1597 the triple subsidy was renewed, again with the accustomed disclaimer of precedent, by a house that sat only a few days after the second invasion fleet in two years had been dispersed by the autumnal storms. The final parliament of the reign met in 1601 almost at the same moment as the Spanish army landed at Kinsale. With this trump card to hand, Cecil was able to persuade the Commons to agree to an unheard-of fourth subsidy, although he also held out a carrot in the form of a hint that peace might be in the offing.[16] All this leaves us with little doubt that, even in the heat of this patriotic war, with its looming threats of actual invasion, the Queen and her ministers felt the need to proceed with the utmost caution and with careful preparation in seeking funds from Parliament. Moreover, there was a keen awareness that, while they might be stretched, there were limits to what could be expected from the taxpayers. The annual burden, which in the 1560's had been about £56,000 and in the 1570's only £33,000, for the years 1590–1601 rose to about £90,000.[17] No less significant than the increase in incidence,

[14] D'Ewes, 431; *Statutes of the Realm*, ed. A. Luders, et al. (11 vols., London, 1810–28), 4(2): 818–34.

[15] D'Ewes, 457–58, 471–74, 477, 491–94; BL, Lansdowne Ms. 104: 78–79, printed in Strype 4: 149ff.

[16] D'Ewes, Simonds, coll, *A Compleat Journal of the Votes, Speeches and Debates, Both of the House of Lords and House of Commons throughout the Whole Reign of Queen Elizabeth*, etc. (London, 1693; reprint, Wilmington, Del., and London, 1974), 599, 623.

[17] Dietz, 389 n. 17.

however, is the fall in yield. In 1564 a single subsidy had brought in £150,000; by the early years of the war a levy at the same rate had yielded little more than £100,000, and in the last subsidy of the reign as little as £67,000 was brought in. The Council complained bitterly but, with assessment and collection in local hands, could do little about it.[18] Signals of increasing war-weariness coming from the localities[19] served to confirm the message that the foot-dragging tax-payers were giving the government.

The royal determination to fight a war of minimal goals, a defensive struggle aimed at securing the *status quo ante*, arose from many different causes, not the least of which were the conservative temperament of the Queen and her most trusted advisors, and their realists' estimate of England's actual resources. Of equal importance was their assessment of the climate of opinion among the political classes. As they saw it, the ancient and deep-rooted convention that limited parliamentary taxation to extraordinary occasions had been widely stretched in the latter sixteenth century, but the underlying conviction that the subjects' liability was a limited one had not disappeared. At the same time the corollary that there was a reciprocal responsibility on the Crown's side had taken deep root, not least because the Crown itself had instilled it in their consciousness. The expectations of the Commons had broadened immensely, had indeed been transformed. They now expected not merely a bare statement of the Crown's needs, adorned with a few ornamental flourishes, but a reasonably detailed explanation of royal purposes. Even more, they looked for a declaration of national—not merely of personal or dynastic—goals, which spoke to that which touched all of them. There was also the assumption that the Crown would stretch its own resources to meet these extraordinary occasions.

The implications of these altered conventions in royal-parliamentary relations were wide-ranging. They bear directly on the whole large question of the development of the state. The acceptance by Parliament of its obligation to assume that part of the cost of government that was used for the public benefit was a long step towards the fleshing out of the new but increasingly familiar

[18] Schofield, 234–35.
[19] For instances, see *CSPD* 6 (1601–3): cclxii, 86 (London) and cclxxxi, 28 (Yorkshire).

phrase, "Queen and state." There was now a public component, apart from the monarch's personal interests, in which the sovereign was to play the role at once of guardian and of symbol. Besides the ancient royal obligation to provide justice, institutionalized and depersonalized in the courts, there was the embryonic notion that the monarch's whole conduct of the public business should be shaped by the interests of the nation as well as those of the ruling house.

All these changes reflected the experience of decades of international tension, followed by open war. What they would mean in an era of peace remained to be seen. Parliament had accepted the need to assume at least a proportion of governmental expenditures during an era of continued stress and obvious external threats. What kind of arguments would be persuasive in the absence of such pressures? Would the commitment hold good in the "ordinary" times of peace? Would the limits, which all agreed to exist, revert to their earlier, narrower, boundaries? Only future events could answer these difficult questions.

There were other long-term consequences of these alterations. The conventions that governed Crown-Parliament relations were increasingly strained by the pressures of war. The government's assumption that its power to raise money from its subjects was ultimately inelastic forced it into economies of operation. No attempt was made to set up the institutional structures necessary for long-term war. The government made do with *ad hoc* improvisations, using the civil magistracies of the shires at home and a ramshackle framework of make-do arrangements abroad. The costs in money and lives were high, but not high enough to lose the war. Similarly in the realm of finance, while relying heavily on taxation to support the war, the government continued to use the increasingly threadbare device of the subsidy, making no effort to exploit indirect taxation—customs or even excises—or to explore the possibilities of large-scale domestic borrowing. There was a disjuncture between the expanding claims of the state on its citizens and the necessary machinery for the successful waging of war. It was, to say the least, an unpromising legacy for the future.

PART II
WAGING THE WAR I:
THE ENEMY—SPAIN

CHAPTER 4

THE PORTUGUESE VOYAGE

1588-1589

As THE AUTUMN of 1588 faded into winter and as the euphoria of the summer's successes waned, the English leadership was compelled to face the cold realities of a major war. Although they had been engaged in hostilities since 1585, the Queen and Burghley had not given up hope of an accommodation. Now not only was that illusion shattered, but the attack of 1588 gave notice that Spain would turn her whole force directly against England. Their goal— as the English saw it—was nothing less than the crushing of the existing regime.

That this was a war of a different kind from those fought earlier in the century was very clear. Burghley gave voice to this realization in a speech in Parliament in 1593:

Not as in former times when the Emperor Charles and the French kings, the great Francis and the warlike Henry, made former wars for towns their greatest wars. . . . For in these wars none of them intended anything more than to be revenged of supposed injuries by burning or winning of some frontier town by besieging. And after revenges mutually had to the satisfaction of their appetites, wherein neither party had any special advantage, they fell to truce and in the end with knots sometimes of intermarriages. And by these kinds of wars none of them did increase in greatness to be dangerous to their enemies. And in these kinds of war the kings of England had their interest of most part to expense of men and money and never to the loss of any small ground in England or Wales nor otherwise. But now the case is altered. The King of Spain maketh these mighty wars by the means only of his Indies, not purposely to burn a town in France or England but to conquer all France, all England, and Ireland.[1]

As Burghley argued, in the reign of Henry VIII the making of war had been treated casually, almost lightly. One could even choose his enemy—the French or the Emperor? The country could usually be cajoled or bullied into providing the money and the men. Miscalculations such as the failed alliance with the Duke of Bourbon or mismanaged campaigns like that of 1524 could be written off on the profit and loss account. And war could be ended as casually as it was begun, at the choice of the English government. But now that England was the defendant, the prospective victim of assault, new modes of thought were imperative. Freedom of choice, more particularly the control of initiative, now lost to the English, lay with an enemy formidably more powerful. Spain had at its disposal a discouragingly wide range of options—naval assault, invasion of France from Flanders, a landing in Brittany, aid to the Irish rebels. The English leaders, on their side, with only limited resources at their disposal, had few opportunities to take the initiative; for the most part their actions had to be reactive responses to immediate crises—the dispatch of an army to the Seine valley or the Breton coast, the reinforcement of the Irish garrison.

Even before the outbreak of war, these uncomfortable novelties fostered a new mode of thought about the conduct of English foreign relations. As old conceptions of dynastic advantage or personal prestige faded, they were replaced with quite other considerations. Roughly speaking, there emerged two schools of thought. One, led by Leicester, was ideological in character and took its origins from the great religious crisis of the century. These men saw England as the citadel and defender of true religion against God's enemies. Dutch Calvinists and French Huguenots were their natural allies and their program was one of intervention on behalf of their Continental co-religionists. Firm believers in a theory of universal Catholic conspiracy, they saw England's safety bound up with that of the whole Protestant world; hence Elizabeth must necessarily support

[1] John Strype, *Annals of the Reformation* (4 vols., Oxford, 1822–24) 4: 149–56.

Protestants wherever they were in danger from the aggressive designs of the Papal-Spanish alliance.

Against this program stood the pragmatists, led by Burghley. They of course shared their opponents' assessment of the threat to the realm but their response was based on quite other considerations. Rejecting the Protestant universalism of the other faction, theirs was a narrowly insular point of view. Their thinking was firmly based on a calculation of English interests. In their eyes the prime consideration was the poverty of English military and financial resources. From these basic propositions they argued for warily cautious measures, diplomatic not military in nature, rejecting any move that risked open confrontation. Any links established with a foreign power must be based on their contribution to English safety rather than their consequences for the general Protestant cause. Up to 1585 these conceptions prevailed in the shaping of English policy. In 1577 the Queen deliberately eschewed open alliance with the States General and in the following years opted for the strategy of the Anjou marriage, hoping by this move to consolidate a diplomatic front strong enough to persuade Philip II to agree to a compromise with his Low Countries subjects.

This policy failed and in 1585 the success of Parma's campaigns forced the Queen to give open assistance to the Dutch rebels. The pragmatists, however reluctantly, accepted alliance with the States, although the Queen and Burghley, by their negotiations with Parma, still struggled for an accommodation. Only the arrival of the Armada in the Channel finally destroyed their hopes.

The two factions now adopted views of war strategy consistent with their prewar positions. The activists—the hawks—pressed for direct assault on Spain's own territories. But they visualized more than a mere repulse of Spanish ambitions. They projected the triumphalist vision of a victory in which the Queen was called to a new role as the foundress of an English dominion both European and oceanic in scope. Long after the Queen's death, Raleigh nostalgically recalled their dreams: "And if the late Queen would have believed her men of war, as she did her scribes, we had in her time beaten that great empire to pieces and made their kings kings of figs and oranges as in old times. But Her Majesty did all by half and by petty invasions taught the Spaniards how to defend himself to see his own weakness which till we taught him was hardly known to himself."[2]

In 1589 their disappointments lay in the future; the issue between them and their pragmatist opponents was still an open one. The latter, now reluctantly committed to the wars, maintained a minimalist position. Victory in their definition was simply the restoration of the European *status quo ante*, not a leap into a new English greatness. In the early 1580's they had tried to persuade the French to alliance by a fully developed balance of power analysis. Spain, it was urged, now threatened to become more powerful than any coalition that could be organized against her. The mission to Paris failed but the pragmatists clung to their conviction that there could not be a satisfactory peace until a continental balance was restored. The collapse of France into civil war dimmed this hope but not their fixed belief that English efforts should not be directed to direct assaults on Spanish power but should make use of those indirect means that would help set the French Humpty-Dumpty in place again, an effective counterweight to Spain. As for the Low Countries, they looked to a return to the "Burgundian" past in which local autonomy would subsist under the umbrella of a Spanish presence strong enough to deter French expansionism. Currently this position obviously involved continued support of the Dutch. In France it meant prodding Henry III into resistance to the Guise and collaboration with Navarre. After his death it meant assistance to the struggling Henry IV. In each case English aid was to be measured out to the allies in just such economical proportions as would insure the continued momentum of their resistance. Such a policy was in the pragmatists' eyes the only reasonable utilization of England's all-too-scanty resources. To risk them in doubtful enterprises against Spain's homeland or her overseas possessions was a recipe for at least frustration and probably disaster.

Yet however much the two factions differed in their conceptions of strategy, they shared a new perception of English foreign policy that left behind the dynastic world of the past. The acute pressure under which England labored forced them to cast their thought in terms of larger interests, of the preservaion of English independence and of the Elizabethan regime, secular and religious. That

[2] Edward Edwards, *The Life of Sir Walter Raleigh*, etc. (2 vols., London, 1868) 2: 273.

new perception reveals itself clearly although un-self-consciously in the terminology that had imperceptibly crept into official correspondence, the recurrent phrase "the Queen and the state." In this perceived distinction between the person of the sovereign and the *res publica* one sees English statesmen, like their Continental counterparts, going through the metamorphosis from personal and dynastic monarchy to the monarchical state.

There was in the comparison with their Continental confreres a paradox. The English ministers, servants to an irenic princess who eschewed the conventional princely ambitions of martial glory and expanded power and who was indifferent to the demands of dynasty, had a freedom to shape their lines of action in ways that changed the very character of statecraft, shifting its horizons to a broader perspective and altering the ingredients that entered into the formation of what can now begin to be called state policy. Too often the Continental ministers found themselves bound by the personal, dynastic, or ideological ambitions of their royal masters. Too often the bellicose pursuit of reputation would oust calmer considerations of interest and constrain them to courses of action that advantaged their sovereigns but at a high cost to their subjects' welfare.[3]

Yet if the English had greater freedom in policy-making, they lacked in large part those means to execute it that were at the disposal of the Continental regimes. During the decades of almost continuous conflict between the Valois and the Habsburgs, both monarchies had developed the necessary institutions for the waging of long-term and large-scale warfare. They had built up a corps of professional soldiers hired for continuous service—a standing army. They had also built the fiscal and bureaucratic apparatus necessary to sustain their war machines. England, on the other hand, still relied, when she went to war, on throwing armies together from scratch, conscripting raw peasants from their farms, and staffing the officer corps with gentlemen amateurs. These forces were designed for short-term service in which there was neither opportunity nor effort to train men to professional standards. Logistical support for these forces had the same *ad hoc* character, making use of the county magistracies and seconding royal servants to temporary service as administrators. The great exception to this generali-

[3] See J. H. Eliot, *Richelieu and Olivarez* (Cambridge, 1984).

zation was of course the navy. England possessed a relatively small but highly competent naval establishment, provided with up-to-date warships and staffed by experienced seamen. A limited but adequate administrative staff provided for maintenance and supply.

The participation of individual Englishmen in foreign service—and particularly that of the captains who served with the Dutch before 1585—provided a small pool of experienced officers who formed the nucleus of a command echelon, but otherwise the English forces sent to the Low Countries were hastily assembled bodies of raw soldiery who had everything to learn about the art of warfare.

England's deficiencies might be offset if she could look for the assistance of more seasoned allies, but in fact England stood almost alone in the latter months of 1588. The Dutch, for the present, were as much dependents as allies, a drain on English resources rather than an augmentation to them. France, the traditional enemy of the Habsburgs, was paralyzed by internal disorder; worse still, her government was, for the moment at least, dominated by Elizabeth's old enemies, the Catholic house of Guise. Perforce England was committed to an all-out war in which the stakes were of the highest and to which in 1588 there seemed no end in sight. As in 1941, three and a half centuries later, the country could do little more than soldier on from day to day with no visible long-term prospect of victory.

Most immediately the problem was how to respond to the situation created by the dispersal of the Armada.[4] The Spanish fleet had been badly battered by the North Atlantic gales, but two-thirds of the ships had in fact returned to Spanish ports and actual losses among the ships that counted—the war galleons—had been minimal. As early as November 1588 rumors that Philip was preparing a new force began to reach England. To the modern observer with a knowledge of the Spanish situation denied to the Elizabethan Council, any early renewal of invasion seems unlikely, but to them, provided with sparse and uncertain intelligence, the probabilities appeared only too real. In any case it was imperative that what re-

---

[4] For a detailed account of English war and diplomacy from this point on to the end of 1594, see the indispensable work of R. B. Wernham, *After the Armada: Elizabethan England and the Struggle for Western Europe, 1588–1595* (Oxford, 1984) [hereafter cited as Wernham].

mained of Spain's naval power be destroyed before it could be refitted for another attempt.

The necessity for preventive action against the remnants of the Armada almost immediately raised larger questions of strategy. The evidence is indirect; the substance of the debate is found in an apologia for the Lisbon expedition, written by a serving officer, Anthony Wingfield, and printed in the aftermath of that unfortunate enterprise. It makes clear that there was wide difference of opinion as to the next step to be taken. The minimalists considered that the war would best be waged by a concentration on Dutch operations, on those "wars in the Low Countries which are in auxiliary manner maintained by Her Majesty." They argued that "it stood more with the safety of our estate to bend all our forces against the Duke of Parma."[5]

Their hawkish opponents among the maximalists agreed that the English effort in the Dutch provinces must be sustained. But they saw in the necessary action against the remaining Spanish ships an opportunity for a bolder and more far-reaching move than a mere cleaning-up operation. Wingfield put the case against an effort limited to the Low Countries, pointing out the difficulties of warfare in that theater. Even in the late 1570's, when the rebels controlled all seventeen provinces and had fielded an army of 20,000 to 30,000 men, they failed to hold their own. Now Parma ruled all but three of the provinces. The best that could be done in this watery country with its fortified towns was a siege a year, with costs equal to those of maintaining an army of 4,000 to 5,000 men in the field. And what had been gained? "Do not ours in these days live obscured in Flanders, either not having wherewithal to manage any war, or not putting on arms but to defend themselves when the enemy shall procure them?" It was of course essential that England support the provinces; their ports controlled the Narrow Seas. But all that could be hoped for was to preserve what the States now held. The expulsion of the Spanish from Flanders was out of the question. If Spain were to be beaten it must be in another quarter.[6]

English effort, so the argument continued, must be focused on Spain, not Flanders. Long ago Philip had "set down in his council that to recover the Low Countries he must bring war to England." The losses of the previous year would only spur him to a renewed

---

[5] See Wingfield.   [6] *Ibid.*, 307–8.

effort, for which he was richly provided. There was no choice for the English but the dispatch of a force not only to prevent the mobilization of another invasion fleet but also to strike a body blow at Spain on her own soil. A force of 20,000 could be landed in one of the many bays of the Spanish coast, establish itself there easily, and pay its costs by plunder. But if nothing so bold was to be risked at least a blockade that choked off the necessary supplies of Eastland grain should be mounted. If this did not bring Spain to her knees, it would in any case divert Spanish forces from the Low Countries. Admittedly such an effort might demand large sacrifice from the ordinary Englishman, but he must recollect the intensity and malignity of Spanish hostility towards his country. Wingfield called for financial contributions from JP's, clergy, lawyers, crown servants, and the country at large. He promised great rewards. The wealth of all Europe lay in two or three Spanish towns. Who would not exchange the fortunes to be found there for 40s. a year and double livery? This pamphlet, written as an apology for the Lisbon expedition, laid out a strategy of offense in its most ambitious form, but calmer voices were also urging the Queen to direct action against Spain on its own coasts.[7]

Those who urged an offensive against the Spanish dominions could point to recent experience in the first years of the war, before the coming of the Armada, as compelling precedents for naval action against Spain. Drake's two voyages in 1585 and 1587 had been the first wartime assaults on Spanish territory, but behind them lay the whole experience of English privateering since Hawkins's voyages in the 1560's and Drake's exploits in the following decades. In 1585, in retaliation for the seizure of the English grain ships in Spanish ports, Elizabeth had loosed Francis Drake against the Spaniards.[8] His fleet was paid for by a kind of joint stock venture in which the Queen contributed two of her ships and the other twenty—armed merchantmen—were financed by private "adventurers," shareholders in the enterprise. This provided a model for future organization of naval enterprises that would be repeatedly followed.

Drake's nominal purpose in 1585 had been to recover the detained grain ships (which had in fact mostly returned before he sailed). After a perfunctory stop at Vigo on the Spanish north coast,

[7] *Ibid.*, 346–50. [8] Corbett, *Spanish War*, 1–27; Monson 1: 121–34.

80

Drake had veered off to the Cape Verdes and thence to the West Indies, plundering, ransoming, and burning as he went. Both Santo Domingo and Cartagena had fallen victim to these blows. Obviously more than simple reprisal for the seized ships had been intended. A "plan of Campaign" ascribed to him at this time[9] proposed the seizure of Havana, to be held as a base, and there had been at least a perfunctory discussion of holding Cartagena after its capture.[10] This would have shifted the theater of war from the Old to the New World, but the problem of supplying and maintaining a base 4,000 miles from home would almost certainly have been beyond the resources of the Elizabethan government. However, the idea had been planted and would in due time germinate.

In the short term Spain had suffered physical damage in its colonies and severe psychological damage to its *amour propre*. The English government could hope that the revelation of Spanish naval and colonial vulnerability might deter Philip from his invasion plans. And if war were to come, this experience gave to the English leaders some clues as to a possible strategy of offense. But to other Englishmen the lesson taught by this venture was a different—and simpler—one. Although the returns of 1585–1586 were disappointing—only 15*s.* on the pound—the temptations of glittering prizes to be won, with minimum effort, by such hit-and-run raids were still compellingly powerful. That golden dream was fatefully to skew every scheme for naval offensives against the enemy for the next decade.

The next expedition, that commanded by Drake in 1587, displayed a variant strategy. Again the financial resources had been provided by a consortium of differing interests. The Queen had sent six of her own ships. London merchants had paid for eleven others, Drake for four, and Lord Admiral Howard for another two. This hybrid fleet had had a more directly military purpose than its predecessor. It was to raid Spanish shipping in its own waters (although not to land on the coasts). The royal instructions were to impeach the Spanish fleet, hinder its provisioning, and, if it sailed towards England or Ireland, to set upon it.[11] Drake had been originally authorized "to distress the ships within the havens themselves." A last-minute attempt by the Queen to revoke this clause

[9] Corbett, *Spanish War*, 69–74.   [10] Monson 1: 132–34.
[11] *Ibid.*, 142, citing Walsingham to Stafford, 21 April 1587.

failed because Drake sailed from Plymouth before the messenger reached him.[12] Nothing if not thorough in carrying out his instructions, Drake had raided Cadiz harbor and destroyed or carried off between twenty and thirty vessels. After scourging shipping along the Portuguese coast, he had sailed for the Azores, intercepted a caravel with a cargo worth £114,000 and returned to England in triumph. The Queen's share of the profits had been £40,000; the London merchants divided the same sum among them and Drake pocketed £17,000.[13] Public purposes had been served in the setback to Spanish naval preparations but, more important to the sponsors, private purses had been well filled. The two voyages had provided models of organization and possible strategies that might be adopted—or adapted—under the new circumstances of all-out war.

Even before the coming of the Armada the activists among Elizabeth's advisors had been pushing for something bolder still, a strategy of offense, aimed at the very heart of Spanish power. As long ago as 1579 John Hawkins had sketched out a general scheme for striking at Spain on the high seas and in the Indies.[14] At the end of 1587 and again in February 1588 Hawkins had spelled out in detail his proposed strategy.[15] In a letter to Walsingham he had insisted there was no choice except between "a dishonorable and uncertain peace" or "such a settled war as may bring forth and command a quiet peace." He had gone on to add, "Therefore in my mind our profit and best assurance is to seek our peace by a determined and resolute war." That war should be ordered "so that we have as little to do in foreign countries as may be but of mere necessity," a reference to the Low Countries. Specifically, what he had proposed was that six of the Queen's large ships should lie off the coast of Spain, attended by six small vessels, "which shall haunt the coast of Spain and the Islands and be a sufficient company to distress anything that goeth through the seas." Charges, amounting to £2,700 a month for 1,800 men, could be covered by prizes. Under

[12] *Ibid.*, 143.   [13] *Ibid.*, 150; *CSPD* 2 (1581–90): cciv, 8, 27–29, 46.
[14] James A. Williamson, *Sir John Hawkins, the Man and His Times* (London, 1969), 396–97.
[15] *State Papers Relating to the Defeat of the Spanish Armada, Anno 1588*, ed. J. K. Laughton, 2 vols., Navy Record Society 1, 2. London, 1894, 1: 58–62 [henceforth cited as *Defeat of the Armada*]; Williamson, *Hawkins*, 317–19; *CSPD* 2 (1581–90): ccvi, 61; ccviii, 47. He sent a copy of the letter to Burghley in July 1589.

these conditions the Spanish "fleet from the Indies and all places can have hard escaping; which if we might once strike, our peace were made with honor, safety and profit." Such a "lawful, open war" would win God's blessing and bring "a most honorable and quiet peace to the honor and glory of the church and to the honor of Her Majesty." The last point, an assault on the treasure fleet, had echoed the sentiment of another correspondent of the Secretary:[16] "Do not think to have any quietness with the King of Spain as long as his money comes out of the Indies. It is easily to be redressed." This proposition had soon become an article of faith among the activist party. Cut off the flow of silver across the Atlantic, which was the very lifeblood of Spanish might, and the giant would be brought to his knees.

Hawkins's advice was not taken in 1588, probably because the Queen thought it too costly.[17] The events of the summer temporarily made such measures irrelevant, but, once the Armada limped home, talk of them soon revived. Tempting as it was, there was a fateful risk in such a strategy, one which the Queen and her less sanguine councillors never forgot. If Spain's coasts were vulnerable to English naval attack, so were England's. In the summer of 1588 the fleets of each realm, outward bound, had nearly passed at sea and only the chances of the winds sent Drake's ships home in time to meet Medina Sidonia. To denude English coasts of a great part of their naval protection would be a risk too great to take.

It was this blend of experience and of theory that was now brought to bear on the immediate post-Armada situation. Even before the Spanish ships had reached home, proposals for retaliatory action were being mooted at the English court. These were the genesis of a counter-armada, no less powerful than its Spanish predecessor—and no more successful. This was the Portugal expedition of 1589, which sailed under instructions to destroy the remnants of the Armada, to enthrone the Portuguese pretender, Don Antonio, at Lisbon, and finally to intercept the plate fleet homebound from America. It was to fail in all three purposes.

It first appears in the record in a cryptic note, uncertainly attributed to July 1588, which refers to articles propounded by Drake and

---

[16] *Defeat of the Armada* 1: 264; *CSPD* 2 (1581–90): ccxii, 57.
[17] *Ibid.*, ccxii, 57.

Norris.[18] More certain evidence comes from September, with a detailed plan for action by Sir John Norris, the premier English soldier, veteran commander in the Low Countries and Ireland. He proposed to finance the expedition by private backing. A sum of £35,000 was to be raised by subscription; the Queen was to contribute £5,000.[19] Additional details followed shortly; 4,000 soldiers were to be obtained by drawing on the English forces in Holland. By mid-October matters were well advanced. Norris and Drake were commissioned to choose officers and levy troops for an assault on Spain that had several objectives in view, including burning the ships at Lisbon and Seville, taking the Portuguese capital, and seizing the Islands—the Azores. Don Antonio, the Portuguese pretender, was to be involved.[20] With some modifications this became the basis on which planning proceeded. A list of investors was drawn up, a treasurer appointed, and disbursement of money began. The Queen agreed to provide six ships; London and other ports added twenty more; the Crown also made available powder and munitions and authorized the levy of 6,000 men.[21] Norris went off to the Low Countries to secure the use of a large part of the English forces there. He returned at the end of December with large promises from the Dutch to release some 3,500 men for the forthcoming enterprise, but in the event this contingent sank to some 1,800. By the beginning of the new year 1589, orders had been sent out for levying soldiers in Essex and Hertfordshire, but they were not to be sent for embarkation until February. In January a pinnace was dispatched to reconnoiter the northern Spanish harbors.[22]

Through March and April preparations went ahead apace. Levies of men were made and ships and men assembled at Plymouth. Some 19,000 soldiers and 4,000 sailors had been assembled. Adverse winds had made for a long and expensive delay, and extra supplies had to be begged from the Queen. It was not until 17 or 18 April that the expedition set sail.[23]

[18] *Ibid.*, ccxvi, 59; see also a letter to the King of Morocco dated in October, referring to an intended expedition, in E. M. Tenison, *Elizabethan England* (10 vols., Leamington, England, 1932–51) 8: 79.

[19] *CSPD* 2 (1581–90): ccxvi, 32.

[20] *Ibid.*, ccxvi, 33; ccxvii, 14, 15; Tenison 8: 9.

[21] *CSPD* 2 (1581–90): ccxxii, 88; ccxvii, 25, 25I, 55, 56, 57, 79; ccxxiii, 64I.

[22] *Ibid.*, ccxix, 23, 37, 45, 47, 54; ccxxii, 5, 6, 79; Wernham, 74.

[23] *Ibid.*, 75, 107; *CSPD* 2 (1581–90): ccxxiii, 24, 59, 75, 70, 71, 72, 73, 91.

What was the intended purpose of these wide-ranging preparations? What was the blow to be struck by this imposing array of ships and men? The first commission issued to Norris and Drake in October spoke of levies "for service to invade and destroy forces of the invaders" of the past summer. Another document, probably to be dated in October, estimates stores and provisions for "the enterprise of Portugal," and the same terminology is used in further papers in February 1589.[24]

The full scope and purpose of the enterprise emerges in the draft instruction dated 23 February 1589. Much interlined and amended, it is certainly an early draft and may have been altered somewhat in later (no longer extant) versions. Two primary purposes are set out—to distress the King of Spain's ships and obtain possession of some of the Azores. Towards the accomplishment of the first the commanders were ordered to "inquire in your way towards the coast of Spain what ships there are of importance in any of the ports, either of Guipuzcoa, of Biscay, or Galicia," which they were to destroy. The English had known since September that the bulk of the Armada ships were at Santander and San Sebastian.[25] They were also to destroy shipping in the Tagus.[26]

The instructions then veer off in a new direction, adding a third and quite different goal for the expedition. The commanders were to take with them Don Antonio, the Portuguese pretender, and if, on inquiry, "the people stand so affected to him as he pretendeth" they were to make a descent upon Portugal in order to place Antonio on the throne. These instructions (or an amended version of later date) were to be the basis for much angry recrimination later in the expedition, and among historians since. Several points require consideration. First, did the initiative for the enterprise come from the two commanders, Drake and Norris? It was they who propounded articles for Burghley's consideration; in another document the whole plan is ascribed to Sir John Norris. It is unlikely that these two men acted solely on their own initiative. Although both were well connected in Council and court, neither had the standing to strike out on his own in so momentous a matter. Who their backers were we cannot say with any precision; the evidence does not survive. That Walsingham was one is a fair guess, given

[24] *Ibid.*, ccxvii, 15; ccxxii, 61, 62, 65, 66.   [25] Wernham, 96.
[26] *CSPD* 2 (1581–90): ccxxii, 89; also Tenison 8: 89.

the activist bent of his whole policy. He certainly figures in the correspondence. His son-in-law to be, the Earl of Essex, was not yet a Privy Councillor, but all the influence of the rising favorite was thrown into backing the enterprise. Burghley's role was obviously a key one; but whatever reservations he may have had, it was difficult to resist a proposal for offensive action, especially as reports of new concentrations of Spanish naval forces began to trickle in. A sour note was struck by Willoughby, the English general in the Low Countries, who dismissed the "windy words" of those who "make the earth, heavens, crown and kingdoms to fall down before him as some do, glorying with Artaxeres over a few ships and not advising with Socrates upon a sound counsel." But his words went unheard. Now that England was fully at war and under threat of a renewed invasion, the more adventurous military commanders acquired a new weight in affairs. No longer adventurers, angling for royal support of some ambitious gamble, they were now professionals whose expertise was urgently in demand.[27]

Exactly what transpired behind the scenes in the winter of 1588–1589 we cannot know; the final decision of course was the Queen's. Some clue to her irritable uncertainty surfaces in a complaint from Burghley to Walsingham in November regarding the intolerable injustice that "all irresolution and lucks" were thrown on the two of them in "all her speeches." A shadowy hint of disagreements comes from a Spanish informant who wrote the Spanish ambassador Mendoza in Paris that there was a rift within the Council and court that lined up Raleigh and Lord Admiral Howard as opponents of the voyage, which was supported by Burghley, Walsingham, Hatton, and (outside the Council) Essex, Norris, and Drake. Certainly Raleigh and Howard are conspicuous by their absence from this enterprise. In the end we must rely on the instructions themselves for clues to interpret the considerations that entered into the making of them.

The directive to destroy the Spanish warships is self-explanatory. Common sense dictated such an action. If all or a substantial part of the remaining war galleons of Spain could be destroyed, her capacity to launch another invasion would be for the time being

---

[27] Monson 1: 195; CSPD 2 (1581–90): ccxvi, 32, 33, 59; *An Apologie of the Earle of Essex . . . Anno 1598* (London, 1603), A4; Georgina Bertie, *Five Generations of a Loyal Family* (London, 1845), 240–43.

wholly destroyed, and an interval of several years would be required to put together another such fleet. This was a strategy on which all could agree whatever their larger strategic views.

The second and third objectives that the Queen set for her commanders represent the goals of the maximalist party, but they also reveal variant strains of opinion among the advocates of a strategy of offense. The Portuguese card was one the Queen had had in her hand for a decade, since the time when the Pretender first fled abroad. She had refused to back Drake in a scheme for establishing Don Antonio in the Azores in 1581 and had declined to join with the French in the Strozzi expedition in the next year. Much English privateering had flourished under the nominal flag of Portugal, and Hawkins had proposed a formal agreement with the pretender for a systematic harassment of Spanish shipping and of the Atlantic islands. Clearly the possibility of utilizing Don Antonio had played a part in the thinking of English naval figures for a decade. What was now proposed took a much grander form. A sizable English fleet and an army were to be used to place him on his ancestral throne. This was a much more far-reaching objective than the destruction of the remaining Spanish ships. If Portugal could be wrested from Spanish control, a substantial part of Philip's naval power would be wiped out; England would acquire an ally on the very doorstep of Spain; and, with Portuguese bases in both the homeland and the Atlantic islands, English naval power could be used to cut the lifeline between the Peruvian silver mines and Spain. The English activists, convinced that Spanish finance depended wholly on these supplies, envisaged not merely a check to Spanish power, but its effective abasement.[28]

The third objective of this enterprise was, of course, related to but separable from the second. The occupation of one or more of the Azores, with or without Portuguese cooperation, would provide the necessary base for intercepting Spanish commerce from both the West and East Indies.

One additional feature of the instructions requires notice. The whole enterprise was to be run, like its predecessors of 1585 and 1587, as a semiprivate joint-stock adventure with most of the capital

[28] Julian S. Corbett, *Drake and the Tudor Navy*, etc. (2 vols., London, 1898) 1: 346–55; *CSPD* 2 (1581–90): cciii, 56; cciv, 53; BL, Cotton Mss., Vespasian C viii, fol. 12.

coming from private sources. The Queen would contribute a few royal warships and a proportion of the military supplies needed, but the main burden of cost was to be borne by the subscribers, who would, so they hoped, recoup their investment in prizes and booty. The restored King of Portugal was also to pay heavily for the English assistance in regaining his throne.[29]

The fleet numbered some eighty-three English and sixty Dutch flyboats. Over 23,000 men, of whom perhaps 19,000 were soldiers, were embarked.[30] Hence the scale of operation was not very much smaller than that of the Spaniard in the previous year. What is to be made of this ambitious, multipurpose enterprise? In many respects it displayed many of the same flaws that had cursed the enemy's great effort in 1588. Like the Spanish enterprise it jostled together an ill-assorted amalgam of disparate—even contradictory—strategies. Almost certainly the instructions reflected a compromise among the competing interests of the various participants.

The first and most important interest was that of the Queen. To her the prime goal was to destroy what was left of the Armada and thus secure her own coasts against the threat of invasion. But there were two matters to be considered. Such an expedition would be costly, too costly for the ill-furnished royal purse.[31] Second, the Queen was loath to risk any more of her precious warships than necessary. These problems were at least in part resolved by the form that the enterprise took. The financial burden was lightened by shifting some of it to the shoulders of the investors, a strategy that in turn meant that the bulk of the fleet would consist of armed merchantmen paid for out of their contributions. Only six Queen's ships would be involved. But there was of course a *quid pro quo*. If the voyage were to make a profit for the backers, conquest in Por-

---

[29] *CSPD* 2 (1581–90): ccxxii, 99; for the contract with Antonio, see Tenison 8: 7–8, dated 23 October 1588. Antonio was to pay three months' wages beginning six days after the landing. He asked to have the right to retain an English force to guard his position.

[30] *CSPD* 2 (1581–90): ccxxiii, 60, 75; see Monson 1: 186 for other estimates of numbers.

[31] A double subsidy had just been levied and a Privy Seal loan raised, so it would be awkward to ask for money; yet even with these sums in hand there was still a substantial debt. Indeed, the Queen was for the first time since 1574 seeking to negotiate a foreign loan. See R. B. Outhwaite, "The Trials of Foreign Borrowing: The English Crown and the Antwerp Money Market in the Mid-Sixteenth Century," *Economic History Review*, 2nd ser. 19 (1966): 288–305.

tugal and the Azores must be included in its aims. This consideration fundamentally altered its character and made the accomplishment of its goals highly problematical if not impossible.

What these instructions reflect is a government divided against itself, torn by conflicting counsels and divergent goals. The ramshackle scheme that was patched together was shaped as much by the straitened circumstances of the Crown and the desire to conciliate domestic factions as by the needs of the military situation. It contained something for everyone—the Queen, her more cautious and defense-minded advisors, the various strands of offense-minded strategists, and the investors whose funds were to float the whole enterprise. That the commanders could carry out all or even a part of these commands was beyond the bounds of reasonable probability. And that probability, such as it was, was further diminished even before the fleet sailed. Only a stroke of good fortune enabled the commanders to find adequate transport for their troops. A fleet of sixty Dutch flyboats, unlucky enough to be passing through the Straits of Dover at the strategic moment, was commandeered. (Twenty-five of them with 3,000 men on board deserted the fleet a few days out of Plymouth.[32]) The Queen reneged on her promise of artillery.[33] Cavalry, once planned for, did not materialize; victuals were in uncertain supply; and there were the usual delays imposed by adverse winds.

The two leaders who shared the command in 1589 were good examples of the new, self-trained professionals on whom the Queen had to rely for the conduct of her wars. Drake had learned his trade as a private adventurer—less politely, as a pirate. Not until 1585 did he sail as the Queen's admiral in a voyage intended to accomplish a public goal (albeit one privately financed). In that year and in 1587 he carried out what were in effect large-scale hit-and-run raids, which were merely grander versions of his earlier piratical exploits. Such habits were not easily broken, and, even in the heat of the Armada pursuit, Drake had turned aside to chase down a prize. How he would perform in the new kind of task now assigned him remained to be seen.

The instructions he was given in 1589 were far more explicit than in either 1585 or 1587, the task to be accomplished measurably

[32] CSPD 2 (1581–90): ccxxiv, 56. See Monson 1: 200; Wingfield 4: 310.
[33] *CSPD* 2 (1581–90): ccxxiv, 22.

greater, but his freedom of action, on paper at least, much more limited. These constraints cannot have been wholly congenial to the great improvisor, used to absolute control of his movements once he left the English shores. Moreover, he now commanded a much larger force than ever before and had to share decision-making with an equal, a soldier no less independent in temper than the admiral.

Norris too had mastered his trade by an apprenticeship outside England, under Coligny in France, Hohenlohe in Holland, and the first Earl of Essex in Ireland.[34] Seasoned by a term as president of the deeply troubled province of Munster, Norris was sent over in 1585 as the commander *pro tem* of the expeditionary force in the Low Countries. He had not taken well to subordinate service under Leicester and was somewhat dubiously regarded by Walsingham.[35] But he was clearly the most experienced of English captains and the one of greatest reputation. He had not enjoyed the unlimited freedoms that the high seas afforded his naval colleague, but he had a high opinion of his own professional skill and judgment, and small regard for the civilian councillors' views on military matters.

Contemporary accounts give us a reasonably clear knowledge of the course of events, but they are not sufficient to elucidate the conduct of the principal actors. Their management of the enterprise led contemporaries to angry recrimination and apologetic justification even before the expedition had returned to England. Historians have continued the debate without coming to settled conclusions.

The expedition did not fare well from the beginning. As we have seen, a persistently contrary wind kept the fleet at Plymouth for over six weeks and the commanders were driven to beg the Queen for an additional month of victual. They finally sailed on April 17 or 18, made a swift crossing, and appeared before the northern Spanish port of Corunna on the twenty-fourth of that month. A successful landing there was followed by the capture and destruction of the lower town and victory over local forces sent against them. However, lacking the artillery once promised by the Queen, they failed to take the fortified upper town. They then sailed to the

---

[34] Wingfield 4: 311–12.
[35] For Walsingham's views of Norris, see W. T. MacCaffrey, *Queen Elizabeth and the Making of Policy, 1572–1588* (Princeton, 1981), 370.

Portuguese coast and landed a force north of Lisbon, which marched on the capital while Drake lay off the mouth of the Tagus. Although the soldiers reached the barricaded gates of Lisbon almost without resistance, the rising of the Portuguese promised by Don Antonio failed utterly to occur. The Spanish, forewarned by Drake's own actions, had made ample preparations for defense and for suppressing any stirring by Portuguese supporters of Don Antonio. Drake lingered with his ships at the river mouth, unwilling to attempt forcing a passage up to the city. Norris, lacking all the means for a siege, had no alternative but to retreat and re-embark. Disciplining troops who were mostly raw conscripts fresh from the shires had proved difficult. At Corunna they were drunk on the local wine, and the same problem reoccurred on the march on Lisbon. Disease, both afloat and ashore, took a terrible toll. Of the 12,000 or so available at Corunna, only 8,500 were left by the time Norris's retreat from Lisbon reached the coast at Cascais, and of these 2,800 were said to be too sick for service. In the next landing, at Vigo on the Spanish Atlantic coast, no more than 2,000 effectives remained. Letters from home brought refusal of the demand for more troops and for artillery.[36] Gales that drove the fleet northward frustrated a sailing for the Azores. Arriving off Vigo, they landed and burned the town.

Drake then made the decision to divide the fleet: he would take twenty ships to the Azores; the rest would return home under Norris. In fact, once they separated, Drake's ships were scattered by another gale; the expedition was abandoned and they made for home. Drake reached Plymouth before Norris. The sole booty of the voyage was some sixty Hanseatic hulks, laden with grain and naval stores, which Drake seized as they approached the Tagus. All his ships returned, but the loss of life, chiefly through disease, was appalling. Almost certainly 8,000 were dead, perhaps as many as 11,000. On one ship, out of 300, there were 114 dead and only 8 able to work the ship when she approached Plymouth.[37]

Almost from the beginning the behavior of the commanders reflected the confusions inherent in their instructions and excited the angry disapprobation of the Queen. Her letters of rebuke began

[36] *CSPD* 2 (1581–90): ccxxiii, 59, 60, 70, 71, 72, 73, 84; ccxxiv, 22, 53; Monson 1: 202–17; Wingfield 4: 306–54; Wernham, 125.

[37] Wingfield 4: 314; *CSPD* 5 (1598–1601): cclxvii, 65; 2 (1581–90): ccxxv, 27; Sir Walter Raleigh, *Works* (8 vols., Oxford, 1829) 8: 480; Wernham, 127.

with the news of the first exploit, the operation at Corunna, but the full gravamen of her disapproval appears in the set of articles to which the commanders were ordered to answer in the fall of 1589. Two central charges were levelled against them. The first dealt with their action at Corunna. Why, the Queen demanded, had they gone to Corunna, where there were few Spanish ships, instead of Santander, where some sixty lay? Her instructions had strictly ordered them to give first priority to destroying Philip's remaining ships. Their answers were evasive. The Queen accused them of putting profit before service. She was probably nearer the mark when she warned them against "[be]haviour of vainglory which obfuscates the eyes of judgment."[38]

What precisely led Drake to his decision at Corunna is not in the record, but a reasonable guess can be made. For Drake and Norris the main goal was always Lisbon. It is noteworthy that, when Essex, in direct defiance of royal command, stole off from England (ahead of the fleet and accompanied by Roger Williams), he made straight for the Portuguese coast. It is highly likely that he participated with the collusion of the commanders. Certainly all his influence would be thrown in favor of the Portuguese venture. That influence would be all the greater when the fleet was far from the reach of royal intervention.[39] It was at Lisbon that fame and fortune could be won. The capture of the Portuguese capital would be a victory far outshining the admiral's exploits at San Domingo, Cartagena, or Cadiz. Its riches were bound to be prodigious, and there was the promise of substantial compensation from the restored Don Antonio. But they could not ignore the royal instructions; there had to be some action against the Spanish ships. Corunna lay most conveniently on the route to Lisbon and was a major port for Spanish naval ventures. It had been reported before their departure that there were two hundred ships at Corunna and neighboring ports. These were tempting prey, but in addition such an attack would be

---

[38] *CSPD* 2 (1581–90): ccxxiv, 50, 53; ccxxvi, 4, 32, 35; ccxxviii, 35; *Calendar of the State Papers and Manuscripts, Relating to English Affairs, Existing in the Archives and Collections of Venice, and in Other Libraries of Northern Italy* 8 (1581–91): 431 (13 March 1589); Monson 1: 197–200; Lodge 2: 396. Others blamed the failure of the expedition on the failure to hold a council of war; others yet alleged that the men were drunk at Corunna and the delays there gave the enemy time to prepare (SP 12/238/45; 225/42).

[39] Wernham, 100–5.

a token fulfillment of their obligations to the Queen to wipe out Spanish ships.[40]

When they were at Corunna, the commanders had written, taking note of other ships at Santander but excusing themselves from going there on the grounds that there was no safe harbor for disembarkation. and then rather contradictorily promising to assault Santander on their return. However, after their experience at Corunna they insisted that the ships in the other ports could not be destroyed without first taking the towns in whose harbors they sheltered. For this they had to have cannon and more soldiers. They wanted twenty companies from the Low Countries and necessary supplies to be sent out to meet them off the Iberian coast on their return. They were in effect telling the Queen they could not carry out the first part of their mission with the means she had provided. These demands were summarily refused in a letter that reached them when they were about to leave Lisbon.[41]

The letter from the commanders had also asserted that the main Spanish preparations were at Lisbon. They had felt free now to seek out their main objective by an assault on the Portuguese capital, although they had, of course, fully alerted the Spanish authorities to their presence on the coast. Their critics at home were to fault them for having landed without any assurance of a Portuguese rising. Their riposte was that they could not destroy the shipping in the Tagus without attacking from land first and that they could only discover the strength of the Portuguese by landing their forces.[42] Certainly the instructions of February were fuzzy to a degree. They were told, "you are very carefully and substantially to inform yourselves before you proceed to attempt anything to this purpose whether the people stand so affected towards him as he pretendeth" and what Spanish forces were on hand. So far as we know, no preliminary attempts had been made to make contact with Don Antonio's putative supporters before the fleet sailed; it is hard to see how they could have tested this support without first landing.

The Queen's cautious and tentative instructions no doubt reflected her own skepticism about the whole Portuguese enterprise and her basic reluctance to back it. The limitations that she imposed

[40] *CSPD* 2 (1581–90): ccxxiii, 64.   [41] *Ibid*., ccxxiv, 53; Wernham, 112–13.
[42] Monson 1: 207; *CSPD* 2 (1581–90): ccxxvii, 35.

were meant to inhibit her commanders from acting at all except under no-risk conditions. Here the royal grasp of tactical realities failed altogether. Any commander would have found it difficult to act upon such instructions, but these men were committed in advance to forceful action and determined to proceed at all costs. The gulf between carefully conditioned royal intentions and the commanders' belligerent resolve was a gaping one.

On another tack Drake's critics assailed him for his failure to enter the Tagus as he had promised Norris when the latter began his march on the capital. The admiral's answer that his men were sick is hard to square with other evidence.[43] He would certainly have had to risk bombardment from the castle guarding the northern shore of the river had he attempted to force his way into Lisbon harbor. Whether such an action would nevertheless have been feasible is hard to judge now; certainly Drake seemed to show less than his accustomed flair and dash. Roger Williams afterwards asserted, "when we arrived, had our navy entered, we would have entered the towns."[44] Drake may have been chary of risking the Queen's precious ships by taking them under the shore batteries. Whatever the reason he made no move. There may have been a second failure of decision when he gave, but then reversed, the order to sail for the Azores. But at the root of the failure was Portuguese apathy and a shrewdly conceived Spanish strategy of resistance. Whatever blame may be attached to the commanders' personal shortcomings during the campaign, the modern observer can only be struck by the lack of foresight or planning and even more by the unrealistic goals that were set.

The commanders and their apologists tried to make the best of it, but the harsh facts were all too apparent. None of the three purposes of the voyage had been attained. The Spanish fleet remained unharmed in the northern harbors, Don Antonio was still a homeless refugee, and the voyage to the Azores had never taken place. Perhaps half the Englishmen who had sailed from Plymouth in April were dead by July. Even the Eastland hulks brought back as prizes had to be handed back to their Hanseatic owners. Some £100,000 had been laid out for the expedition with nil return.[45]

---

[43] Monson 1: 217–23, but see also Lodge 2: 406–8.

[44] Roger Williams, *The Works of Roger Williams*, ed. J. X. Evans (Oxford, 1972), 13.

[45] Wernham, 140, 129.

The failure of this ambitious enterprise illustrates in too vivid detail the tissue of constraints and contradictions that enmeshed the Elizabethan government's efforts to wage war. First of all there was the failure to establish coherent goals. Initial agreement on the need to eliminate the remnants of the Armada had soon dissolved into muddled confusion. Three disparate goals were set forth, any one of which would by itself have exhausted most of the available force at England's disposal.

Moreover, Elizabeth's parsimony in these matters went far towards cancelling out her own strategic intentions. A contemporary seaman, commenting on the voyage, roundly declared that anyone who undertook "so great an enterprise without a prince's purse shall be deceived." The two commanders should never have attempted "so great a charge with so little means."[46]

The Queen's inability to find money of her own to float the enterprise, coupled with her unwillingness to risk any large number of her own warships, necessarily altered its character. The private adventurers who financed the armed merchantmen would not risk their ships without hope of compensation in prizes and plunder. For them the seizure of Lisbon was clearly the primary objective of the whole expedition. In this diversion from the Queen's main purposes they had the hearty cooperation of the commanders themselves. The paper restrictions that Elizabeth laid on her commanders were unlikely to restrain them from a gamble that promised both fame and fortune. In the best of all possible worlds the Queen could have wished for commanders with more experience in large-scale operations, more amenable to the disciplines of an ordered command system and more sensitive to the larger strategic goals of the war. But she could only take what the patchy and amateurish English military experience of the past few years provided her. These men, panting for the chance for action, gave less than half-hearted attention to obeying the Queen's directions to attack the Armada ships. The futile assault on Corunna wasted their resources and forewarned the enemy. Their own tactical errors at Lisbon completed the disaster.

The third mission of the voyage, whose realization would have taken them to the Azores, was only halfheartedly attempted. It's undertaking was quite unrealistic without a base at Lisbon, which

[46] Monson 1: 177.

could have provided for revictualling and refitting. Even had the winds been favorable, with a fleet that had already been at sea for nearly three months and was riddled with disease, there was little chance of a serious assault. This became painfully evident when it reached Plymouth. The Queen's lingering hope that the fleet could put to sea again was speedily proved vain.

The fleet's arrival in England coincided almost to the moment with the assassination of Henry III, which altered the whole character of England's war plans overnight. Even apart from the new French commitment, however, the Queen was probably as disillusioned by this disastrous essay in the offensive as she had been in 1563 after the loss of Le Havre. It would be six years before the party favoring a major offensive against the Spanish on their own soil would have a second inning—and under much changed circumstances.

CHAPTER 5

WAR ON THE HIGH SEAS AND IN

THE INDIES, 1589-1595

THE LACK of success of the Lisbon expedition discredited the strategy of direct assault, and its principal exponent, Drake, was in disfavor for the next half-dozen years, relegated to routine defense tasks. Norris returned to his duties in the Low Countries until he took command of the English force in Brittany. At the same time events elsewhere compelled the Queen to divert her attention and her resources to land campaigns rather than naval enterprises. The assassination of Henry III at the end of July 1589 and the hotly disputed succession of Henry of Bourbon forced her willy-nilly to give him the aid in men and money that he so urgently demanded. For the next five years the English military presence in France would consume a great proportion of their war effort.

Nevertheless, during these years naval action against Spanish shipping continued, albeit as a sideshow compared to the English efforts on the Continent. Royal participation was very limited; the bulk of the ships and money involved came from private sources. The objective of these enterprises was once again the interception of either the plate fleet or the great East Indian carracks. With one significant exception—the capture of the East Indian *Madre di Dios* in 1592—English hopes were disappointed. But apart from these major, semipublic voyages the war had loosed a whole swarm of individual venturers who relentlessly hunted down their Spanish prey wherever they could find it. Their largely unchronicled voyages inflicted a cumulative damage on the Spanish economy considerably greater than the more publicized activities of the royally sponsored ventures.

The potential profits were immensely attractive to the private entrepreneur, and these years saw the explosion of privateering into a major economic activity.[1] It had, of course, begun as outright piracy in the Caribbean in the 1570's. Drake is only the most famous of the names associated with these exploits. After 1585 letters of reprisal issued by the Crown to merchants who suffered loss legitimized such activity. As the war spread the issuance of such letters became a mere formality, which many did not even trouble to fulfill.

By 1593 the Venetian ambassador at Madrid could write of fifty English private ships operating in Spanish waters. A seventeenth-century English writer claimed there were no fewer than 200 on the enemy's coast at any one time. Recent scholarship has largely confirmed these boasts. At least 236 ships can be identified as operating in Spanish waters in Europe or the New World in the years 1589–91; in 1598 the total number for that year was no fewer than 86.[2]

The seas were not left solely to the profit-seeking initiatives of private venturers. In every year from 1589 through 1594 naval expeditions backed by the Crown and the inner circle of court magnates were launched against the enemy. Virtually all of them combined royal and private resources in ships and money, as in 1585, 1587, and 1589. And, as in these earlier years, there was a similar mingling of motives among the participants. Two of these voyages, those in 1590 and 1591, were primarily royal enterprises in which strategic war aims were given priority (although they were financed as far as possible by the taking of prizes). The others were much more straightforwardly entrepreneurial operations with profit as their main goal. Obviously damage would be inflicted on the Spanish war effort by the loss of shipping, but the great hope of their backers was, if not the capture of a part of the West Indian treasure fleet or an East Indian carrack, at least a profitable haul of less exotic cargoes and workaday ships.

---

[1] See Theodore K. Rabb, *Enterprise and Empire* (Cambridge, Mass., 1967); Kenneth R. Andrews, *Elizabethan Privateering* (Cambridge, 1964).

[2] *CSPVen* 9 (1592–1603): 67 (17 April 1593); Andrews, *Privateering*, 4, quoting John Hagthorpe; see also Kenneth R. Andrews, *English Privateering Voyages to the West Indies*, Hakluyt Soc., 2nd ser. 111 (1959), introduction.

The pattern of the royally backed expeditions was one followed on each successive occasion. The squadrons sailed out to the Azores to wait for ships arriving from either the East or the West Indies, hoping both to serve public strategic purposes and to fill private pockets with spoil. The record of success was a checkered one. In 1589 the great effort at Lisbon was paralleled by two smaller enterprises. In June the Earl of Cumberland, a gentleman amateur, with two unsuccessful ventures behind him, sailed with one royal ship and three private vessels. (Others joined him from time to time.) After a summer of cruising in the Azores, burning and plundering the island towns, he missed the flota, but the thirteen prizes he picked up left him—even after the shipwreck of the richest—with enough to discharge his debts.[3] Sir Martin Frobisher, sailing in September with a fleet of four Queen's ships, captured four prizes, losing two by shipwreck, but covering the Queen's costs with a few thousand pounds to spare.[4]

In 1590 and 1591 a serious effort seems to have been made to implement the strategy that John Hawkins had been advocating for years—to lay hands on the American plate fleet and so disrupt Spanish overseas commerce. Hawkins had been conspicuously absent from the 1589 expedition and may have disapproved of it. The third objective laid out in the instructions to Drake and Norris may have been a nod in his direction. In any case, in the aftermath of the Lisbon fiasco Hawkins seems to have gotten a hearing for his scheme. Certainly as early as December 1589 plans to send him out with six ships were being made. In February the number was apparently increased to thirteen. Then on the 23rd of that month, when all was ready, the Privy Council halted their departure because of sudden fears of invasion, triggered by Philip's move to send a force to assist the Catholic Leaguers in Brittany. As late as 24 April there were reports of Spanish ships off Wales, and orders for an alert were sent to the West Country. Hawkins was bitterly disappointed at this check to his ambitions. "Now being out of hope

[3] Andrews, *Privateering*, 72; Monson 1: 226–37; Edward Wright, "The Voiage of the Right Honorable George Erle of Cumberland to the Azores," in Richard Hakluyt, *The Principal Navigations, Voyages, Traffiques of Discoveries of the English Nation*, etc., ed. Walter Raleigh. (10 vols., London and New York, 1927) 4: 355–80; G. C. Williamson, *The Third Earl of Cumberland* (London, 1920), 70–83.

[4] Monson 1: 237–39; see also Frank F. Jones, *The Life of Martin Frobisher*, etc. (London, 1878).

that ever I shall perform any royal thing, I do put on a mean mind."[5]

In the upshot the fleet was divided, with six ships assigned to Hawkins and seven to Frobisher. In June the Privy Council warned the admirals that a Spanish fleet had sailed and told them that they were to guard the English Channel until the end of the month in case the fleet was destined for Brittany. Later they were released to go to sea—Hawkins to cruise off the Spanish coast and return home disconsolate in October, having little or nothing to show for his efforts, and Frobisher, his supplies exhausted, to return home a month before Hawkins. These expeditions had cost over £17,000 and had brought little, if anything, in the way of prizes. They had, of course, missed both the plate ships and the carracks. The first delay had cancelled out any possibility of intercepting the delayed 1589 flota, which reached Spain in March. A second fleet of treasure ships eluded Frobisher in August. The priorities of defense against the apparent threat of invasion had taken precedence over the strategy of offense. The circumstances displayed once again the contradictions in action that England's limited resources imposed on her policy.[6]

The disappointments of 1590 did not discourage another effort in 1591. This operation, quite grandly conceived in its initial form, did envisage the employment of a large part of the royal navy and was the most considerable effort undertaken between 1589 and 1595. However, there was a significant shift in leadership. Two men of a younger generation now took charge—Sir Walter Raleigh and Lord Thomas Howard, in conjunction with Lord Admiral Howard. Raleigh, then at the peak of his influence with the Queen, had not of course commanded a fleet and could not compare in experience to the veterans Drake, Hawkins, and Frobisher. In fact, he was to remain at home, a sleeping partner in the enterprise. Lord Thomas was also a newcomer to high command. This thirty-year-old younger son of the fourth Duke of Norfolk, executed in 1572, had been restored in blood in 1584, had served as a volunteer in the Armada, and had commanded a ship. The aim of this enterprise

---

[5] Williamson, *Hawkins*, 450; *CSPD* 2 (1581–90): ccxxix, 2, 3; ccxxx, 66, 80; ccxxxi, 2, 88, 94; BL, Lansdowne Ms. 58/169–73.

[6] *CSPD* 2 (1581–90): ccxxxii, 13, 14, 15, 24; ccxxxiii, 118; *APC* 1590: 209–10. There may have been some booty from Hawkins's voyage; see *CSPD* 2 (1581–90): ccxxxiii, 118; Monson 1: 249–50.

was to waylay the plate fleet on its way home. Although this was a naval rather than a privateering enterprise, costs were to be shared among the Queen, Lord Admiral Howard, Raleigh, and ultimately a group of London merchants. The court backing was obviously that of the Howards in alliance with the favored Raleigh. Essex was away in France that summer, Drake and Hawkins relegated to routine duties.[7]

The scheme was first broached in January 1591 when there was talk of twenty ships being assembled. It was in fact a much scaled-down force that sailed in April. Lord Thomas commanded six royal ships and three pinnaces. He was warned that a Spanish fleet waiting to sail westward lay somewhere off Portugal; it was left to his judgment whether to lie in wait near Cape St. Mary (on the southern coast of Portugal) or off the Azores. The admiral chose the latter tactic and sailed for the islands. In June arrangements were made to send two months' victual to him, convoyed by two warships that would join his flotilla. The Queen had in addition come to an arrangement with a London merchant consortium to send an additional six armed merchantmen. There was also a scheme to enlarge his fleet with an additional eight Queen's ships and fifteen armed merchantmen provided by the outports, with the possible addition of a Dutch squadron. This fell through when the outports begged off and the Dutch declined to participate. Instead of the forty or so ships that were meant to accost the Spaniards, Howard had but eight. The victuallers and the two extra royal ships had reached him before he encountered the Spanish fleet; the Londoners had not.[8]

The Spanish government, now thoroughly alarmed by the English menace, had at last been able to mobilize an effective fleet to protect its ocean shipping. The treasure ships waiting at Havana were alerted and at the same time some fifty-five ships sailed from Ferrol to encounter Howard's six warships off Terceira. The English admiral, warned only hours before of the Spaniards' approach, prudently retreated with all but one of his ships, Sir Richard Grenville's *Revenge*. Grenville's decision to remain behind—whether by choice or by constraint of circumstance—was to elevate him to the

[7] *CSPD* 12 (Addenda, 1580–1625): xxxii, 7.

[8] Monson 1: 257; Wernham, 298–99; *CSPD* 3 (1591–94): ccxxxviii, 18, 19, 63, 82, 150, 152, 154; ccxxxix, 20, 52.

pantheon of English naval heroes and to provide a new chapter in the nation's patriotic mythology. But most immediately it took all the skill of Raleigh's accomplished pen to mask the bare facts of English ill-success. The only profits of the voyage came from seven ships taken by the London contingent during their return. The London adventurers had £6,000 on an interim dividend (which they were persuaded to invest in another enterprise planned for 1592). The Queen seems to have covered her investment, a sum approaching £18,000; Raleigh seems to have had nothing.[9]

The two successive seasons in which the strategy of intervention had been applied with some consistency of effort had left disappointing results. In 1590 command of the forces had been in the hands of two veteran professionals who, however, lacked political clout. (Conceivably the death of Walsingham early in the year deprived them of their most influential advocate.) At any rate they had to yield to the Queen's nervous fear of invasion. Later the Spanish move on Brittany distracted attention in another direction and most of Hawkins's time was spent watching the Breton coast. Frobisher was able to reach the Azores, but after two months of vain waiting was forced to return when his victuals ran out. In 1591 the backing of two great figures, the lord admiral and Raleigh, insured a more carefully planned and generously supplied operation. Howard, once at the islands, was revictualled, reinforced, and warned of the approach of the Ferrol fleet. Yet, even with his reinforcements, he was far inferior to the fleet sent against him.

A retrospective view of these two campaigns suggests several considerations. Most obvious is the Queen's clear reluctance to commit her forces to action in distant waters. She was beset by fears of another invasion even though Parma's involvement in France and the Spanish preoccupation with protecting their commerce rendered this possibility unlikely. But in these years—as in the future—Elizabeth could hardly be brought to more than a grudging support of an oceanic strategy. The corollary of this was that the resources committed to these schemes were inadequate to the proposed goals. Frobisher had perspicaciously pointed out, in a letter surviving only in a fragment, that the naval force necessary to seize the plate fleet must be large enough not only to beat the Spanish warships but also to pursue and capture the cargo ships. "For when

---

[9] Monson 1: 261, 283; *CSPD* 3 (1591–94): ccxl, 55; ccxli, 9.

they come to fly it is the number that takes them for when every ship make shift for her[self it is the] multitude must perform the chase." And this letter did not take into account the formidable war fleet the Spaniards could muster for service from 1591 on. If the strategy of intervention were to work it would require a larger commitment of English naval power than the Queen was disposed to grant or, indeed, could muster on her own.[10]

Indeed, one may question whether the oceanic strategy was a viable one at all. Modern commentators have applauded its intelligent assessment of Spanish weakness and the English potential for striking at Spain's soft underbelly. But, however appealing in grand outline, it presented severe practical problems for contemporaries seeking to execute it. As suggested previously, the size of the naval forces would have strained English resources to their limit. Regular revictualling measures (such as there were in 1591) would have been essential, as would have been a rotation of ships. There was also the question of where the point of pressure should be. Hawkins wanted two squadrons, one to hold the Spanish fleet in check in its home waters and another to intercept the flota. Frobisher preferred a different scheme—a station off Cape St. Vincent or, better still, one in the West Indies. The latter plan raised the further problem of a base—the capture of one of the Azores or the occupation of an American site. But this in turn would have required more support, in men, money, and supplies—all in scant supply. Last, there were the inevitable contingencies of wind and weather that beset all sixteenth-century operations but were especially important in the storm-swept seas of the Atlantic and Caribbean. The best laid plans of governments or of high commands were at the mercy of such gales as decimated the Spanish fleet after the *Revenge* encounter or fatally delayed Essex in 1597.

In any case Elizabeth's experience in the two years in which she had given her admirals their head and allowed them to use her navy on the Atlantic seas to strike at Philip's treasure fleet had left her unconvinced. Not until 1595 would there be another royal naval enterprise, and its objective would be the nodal point in Spain's lifeline: land transit at the isthmus of Panama.

Even though no major assaults on Spanish commerce were made by the royal navy after 1591, the Crown did not remain inactive.

[10] BL, Cotton Mss., Otho E viii, 8, fol. 266.

Through a working partnership with two great entrepreneurs it continued to harass Spanish shipping while filling the Exchequer with the profits of large-scale plundering. The first of these partners was George Clifford, third Earl of Cumberland. This nobleman, the heir to embarrassed North Country estates, had quite deliberately set out to recoup his fortunes by large-scale privateering. His first two ventures were unsuccessful, but in the summer of 1589 he was at least successful enough to discharge his outstanding debts. After a thin year in 1590 Cumberland had a share in the events of 1591 when he sailed with one royal ship and four of his own. The cost was considerable, the returns meager. The prizes taken were almost all lost; but at least it was his pinnace that gave warning to Thomas Howard off Terceira and enabled the latter to escape the formidable enemy fleet.[11]

For Cumberland 1592 was a year of great good fortune even though he had to share it with others. Raleigh had, of course, played a large role in the expedition of 1591, which left him heavily in debt. Already in December of that year a new scheme was afoot. It was to be financed in part out of the £6,000 profit earned by the Londoners in 1591 and in part out of the £2,000 owed Raleigh by the Queen. Raleigh's initial intentions were to sail to the West Indies, possibly to Panama, but in the end he set his sights on the East Indian carracks. When his secret marriage forfeited the Queen's favor, it was Frobisher who led the fleet. Frobisher was a great seaman but an unpopular disciplinarian, and Raleigh had to sail as far as Cape Finisterre to assure the loyalty of the sailors. There he divided a fleet that consisted of two Queen's ships, ten merchantmen, and four pinnaces; six went with Frobisher to remain off Cape St. Vincent, and the rest under Sir John Burgh to the Azores. Frobisher took at least one prize, a sugar-laden ship from Brazil.[12]

Burgh's squadron arrived in the Azores, where it was augmented by two London vessels, a ship belonging to Hawkins, and five ships owned by Cumberland. The earl had mounted an expedition of his own but left command to John Norton. This combined

---

[11] Andrews, *Privateering*, 71–72; Monson 1: 269–76; Williamson, *Cumberland*, 70–82; *CSPD* 3 (1591–94): ccxxxviii, 63, 86, 102, 117, 159.

[12] BL, Lansdowne Ms. 69, fols. 54, 55; William Cecil, Lord Burghley, *A Collection of State Papers ... Left by William Cecil, Lord Burghley*, ed. Samuel Haynes and William Murdin (2 vols., London, 1740–59) 2: 663 [hereafter cited as Cecil Papers]; HMC, *Hatfield* 4: 200.

fleet enjoyed the great privateering success of the war years when it captured the East Indian carrack *Madre di Dios*, with a cargo worth perhaps half a million pounds. Even after extensive looting by officers and men alike, the cargo alone realized at least £140,000, and probably more. The Queen, who had invested about £3,000, realized about £80,000 of the returns; Cumberland saw £36,000 gross but only £5,000 net, and that had to be shared with other adventurers. The Londoners got £12,000 (a net of £6,000); Hawkins and his associates made £7,000 to £8,000, while Raleigh with £24,000 gross was left with a net loss.[13]

In 1593 Cumberland borrowed two Queen's ships for a venture to the West Indies, with four of his own. Part of the fleet operated in the Azores, part in the Indies. The returns were large—perhaps "the most gainful he made before or after." A venture the next year was less successful. A fleet of three ships sent out by the earl to the Azores encountered two carracks; the first burned and sank, while the second escaped. In that year Cumberland's debts had mounted to £11,200, largely though not entirely through his maritime expenditures.[14]

These semiprivate, semipublic ventures had a mixed record and, except for the *Madre di Dios*, failed to catch any of the great prizes they sought. The Crown profited by virtue of the Queen's pre-emptive claim on the profits, but these gains have to be offset by the heavy and unrecompensed expenses of 1589 and 1591. The great gentlemen entrepreneurs, such as Cumberland or Raleigh, were net losers, but the much larger body of private adventurers who were operating on their own in these years were doing very well indeed. A modern historian's calculations, based on the Admiralty records for the three years following the Armada, suggest that 299 prizes brought in something like £400,000. These may have been unusually profitable years, but a calculation from other available data indicates an annual average for the war years of between £100,000 and £200,000, something like 10 to 15 percent of total national import value and a sum probably equal to annual Iberian imports in peacetime. Individual participants, like the London merchants Myddleton, Watts, or Bayning, made a substantial part of their con-

---

[13] Monson 1: 295; Andrews, *Privateering*, 73.
[14] *Ibid.*, 75–76; Williamson, *Cumberland*, 93–94, 126–39.

siderable fortunes out of privateering and such associated operations as the purchase of prize goods.[15]

How much influence the activities of the commerce raiders, public and private, had on the Spanish war effort is a question difficult to resolve. Obviously little precious metal (in relation to the total value of American production) was lost. Nor could the private raiders much affect the essential imports of grain and naval stores from the Baltic, since the hulks carrying them were too large a prey for the ordinary privateering ship. The loss of sugar imports from Brazil did not directly affect the war effort except as it reduced customs revenues on re-export profits.[16]

One clear—although unmeasurable—advantage did in fact accrue to the English. Spain was forced to divert some of its increasingly overstrained resources to an oceanic fleet and to fortifications in the colonies. Coming at a time when Philip was expending every effort to assist the French Catholic Leaguers with men, money and (in Brittany) ships, the English diversion was significant. For contemporary English military leaders and their backers at court, the lack of any obvious victory was no doubt a deep disappointment and a lasting frustration. In a much larger perspective, however, the interested observer might argue that a strategy of harassment— by nibbling at the maritime commerce of Spain and forcing its rulers onto a constant alert as well as to a diversion of their resources— was the only strategy that comfortably matched England's limited capabilities in men, ships, and money.

[15] Andrews, *Privateering*, 100–23, 125, 128.   [16] *Ibid.*, 131.

CHAPTER 6

WAR ON THE SPANISH COASTS

1596-1597

IN THE SUMMER of 1594 Sir John Norris, with naval auxiliaries commanded by Sir Martin Frobisher, assailed the fort the Spaniards had built at the entrance to Brest haven. The English stormed the fort and massacred the defenders, although their victory was marred by the ensuing death of Frobisher. From the government's point of view this was a crucially important action. Had the Spanish won complete control of this well-protected and capacious harbor, they would have had just the kind of base they needed for large-scale naval operations against England. Their expulsion manifestly eased the much-feared threat of Spanish enemy action in England's home waters. Since this victory coincided with the crushing of League resistance in much of Brittany, the threat of a Spanish presence in that province was fast fading. Elizabeth was free to do what she had long desired, to withdraw the substantial forces she had committed in France since 1591 and thus liquidate her participation in the French war. Some of the forces thus released were sent to Ireland, where unrest seemed about to transmute itself into rebellion. But with the liberation of English forces in France, there was a new opportunity for the proponents of a forward policy against Spain itself to win another hearing and perhaps even another inning.

During the next three years the English would make three major efforts to assault Spanish power, either on its home soil or in the overseas possessions. In 1595 the attack was aimed at the West Indies; in 1596, at the great port of Cadiz; and in 1597 the plan was to wipe out the Spanish ships in the northern Spanish ports as a prelude to the capture of one of the Azores. Two of these campaigns, the first and the last, failed—one by bad management, the other by bad luck. The second achieved spectacular success, although (for different reasons) it disappointed both its leading spirit, the Earl of Essex, and his royal mistress. These enterprises had offered a supreme opportunity to the hawkish party to carry out its strategy. Their lack of success brought an end to any serious attempt to break Spanish power. The last of them was speedily followed by French withdrawal from the war and the faltering initiation of English peace negotiations with Spain.

In the first of these offensives the English chose to push a variation of the strategy of offense last used in 1585. The venue of action was now to move from the Iberian homeland and the Atlantic islands to the other side of the ocean, to the Caribbean Sea, unvisited by the Queen's navy since Drake's voyage of 1585. A raid on the West Indies had been part of Raleigh's original plan in 1591–1592, but by the time his fleet had sailed its goals had been reduced to the now conventional ploy of a voyage to the Azores.

Just what caused this shift in tactics in 1595 is not immediately evident. One may guess that the repeated failures to achieve anything significant in the middle Atlantic had discredited the concept of interception. The goal of the new enterprise remained the same as in the past—disruption of the Spanish lines of communication—but now the assault was to be aimed not at the fleet but at the nexus of the whole communication system, the isthmus of Panama, the corridor through which the Peruvian silver had to pass when it was transshipped from the Pacific to the Atlantic. Close that door and the whole flow of bullion was halted—not just for a single season but until the choking giant could be brought to its knees. This sweeping strategy, aimed not only at a telling blow to Spanish power but at ultimate victory, was the brainchild of Drake; however, the path that led from conception to execution was long and tortuous.[1]

There had been a preliminary move as early as January 1593, when Drake and Hawkins had been authorized to mobilize three

[1] Kenneth R. Andrews, ed., *The Last Voyage of Drake and Hawkins*, Hakluyt Soc., 2nd ser. 142 (1972), 15–16.

royal and twenty private ships, but nothing further had come of this. It was being talked of again in the summer of 1594, but not until late in that year did matters begin to move, with the authorization for money, and by March 1595 £22,000 had been laid out for a voyage that was supposed to start at the latest by 1 May.[2]

The plans for the new enterprise reflect not only a change of policy but also the shifting currents of court politics. Neither Drake nor Hawkins had sufficient status at court to take the initiative on his own. The former, moreover, had been discredited by the failure of 1589, and the latter had lost the opportunity to prove his favorite strategy in the frustrations of 1590. Drake's re-emergence in 1595 and the adoption of his plan for a West Indian assault mirror the influence of that rising star, the Earl of Essex. Essex, always the advocate of vigorous action against Spain, now became the patron of Drake's scheme and threw his weight behind the seaman. The earl's influence on the expedition is evident in the military dispositions for the voyage. An army of about 1,000 soldiers was to sail with the fleet. Their commander was Essex's dependent (and kinsman), Sir Thomas Baskerville; the lieutenant-general, the sergeant-major, and seven of the fourteen captains were known followers of the earl.[3]

Drake was not to have undivided naval command: he was to share responsibility with Hawkins. This appointment may well reflect the apprehensions of the more conservative councillors about the naval hero. As one of the officers on the voyage wrote, Drake was "better able to conduct forces and discreetly govern in conducting them to places where service was to be done than to command in the execution there," and he added, "but entering into them as the child of fortune it may be his self will and peremptory command was doubted." The sober and cautious Hawkins was probably intended to be a check on his impetuous colleague; he may even have owed his place to the court party led by the Cecils, whose suspicions of Drake's willful independence remained. (Hawkins bequeathed £100 to Burghley and £500 to Burghley's grandson in his will, made just before he sailed).[4]

The fleet consisted of six royal ships and thirteen merchantmen.

[2] *Ibid.*, 12, 86; SP 12/4/94; Monson 1: 317, 321.
[3] Andrews, *Last Voyage*, 44, 45–48, 90.
[4] *Ibid.*, 86; Williamson, *Hawkins*, 474; HMC, Hatfield 5: 495–96; Monson 2: 329; Tenison 10: 558.

The financial arrangements for the voyage followed the pattern set in previous enterprises. The Crown was to bear two-thirds of the cost; the rest of the money was to come from Drake, Hawkins, and their backers. The owners of the merchantmen and the soldiers were to be shareholders in the booty in lieu of ship-hire or wages. Something like £28,000 was laid out by the Crown out of a total of £43,000 in direct costs.[5]

The departure of the expedition was delayed from 1 May 1595 to late summer. The causes for delay may have been in part of the admirals' making, but it was the Queen's decision that held up the sailing during August. In July four galleys had appeared off the Cornish coast and, in a brief raid, burned several villages. More important was the government's information on two impending threats from Spain. The first was in the shape of a Spanish fleet expected to sail for Ireland before winter; the latter, less immediate but more menacing still, was an armada reportedly greater than that of 1588, whose sailing was planned for June or July of 1596. These threats deeply alarmed the Queen and led her to order a radical change in the admirals' plans. They were to reorder their priorities, first by a preventive raid on the Spanish ports, on the model of 1587, destroying whatever they could so as "to impeach the issue of the Spanish army at this present." Second, they were to intercept the plate fleet; only after accomplishing these missions were they to be free to sail to the West Indies. And even then they must give an ironclad guarantee that they would be home again not later than May 1596. For the moment, pending the dispatch of a naval force under Sir Henry Palmer to Ireland, they were to remain off the English coast keeping watch for the putative invaders of Ireland.[6]

The response of the admirals to these alterations was a wail of anguished protest. Writing to Essex, they insisted that, if the purposes of the expedition were to be changed, the Queen must bear the burden of all charges, for ships, victuals, and wages of soldiers and sailors. Baskerville, general of the land forces, added his voice, urging the earl to "second this our journey in such sort that we may go forward in our first pretended course without being limited to

[5] Andrews, *Last Voyage*, 48, 77–78; the Maynard narrative (*ibid.*, 87) gives a total of twenty-seven ships.

[6] *CSPD* 4 (1595–97): cclii, 28; ccliii, 30, 31, 70, 76; HMC, *Hatfield* 5: 285, 290, 307.

so short a time ... for who is he so unadvised to undertake the performance of such a 'viage' wherein there is so great expectations of so great things to be done in so short a time."[7]

The proposed change in plans also triggered a vigorous debate in the Council in which these opposing strategies were argued out. The conservatives stressed the great risks of a voyage "into hott cuntryes" with the loss of many mariners and the absence of ships from the English coasts. Their opponents retorted by pointing out the financial loss to the investors and the Queen and the dishonor "because it would be imputed to fear." The reporter goes on to add, "Some proposition was made by the active sort (you may guess whom) to convert this fleet, assembled with some enforcement, to an offensive course upon the ports of Spain, but checked from above or crossed underhand not without a great distemper of humor on both sides for a few days."[8]

The deadlock may have been resolved by a lucky chance—the report that a great plate ship had been disabled at sea, had made for Puerto Rico, and had there unloaded its cargo of two and a half million pesos in treasure (in fact 3 million). Apparently it was the news of this glittering prospect that finally dissolved the Queen's objections, and by 18 August the admirals had the royal consent to their sailing. But now their goal was Puerto Rico, and their prey the treasure at San Juan. Offered a choice between a great privateering enterprise with prospects of handsome profit and a mere workaday naval action designed to cripple the enemy's offensive power before it could be launched, the Queen opted for the former. The hope of immense gain overcame her fears of invasion.[9]

The history of the voyage has been often and well told. It is a sad story. The two admirals were bitterly at odds from the beginning. Drake's insistence on raiding in the Canaries gave the Spanish an opportunity to warn the authorities in Puerto Rico. There were further delays in the Caribbean, and when they finally arrived off San Juan, Drake, viewing its fortifications, was for once cautious. Indeed he may have been overly cautious but in any case declined to attack the place. At that moment Hawkins, full of sorrowful anger,

[7] *Ibid.*, 5: 319; *CSPD* 4 (1595–97): ccliii, 79, 87.
[8] Sir Henry Sidney, *Letters and Memorials of State ... Written and Collected by Sir Henry Sydney*, etc., ed. Arthur Collins (2 vols., London, 1746) 1, pt. 2: 343–44 [hereafter cited as Sidney Papers].
[9] Monson 1: 325; HMC, *Hatfield* 5: 324–25, 332.

died. Frustrated in Puerto Rico, Drake reverted to his original intention and made for the isthmus of Panama. Again there were unaccountable delays off the mainland coast before Baskerville marched across the isthmus in an attempt to reach Panama City. Turned back by Spanish resistance and by the utter exhaustion of his men, Drake retreated to the fleet. In one last desperate fling, he proposed an attack on the Nicaraguan lake towns. But before a landing could be effected, Drake too was dead, struck down by dysentery. In this last episode in his career, the once bold leader had clearly lost his touch. Impetuous and careless in the Canaries, over-cautious at San Juan, reckless on the mainland—his every move was disastrous. There was nothing for Baskerville, who succeeded to command, but to make for home. He was at least successful in beating off a Spanish fleet west of Cuba. His fleet limped home with a fifth of his force dead and some £5,000 in booty to offset the costs of the voyage.[10]

The deaths of the two admirals and that of Frobisher in the preceding year ended the generation of the great sea-dogs, the pioneers of the buccaneering voyages. In Hawkins they had produced not only a commander but also a strategist, the first exponent of a systematic exploitation of sea-power. But after 1569 he had had little opportunity to command at sea. It was Drake to whom these opportunities fell but who failed to exploit them. The haze of patriotic myth that enveloped him in his lifetime—and has pretty much ever since—veils the fact that he was essentially throughout his career a buccaneer: a master of the smash-and-grab technique but altogether ill-suited to the tasks of high naval strategy, especially the command of expeditions combining military and naval elements (except of course in 1587). This unlucky mismatch of talents and purposes foredoomed those enterprises that were entrusted to his command after 1588.

Since 1589 the English had made a series of attacks, more or less royally supported, on Spanish naval might, aimed at the communications lines with South America. Not one could be considered a success, although none had been a catastrophe of the kind Spain had suffered in 1588. Only one English warship, the *Revenge*, had been lost. The costs to the Crown were barely offset by booty, even

[10] See Andrews, *Last Voyage*, for a full contemporary account; see also Monson 1: 328; Williamson, *Hawkins*, 489.

allowing for the windfall of the *Madre de Dios*. Private enterprise, on the other hand, had flourished and the income from prize goods may well have equalled the peacetime profits of the Iberian trade.[11] The policy of the activist party seemed largely discredited; each of their proposed strategies—the scourging of the Iberian coasts, attack on the Indian fleets in the Atlantic, assault on the West Indian colonies—had been tried and had failed. Yet in fact the Queen was about to be persuaded to concede to the forward party a new and grander opportunity.

Even while Drake and Hawkins were at sea (and their fate unknown in England) the first stirrings of a new enterprise were in motion. This time English efforts were to revert to the earlier models of 1587 and 1589, an assault on the Spanish homeland. Such a scheme may have been mooted in 1592 and 1594. Antonio Perez, the fugitive minister of Philip II, had been urging such a move since 1593, and rumors of another descent on Spain by Drake had circulated in that year. In 1594 Drake was in the Low Countries seeking to obtain the use of English troops. In the event, the Queen was sidetracked by renewed fears of invasion and by the problems of Henry IV. In 1595, however, the government pushed ahead with serious plans for a large-scale expedition involving the use of land forces. By November of that year the Dutch had agreed to provide thirty ships for such a scheme, and in December the Londoners promised twelve ships and six pinnaces. As early as November plans had been made for victualling 12,000 men at sea for five months, beginning 31 March. By the end of the year this had been scaled down to a fleet of seventeen Queen's ships and twelve merchantmen. Sixty transports would be provided by London and twelve maritime counties. They would carry more than 6,800 soldiers.[12] Total costs for outfitting the expedition were estimated at about £50,000. Burghley reckoned future known costs would reach a total of £78,000. Part of the wages bill was to be borne by Howard and Essex.

The much-enhanced scale of the enterprise in comparison with

[11] Andrews, *Privateering*, 128.

[12] Corbett, *Drake*, 2: 398; Monson 1: 319–20; Thomas Birch, *Memoirs of the Reign of Queen Elizabeth, from the Year 1581 till her Death*, etc. (2 vols., London, 1754) 1: 107, 331, 367, 387–88; HMC, *Hatfield* 6: 6; *CSPD* 4 (1595–97): ccliv, 53; cclv, 8, 12, 13; cclvi, 10, 23, 63, 103; cclvii, 60, 106, 107; cclix, 2; Monson 1: 358–60, quoting Pipe Office Declared Accounts.

that of its predecessors is obvious; no less than seventeen royal ships would sail (against six in 1589). Counting the six with Drake and Hawkins, the Queen was risking the great bulk of her navy in this year. The Dutch were called upon as allies (in 1589 the flyboats had been commandeered) and their contingent of eighteen warships (and six others) doubled the fighting strength of the expedition. The total number of participants, English and Dutch, was between 12,000 and 15,000. With the transports and auxiliary vessels the whole armada numbered well over 100, perhaps 120, ships.[13]

The purposes for which this great fleet was assembled remained publicly uncertain. Essex wrote to the Scottish Earl of Mar in January 1596 of a Channel squadron; Burghley told the English diplomatic agent Palavicino in early March that a fleet would put to sea to meet Drake and protect his return. Various employments were intended for Essex, depending on circumstances—possibly as army commander in Brittany or as a naval leader at sea or in a command off the Irish coast. A general commission "for this great action" was issued to Lord Admiral Howard and Essex before the end of March.[14]

By 20 March the government had at last focused its sights; Burghley was writing of a voyage to the coasts of Spain and Portugal with soldiers for a landing force, but he was still uncertain where on the coasts they should land and how far west or south the ships should proceed (presumably against the plate fleet or the Portuguese carracks). The English commander in the Low Countries, Sir Francis Vere, in the same month urged that, if a port were to be seized, it should be Cadiz or Corunna, preferably the former. The Queen, alarmed at the cost estimates, was still unconvinced.[15]

All these preparations were rudely interrupted at the beginning of April when the new governor of the Spanish Low Countries, the Archduke Albert, attacked and captured Calais. There was panic

[13] HMC, *Hatfield* 6: 201, 205–6; Birch 2: 15; Monson 1: 358–61, citing [1] BL, Cotton Mss., Julius F vi, fol. 278; [2] Otho E ix, fol. 377; [3] Pipe Office Declared Accounts 2234; William Slingsby, "Relation of the Voyage to Cadiz, 1596," ed. J. S. Corbett, Navy Record Society, *Miscellany* 1 (1902): 37, 50 n. 1; list of 5/30 in *CSPD* 4 (1595–97): cclvii, 60; cclix, 2; Pipe Office Declared Accounts 2234; and Cotton Mss., Otho E ix, fol. 377.

[14] Monson 1: 363; Birch 1: 378; *CSPD* 4 (1595–97): cclvi, 77, 95; cclvii, 45, dated 24 April, for articles published by the admirals.

[15] *Ibid.*, cclvi, 99; HMC, *Hatfield* 6: 86–88; Birch 1: 440.

in London; Essex was given a commission to raise troops for the relief of the town; in a flurry of confusion and indecision orders were given, only to be revoked, then reissued. But all was to no avail; by 14 April Calais was in Spanish hands. The French sought anxiously to persuade the English to redeploy their assembled forces to France, and Essex found himself in oppposition to his accustomed ally, Henry IV.[16] The Queen wavered and the earl, with his whole armada poised at Plymouth, was beside himself with anxiety. In a candid outburst to his secretary, Reynolds, he asserted that

> the Queen wrangles with our action for no cause but because that it is at hand. If this force were going to France she would fear as much the issue there as she doth in our intended journey. I know I shall never do her service but against her will and since I have wracked my wits to get this commission and my means to carry that which should do the feat, as they say, I will either against the hair go through with it or of a general become a monk upon an hour's warning.[17]

The Queen in her indecision next proposed to recall the two commanders at Plymouth and replace them with inferior officers. This evoked an anguished response from the ranking officers that revealed how much the whole venture pivoted on the initiative of Howard and Essex. The numerous aristocratic volunteers whom they had recruited, in Essex's expression, his "friends, servants and followers," would decamp and so cut the very heart out of the enterprise while the common soldiers would be demoralized. A proposal emanating from the group later termed the "sea-faction" went further still, proposing that only the ships but no soldiers be sent. Vere, writing separately and as Essex's designated successor as general of the soldiers, emphatically backed his commander. However, the Queen at last gave way to the activists' persuasion, and the weeks of waiting, lengthened by the weather, finally ended. On 1 June they put to sea. An official declaration was published, asserting that the purposes of the enterprise were defensive and reassuring neutrals that their lawful interests would be respected.[18]

The fleet was on the high seas, but what was its goal? The official

---

[16] See Chapter 10.

[17] *CSPD* 4 (1595–97): cclii, 110 (misdated June 1595); cclvii; Monson 1: 369–70; Birch 1: 467, 483, 484.

[18] HMC, *Hatfield* 6: 188–89; Birch 2: 8.

instructions from the Queen, issued sometime after the end of March, are full and explicit. They recite her fears of an impending invasion on the scale of 1588, partially abated when the Spanish detached ships to pursue Hawkins and Drake, but not eliminated. She anticipated now that there would be an expedition to Ireland about May 1597 with men and money to aid Tyrone. In order to scotch these designs she had "upon the motion of you two, offering your service in this purpose" and with her Council's advice, commissioned Howard and Essex to use all means to destroy Spain's ships and supplies. These orders were promptly hedged by exhortations to avoid danger to her ships and subjects; there were to be "no desperate or doubtful actions of offense in a strange country." If, after destroying the ships and supplies, they were to find a town incapable of defense and from which all riches had not been removed, then they might attempt its capture—but only after taking counsel with their inferior officers and finding the attempt "sperable to be achieved without hazarding either your own lives or the lives of our subjects." Unless these conditions were met there was to be no such attempt for mere hopes of gain. And then, as yet another check on impetuous action, the generals were hobbled by a council of officers, appointed by the Queen, with considerable blocking powers. Finally, if "after service done" there were news of approaching carracks, ships could be detached to pursue them.[19]

These instructions echo those given to Drake and Norris in 1589 and to Drake and Hawkins in 1595. There was the same multiplicity of incompatible goals, reflecting the same divisions of opinion in the Council and the Queen's invariable indecisiveness. The leaders of the earlier expeditions, although professionals of high reputation, were in a political sense secondary figures, officials rather than councillors or courtiers. The leaders of 1596 were both noblemen and Privy Councillors, intimates of the sovereign, and their principal coadjutors were a great courtier, Sir Walter Raleigh, and another nobleman, Lord Thomas Howard. However, with respect to command experience, they were all gentlemen amateurs. Lord Admiral Howard had, of course, by virtue of his office, commanded against the Armada, but he was neither a professional nor widely experienced at sea. Essex had served in the Low Countries and commanded the small expeditionary force sent to Normandy in

---

[19] BL, Cotton Mss., Otho E ix, fol. 343; *APC* xxvii, 84–89.

1591, but again his professional qualifications were limited and his naval experience nil. Raleigh had been at sea a number of times but always in small expeditions and without high command; Lord Thomas Howard's command experience was confined to the cruise of 1591, made famous by the *Revenge*.

A high command consisting of two lords of Council—members of the inner circle of high politics, where men jostled and fought for the royal favor—was a recipe for divided counsel. Just how fragile the Devereux-Howard alliance was became apparent in an episode of April 1596, when Essex was assigned overall command of the forces hastily levied for the relief of Calais. The lord admiral, in a perfect spasm of injured vanity, sent off what Cecil's secretary discreetly labelled a "passionate letter." Howard furiously insisted that by virtue of his office only the Lord Admiral could command any force sent overseas. He announced his withdrawal from the Spanish enterprise with a declaration that "I leave forever farther to deal in martial causes." These troubled waters were quieted, presumably by the Queen or Robert Cecil, but observers watched apprehensively for further signs of friction.[20]

The alliance, however, held long enough to achieve the most spectacular English victory of the war, the capture and sack of Cadiz. The leaders' cooperation during the attack was fitful and, as one historian has written, they behaved like schoolboys scrambling for first place. Still, in spite of the confusions engendered by this rivalry, they were able to shatter Spanish naval resistance and to capture the city. Once the city was entered the attention of the soldiery—and of their officers—was given solely to plundering. Although Essex reminded Howard of the Spanish merchant fleet sheltering in the upper bay, laden with cargoes for America, nothing was done. The Spanish temporized with an offer of ransom, which gave them time to unload the most valuable goods and then to burn the ships with their remaining cargo.[21]

Having secured the town and bargained for the ransom of the inhabitants (a ransom that went unpaid), the commanders had to determine their next move. The initial determination of the council they summoned was to hold the city, and preparations were made

---

[20] HMC, *Hatfield* 6: 144, 199–200; BL, Stowe Ms. 159, fol. 353.

[21] Clements R. Markham, "*The Fighting Veres.*" Lives of Sir Francis Vere, etc. (Boston and New York, 1888), 226, quoted in Monson 1: 386; Slingsby, 77–79.

accordingly. At a second consultation of the commanders it was agreed that 3,000 to 4,000 men could be supplied from what was in the town and what the fleet could spare, for a period of two months. That would give time to bring fresh supplies from England, the Low Countries, and North Africa. Part of the fleet, under Lord Admiral Howard, was to return to England while Thomas Howard and Raleigh sailed with a squadron to the Atlantic islands to await the Indian fleets. What happened next is less certain.[22]

What had been agreed upon up to this point was Essex's plan. Initially it was accepted by Lord Admiral Howard and the leading officers. How the ensuing change of mind that reversed the plan to hold Cadiz came about is not clear. In one account—that of Slingsby—Essex is reported to have insisted that he and only he must command the garrison at Cadiz since only his presence there would move the Queen to grant the necessary supplies. Lord Admiral Howard refused to return without the earl, pleading the Queen's absolute command for the latter's return. Howard's own version repeats the latter argument as well as the Admiral's insistence that he had no commission to hold the town (a plea consonant with the surviving instructions cited earlier). The earl's own account states that when the question of victuals for the Cadiz garrison pending the arrival of new supplies was raised, the officers all pleaded shortages—or, as Essex scornfully put it, "the victuals were for the most part hidden and embezzled." He threw the full blame on his fellows. "I was forced to leave Cales and did not choose to abandon it."[23]

Essex's proposal to hold the port was no sudden impulse on his part. It formed part of his larger strategic vision, laid out in a letter dispatched to the Privy Council after the fleet sailed in June. He began with the general proposition that "it is better to do something in another country than to attend the enemy" in one's own, a rule particularly cogent for a state "little in territory, not extraordinarily rich, and defended only by itself." A prolonged war would be to England's disadvantage, hence the need to strike now by intercepting Spain's treasure "whereby we shall cut his sinews and make war upon him with his own money." Spanish sea-power broken, the

[22] Slingsby, 80, 85; Stephen and Elizabeth Usherwood, *The Counter-Armada, 1596: The Journall of the "Mary Rose"* (London, 1983), 85, 88–89.

[23] Slingsby, 83; Essex, Robert Devereux, Second Earl of, "Omissions of the Cales Voyage," in Lediard 1: 338; SP 12/259/60, 114.

Queen would not only be safe from invasion but herself mistress of the sea, "which is what the queen of an island should aspire to." This is the moment "if we ever allow the counsel of prevention [i.e., the strategy of attack] to be reasonable we must confess it now opportune."[24]

From these premises he urged not only a seizure of Spanish wealth on the high seas but something more—"to have made a continual diversion" leaving "a thorn sticking in his foot." Such a move would not only deliver the Queen from any fear of invasion of her dominions but would in fact place her at the head of the whole anti-Spanish party in Europe, having "delivered all Christendom from the fearful usurpation." It was the goal of his stepfather, recast, with Elizabeth playing a female St. George to the Spanish dragon—or, less fancifully, a European leader.

As for the immediate bread-and-butter problems—in Essex's language "hazard" and "change"—Essex was optimistic. A place well fortified on the landward side and supplied by sea would be impregnable (a faint foreshadowing of Wellington and the Lines of Torres Vedras). Less convincingly he argued that the cost could be recovered by turning "a part of the golden Indian stream" into English coffers. He named no particular port but promised details if the Privy Councillors could persuade the Queen to his views.

Essex could not persuade his fellow commander and the other officers of the fleet; it is even less likely that the Queen would ever have assented to the scheme. What followed after the fleet left Cadiz was protracted anticlimax. Although defeated in his immediate plan to hold the port, Essex continued to press for more offensive action. After the rather pointless capture and sack of the little port of Faro, while the fleet was doubling Cape St. Vincent, and again off Lisbon, he urged that the fleet be divided, the army and the sick to be sent home while the rest, stocked with the fleet's remaining victuals, made for the Azores. There, at first landfall for both West and East Indian ships, they might stalk their prey. The Spanish, after Cadiz, would probably order their ships to be held at the islands but they would not expect to find the English there. To this proposal to divide the fleet both Howard and Raleigh de-

[24] *CSPD* 4 (1595–97): cclix, 12, in Walter Devereux, *Lives and Letters of the Devereux, Earls of Essex, 1540–1646* (2 vols., London, 1853) 1: 349–56, with notes by Robert Cecil.

murred; only Lord Thomas Howard backed the earl. The lesser councillors proposed that Essex be given two Queen's ships with eight or ten merchantmen, but this the Lord Admiral refused.[25]

Finally, in desperation, Essex played his last card, a proposal to look into the Biscayan ports for Spanish shipping that could be destroyed. "To the Groyne with cart-ropes I drew them" but a glimpse of the empty harbors of Corunna and Ferrol was all he could win from them. They absolutely refused a further excursion to Santander or Pasages for dread of being "embayed," trapped in the angle between the French and Spanish coasts with the winds against them. Added to the commanders' reluctance for further action was the clamor of the sailors and soldiers to take their booty-laden ships home as fast as possible. Essex could do nothing but reluctantly follow the rest home.

In the meantime Ashley, secretary to the commanders, had returned home with the first official dispatches. The royally dictated response, far from congratulatory in tone, irritably inquired as to their future plans. Unofficial news of the landing at Faro was circulating in London. These tidings provoked a sour comment on the doubtful advisability of a long, hot, and inconvenient march "without any profit arising thereby as is reported." Their original instructions were then rehearsed and their attention drawn to the second major heading—the interception of the Spanish plate fleet. They were ordered to prepare a squadron for this mission, shifting all the victuals to these ships and sending the army home. Emphasis was laid on the prospective profits that would enable the Queen to maintain her wars against Spain and in Ireland. If this letter reached them after their return, they would find victuals waiting at Plymouth to insure a speedy return to sea en route to the islands.[26]

They were indeed at Plymouth before this letter came, and there they found another communication from the Queen herself in which she vented her spleen at full length. With gloomy self-satisfaction she noted that the "inconvenience which we suspected would follow this journey" had ensued "namely that it would rather be an action of honor and victory against the enemy and particular spoil and profit to the army than any way profitable to ourself." The "actions of hope" were over without paying the bills

[25] Essex, "Omissions," in Lediard 1: 338.
[26] *APC* 1596–97: 84–89, dated 7 August.

already incurred or those now coming in (for wages). She could not "forbear to remember you first of that which is past ... for we did lay before you (if we might be believed) that so great forces of land would serve for nothing but to increase charge" and after the first exploit, by consuming victuals render a later sea action impossible. "But in these you were ever so confident as when we reasoned against uncertainties for intercepting the fleet. ... Nothing would be admitted to reason but all things were answered by strong affirmations and assurances." She was surprised that they were short of victuals, considering the opportunities they had had to be "refreshed with infinite magazines of oil, corn, wine and all things." Had they done their duty she and her people might have been relieved of the huge fiscal burdens they bore. "All of which matters were not overseen [unforeseen] by us, if you can both remember, but were, as divers other things, neglected and contradicted both by yourself and soothed by others to our no small discontentation." After this final assertion of superior wisdom, she descended to particulars—for paying and discharging the troops—and ended on a forgiving note: "We do forbear to trouble ourselves with this matter." A letter of the same week gave strict orders to search the ships and men for plunder. Was it really necessary to pay them, considering how much had been pilfered?[27]

After this withering rebuke for their past incompetence the Queen turned to the future. The fleet was to be made ready to sail again with all possible speed. The carracks from the East Indies had been delayed and the West Indian ships would not arrive until mid-September; it might still be possible to garner in some of them, returning scattered and unprotected. But even the Queen soon had to accept the fact that her sea-worn ships and their disease-ridden crews were in no condition to be sent to sea again on short notice. In the end no such fleet as the Queen envisaged sailed, and she had to swallow the cost of £78,000 against which there was very little offset in recoverable booty.[28]

The Queen's sour dissatisfaction at the time of the fleet's return had some justification. Neither of the goals laid out in her instructions had been realized. The Spanish war fleet was still intact—the Indian fleets, eastern and western, soon safely at home. There was

---

[27] BL, Cotton Mss., Otho E ix, fols. 363–64, 368–70.
[28] *Ibid.*, fols. 370–71; Monson 2: 14; *CSPD* 4 (1595–97): cclvi, 107.

little or nothing to offset the costs of the expedition, let alone to enrich her starved exchequer. Yet it was by no means a barren victory. The deed spoke for itself: the King of Spain's principal port had been taken, sacked and held to ransom and two of his war galleons carried off in triumph. Philip was humiliated in the eyes of all Europe. There were also very tangible gains. The loss of the merchantmen laden for their West Indian voyage had been a body blow to Spanish credit. The archduke-governor's bills of exchange were being refused in Italy, and before the end of the year the Spanish treasury had once again resorted to one of its periodic repudiations of debt. More important still was the unwise riposte into which Philip was stung by the summer's events. He ordered his fleet into an ill-timed assault on England, only to see it perish in the autumnal storms of Biscay. The angry seas accomplished what Elizabeth had hoped her fleet might have; for a season at least the threat of renewed Spanish invasion was allayed.[29]

What the whole affair reveals to a more distant observer is the muddle of contradictory purposes, as apparent here as they had been eight years earlier in the Lisbon enterprise. Initially the Queen seemed to display a clear-headed strategic sense in giving priority to the destruction of the Spanish ships. Yet in her reproaches against her commanders on their return, it is their failure to intercept the rich cargoes—which would have paid for the war had they been seized—that she emphasizes. And the commanders themselves—at least Essex and Raleigh—were so carried away by the immediate excitements of battle and the hot-headed rivalries of the attack itself as to neglect their most urgent military responsibilities. In their haste to beat out one another in the capture of the town, they neglected the whole body of shipping in the upper bay, giving the Spaniards time to unload the more valuable cargo and to destroy the ships. If Essex had displayed a larger strategic grasp in his scheme for holding the port, he had shown little understanding of the tactical preliminaries for such a project, the cooperation of his officers, or the logistics of a sustained operation. As in 1589 the inner contradictions of the English leadership are all too manifest. The confusions of the original instructions with their quite unrealistic combination of incompatible goals were compounded by the commanders' own disagreements. Both reflect something deeper:

[29] HMC, *Hatfield* 7: 109–11; Monson 2: 15.

the inherent limitations on all military operations imposed by the Crown's scanty financial resources. The necessity of financing these expeditions by a large infusion of private money forced the Crown into a kind of bargain with the commanders. The resulting instructions strung together the very different purposes of a warily defensive royal strategy and the soaring ambitions of a clique of adventurers who dreamed of an imperial destiny for the Queen, chivalric fame for themselves, and, more sordidly, the rich plunder of Spain's treasure.

The return of the booty-laden English fleet, fresh from the sack of Cadiz, was occasion for much congratulation, but in fact the most important goals of the enterprise had gone unachieved. Its initial purpose had been to destroy the Spanish warships assembled at Lisbon and in the northern ports in preparation for another assault on their foe. In spite of the destruction at Cadiz and the capture of two galleons, the bulk of the Spanish war fleet and its auxiliaries was still intact. Moreover, the shock of Cadiz galvanized the hitherto sluggish Spanish preparations into hasty improvisations for an immediate assault. Ireland was apparently to be the destination, with a fallback on Milford Haven if a landing on the other side of St. George's Channel proved impossible.[30]

The English were in a general way aware of Spanish preparation but had no certain knowledge of the impending attack. Pinnaces were sent out in November to reconnoiter off the northwest Spanish coast. Warnings came from Holland in late October and from Madrid in November. The latter included the information that an Irish bishop was on board, a pointer to the fleet's destination. The fleet was said to number more ships than the 1588 Armada, although with a smaller army on board.[31]

The Queen was alarmed enough to summon a meeting of leading military experts under Burghley's chairmanship. Besides Essex it included Lords Burgh, Willoughby, and North; Norris; Vere; and others—the collective military wisdom of the country. They met on 4 November, aware that the Lisbon squadron had sailed, but quite uncertain as to the further movements of the whole fleet. Essex posed a series of questions, the first asking whether the enemy

[30] Ibid., 17–19.
[31] HMC, Hatfield 6: 444–45, 469; CSPD 4 (1595–97): cclx, 91, 110, 119; Tenison 10: 143–44.

would sail now or wait until later. There was division of opinion: Essex thought invasion, not a raid, was intended; Burghley agreed that England, not Ireland, was the goal; Raleigh insisted the attack would not come until next summer. All agreed that England must be ready. If the enemy landed, a pitched battle was to be avoided; Fabian tactics should be employed. Within the next few days measures were taken to mobilize men and ships. London was ordered to mobilize 3,000 men and three ships.[32] But as early as 1 December Cecil had a letter from Robert Sidney reporting a great shipwreck of the Spanish fleet in the Bay of Biscay, and more news trickled in during the following weeks. In fact the disaster had occurred as early as 17 November. By 28 December the men mobilized on the Isle of Wight were being sent home. Once again the Lord had blown upon the water and scattered His enemies. In this oblique way Essex's expedition had accomplished its original intention of dispersing the Spanish fleet.[33]

In January there was news from Galicia that as many as twenty-four out of one hundred ships in the armada had been lost. Nevertheless, as early as Christmas Eve the English government had begun to think of another naval expedition. The nervousness of the government, faced with rapidly growing rebellion in Ireland and well aware of Tyrone's correspondence with the Spanish, was unabated. The city of London was approached to provide ten ships for the royal navy for defense against Spanish invasion. They gave a dusty answer. Three years of dearth, the ensuing burdens of providing grain for the poor, plus the £11,000 deficit on the Londoners' investment in the Cadiz exploit made them very unwilling to assume new commitments.[34]

Consideration of a voyage went forward, nevertheless. By early January Robert Cecil had produced a memorandum for things to be done by Essex and the lord admiral for a sea journey. He envisaged a force of 4,490 men to serve for five months. This was fol-

[32] *Ibid.*, 133, quoting Guildhall Remembrancia 2: 56.

[33] HMC, *Hatfield* 6: 444–45, 469, 499, 533; *CSPD* 4 (1595–97): cclx, 110, 119, 94, 101, 102; cclxi, 26; Birch 2: 207; Monson 2: 17; *CSPD* 4 (1595–97): cclx, 82, 83, dated October by the editor, but note reference to their being off Finisterre 18 last month; Monson says the Adelantado left Lisbon on 18 October; probably these documents belong to the November meeting.

[34] CSPD 4 (1595–97): cclxii, 3; Monson 2: 17; HMC, *Hatfield* 6: 534–36; for Londoners, see Monson 2: 17.

lowed by another paper, by his father, urgently pressing for some enterprise against the Spanish ships at Ferrol, to hinder their plans for Ireland. Two proposals were on the table. The more modest, the Earl of Cumberland's, would require only two Queen's ships plus twenty Dutch and some of his own, but he could not insure that he could destroy the Spanish ships. The larger scheme (Essex's product, at the Queen's request) called for ten to a dozen royal ships, twenty Dutch and twelve from London with a force of 5,000 soldiers. Burghley's comment on the proposal echoed the enduring nightmare of the English government throughout the war. What if the two fleets passed at sea, leaving England open to invasion? Hedging his bets, the treasurer would prepare ships and victuals for 5,000 men but made no final commitment to the bolder plan.[35]

Within a week warrants had been issued for the arraying of twelve ships for sea service for four months, and the Queen had written to the States-General for ships to join her navy in preventing the threatened invasion of Ireland. An intelligence report of early February listed seventy ships at Ferrol, including six great men-of-war; they were predicted to sail for Ireland in April. For the next several months the government's intelligence reports from every quarter reported the growing strength of the Spanish preparations.[36]

Then there was a lull in further preparations. Probably it was owing to two circumstances. The first was another squabble between the Cecils and Essex, occasioned this time by a tussle over the appointment of a new Lord Warden of the Cinque Ports. It eased when Essex was given the mastership of the ordnance,[37] and there followed an entente among Essex, Cecil, and Raleigh. (see Chapter 25). Second, there was the prolonged negotiation with France over a possible English expeditionary force there, occasioned by the fall of Amiens (see Chapter 10).

The domestic settlement bore fruit quickly in collaboration for a new enterprise. By early May Anthony Bacon could write that his patron would command either in Picardy or at sea. The French

---

[35] *CSPD* 4 (1595–97): cclxii, 9, 16; Birch 2: 266.

[36] *CSPD* 4 (1595–97): cclxii, 32, 36, 37, 50, 67, 72, 76, 91, 111; HMC, *Hatfield* 7: 6, 14–15, 33, 121–23, 131, 152, 176. See also *Apologie*, Bv B3.

[37] Essex's patent as master of the ordnance is dated 19 March, and his commission as commander of the expedition 4 June (Tenison 10: 183, 201).

alternative foundered on the French suspicions as to English intentions towards Calais. The English government, convinced that the risks to Ireland's security were greater than those of a Spanish move in Picardy, opted for another naval campaign against Spain. The Queen remained skeptical that there was real danger and insisted that she would not make war but would arm for defense. In late May she went so far as to stay all preparations, but in the end she was persuaded to allow the expedition to go forward.[38]

Various plans were bruited in Council. The final arrangements provided for 6,000 men, including 1,000 veterans from the Low Countries, with Essex as commander of both army and navy, assisted by Lord Thomas Howard and Raleigh as admirals. Essex was to choose the captains and, unusually, men from the trained bands were to be used. Sixteen Queen's ships (ultimately nineteen) were assigned to the enterprise. Burghley gave his blessing: "I like so well to attempt something against our Spanish enemy that I hope God will prosper the purpose." Robert Cecil added his endorsement in a cordial letter written on the eve of departure. In June a council was appointed to assist Essex. Two of the members, Thomas Howard and Walter Raleigh, men of his generation, had some experience of sea warfare. Vere brought his experience and reputation as the most professional of English soldiers. Carew (as master of ordnance) and Gorges (as sergeant major) were Cecilian dependents. A newcomer of rank and some experience was Lord Mountjoy, possibly added at the Queen's insistence. A host of volunteers, perhaps as many as five hundred, joined the fleet. Even as late as 11 June the well-informed court gossip Chamberlain thought the expedition might go to Calais, the Channel Islands, Spain, or the Indies.[39]

The Queen's instructions, dated 15 June, rehearsed the basically defensive objectives of the campaign, i.e., to avert a series of impending threats to English security: aid to the Irish rebels, a descent on the Channel Islands, or a renewed effort to make use of Brest as a base. These offensive intentions of the Spaniards must be checked by the destruction of their fleet, lying now at Ferrol. An attack by land and by sea on that base was ordered, although, with character-

---

[38] Birch 2: 343; Sidney Papers 2: 52–53.

[39] *CSPD* 4 (1595–97): cclxii, 19, 4/13 unnumbered, 120, 124, 4/20 unnumbered, 140, 145, 150, 150, 199; cclxiii, 50, 74, 99; cclxiv, 3, 5, 19; HMC, *Hatfield* 7, 248–49; Monson 2: 38–40, quoting Pipe Office Declared Accounts.

istic irresolution, Elizabeth insisted that none of her ships were to enter the harbor to "their manifest danger."[40]

If the Spanish had already sailed from Ferrol, Essex was to follow them wherever they went. Assuming that he was able to accomplish their destruction at Ferrol, he was then to proceed to the Azores to intercept the homecoming ships from both the Indies. He could attack the islands by land or by sea but he must be home by winter. Specific permission was given to capture Terceira, the largest of the Azores, but as to holding it permanently the Queen was very doubtful. A succession of annual relief expeditions to sustain the occupation would be a burden the country could not bear. Behind this caution lay the understanding that no overseas base could be held without permanent command of the seas. Even if the ships at Ferrol were destroyed, Spanish sea power would still be formidable.

Essex's view of his mission was both grander and more optimistic. For him the operation was a strategic whole, with the most far-reaching consequences. Everything hinged, of course, on the destruction of Spanish sea power at Ferrol. With that accomplished, invasion would be forestalled, the Indies fleet unguarded, the conquest of the island made easy, and the possibility of a West Indies venture opened up. "To conclude Her Majesty would be absolute Queen of the Seas." An initially defensive operation would be transformed into an offensive against the very bases of Spanish power. The English could turn from a strategy of preservation to one of aggression.[41]

Essex's grasp of the grand strategy of sea power was sound. He saw that the enemy's naval force must first be wiped out before the English attempted to establish an overseas foothold in the islands or America. The objective was clear enough, but the Spanish position at Ferrol was likely to prove a very tough nut to crack. The veteran Vere, who thought an attack on Calais would afford greater overall results, expressed his grave doubts about the possibility of success at Ferrol. The port lay at the end of a fjord-like bay, long, narrow, and heavily defended by forts on the hills at the entrance. As Vere pointed out, and Essex recognized, a military victory was necessary before the ships could be destroyed. Just how an army was to be landed and deployed remained to be seen. Perhaps Essex

[40] *CSPD* 4 (1595–97): cclxiii, 102, for instructions. [41] *Apologie*, Bv–B3.

was given encouragement by the success of Drake and Norris in a similar situation at Corunna in 1589. Certainly the earl hoped that the defending forces would be a mere country militia.[42]

There were the usual cliff-hanging uncertainties before the fleet sailed. The Queen got cold feet when she contemplated the possibility that both fleets might be at sea at the same time, missing one another and leaving England naked to attack. She had to be reassured. Second, the long delays in assembling and manning the fleet exhausted the victuals, and the Queen had to be cajoled into granting another month's supply.[43]

The fleet departed on 10 July. The weather worsened immediately and, of the three squadrons, only Thomas Howard's saw the Spanish coast (off Corunna). Essex and Raleigh limped back to Plymouth and Howard, after vainly waiting off Corunna, followed the others home, arriving by 31 July. Whether the English could repeat at Ferrol the success at Corunna in 1589 would never be determined.

There followed weeks of confusion. The Queen was reasonably doubtful that anything could be accomplished now that the Spanish were alerted to English intentions, but left the decision up to Essex and his colleagues. The English knew that Philip's commander in northern Spain, the Adelantado, was frantically strengthening his defenses now, but the earl and his counsellors were still insistent they could accomplish their mission. Doubts there must have been, for suddenly on Raleigh's instigation Essex and the others (except for Vere) proposed that the fleet sail for the West Indies. This radical shift in plans has about it an air of desperation; in any case, when Essex and Raleigh took this scheme to court, the Queen promptly vetoed it.[44]

By 11 August Lord Thomas Howard was reluctantly advising that the soldiers, who were eating up their rations and who were visited by infection, should be reduced to a force of 1,000 veterans; the Queen assented. This decision ended all possibility of a military

[42] HMC, *Hatfield* 7: 211–12, 236–37.

[43] *CSPD* 4 (1595–97): cclxiv, 11, 21; HMC, *Hatfield* 7: 291.

[44] *CSPD* 4 (1595–97): cclxiv, 50; Monson 2: 53, 54, citing *CSPD* 4 (1595–97): cclxvi, 69; Francis Vere, *The Commentaries of Sir Francis Vere* (London, 1657), 45–67; BL, Cotton Mss., Otho E ix, fols. 377, 382–83; Birch 2: 353; Edwards 2: 191–93.

assault on Ferrol, which both Vere and Essex held to be a necessary prelude to the destruction of the fleet. Yet in the same letter the Queen approved a revised scheme for a renewed attempt at Ferrol, devised by Essex. He proposed to assail it with fireships, backed by the two captured Spanish galleons in his squadron and by merchant ships. (This tactic would meet the Queen's condition that none of her ships be risked in the operation.)[45]

Once again, in the same letter, Essex used the opportunity to reiterate his sense of the Queen's European mission, as defender of religion and liberty, and the strategic necessity for keeping the Spaniard from strengthening himself at sea or bringing home the Indian fleet. He knew of course that without an adequate army it was impossible "to beat the land army there and take in the forces, which was the certain way to command the Adelantado's fleet." How seriously we are to take Essex's announced intention of assaulting Ferrol we cannot tell. At least one of his officers thought it a matter of mere "pretenses and speeches," given out "to amaze the world of false alarms." "Both our general and the wisest of his council of war did well enough know that the Groyne or Ferrol were no morsels fit for our mouths." Nor was Robert Cecil any more sanguine in his expectations. Writing to the Deputy of Ireland he reported the Queen's warm favor to Essex and Raleigh in their brief visit to court between the two voyages, but as for the second of these he hoped for nothing but "the keeping up of the journey's reputation by keeping the sea as long as the time of year for the Spaniard to come out doth serve and to lie off the island and interrupt the Indian fleet." But in fact the fleet at Ferrol would not be burned, the carracks had come home, and the islands could not be taken, "so that their weak watery hopes do but faintly nourish that noble earl's comfort."[46]

Cecil's forebodings were borne out. Perverse winds drove the English too far westward, while mishaps beset their ships, driving one of the two captured galleons back home. A council of war concluded "that the enterprise of Ferrol was overthrown." The wind

---

[45] HMC, *Hatfield* 7: 346, 349; Birch 2: 357; Gorges's narrative in Samuel Purchas, *Hakluytus Posthumus or Purchas His Pilgrimes* (London, 1625; reprint, 20 vols., Glasgow, 1905–7) 20: 25–26; Devereux 1: 445–46; *Apologie*, Biv; *CSPD* 4 (1595–97): cclxiv, unnumbered [July ?], p. 481.

[46] *Apologie*, Biv; Purchas 20: 49; HMC, *Hatfield* 7: 361–62.

blowing strongly from the east drove them away from their target, but, even had it served, they lacked the ships needed for attack.[47]

This left no hope of effective action but the interception of the plate fleet or the defeat of the Adelantado, should he put to sea. The conquest of Terceira was impossible with the reduced land force. The English force's next move was triggered by a delusive report that the Spanish had indeed sailed for the Indies. This led to a prolonged game of blindman's buff on the seas around the Azores. While the separated squadrons of the English fleet dodged frustratedly about the islands, the West Indian fleet, although detected by their foes, sheltered safely under the guns of Terceira. In the end—in mid-October—the decision to return home was reluctantly taken with nothing to show but a few prizes. Even as the fleet was sailing from the Azores the Queen was writing to express her disappointment in the year's action at Ferrol and in the failure to intercept the East Indian carracks. Unless the plate fleet were intercepted the Queen would be worse off than when she had launched the action. She ordered Essex to leave some warships and merchant vessels to lie off the islands in the hope of intercepting the treasure ships. Neither he nor any of the other principal commanders were to stay with the fleet.[48]

The crowning irony came in the circumstances of their arrival home. Battered by a storm and scattered over the waters off the Scillies, some of the English vessels fell in with the remnants of the Adelantado's invasion fleet. The Spanish admiral had finally put to sea just as Essex left the Azores. The same storm that scattered Essex's ships as it neared the home coast utterly routed the enemy fleet, although some Spanish vessels were seen off Falmouth, the intended goal of the expedition. By the time the English government was aware of the attack, the enemy fleet was already dispersed. In 1597, as in the preceding year, the winds proved to be England's best defense. Once again Spanish anxiety to strike a retaliatory blow had led to fatally unwise decisions. There was a short-lived flurry of activity as the English became aware of the threat, but by 31 October the extra ships hastily commissioned could be paid off.[49]

[47] Purchas 20: 27 (official report) and 71–72 (Gorges account).

[48] HMC, *Hatfield* 7: 433–34.

[49] Sir Arthur Gorges, "A Larger Relation of the said Iland Voyage, Written by Sir Arthur Gorges Knight, Collected in the Queenes Ship Called the West Spite,"

The campaigns of 1596 and 1597 were landmarks in England's military history. The activist faction, which had long urged an offensive strategy, was given its head. There followed considered efforts aiming at a deliberate use of English sea power against Spain. The more moderate hopes of its sponsors aimed at crippling the enemy's power to strike at England, while their more ambitious expectations looked to a successful capture of Spanish strong points. Unlike the muddled effort of 1589 these enterprises had been directed by leaders with a clear-headed sense of the strategic goals they sought. They were in important ways a different breed from the half-tamed buccaneers of earlier years.

Yet, in spite of the intelligence of their strategic insights, these leaders largely failed in the enterprises to which they set their hands. Much responsibility must be laid at the door of their royal commander-in-chief. Her timidities, her hesitations, and her irresolution clogged their best efforts, and her ingrained parsimony often deprived her captains of essential supplies. Yet they in turn betrayed their own goals when they allowed personal rivalry to override urgent military considerations, as at Cadiz. They had very imperfect control over their own passions and over the untrained troops they commanded.

The shortcomings begotten by inexperience were painfully reflected in the frequent gap between ends and means, which was apparent in every one of the overseas expeditions of the decade. A glaring example was the 1597 attack on Ferrol. Given the known probabilities of wind and weather, the strength of Spanish fortifications, and the intrinsic topographical characteristics of the site, the chance of success, even on the first voyage, was poor (as Vere pointed out). The outcome of the second voyage, undertaken with a mere 1,000 soldiers, was a foregone conclusion. And, indeed, Essex's basic strategic scheme, the seizure of a key Spanish position such as Cadiz or Terceira in order to hold the Spanish empire to ransom, demanded, as the Queen's instructions implied, resources sufficient to keep open the sea lanes to England so as to maintain a continuous reinforcement of men and supplies.

There was more involved, however, than a clash of personalities

in Samuel Purchas, *Hakluytus Posthumus or Purchas His Pilgrimes*, 20: 34–129 (Glasgow, 1907), 124; Monson 2: 77, 78; *CSPVen* 9 (1592–1603): 112 (8 November 1597); HMC, *Hatfield* 7: 494–95; Tenison 10: 293–94.

or a deficiency of judgment. To sustain the enterprises advocated by the hawkish faction would have required a larger, more permanent, more professional, and certainly more costly naval establishment than the Elizabethan government possessed. To have obtained any of these desiderata would have required a leap of the royal imagination, indeed a miraculous transformation in the persona of their royal mistress that was quite beyond the realm of possibility. As is argued in Chapter 1, the state over which the Queen presided was a minimalist one, designed almost entirely in terms of peacetime needs. Its war-making machinery, such as it was, was designed solely for short-term purposes and its fiscal structure, correspondingly organized, provided inadequate and inelastic revenue for large-scale or prolonged warfare. It would require not only another ruler but also a wholesale revolution both of ideas and of institutions to render the English state capable of realizing the potentiality of its newly developed sea power.

The year 1597 saw the last attempt to use the royal navy for a grand assault on Spanish power, but during the remaining five years of the reign there was continuing naval activity, although at a reduced level. In 1598 English attention was focused on the peace negotiations between Spain and France and on the growing crisis in Ireland. Public funds were not available for a naval enterprise, but the year witnessed the largest private venture of the war.[50]

The Earl of Cumberland had invested his fortune in privateering and had acquired a reputation as a great sea commander. He now assembled a fleet of some eighteen ships and 1,000 soldiers under a royal commission with power to impress men and to enforce discipline. The profits were to go wholly to the adventurers, paying only the Queen's custom. The objective, however, was more than mere plunder. One of the various aims of the strategists of the offensive had always been the seizure of a Spanish New World possession. Cumberland set his sights on Puerto Rico, a small, sparsely peopled island, flanking Spanish lines of communication and with a secure and defensible port. The earl made the usual preliminary canter down the Portuguese coast and so frightened the carracks waiting to sail from Lisbon that they postponed their voyage. Cumberland then pressed on to his destination and after some fighting secured

[50] Monson 2: 204–25; Purchas 20: 34–135; Gorges narrative in BL, Sloane Ms. 3289.

the island with its port of San Juan. Any hopes of holding on to it turned to dust and ashes, however, as dysentery felled his men, killing four hundred of them before he left for home. Financially the profits were not equal to half the cost; militarily it was a striking success—strategically, a failure. It displayed once more the potential of English strking power and the fatal flaws that made impossible any exploitation of that power.[51]

The year 1599 was marked not by any further English offensives but by a panic reaction that triggered the largest English mobilization since 1588. It illuminates all too fully the inadequacies of English intelligence. Just possibly it may owe something to a fear of Essex, then in command in Ireland but thought in some quarters to be considering a descent on England. Initially the circumstances of the year seemed to promise tranquillity to England since the Dutch had launched a formidable fleet that would remain off the Iberian coasts for the whole season. In fact, after a reconnaissance the Dutch sailed on south to the Canaries.[52]

Then in July the government had a report of an impending invasion, followed by a letter from Brest that the Spanish were asking leave to anchor ships there. This led to a fury of preparation. A fleet was commissioned and London called on to supplement it with more ships. At the same time no less than 25,000 soldiers were called to arms. Vere was summoned home with 2,000 veterans; preparations were made for blocking the Thames. After a few weeks reassuring reports from Brest and from the Spanish coast lowered the temperature. First the army and then the fleet were demobilized. Cecil rather shamefacedly explained that the reports came "with a whirlwind" and he had chosen "to run rather with the stream of providence than of too much confidence on my own intelligences." While the episode reveals the breakdown of effective intelligence services (possibly due to the absence of Essex and the loss of his network of intelligencers), it also highlights the state of tension under which the Elizabethan government labored. Twice, in 1596 and 1597, the enemy had come unexpectedly, detected only at the last minute, and only the winds of providence had staved off

---

[51] Williamson, *Cumberland*, 174–218; *The Egerton Papers*, ed. J. P. Collier, Camden Soc. 12 (1840), 263; Monson 2: 216; *CSPD* 5 (1598–1601): cclxviii, 71, where the returns are noted as £15,000 to £16,000, half of the charges.

[52] Monson 2: 97–111; HMC, *The Manuscripts of the Right Honourable F. J. Savile Foljambe, of Osberton* (15th rpt., app., pt. 5, London, 1897), 69.

a landing. The government could not risk a third tempting of the fates.[53]

In 1600 there was a modest venture by the English. Four ships under Sir Richard Leveson were sent out in the hope of intercepting the East Indian carracks off the Azores, but they evaded him and he returned home in September empty-handed. Naval action in 1601–1602 was dominated by the Kinsale landing, in which the navy played an effectual role in blockading the invaders. In the spring of 1603 a squadron putting to sea under Leveson was halted by news of the Queen's death. The fighting was over.[54]

[53] *CSPD* 5 (1598–1601): cclxxi, 94; Ralph Winwood, *Memorials of State in the Reigns of Queen Elizabeth and King James I*, ed. Edmund Sawyer (3 vols., London, 1925) 1: 19; Monson 2: 102, 103; 101 reports the Cecil letter but gives no reference.
[54] Monson 2: 196–98.

PART III

WAGING THE WAR II:

THE ALLIES—FRANCE

CHAPTER 7

THE WILLOUGHBY EXPEDITION

1589

On 1 August 1589 Henry III of France was stabbed to death by a Catholic zealot. That event immediately precipitated an alliance between the English Queen and the new French King, faced as they now were by a common enemy. England now had an ally who, potentially, might reestablish a counterbalance powerful enough to hold the Habsburg power in check and bring its ruler to the negotiating table. For the first time since the war began, some prospect of peace flickered on the horizon. More immediately, however, there loomed a mighty struggle as Henry IV fought for a throne that as yet eluded his grasp. Throughout this struggle England would be under constant pressure to provide money and men on at least as large a scale as her Netherlands commitment. Elizabeth was to respond grumblingly but not ungenerously to Henry's urgencies, yet by far the greater part of her contribution resulted in nothing but the loss of life and the waste of treasure. In the end it was Henry's own efforts, political rather than military, that would win him his throne. Consequently the chronicle of English participation in the French struggle that follows is one of endless frustration, in which a series of defeats and disappointments was paradoxically to end in the realization of a major English war aim: the re-establishment of a European balance of power that would bring Spanish aggression to a halt.

In long perspective the assassination of Henry III ended one phase of French history and brought to the throne a new king and a new dynasty who would re-establish French unity, revive French greatness, and initiate a new epoch of European history. In the short term, however, the assassination was only one more link in a chain of events that had been being forged for a generation. The childlessness of the Valois kings had cast a shadow over French politics for at least a decade. The death of the Duke of Anjou, the last Valois prince, in 1584 made certain that the problems of religion and of the succession would merge, now that Henry of Navarre stood next to the throne. At the end of 1584 the treaty of Joinville sealed a pact between the Catholic Guise princes and the King of Spain for the defense of the Catholic faith, in which they proclaimed the heretic Henry of Navarre ineligible for the succession and set forth the claim of his uncle, the Cardinal of Bourbon. The treaty insured that ultimately the ensuing struggle would be international as well as merely domestic in nature.

For the present there unfolded a three-cornered struggle for control of the country among the King, the Guises, and Navarre. In 1588 the Day of Barricades made the King a virtual prisoner of the Guises until Henry III, acting with unwonted determination, turned the tables by killing the Duke and Cardinal of Guise in December of that year. But the snake was not scotched; the vigor of continuing League resistance under its new leader, the Duke of Mayenne, drove the King into the arms of Navarre in April 1589, and for the short remainder of his life the two Henrys worked in harness. This meant that many of the royalist faction who backed the last Valois were ready on his death to join with the Huguenots in support of the new king. Even with this backing, however, Henry IV controlled barely half the country. Paris and nearly every city of size as well as whole provinces from the Mediterranean to the English Channel were in League hands. Since 1585 the Catholic party had received Spanish subventions; they could stand assured of continued Spanish aid, even, when the need arose, the assistance of Parma and his army from the Low Countries. Henry IV, menaced by this threatening combination, necessarily sought to redress the balance by summoning foreign assistance. Within a week of his accession his agents were soliciting a loan from Elizabeth; within another month the Queen was levying troops to send to France.

In England, as in France, the events of 1589 were only a new chapter in an old story. Elizabeth's relations with the Huguenots went back even before the ill-advised intervention at LeHavre

(Newhaven) in 1562–1563. Later dealings with the French Protestants were more reserved in character, but they had always been able to count upon a base in English ports, representations in their behalf at the French court, and various kinds of clandestine aid (for which they had to pay). At the same time the Queen had carefully cultivated friendly relations with the Valois court, based on the treaty of alliance signed at Blois in 1572, which, however tattered and torn, survived the attempted extinction of French Protestantism in the Massacre of St. Bartholomew. From 1579 to 1581 Elizabeth had made a supreme effort to secure a working alliance aimed at checking Spanish recovery of full power in the Low Countries. She failed and had to settle for a poor second-best: Anglo-French backing for the feckless Duke of Anjou as governor of the Low Countries. When that episode petered out in dismal disarray, Anglo-French relations drifted uncertainly. With the temporary triumph of the Guises English influence at Paris was virtually nil. After Henry of Navarre moved into open opposition to the Crown in 1585 the Queen provided (in 1587) a modest loan of £30,000 to pay for the services of German mercenaries.[1] Although the German army was defeated by the royal forces, Navarre managed to keep afloat in the provinces south of the Loire. He kept his lines to the English government open, looking to Walsingham as his intermediary there.[2] In 1588 Buzanval, his agent in London, was pressing for English help in negotiating a loan in Germany.[3] In the spring of 1589 he was busily recruiting men and buying weapons in London.[4]

As far as Henry III was concerned, Elizabeth's role was necessarily limited as long as he was under Guise's thumb. The most she could do was to urge him—vainly—to resistance, but once he had broken free she could exert her influence to bring about cooperation with Navarre. A request for a direct loan was turned down in June 1589,[5] but in July Burghley was advancing a plan for a loan to Henry III as bait to draw him into a general anti-Spanish league.[6] Thus his death at the end of the month served to reshuffle a group of actors already on the stage and to intensify a drama already being

[1] *Calendar of State Papers, Foreign Series, of the Reign of Elizabeth*, ed. Joseph Stevenson et al. (London, 1863–1950) 21(1) (June 1586–June 1588): 186, 200.
[2] *CSPF* 1588(2): 63.   [3] *Ibid.*, 53–54.
[4] *CSPF* 1589(1): 260, 262, 263, 275.   [5] *Ibid.*, 340–41.
[6] *Ibid.*, 349; BL, Lansdowne Ms. 104, 26/57–59.

played. Even before the assassination Elizabeth was moving towards intervention in French affairs, but the death of the king catapulted her into an active participation.[7]

The sudden appearance of a new ally was a mixed blessing. In the past Elizabeth had striven with all her resources to win French support against Spain; now it had come, but in a form that made France as much a liability as an asset. If war in France led to the diversion of Parma's armies from the Low Countries, the advantage to the Queen's Dutch allies was all to the good and might even permit some reduction in English commitments there. But a heavy price had to be paid since Henry's poverty and his weakness in the field put pressure on the Queen to provide both money and men to assure the new King's survival. He was an ally who, at least for the present, made heavy demands on English resources without offering much compensatory strength that might ease the English burden. If Henry could achieve mastery in France he might make the kingdom once again a counterweight to Habsburg power in Europe and thus restore the balance between the two great powers on which English policy had counted for decades past.

The dispatch of English forces was a direct response to Henry's plight in the fall of 1589. With an army less than half the size of his opponent's, he had fallen back on Normandy, where a loyal supporter kept Dieppe for him, at once a place of refuge and a gateway for English aid. But he was in great risk of being trapped with his back against the sea. By 24 August was asking for troops,[8] and as early as 9 September orders for levying forces were being sent to the Lord Lieutenants of the southeastern counties.[9] As commander of the expedition the Queen chose Lord Willoughby, Leicester's successor as the English general in the Low Countries. His commission, signed 20 September,[10] explained that because of her commitments in the Netherlands and Ireland she could provide only one month's pay. If her forces were needed for a longer time, Henry would have to pay out of his own pocket—at English rates. She dispatched 4,000 men (actually 3,600 after allowance for 10% dead pays).

The Queen was loath to send any "unless there shall be very

---

[7] For Wotton's mission in February 1589, see *CSPF* 1589(1): 91.

[8] *List and Analysis of State Papers, Foreign Series: Elizabeth I*, ed. Richard Bruce Wernham (5 vols. to date, London, 1964–89) 1589–90: 470.

[9] SP 12/226/13, 14, 18, 19, and September 1589.   [10] SP 78/20/52.

apparent and urgent necessity to employ them,"[11] and on the news of Henry's brilliant and unexpected victory at Arques (20–21 September) she held back her men from embarkation. Walsingham warned Ambassador Stafford to be "very wary in putting them in comfort there." Indeed, the expedition was very nearly revoked. Ambassador Stafford, faithful to instructions, wrote to Willoughby after Arques that the King was out of danger and the English general should not sail. Willoughby ignored this advice and crossed to France. The Queen, enraged,[12] ordered him to return unless Henry desperately needed his help. Henry, rejoicing in Willoughby's arrival after hearing he was not to come, naturally found reason to keep the English forces.[13]

The English had been ferried to Dieppe during the last week of September and the first of October. On 11 October they set off to join the King outside Paris and underwent their baptism of fire in a vain attempt on one of the city gates. Henry abandoned his siege of the capital for a sweep through Normandy and Maine that effectively asserted royal authority in the provinces north of the Loire. The English accompanied him in this campaign, which lasted until the end of the year. Active participants in many of the military actions of these months, they provided an augmentation to the royal forces, which on several occasions was crucial to Henry's success.[14] The march was one of great hardship in the wet weather of late fall. They lived off the country and had no pay from the King. Inevitably the list of sick grew as the weeks went by. Although only about one hundred were killed fighting, barely eight hundred were fit for service by the end of December, and only about three thousand returned.[15]

The first venture of the English in cooperation with their new ally was a novel experience for the Queen's government. When they had gone to the assistance of the Dutch in 1585 the relation was of a different kind. England was very much the senior partner; the suppliant provinces were as yet a quite inchoate state and accepted—indeed solicited—a kind of protectoral role by the Queen. This was institutionalized by giving English officials membership

---

[11] *L&A* 1589–90: 473.
[12] *APC* 1589–90: 144–46.
[13] *L&A* 1589–90: 478.
[14] Wernham, 162–64, 172–73.
[15] *L&A* 1589–90: 478, 551, 556, 558, 561; *CSPD* 2 (1581–90): ccxxix, 35. See Cruickshank, chap. 13 (B).

in the Council of State and the English commander authority over the States' army.

In 1589 the new partner was a sovereign prince at once head of state and commander in the field. The urgency of his circumstances was so great that no time could be spared for drawing up a contract of partnership, a formal alliance similar to the 1585 Treaty of Nonsuch with the Dutch. Willoughby's instructions were simple and to the point:[16] he was at the disposition of the King, who had a carte blanche to make use of the English forces as seemed best to him. Moreover, the virtual breakdown of communications with a peripatetic monarch, whose seat of government was the camp, made impossible coherent dealings between the sovereigns. The English ambassador, unable to find horse at Dieppe, returned home, at the urging of the King, who thought him more useful as an intermediary with the Queen if he were at her court.[17] Burghley complained that it was easier to hear from Venice than from Willoughby, to which the latter retorted he would rather travel from Venice than across the terrifyingly unsafe roads of northern France.[18]

The Queen had been hustled into this expedition by the urgency of Henry's plea for help. She would have backed out after the victory of Arques eased his situation, but Willoughby and the King between them thwarted her will. The campaign proved both fruitful and brief. Henry's assertion of his effective presence in the Seine valley was essential to the continued functioning of the alliance, so Elizabeth could feel her money and men were not thrown away.

The clamorous necessity of the first months of Henry's reign was now ended, and with it the moment of enforced cooperation. The year 1590 was one of checkered fortunes for the King. In March he defeated the Leaguers at Ivry, but the ensuing siege of Paris was broken by Parma's bloodless intervention in the early fall. In these events the English played no role. Now that Henry's survival was insured and a breathing space secured, Elizabeth had time to consider her position more deliberately. It soon became apparent that, although the two sovereigns (along with the States General) shared a common foe, this by no means insured identity of other interests

[16] *L&A* 1589–90: 479, 532.   [17] *Ibid.*, 479.
[18] *Ibid.*, 549.

or agreement as to the best strategies to be used against the Spaniards.

In 1589 Henry's enemies were his own countrymen, the Catholic Leaguers. His very successes against them in the fall of that year led to an influx of foreign auxiliaries to their ranks. At Ivry there was already a contingent of 1,700 troops sent by Parma to assist the League commander Mayenne in the struggle for Normandy. Later in the year Parma himself intervened to relieve Paris from the royal besieger. Henceforth the King had to reckon not only with his Catholic countrymen but also with the formidable Duke and his veteran soldiers. Anxious to strengthen his own unstable army, fluctuating in number and quality, ill-paid and ill-provisioned, Henry sought to increase his strength with a corps of German mercenaries. Perpetually short of funds himself, the King now turned to the Queen for financial aid. She had already loaned him some £40,000 in late 1589, and another £10,000 followed in September 1590. (There had been an earlier loan to him as King of Navarre of about £30,000, which, with some other small sums and accrued interest, made a total of £81,000 owing from Henry to Elizabeth.[19])

In November 1590 Henry proposed that the Queen participate with the German princes in a loan designed to pay for a mercenary force, and shortly thereafter he escalated that demand to include a force of 4,000 English soldiers.[20] Hence, by late 1590 the Queen was under strong pressure from Henry's envoys, seeking to persuade her that England's interests would be served by a large diversion of English resources to France and that the safety of her island realm could be secured on the battlefields of Normandy and Picardy. Concretely this meant more cash from the Queen's scanty coffers and the service of 4,000 Englishmen. Money and men were to be wholly at the French King's disposal. Such a role, that of a sleeping partner, docilely contributing at the active partner's behest, was not likely to appeal to the English Queen.

This force was intended to deal with Parma's threatened intervention from the Low Countries, but this was only one aspect of Spanish strategy. They sought also to distract the King's attention and to fragment his authority by stirring up local disturbance wherever they could. The Duke of Savoy was encouraged to mount an

[19] *CSPF* 1588(1): 186, 200; *L&A* 1589–90: 471, 483; 1590–91: 455.
[20] *Ibid.*, 496, 497.

invasion of Provence and ambitious regional satraps everywhere aided in setting up shop as autonomous warlords. In one province the Spaniards went even further, sending in forces of their own. In Brittany the Duke of Mercoeur, exploiting his wife's claims, sought to build a fiefdom for himself.[21] The Spanish offered both money and men, for their goals in this province were not limited to the French theater of war. Control of Breton ports and Breton waters would provide an excellent staging post for an invasion of England, better in many respects than Flanders. This development meant that henceforth Elizabeth and Henry had widely divergent perspectives on the French theater of war and consequently a different order of priorities in the strategy to be pursued there. For the English the arrival of Spanish troops at the Breton port of Blavet in October 1590 was cause for serious alarm. Indeed, they had sought unsuccessfully to prevent this occurrence by naval intervention.[22] But Henry saw this episode in a less serious light. What to Elizabeth was a looming threat to the security of her realm was to Henry only yet another harassment, in this case on the periphery of his kingdom and far removed from what he saw as the main theaters of action.

Elizabeth, her attention divided among the Low Countries, the Breton coast, and the Spanish ports, could not afford to ignore any of these theaters. Although she did not dispatch another expeditionary force against Spain like that of 1589, she did maintain a substantial fleet at sea in 1590 (in part to check Spanish access to Brittany). In the Low Countries the English forces under Sir Francis Vere formed a veteran core of experienced soldiery, the largest body of Englishmen under arms and the nearest approximation to an English professional army. Some of the Queen's counsellors would argue that it was in the Low Countries and with these men that England could most effectively strike at its enemy.[23] Indeed, Elizabeth herself had proposed to the States in 1590 that she should land 4,000 men to cooperate with the Dutch commander, Count Maurice of Nassau, in a strike against Dunkirk. She had gone so far as to

[21] For Breton history in the 1590's, see L. Gregoire, *La ligue en Bretagne* (Paris and Nantes, 1856).
[22] Lodge 3: 10–12; see also Chapter 2.
[23] See Wingfield's pamphlet, cited in Chapter 1.

order forces put in readiness in the counties for dispatch to the Low Countries.[24]

Such was the situation in November 1590 when a high-ranking ambassador, the Viscount Turenne, came to press support for the proposed German subsidy. Hardly had he left before another French mission, this one from the royalist governor in Brittany, the Prince of Dombes, arrived at the English court, urgently clamoring for 2,000 men, plus supplies, to resist the Spanish at Blavet. These were the alternatives of action that faced the Queen and her ministers at the opening of 1591. That some action should be undertaken seems to have been the common assumption of all, but which could would best serve English interests?[25]

Most pressing were the proposals brought by the French ambassador Turenne. The eminence of this high-born Protestant leader,[26] kin to the great dynasties of Montmorency and the Chatillon, bore witness to the urgency of the King's request. He came to pursue a proposal broached in the previous year. Henry was anxious to secure a German mercenary force to be backed by a consortium of German princes, who would foot the bill for initial costs. England's role was to prime the princely pumps by a sizable contribution. Elizabeth responded by dispatching the naturalized Italian Horatio Palavicino, an experienced intermediary with continental rulers, to Germany with instructions to exhort the princes to a concerted support of Henry. However, since the most he was allowed to offer as bait was a vague half-promise of an English contribution, the mission came to nothing.[27] On his return she sent him on a second mission, this time to France.[28] Although he was forbidden to commit the Queen to further expense and could do little more than make encouraging noises, Henry had shrewdly manipulated the situation by choosing to assume blandly that Palavicino's mission was a proposal by the Queen for the furtherance of the loan. The purpose settled, all that Turenne needed to do in England was to work

[24] HMC, *Hatfield* 4: 57–58. See also Sidney Papers 1: 312.

[25] *L&A* 1589–90: 468, 471.

[26] Howell A. Lloyd, *The Rouen Campaign, 1590–1592: Politics, Warfare and the Early-Modern State* (Oxford, 1973), 31–32.

[27] *L&A* 1589–90: 714; Lawrence Stone, *An Elizabethan: Sir Horatio Palavicino* (London, 1956), 149–62.

[28] Stone, 164.

out the details of execution. He could then proceed to Germany in company with Palavicino, armed with a letter of credit that would persuade the princes to fill up the subscription.[29]

Elizabeth's reaction was predictably cold. She had had some experience with the use of German mercenaries. There was Count Casimir's futile enterprise in the Netherlands in 1578 and, more recently, and very much to the point, the fruitless German expedition to aid Henry of Navarre in 1587 on which she had wasted £30,000. At first she refused any money at all, offering only moral suasion,[30] but eventually she came around to a limited commitment. Palavicino was sent off to Germany with power to offer £10,000 (and just possibly £5,000 more) towards a total of £60,000.[31] It was uphill work to persuade the princes to act, and Palavicino stretched his instructions by offering an extra £5,000, only to be repudiated at home. However, Turenne did get his army (some 15,000 men) and by the beginning of 1591 its projected arrival was a major factor in all strategic calculations.

The approach of a German force of such size opened up new possibilities for offensive action, and at the end of 1590 the Queen's government was canvassing available options. Robert Sidney's agent in London reported to his employer at Flushing a rumor that the Queen had agreed to send 4,000 men to check Parma in October 1590 but then had reversed her decision.[32] A paper of the veteran Low Countries commander, Sir Roger Williams, dated in November, surveys the Continental scene.[33] Optimistic about the French potential once the mercenaries arrived, he believed Parma could be starved out or beaten in the field, but it would be six months before the German succor reached France. In the meantime the King was woefully weak and his weakness threatened England's safety. The French could not check the Spanish in Brittany and, if the latter were allowed to consolidate themselves at Blavet, England would

[29] Lloyd, *Rouen*, 36; Thomas Egerton, Baron Ellesmere, *A Compilation . . . of Evidence . . . to Illustrate the Life and Character of Thomas Egerton, Lord Ellesmere* (Paris, 1812), prints Turenne's instructions (29–30).

[30] Lloyd, *Rouen*, 40–41.

[31] *Ibid.*, 42–47; *L&A* 1589–90: 725–28; *APC* 1588–89: 419; *CSPD* 2 (1581–90): ccxxx, 68, 84.

[32] Sidney Papers 1: 312.

[33] SP 78/22/134. See Vere's doubts about using the Germans in the Low Countries, SP 84/41/36.

be in the gravest danger. Most to be feared was a junction between Parma and the Spanish forces already in Brittany. Hence the Queen must be ready to succor Henry. At least 8,000 men must be sent, either to Brittany or to the Low Countries; Williams seemed to favor the latter alternative since it would force Parma to draw away from France altogether, and that was the great desideratum. "All is nothing without dislodging the Spaniard out of France."

In closing, however, Williams lifted his gaze from the Continent to sound the clarion call of the activist party—Spain's power could be broken only on the seas. "Neither shall we nor our friends give them the law as we should do without ransacking his Indies, for his treasure comes unto him as our saletts to us. When we eat all we fetch more out of our gardens, so doth he fetch his treasure out of the ground after spending all that is coined."

Williams's recommendations did not go unheard. In the same month Burghley was writing to Palavicino with a scheme that the Queen pressed on Turenne for bringing the German mercenaries by way of Cologne into Brabant and Flanders, where in collaboration with the Anglo-Dutch-French forces they could pen up Parma so straitly that he could not risk leaving his vulnerable Low Country bases undefended while he entered France.[34] This proposal was forcefully urged by the Queen, for whom it had the particular attraction of economy. The English troops in the Low Countries could be used and there would be no need for levying new forces. But Sir John Norris, when consulted as to the feasibility of this scheme, put a damper on it.[35] It would certainly require more forces than those currently available in the Netherlands. Would the Queen find men for both Brittany and Flanders? In Norris's view the Breton enterprise was more urgently necessary; the Germans, even if not strong enough to break through, would by their very presence inhibit Parma's movements and prevent a junction with the Spaniards in Brittany. In pressing these views he was, of course, taking a narrowly English outlook. Action in the Low Countries would have required allied cooperation; it would also have benefitted all three parties if the enemy's principal army in northern Europe could be crippled. A Breton campaign, on the other hand, would largely serve specifically English interests.

For a moment the prospect of a large-scale coordinated effort,

[34] SP 78/22/143, 163.   [35] SP 84/41/52. See also Vere in SP 84/41/36.

Anglo-Dutch-French in the Low Countries and Anglo-French in Brittany, seemed a possibility, but the Queen's reluctance to launch so expensive an operation aborted it. Her attention more and more turned to Britanny.[36] At the beginning of 1591 Williams once again pressed his views. While reiterating the dangers of a Spanish occupation of Blavet, with a harbor as ample and useful as those at Falmouth or Milford Haven, he shifted his prescription for action away from Brittany to the French royal army.[37] He now argued that the correct strategy was to reinforce Henry with an English army, even if it meant withdrawing the whole English field force from the Low Countries. Parma would in any case have to go on the defensive there. The French horse, he held, were the best in the world and, with the support of 3,000 English foot, could handily beat Parma in the field. His voice was not unheard, and the possibility of intervention in Flanders, but without adding any English forces there, was still in the air in March.[38] However, by this time the government had moved decisively to intervention in Brittany.

This was not the only decision made in this spring. At almost the same moment as Sir John Norris embarked for Brittany, another force, under Sir Roger Williams, sailed for Dieppe in Normandy, and by early summer Elizabeth had committed herself to two major operations in France. Nearly 8,000 men were involved, financed entirely by English funds. The first phase of the Norman venture, the siege of Rouen, ended after some eight months in the abandonment of the enterprise. A small contingent of English soldiers (less than 2,000) remained in service under Henry IV until his conversion to Catholicism in 1593. Their service as auxiliaries made some small contribution to Henry's military operations in these months but their effect on the French situation was marginal.

The Breton contingent was to spend three unhappy years of fruitless inactivity, vainly hoping for an effective French collaboration that never materialized. Only at the very end of their stay did they realize any success. When the Spanish, faced by the disintegration of the Leaguer cause, set out to build a base that could control the haven of Brest, Norris's forces assaulted the fort and wiped out the garrison. They then departed, content that Brittany was no

[36] Wernham, 272.   [37] SP 78/23/28.
[38] SP 78/23/161–62.

longer a menace to English security but bitterly resentful of the total failure of the French royalists to give them support.

The Breton intervention began with an initial plea from the royalist governor of that province in November 1590. At the time he had been turned down on the grounds that the King, free of Parma's presence, could now take action in the western province.[39] But the warnings of Williams and Norris as to the dangers from a Spanish-occupied Brittany obviously began to sink in, and early in December Norris was commissioned to secure the withdrawal of troops from the United Provinces for use in Brittany.[40] The States objected strenuously to this, and in the end a compromise was effected. Half of a force of 3,000 for service in Brittany would be made up of veterans (to be replaced by draftees from England).[41]

In the meantime the Queen had sent an agent, Edmund Yorke, to the King, who was besieging Chartres.[42] He was to reproach Henry for his neglect of his western coasts and to paint a grim picture of Parma marching into Brittany to form a junction with the Spaniards already there. To avert this calamity the Queen offered 3,000 English troops for Breton service, provided there were assurances of strong French support. Henry's response was one of prompt acceptance. Full of facile promises, he assured the envoy that an equal number of French would be sent and that the ports would be thrown open and supplies provided; there was even a carefully hedged offer of Brest as an English base. The Queen, moved not only by the appeals of the Bretons and the persuasions of her military advisors, but also by reports of new Spanish forces for Brittany, accepted Henry's promises at face value.[43] In April 1591 a contract was drawn up for the dispatch of 3,000 foot at a monthly charge of £3,500, to be repaid by France at the end of twelve months. A force of this modest size could play only a defensive role.[44]

---

[39] L&A 1590–91: 476.   [40] Ibid., 262.
[41] APC 1590–91: 206, 361–63; SP 84/41/168.   [42] SP 78/23/48–58.
[43] SP 78/23/161; Lloyd, Rouen, 60.   [44] L&A 1590–91: 529.

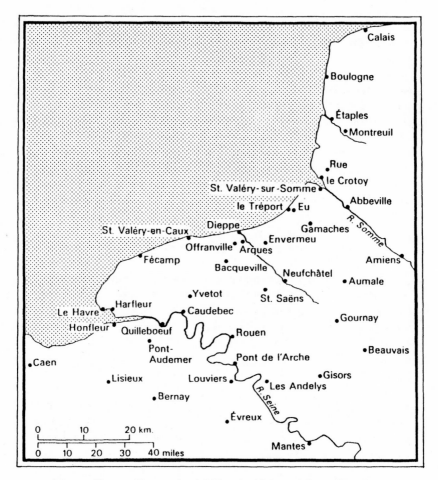

MAP 1. *Eastern Normandy and Picardy.* (Adapted from Wernham)

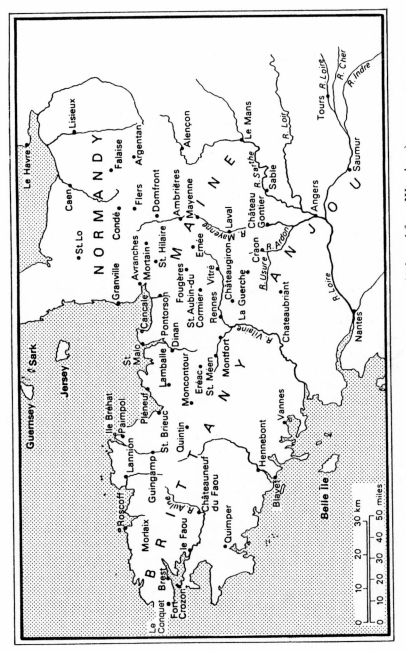

MAP 2. *Brittany and its borders, 1591–1595.* (Adapted from Wernham)

CHAPTER 8

BRITTANY AND

ROUEN

COMMAND of the Breton expedition was given to the veteran Sir John Norris.[1] His instructions bear witness to the uncertainties, confusions, and sheer ignorance that surrounded the enterprise. The port of disembarkation was left uncertain—either Granville in Normandy or Cancale on the other side of the Bay of Mont St. Michel, a few miles from St. Malo. (In fact, they landed at Paimpol, some sixty miles to the west, on the western side of the Gulf of St. Malo.) No doubt, the instructions indicated, someone in authority would meet him. Once landed, he was to ascertain the state of the King's forces in the province and that of his foes, native and foreign. Norris was empowered to join in any enterprise proposed by the French that was within the capability of the combined forces, but if they were too weak, he was to urge against taking action. It was taken for granted that until the King sent larger forces to the scene no definitive engagement was likely.

Norris himself, before he left Southampton, surveyed the possibilities as laid out by the Breton agents in England.[2] Of the three alternative actions proposed, two were not feasible and the third not worth the effort; Norris's conclusion was that it would be better for the present to employ the whole force in Normandy (where Williams had been hastily dispatched with six hundred of Norris's bands to the endangered port of Dieppe) until better arrangements

[1] SP 78/24, 26.　　　　　　　[2] SP 78/24/66–67.

could be made in Brittany. Nevertheless Norris followed his
Queen's instructions, went his way with his regiments, and landed
in Brittany at the beginning of May 1591.[3]

When Norris set out, he faced an uncertain and unpromising
prospect in the province in which he was about to land. Well before
the death of Henry III, Brittany had fallen firmly into the grip of
the Guisan party. Its governor, the Duke of Mercoeur, appointed
in 1582, was a cadet of the House of Guise, and by marrying a
descendant of the ancient Breton ducal family he had secured a
claim on the loyalties of the Bretons, who retained a lively sense of
their special identity and were anxious to preserve as much as possible of their own institutions.[4] They were also enthusiastically
Catholic, and the Duke had little difficulty in suppressing the Protestant movement in the province, driving its clergy into exile. A
program of preaching and processions and the careful organization
of a Catholic party structure secured the ducal position on both the
political and the religious fronts. Although there was some support
for Henry III in his last months, after he had broken with the
Guises, on his death it was not difficult for Mercoeur to assert his
mastery over almost all the province. The scattered royalist strongholds were seized; Nantes was firmly secured; and among the principal towns only Rennes on the eastern frontier of the province remained loyal to Henry IV. Other than this there were royalist
pockets widely separated, such as Brest, where a local coup put in
power a royalist governor, the Marquis de Sourdeac. St. Malo, initially royalist, fell to the Leaguers but the local leadership carefully
protected local interests, almost to the point of neutrality.[5]

On landing, Norris made contact with the Prince of Dombes,
Henry's lieutenant in maritime Brittany, and the two collaborated
in the successful siege of Guingamp, a town a few miles from Norris's landing place.[6] Norris was soon asking for reinforcements and
more artillery,[7] but the Queen, disgusted at the smallness of the
royal forces in Brittany, not only refused them but hinted at the
withdrawal of her own soldiers unless the King made more effort
on his side.[8] After the initial success at Guingamp the Anglo-

[3] *L&A* 1590–91: 560.   [4] Gregoire, 3–12.
[5] *Ibid.*, 105–10.   [6] *L&A* 1590–91: 560, 579.
[7] *Ibid.*, 562.
[8] *L&A* 1590–91: 582; Sir Henry Unton, *The Correspondence of Sir Henry Unton
. . . in the Years 1591 and 1592*, ed. J. Stevenson (London, 1847), 12–14, 17–18.

French army remained pretty much on the defensive.[9] Norris's forces gradually dwindled from sickness and desertion in spite of a reinforcement of 600 men from the western counties.[10] By July 1591 Norris had lost much hope of any effective action; even if there were troops, there was no money to pay them. French forces came and went as the harvest or other domestic duties moved them.[11]

The story from then on, for month after weary month, was one of utter frustration. By the end of the summer the French commander, Dombes, was pressing for a move into the interior of the province, to the vicinity of Rennes, having lost any hope of securing ground in the coastal areas around St. Malo. Such a move contradicted the whole purpose of English intervention, which was to deny the vital coastal areas to the Spaniard.[12] Both Norris and the Queen protested, but in the end the English commander, too weak to subsist on his own, had no choice but to follow his French colleague in a meandering march across country to the borders of Anjou, skirmishing futilely and losing men to disease and desertion as he went.[13] In November Norris could still muster about 2,000 men; by February 1592 he was down to less than 1,700, of whom a large proportion were sick. In December the French had broken up their army altogether and the English were left to fend for themselves as best they could, living off the country.[14] Norris's stream of requests for reinforcements, supply, and money went largely unanswered. The Queen, by now deeply engaged in Normandy, was in no mood to risk more men in Brittany.

Her vexation at the failure of the French to live up to their promises flared up in reproaches to Henry and his ambassadors, and she made frequent threats of withdrawal,[15] but Elizabeth was caught on the horns of a dilemma.[16] Given royalist weakness in the province, the Queen's withdrawal of her forces would only serve to confirm Spanish/Leaguer control. On the other hand if she left her

---

[9] See *L&A* 1591–92: 416–477.   [10] *Ibid.*, 428, 433.

[11] *Ibid.*, 429, 430.

[12] *Ibid.*, 435, 438, 440. For English movements in this summer, see also *Advertisements from Brittany and from the Low Countries in September and October* (London 1591), STC 3802.5, and *A Journal or Brief Report of the Late Service in Brittany by the Prince de Dombes Assisted with Her Majesty's Forces under Sir John Norris*, etc. (London, 1591), STC 13156.

[13] *L&A* 1591–92: 453, 457.   [14] *Ibid.*, 459, 464.

[15] *Ibid.*, 439, 451, 466; Unton, 35–39, 48–49.   [16] *L&A* 1591–92: 441.

forces there, unsupported as they were by the French, she might well lose her soldiers altogether. Lacking any effective leverage against the French, she could do little but fire off alternating reproaches and threats, neither of which had any effect. The one resolute decision the Queen made was a negative one—to turn a deaf ear to all of Norris's requests for men or supplies. She was not going to throw good money after bad in so hopeless a cause. Indeed, even if a firm decision to withdraw had been made, it would have been very difficult to implement since the enemy largely controlled the coast. So Norris was left through the long winter to soldier on as best he could, watching his troops dwindle away. His little army was getting the worst of both worlds, neglected by its home government and by its allies. By March 1592, some ten months after his arrival, Norris was encamped with the remnant of his forces near the key junction town of Craon on the Angevin borders, hoping against hope for some substantial backing from the French. He was pessimistic in the extreme; no help could be expected from the King, and unless the Queen acted to replenish her decayed forces, the whole province would be lost.[17] He was finally summoned home for consultation.

In his absence in April 1592 the French managed to put together a force large enough to besiege Craon. The siege, pressed for some weeks, ended in mid-May in a disastrous defeat for the royalists and their allies when Mercoeur assailed the besiegers. The English forces were under the command of Anthony Wingfield.[18] Some 800 English soldiers survived, of whom only about 600 were still able to serve. Seven captains were taken or slain, and there had been serious losses among the junior officers. The Queen, aware of the defeat but lacking certain information, sent off Norris's brother, Sir Henry, on 27 May to report on the situation of her troops and secure French assistance for their welfare.[19]

It was time now for a major reconsideration of the whole English strategy in France. Not only the feeble response in Brittany but also the competing demands of the parallel enterprise in France, the siege of Rouen, had contributed to the lack of support from Norris from home. He and his army had had to play second fiddle to the rival enterprise. The first contingent to be sent to Normandy under

---

[17] *Ibid.*, 478. [18] *L&A* 1592–93: 318–23.
[19] *Ibid.*, 325; Unton, 460–64, 467–68.

Williams had landed at Dieppe at the same time as Norris at Paimpol, and Essex with the main force had arrived in August 1591. Until the spring of 1592 English attention had focused on Rouen and on the threat posed by Parma's advance into France. That crisis past, the bulk of the English troops were withdrawn, but Henry was still urgent in his demands for renewed English assistance. So in the summer of 1592 it was imperative for the English to rethink their strategy. What resources were they prepared to commit to France? What use should be made of them? To understand the decisions that were made at this time we need to turn back to the origins of the Norman expedition and the siege of Rouen.[20]

The possibility of English action in Normandy had first been suggested by Henry IV in October 1590 and then again in September 1591 when the retiring ambassador, Stafford, forwarded a request for 6,000 English soldiers to serve in the siege of Rouen. Stafford pressed this as a better scheme than subsidizing German mercenaries since the advantages would be immediately and directly useful to England. Rouen was the focus of Leaguer power in Normandy; with its outlier, Le Havre, it controlled the commerce of the Seine valley, and it had been a major center for English traders in peacetime. Nothing came of this scheme at the time. Henry's attention was fixed on Paris; after the capital was relieved and supplied by Parma, he concentrated his efforts on blocking its food supplies and to that end besieged Chartres in the winter of 1590–1591.

The prospect of Parma's return to France continued to be a haunting worry for the King. The German mercenaries were being called in to check him but they would not enter France for some months at the earliest and the Duke might well arrive before they did. Elizabeth's proposal to forestall Parma by action in the Low Countries drew only a lukewarm response from the King. What he wanted was reinforcements for the army directly under his control. He took the opportunity of the English agent Yorke's mission on behalf of the Breton enterprise in late February 1591.[21] Yorke returned not only with Henry's assent to the Breton expedition but also with a request for 4,000 to 5,000 soldiers for service in Normandy with a substantial amount of military supplies and some

[20] *L&A* 1589–90: 480; 1590–91: 458.
[21] *Ibid.*, 490–93, 511; SP 78/23/231–32.

naval support. He wanted these in case Parma arrived before the Germans; in that event he planned to deploy his forces on the Somme, but while awaiting the Duke's approach, they could be used to clear the Leaguers out of Normandy. The Queen herself, in a preliminary memorandum to Beauvoir, the French ambassador, offering 3,000 men for Brittany, had suggested Normandy as an alternative destination if the King so wished.[22]

These converging Anglo-French interests in Normandy received a new and definitive stimulus from events at Dieppe. That town, which had been steadfastly royalist throughout and the port of entry for English aid, was now under threat from the local Leaguer forces. (Since the King had returned from Paris much of Normandy, which had submitted to him in the fall of 1589, had been recovered by his enemies.) At the end of March urgent appeals for help were sent by the governor and by the unofficial English agent there, the merchant Ottywell Smith.[23] At first 3,000 more were asked for; then the demand was lowered to 600. Surprisingly, the Queen's response was immediately favorable; the 600, taken from Norris's bands, were sent over in early April under Sir Roger Williams, with one month's pay. Williams's instructions[24] limited him to defending the town but gave him some leeway to cooperate with the royalists in establishing control over local areas.

During the next few weeks Williams, Smith, and the French agents bombarded the Queen with letters painting the importance of capturing Rouen.[25] The most comprehensive of these was written by Williams in a sweeping survey of the war situation. He dismissed Henry's current campaign as pointless, a mere conquest of empty country. The Queen must persuade him to undertake an assault on his principal towns; otherwise in a protracted contest Spain's superior financial resources would insure victory for Philip. But then, shifting to a more narrowly English point of view, Williams urged the Queen to press Henry to clear his sea-coast, "which is dearer unto England than the main land." If he lost his ports, how could they succor him? More particularly, Henry must be drawn to besiege Rouen. Either it would fall—and with it all Normandy—or Parma would be forced to battle, and beaten. The King's Papist councillors would dissuade him from this; there was

[22] *L&A* 1590–91: 513. [23] SP 78/23/177, 181, 188; Lloyd, *Rouen*, 64.
[24] SP 78/24/49, 53. [25] SP 78/24/53, 55, 78.

all the more need for pressure from the English court. Williams could not resist reiterating his dicta on overall strategy:

> Believe me unless you can give great blows, either on the Indian navy or in those countries where his treasure comes or on the disciplined army, I mean on the Duke of Parma, or in the main of Spain or Portugal, be assured all the rest is but consuming of little fires. Do what you can without putting the Spanish King in hazard of one of three, Your Lordships shall never bring him to any reason.... Let him be thoroughly warmed in any of the three actions, be assured his own estate will force him to any peace or condition you can desire, for necessity hath no law.

Coming back to the immediate situation he argued that Parma could be hit only through the French King. With 3,000 of the best horse anywhere, and with 4,000 English foot, he could beat Parma in the field or, if the Duke refused battle, take the principal towns. And—a great lure for Elizabeth—if Henry granted her the customs of Rouen for a period of years it would pay off all his debts to her. At this very time the Earl of Essex was entertaining DeReau, the envoy sent by Henry to follow up his first approaches through Yorke, with a request for men to be used both in Brittany and against Parma if he crossed the frontiers again.[26] He got more than he bargained for: not only the Breton contingent but also an offer of 3,000 to 4,000 men for the siege of Rouen, an enterprise to which the Queen strongly urged him.[27]

This hopeful beginning was clouded over when the Queen, alarmed by a report of Spanish reinforcements landed at Blavet,[28] suddenly ordered Williams to join Norris in Brittany. Even now, in advising Beauvoir of this change, she dangled the bait of a 4,000-man force for the siege of Rouen if the King would undertake it. It has been suggested[29] that Elizabeth's revocation of Williams from Dieppe was a ploy to prod Henry into a real commitment to a siege of Rouen. Certainly it was not his first priority; he still sought most anxiously the services of an English contingent in resisting Parma.

During the next few weeks the royalist officers in Normandy, with Williams's assistance, made a siege far more feasible. The Parlements of Caen and Tours and the townsmen of Dieppe pro-

---

[26] L&A 1590–91: 536, 537. [27] Ibid., 566.
[28] Ibid. [29] Lloyd, Rouen, 69–73.

vided money[30] while Williams and the local royalist commanders engineered the capture of Louviers, a key position for possible siege operations. Henry finally took the proferred bait and DeReau formally presented the King's demands to the Queen.[31] He now wanted 5,000 to 6,000 foot with 200 to 300 horse, 1,000 sappers with artillery, and naval vessels to serve in the Seine. In the bargain that was then swiftly struck, the Queen conceded 4,000 foot (or 3,750 foot and 100 horse), leaving the other requests open to negotiation. Ultimately the costs were to be borne by the King, secured on the yet-to-be-conquered tax revenues of Rouen and LeHavre, but present funds would be provided by the Queen.[32] The necessary documents were signed and sealed by early July. In August Essex landed at Dieppe. With his arrival England had committed two major armies to action on the Continent.

These decisions by the English government in this summer of 1591 had opened a new phase in England's involvement in the war against Spain. The two armies now in France numbered together rather more than the English contingents fighting with the States and the monthly charge was roughly equivalent to the outlay in the Low Countries. The contrast with the Willoughby expedition of 1589 was striking. Then intervention had taken place at French insistence and under the pressure of urgent events. This time in both cases the initiative for action was taken by the English government, although the circumstances varied considerably. In Brittany the pressure of events locally provided a general impetus, but it was the threat posed to immediate English interests that triggered the Queen's decision as much as the appeal of the provincial leaders. In Normandy the English government took the lead in pressing its case upon a somewhat reluctant, or at least lukewarm, French monarch. In both cases the decision was taken deliberately, after a period of hesitation and deliberation. Expert advice, in which large strategic issues were aired, was pressed on the Queen. What are we to make of this important step in English war policy?

First of all, it seems clear that there was a general consensus among the English leaders that a major offensive action should be mounted. Both the opportunities and the risks of war had been changed by the assassination of Henry III. The addition of France

---

[30] *Ibid.*, 72.   [31] *L&A* 1590–91: 519.
[32] BL, Lansdowne Ms. 149, fols. 24–24v; Lloyd, *Rouen*, 75; Unton, 8–10.

to the ranks of Spain's enemies made possible a direct assault on the Spanish position in the Low Countries. If English, Dutch, and French forces (aided by German mercenaries) could be coordinated, it might be possible to destroy—or at least to weaken—Spanish power in that vital area. After all, it was just that goal that had drawn England to her original involvement in Low Countries in the years before the actual outbreak of war with Spain. And the Queen's first instinct seems to have been to mount an attack on Parma on his home ground—specifically at Dunkirk. We have seen that she failed to convince her allies and it was only very reluctantly that she abandoned a project that she hoped could have been carried out without augmenting English forces. But her allies' indifference and Norris's warning that it would in fact require larger English armies finally discouraged her.

Roger Williams's appreciation of the general strategic situation had pinpointed both the Flemish and the Breton coasts as key areas, either of which could be a launching pad for an invasion of England. Thwarted in the former, the Queen's hand was forced by the enemy initiative. Her admirals had failed to prevent the Spanish occupation of Blavet in the preceding fall, and by the spring of 1591 it was clear that the French king could not be counted on to act in the coastal province. Fearful of Spanish reinforcements, the Queen was pushed into accepting Henry's doubtful promises of action and to send off an expeditionary force with minimal preparation.

The Norman expedition was quite another case. Here the thrust for action came first from the captains on the scene and then from the Queen herself. The first step, the threat to Dieppe—perhaps exaggerated by Williams and Smith—frightened the Queen into an unaccustomed alacrity in dispatching a force there. This gave Williams and his collaborators a golden opportunity to press the advantages of a siege.[33] Williams, who had forcefully argued a short time ago for the necessity of intervention in Brittany, now produced an eloquent demonstration of the overwhelming advantages of besieging Rouen, while giving Brittany a back seat in his arguments.[34] Even more efficacious was the prospect that a lien on the Rouen tax revenues would clear the French debt within a short time. Eliza-

[33] See also Birch, 1: 65, for Burghley's role in pushing for a siege of Rouen.
[34] SP 78/24/234.

beth, haunted by the spectre of an empty exchequer, was always an exigent creditor.

Another—and novel—factor in bringing the Queen to this decision must have been the urgings of the favorite, the Earl of Essex, who was moving heaven and earth not only to persuade his mistress to authorize the Norman adventure but also to give him the command. (His appointment to the Norman command was rumored as early as February 1591.[35]) He longed passionately for the chance to hoist his standard as a great captain and to enter on the military stage in a leading role. Probably even more potent in the Queen's calculations, however, was the opportunity to control the movements of her royal ally more effectively and to make herself mistress of events. She had lectured Henry on his shortcomings in a hectoring letter written in the spring,[36] rebuking him for the neglect of his ports (Dieppe and the Breton ports). "He must pardon the simplicity of her sex; but from her experience of government she knew what became a king and that Henry would conquer his enemies if he followed her advice." The beauty of the Rouen scheme from Elizabeth's point of view was that it would not only bring the King to the Seine ports but would also pin him down to a specific goal that he could attain only with English aid and that would redound to English advantage. No doubt she took pleasure in the hard bargain she drove with him, reducing the number of troops she would provide and ignoring his reasonable requests for the special needs of a siege—heavy cannon and pioneers. Still, even here, as in the Breton contract, she was willing to take Henry at his word and displayed a somewhat naive trust in the power of signed agreements, properly sealed and registered in all the appropriate bureaus of the French monarchy.

What was not clear in the Queen's calculations was any understanding of the quite different strategic priorities of the King. His eye was always fixed on the one great conquest he must make if he was to be a king in deed—his capital. He was also warily waiting for the arrival of Parma, that elusive commander whom Henry so ardently hoped to draw into battle, in an arena where the King's military skills might win not only the day but the war as well. The siege of Rouen was useful for him so far as it might serve these purposes; English troops on hand would be a major reinforcement

[35] Sidney Papers 1: 316–17.   [36] L&A 1590–91: 514.

if he were to meet the Duke in the field. In the wily and slippery French king with his plausible promises and smooth tongue Elizabeth had met an adversary worthy of her steel. She had a good hand to play, but the cards were not quite good enough to assure the mastery of events for which she strove.

The expedition to Normandy was now inaugurated; 3,400 foot were to join Williams's 600. Henry on his part had formally assigned the *taille* and the customs of Rouen to pay off his debt.[37] At the same time Sir Henry Unton replaced Sir Edward Stafford as resident ambassador to France (after a hiatus of nearly a year). He like his predecessor was a client of the Cecils.[38] His instructions reflected the novel conditions of this expedition. This time command was being given not to a hardened veteran of the Low Country wars, like Norris or Williams, but to a noble amateur, whose principal recommendation was his credit with the Queen and whose military experience was limited to a season with Leicester in the Low Countries and a volunteer's role in the Lisbon venture. The Queen brought herself to consent to the earl's command, but she determined to hedge in his freedom of action as much as possible. Ambassador Unton was to be both ambassador and a kind of tutor to Essex. Unton was to praise or criticize as occasion demanded even though "commonly young noblemen at the first do not embrace advertisements of things to be reformed," a caveat that must have given pause to Sir Henry.

Essex was further to be counselled by two veterans: Sir Henry Killigrew, a long-time diplomat with experience in Scotland and the Low Countries, and his uncle, Sir Thomas Leighton, governor of Jersey, a distant connection of the Queen through his wife and also a former envoy to France. Essex's instructions were to submit to the commands of the French king, but he could discreetly object to particular orders. He was directed to husband his forces so that they might not be unprofitably employed.

[37] *L&A* 1591–92: 520, 525–28, 532, 551; Lloyd, *Rouen*, 76; BL., Lansdowne Ms. 102/200–3.

[38] *L&A* 1591–92: 550, 551; see his instructions BL, Lansdowne Ms. 102/288–89. For his dependence on the Cecils, see for instance Unton, 26–27, 62–63, 153–54.

CHAPTER 9

BRITTANY AND ROUEN:

THE SECOND ROUND

ESSEX'S FORCES landed at Dieppe at the beginning of August and on 7 August mustered about 3,150 men. Essex himself was attended by the usual entourage of volunteer gentlemen-officers, some sixty-one in all, serving at his expense.[1] All the soldiers were newly levied (except for one company from Brill), straight from the farm or shop; they came from London and from some nineteen counties reaching from the Midlands to East Anglia. With Williams's 600 the English forces fell not far short of the promised 4,000.[2]

Henry had just received the surrender of Noyon and had been preparing to meet the German mercenaries in Champagne. The King still planned to besiege Rouen, but first several key outlying places had to be taken. And—more important—the siege itself would have to wait on Parma's movements.[3] When the Duke was reported as already having crossed the frontier, the King cancelled his trip to Champagne so as to ready his forces to face his opponent. This meant delaying the siege and persuading the Queen to allow Essex to join Henry in opposing Parma's advance. Even before the arrival of DeReau, the French agent, in England the Queen was protesting the delay in initiating the siege and leaving her forces,

[1] L&A 1591–92: 258.
[2] APC 1591: 241–42; L&A 1591–92: 547, 576; note the reference in 576 to troops who were peasants two months ago.
[3] L&A 1591–92: 556.

hurried across in great haste, "inutile."[4] When DeReau presented his master's letters, the Queen exploded and at first threatened withdrawal of her forces unless the King opened the siege; then, relenting a little, she consented to allow her troops to fill out their two months—and to stay forty days longer (at Henry's expense), but only for the siege of Rouen.[5]

In the meantime the King had summoned the earl to meet him near Noyon,[6] and Essex set off, accompanied by Roger Williams and attended by 300 horse. He was received with great warmth, and a rapport was established between the two men that would deeply affect Anglo-French relations for some years to come. Essex's return at the end of August was a dangerous journey, plagued by a bout of fever and by a pursuing force of Leaguers. Then in early September a "bravado" against the French commander in the suburbs of Rouen baptized the English in action, but at the cost of the life of Walter Devereux, the earl's younger brother. The Queen's unbridled anger over Essex's unauthorized journey to the King, combined with the death of his brother, drove the earl into hysteria.[7] Nevertheless, when urged by Marshal Biron to join with him in an assault on Gournay, the English commander (with the assent of his advisors) agreed, and by 26 September they were masters of this strategically placed town, which commanded the approaches from Picardy.[8]

The Queen, in the meantime, unconvinced by Essex's excuses for his visit to the King, reiterated her displeasure in the strongest terms and contemptuously rejected his optimistic expectations of Henry's prompt arrival before Rouen. She ended by commanding his return to England, leaving behind some part of her forces for a month or so, to be used solely against Rouen or LeHavre.[9] The earl's anguished response defended his actions up through the siege of Gournay and warned the Queen in the most solemn tones that withdrawal of her forces now would insure the loss of all Normandy, drive the King to Tours, and bring about the "greatest alterations in these parts of Christendom that hath been seen these hundred years." For himself he asked only leave to keep twenty

[4] *Ibid.*, 560, 561; Unton, 39–40.   [5] *L&A* 1591–92: 563; Unton, 55–57.

[6] *L&A* 1591–92: 264; Unton, 32.

[7] *L&A* 1591–92: 278; Unton, 61–62, 86–88.

[8] *L&A* 1591–92: 280, 284; Unton, 96–98.

[9] *L&A* 1591–92: 573, 574; Unton, 72–76.

men "to see the catastrophe of this miserable tragedy."[10] Leighton and Killigrew added their voices to the commander's, confirming his view that his departure would demoralize all the French auxiliary forces.

By 24 September the Queen had already determined on Essex's return, to be followed as soon as feasible by that of her forces. A declaration was prepared that laid out at length her dealings with Henry, her angry dissatisfaction, and her conviction that she had been treated with carelessness and unkindness, indeed with contempt and mockery.[11] The arrival of Essex's defense of his actions did not change her mind and Burghley conveyed the royal command that Essex should sail for Rye immediately.[12] Elizabeth was in fact softening; first she consented that the army should remain, provided Henry found their weekly pay, but this arrangement was to be kept a secret until Essex had returned. Then by 3 October she relented altogether and agreed to Essex's remaining in France.[13] But the chances of wind and weather had so tangled communications that Essex had already arrived in England before he knew of the Queen's change of mind. During a week's stay at court he was reconciled to his mistress and returned with renewed confidence to his Norman task. The reconciliation had lasting effects; the Queen's tone in her communications to her commander notably moderated in the following weeks.[14]

Essex's return came none too soon; the usual casualties of a campaign had reduced his effectives to less than half his original force, and he asked the Queen for another 1,000 conscripts to be ready to come over as soon as the King arrived at Rouen. Sickness continued to decimate their ranks, but at least the French were finding money for their pay.[15] By 30 October Biron had invested Rouen, and Essex had taken up his quarters in a suburb of the city. His forces by now numbered barely 1,000, but at the end of November some 300 pioneers arrived from England.[16] By 13 November the King had finally appeared and began to press the siege. Neither Norris nor Essex's lieutenant, Baskerville, thought well of his tactics or his

---

[10] HMC, *Hatfield* 4: 139–41; *L&A* 1591–92: 575.

[11] *Ibid.*, 579–81; Unton, 88–93. The ambassador added his voice in support of Essex, as did Leighton and Killigrew (*ibid.*, 76–81).

[12] *L&A* 1591–92: 584.   [13] *Ibid.*, 588, 591.

[14] Lloyd, *Rouen*, 124.   [15] *L&A* 1591–92: 296, 300, 301.

[16] *Ibid.*, 306, 309, 319.

chances of success.[17] Parma was now stirring on the frontiers and Henry, anticipating his arrival on the Seine, was pressing the Queen for aid in ships, weapons, and men.[18] She committed herself to an additional 1,000 men, veterans from the Low Countries, plus 400 pioneers and 50 miners from England, while calling Essex home for consultation.[19]

Henry was simultaneously seeking even more assistance— enough troops to make the English total 5,000, with their pay for six weeks. The Queen absolutely refused further financial aid while Essex (now back in France) was commanded to remain at Rouen if the King marched to meet Parma; if the besieging forces were insufficient, he was to return home.[20] And from court Burghley, Howard, and Hunsdon wrote to the earl urging his return; they reckoned there were no more than 1,000 English left in his force; the Queen would certainly send no more. It was not to his honor to remain in command of such a pitiful remnant. The Queen added her voice to theirs.[21] Yet Henry was nothing if not persistent, and yet another of his servants, Philippe DuPlessis, was dispatched to London to press the Queen in his master's behalf. Their importunities only evoked a long, circumstantial declaration from her, detailing the King's delinquencies since the Norman expedition had first been initiated, a lengthy list of broken promises and dilatory action.[22] In January 1592 Essex departed for the last time from France, leaving behind the remnants of his forces under Roger Williams's command.

In the meantime—in early March 1592—the veteran diplomat Sir Thomas Wilkes was sent off on a special mission to the French King.[23] He was to detail the sorry tale of the English expeditions in Normandy and Brittany—a litany of waste and muddle that left the Queen with nothing to show for her sacrifice of men and money. The tone was sober and businesslike, the Queen's inclination plain enough. Unless Henry could make a case—which she wholly doubted—for the imminent fall of Rouen, she could see no

[17] *Ibid.*, 322. [18] *Ibid.*, 310, 602, 605, 608; Unton, 150–51.

[19] There were now 1,018 soldiers and 336 pioneers on hand (Lloyd, *Rouen*, 156 n. 40); *L&A* 1591–92: 332, 609; Unton, 140–42, 175–76.

[20] *L&A* 1591–92: 623, 624, 627; Unton, 186–88, 198–200.

[21] *L&A* 1591–92: 629, 630; Unton, 211–12, 230. [22] *L&A* 1591–92: 635–38.

[23] For his instructions, see *L&A* 1591–92: 651, 654–58 (12–16 March); Unton, 387–88.

reason to keep her troops there. "For Her Majesty plainly mindeth, except she may receive good satisfaction for these her doubts, she mindeth to revoke her forces from thence." The same sober list of indictments of French failures was presented for the Breton campaign, but here the Queen stopped short of threatening withdrawal. Instead Wilkes was to press for a port, preferably Brest, to be handed over to the English as a base for action. An unsigned note attached to a list of the forces at Rouen[24] sums up English hopes. If Rouen were to fall, all the royal forces except those in Brittany should be withdrawn, providing the King went to that province. But henceforth "if ever the Queen succor the King again, let it be with money whereby she saveth armor [and] men, thereby easeth the countries and the King obtain more service from his own nation paid than from the English, their infirmities being so great with their want of discipline."

Wilkes and Unton saw the King and pressed on him the Queen's instructions. He defended his action in detail but admitted that he had been persuaded into besieging Rouen against his own judgment.[25] He intended now, if Parma did not return soon, to batter Rouen and force its surrender. Quizzed on overtures the Leaguers purportedly were making for peace, he admitted their existence and a subsequent negotiation. He doubted success but promised the Queen prompt knowledge of any developments. The Leaguers had demanded, and Henry had agreed, to exclude the English and Dutch, limiting the discussions to the two French parties.[26] In response to her complaints about his failures, the King gave the Queen as good as he took. She "made war at this time good cheap against so great an enemy . . . and he wished he had such another fool as Her Majesty had of him to make wars against the King of Spain, that he might look out the window, as she doth now, and behold the tragedies betweeen him and his enemies now in action." He could not assent to yielding Brest or St. Malo but vaguely promised that the first port town to be taken would be handed over to the English as a base.[27] Wilkes returned early in April; Unton secured through Burghley a promise that his revocation would soon follow.[28]

[24] *L&A* 1591–92: 659. [25] *Ibid.*, 663–64.
[26] *Ibid.*, 664. [27] *Ibid.*, 669.
[28] *Ibid.*, 674.

Before Wilkes's departure the Queen had yielded to Henry's plea for money and men and authorized a levy of 1,600 soldiers. These men were mustered at Dover, waiting for a wind.[29] By now, the force remaining in France was reduced to a bare 1,000, of whom 315 were sick or hurt and others absent from their companies. When the newcomers were mustered at Dieppe on 20 March they added about 1,400 to English strength in France. They arrived only to join the King's retreat from Rouen; he had raised the siege on 10 April. The English forces under Williams then accompanied the King during the abortive campaign in which Parma skillfully eluded battle after having victualled Rouen.[30]

The Norman expedition was in its beginning a hopeful enterprise. Rouen and the Seine valley would have been cleared of the Leaguers; the Channel coasts of France, so vital to the English, would have been secured against a Spanish threat; the tax revenues of Rouen would have gone to liquidate the ever-growing debt owed by the French King to his English sister. None of this had come to pass; the League was still in full control of the strategic centers of Normandy. Some 6,000 to 8,000 English soldiers had been committed to the struggle; the bulk of them were dead or had been invalided home. Thousands of pounds of the Queen's scanty funds had been effectually wasted.[31] And besides the human and material losses there was the intangible damage to Elizabeth's role in her partnership with Henry. The hopes of bending his efforts to her will and engaging his energies in an enterprise that, while advantageous to him, was primarily designed to serve English interests were utterly dashed. The reasons for the Queen's ill-tempered reproaches and her grumpily ungracious reception of Henry's further solicitations were not far to seek.

From a more detached point of view the whole episode goes far to highlight the special and peculiar conditions under which the Anglo-French partnership labored. The strategy assumed by Henry was a simple enough one: the English should provide auxiliary forces, fully equipped and paid for by the Queen (indirectly through a loan to Henry). These troops would be available for joint

[29] *L&A* 1590–91: 377, 645, 646, 647; Unton, 316–17, 336–37, 349–50. The King ascribed the dispatch of the reinforcements to the influence of Essex.

[30] *L&A* 1591–92: 385, 398, 403–13; Unton, 413–16, 433–34, 436–37.

[31] According to SP 78/28/228, £35,369 had been spent between June 1591 and June 1592.

operations, primarily designed, of course, to further the King's cause. But what role were the English to play in deciding strategy? The terms of Essex's instructions were vague; he was to be at the disposal of the French monarch, yet with some margin of freedom, since he could object to the proposals made by Henry. In fact, quite basic differences of outlook divided the two courts. Henry, desperate to hold together an army that was largely a coalition in which aliens were as numerous as natives, looked on the English as just another contingent of foreign auxiliaries, not much different from the Swiss or Germans and to be used as freely as his own mercenaries wherever and for whatever purpose military necessity dictated.

Elizabeth, on the other hand, insisted that the alliance must serve her needs as much as those of the French. Her forces should be used in collaboration with the French, but only towards objectives that would directly serve English interests. The gap between these conceptions is readily apparent. A king fighting a highly fluid war had to be ready to respond wherever pressure was felt, especially that of Parma and his formidable tercios. This ran wholly contrary to Elizabeth's plans for a tidy, neatly defined campaign in one particular corner of the King's domains. Within his or her own terms each was pursuing a rational strategy; but only occasionally were those strategies likely to be congruent with one another.

The effort to square the circle by bringing royal commands into line with the realities of the battlefield put an often intolerable strain on all the actors. This summary (and simplified) account of events hardly does justice to the baffled fury of the Queen as she looked on helplessly while her men and money were wasted—a fury only heightened by the importunate clamor of the French King for yet more assistance. The King himself was quite literally beyond her reach; it took weeks before her ambassador, Unton, reached him. First Unton's illness, and then the great dangers and difficulties of crossing a war-torn countryside in pursuit of the elusive Henry, meant that it was very difficult even to communicate her displeasure to her ally. Not surprisingly, much of her wrath was visited on her commanders, especially Essex, who at one stage was so beside himself with vexation that he burst his buttons, rolling on his bed in inarticulate misery. Killigrew, Leighton, and Unton all shared in the royal displeasure, although after Essex's enforced visit to England the royal irritation subsided somewhat.

The army leaders may well have envied their naval comrades, who, at least during their campaigns, were beyond the reach of the Queen's anger. And in fact all too often, by the time the royal letters arrived after the delays imposed by weather and unsafe roads, they were already hopelessly out of date, so fast did the situation change. The commanders on the scene had to make decisions that they knew would be ill seen at home. The diversion of English forces to local actions in Normandy made militarily good sense either in relieving some immediate pressure on their French allies or in organizing the preliminaries of a major siege.[32] And the King's demands that the English forces be available for a battle with Parma were reasonable enough; if the Duke overran Normandy the dangers to the English were obvious. Hence Essex and Williams, anxious in any case to gain the laurels of victory, bowed to French demands, counting on the chances of time, fortune, and weather to appease their mistress in London. Nor, in the largest sense, were their decisions unsound. Rouen remained untaken, but the King had not been driven from Normandy; the Leaguers' military position was not stronger; Parma's intervention had had only temporary effects.

Although the King's failure to take Rouen was an immediate disappointment, it proved to be a turning point in the war, although admittedly one not immediately visible to contemporaries. The expedition of 1592 proved to be Parma's last intervention in France. He withdrew to the Low Countries already an ill man, and his death followed at the end of that year. The immediate aftermath was a time of confused and aimless maneuvering. Henry would have liked to resume the siege of Rouen but his forces dissolved as his followers returned home. The chances of another Spanish invasion still seemed great.[33]

In the year between the end of the siege (April 1592) and the definitive shift in Henry's fortunes upon his conversion to Catholicism (summer 1593) the role of the English forces continued to be highly uncertain. Williams, now in command, wrote pessimistically of their condition at the beginning of May 1592. No more than 600 remained in fighting trim and these were men weary of the war. They were neglected both by their government and by the French,

[32] See Roger Williams's comments in SP 78/28/286.
[33] SP 78/28/54, 60.

and it was Williams's view that the best thing would be their with-drawal; in any case he begged for some directive from the Queen. For the time being they remained encamped at Neufchatel near Dieppe. Williams was urging on the government the acquisition of a seaport base that could be the "Flushing" of Normandy, a gage for the French debt, in short a cautionary town on the Dutch model. But for the present their energies were being wasted as the French devoted themselves to the siege of various small towns in the Seine valley.[34]

At home a familiar scenario was being re-enacted. Beauvoir was asking for another contingent of English soldiers.[35] At this juncture, however, the attention of both the English and French leaders was suddenly jerked away from the Norman scene to the Breton. Bad news arrived from the western province: the royalist forces had been mauled at Craon on the borders of Anjou, and the English had suffered very heavily; 1,400 men were lost, including 7 cap-tains; only 800 remained. Beauvoir was already seeking English help by 26 May and stressing the risks to the whole allied cause if the Spanish were not checked in Brittany. Elizabeth immediately dispatched Sir Henry Norris (John Norris was then in England) to investigate, with orders that the remaining troops should stay where they were until a decision about their future was made.[36] In Normandy Williams held his forces in readiness for a possible move to Brittany. The Queen, in the meantime, having tentatively agreed to send 2,000 of her Low Countries forces to reinforce Norris's con-tingent, then countermanded the order. Henry pressed the Queen further through yet another envoy, DeSancy, with a demand for 4,000 men for the Breton front. As a stopgap measure he proposed that the Norman contingent under Williams be sent off immedi-ately. As a carrot the Queen was to be offered one of the first two places taken by her forces in Brittany as a base (but under a French officer nominated by the English ruler).[37]

The Queen's response to DeSancy raised a new issue that was agitating the English leadership—rumors of peace talks between Henry and the Leaguers. The envoy brought Henry's assurance that the Spanish were not included in these talks and that no peace

[34] SP 78/28/1, 3, 75; Unton, 457–58; SP 78/28/54, 58, 81; *The Edmondes Papers*, ed. C. G. Butler (London, 1913), 1–4, 7–9.

[35] SP 78/28/38.   [36] SP 78/28/66, 117, 157.

[37] SP 78/28/121, 133, 154, 180; Unton, 457–58; *Edmondes*, 21–22.

with Philip would be concluded without English knowledge, but the Queen was obviously uneasy. Once Henry gained control of his own kingdom, would he still wage war on the Spaniard? Elizabeth's view was that Henry was bound to aid the English under the inclusive terms laid out in the Treaty of Blois of 1572. No newer pact had been concluded at the beginning of their active cooperation, so the legal situation was cloudy.[38]

These considerations much influenced the Queen's reaction to Henry's demands. They were on a very large scale: 6,000 foot and 100 horse for Brittany; 1,000 more to join Henry in the Ile de France; 10 ships to lie off Bordeaux; 400 pioneers for Picardy; a contingent to go from Ostend for an exploit in Artois—and all at the Queen's expense! The Queen declared that she would not have believed such demands could be made had she not seen the letters of credence. She was all the more astonished in view of the current negotiations with the League. Under the circumstances she could give no answer to the French demands until she knew more about these negotiations.[39] This led to acrimonious correspondence with Beauvoir, who suggested that the English would use the peace negotiations as an excuse for inaction and strongly hinted that the King would be justified in making whatever terms he could, given the lack of support from his ally. He reiterated Henry's requests, particularly those designed to check Parma and to defend the traffic of Bordeaux, which, he argued, were as beneficial to the Queen as to Henry.

This led to some hard but indecisive bargaining. The Queen agreed to send forces to Brittany—as soon as the King made peace with his rebel subjects and they agreed to aid in expelling the Spaniards or at least to remain neutral. The King must also promise not to make peace with Spain without English consent. Elizabeth would send 4,000 (not 6,000) newly conscripted troops to Brittany if Henry would provide for the English a base port with the right to collect all taxes and impositions there and would send 10,000 soldiers to fight along with the English. The desperate Beauvoir countered with a plea for 7,000 English, since Henry had candidly to admit that he could supply no more than 2,000 foot and 1,000 horse, and at least 10,000 were needed to counter Mercoeur. Again

[38] SP 78/186, 190, 192, 193, 199, 206, 232. [39] SP 78/28/186, 192.

he proposed that the companies in Normandy be borrowed for a six-week fill-in.[40]

In France the negotiations for peace between the King and the League had fallen through by the end of June 1592. This issue laid aside, at least for the present, the Queen finally consented to an agreement on Brittany, and a contract was signed for the dispatch of English foot; the question of filling up the English force in Normandy went unsettled. A sudden crisis in the Seine valley when Quilleboeuf on the estuary seemed about to fall persuaded the Queen to give Henry the loan of Williams's forces for the time being.[41] Williams arrived to find the crisis past, and a month later he was complaining of the conflicting demands on his services—from the King, the governor of Dieppe, and the local commander, the Count of St.Pol. "I know not what to do but I protest unto Your Lordship **if** I knew which way to do Her Majesty and my country any course my carcase should not be spared." But he continued to wander from village to village between Dieppe and the mouth of the Somme. In fact plans were being drawn up to divide his forces between Brittany and the Low Countries.[42]

The contract for Brittany had been signed on 1 July but the delays of mobilization as well as the Queen's continuing insistence that the King should go to the province in person delayed action until late August. Norris himself was pessimistic, given French weakness and growing Spanish strength; the Queen might well opt even yet to withdraw altogether. The French in lieu of a royal presence offered a trio of leaders—the Duke of Montpensier to govern Normandy, St. Luc and Marshal d'Aumont to command in Brittany. Henry's departure from the main theater of conflict would only lead to the loss of Champagne, Picardy, and Burgundy. There was also news of a royalist success in Brittany.[43]

The Queen finally moved to a decision in late August when she issued instructions to Norris that he was to lead a force of 4,000, made up of a draft of Low Countries veterans, Williams's men, and 600 raw conscripts from England. His first priority was to secure French assistance in capturing maritime towns, one of which was to be handed over to the English as a base and place of retreat. The

[40] SP 78/28/206, 215.   [41] SP 78/28/206, 215.

[42] SP 78/29/20, 27, 29, 52.

[43] SP 78/29/29, 31, 34, 35, 51, 52; *Edmondes*, 25–28.

King, for his part, according to the contract signed on 1 July (but not ratified until 4 September), was to provide 4,000 foot and 1,000 horse. Norris himself had gone so far as to offer to find the wages of another 1,000 men for two months; with such a force he could secure a base without French aid; the Queen looked favorably on this scheme.[44]

With this decision the Queen re-launched the Breton enterprise. The auspices were not favorable. None of the obstacles that had impeded the first phase of the operation had been removed, and for some time events merely recapitulated previous experience. In the end it was larger movements within French domestic politics that broke the stalemate in Brittany and lessened the Spanish threat. However, the English were to have the satisfaction of ending their Breton expedition with a final moment of success against the Spanish.

Norris's offer to raise troops on his own arose from his skepticism about French promises. Specifically he proposed that he be allowed to secure either Morlaix or St. Malo to be held as an English base. Elizabeth was willing to go halfway; she wanted the base but insisted that no move be made without French participation. The tangle of suspicion and bad faith and the ensuing muddle in English policy were never more apparent. The Queen was willing to risk a second contingent of 4,000 men in Brittany on the dubious strength of French promises. She listened to the warnings of her commander and to his proposals for independent English action, but then hesitated to give him freedom to act on his own.[45]

Before Norris, delayed by contrary winds, could set sail, news came of another English defeat with the loss of 500 to 600 men by death or capture. He arrived in France in November with the English contingent, but the Low Countries companies did not join him until January 1593.[46] In the meantime the government at home was distracted by a new clamor from France for more aid—this time on the northern frontier. As early as September Williams had reported menacing moves by Parma, who, now in the last months of his life, was planning another invasion of France. He wanted 4,000 men and explained that the need in the north was more ur-

[44] SP 78/29, 59, 68, 72, 78, 132.   [45] SP 78/29/351, 364, 404–5; 30/170.
[46] SP 78/29/197, 218, 267; 30/15.

gent than that in Brittany. In early November the French added their voices to this demand.[47] Beauvoir was now asking for 3,000 men as well as the remnant left under Williams's command and declaring that nothing less than the loss of Normandy threatened. Local Leaguer successes in the province led the royalist commanders to seek immediate assistance from Williams. The Queen's response was a chilly negative, citing the King's absence from the danger points in Normandy and Brittany as signs of his neglect. By early December, in spite of Parma's death, the French ambassador had become almost hysterical in his representations. How could so wise and sage a princess allow her ally to go to his ruin and thereby lose all she had gained in the past? Where were Burghley's wisdom and fidelity if for the lack of 50,000 lasts of powder and 2,000 pikemen all his life's work would be sacrificed? Beauvoir went on to hint that the King's position was so desperate that he might have to yield to Catholic demands.[48]

These exhortations had their effect; in January 1593 the Queen agreed to a general reinforcement of the English forces in France, in both Normandy and Brittany. A total of 5,000 men would be divided unequally, two-thirds for Norris and the other third for Williams. But this augmentation would take time; in the immediate future it would merely add about 800 men to Williams's forces, bringing his contingent to about 1,500 by the end of February.[49] Williams had joined with the local royalist commander in a successful assault on a fort at the mouth of the Somme in February and for a time held St. Valery-sur-Somme. Although Williams wanted reinforcements, he was highly critical of the French leadership in the area. He urged that no agreement be made that placed him under French commanders who could "command us hither and thither"[50] and at the same time balked at a French proposal to assist in the siege of Neufchatel unless the Queen commanded him.

In fact, Williams was toying with a scheme for independent English action to seize Le Havre or St. Valery-sur-Somme with the intent of holding it as a cautionary town. This plan would both give a gage for the French and assure that France would not negotiate

[47] SP 78/29/157, 312; Leon van der Essen, *Alexandre Farnese* (5 vols., Brussels, 1937) 5: 376–78.

[48] SP 78/29/312, 326, 394.   [49] SP 78/30/42, 95, 116, 142, 232.

[50] SP 78/30/98, 124, 149.

separately for peace.[51] Shortly thereafter Williams did in fact occupy St. Valery-sur-Caux, where his hanging of a miller for betraying the English to the enemy aroused French indignation and suspicion of English intentions. But now Williams was summoned by
the King to join his main army, and in early April was with him at
the siege of Dreux with about 1,300 to 1,400 men.[52] In June Elizabeth authorized another levy of 1500 men to strengthen Williams's
force.[53] The English commander reached the King just as the pressure on Henry to change his faith began to reach its climax. Before
examining this crucial development, however, it is necessary to follow the fortunes of Elizabeth's other expeditionary force, Norris's
companies in Brittany.

For the English companies in Brittany the winter of 1592–1593
was a miserable one. As Norris put it, they "have continually
walked about the country receiving every day alarm of the enemy's
intentions" but no assistance from the royalists. The Queen might
as well revoke her forces for any good they were doing. He was
cheered somewhat by the arrival of the Low Country veterans,[54]
but there was little possibility of action at least until the spring. In
March the French announced the appointment of the Duke of
Montpensier as governor, to be assisted by Marshal d'Aumale and
St. Luc, and a plan of campaign that would be initiated by the siege
of Laval in Maine. Norris, apprised of these plans, was duly skeptical of their fulfillment, but he did agree to take his forces to Maine,
as much for his own protection as for the advantage of the French.
Norris's apprehensions were borne out; Montpensier remained
with the King; d'Aumale stayed in Berry and St. Luc arrived with
only 800 harquebusiers and 100 horse.[55]

This continued French inaction provoked the Queen into yet another indignant outburst at her ally's failure to keep his promises.
It also offered Norris the chance to press again a strategy that he
had been urging for some time: the occupation of a French port as
a retreat and bridgehead. The French had tentatively offered the
little port of Paimpol (and the neighboring island of Brehac) when
Norris was waiting for his Low Countries reinforcements. The

[51] SP 78/30/151, 165, 222. Williams proposed 6,000 men under a nobleman to
take Newhaven.
[52] SP 78/30/165, 172, 179, 197, 210, 213, 222, 260, 262, 287; *Edmondes*, 57–59.
[53] Wernham, 495.   [54] SP 78/30/7, 15, 30.
[55] SP 78/30/161, 170, 189–90, 237; *Edmondes*, 51–57.

Queen had earlier vetoed such a proposal but she was now more favorably inclined. So was Burghley, who was worried about the security of the Channel Islands if the Spaniards should seize a port on the northern shore of Brittany (where Paimpol lay).[56] Norris hoped for sufficient reinforcements (1,000 men) so that he could both garrison Paimpol and keep the field with the French.[57] What he got from home was an absolute refusal to send more troops and deliberately ambiguous commands from both Queen and Council, throwing on him the onus of a decision to withdraw or stay. If he moved to Paimpol, it was to be only for a temporary stay and he would be given no means to fortify it.[58]

Norris hung on. Responding to the Queen and the Privy Council, he argued that withdrawal was virtually impossible either by land or by sea; the dangers were too great. French prospects were improving, and if the Queen would only live up to the promise of reinforcements that she had made (but then revoked) in January, Norris could hold out hopes of establishing himself in Lower Brittany. But the French would not move unless more English were sent.[59] He had now only 1,400 able-bodied men; he must have 2,000 more and a garrison for Paimpol. The situation improved as the Leaguers drew back from a threat to the north coast ports, but d'Aumale remained immobile waiting for some decision from the Queen. In the fourth letter of a series Norris once again pressed for an English contingent of 4,000 and again offered to pay for an additional 1,000. All he got was a firm refusal. "We see no cause at all why upon these your former promises and requests we should suffer ourselves to be further abused or rather (as surely we may term it) mocked." As it was, the French proposed to take two towns in Maine before even entering Brittany. There was no possibility of service in Brittany this summer. "We determine to revoke our forces and have so told Norris."[60] Even before the final refusal Norris had so sunk into despair that he asked for leave to go to the Low Countries to collect debts owed him and then to depart for the Indies with as many soldiers as possible.[61]

This royal order, for all its peremptory tone, was as much a paper tiger as the Queen's past pronouncements. The record of the past

[56] SP 78/30/15, 241–44, 246.   [57] SP 78/30/258.
[58] SP 78/30/275, 279, 295.   [59] SP 78/31/56, 136.
[60] SP 78/31/134, 136, 211, 216, 233–34.   [61] SP 78/31/134, 138.

year highlighted the utter confusion of English policy in Brittany. In summer 1592 the Queen had faced the bitter truth that her forces in the province had wasted away to a feeble remnant with nothing to show for their endeavor. Yet with the strong Spanish presence in Brittany she hesitated to withdraw altogether. Once again she brought herself to accept Henry's promises and dispatched another expeditionary force. The earlier history simply repeated itself. The promised French army failed to appear, and once again English strength dribbled away while their army drifted purposelessly across the countryside. The Queen stormed at Henry, threatening withdrawal. And in fact the threat might have become fact were it not for the delaying tactics of Norris. He was determined to stay on. Aided by the difficulties and delays of communication with home, he stalled at each proposal for retreat, finding excuses for his continued presence. He was able to hang on, but his repeated efforts to secure reinforcements were invariably rejected and his power to act correspondingly reduced. The Queen, in a long agony of indecision, would neither fish nor cut bait, neither send reinforcements nor decisively end the campaign. As always, it was events beyond her control that would force her hand.[62] So things stood in the spring of 1593; the residue of the Normandy force still attended the King as auxiliaries in his further campaigns; the English in Brittany rusted away in futile inaction. Events in the French court would soon overtake those in Brittany and transform the stage on which all these actions were set.

As early as late April 1593 reports began to arrive of negotiations over the vital question of the King's faith. Edmondes, the English agent with the King, warned Burghley that Henry's old ploy of offering to be instructed would no longer serve. "I fear Your Lordship shall shortly hear he is forced to make that metamorphosis."[63] With the conversion of Henry to Catholicism Anglo-French relations sustained a shock that transformed their character. That such an event might occur may have been in the long-term calculations of the English leadership. In September 1592 Smith at Dieppe was relaying rumors of pressure from Henry's Catholic supporters to attend mass, and this may have been in Burghley's mind in a letter to the Duke of Bouillon in the following month. Reflecting on the

---

[62] For a rather different view of events in 1592–1594, see Wernham, 414.
[63] SP 78/30/287, 290, 300; *Edmondes*, 66–68, 70–73.

harsh necessities of the King's situation, he preached a doctrine of mutual toleration, piously asserting that the Christian faith was never established by the sword.[64]

After Edmondes's initial letters in April a string of others from him and from Williams and Smith tracked the rapid progress of events in the early summer.[65] Although a conference between the two parties was broken off, preparations for the conversion went forward apace. It was at this time that the King wrote a letter to Beauvoir, the main thrust of which was a hysterical plea for English reinforcements, but which also more than hinted at his forthcoming conversion. His affairs, he argued, were at a grand crisis: the Leaguers were meeting in Paris to elect a new king, and a threatening Spanish force was hovering on the Flemish borders to back them up; endless war seemed to loom ahead. English aid was essential to his very survival, but it was also clear that "without the hope that my good subjects have taken of contentment that I may give them on the fact of religion," his estate was hopeless. He soon acted on these words and was received into the Catholic fold. By the time the King reached St. Denis for the ceremony of reconciliation to the Roman Church, an intercepted letter gave him the information that the Spanish commander, Mansfeld, was not sufficiently strong to reach Paris so the immediate military pressure was relaxed. Soon after, a special envoy arrived from France to make his master's case to the English Queen.[66]

The King's strategy was outlined in a message borne by his most recent emissary. His conversion achieved, he needed now to deal with the League. He hoped to put together a combined force of Swiss, French, and 6,000 English; he wanted also a 10,000-crown loan, the use of English ships off the western coast and an assurance of a continued English presence in Brittany. But above all he was anxious to secure public assurance of continuing English support during the delicate negotiations for a truce with the League. He must have this card if his hand was to be good enough to take the trick.[67]

The English had now to accept the inevitable. Their reactions appear first in a survey of the problem by Burghley that took its

[64] SP 78/29/95, 189. [65] SP 78/31/7, 23, 32, 201; *Edmondes*, 70–79.
[66] SP 78/31/201, 204, 208, 236, 248; HMC, *Hatfield* 4: 343; *Edmondes*, 90–91.
[67] SP 78/32/28.

tone from the first sentence—"the affairs of France being more to be lamented than remedied."[68] He went on to insist on the irreconcilable differences between the Church of England and Rome. The Petrine claims, the doctrine of sacerdotal absolution, transubstantiation and the sacrificial character of the mass were all cited. Hence the Queen, "misliking and disallowing of the conversion even for her own conscience in not allowing anything against the truth of Christian faith," could no longer share the bonds of amity that led her to sacrifice treasure and lives now that Henry was bound to obey the Queen's perpetual enemy, the Pope, who had deposed her. "And yet though Her Majesty shall do well in this sort to censure the French king yet it is to be considered what shall be meet in policy for Her Majesty to do to help the King against the King of Spain, the Guises, and such as will not submit themselves upon his conversion."

Burghley then came down to cases. How and by what means would a Catholic Henry oppose the enemy and, especially, what would he do about Brittany? Until the Queen knew his plans for that province and also his own plans for taking Paris, she should reserve judgment as to her own action. Brittany, he pointed out, was crucial for both rulers since it afforded the easiest way for Spain to send forces into France without resistance as well as providing an excellent base for invading England.

By mid-July it had already been decided to send off the veteran diplomat Thomas Wilkes on a special mission to the King, the princes of the blood, and the officers of the French crown. He was to respond to the arguments offered by Henry's own special envoy. Since the English court was not certain whether the act of conversion had actually taken place, Wilkes was given alternative instructions. If it had not yet occurred, the King was to be solemnly adjured not to betray the true faith in which he had been brought up, while the Catholic party was to be wooed with a program of Burghley's design for a general reconciliation with France. Both sides should sink their differences in a common patriotic resistance to Spanish aggression, which assailed the fundamental laws of the kingdom in seeking to alter the succession. He was to put forward an irenic scheme for a council to reform abuses and reconcile dif-

[68] SP 78/31/222–23.

ferences and urge that the King's conscience not be constrained by pressure but left free to persuasion.[69]

If the act had been accomplished, then Wilkes, having ritually expressed the Queen's disapproval, was to accept the fact. Elizabeth presumed that the conversion would have consequences for good or evil; she hoped they would be for the better. Concretely, what would Henry do with her in offensive and defensive actions against Spain? She wanted to pin him down to the specific terms of a treaty under his hand and the Great Seal of France guaranteeing active alliance against Spain so long as Philip remained hostile to the English. She was prepared to continue her force in Brittany but she would not commit any more men there until she had firm assurances of French action in the province. She also wanted Brest or St. Malo as a cautionary town. But as encouragement to Henry she promised the prompt dispatch of 1,500 men. Along with the envoy there went two personal letters to the King from Elizabeth, recommending Wilkes to his attention. Written in a high rhetorical style appropriate to the solemnity of the occasion, they expressed her grief at his decision; yet the tone was as much one of reproach as of anger, the reproaches of an ally and friend whose advice had not been sought at this crucial moment and who was full of apprehension as to the consequences of Henry's grave decision.[70]

Wilkes crossed to Dieppe and went to seek the King at Argentan. A truce had been proclaimed between the King and the League, and since it prohibited the presence of foreign troops Wilkes queried whether the promise to augment Williams's force now held. Once Wilkes saw the King it became clear that he had chosen conversion because there was absolutely no alternative. But the King was equally resolved to wage war on Spain and indeed issued a formal proclamation that he would continue in alliance with the Queen and would not make peace without her consent and her inclusion in its terms. On Brittany he hedged, vaguely promising more French forces but eluding any commitment to an English base.[71]

The Queen in the meantime, abandoning her offer of reinforcements, had notified the French ambassador of her intention to withdraw all her forces, and an order was sent to Williams, who had

[69] SP 78/31/224–27, 248–51.   [70] HMC, *Hatfield* 4: 342, 343.
[71] SP 78/32/15, 34, 51–52, 58.

already retired to Dieppe, to prepare for return home. Norris received a similar command. Wilkes was home by 30 August.[72] Within the week the Queen had been persuaded to retract her decisions, at least to the extent of staying the revocation of the Normandy forces on condition that they be given a seaside base at the mouth of the Somme. The King, although anxious to retain English support, desperately tried to explain that the base that Elizabeth wanted was the property of the Duke of Nevers, who would be mortally offended it it were turned over to the English, and offered an alternative at Dieppe. When the English agent refused this offer, he was warned against making the King so desperate that he would have to turn to new friends.[73]

This hint took on more significance when Edmondes relayed the report that Henry had secretly sent an emissary to Madrid. The King, pressed by the English agent, admitted the fact, although minimizing its importance, passing it off as a maneuver in the game he was playing with his domestic adversaries. The Queen remained determined to withdraw her forces, and when transports appeared at Dieppe, Henry's anguish overflowed. At a time when the response of the French Catholics hung in the balance between the solicitations of Henry and those of the Spanish, he desperately needed at least the appearance of continued English support; the withdrawal of their forces would have a disastrous moral effect and might well tip the balance in Spain's favor. In his desperation Henry went so far as to offer Harfleur as a base, provided the Queen filled up her complements to 3,000 in Normandy and 4,000 in Brittany; he also offered the Ile de Brehat off Paimpol. Henry made it clear that English aid was needed not merely as a counter in the domestic diplomatic chess game but as an active force to be used when the truce came to an end and Henry launched a campaign in the Spanish provinces that would benefit both England and the States.[74] Elizabeth remained unyielding, and her forces in Normandy departed for home. Their return liquidated direct English efforts to cooperate with the King and the armies under his direct command. Elizabeth now restricted her participation in French affairs to Brittany.

[72] SP 78/32/3,66, 72, 78, 85.
[73] SP 78/32/156, 158–59; *Edmondes*, 97–99.
[74] SP 78/32/193, 211, 277–80, 294, 306; *Edmondes*, 117–19.

On the diplomatic front the Queen still hesitated. For the moment she stalled by sending off another envoy, Robert Sidney, Governor of Flushing, whose main task was to mediate between the Protestants and the King. In addition, he was to urge on the King that he go ahead and settle with the Leaguers without waiting for Papal absolution; it was more than hinted that a Gallican stance might serve to draw Frenchmen together in a common purpose (and at the same time widen the rift with Spain).[75]

[75] *Edmondes*, 100–2, 109; SP 78/32/287.

CHAPTER 10

BRITTANY AND

PICARDY

THE TOP-LEVEL negotiations between the Queen and the King of course included Brittany among the topics at issue, but there was a parallel and to some extent separate line of action that involved the Queen, Norris, and the local royalist leaders in Brittany. As in Normandy the French truce was taken as an excuse for an order to evacuate, dispatched from the Council on 12 August. A week earlier Norris had been solicited by Marshal d'Aumont to join him in the succor of Moncontour, southward well below the Loire. (The truce had not taken hold here.) Without a letter from home for two months, Norris knew not which way to turn. When such a letter came, he may well have regretted it. In the Queen's best sarcastic vein she acidly pointed up the discrepancy between his pay list of 3,350 and the 800 reinforcements for which he now pleaded as necessary to fill up his depleted ranks. She ended, however, after her usual condemnation of the French, with a grudging permission to complete his service at Moncontour with the Marshal before actually embarking for England. (In fact the Leaguer Mercoeur, pressured by the Breton gentry who wanted to go home for the harvest, had accepted the truce and d'Aumont had dispersed his men in garrison.[1])

Norris had then pressed the French to deliver up Paimpol as promised. Determined to stay he warned Burghley that if the En-

[1] SP 78/32/5, 21, 36, 42.

glish departed the province would be in the hands of the Spanish within a month. This view was shared in the Privy Council, and in an interesting letter the treasurer described the way in which they had persuaded the Queen to change her mind, to revoke her firm orders for evacuation and consent to Norris's remaining there at least as long as the truce held. We have a rare glimpse of decision-making in the Elizabethan government, Queen and Councillors in disagreement, the former yielding to their persuasions. But as usual the very next day Elizabeth shifted ground again; Norris was to remain at Paimpol only if it could be had without any contention and if the port were fully at English disposal. Her own disposition was for immediate return "and yet, she saieth, she yieldeth unto your tarrying because she findeth us that be of her Council to be of that mind."[2]

Norris did in fact occupy Paimpol but immediately encountered French intransigence in their refusal to let him have the neighboring Ile de Brehat, and in mid-September he was writing doubtfully about the insecurity of Paimpol. The Queen, turning as rapidly as a weathervane in a gale, first ordered Norris to leave as soon as possible because of the French refusal of the island. Then within four days she reversed herself and commanded him to remain there at least for the time being. Norris's response to these dizzying changes of the royal mind was forthright and more than usually candid. Writing to Burghley, he bluntly pointed out that the ill success of the Breton venture was owing to the Queen; she had always been warned that French participation would be minimal and only her own efforts would effect any real achievement. His claim was that even with their inadequate resources the very presence of the English had paralyzed the movements of Mercoeur. When the latter had finally made a move against Moncontour the mere approach of the English had frightened him away. So there was much to show even with present inadequacies; how much more could be done with real royal support! But the Queen continued to waver uncertainly, and Norris to beg for reinforcements or withdrawal.[3]

The extension of the truce by a month gave the Queen more time for decision. In early December the compass swerved around again and the Queen, writing directly to Norris, gave the order for his return; ships were being sent to take his men to the Channel Is-

---

[2] SP 78/32/78, 81, 82, 83.   [3] SP 78/32/103, 147, 178–82, 195–97, 231.

lands. But just at this juncture her attention was drawn in another direction. In September there had been a letter from Sourdeac, the governor of Brest, warning of a Spanish threat to his security and asking for 300 men. Now in December he wrote of Spanish forces on Belle-Isle and again asked for English help. Realizing that the loss of this great port and harbor to the Spanish would be highly dangerous, reluctantly, and with many misgivings, the Queen authorized Norris to yield to the governor's request, provided he permitted enough English into the town to make them capable of self-defense. These alarms were heightened by the news of Spanish reinforcements arriving at Blavet in the first days of the new year 1594. The Spanish, alarmed by the effects of the truce, were finally moving on their own to establish a firm base in Brittany.[4]

On a broader front the new year would bring sweeping change, a new and triumphant phase in the reign of Henry IV and a consequent major alteration in Anglo-French relations. In its very first days there was news of the defection of Orleans and other major towns from the League cause. But the King, while increasingly hopeful, was also concerned about Spanish forces gathering on his Flemish frontier and once again pressed the Queen for a reinforcement of 3,000 men to join him. Now that he faced direct war with Spain both on the eastern frontier and in Brittany, he more than ever needed English support. The Queen's view of the situation had a different slant to it; she had in fact just withdrawn her Norman contingent and sent them to Ostend to satisfy the demands of her other ally, the States. She was continuing her forces in Brittany and had been in touch with the governor of Brest, now clearly the key position. She would send succors there if she was given access to the town; she had no territorial ambitions, merely a desire to expel the common enemy from an area so sensitive to both sovereigns.[5]

The King's attention was now riveted on a climactic event, the occupation of his capital on 22 March, followed a few days later by the submission of Rouen and LeHavre. Even before that event Robert Sidney was pointing out to Burghley the changing character of the war, as it ceased to be a civil conflict and reshaped itself into an international struggle between the two great Continental rulers. He

---

[4] SP 78/32/234, 287 (a treatise against English withdrawal from France), 123, 366, 370–71, 386; SP 78/33/5, 7.

[5] SP 78/33/5, 12, 26, 90, 101, 114.

warned that Elizabeth would be urged to a tighter alliance with Henry and to participation in a general anti-Spanish coalition including the States and the German princes. The King saw the coming summer as the testing time of his fortunes, and his need for English aid was greater than ever. Some around him were saying that Elizabeth's assistance had never been intended to do more than prevent his sinking; coming events would also test her intentions most seriously. The King held out the bait of 1,500 Swiss mercenaries to be sent to Brittany. These exchanges set the pattern that would obtain for several months to come, in which Henry stubbornly pleaded for his 3,000 English foot while the Queen with equal obstinacy insisted on the priority of the Breton campaign.[6]

In that distant province events followed their usual confused and indeterminate course. Norris, now insecurely based on Paimpol, narrowly watched Mercoeur and his Spanish allies, fended off French proposals for action in various parts of the province, and waited anxiously for a firm decision from home. Both his attention and that of his government were being drawn to an unfolding crisis at Brest, now seriously threatened by Spanish forces on the scene. The latter, fearing the desertion of their Leaguer ally, Mercoeur, were moving on their own.

In January 1594 Norris, in accordance with the latest royal command, was waiting for the ships from the Channel Islands to take away his forces. While waiting he had written to Sourdeac, the governor of Brest, but expected little that would give the Queen contentment. The governor wanted 200 men, a request Norris refused because this was too few to do any good, and in any case they would not be admitted to the castle, the core of the town's defenses. The Queen was herself in direct contact with Brest through an agent dispatched by her, while the Breton estates had dispatched an envoy to England to press their case. They offered Paimpol and the Ile de Brehac as bases and the customs of the port as revenue; in return they sought an army of 4,000 and military supplies as well as money. Norris had already written that it would take a year to make the island a fortified place and that the local customs would come nowhere near paying his costs.[7]

The Queen was hesitating in her usual way. The governor of the

[6] SP 78/33/114, 18, 124, 126, 129, 160.
[7] SP 78/33/36, 40, 56, 58, 77, 80, 86, 98, 139, 167, 172.

Channel Islands had been unable to find victuals for the evacuation and had sent his ships back to England so Norris was still at Paimpol. However, these ships, now victualled, had returned and were waiting to fulfill their mission. The Queen's initial impulse was evacuation to the islands; the Breton deputies had been repelled. But then with the news of the fall of Paris and the prospect of some aid from Henry, she relented so far as to allow Norris to remain until the King's proposals were made concrete. At the same time she managed to shift ultimate responsibility to her commander by instructing him to stay only if he could defend himself with his present force. Norris in his distant camp struggled to understand the royal intentions and especially to avoid the burden of ultimate decision on withdrawal. His experience was that any step he took, of whatever character, inevitably drew down royal displeasure.[8]

In the instructions that he gave his brother Sir Henry Norris, who had been sent to court to winkle out the royal intentions, he asked for reinforcements and urged a bolder course. The neck of the League was now broken; what lay ahead was straightforward war between France and Spain. Would not the Queen consider "that if Her Majesty were so settled here that she might be able to balance the matter as might seem good unto her, then it were not amiss to let the two kings try their strengths together for a time"?[9] For the time being he held on at Paimpol; he continued to oppose sending a small contingent to Brest, where the Queen had sent Roger Williams to gather more information. The situation there began to grow urgent with a report in March of Spanish reinforcements approaching and of the building of a new fort near the port, now nearing completion. It was presumably this last news of a move that threatened Spanish control of the waters off the port that galvanized the government at home into action. In early May Burghley was busy arranging for 1,500 veterans from the Low Countries to join Norris's remaining 900 men while a fleet under the Lord Admiral would bring another 600. Norris insisted that the action be a joint one with the French, that the reinforcements join him, and that they all march to a junction with the French.[10]

The Queen, shifting ground again, now ordered Norris to leave Paimpol for the islands, where he could wait to see if the King

[8] SP 78/33/148, 152, 158, 177, 179, 181.   [9] SP 78/33/183–87.
[10] SP 78/33/177, 191, 195, 214, 217, 223, 226, 229, 247, 249.

would make an effort to save Brest in which the English could join. Williams was sent off to France to demand 3,000 French troops for Brittany while offering both ships and more soldiers. Henry's response was a very candid one: acknowledging the great advantage offered him, he nevertheless argued that of the three pressure points at the present—Flanders, Italy, and Brittany—it was the last that was least urgent. The Spanish there had a long supply line but on the other fronts they had ample support at hand. The most he could do was to send Montpensier with perhaps 700 to 800 horse and 2,000 foot.[11]

By June the Queen had at last begun to accept the need for action and had dispatched a force to Guernsey; Norris, acting on his own, summoned it to Paimpol, and the whole body of men set off by land for Brest. Elizabeth after another spasm of hesitation applauded Norris's decision and gave him full authority to do as seemed best on the spot to relieve the pressure on Brest while summoning him home for consultation. The English move towards the port had frightened the Spaniards into a retreat but the French provincial commander, d'Aumont, had prohibited his forces from joining the English in their march and urged the English to join him at Lannion in the opposite direction from Brest. However, a serious threat now loomed. The Spanish fort threatening the haven was now far advanced; once finished it would be used to blockade the port. Norris was insistent that an attack not be delayed. The Queen was now fully committed to action and promised Norris 2,000 soldiers out of England (plus 20 Cornish miners) with 100 horse, bringing his total forces to some 4,000. Frobisher would accompany him with a fleet to serve in the haven of Brest.[12]

Negotiations with the French were pushed; the Queen had offered both the men and the ships but she wanted ironclad guarantees from the King that there would be reciprocal forces (beyond the provincial levies) to collaborate with Norris. She reserved the right to withdraw if the French did not live up to their side of the bargain. The King offered a force of Swiss (if he could find the money to pay them) but balked at Elizabeth's request that the Duke of Montpensier command the forces. The strains of internal French

---

[11] SP 78/33/261, 285.
[12] SP 78/33/298, 301, 309, 317, 319, 331, 356, 369, 379; see Raleigh's warning of the dangers at Brest, in Edwards 2:93.

politics made it imperative that the duke remain with the King.[13] This inconclusive diplomatic sparring faded into the background as the arena of decision shifted to Brittany itself. The English government moved with unaccustomed speed once the decision to reinforce Norris was made. The royal instructions made it clear that these new forces were to be limited to action around Brest, in collaboration with the governor there. Given past performance, the Queen had few illusions about French promises and clearly saw Norris's role as pinpointed on the relief of Brest, putting aside any general cooperation with the royalist forces in the province.[14] The English commander at last had freedom to act on his own without waiting for French cooperation.

The first levies from the West Country arrived at Guernsey as early as 23 August, and by the beginning of September Norris had returned to Paimpol with his troops. In the interval of his absence in England the local royalists had scored some notable successes, having secured the town of Morlaix although the castle still held out. Norris's deputy, Baskerville was already with the royalists; Norris himself now followed, and together they drove off a relieving force and the castle capitulated promptly. Norris pressured the French commander to fulfill an old French promise to provide an English base by handing over Morlaix; he met with a refusal and the whole matter was referred to the French court, where Henry attempted to wriggle out of the commitment.[15]

Norris now turned to his main business, the siege of the Spanish fort at Crozon, which threatened to dominate the haven of Brest. D'Aumont with a part of the English forces had gone off to lay hands on Quimper and negotiate a truce with Mercoeur. The promised royal succors under St. Luc were no nearer than Rennes. Norris with the remainder of his force opened the siege on 1 October, and a few days later the French joined him. Frobisher played his role off the coast. The siege proved more difficult than anticipated, and the Queen as usual got cold feet and proposed abandonment of the enterprise, using the absence of royal support as an excuse for honorable retreat. Only under determined pressure did she reluctantly allow Norris to continue. Anxious for her ships in the stormy autumnal weather, she extended their rations for only

---

[13] SP 78/34/7, 9, 13, 29, 61, 103, 118, 149.   [14] SP 78/34/38, 40.
[15] SP 78/34/59, 63, 66, 94, 111, 115, 136, 149, 151; *Edmondes*, 170–74.

one additional month. An attack on 31 October failed, but less than a fortnight later came the news of victory. The fort had fallen to assault, preceded by the explosion of a mine.[16]

The Queen's response was prompt; she praised the achievement of her commander and his soldiers in vanquishing the proud Spaniard but then went on to order immediate withdrawal from Brittany. Two thousand of the veterans drawn from the Low Countries forces were to go directly to Ireland to serve under Norris in Ulster. The balance of the troops were to be returned to the counties from which they had been levied. Beauvoir, of course, protested indignantly, but the Queen's decision was absolute and Burghley could hold out no hope of a change of heart. Norris's reactions were not much more favorable than Beauvoir's; he doubted his ability to evacuate his forces at so late a season but would do his best. He continued to insist that keeping the Spaniards out of Brittany was as high a priority as keeping them from Ireland.[17]

With the withdrawal of Norris's forces from Brittany a long and unsatisfactory chapter of the war drew to a close. From the beginning the English intervention in the province had been aborted by the iron grip of the intractable circumstances within which it operated. Ends and means were constantly at odds with one another. The English motives in undertaking the intervention were straightforward enough—to crush the Spanish presence before it could become a menace to England by the establishment of an effective Spanish base for operations against the island. The Queen proposed to accomplish this by sending an auxiliary force of some 3,000–4,000 men to join with the royalists in ousting the foreigners and containing the Leaguers. In actual fact royalist forces in the province were negligible and based largely in the inland districts, well away from the northern coast, the focus of English concern. The English, sent to expel the Spaniard, found themselves instead involved in a local civil conflict, compelled to come and go at the French leaders' beck and call. And since the royalist forces were small and badly organized, this meant the English were largely inactive. When they were called on to act, it was in assisting their allies on the inland borders of Brittany or even in the neighboring provinces of Maine or Poitou.

[16] SP 78/34/ 129, 131, 162, 164, 169, 173, 198, 213, 217, 237, 252, 254, 262.
[17] SP 78/32/262, 274, 310, 320; *Edmondes*, 190–93, 196–202.

Under these circumstances both the Queen and her general were filled with frustrated anger as their men wasted away from disease and neglect. These views were shared in her court. Burghley's comment was, "unhappy is the time when Her Majesty is forced to join with such as have no other regard of her state but to ease themsevles with throwing their burdens upon her."[18] Raleigh was in full agreement. "We are so busy and dandled in these French wars, which are endless, as we forget the defense next the heart." The Queen's consistent impulse was to withdraw her forces altogether, hence the stream of peremptory orders for revocation that bombarded the distracted Norris. He, equally angered by French incompetence, sought to resolve the situation by more vigorous English action. Repeatedly he assured the home government that larger forces, some of which he even offered to pay for himself, would enable the English not only to establish a strong base on the northern coast of Brittany (which could then be held as a gage for French debts) but also to become the arbiters of affairs in this sensitive area. By dragging his feet at the appropriate moment or even by ignoring royal orders, he was able to ride out the successive waves of royal anger when the Queen's disgust with the French got the better of cooler calculation. Although her basic instinct was to wash her hands of the whole infuriating business as soon as possible, her own sober judgment and the counsels of her ministers warned her that the Spanish menace on the Breton coast was a real one and that she could not run away from her responsibilities in the province. Consequently, torn by conflicting choices, she was consistent only in her indecision. While she steadily refused to give Norris the reinforcements he demanded or to back his strategy of an independent English initiative in the province, she never quite lost hope that Henry, bombarded by her angry reproaches and pressured by her threats to withdraw, would eventually produce the additional royal armies that would tip the balance against Mercoeur and his Spanish allies.

It took the Spanish initiative at Crozon to jar the Queen into decisive action. The Spanish, seeing the League in dissolution, took steps to secure a firm naval base of their own. At this juncture Elizabeth abandoned her insistence on French support and allowed independent English initiative. Reinforcements for Norris's army and

[18] See Cecil Papers, 666–67; Raleigh's is on 664–65.

a squadron under Frobisher were rushed to the scene, and the Spanish hold at Crozon was quickly overwhelmed.

Then without hesitation the Queen moved to liquidate her whole Breton commitment. Already before the fall of the Spanish fort the solvent effect of Henry's conversion and the succeeding truce had begun to be felt in Brittany. The crucial ports of the northern and western coast had fallen or were about to fall into royal control—Morlaix, St. Malo, Quimper. With this shift in the Breton situation the English could begin to breathe more easily. The disappointed Norris, deprived of the chance for enhanced military glory just as it seemed within his grasp, was called away to more urgent but less glittering tasks in Ireland. As in the main theater of action, it was domestic French developments that altered the situation in England's favor. But in Brittany there was at least the gratification of one decisive English victory, which assured that the Spanish would not be able to establish an independent base in the province.

Some of Henry's Catholic advisors had insinuated to the King that Elizabeth would support him just enough to keep him from sinking—but no more. They were not far wrong. As long as Henry's survival hung in the balance she was willing to listen to his pleas for aid and grudgingly and stingily dole out men and money in his behalf. Successive infusions of men and money had gone for nought, yet to abandon Henry to his own resources was to give far too many hostages to fortune. But now, with the crumbling of League resistance, Henry could stand on his own feet and it was possible to extricate the English government from what had been from the beginning a vexing and fruitless commitment.

The conclusion of the Breton enterprise and the uncertainties of future Anglo-French relations more or less coincided with and perhaps led to a curious and revealing diplomatic initiative by the English government.[19] The immediate circumstances were the spate of accusations that the English envoy at Constantinople was encouraging Turkish attacks on the Empire, which in turn had led to a demand that German ports be closed to English trade. The arrival of the Austrian Archduke Ernest as governor-general in the Low

[19] For what follows, see R. B. Wernham, "Queen Elizabeth I, the Emperor Rudolph, and Archduke Ernest, 1593–94," in *Politics and Society in Reformation Europe*, ed. E. I. Kouri and Tom Scott (London, 1987), 437–49.

Countries, in early 1594, gave an opportunity to send an agent who could repudiate these libels on English policy.

In such a mission there lay a second purpose. Burghley (and probably the Queen) had never quite lost hope that the Spanish-controlled provinces of the Low Countries might be induced to separate from their Spanish masters and make peace. The negotiations with Parma in 1588 were the major such effort. They had failed, but from time to time feelers had been thrown out, particularly after the death of Parma.[20] The arrival of an imperial prince at Brussels seemed to open another window of opportunity. A memorandum of spring 1594[21] suggested that the archduke would not have come unless it was with commission for a peace that would free Spanish forces for service against the Turk. An unexpressed hope was that such a settlement would obviate French intervention in the Low Countries.

Before an agent could be sent to Brussels, the picture was clouded in another way, with the discovery of the Lopez plot, the alleged conspiracy of the exiled Jewish/Portuguese doctor Lopez to poison the Queen. The instructions for Sir Thomas Wilkes, the agent to be sent to Brussels, were altered.[22] He was to rehearse the doctor's confession, which implicated the Count of Fuentes, the highest-ranking Spanish councillor at Brussels, as the mastermind of the plot. He was to demand his arrest, along with that of some other Spanish officials and a group of English exiles. (The latter were accused of a second, more recent, plot against the Queen's life.) While Philip himself was not directly attacked, he was in fact invited to clear himself from the imputations of tacit involvement in the plot. The archduke did, on request, issue a passport for Wilkes, but the style of address he used to the Queen was declared to be incorrect and the passport was returned unused.[23] A few months later Archduke Ernest died, and in the following November the English published an account of the conspiracies.[24]

It is not altogether easy to understand this episode. The initial intention was obviously to throw out a peace feeler to a new ruler who might be expected to be detachable from Spanish control. It was queered by the discovery of the plot, which impugned the King

[20] *Ibid.*, 443; Thomas Wright, *Queen Elizabeth and Her Times* (2 vols., London, 1838) 2: 423–24.

[21] SP 77/5/108–13.   [22] SP 77/5/132–36.

[23] SP 77/5/152, 155–56.   [24] Wernham, "Queen Elizabeth," 449.

of Spain. One can detect in the instructions to Wilkes a personal note. They spoke with horror of "unnatural and beastly actions," condemned even by the heathen, which would stain the honor or a prince. To Elizabeth there was something particularly abhorrent in the notion of royalty stooping to such villainy. Whatever the intentions the initiative petered out, and Burghley would not again attempt to lure the ruler of the Spanish Low Countries into an act of revolt. The episode says something about his reluctance to continue a war he never wanted and his lingering hope that somehow, by finding a crack in the enemy's armor, the fighting could be terminated.

CHAPTER 11

THE CECIL MISSION

AND VERVINS

THE ENGLISH withdrawal from Brittany was directly linked to other, larger events that soon began to work a radical change in Anglo-French relations. Most important was the rapid dissolution of the League, as one magnate after another and one town after another fell away from its ranks and hastened to make terms with the new master of France. Henry was no longer fighting a civil war against his fellow Frenchmen; the enemy was now a foreign power, the King of Spain, the war an international one. For the English this meant a major shift in their role. They were no longer party to a civil war, shoring up the uncertain fortunes of a claimant to power against his domestic rivals. They were now partners in an alliance with a great power, an alliance in which they were the lesser member. The strategy of conflict and the hoped-for goals of victory had to be adjusted accordingly.

In one sense this was cause for English rejoicing; the power of France, no longer absorbed in civil strife, could be fully marshalled against Spanish might. The European scene, as viewed from London, was returning to its normal—one might say its natural—condition as France once more assumed her place as an effective counterbalance to Habsburg power. The possibility of realizing the basic aim of the war as the English perceived it—the restraint of Spanish ambitions—seemed to be in sight. It was now possible that Philip II could be forced to the peace table.

However, this fair prospect was marred by a small but menacing cloud of doubt. Now that Henry had established his authority at home, how much interest would he have in the vigorous pursuit of foreign war? What was the value of the English alliance to Henry under these new conditions? His crown was laden with debt; his country was exhausted by a generation of war; his people longed for a surcease of strife. Would he not be tempted by offers of peace—offers all the more likely to be made if the Spanish government decided to cut its losses in France and turn its energies once again to the central problem of crushing the Netherlands revolt?

On the French side, too, similar doubts began to surface. In 1589 when the alliance was forged, the Queen had had no more choice than did her successors in June 1941. The risks posed by a pro-Spanish regime at Paris were appalling; England must do all she could to prevent such an outcome. But now the struggle had reassumed the more familiar lineaments of a contest between Bourbon and Habsburg, and England's interests had correspondingly changed. It was immensely to her advantage to see two rival giants once more pitted against one another; their mutual animosities were the best guarantee of English safety. How much should England contribute to the advancement of French interests in such a struggle? War between the two continental monarchs would be principally fought out on the Low Countries frontier; French success might amplify French power in that area; links with the States General were already fairly strong. At the very beginning of the revolt in 1572 fear of French encroachment in the Low Countries had been as great as apprehension of Spanish recovery.

These larger issues were still veiled in an uncertain future, but the English had very immediate decisions to make. Now that the French clamors for assistance had lost their edge of desperation Elizabeth and her ministers were free to reconsider the best deployment of her limited military resources. The pressures of the Irish revolt were now increasingly urgent; carefully considered priorities would have to be established for England's scanty resources. A signal as to Elizabeth's intentions was given by the prompt liquidation of the Breton enterprise as soon as the Crozon fort was captured. Within a matter of weeks Norris's men had departed, some of them bound for immediate service in Ireland.

In the months that followed the English withdrawal from Brittany the French steadily pressured Elizabeth to make a wholesale commitment to war with Spain. In January 1595 Henry formally declared war on Spain and proposed that the English Queen should join in a common enterprise; he would submit to any reasonable conditions she proposed and give ample opportunity for her subjects to share the glory of those who espoused this cause. Beauvoir pressed the same argument with Robert Cecil, declaring that the whole fate of Christianity depended on the cooperation of the two monarchs.[1]

The Queen's reponse was sent via both Edmondes, the agent in Paris, and Beauvoir, the returning French ambassador. She was eloquent in the expression of her continued goodwill to the King but insistent that she had done more than her share and that it was now his turn to bear the burden. She had spent 600,000 crowns in Brittany and 200,000 in Normandy while the French had consistently fallen down in their oft-promised cooperation. She would continue to assail the King of Spain when and where, in her judgment, the best opportunity offered. (She was in fact already planning the Drake/Hawkins expedition to the Indies.)

Relations between the two courts drifted aimlessly through the spring and summer months of 1595, varied by a Scottish attempt to forge an alliance with France (coolly rebuffed) and a spat over the behavior of the English ambassador at Constantinople,[2] who was reported to be urging the Turk not to arm against Spain. Henry, now in Burgundy, saw little of the English agent, as he continued his successes in winning over League magnates to his cause.

In late summer Anglo-French relations took on a new urgency when the archduke's forces suddenly surged into Picardy, taking first Doullens and then Cambrai, thereby endangering the Channel ports.[3] Henry begged for the immediate dispatch of 4,000 soldiers to the Picard front; the Queen expressed her great distress at the French plight but was firm in her regret that her own affairs made it impossible to give aid.[4] Henry was not so easily put off; no fewer than three special French emissaries crossed the Channel in quick succession in these months while two special English missions (another was aborted) passed in the opposite direction.[5]

The cross-purposes of the two monarchs became rapidly visible. Elizabeth had her eyes fixed on Calais and the threat to the Narrow

---

[1] SP 78/35/31, 50, 57; *Edmondes*, 207–11, 219–22.
[2] SP 78/35/57, 76; *Edmondes*, 246–49.
[3] SP 78/35/198, 199, 219; *Edmondes*, 258–61, 268–70.
[4] SP 78/35/226.   [5] SP 78/35/223; 36/1–7, 113; *Edmondes*, 283–85.

Seas. Henry's were fastened on the Picard front, where he was desperate to avoid a further breakthrough. At the very first news of Spanish success the Queen had offered to send troops to defend Calais and Dieppe, and had made preparations for levying troops, but Henry had preferred to call on Dutch help to protect these towns.[6] Roger Williams was sent off to give the Queen's views to Henry. After noting "that we have employed our forces all these years in such places as he desired," she declared that "[we] did never find ourselves in greater expectation than now [of] the enemy's full possession" of the areas most dangerous to England, Brittany and the Channel coasts. Calais, she insisted, was the next object of the archduke, a place of great importance "to the dominion of the Narrow Seas where we can suffer no companion." Williams was to tell Henry that she absolutely refused to lift a finger unless her forces were admitted to that town in sufficient number to assure its safety—and their own. These conditions met, she would send 3,000 men. She ended by hinting at hostile advisors around the King who impugned English motives.[7]

The fall of the citadel of Cambrai precipitated the arrival of another French envoy, Lomenie, clamoring for assistance on the Picard front, declaring that Cambrai need not have fallen if such aid had been forthcoming. He unwisely suggested that the Queen's judgment was being swayed by advisors unfriendly to the French. There followed an angry royal outburst: the king ought not to doubt "our inviolated conscience nor yet mistrust that either we would incline to any counsel adverse to his estate if it were given us or suffer any about us that durst presume to open themselves in factious humor of any or practice against his prosperity." The King could count on her in any emergency (just as she had mobilized in the recent crisis at Calais), but she refused any assistance now when his own strength was sufficient to repel the enemy. She on the other hand faced a winter attack by a fleet larger than that of 1588. In short, the Queen would provide help for the French when she saw immediate threats to English security but not otherwise.[8]

Relations soured rapidly; Henry intimated in Lomenie's message that unless English aid were forthcoming he would have to consider peace with Spain. News came too of an impending truce in Brittany

---

[6] SP 78/36/5, 23, 52–55.   [7] SP 78/36/1–4; 36/8.
[8] SP 78/36/32–35, 39, 52–55; *Edmondes*, 268–71.

that would include the Spanish.[9] To quell this rising tide of ill-feeling the Queen resolved to send a new envoy, Sir Henry Unton, a veteran of earlier service at the French court. His instructions struck a conciliatory note, restating Elizabeth's good will and blaming the conduct of Lomenie for much misunderstanding. But they further emphasized the heavy cost of war (each year equal to seven under Henry VIII) and the urgency of the Irish problem. All these considerations precluded any joint action with Henry so long as the threat of invasion or pressures in Ireland existed. The Queen was giving clear notice that the phase of Anglo-French relations that had begun in 1589 was now at an end; joint action was ruled out; aid would be provided only when English security was directly at stake.[10]

The new ambassador's task was no easy one. Elizabeth was plainly worried about the rumors of a possible peace, and Unton was directed to use all possible contacts in the French court to probe the truth of these rumors and to find out if it was intended that England should participate in any negotiations. He was also to dissuade the King from listening to the siren voice of Spain, but the arguments he could use to influence the King were feeble, not much more than reminders of the ancient enmity of the Habsburgs to France or reports of the Dorman book, published by English Catholic exiles, asserting Spanish rights to the English succession.[11]

On his arrival in France in the new year of 1596 Unton heard much to discourage him even before he reached the court. The Duke of Montpensier, the Protestant leaders, and the English resident, Edmondes, all recited the same doleful rumors of an impending truce with Spain that would be the prelude to a peace. The reliable facts were that Mercoeur had made a truce in Brittany on Spanish instructions and that a truce on the Champagne/Luxemburg frontier was also about to be proclaimed.[12]

The first audience with the King went far to confirm Unton's first impressions. He bluntly pressed Henry by speaking of that new amity the King seemed to be seeking "whereof the world did not spare to speak liberally," especially in light of the coming visit of the Cardinal deJoyeux from Rome. The King responded by listing his grievances against England—the abandonment of Brittany and

[9] SP 78/36/88, 90. [10] SP 78/36/113, 115, 119–28.
[11] SP 78/36/149, 162, 169–70. [12] SP 78/37/2.

Normandy, the refusal of aid or even of conference, the strange demands for Calais—and imputed this to the Queen's ministers, who sought to break the harmony betweeen the monarchs. Then in a tone of dispassionate sorrow, he accepted the Queen's decision to withdraw from active collaboration. He on his part would have to put aside his natural preference for an English alliance since the Spanish pressure on his maritime provinces was too great to be resisted with his own resources. Necessity must govern "election and counsel." And when Unton raised the delicate question of possible English inclusion in peace talks, Henry regretfully explained that the Pope—the intermediary—had ruled out English participation.[13]

Unton's pessimistic conclusions from these conversations were that peace would follow the truce that already existed on all fronts except Picardy. Papal pressure, popular war weariness, and sheer exhaustion of resources would force its conclusion. He urged as an immediate measure the dispatch of troops to Picardy and acceptance of a conference. He relayed more rumors about DeJoyeux's mission and of overtures to the States to join in the talks. French distrust of English intentions was bluntly summed up by the Constable de Montmorency, who asserted that were there an alliance with the Queen, she would take the first opportunity to become a mere observer, leaving Henry to fight the enemy. Privately Unton wrote, "I am so nakedly instructed and the instructions so contradicting unto the former letters and assurances given them as I was ashamed of my message and forced to wrest my wits and encounter their directions."[14]

The weeks that followed brought nothing but stale reiterations of the same arguments. Henry continued to insist that the best strategy to counter a Spanish invasion of England was a campaign in Picardy and ascribed the Queen's apparent blindness to evil-wishers in her council. He himself was engaged in the siege of LaFere, which had recently been added to the Spanish acquisitions on his frontiers. It was while attending him there that ambassador Unton fell ill and died in late March 1596.[15] In the meantime English intentions to pursue an independent military strategy against Spain became clear when Vere in early 1596 began drafting English vet-

[13] SP 78/37/25, 50.   [14] SP 78/37/37, 39–42, 52.
[15] SP 78/37/46, 63, 64, 65, 67–68, 117, 122.

erans in the Low Countries for what would ultimately be the Cadiz expedition. Hearing they would be used in Spain, Henry exploded angrily at this act of mere private utility (and public futility), as he saw it. Elizabeth defended her policy, arguing that the weakening of Spain anywhere was a contribution to the common cause.[16]

A new impetus was given to events with the appearance of a Spanish besieging force outside Calais at the end of March. The States had readily responded to this threat with land and sea forces; Vere, the English commander, had excused himself. But Henry used the crisis, much heightened when the port actually fell to the Spanish, to break out of the stalemate by an initiative of major importance. Earlier he had suggested through LaFontaine, minister of the French church in London, that a conference be held to discuss military cooperation, to renew the treaty of 1572, and to settle the question of peace negotiations. This would end the rumors of peace and an agent could go on to Holland to confirm a treaty that would include the States.[17] Now the King sent a new mission to London, headed by the Huguenot magnate Bouillon. Their initial charge to obtain help for Calais became irrelevant with the fall of that port. And in fact they were charged with weightier and more far-reaching matters.[18]

Henry sought nothing less than a full alliance, offensive and defensive, in which the Queen was to provide 4,000 men for six months of each year, to serve in Picardy, Normandy, and Champagne; the King, more vaguely, would provide 6,000 for the Queen's service if she needed them. The object of this alliance was a specific one—to assure common action in those areas where English, French, and Dutch interests coincided. (The States were to be included in the treaty.) It was to be a regional pact, locally confined to the North Sea coasts and the adjoining frontiers. The French representatives warned the Queen that if she refused this offer the King, left without hope, would have to consult his own interests.[19]

Elizabeth's response was, on paper, enthusiastically wholehearted; she agreed to provide 4,000 men on the King's request. But this "league general" was immediately "retracted," at least for the coming twelve-months. Because of the exigencies of Ireland she

[16] SP 78/37/128.   [17] SP 78/37/121.
[18] SP 78/37/110, 150–53, 180, 182.   [19] SP 78/37/152.

could provide only 2,000 men this year and then for the specific purpose of garrisoning Boulogne and Montreuil *if* the Spanish approached from Flanders and *if* Henry himself were present with an army. Moreover, the Queen would pay only four months' wages. Bouillon urged acceptance of this half loaf with as much enthusiasm as he could muster, especially since it was sweetened by a loan of 20,000 ecus. The Queen wrote a self-congratulatory letter to the King, preening herself on her generosity: "a better sister than a queen"—who forgot the adage that charity began at home.[20]

The King on his side was something less than enthusiastic about an agreement that barely yielded him a half loaf, nothing for his immediate needs beyond a few thousand pounds. He indicated he would consult his counsellors, although he promised ultimate signature of the general league. He hinted at continuing moves for peace; he was renewing the Breton truce until late summer, and the Archduke at Brussels was still throwing out feelers for a treaty. In fact the King's situation was a difficult one: the Spanish advance had continued; they had taken LaFere, which Henry in turn now besieged, more, as he ruefully commented, to advance the peace with the enemy than to take the town.[21]

The long delays in ratifying the treaty were a clear sign that Henry's impetus to revive active Anglo-French cooperation had failed. It was initialled in late May, but it was August before Shrewsbury was dispatched as ambassador of honor for the ratification, accompanied by a new resident ambassador, Sir Anthony Mildmay. There were two treaties, a general league "for sight of the world" and a particular pact that abridged most of the first and was the only one binding on the Queen. Shrewsbury was to insist on having a copy of Henry's letters patent of 29 August 1593 in which the King bound himself not to make peace without the Queen's contentment. He was to refer in his speech to the rumors of peace negotiations and to assure the King that the Queen did not believe them. From Elizabeth's point of view the treaties served mainly to prevent Henry's making a separate peace. For the rest she intended the treaty to be virtually inoperative—unless some vital English interest was touched by a Continental event.[22]

[20] SP 78/37/157, 160, 169, 176.   [21] SP 78/37/202, 209, 226.
[22] SP 78/37/261, 288.

Sir Anthony Mildmay, the new resident, was faced with the onerous task of dishonoring the treaty while somehow retaining am-
icable relations with Henry. It is not surprising that he failed. The
Queen had promised 2,000 men for Picardy whenever the King
went there with his army; they would be ready by the end of the
month. But the Queen was alarmed by reports of pestilence in Picardy and, remembering the experience of 1562, when the English
returning from Le Harve had infected the whole realm with the
plague, she ordered Mildmay to urge the King not to press for the
service of these soldiers. His more general instructions reflected the
same reserved attitude. He was to insinuate that in inclining to
peace the King had fallen under Catholic and clerical influence so
deeply as to distress such Catholic friends as the Tuscan Grand
Duke. He was being drawn on by Rome into a peace that would
abandon the claims of the Gallican church. His whole effort was to
aim at impeaching as much as possible any peace moves. The English troops, even if they were sent, were to serve only on the Norman coast and under a Reformed commander. In short, the ambassador was instructed to pursue a policy of chilly cooperation and
maximum obstructiveness. Similar attitudes prevailed in London,
where difficulties were raised about payment of the 20,000 ecus.
The promised contingent would be sent only if the King's arrival
with his army was confirmed by special messenger or by an ambassador. Hostages were required as security for the loan. Bouillon's
dismay at all these delays was understandable. On the larger
scheme of the proposed general league that was to include not only
the States but German princes as well, the Queen dragged her
feet.[23]

More unexpected and less explicable was the King's behavior. At
first he continued to urge the dispatch of the English forces and
declared that he would open the campaign in spite of the lateness
of the season (October). But then, startlingly, in his first audience
with Mildmay he caved in to the ambassador's request for a three-
month delay (because of the plague) and on his own extended it to
six months. Now it was Elizabeth's turn to reverse her signals; the
troops she had promised were embarked and by 5 November were
at Dieppe. The King, taken by surprise, could only stammer out

[23] SP 78/37/294; 38/19, 87.

embarrassed thanks and then, having no use for them, send them off to winter quarters in the Somme valley, where they were left without adequate shelter to make the best of it.[24]

The King had, in fact, subsided into a season of unaccustomed lethargy. Since the Spaniards showed no signs of pressing their advantage he could settle down to the enjoyment of his mistress and the excitements of the hunt. Diplomatic activity now ebbed to a virtual halt. The King continued to hint at the need for peace with Spain. But English attention, in the fall after Cadiz, was riveted by reports of an approaching invasion fleet. General mobilization was ordered in mid-November; forces were sent to the Channel Islands and the Isle of Wight; Essex was put in charge of a fleet. But once again providential intervention scattered the Spanish ships across the Bay of Biscay and drove them battered and broken back to their home ports.[25]

The sudden switch in Elizabeth's policy when, after weeks of sullen obstruction, she sent her troops off to France in the face of French indifference, needs explanation. Probably the immediate cause of her action was concern that Calais might be used as a base by the approaching invaders. She hoped to galvanize the King into an assault on the port. But even when the danger had passed, her worried concern remained. Early in December she revived the scheme of an attack on Calais, this time to be mounted by joint Anglo-French-Dutch forces. But the price of English participation was to be nothing less than the retention of Calais after its capture. This aroused Henry to declare that he would rather have his enemies take the town than his friends.[26]

Mildmay was by this time on the worst terms with the King and his ministers. Hating his job, disliking the country, he longed only for a speedy recall. To the King he took a particular dislike, which Henry reciprocated, and their relations deteriorated to the level of bare civility. In the ambassador's opinion the old Leaguers at court were coming to dominate the scene, pushing aside both the Protestants and the old royalists and urging Henry to a pro-Spanish and pro-papal policy. Consequently Mildmay's dispatches emphasized

[24] SP 78/38/113, 133, 199, 208, 211.   [25] SP 78/38/189, 191, 213, 216.
[26] SP 78/38/199, 237–38; 39/3, 21, 58, 62.

the unreliability of the French as allies, their internal weakness, and the virtual certainty of a peace with Spain.[27]

These increasingly ill-tempered relations came to an abrupt end, and the King was shocked out the self-indulgent round of pleasure into which he had sunk in the winter by the sudden capture of Amiens by the Spanish on 12 March 1597. The Flemish front, dormant for months, now sprang to life and the English troops who had been wasting away in the miseries of a Picard winter were suddenly summoned to action as the King moved hastily to mount a siege for recapture of the town. War was renewed also on other fronts: Mercoeur resumed action in Brittany; a Spanish fleet was prepared to assail Brest; Savoy threatened to break relations. Talk of peace receded into the background.[28]

In a flurry of reaction to these new dangers, Henry pressed the Queen for an additional 2,000 men, but she would grant this only if the King paid their wages. Lacking the funds, he could not accept this proposal. He now tried another tack, offering nothing less than Calais, to be held once an Anglo-Dutch force had captured it, as a cautionary town until the French debt was repaid.[29] In return he sought his 2,000 extra Englishmen. The Queen pleaded that her situation was as precarious as Henry's. She could take no risks "lest by hazarding uncertainties at unfit times we should lose our own certainty, being a prince that never hath yet had fortune to receive any blows or affront from our enemies." The most she could offer—and very little it was—was to extend the service of the present contingent for six months and to offer once again another 2,000 if Henry paid their wages. This same letter contained a rather uncharacteristic *cri de coeur* that revealed something of her underlying anxieties. If only there could be plain and frank speaking so that she might know what Spain was offering, or what Henry intended in Brittany, an area so sensitive to England. What were Henry's general intentions? Were his demands on her, the Queen wondered, merely meant to serve his present turn, to give him time to make a separate peace with Spain? If only she were convinced of Henry's good faith, she would strain herself to give him the extra men to take Amiens.[30]

[27] SP 78/39/23, 25, 50, 58, 97.   [28] SP 78/39/74, 79, 85.
[29] SP 78/39/127–32, 137, 167, 169, 172–75, 176–79, 201, 216.
[30] SP 78/172–75.

The King was not to be wooed. Lacking funds, he thankfully declined an offer that was useless to him. If she would pay the men until the end of summer, he would hope to be in a better position; that was the best he could say. Otherwise he would have to sue for such a peace as Spain would give. But, indefatigable, Henry was not prepared to give up so he again offered the bait of Calais through yet another emissary, DeReaulx. Mildmay in a thoughtful memorandum urged rejection. Elizabeth's whole policy had been founded on a scrupulously defensive stance. "Because she hath not ambitiously sought to enlarge her dominion by the ruin of her neighbors," a posture, "pleasing both to God and man," she had limited the number of her enemies and maintained the image of a peaceful and nonaggressive neighbor. To attack Calais—in itself a militarily doubtful enterprise—would only give scope to "many who envy her virtue and felicity" and "who would be glad of an opportunity to express malice." It was a good exposition of Elizabethan policy, although clearly, in the past, the Queen had been tempted by the thought of recovering Calais.[31]

During these months there was virtual military stalemate, since Henry's forces were inadequate to the capture of Amiens while the Spanish impetus to attack seemed exhausted. His English contingent could only endure their plight, unpaid, underfed, and unused. Their commander, Baskerville, died and so did his immediate successor. The diplomatic front was stirred into life by the arrival of the General of the Cordeliers, bearing, it was said, the offer of a seven-year truce.[32]

Finally the Queen acceded to the French pressure so far as to agree to fill up the complement of 2,000 men at Amiens, now sadly depleted. Four hundred Englishmen landed at St. Valery; 300 more were needed. The siege at last showed signs of success; the Cardinal of Austria failed to relieve the town, and by 19 September 1597 it had fallen. The English prepared to go home. This ended military activity on the Picard front for the year; the King now turned his attention to Brittany. It also opened the way for renewed and much more serious Franco-Spanish negotiations. As early as August the King had asked Elizabeth for advice on how to view the Spanish overtures. (He had just sent his secretaries, Villeroy and Bellievre, to Brussels.) Her advice was mildly encouraging, pointing out that

[31] SP 78/39/167, 169, 172–75, 267.　　[32] SP 78/39/254, 256, 279, 323, 330.

Anglo-French war aims were defensive—the checking of Spanish ambitions—and hinting that she looked forward to a joint exploration of these Spanish advances.[33]

The French reconquest of Amiens did indeed mark a definitive turn in the road to a Franco-Spanish peace. It was reflected in Henry's relations with England in the appointment of a new French ambassador to London. Significantly DeMaisse, unlike his predecessors, was a Catholic, a moderate and a councillor. They had come armed with urgent demands for further aid; his mission was to take soundings as to England's disposition to peace. The King in a letter to the Queen in November 1597 asserted that the enemy now sought peace and that he and she must be united in their purposes. Edmondes, now back in Paris as the English representative, believed the Spanish were making sweeping concessions in a real effort to end the war. As he saw it, the French believed Elizabeth would join in a treaty, even if it meant excluding the States, who would be fobbed off with a truce for a term of years. In any case they were anxious for English participation in the negotiations, to give weight to the French case. For the moment there was a slight cooling in the exchanges and lingering doubts as to Spanish sincerity—were they playing for time or were they truly exhausted? But this slowed the pace only momentarily.[34]

DeMaisse, arriving in London in November 1597, resolutely asserted that his task was to resolve the question of war or peace. If it were to be the former, Henry proposed a grand coalition of English, French and Dutch forces to assault Calais in the spring, an action that, in the weakened state of Spanish power, would pay off handsomely. At this point the Queen resolved to shift the venue of discussion from England to France. She determined to send a formal and weighty embassy to wait on the King, to deal face to face with him. To head this mission she chose Robert Cecil, secretary since 1596 and now about to succeed his failing father as "first minister." To Henry she playfully wrote that she was sending "mes petites tablettes, que vous mande pour embassadeurs qui portent en elles beaucoup de mon esprit."[35] Cecil was accompanied by the veteran diplomat Sir Thomas Wilkes and by the second secretary, Herbert,

[33] SP 78/40/33, 41, 126, 135, 137, 204, 213, 233.
[34] SP 78/40/223, 236, 238, 254; *Edmondes*, 296–302, 304–11.
[35] SP 78/40/272, 274, 291; 41/48–54, 195; *Edmondes*, 320–24.

along with a staff of eighteen gentlemen and an appropriate number of servants. During his absence from court heavy responsibility would fall on the Earl of Essex since Burghley, now in the last months of his life, was virtually *hors de combat*. Essex gave every sign of goodwill and cooperativeness towards his rival.[36]

The voluminous instructions prepared for the embassy reflect the jostling suspicions, fears, and uncertainties that beset the English leadership at this awkward juncture. For the past year or so it had been possible to reassure themselves that the Franco-Spanish conversations, although worrying, would not eventuate in any solid agreement. But now the Spanish failure to resume activity on the Flemish frontier, even after being reinforced from Spain, and their indifference towards the fate of their Breton ally, Mercoeur, were conspicuous signals of a change of heart. The French king, on his side, with the recovery of Brittany, was about to eliminate the last major center of opposition to his sovereignty, and his bargaining position was a strong one.[37]

The Secretary was to confer not only with Henry but also with a Dutch delegation, headed by Oldenbarnevelt, which the States were sending to France. His primary purpose was to gather information. "The chiefest end of our journey is inquisition," as Sir Robert wrote to his father. Three central questions needed answering: how serious were Spanish intentions, how serious French inclination to peace, and what was the attitude of the States? With this information in hand the crucial English decision—whether to join in the negotiations—would be made at home.[38]

Although the mission's task was to seek information, much of the thinking about the decisions that lay before the Queen and her ministers is reflected in the lengthy memoranda that form part of the instructions. They reiterate the Queen's besetting memories of the 1588 negotiations with Parma. Her betrayal then had been indelibly graven in her mind; it haunted her thoughts in the present situation and made her (and her councillors) deeply doubtful about trusting any Spanish offers.

A second theme that runs through the memoranda is Elizabeth's insistence that any peace settlement must provide for the security of the States. What this meant concretely is at least sketched out. Echo-

[36] SP 78/41/93, 141.   [37] SP 78/41/149.
[38] SP 78/41/48–54, 59–68, 120.

ing a constantly reiterated policy that dated back to the 1570's, the Queen wanted a return to the *status quo ante* of Charles V's early years, a restoration of the liberties of the *Joyeuse Entrée* of 1477, with an addendum providing for the toleration of Protestants. In short, the Dutch were to return to their allegiance to the Habsburg dynasty, but the Spanish were to remove their troops and officials, from the Low Countries, becoming absentee landlords and leaving to the provinces their autonomy. If the States refused such terms, England would then be free to consult her own interests.

If the negotiations failed and war continued, the English would expect the Dutch to assume full financial responsibility and to promise reciprocal aid to the English. The French were to be warned not to expect any military aid from England except in the direst emergencies (and in practice only when English interests were directly affected, as in Brittany or Picardy). In addition, both allies were to be dunned for their accumulated debts to the English crown; it was even suggested—but merely as a bargaining point— that Calais be handed over in lieu of monetary repayment by France.

By 12 February 1598 Cecil and his company were at Dover waiting for the wind. He wrote from there proposing to deal first with the French ministers, then with the States deputies, and finally with the King himself. The Queen, standing on her dignity, ordered him not to proceed beyond Rouen except to meet the sovereign himself. Under Essex's persuasions she gave in to Cecil's scheme. The Secretary, meditating on these matters while waiting for the wind, came to the conclusion that the suggestion that Spain would treat with the English was mere moonshine; imbued with the deepest suspicion of Spanish motives, he was now certain there was no commission from Spain to deal with England. The French were using this fiction so that when the Queen refused to join in they would have a justification for making a separate peace. Would it not be better, Cecil argued, to concentrate all their efforts, with Dutch assistance, on dissuading the King from treating? Perhaps the Huguenots could be stirred up to pressure him. The Queen's reaction to this assertion that there was no Spanish commission was to recall the embassy, and it took the combined art of Essex and Burghley to quiet her. The absence of such a commission would mean continued war and eliminate the leverage the Queen hoped to exercise upon the States. Moreover, the arrival of reinforcements (4,000

Spanish soldiers at Calais) would be an added inducement to Henry to sign a peace treaty.[39] These exchanges reveal the nervous uncertainty of the English leaders as they edged into negotiation with the French king.

It was not until the very end of February, fully a fortnight after their arrival at Dover, that the mission reached Dieppe, where they glumly concluded "it is such as we have all thought fit to return." However, they decided to go on to Paris but, reverting to the Queen's earlier intentions, to do no business with the ministers until they had seen the King. They were determined not to be fobbed off with time-wasting sessions with subordinates; they must deal directly with the maker of policy. This would mean a longish journey across France, since Henry was on the borders of Brittany. There was pressure of time also; the arrival of the English had stimulated the Spanish to the final concession of Calais and Ardres, and they now pressed for instant signature. Henry resisted, but clearly he was now within reach of all his goals for a satisfactory peace.[40]

At home Essex set his prolix pen to paper and in a meandering letter reflected on the crisis. He emphasized the continuing Spanish threat, with 4,000 men newly arrived at Calais and a fleet of galleys in the Flemish ports that could elude the wind-bound English ships in an attack on Sheppey or the Isle of Wight. Essex went on to sketch another scenario of Spanish intrigue in which they established themselves in Scotland and Ireland. In any case, the Earl reckoned that from Spain no true peace could be meant. He doubted the States would ever consent to a truce (and if they did they would be ruined). Thus Essex, doubtful of any viable peace, declared he "would seek peace, that is to say, safety," by war. It would be easy to clear the Flemish coast from Boulogne to Flushing within a year.[41]

In the meantime Cecil and his colleagues (except for Wilkes, who fell mortally ill at Rouen) moved on to Paris, to be met with a letter from the King inviting them to meet him at Angers and announcing the collapse of Mercoeur's resistance. This meant a long journey for the envoys, but it was also a chance to observe something of the country. Cecil was appalled by what he saw: whatever Spain's condition might be, France's was clearly desperate. More than ever the

---

[39] SP 78/41/120, 122, 135–36, 141, 143, 149.
[40] SP 78/41/157, 172.   [41] SP 78/41/177.

Secretary was convinced that, as soon as Spain offered reasonable terms, France would thrust aside all previous commitments in order to make peace. The English had come prepared for the option of continuing war or negotiating peace; the former had now vanished. They could do little more than justify the Queen to the world as a Christian and peace-loving princess. By insisting that the Queen, given her past successes and present strength, could not make peace without securing honor and safety, they could undercut French allegations that she could have had peace if she wished. Cecil had little hope that either English or Dutch persuasions would divert the King from his purpose; none of the arguments they could bring would have any effect. He took it as "a maxim that it shall not be by the French that peace is not made."[42]

While the mission made its slow way across France, the English Council had come into possession of crucial documents—nothing less than the proceedings at Vervins, where the French and Spanish negotiators were meeting. These contained the dramatic revelation that a preliminary peace had already been agreed upon, but that it was being kept secret until an additional commission could be obtained from Madrid to deal with the Queen. That commission, however, was a mere pretense, intended only as a gesture to absolve the King from blame. He intended to go ahead with the treaty now without regard to England or the States. English knowledge of these dealings, the Queen instructed, was to be sprung upon Henry in such a way as to trap him and force out of him a confession of their truth.[43]

Cecil was still ignorant of these revelations when he arrived at Angers and had his initial audience with the King. It was very much a sparring match. The King got in the first blow by reproaching the Queen for her secrecy about her own naval expeditions, and then by decrying the futility of the English strategy. While her feats were nobly begun and ended, unless the Queen made war of another fashion, to follow a more constant resolution, the greater purse must outspend the lesser. Shifting ground, he repeated the familiar French line that the distress of his people forced him to seek peace. Cecil in turn rehearsed the well-worn English argu-

[42] SP 78/41/186, 203–6, 226.
[43] SP 78/41/236–38, 239–41, 246–48, 251, 253. For copies of French correspondence, see 255, 256b.

ments: that Spain sought only to separate the allies, that England by past performance had demonstrated her commitment to war, that Cadiz had weakened Spain by diverting his forces from other fronts. To this the King suddenly yielded—"Je confesse tout, vous avez raison"—and ended the audience.

At a later audience there was more plain speaking. Cecil insisted he did not come to dissuade the King from peace, provided he were persuaded of Spanish sincerity, but to inquire what the Spanish intentions towards England were, indeed, to make Henry a mediator for England. Could he authenticate the Spanish claim that they had power to treat?[44]

The King now showed at least some of his cards; the Spanish were offering all he asked, even Calais. As for England, he hedged. She had hurt Spain more than France, he pointed out, but Henry at least was showing himself an honest man by insisting on the commission to treat (which he was sure would soon arrive). He warned again that if there were no settlement, Spain's "council and his purse will eat out the Queen of England and all of us." Then, swinging to the offensive, "I am told that your drift is only to amuse me, to leave me in the war ever and to account that your safety, but I am not of that faith."[45]

The conversation then turned to the Dutch problem. "For whom," the King said, "must we be miserable in perpetuity?" To which Cecil riposted that it was a strange apprehension to all his neighbors to behold a King of Spain by conquest or contract absolute master of all seventeen provinces. Henry then challenged Cecil directly: "since you will not let me make peace alone nor you may not make peace without the States," is there a third way? What about peace among the monarchs, with a truce for the States? Cecil returned the ball by asserting that the Dutch were as opposed to a truce as to peace. Very well then, what about a peace without the States, leaving them to continue the war? Here Cecil hedged, "so they might not perish by it, it was less harmful." "Well, saieth the King, will nothing content your Queen?" On that uncertain note the encounter ended.

Cecil now advised that the mission return home. Obviously

44 SP 78/41/263–68, 269–86.
45 For details of Franco–Spanish negotiations over the past few months, see SP 78/41/319.

war—for the English and the Dutch—was to continue. Decisions for the future could only be made at home. But the Dutch mission, headed by Oldenbarneveldt, had now arrived, and Cecil talked with them at length. He reassured them that the Queen would not make peace without them but pressed them hard as to why they were unwilling to accept as a basis for settlement the general conditions that all strangers should leave the Low Countries, i.e., a return to the *status quo ante* that Elizabeth favored. The Dutch reply summed up the fundamental principles of the new state. Their constitution, they said, was incompatible with monarchy whether under the King of Spain or a Duke of Burgundy (i.e., the archdukes). Moreover, they argued, the problem was not one of strangers only but also of Spaniolized natives. The English response was a reserved one, once again urging pressure on Henry to continue the war in Flanders, to which the Dutch countered with a request for an English army of 12,000 to 13,000 men. Cecil hastily backed away from this by raising the issue of the Dutch debt. The unresolvable dilemma of the English was never more plain; they wanted each of their allies to continue fighting but were resolutely determined not to give either any additional assistance.[46]

Cecil had now received news of the intercepted documents from Vervins. A dramatic interview followed in which the Secretary taxed the King with a breach of public faith. Henry responded in a letter to the Queen, blandly asserting that she had nothing to fear. Carefully avoiding any forthright denial of the documents' authenticity, he emphasized that the commission from Spain would certainly arrive and asked for patience. If his agents had signed any draft treaty, they had gone beyond their powers, but he warned that affairs could not long remain so fluid.[47]

Cecil followed the King to Nantes and there had the most stormy interview of the mission. Sir Robert tried to smoke out the King— did he favor war or did he favor peace? Henry forthrightly answered that his necessities would not let him stand out and that he would get no more by hazard of war than he thought to have by peace. He compared himself to a man clothed in velvet but lacking food to eat. There was an unseemly wrangle in which Cecil blamed the King's plight on the disorder of his servants and Henry dismissed English aid as always too little and too late. When tempers

[46] SP 78/41/319.   [47] SP 78/41/359, 364.

had cooled a little, Cecil declared that there was no point in continued discussion, so they should proceed on the assumption of a
French peace. In that case, what about the States? The King asserted they could defend themselves. And he in turn demanded of
Cecil what the English reaction would be, now that the Spanish
commission to treat had arrived.[48]

The English evaded this demand by explaining that their commission was only to consider continuation of the war. There was
further squabbling between the King and the envoy in which
Henry reproachfully told Cecil he had not treated him like an ordinary ambassador. To which the Englishman replied that he
served "an extraordinary prince, a prince that ought to be extraordinarily respected . . . and if without arrogancy I might speak it I
might take myself (considering my place) as no ordinary ambassador." In the end, after a few more such volleys, they parted, Cecil
flinging reproaches at Henry, the King insisting he would still be
Elizabeth's friend. The Secretary may have had the better of the
exchange, but he had to face the fact that his mission had failed in
its hope of diverting the King from peace. In a weary letter to his
father, Cecil revealed the deepest anxiety that troubled his government. If only Ireland were settled, "I protest I would not in my
poor judgment care what France did." If England's back door were
securely locked against any intruder, Cecil reckoned that Spain, excluded from France and tied down in the Netherlands, could do
England no real harm.[49]

In the final stages of the mission the English tried at least to
salvage as much moral and psychological advantage as they could.
They did their best to shift the onus for choosing peace on to Henry's shoulders. They continued to insist that they had come for serious discussion of the options before them, not merely to gain time,
as the French alleged. The French were reproached for their haste
in coming to a decision without giving the allies a fair hearing.
Henry, in his turn, declared it was the refusal of these allies to make
any firm commitment for the future that drove him to sign the
treaty. In mid-April the mission returned home, soon to be followed to England by the Dutch, whose hope for a rapprochment
with the French had been finally shattered. On 2 May 1598 the

[48] SP 78/42/1–5.　　　　[49] SP 78/42/13.

commissioners at Vervins signed the treaty ending war between France and Spain.[50]

That event ended the phase of uncertainty that had begun with the English withdrawal from Normandy and Brittany three years before. That withdrawal had coincided with the collapse of the League and Henry's bloodless conquest of his troubled realm. He was then no longer the beleaguered claimant fighting desperately for his throne against a formidable party of his own countrymen backed by a great foreign power. The war now assumed the lineaments—so familiar for the past century—of a straightforward contest between the French and the Spanish monarchies. This freed Henry IV from the narrow constraints of his first years and gave him for the first time a range of options. His choices stretched from full-scale, all-out war on the one hand to a peace of accommodation on the other, and in between flexible combinations aimed at either goal could be explored, as conditions dictated.

If war were continued, Henry quite plainly saw that it had to be determinedly offensive, aimed at a prompt and crushing assault on Spanish power in the Low Countries. It needed to be of short duration, for his country, exhausted by decades of civil war, could not face a prolonged defensive struggle. Such a war had necessarily to entail large-scale cooperation with his English and Dutch allies. The other possibility, a negotiated peace, seemed increasingly a real option, as Savoy came to terms with France, and papally mediated feelers came from the Spanish side. Until one could assess the sincerity of these overtures, however, France had to remain in as strong a posture as possible. She needed to have the apparent and active support of her allies so as to strengthen her hand when she came to the bargaining table. Hence the French King worked hard to keep all these options open. He sought to keep his lines open to Brussels while at the same time maintaining live—and visible—cooperation with England and the States. The threat of a separate peace served to prod the latter to effective support of the French, while the dangers of a tripartite offensive in the Low Countries pushed the Spanish to larger concessions in the cause of peace.

Elizabeth's perceptions of the scene were, of course, radically different. She had assisted Henry when he seemed about to be overwhelmed by a Guisan regime, Spanish-dominated and vociferously

[50] SP 78/42/18–25, 70, 82.

anti-Protestant. With the establishment of Bourbon authority, that danger was past; once again there was a continental balance; a restored French monarchy glared menacingly at its Hispano-Burgundian rival. For Elizabeth it had been highly important that this hostility remain glowingly active. She did not have the options that Henry enjoyed. Once his realm was cleared of the Spanish intruder, only negotiable details needed to be settled before peace was achieved. For the Queen, however, the prospects of a viable peace seemed dim.

Two sticking points halted all progress towards a settlement. It was imperative for England that the security, both of Ireland and of the States, be assured. As long as there was any threat of renewed invasion of either of the British Isles or danger that the United Provinces, left alone, would be overwhelmed, Elizabeth could not end the war. Moreover, her ineradicable distrust of Spanish intentions, based on her experience with Parma in 1588, made her suspicious of every olive branch that was tendered and quite unwilling to risk the future on Spanish promises. Hence her anxiety to keep Franco-Spanish hostilities ablaze as long as possible. But at the same time she refused to give any additional help to a power that she felt could now stand on its own feet. Only a direct threat to English interests, such as Calais, would move her to intervene again.

This policy was entirely consistent with that pursued by the Queen in the years before war began, when she had striven for maximum English independence of action. English resources were to be committed only in the most necessary—and desperate—conditions, and then for the shortest period of time possible. This fundamental isolationism of the Queen was immeasurably strengthened by her experience in Normandy and Brittany, where her forces rusted away in futile inaction. She saw no reason to repeat this frustrating and wasteful experience now that France could stand on its own feet. The insatiable demands of her commanders in Ireland as they struggled fruitlessly with rebellion reinforced her position even more. Coupled with the fear that Ireland might become to England what the Low Countries were to Spain, along with the threat of another Armada, the Ulster risings from 1595 onward became the overriding preoccupation of the Queen and her ministers. England, laboring under these compelling dangers, could spare no men or money for a France that now commanded ample resources for its own defense.

Thus in these years English and French interests had slowly but steadily diverged as Henry moved gropingly towards the peace that his exhausted realm desperately needed while Elizabeth, despairing of peace, sought to maintain the broadest and strongest anti-Spanish coalition possible. The incompatibility of these goals was ever more apparent as peace became more and more a real prospect and the Queen's resolute refusal to enter into active military cooperation hardened into rock-like firmness.

Before Cecil left France the expected Spanish commission to treat with England arrived, and the French secretaries affirmed its sufficiency. It empowered the Spanish representatives to negotiate at any time within the next six months. A memoir was prepared by the English for the use of the French intermediaries that demanded among other things repayment by Spain of the loan made to the States-General in 1577. A more fundamental difficulty was that of Flushing, which the Queen proposed to return to the States; the Spanish expected the return of that port and of Brill to their hands. All this suggests delaying tactics on the part of the English, along lines proposed by Cecil,[51] but in fact the first hesitating steps were being taken towards dealings with the Spanish.

The conclusion of peace and the end of the Anglo-French wartime alliance worked a wholesale alteration in their diplomatic relations. The hectic pace of wartime business, punctuated by successive crises and dominated by the incessant French demands for aid, now subsided into a humdrum routine. Diplomatic representation became better organized. Boissise, sent by Henry in September 1598, was to remain in England until early 1602. The English representation at Paris was also regularized, beginning with the dispatch of Sir Henry Neville in January 1599. He later blotted his copybook by his peripheral involvement in the Essex rebellion. An effort was made to continue representation at the ambassadorial level, rather than merely through an agent, but neither Sir Anthony Mildmay nor Ralph Winwood were happy in their relations with the King. Nevertheless, at least there was a continuous English presence at the French court.[52]

---

[51] SP 78/42/9, 124, 171–76.

[52] P. Laffleur de Kermaingant, *L'ambassade de France en Angleterre sous Henri IV: Mission de Jean de Thumery, sieur de Boissise (1598–1602)* (2 vols., Paris, 1886) 2: 8–9 [Vol. 1 hereafter cited as Boissise. Vol. 2 subtitle: *Pièces justificatives*; hereafter cited as Boissise, *Pièces*].

In the immediate aftermath of Vervins attention was centered on the attempted French mediation between London and Brussels. Edmondes, interim agent at Paris in late 1598, was under considerable pressure from the King to further negotiations with the archduke. But the death of Philip II in August and the subsequent departure of the archduke-governor for Spain served to slow down what was already a half-hearted process. When more serious negotiations came to life in the following year, the contacts were directly between London and Brussels, although the ill-fated conference of summer 1600 was held on French soil.[53]

The instructions that were provided for Neville in January 1599 provide an overview of Anglo-French relations as seen from London. First priority was given to trade relations. English ships, both royal and private, lay in wait for hulks bringing grain and naval supplies and other cargo from the Baltic to supply Spanish demand. Now that peace had come and French trade with Iberia was renewed, their merchants were among the sufferers who saw their ships and cargoes confiscated by the English as contraband. Efforts to obtain redress in the English courts were highly unsuccessful; the volume of protest grew steadily. At the same time the French government, able at last to devote itself to peacetime tasks, was taking measures to restrict the import of English cloth. The claims and counterclaims of their respective merchant communities would keep both ambassadors busy for the remainder of Elizabeth's reign.[54]

[53] SP 78/42/171–76.
[54] SP 78/43/5, 25–31; Boissise, *Pièces*, 19–20, 22–24, 25–27, 55–58.

CHAPTER 12

SHUFFLING TOWARDS PEACE

1598-1603

THE CADIZ EXPEDITION of 1596 and the abortive enterprise of the succeeding year were to be the last major offensive efforts the royal navy would make against the enemy. It was political rather than military or strategic circumstances that led to the end of an offensive strategy. The success of Henry IV in overpowering the League and establishing his full royal authority transformed the international scene and profoundly affected the calculations of the other protagonists in the European struggle. Philip II, near the end of his life, had reluctantly to accept defeat, recognize the Bourbon dynasty, and withdraw from intervention in French affairs. Spanish attention was now, once again, focused on the Low Countries, where a radical shift of Spanish strategy was under way. The Cardinal Archduke, Albert of Austria, newly matched with Philip's daughter, the Infanta Isabella Clara Eugenia, was set up with his wife as rulers of a revived Burgundy. On paper at least the Habsburg Low Countries provinces were to be autonomous, with the prospect—if the marriage bore issue—of a separate branch of the dynasty. This was a strategy designed to rally the flagging loyalties of the southern provinces while providing the umbrella under which war-weary and discontented elements in the United Provinces might find a tolerable alternative to endless conflict. A States-General of the Habsburg provinces met at Brussels in August 1598 and insisted politely but firmly that their new rulers listen to their voices of advice and grievance, a request to which Albert had to accede.[1]

The archduke's first task was to negotiate a peace with France, which was achieved by May 1598, some months before the death of Philip II swept off the stage the greatest actor in European politics. Obviously these events profoundly affected Anglo-French relations; equally they altered those of England and Spain. For the first time since 1588 there opened up the glimmering prospect of a settlement. At Vervins the French had pressed for English—and Dutch—inclusion in the negotiations. While this insistence was largely tactical, designed to serve French interests in justifying their withdrawal to their allies, it did result in a Spanish commission to treat with the English and half-hearted agreement by Elizabeth to a French mediation.[2]

The English Council now had seriously to consider what response to make to the Spanish overtures. There was initial skepticism as to the sincerity of the offer, the Queen remembering the experience of 1588 and "doubting of some like accident to accompany this bare offer in the name of the Cardinal." These doubts overcome through French mediation, the English had then to consider their own position. The immediate response was a very reserved one. There could be no peace without the agreement of the States, and the Dutch were firm in their refusal to negotiate. The French king was to be thanked but the Queen would appoint no commission to treat. However, a door was kept open; England was by no means unwilling to seek peace. The Queen was prepared to listen to any overtures that the enemy might make, but she herself would take no initiatives. It was up to the new rulers of Spain and the Burgundian provinces to come forward with the first move.[3]

Supposing such a move should be made what should the English response be? There was much debate both inside and outside the

[1] *Actes des Etats Généraux de 1600*, ed. M. L. Gachard (Brussels, 1849), introduction.

[2] SP 78/42/9, 171–76; Boissise, *Pièces*, 14–16.

[3] SP 78/43/25–31. For this and the following paragraphs, see also BL, Lansdowne Ms. 103: 87/243–51, 252–56. For further discussions of the English response, see BL, Harleian Ms. 6798: 76–79, 163–69; Lansdowne Ms. 87: 8/31/–32 and 160: 89–92; Strype 4: 451–64; William Camden, *Annals of Queen Elizabeth* (London, 1675), 546–47. See also Lodge 3: 92–94, for Edmondes's views at this juncture, as reported to Shrewsbury.

Council. Opposition to peace emphasized the immediate question of Spanish good faith. The example of the Bourburg negotiations in 1588 was much cited, as well as the familiar argument that Catholic kings would not keep faith with heretics even if they signed a peace. They would amass more treasure and when they were ready resume the war. There was also the practical difficulty of the cautionary towns; these could not be surrendered without betraying the Dutch.

Proponents of a peace settlement pressed the argument more deeply. Harking back to 1585, they pointed out that the Queen had embarked on war not for her own aggrandizement but to protect the ancient liberties of the Low Countries, of a people closely associated with the English and oppressed by a tyrant king. Her objective was to restore the *status quo ante* of the era of Charles V. These goals were now realizable; an autonomous United Provinces, free from external political or religious domination, was now in being. With the revival of French power the provinces had nothing to fear; in alliance with France they would be secure against Spanish threats. England's basic war aims would thus be obtained. There was no need to further the greatness of a state that already rivalled England on the seas.

Spain, exhausted by war and faced by a resurgent France, gave no cause for fear. However, she was still too strong to be successfully assailed by England (or an Anglo-Dutch navy); further offensives would be mere waste. More important, the end of hostilities would crush Irish hopes of Spanish succor and open the way for extinguishing the rebellion. Burghley, now in the last weeks of his life, threw his weight on the side of peace for rather different reasons. In a revealing sentence he warned of "the nature of the common people of England, inclinable to sedition if they be oppressed with extraordinary payments," and further "that there was an inbred disaffection in the vulgar towards the nobility." It tells us a great deal about the English government's underlying uncertainties as to the limits of its power to coerce its subjects.

To such arguments the advocates of continuing war could only insist on Spanish treachery and on their unappeasable appetite for universal dominion. To the argument that further offensives were impossible, they admitted that this was so in Europe but claimed that a successful effort was still possible in the Indies, where an army of 10,000 might seize Panama. But they had lost the argument. The English government was prepared to hear the Spanish proposals and, if feasible, to deal with them at the negotiating table.

To clear the ground for such negotiations the English laid out a set of demands. They would first propose a return to the *status quo ante* of Anglo-Burgundian relations, the treaties of 1520 and 1542; there should be a mutual act of oblivion for all the events of the war years. Then the substantive questions, last discussed at Bourburg in 1588, could be raised. The English would demand for themselves renunciation of Spanish claims to the English crown, severance of relations with the English Catholic exiles, approval of English aid to the States, and English retention of the cautionary towns until the Queen was repaid for her outlay on the war. Trade should be free of both economic and religious restrictions; English merchants should have access to the Spanish Indies. For the Low Countries there was to be a restoration of the *status quo ante* of Charles V, but with freedom of religion in the northern provinces and of conscience in the southern provinces. There would be a board of guarantors chosen from French, Dutch, and English nobles to insure performance of the treaty, and an international treaty as a further guarantee. These proposals echoed English policy since the first days of intervention. The flimsy fiction of Philip's sovereignty would appease Spanish pride while easing Elizabeth's qualms about legitimizing rebellion. Realistically it would be a peace that recognized the essential English war aims.

The nature of these aims emphasized most of the concerns rehearsed above. The cardinal English concern was the Spanish threat to England's security. Suspicion of Spanish intentions towards England ran deep; memories of Alva and his successors and of their scheme to make of the Low Countries "as it were, a bridge to come into this realm" were recalled, and Philip's backing for the attempts on the Queen's life cited. It was imperative that the present regime continue in power at The Hague, strong, armed, Protestant, with free access to all Spanish territories. In the southern provinces all foreign troops were to leave; only natives were to be employed as soldiers. The States would continue to recruit in England; the English would hold on to the cautionary towns. These terms presumably represented the maximum English program for a stable peace. Compromise on some conditions might well follow, but the central condition of effective Dutch independence was a *sine qua non*.

The English strategy of pushing the initiative on to the Spanish was a successful one. At the end of the year the first overtures for negotiation were put forward by the Brussels government. (The Archduke Albert was absent in Spain; his cousin, Cardinal Andreas of Austria, was acting governor.) An Antwerp juriconsult, Jerome Coomans, chosen to make the first contacts, was sent to London in January 1599. He was dispatched in the greatest secrecy; only two councillors were informed, but the French ambassador was made aware of the mission. Coomans was instructed to seek an interview with the Queen through Cecil or other ministers. His message was simple: Cardinal Andreas, distressed by the miseries of the war, offered his services as a mediator. If the Queen agreed, he would write to Archduke Albert and Philip III, to gain their consent to conversations with the English. Coomans was to confine himself to generalities, avoiding all specific issues, and to take pains to quench any notion of a rift between archduke and king.[4]

The Queen received the agent and expressed a cautious interest in the cardinal's proposal. She shared his concern for peace and was willing to listen to whatever offers the Spanish had to make. Coomans returned for a second visit with the proposal that each side appoint deputies for a meeting. To this the Queen agreed, provided full powers to negotiate were given the Spanish commissioners by Madrid.[5] This took some time to arrange and the whole matter was postponed until the archduke's return to the Low Countries in the late summer of 1599. The anticipated arrival of a Spanish invasion fleet threatened to kill the negotiations altogether. But when the fleet was first diverted and then shipwrecked, Coomans reappeared and by October was shuttling back and forth again.[6]

During these months the matter was much discussed in the Council. The French ambassador, Boissise, thought the Queen favored a peace, although she still doubted Spanish sincerity, and the English ambassador at Paris was told that England would welcome peace in certain circumstances. Essex was forthrightly opposed, asserting that the overtures were mere trumpery and that such a peace would be the ruin of the kingdom. The French ambassador

---

[4] Boissise, *Pièces*, 16–18, 29–31, 40–42; *Actes*, introduction, xxff.

[5] SP 77/6/7.

[6] *Actes*, xxiv; PRO 31/3/30: [1599] 3/18, 3/26, 5/12, 7/4, 8/13, 9/1, 10/13, 10/17; Winwood 1: 68–73, 90–92, 95–97; Boissise, *Pièces*, 43–45, 50–53, 72–73; *CSPVen* 9 (1592–1603): 382, 385, 386; SP 77/6/46, 59, 71.

even believed that the treaty was supported by those who sought peace as a means to abase the greatness and authority of Essex. In any case, the earl departed on his ill-fated Irish venture in April. The Queen's attitude towards the proposals gradually warmed, although she was emphatic that any treaty must protect the interests of the States. Henry IV, a shrewd observer, thought a settlement possible if the States suffered no more setbacks.[7]

The Queen had in fact consulted the States. Late in 1599 Caron, their agent in London, was sent home to persuade his masters to join in the treaty. He returned in December with their refusal, and Elizabeth decided to negotiate on her own. In January 1600 she sent off an English emissary, the much-travelled Edmondes, to Brussels to discuss a possible venue for the meeting of deputies. He was enthusiastically welcomed as a harbinger of peace; in some towns bells were rung as he passed through; at the capital he was feted.[8] In Brussels it was agreed that Boulogne should be the site of the meeting. (Henry IV had already been approached and had consented to use of the site.) By the end of February a Flemish envoy (this time of official rank), the audiencer Louis Verreykens, arrived in London. He was handsomely and publicly entertained.[9]

With his arrival, serious negotiation over matters of substance got under way. At this first audience with the Queen he was given a cordial welcome. She declared she had always wanted peace; indeed, she would have gone to Spain in person to seek it had not religious differences deterred her. Philip II, she was certain, had been led astray by evil advisers, but, as she pointedly asserted, her desire for peace was not dictated by fear or necessity. Verreykens was closeted with a committee of Privy Councillors—Cecil, Nottingham, Buckhurst, and Hunsdon—to whom he presented the archduke's terms. He offered a renewal of the old Burgundian treaties of alliance; archduke and Queen were to be "amis des amis et ennemis des ennemis," a defensive and offensive pact. Its necessary corollary would be the rupture of the treaties with the States and a prohibition of trade with them. Finally, Brill and Flushing were to be handed over to the archduke. These terms were presented solely

[7] PRO 31/3/30: [1599] 2/8, 2/16, 3/18, 3/26, 4/13, 4/29; Winwood 1: 56.

[8] SP 77/6/79, 83, 85, 91, 101, 102, 104–30.

[9] Winwood 1: 139–40, 156–57; PRO 31/8/31: [1600] 1/1, 2/1, 2/12, 2/19, 3/6; SP 78/43/411; Actes, xxvi; CSPVen 9 (1592–1603): 390, 395, 399–400; Boissise, Pièces, 98–99.

for discussion at this level; conclusions would be reached at Boulogne.[10]

The English response was a vigorous denial of each of the Spanish demands. An alliance was impossible because it would entail
war against co-religionists. Freedom of trade rested on ancient
treaty commitments. And the English, on their part, had a set of
demands. They wanted repayment of the loan of £100,000 made to
the States-General in 1577; a delay of six months in implementing
the treaty to allow inclusion of the States; and finally, if the latter
refused to treat, assurances against any fleet sent from Spain to conquer the provinces.

The Queen, irritated by the impasse at London, determined to
send Edmondes to Brussels to deal directly with the archduke. His
message was an emphatic one. The Queen would not give way on
any of the three major Spanish demands "as being things of extreme and exalted nature that Her Majesty can in no wise yield to
them." The archduke avoided a direct reply by referring all these
matters to the conference; clearly the Spaniards wanted the meeting
to go forward. Cecil, figuratively shrugging his shoulders, supposed
"that seeing they desire to meet we ought to imagine they have a
purpose to accommodate." Presumably they would be sensible of
the futility of a "vain colloquy."[11]

On 10 May the English commission for the conference was issued. The delegation was headed by Sir Henry Neville, the ambassador to France, Cecil's enthusiastic choice as a man without "private passion or prejudicate disposition either violently to war or
blindly to peace." The Earl of Northumberland would have been
chief commissioner in order to match the dignity of the Admiral of
Aragon, but that dignitary had been dropped from the Spanish list,
which now consisted of two Flemings—Richardot, president of the
archduke's council, and the audiencer Verreykens—and one Spaniard—the councillor Carrillo. The remaining three Englishmen
were John Herbert, second Secretary, and Robert Beale, Clerk of
the Council in the North, along with Edmondes, the veteran of the
earlier exchanges. Cecil had evaded the task, loath to undergo ei-

[10] *Actes*, xxvi, xxviii; PRO 31/3/31: [1600] 3/15, 3/22, 3/31; *CSPVen* 9 (1592–1603):
387; SP 77/6/241.

[11] PRO 31/3/31: 3/31/1600; *Actes*, xxix; Winwood 1: 139–57, 171–75; SP 77/6/142,
146, 158.

ther the burden or the charges. His absence may also hint at his skepticism as to final results.[12]

Their instructions, drawn up by the Queen on 12 May, began by reminding the commissioners that these negotiations represented a complete turnaround of Spanish policy and required the closest attention to every detail. The first detail—no mean one—was "precedency, which admits a possession of pre-eminence and dignity." On this claim, that the English were to take first place in all matters of protocol, there was to be a firm stand; the commissioners were well armed with ample historical proofs to substantiate the Queen's position. However, in the end, they were given some flexibility. If the Spanish proved stiff, they could propose a compromise of equality, in which there would be daily alternation of "preseance," the first day to be chosen by lot. Elizabeth's insistence on this matter of protocol was not mere royal vanity or dynastic amour propre, but a determination to make a point of consequence. She wanted it to be perfectly clear that she came to the bargaining table not as a suppliant or out of weakness. In lands and population she might be inferior to Philip III, but as an opponent whose might was unshaken by the war, she stood on terms of absolute equality, and it was as an equal that she proposed to bargain with the Spanish king and his subordinate, the archduke.[13]

The commissioners were to seek a treaty of amity (as distinguished from a treaty of alliance), i.e., peace but no alliance. These instructions reflected the underlying English strategy in the whole negotiation. They wanted to disengage from the head-on struggle with Spain, but not in such a way as to endanger the security of the States. The latter's survival, free from a Spanish presence, was a *sine qua non* of English policy. Their very existence, as a new fact in European life, made impossible a return to the old days of the Burgundian alliance. The Spanish must accept that that political order no longer existed.

In conducting the business of the conference the English were to be careful, in every case, to force the Spaniard to the initiative. They were to stand on England's defensive and conservative goals, her desire for nothing more than the restoration of peace and the ab-

---

[12] SP 77/6/203; Winwood 1: 186, 156–57, 166–67, 171–75; Camden, 586.

[13] SP 78/44/113–17. For the instructions, see also BL, Harleian Ms. 1858, 11–28, and Camden, 586–87.

sence of all territorial claims. It was Spain who had provoked the war and it was up to her to lead the way to restored peace. The English had a pretty clear idea from the discussions with Verreykens what the Spanish demands would be, and their deputies were provided with specific answers for each case. The Spanish proposal for an offensive and defensive alliance was a trap designed to set England at war with the States. The claim for the cautionary towns must be refused as contrary to the treaty with the States. Even if the Spanish offered to pay the debt secured by these towns, they must be denied; honor forbade such a concession. Again the Spanish request to restrict Dutch trade was contrary to existing treaty obligations. The English were to stand firmly on a free-market doctrine, assuming merchants would not trade where goods were at risk. Faced with a demand that English troops be withdrawn from the provinces, they were to give the airy reply that the sovereign could not restrict young men who wanted to volunteer for military employment, but that the Queen would graciously consent not to pay any troops except those in the cautionary towns. The English should demand entry to the Indies trade but be willing to compromise by agreeing to stay away from settled lands—but not from those yet unoccupied.

The conference opened with the arrival of the English commissioners at Boulogne on 20 May. Instruments were exchanged and there followed a fencing match over matters of protocol, such as the terminology of the Spanish commission, the use of the Spanish privy seal, and the titles assigned the archduke. After a flurry of such exchanges with the Spaniards, the English deputies turned to the Queen for instructions. Her response was coolly pragmatic. While she saw matter to which she might take exception, she was content to pass over it, more concerned in pressing ahead with items of substance than those of mere detail.[14]

It was on another issue of protocol, however, that the conference speedily became stuck—that of precedency. By 29 May the commissioners were sending home a whole sheaf of letters dealing with this vexing question. There was much learned discussion on Gothic kingship, early Dukes of Britain, and such antiquarian lore, but the Spanish refusal to budge was unyielding. They insisted on the pre-

[14] Winwood 1: 188–201; BL, Harleian Ms. 1858, 31–37, 46–47 (dated 20 June, but more probably May), 47–50 (no date).

cedence of their sovereign. In private conversation they made the excuse that they had wrestled with the French at Vervins over the same problem. If they assented even to equality with the English, they would concede the French case since England allowed precedence to France.[15]

The English had offered the compromise of daily alternation but had had no answer yet. The Spanish response when it came was for a meeting on the sands with the Flemish delegates, Richardot and Verreykens, to which the English objected on the grounds that this implied equality with the archduke and reiterated their motion for alternation. In the end the Spaniards asked for time to consult Brussels, first by letter and then by sending Verreykens in person with a promise that he would return within fourteen days.[16] The English councillors (Egerton, Buckhurst, Cecil), alarmed by these delays, scented some ulterior purpose and instructed their representatives to smoke out the Spaniard by making noises about leaving. If there were any talk of reference back to Spain they were to refuse to wait.[17]

Informal conversations between the commissioners continued while they waited, and it was in one of these that Richardot, the president of the archduke's council, showed his hand. He played his card as a "private conceit," of which his master had no knowledge. Since, he said, there could be no entire peace with England until Holland and Zealand were reduced, the only road to peace lay in amity with the provinces. And a perfect opportunity to accomplish this was at hand in the meeting now being held at Bergen op Zoom between the United Provinces and the deputies of the southern provinces. Would not the Queen be willing to mediate, by inviting the Dutch to Boulogne, or even by sending her commissioners to Holland, where precedency could be granted? To understand this turn in the play we need to look back a little into Flemish developments.[18]

In 1598, when the southern estates were summoned to swear allegiance to their new governor, they asked for further such sessions to advise broadly on questions of general concern. The archduke agreed and the same body was reassembled in the spring of 1600. One of their first moves was to ask for authority to deal for a peace

[15] Winwood 1: 202–5; SP 78/44/147.   [16] Winwood 1: 205–6, 208.
[17] SP 78/44/192.   [18] Winwood 1: 216–19; SP 78/44/228.

treaty with the United Provinces. The archduke was loath to permit this but allowed them to open a correspondence with The Hague. At first their overtures were sturdily rejected, but after the disappointing results of the battle of Nieuport and Maurice's failure to relieve Ostend, the northern estates agreed to send deputies to Bergen, to a meeting that took place in mid-July just as the English and Spanish commissioners were about to open their negotiation. (The Queen was annoyed that the States had not given due notice of their acceptance of this invitation.)[19]

These were the circumstances that lay behind Richardot's trial balloon. As the English saw it, they were to be a decoy to draw the States—the game that the Spanish wished to bag—into a net of negotiation. The threat of English defection would be sufficient stimulus to bring them to heel. Their prime interest was not so much peace with England as a settlement with their rebellious provinces. The immediate bait for the English was a resolution of the precedence question. In a meeting on Dutch or Flemish soil the rules of protocol automatically gave Elizabeth the "preseance." Edmondes reluctantly took the proposal back to his colleagues. They were unanimous in refusing to transmit it to the Queen, saying she would dismiss it as merely another delaying action. Richardot, pressed as to whether his master would refuse to negotiate with the English alone, hastily retreated, declaring the whole "conceit" to have been his alone.[20] The Queen, apprised of this initiative, entirely approved of the commissioners' answer. By now Verreykens had more than overstayed his fortnight, and she was growing very impatient. If he did not return by the end of the next week with a compromise on the precedence issue, they were to leave.[21]

For Robert Cecil the Richardot ploy merely confirmed what he had already supposed, "that howsoever they may resolve to conclude with England rather with neither yet the main point they most affect is to draw the Low Countries to a tripartite covenant wherein for my part I will never be brought to believe that they that have raised themselves to such a height will ever become servants." The Spanish, as Cecil saw it, hoped to open a rift between England and the States, each fearing the other would settle sepa-

[19] *Actes*, introduction; PRO 31/3/31: 8/17/1600.
[20] See Neville in SP 78/44/234; PRO 31/3/31: 8/17/1600.
[21] Winwood 1: 219–20; SP 77/6/184, 185.

rately. But the hope that the States would negotiate was the merest will-o'-the-wisp. The United Provinces had accepted the invitation to Bergen as an act solely of their fellow estates, firmly refusing to acknowledge the authority of king or archduke. In the end, Cecil believed, the archduke would "be glad to retain superiority only over those that he now possessed and to suffer the other states to keep in a body as they are. Not that he will either surrender or covenant but be content with a temporary quietness which is the best he can look for."[22]

The Queen's analysis was on similar lines. Spanish recalcitrance, she thought, was owed either to "bravery" or to some ulterior design such as an impending attack, but these explanations she dismissed. Interest in peace with the United Provinces was Spain's central aim; either they were desperate for a treaty with the States and therefore England was no longer useful to them or, hopeful of some agreement, they were losing interest in peace with England. If it were a choice "whether to have the Low Countries without the Queen or Her Majesty's amity without them, they will leave her to take them."[23]

At last the audiencer returned from Brussels with the bleak message that the Spanish could not proceed further without receiving the honor of precedency due them. The most they would concede was to meet in some third place (not the Spanish or English quarters) but still with precedency to Spain. The English offered as a compromise that they would negotiate by writing only, without meeting in person, but this too was rejected. The English agreed to consult their government.[24]

The response of the Privy Council (Buckhurst, Nottingham, Cecil) is interesting; their commissioners were given a number of ploys by which the negotiations might be revived or at least kept alive. One was a proposal to deal through informal conversations among the delegates. Or the English could—as of their own volition—offer to submit the Richardot scheme to the Queen, asking the Spanish to wait while Edmondes went to England. Or again, the Spaniards could be invited to England, where by the rules of protocol they would have precedence. (This proposal was rescinded in a later letter.) As a last resort the English could offer to conclude

[22] Winwood 1: 220.   [23] *Ibid.*, 222–24.
[24] *Ibid.*, 221–22.

at least a truce, an armistice.[25] But if all these initiatives failed and the conference must break up, then the departure was to be such as to suggest "that there is a discontinuance rather than an absolute dissolution." And a statement must be issued, proclaiming the Queen's commitment to the continued search for peace and hinting at Spanish insincerity.

The last scene followed swiftly; when the English proposed to send home to hear the Queen's decision on an adjournment to Holland or Flanders, the Spaniards refused to wait. The most they would concede was that the archduke or Richardot write with a proposal for shifting the venue, and the Queen would have up to sixty days in which to answer. Thus, even though the conference was at an end, the fiction of a continuing ghostly life was maintained.[26]

Some eighteen months of active negotiation, which had given lively hope for peace, had now with the failure of the conference ground to a halt. Out of a retrospect of those months emerge some fairly clear impressions. First, there is the genuine and sustained effort of the English to bring about an end to the war with Spain. Internal discussions, the tenor of the instructions, the Queen's willingness to compromise on the nonessentials of protocol, and above all the desperate effort to keep the conference afloat at almost any cost—all bear witness to the sincerity of English intentions.

England undoubtedly sought an end to the direct confrontation with Spain. This would lift the constant threat of invasion and eliminate the burdensome cost of naval and military preparations, defensive and offensive. It would reopen important trade channels. Even more important, it would close off the possibility of Spanish aid to the Irish rebels and leave England free to deal with them, unhindered by other cares. Peace with Spain would terminate a war that Elizabeth had never sought, which (in her eyes) had been forced on her and in which she had no goal other than its mere cessation. Such a peace settlement would place England in the comfortable position envisioned by a French commentator. England at peace with Spain would recover leverage with both of the great powers, who, in their rivalry—which would almost certainly lead to war—would bid handsomely for English support. Nevertheless

---

[25] *Ibid.*, 222–24, 225; BL, Harleian Ms. 1858, 50–56.
[26] Winwood 1: 225–26.

England's ardent desire for peace was conditioned by several strongly held premises that made its achievement more difficult.

Spanish goals, on paper at least, seemed not so far from the Queen's. They offered in effect to wipe out the recent past, to return to the "good old days" of the Burgundian alliance, the loose partnership based on shared trading interests and a common distrust of France. But such wishful thinking ignored the fact that there was another war in progress—between Spain and the United Provinces—in which England had a vital stake and that altered the whole equation of Anglo-Spanish relations. Ever since the fateful rising at Brill, England and Spain had moved apart, on ever more divergent tracks. England's cautious yet persistent aid to the rebels had eventually convinced Philip that only by striking first—and hard—at England could he hope ultimately to recover the Low Countries.

Spanish contentions were not without justice. Although towards Spain itself the English could honestly claim to have no offensive aims, to be fighting for entirely defensive goals, this was something less than the whole truth. In 1585 the English had asserted that the Queen was going to the assistance of the States solely to safeguard their ancient liberties against the encroachments of a would-be tyrant. In more blunt terms this manifesto expressed the anxiety of the English government that the Netherlands should remain semi-autonomous, ruled by an absentee—and undemanding—suzerain, on the model familiar since the late fifteenth century. The circumstances of the war, the fierce assault of 1588 and the tenacious effort to repeat it, had hardened these convictions to a firm determination that the *de facto* independence of the United Provinces must be maintained. Whether the States were to be entirely sovereign or to retain some shadowy Spanish suzerainty was immaterial, but there must be no re-establishment of effective Spanish power in the liberated provinces. The existence of the Dutch Republic had become a bulwark of England's security.

Obviously the contrasting goals of English policy—peace with Spain and the independence of the States—could be achieved only if there was a general peace to which all three powers acceded. The negotiations of 1600 showed how far from realization these hopes were. Spain had by no means given up hope of some kind of reincorporation of the rebellious provinces into the Habsburg Empire, while the States were resolute in their refusal to acknowledge any shadow of Spanish sovereignty in their territories. As long as these conditions obtained, the war must continue, and with some degree of English involvement. The Queen was asking to have her cake and eat it too—that the Spanish should cease to trouble her in England or Ireland, but that they should turn a blind eye to her continuing and active support of the States.

The very figure of speech employed suggests that Elizabeth's policy was an unrealistic one. Is this a justifiable judgment? We need to look at the assumption underlying the English government's approach to the problem of peace with Spain in 1600. It has been argued that the Queen and her ministers seriously sought peace with Spain at this juncture. Whatever vestiges of the forward policy espoused by Essex or Raleigh yet remained had vanished with the first hope of peace and with the disappearance of the earl from the royal councils. Was it realistic to seek peace and yet keep active the alliance with the States?

The level-headed Robert Cecil evidently thought so, and he had reasonable grounds for his hopes. For several years past the intelligencers who served his government had been reporting news of gathering distress in Spain itself, of war weariness in the Habsburg Netherlands, mutinies in the armies there, shortages of money everywhere. The actions of the Spanish government seemed to bear out these reports. Philip II had sued for peace with France and cut his losses by conceding all that the French demanded. The new regime in the Low Countries loosened Spanish control and gave vent to the urgent clamor of the southern provinces for peace. As we have seen, their estates were even allowed to open up negotiations with The Hague. And it was Spain that had made overtures to the English. All these considerations seemed to point to an urgent Spanish need for peace.

Over against them there were other reckonings to be made. The young king was reported to be warlike in his ambitions and opinion in the Council at Madrid to be bellicose, much more so than in the weary councils of Brussels.[27] The Spanish might well hope to separate the allies and, by isolating one or the other, leave themselves free to concentrate their attack. Or they might make a peace merely to gain a breathing space before resuming the struggle. The endless

[27] Boissise, Pièces, 29–31, 55–58, 98–99, 116–18.

supply of American silver provided a bottomless purse and an easy resilience.

On balance Cecil was a hopeful man in the summer of 1600. His views are summed up in the letter to Neville quoted earlier.[28] He did not believe that the States would treat with Spain or that the archduke could subdue them. Sooner or later there would have to be a suspension of arms; Spanish pride would probably not tolerate more than a bare truce for a term of years. These opinions were bolstered by Cecil's expectation of renewed war betweeen Spain and France. Relations were always tense and at the moment English hopes ran high. With France threatening war against Savoy, a client of Spain, the latter's involvement seemed highly probable.[29]

These high hopes were soon disappointed with the collapse of the conference and with the peace concluded with Savoy at the end of the year. The Spanish were not yet ready for peace. They still hoped to use the Irish rebellion as a stick with which to beat the English into more favorable terms.[30] A Spanish descent on Ireland might be expected. But if this could be repelled and Tyrone brought to his knees, Madrid might be more amenable to a treaty. In the meantime the English determined to keep alive their contacts with Brussels. That door was not wholly closed, and it was important that it should remain open.

When the negotiators left Boulogne it was understood that either the archduke or Richardot would write with a formal proposal for joint negotiations with the States, and the Queen would have sixty days to answer. Neville treated this as mere face-saving, but his masters took it more seriously. The Queen asserted as early as 3 September that she had had a letter, but in fact nothing had been heard from Belgium, and Edmondes had been primed to write to Richardot while Caron, the States' agent in London, was enlisted as a lobbyist to go home and persuade the States-General into negotiations. It was not until 15 October that an answer came from Brussels, and that an unsatisfactory one. General in tone, it evaded any firm reply. Further exchanges revealed the Spaniards' continuing hope that the States might be persuaded to join the English. By now they had, through Caron, once again made plain their re-

[28] Winwood 1: 220. [29] *Ibid.*, 234–35; BL, Harleian Ms. 6798, 78–79.
[30] Winwood 1: 231.

fusal. If the archduke insisted on joint negotiations, all dealings would be at an end.[31]

Nevertheless, exchanges continued. We lack evidence as to their content and can do little more than track their sequence. In mid-winter 1601 Neville thought negotiations would reopen in the spring. The disturbance of the Essex rising distracted the government and, according to Neville, left Cecil worried lest Essex's accusations of his dealings with Spain be thought true. Just before the rising the Spanish proposed that the conference should reassemble in Flanders (where the precedency question would automatically solve itself). In late March the Queen had still to answer, and correspondence was not resumed until May. The Queen was willing to reopen the conference but only as a kind of summit meeting, which would simply give formal assent to conclusions already agreed upon. To this the archduke, after some hesitation, assented. Each party would send two delegates to meet somewhere between Brussels and Calais. The Queen, however, balked at this; two delegates would make the meetings public; absolute secrecy must be preserved, and this required only one representative on each side. She wanted no more public fiascos such as Boulogne. After this, negotiations seem to have trailed off. In October Coomans was again in London, being sent, as Cecil contemptuously put it, "to set a new vernice upon his former table." He was sent home answerless. Events intervened at this stage. The siege of Ostend called forth substantial English reinforcements for the States. In any case the arrival of the Spanish at Kinsale, anticipated through the summer of 1601, choked off further dealings for some months.[32]

They resumed in the spring of 1602 with a letter brought by a Portuguese named Fortado. In it was another proposal by Richardot for a conference that would include the States. The answer he carried back, after some recriminations about the failure at Boulogne and the Irish invasion, left the door open—neither yes nor no. Henry IV thought that the archduke, in these months, was hamstrung by a bellicose council at Madrid. The English government was not going to move until it was clear that Spain as well as

[31] *Ibid.*, 232, 272–73; PRO 31/3/31: [1600] 9/3, 9/11, 9/30, 10/30, 11/7; SP 77/6/213, 225–27, 242; BL, Additional Ms. 48, 152, fol. 173.

[32] Winwood 1: 291, 314–15, 350–51; PRO 31/3/32: [1601] 1/28, 3/24, 5/10, 6/19, 6/26, 6/30, 7/9, 7/22, 8/8, 8/26, 9/18, 10/13; SP 84/61/77–78; SP 77/6/275, 283–84, 301–2, 328.

the archduke really wanted peace. Fortado went on to Paris and then to Spain. Renewed English support for the States chilled further progress. Boissise thought that Cecil and Nottingham were pleased to see these dealings checked, and in early 1603 Edmondes could write in passing, "since we have resolved against peace with Spain."[33]

These desultory negotiations suggest that, although the English would have welcomed peace, they were not prepared to yield on the terms they had set out at Boulogne. The very uncertain notes sounded on the other side made them even more wary and skeptical of a genuine peace. Cecil's view of Spanish intentions in the aftermath of the Kinsale disaster was spelled out in a letter of August 1602. Although the Spanish would make no major effort in Ireland, they would feed the embers of rebellion. A force of 1,000 men strategically placed on a neck of land could cause as much trouble as 5,000 in the field. The King of Spain could not carry the island but he could "maintain a continual fire in that kingdom so that the Queen should be eaten out with charges so long as the Spaniard was lodged there." Until the English had entirely suppressed the Irish rising, Spain would continue to fish in these troubled waters and the conclusion of a peace would be correspondingly delayed. The English riposte should be strong support of the Dutch at Ostend and a resolute posture at sea. Amidst these uncertainties, with the hope of peace still clouded over by suspicion, the reign came to end, the final conclusion of the war still unresolved.[34]

The peace of Vervins worked a wholesale alteration in Anglo-French relations. No longer allies, they were nevertheless still close neighbors caught up in a network of intersecting interests. In the continuing war that still swirled around France, she was far from a disinterested observer or detached neutral. Her relations with Spain were barely civil, and observers confidently predicted a speedy resumption of hostilities. French interest in the fate of the States was as strong as England's, and Henry barely took the trouble to conceal his clandestine assistance to the Dutch. French interest in the proposed Anglo-Spanish peace was equally keen, and they kept close

---

[33] PRO 31/3/33: [1602] 3/26, 4/14, 4/18, 5/9, 5/30, 6/6; SP 78/46/109–12, 120; 48/68; SP 77/6/328; also SP 77/6/436–37, for parallel negotiations through a Liegeois named Boulant. There is some suggestion here that the English were hinting at peace but that their signals were misread.

[34] Winwood 1: 428–29; SP 78/46/109–12.

and anxious watch on the progress of negotiations. These underlying tensions, half hidden but frequently surfacing, made for a tense,
suspicion-laden atmosphere in which to carry on the day-to-day relations of two neighbors. These in turn were aggravated by a range
of quarrels arising as byproducts of war.

The coming of peace had reopened a lucrative trade between
France and Spain, all the richer in possibilities because of the rupture of Anglo-Spanish commercial relationships. This trade revival
immediately spawned an ill-tempered dispute between France and
England. The English, as a part of their overall strategy, preyed
continually on the shipping that, passing southward through the
North Sea, much of it from the Baltic, supplied the needs of that
hungry importer, Spain. The ships traversing these troubled waters
were prime targets of English privateers. Not only did these cap-
tures weaken the Spanish war effort, but they also put money in
the pockets of the privateers, who hauled in a steady array of prizes.
Legally they were entitled to seize only contraband goods, i.e., military and naval supplies, but this was an ill-defined category and
they were not particular in their habits. In practice the French merchants found themselves heavy losers, deprived of their cargoes and
unable to make legal recovery in the English admiralty courts.
What was from the English point of view justifiable stop-and-
search for contraband goods was to the French simple piracy. From
1598 on, the complaints of the French merchants formed the staple
of ambassadorial business. In audience after audience Boissise, the
ambassador in London from 1598 to 1602, the retailed their grievances; he was invariably met by denial, excuses, promises, or outright indifference, but seldom obtained effective remedy.

By the beginning of 1599, after six months of peace, the Queen
was already demanding that all French ships trading to Spain be
stopped, while Secretary Villeroy was threatening a break with England if what he termed piracy did not cease. In the spring cooling
tempers prevailed and a tentative agreement was reached by which
Henry was to ban munitions trade while the Queen would overlook
the grain cargoes. In April Boissise recommended a draft treaty to
Villeroy that won guarded royal approval, and negotiations continued over specific terms, but nothing was settled. Accusations and
denials were still being bandied about in late May. Secretary Villeroy and Boissise in London were all for strong measures in reprisal,
but Henry, cooler headed, took a longer view of the problem. First

of all, he lacked the necessary naval forces to act effectively. More-over, to embroil himself with the English would only benefit the Spanish and harm the States. On balance, he told Boissise, the French would have to temporize and swallow their grievances for the present. Depredations continued; the flow of French complaint was unceasing, but not until 1601 were there any real moves to-wards attempted settlement. By then the quarrel had become en-tangled with another in which the English merchants were the complainants.[35]

Their grievances arose from a series of royal decrees, especially one of April 1600, which effectively banned the importation of a wide variety of cloths that formed the staple of English exports to France. Ostensibly the ban was introduced because of the poor quality of these cloths, but it was clearly a protectionist device to safeguard the interests of the French producers. It was in fact part of Henry's larger scheme for the rehabilitation of French industry after the disasters of prolonged civil war.[36]

These matched grievances provided pressure sufficient to bring both sides to the bargaining table in 1601. It was not until Decem-ber of that year that a joint commission was set up; meetings began in early 1602. In March a tentative accord was put forward by the commissioners to their respective governments, and in July they adjourned. There is no evidence that either government accepted these proposals; in October 1602 Cecil was writing of a proposed total embargo on French trade with Spain while the vexing ques-tion of customs duties at Rouen still preoccupied the English am-bassador. The coming of peace would resolve the first dispute; the second would be a legacy to the new regime.[37]

Ambassadorial time and energy were spent in vain in these futile exchanges over intractable issues. Clearly, English depredations on French shipping would continue as long as the war lasted, unless the French could provide naval protection, which in turn might result in uncomfortable confrontations. French protectionism was part of a long-term policy that would be pushed with increasing

---

[35] PRO 31/3/30: [1599] 1/6, 1/25, 3/26, 4/13, 4/29, 5/7, 5/21, 5/29; SP 78/43/61, 79, 126.

[36] SP 78/44/61, 85; Boissise, 454ff.

[37] SP 78/45/162, 151, 239, 284, 303; PRO 31/3/32: [1601] 8/15, 11/16; [1602] 2/20, 3/21; Winwood 1: 389–94.

zeal by successive French governments and against which the English could do little more than protest.

Another source of dispute and ill-temper preoccupying the ambassadors in these years was that of the French debt. The sum total was about £400,000. In part it represented direct loans, the first of which had been made when Henry was merely King of Navarre. But the larger portion had accumulated as direct expenditure by the English government in support of its forces in Normandy, Picardy, and Brittany. The correspondence of the respective ambassadors is filled with the repeated demands of the English for regular repayment installments and with the excuses of the French for failing to make them. The Queen missed no opportunity to vent her angry reproaches on the king or on his hapless ambassador, and her genuine anger on the subject was more than a mere diplomatic ploy.[38]

In 1599 the French reluctantly, and after many delays, paid the derisory sum of 20,000 crowns (about £6,600) but would offer no promises for the following year. In 1601 Henry evaded the representations of the English agents in audience after audience, and there seems to have been no payment at all. In May 1602 a payment of 50,000 crowns was transmitted, but with a proposal that a third of it should be paid in brass coin. In September something was promised for the next year, but in October Cecil admitted that nothing could be done to enforce payment. He had some reason to be cheered in January 1603 when a larger installment of £20,000 was promised.[39]

These dribbles of repayment were all the more galling in that the French were making large and regular payments on their debts to the States and to the Swiss. The brute fact was that here, as in the ban on cloth, England had little bargaining power. The assurance of Swiss mercenaries' service, now and in the future, was a matter of great moment to the French government while the continued resistance of the States and their ultimate survival as an independent body were a *sine qua non* of French policy. Relations with England might be soured by French refusal to pay up, but they would not be ruptured.

[38] Winwood 1: 18, 27–28. For the French debt, see BL, Cotton Mss., Titus C VIII, fol. 242.

[39] SP 78/43/173, 220, 260; 45/48, 148–53, 180, 234; 46/119, 141; 47/100, 119, 157; 48/6.

Vexing and time-consuming as these quarrels were, they were mere surface phenomena. Deep-lying and more significant were the uneasy suspicion and distrust that disturbed relations between the ex-allies. Elizabeth was never reconciled to the peace of Vervins, which she insisted was as unwise from France's point of view as it was damaging to English and Dutch security. She and her councillors never gave up hope that hostilities would be renewed and lost no opportunity to stir up French fears of the Spanish intentions. The first opportunity arose with the Savoyard war over the marquisate of Saluzzo in 1600. The disposition of the marquisate had been a question left open by the Vervins treaty. Savoy was of course a client of Spain and could look for backing by her patron in any dispute with France. Already in July 1600 Boissise was speculating that, if there were no peace with Savoy, his king would need to seek the support of England and the States.

In September war did in fact break out. Cecil was quoted as saying that the war was the best news possible. At the end of October Henry flattered the Queen by asking her advice on his Savoyard policy, probably a prelude to more definite advances. Converging interests drew the two powers together: France was threatened with a Spanish war; the English saw their hopes of peace fading in the disappointing aftermath of the Boulogne conference. Possibilities of compromise on the piracy issue and renewal of the 1572 treaty were in the air. (Boissise warned that any talk of including debt repayments in the settlement must be politely evaded.) In early December the Queen was talking of giving the special wedding embassy to France special powers to confirm the Treaty of Blois but was disappointed to hear of French successes in the field. Disappointment turned to chagrin when a Franco-Savoyard peace was concluded at the end of the year.[40]

In the new year 1601 English hopes revived when a violation of the residence of the French ambassador at Madrid again threatened a rupture between the Continental rivals. This led, as in the Savoyard episode, to renewed discussions on settling the piracy dispute. It also coincided with heavy Spanish pressure on Ostend. The alarmed King, fearing the port's fall, urged Elizabeth to prepare a sizable relief force. He also announced his intention of going to

---

[40] Boissise, 313–15; PRO 31/3/31: [1600] 7/15, 9/3, 10/5, 11/18, 12/6; 1/28/1601. For Elizabeth's views on Vervins, see for instance PRO 33/3/33: 1/29/1602.

Calais and asked that the English envoy, Edmondes, meet him there. The English, also alarmed by bad news from Ostend, jumped at what they took to be an offer of French aid in relieving the town. Elizabeth professed herself to be ready to send 4,000 troops if Henry could give active support. He now hastily denied having made any offer of military aid, and restricted his assistance to a month's pay for not less than 7,000 to 8,000 English soldiers. There was an aftermath of mutual recrimination. As late as October the Queen was still inquiring whether Henry would respond to the insult to his ambassador at Madrid, and Cecil was suggesting that if the English sent 6,000 men to Ostend the King should pay for them.[41]

Attempts to exploit the renewed Franco-Spanish tension ended as the dispute was brought to settlement at the end of the year, much to the disgust of Elizabeth, who declared she would never have accepted such a compromise to her honor. She herself was preoccupied with the Spanish expedition to Kinsale. Henry was generous in expressions of sympathy, shrewdly confident of English success, and quite determined to offer no material aid—not even an enlarged installment on his debt.[42]

In the early spring of 1602, while the Anglo-French conference on piracy and trade was proceeding in London, Winwood in Paris suddenly proposed to the king a joint military action in Flanders, aimed at nothing less than the expulsion of the Spaniard altogether from the Low Countries. He coupled the proposal with a suggestion that the Queen was in a position to make a free choice between peace and continued war. Rosny (Sully) and Villeroy, the two leading French ministers, took up the proposal with some enthusiasm, urging the advantages of such a move over a naval demonstration on the Spanish coast, which the English were preparing. Probably the French ministers were simply probing to find out more about this sudden English move; their master was very skeptical of English intentions and suspected some ulterior scheme. Boissise agreed, seeing it as yet another effort to bait France into war with Spain; indeed the lord admiral and Cecil had both told him they thought war between the two powers was inevitable. Cecil also re-

[41] Boissise, 541–42; PRO 31/3/32: 8/15/01, 8/18/01; SP 78/45/180. For the whole confused episode of the Calais enterprise, see PRO 31/3/32: [1601] 8/26, 9/1, 9/4, 10/13, 10/25; 3/33: 1/29/02, and SP 78/45/184.

[42] PRO 31/3/32: 11/16/01; 31/3/33: [1602] 1/13, 1/29, 3/23.

vealed something of immediate English aims by confessing that the Queen could not find the 6,000 men necessary for relieving Ostend without French aid. In the end she did in fact send 3,000 men, and pressure for immediate French action slacked off.[43]

Then, in a sudden *volte-face*, Henry shifted his policy. The revelations of the Biron conspirators (Biron was executed 31 July) made all too evident the active participation of Spain in the plot, and it was presumably this fresh evidence of Spanish hostility that moved the king to instruct Boissise to sound out the English for an alliance. Henry himself, lamenting the perpetual distrust that haunted his relations with the Queen, was not hopeful; Boissise was more optimistic since English fears for the fate of the States, should Ostend fall, ran high. The peace negotiations with Spain had faltered, another attack on Ireland seemed in prospect, and Boissise's initial soundings were favorably received. The Queen herself urged that the revelations of the late conspiracy justified war; she had even rejected the latest peace offers because she distrusted a court whose friendship was more dangerous than its enmity. But Boissise warned that the Queen would insist on watertight assurances that once an alliance was sealed, there would be no peace with the enemy. She wanted no repetition of Vervins.[44]

The king, having made the first advances and having had a hopeful response, now began to have reservations. While asserting that Spain would certainly make war on him if the States were beaten, and admitting that the Spaniard plotted all over Europe against the French and the English, he did not want to precipitate a crisis. Ostend seemed safe for the present and, if Maurice captured Grave, the fortress he was then besieging, the archduke's reputation would be sunk. Hence he declined the urgent invitation of the English that he meet Cecil at Calais. Boissise's correspondence with the king throws more light on French intentions in these ambivalent overtures. As they saw it, the insecurities that had restrained the English from making peace at Vervins had now vanished; in Holland, in Ireland, and at home the situation was much improved and a secure peace was now possible for the Queen. Hence the need for French exertions to prevent such a peace by offers of alliance,

[43] PRO 31/3/33: [1602] 2/26, 3/12, 3/16, 3/26, 5/162; Winwood 1: 381–85.
[44] PRO 31/3/33: [1602] 7/8, 7/25, 7/30, 8/2, 8/3, 8/13, 8/20.

firm enough to be attractive but too vague to commit the king to present action.[45]

These tedious and inconclusive dealings between England and France in the years after Vervins are worthy of attention because of what they reveal about the basic nature of the two states' relations in this difficult era. Although no longer active allies, they still had important common interests. For both, Spain was a dangerous enemy; for both, the survival of the United Provinces was essential to their security. But the difference was that France, now at least formally at peace with her rival, had wide room for diplomatic maneuver, while England, still at war, was bound by the iron chains of military necessity. Resentful of her neighbor's freedom, England used every opportunity to draw her former ally back into the fray. At times the English government hoped Spain would do their work for them; failing that, they sought to achieve their goal by playing on French fears for the States. They were disappointed in all these hopes.

English anxiety to draw the French back into the struggle was matched by the latter's determination to prevent an Anglo-Spanish peace. Henry was quite certain that war with Spain would come sooner or later, but he intended that the time and the circumstances should be of his making. Until that time it was imperative that Spain should remain entangled in war against England. Hence his instruction to Boissise in May 1602 to do all he could to prevent a peace settlement. Henry was more successful in his aims than the English were in theirs.[46]

Peace could come only when Spanish power to do mischief to England had been neutralized. After so many Spanish failures the fear of invasion was dwindling; the power of the Dutch to survive (given the patronage but not the alliance of England and France) seemed beyond question. But as long as Spain could hope to keep the fires of rebellion burning in Ireland, a stable peace was beyond England's grasp. As Boissise had observed,[47] these conditions were now nearly but not quite obtainable. The fate of Ostend was still grave cause for concern in the Low Countries; Tyrone was on the run but still dangerously at large, and until he was captured or

[45] PRO 31/3/33: [1602] 8/29, 9/8, 9/13.
[46] PRO 31/3/33: [1602] 4/11, 5/13, 8/29.
[47] PRO 31/3/33: 8/29/02.

submitted, rebellion was still alight. And so for the time being the English remained frustrated of their hopes of peace and forced to bear the burden of continuing war, while the French, reassured by the continuing engagement of Spanish force and confident in the security of the States, could look on with a smug sense of satisfaction.

Circumstances dictated that a renewal of the alliance remain a mere possibility. Had it become a certainty—or near certainty—another problem would have reared its head: the endemic distrust of each sovereign for the other. Henry complained of his "grande peine et géhenne insufferable"[48] when faced with such lack of trust. Elizabeth's view of her royal brother was no more charitable. At bottom each feared that, were an alliance made, the other partner would take the earliest opportunity to slip his bond and make peace, shifting the burden of resisting Spain on to the other's shoulders and thereby providing the best possible security for the defector. Both sides were quite candid in voicing these suspicions. French distrust went back twenty years to the days of the Anjou marriage; for Elizabeth, Vervins was an all-too-convincing proof of her suspicions.

Buried more deeply was yet another and older fear. However much the Spanish power in the Low Countries was feared, its total removal raised the fear of intervention by another great power.[49] Fear of French intrusion had been as much a preoccupation of English policy in the 1570's as Spanish reconquest. Henry's patronage of the States was aimed at countering not only Spanish power but also English influence. Given such worries, a continuing although weakened Spanish presence in the Netherlands was useful to both sides.

When the Queen died in March 1603 the war with Spain was still alight, but just barely. Except at Ostend active hostility between English and Spanish had ceased. Neither side any longer contemplated a direct attack on the other. The survival of the United Provinces was assured. The rebellion in Ireland was finally crushed. The goals pursued since 1585 had been realized. It remained only to make a formal declaration of peace, and this proved an easy task for the new king and his ministers.

[48] PRO 31/3/33: 8/2/02.   [49] BL, Harleian Ms. 6798, 78–79.

PART IV

WAGING THE WAR III:
THE ALLIES—THE
STATES GENERAL

Town regained for good by Dutch
Town gained by Dutch but retaken by Spain
Battle
Frontier, 1607-21
Line of redoubts, built 1605-6

Map 3. *The Dutch reconquest, 1590–1607*. (Adapted from Parker)

CHAPTER 13

FROM DEPENDENCY TO

ALLIANCE, 1588-1594

THE ALLIANCE with the States-General entered into in 1585 was, like that with Henry IV, another chapter in a long history of earlier involvement, reaching back to the beginning of the revolt. The terms of that relationship were radically altered by the events of 1588. It had grown up in the early years of the revolt when the rebels were suppliants for English aid. That aid had been given circumspectly and grudgingly, and always with an eye to retaining civil relations with Spain. In the end, in spite of all the Queen's best efforts, patronage had slid into protection and, in the 1585 Treaty of Nonsuch, into open alliance. Leicester's army crossed to the Netherlands, where the earl, to the Queen's fury, accepted the governor-generalship. In doing so he was countering her determination to evade any assertion of sovereignty over the provinces. Yet, however much she rejected such a role, she plainly regarded the provinces as her dependents and insisted on the active role of her commander in all their decision-making.

The Dutch, on their side, having turned to the Queen at the nadir of their fortunes, were deeply disillusioned by the actual experience of alliance. Leicester's military leadership yielded only modest results in his first campaign, and the second ended with the disastrous loss of the strategically important port of Sluys. His clumsy intervention in domestic politics set faction against faction and alienated the most active and effective leadership group, that led by Oldenbarnevelt and Count Maurice. Worse still was the

Queen's obvious reluctance to support the alliance wholeheartedly and her wayward pursuit of an English settlement with Spain through the mediation of Parma, in which she was haughtily disregardful of the interests of the provinces.

With the approach of the Armada, roles were reversed. It was the English who now needed Dutch assistance, particularly in the blockading of the Flemish embarkation ports from which Parma's troops would issue forth, once the fleet arrived. The Dutch were ready and responsive in the performance of this task, although the promised auxiliary ships that were to join Seymour's squadron in the Narrow Seas arrived too late to join in the naval battle off Gravelines.[1]

Even before the Armada, relations between the allies had been undergoing change. The abrasive presence of Leicester had ended with his departure in the fall of 1587 and his subsequent resignation. His influence on English policy ceased with his death in September 1588. But the experience of his regime had administered a salutary shock to the Dutch leadership, and the lessons they learned from it were quickly put into practice in a major reorientation of their past policy. In previous decades William the Silent had consistently sought to obtain the protection of some great foreign prince who could provide the necessary backing to repel the Spaniards, at the same time leaving the provinces with the loose autonomy they had enjoyed under the Austrian Habsburgs. The unhappy flirtation with the Archduke Matthias, the disastrous episode of Anjou's intervention, the solicitation of Henry III after the death of William, and the Treaty of Nonsuch itself were all part and parcel of this policy. But now under the strong leadership of Oldenbarnevelt, Advocate of Holland, acting in alliance with the Orange interest represented by the young Count Maurice of Nassau, second son to William the Silent, the provinces moved rapidly towards a straightforward assertion of the sovereignty of the States-General and to the erection of a fully independent state. This, more than the Union of Utrecht in 1579, was the true moment of a Dutch declaration of independence.

The first concrete manifestation of this new orientation was displayed in the months immediately following Leicester's departure.

[1] Jan den Tex, *Oldenbarnevelt*, trans. R. B. Powell (2 vols., Cambridge, 1973) 1: 133–36.

The Oldenbarnevelt faction moved quickly to seize control of all the key positions, military and civil, in the provinces. This meant sharp conflict with the factions that had been patronized by Leicester. These men naturally turned to the new English commander, Lord Willoughby, and to his government at home for support. All they received was fair words; the Queen, preoccupied first with the Armada and then with the Lisbon expedition, was quite content to stand aside and allow the liquidation of the Leicester faction in Dutch politics. By the end of the year these elements, in Holland and Utrecht, had vanished from the scene and the Oldenbarnevelt-Nassau party was in full control of the Dutch machinery of power.[2]

This was the way things stood when the new English envoy, Thomas Bodley, arrived in Holland in January 1589 to take up his office as senior English member of the Council of State. His role was a novel and difficult one. The English government had tacitly accepted the elimination of the pro-English faction in the provinces and now, on the departure of the English commander Willoughby in early spring 1589, made what at first was an interim appointment as his replacement. A young and inexperienced officer of lower rank, Sir Francis Vere, was given the more modest title of sergeant-major-general. This meant that he lacked equality with the Dutch generals although he was something more than a mere subordinate to them. These changes recognized in some degree the alterations on the Dutch scene, but the English government had by no means relinquished its determination to maintain firm control over the disposition of its forces in the Low Countries. Here, as in the French case, the English faced the awkward problem posed by an alliance in which their role was mainly as provider of soldiers for a partner, without having effective determination of military decision-making. In the case of Henry IV there was little they could do to check his actions, but in the Dutch instance the terms of the 1585 treaty gave them much more leverage. With two seats on the executive Council of State they presumably had a determinative voice in all decisions. It was precisely this position of strength that Oldenbarnevelt had already set out to erode by reducing the Council to the mere agent of the States-General in which sovereign authority was firmly vested.[3]

No one in England had yet grasped just how far this sea change

---

[2] See *ibid.*, 126–39.   [3] *Ibid.*, 130ff.

in Dutch politics had gone. It was left to the new English agent, Thomas Bodley, to grapple with the new situation. His task was made the more difficult by a crucial move by his government. Faced in the aftermath of the Armada with the necessity for direct action against Spain, they now proposed to draft a considerable part of the English forces in Holland into the expedition to Portugal, leaving a bare 1,000 foot and 250 horse in the States' service. The English government, now waging war on more than one front, was giving priority to its own needs. Moreover, it was treating the English expeditionary force in the Low Countries as a kind of reservoir of seasoned troops, on which it could draw as needed. Thus, with the entry of France into the picture later in 1589, the Dutch found themselves one of a queue of claimants for English assistance. Although this circumstance entailed some obvious disadvantages, it was offset by their role as trainers of the English forces. With this asset in hand they now had room for bargaining and an opportunity for shifting away from the status of mere supplicant towards that of ally.[4]

Bodley quickly encountered the new spirit that animated the Dutch leadership. To a set of proposals that he presented to the States-General in mid-January he was answered "with undecent and malepert terms wherein they offend in several places." He had asked for an enlargement of the authority of the Council of State and in particular that the English councillors be informed of all martial affairs. The States-General retorted that the Council of State was an instrument for executing the views of the provincial states as given to the States-General. In another answer later in the month they spelled out very clearly their view that the Councillors of State had no more right to quarrel with their instructions than royal councillors to question those of a king. The States-General was to be as sovereign as Queen Elizabeth.[5]

In the same despatch Bodley withheld, until further acquaintance, his view of Oldenbarnevelt, "by whom they are strangely ruled and overruled." Within another week or so he had concluded that Oldenbarnevelt had no confidence in English promises or the Queen's proceedings. These exchanges set the tone and dominated

[4] *CSPF* 22: 221, 232, 327–29; 23: 23, 29–30, 110–11.
[5] *CSPF* 23: 51, 75–76.

the substance of Bodley's dealings with the States for some months to come.[6]

In February he reiterated the view that the English commander was to have the same preeminence over other governors as previous governors-general, and hence that his authority was not limited to the command of the English troops. Gilpin, the Merchant Adventurers' agent, a long-time resident in the Low Countries and the veteran English observer on the scene, quite bluntly told Lord Buckhurst, the Privy Councillor most knowledgeable about Dutch affairs, that the agents of Holland and especially the Advocate could tell the Council of State what they pleased; "the said Council are in government *nomine sed non re*." The English showed signs of a more conciliatory stance.[7]

The predominance of Oldenbarnevelt and the impotence of the Council of State had been brought home to the English in the painful episode of the garrison in Gertruydenberg. Its men had been mutinous since the previous year and even the offer of 200,000 guilders taken from the funds raised by the States to fight the Armada failed to appease them. Willoughby had been made responsible for suppressing the mutiny. His failure and the continuing threat that the garrison would defect to Parma aroused Dutch suspicions, and in the end they took action on their own without informing or consulting the English. In March, after secret preparations, Maurice had opened the siege of the town. Willoughby had protested volubly, as had Bodley, at their failure to include the English in their plans. The latter saw the whole affair as an example of Dutch suspicion and dislike. Gilpin pointed to the Holland leaders, especially Oldenbarnevelt ("the man you know of") as the promoters of the enterprise. There was an exchange between the English government and Count Maurice, the latter defensive but unrepentant, the former reproachful but also defensive. In the end the English had the doubtful satisfaction of seeing their prophecy of disaster come true, when the mutineers compounded with Parma. But the episode made clear the willful determination of the Dutch to act on their own and the powerlessness of the English to check them.[8]

In some sense this affair, unpleasant though it was, served to clear the air. The loss of Gertruydenburg proved in fact less dam-

[6] *Ibid.*, 79–80.　　　　　　　　　　[7] *Ibid.*, 119–22, 140, 143–47.
[8] Tex 1: 136, 134; *CSPF* 23: 148, 154, 155, 172, 186–87, 205–8.

aging than had been feared. Willoughby, against whose head much of the Dutch wrath had been hurled, had now gone home, angry and disappointed, but no longer a figure on the Dutch scene. At the same time the English gave proof of their continued interest in the Low Countries by reinforcing the Ostend garrison, weakened by withdrawals for Portugal and threatened by enemy action, with 1,500 men. Here of course direct English interest was at stake, in the isolated but strategically important Channel port. The States-General, characteristically, asserted themselves by refusing to contribute to the costs of this reinforcement. The rest of the spring was spent in continued bickering between the English government and the States, but the Dutch did accept the withdrawal of troops for the Portugal expedition. The English continued to insist on the authority of the Council of State and on a major voice in decisions. Secretary Walsingham probably echoed others' sentiments in a draft scheme for a new government of the provinces that would have shifted power to the Council of State and reduced the States-General to a single annual meeting. The Dutch on their side complained bitterly of the English depredations on their shipping bound for Spain, an issue that divided the allies as long as the war lasted. But by June 1589 the Queen had been brought to consider a declaration disavowing all who sought to sow dissension between her and the States-General or the provincial states. A delegation sent to London wrangled with the English Council over current issues; not much was settled, but the envoys returned home in a more hopeful frame of mind, a mood echoed by Bodley at the end of the summer.[9]

The controversy that raged through the fall and winter of 1589–1590 in the English Council as to what policy to adopt towards the assertive provinces was reflected in a sheaf of position papers. They all revolved around a proposed mission to The Hague, initially to be headed by Buckhurst, then later by Sir Thomas Wilkes. Opinion traversed a wide spectrum; some reiterated the familiar demand for a governor-general (possibly Maurice) governing in tandem with a powerful Council of State; others wanted a separation of powers with a governor for civil affairs and a general (Norris is mentioned) for military matters. A few despairing spirits took a more radical

---

[9] *CSPF* 23: 199, 278, 283, 284, 288, 352; *L&A* 1589–90: 268, 273, 283, 290; Tex 1: 182.

line and suggested a reduction in the English forces or even a complete withdrawal, leaving the Dutch to fend for themselves.[10]

The instructions that were finally drafted for Wilkes suggest a compromise among the various views, but weighted in favor of continuing English authority. Although the Queen was to disavow all patronage of any faction, the Council of State was to have unquestioned control over troop movements and the garrisons. The governor-general (unnamed) would enjoy the same powers as in the time of Charles V or "Philip, their late King," but a negative voice in matters touching the Queen's interest; trade with Spain was to be controlled by license. Wilkes was to woo Oldenbarnevelt. The hidden purposes of this mission were to investigate rumors of a French overture and even more alarming reports of a conciliatory offer by Philip. When the envoy arrived in June 1590 the Advocate received him with courtesy and some warmth but was critical of both Leicester and Willoughby and noncommital about treaty changes.[11]

The rest of the summer was consumed by protracted discussion between the English commissioners and the States-General. The latter deployed the commissioners' whole panoply of delaying tactics, above all their insistence on referring back to their principals, i.e., the provincial states. The English stuck to their instructions, offering a continuance of the present auxiliary force of 5,000 foot and 1,000 horse, but otherwise adhering closely to the terms of their instructions. The States-General reiterated that final authority rested with them, the body in which power resided "by tradition from the people." This led to a very ill-tempered exchange in which the English intimated that the Queen could manage well enough without Dutch aid, while the States retorted that they were more necessary to her than she to them. Tempers cooled later, but the States made it clear that they could not give an authoritative answer until they consulted the provinces, and the meetings with the English were adjourned. Weeks, possibly months, would pass before a reply came, so Wilkes asked for and received his recall. He was at least able to reassure his government that there was nothing to fear from the French and Spanish overtures.[12]

[10] *L&A* 1589–90: 296, 297, 300, 306, 309, 315–18, 325–26, 329, 330, 331, 334–37, 338, 340, 341–42.
[11] *L&A* 1589–90: 340, 348–57; Wernham, 224–25.
[12] *L&A* 1590–91: 220, 223, 231.

It was not until December that the States produced a response to Wilkes's proposals; it was entirely negative, bearing out Sir Thomas's earlier predictions. This first English effort to change the terms of the treaty had come to a dead end. It foundered in large part on Dutch determination to hold the English to the succor promised in 1585 without yielding to them any substantial authority over Dutch affairs. Against this resolution the English had no effective leverage. So long as the Dutch military position remained as fragile as it still was in 1590, the English could hardly implement threats of withdrawal, or even reduction, of aid without damaging their own all-too-vulnerable situation.[13]

The failure also owed something to the uncertainties of the English themselves. On the one hand many were apprehensive that the provinces, liberated from English tutelage, would weaken or even dissolve the tenuous alliance, by collaborating with the new French king or even making terms with Philip. Others, above all Burghley, saw the alliance as something of an albatross and sought to lessen the burden by reducing English commitments as much as possible. The Lord Treasurer was prepared to yield a good deal of power to Maurice as a *quid pro quo* for a reduced subsidy. In this tangle of motives, ancient fears of revived French ambitions in the Low Countries played against the more immediate threat of Spanish power. One senses in Burghley the "little Englander's" instinctive distaste for the entangling obligations and the heavy burdens of foreign alliances—from "this unhappy war with its infinite charges and end that no man could see."[14] Nevertheless, these exchanges had led the English government to a recognition of the strength of Dutch leadership and to an increasing respect for their initiatives in Low Countries matters.

While the diplomats and politicians warily fenced with one another in a static ritual, the soldiers were on the move. The immediate post-Armada interval had been one of uncertain and limited maneuver in the Low Countries. In the fall of 1588 Parma had made an attempt to follow up his conquest of Sluys by securing one of the last Dutch strongholds south of the Scheldt, Bergen op Zoom. Relying on treachery rather than force, he had been outwitted and outfought and had to retire in some disorder. In this episode the English forces, led by Willoughby, had performed with credit and

[13] *Ibid.*, 252.   [14] *Ibid.*, 197.

had provided a substantial portion of the manpower. But a few months later the defection of the Gertruydenberg garrison had damaged their reputation badly and brought Anglo-Dutch military relations to a nadir. Before the curtain lifted on the next bout of purposeful military action, Vere had replaced Willoughy. He did not wield either the personal or the official authority of his predecessors, but, more important, this highly professional young soldier early on established close and harmonious relations with Count Maurice. It marked another stage in the retreat of the English from the role of protector/patron to that of ally.[15]

Through most of 1589 the Spanish remained quiescent. The assassination of Guise in December 1588 had led to the abandonment of the Rhine campaign; an abortive move against Ostend in April of that year was the last action of the Duke before he left for Spa on sick leave in May. He would remain there until October. The death of Henry III in August led to a royal order from Madrid to Parma to prepare for a French campaign, meanwhile falling back on the defensive in the Low Countries.[16]

In the allied camp there was little movement during 1589. The English were preoccupied with the Lisbon expedition, and when Willoughby, home since March, resigned, the appointment of a new commander was second-order business. Various names were mentioned, including those of Grey (too poor) or Norris (out of favor after the Portuguese fiasco). In the end, in August, command of the field forces went to Vere, the 29-year-old cadet of a great noble house with three years' hard-won experience in the Low Countries wars. With the title of sergeant-major-general he was technically third in rank after a nonexistent lord general and his lieutenant. Command of the garrisons was left to their governors. Working in comfortable harness with Count Maurice, Vere won Dutch confidence in the actions at Bommel-wart in July 1589, and later in the year he took the lead in two expeditions to relieve Rheinberg.[17]

In the following winter Vere was associated with Maurice of Nassau in an exploit that proved to be a turning point in the war—the Trojan horse operations that captured Breda in March 1590. After years of a desperately defensive strategy the Dutch had now chalked up a spectacular offensive success. It coincided, of course,

---

[15] *CSPF* 21: 187–280; Tex 1: 144.   [16] Essen 5: 276–78.
[17] *L&A* 1589–90: 268; Markham, 144; Vere, 1–2, 3–4.

with Parma's preparations for a French expedition. A Spanish contingent was already present at Ivry in March, but it was not until August that the Duke crossed into France. At this point the English government took the initiative and began to press for action in Brabant or Flanders to relieve the pressure on the French king. The States' initial response was lukewarm; they pointed to the plundering raids with which they were harassing the hapless villages of the two provinces. Finally in September the Queen offered to send 3,000 troops to Ostend if the States would take action, and there was talk of a plot to seize Dunkirk with inside help. This scheme was part of the larger strategy discussions of that year, as the English moved rather uncertainly towards basic decisions as to how best to utilize their forces against an enemy now facing them on several fronts (see Chapter 8).[18]

In the end the English decision was to move in France rather than in Flanders; Brittany, threatened by a Spanish occupation, was the chosen theater of action. Just before Christmas 1590 Elizabeth sent Sir John Norris to Holland with orders to draw off some 3,000 soldiers (roughly half of the English strength in the Low Countries). The men were to be taken first from the field forces, leaving the four garrisons as far as possible intact. (There were English garrisons in Ostend and Bergen op Zoom as well as the two cautionary towns.) Norris's instructions foresaw the possibility of a Dutch refusal and authorized him to use extreme measures. If necessary he was to dissolve the existing companies, allow the men to proceed to the English-held ports, and there reenlist them. Clearly the English government envisaged strong Dutch objections to this diversion of manpower from the Low Countries. An olive branch of sorts was offered them in the form of concessions on trade with Spain. Anxious to block the shipment of grain from the Eastland, so essential to Spanish survival but so profitable to the Dutch, the English even proposed to find alternative trading opportunities for the latter in France, Italy, or England itself.[19]

The first Dutch reaction was, as anticipated, a refusal to let the troops go, for the soldiers' departure was tantamount to a revocation of the English expeditionary force. The French king, they

---

[18] Essen 5: 284–93; *L&A* 1590–91: 229, 233–36, 245, 246, 196–97.
[19] *L&A* 1590–91: 258, 260, 262–63, 265, 268.

urged, could best be helped by a campaign in the Low Countries, for which the English were needed. Norris, acting on his orders, summoned the English forces in Gelderland in February 1590. The resulting Dutch obstruction (they had plans laid already for a spring offensive) induced the Queen to accept a compromise. When the numbers to be drawn from the Low Countries were reduced and replacements promised, the States-General agreed to the amended terms. The required contingents departed for France (by now their destination was Normandy rather than Brittany). They were to join Essex's army in the siege of Rouen. This arrangement, hammered out between the two governments, provided an important precedent for the future. It implicitly acknowledged that the English forces in the Low Countries were not only auxiliaries to the Dutch but also a reserve of seasoned soldiers on which the English could draw for their own needs on other fronts.[20]

During the spring of 1591, while English attention was fixed on Essex and his army in the Seine valley and on Norris's forces in Brittany, Count Maurice embarked on his first campaign to drive the Spaniard out of the inland provinces of the north. The first step was to secure the line of the Yssel. Zutphen fell on 20 May after a five-day investment, a victory eased by Vere's brilliant ruse in seizing the sconces across the river from the city. This was rapidly followed up by the capture of Deventer in June, where again Vere and his companies played a key role.[21] Parma, who had returned from France in late 1590, now stirred himself to action. He moved against the fort on the Betuwe, at Knodsenberg, which the Anglo-Dutch had erected in the previous year as a preliminary to the siege of Nijmegen. But his faltering siege came to an abrupt end with the arrival of an order from Philip to march into France to the aid of the League. The Dutch went on to crown this season of triumphs with the capture of Nijmegen in October.[22]

During these months of activity, the English, not quite able to throw off old habits, were still intriguing behind the backs of the Dutch authorities. Bodley entered into correspondence with dissident elements in the city of Groeningen without letting the States-General know what he was up to. And the ever-busy Sir Robert

---

[20] *Ibid.*, 271, 277, 287, 292.   [21] Essen 5: 316–17; Vere, 17–18, 18–19.
[22] Essen 5: 319; Wernham, 348.

Sidney, the garrison commander at Flushing, was pressing a scheme for the seizure of Dunkirk without the privity of the States (although he was keeping Maurice informed). The object of the exercise would be to bring Dunkirk under English control. Through these months, of course, the perpetual row between the allies over contraband trade rumbled on, unsettled. At home that shrewd and knowledgeable observer, Sir Thomas Wilkes, instructed by the Privy Council to press again for an answer to the English proposals of the previous year, urged patience. The States would not yield unless the Queen actually withdrew some part of her aid. "God of late hath blessed their martial endeavors in a wonderful manner." In another year they would seek to recover more of Groningen and Brabant, and if that came to pass (or the French king prospered) the provinces would be secure and then the Queen could safely withdraw all or part of her auxiliaries, for the States would be strong enough to defend themselves.[23]

The relative amity that prevailed between the allies in these months was made evident when the Queen urgently sought the dispatch of another contingent for Rouen and also asked for Dutch naval aid in the Seine estuary. This time the Dutch had no hesitation in consenting to both requests, and some 1,800 out of the total 5,700 English in the Low Countries had departed by January 1592.[24]

The priority that the English accorded the French campaign, and their continuing underestimation of the Dutch achievements of the past year, are reflected in the advice Bodley was urging on his government. The Dutch were planning a major effort for 1592, fielding not less than 12,500 troops. This included the English contingent now in Normandy, which the States expected to return in the spring. Bodley urged that they remain in France, where the King's needs were desperate. He went on to cast doubt on the Dutch plans for 1592. Last year's victories had only been a fluke. It had been God's good pleasure that "the enemy should be abused and should want at that time the common use of his sense for preventing their attempts." In March he went a step further and broached the idea of a force to go to France in the summer. (Oldenbarnevelt for a moment responded favorably but later, realizing its possible effects on Maurice's plans, backed away.) Vere, on the other hand, was

[23] *L&A* 1591–92: 168, 173, 185, 186; 1590–91: 274, 296, 300–1.
[24] *L&A* 1591–92: 188, 189; SP 84/44/10–12, 21, 55.

working hand in glove with Count Maurice. He explained the strategy in letters to his masters at home. Steenwyck and Coeverden, the keys to the inner provinces of Groningen, Friesland, and Drenthe, would be assailed in sequence. The city of Groningen would follow automatically once they had fallen, and Spanish power north of the Rhine would be liquidated. Parma, tied up in France, would be helpless to intervene. English participation, however, would be limited because of the absentees in France and the delinquency of his captains, all too often at home in England.[25]

In the meantime the Queen had taken up Bodley's scheme for a Dutch expedition to France, although Buzenval, the French envoy at The Hague, had turned against the plan, fearing that, if the Dutch aided France, the Queen would conclude they no longer needed her assistance and would slacken her efforts accordingly. Bodley continued to emphasize his view that the main front was in France; it was there that Spanish power must be broken. In April 1592 the Queen, in a letter to the States transmitting Henry's request for more men in Normandy, echoed Bodley's arguments. She herself was sending 2,000 foot and 100 horse; she asked that the four companies of English foot the States wanted for the Ostend and Bergen garrisons, plus a company of horse, be diverted to France. A flutter of French success had raised high hopes in England. Burghley excitedly wrote Vere that "the hastening of his [Henry's] victory and his enemy's total ruin in France whereof God hath given apparent tokens of his favor in sundry late overthrows given to the Duke of Parma and his army" was of greater consequence than the capture of four or five small towns. He wanted to increase the contingent from the Low Countries to six companies from Bergen and eight from Vere's field forces. The Dutch, who had in fact sent some twenty companies under Philip of Nassau to aid the French, saw the French successes as sound reason for rejecting the English proposals and concentrating their efforts at home. In May Maurice forthrightly rejected any more aid to France.[26]

In the same month the count opened his campaign in the north. Vere was present with some 1,350 English soldiers. The siege of Steenwyck proceeded according to plan, which naturally strength-

[25] SP 84/44/64–65, 97–99, 161–62, 169–70, 167–68, 171.
[26] SP 84/44/178–79, 207–9, 278, 286, 288, 318; 45/79–80; Tex 1: 174–75.

ened Dutch obstinacy in refusing Elizabeth's request. Vere received the royal orders to pull out his troops before the siege ended; he delayed immediate action by going to The Hague to deal with the States-General. The States of Zealand refused to part with the Bergen companies unless the Queen sent replacements before they left. Both Maurice and the Council of State fended off the Queen's request by referring the matter to the States-General. Bodley loyally did his best to persuade the Dutch but privately, in his dispatches home, he warned Burghley that after the casualties of the siege and normal attrition the forces available for France would not exceed 1,100 to 1,300 (instead of the 2,000 of which the Queen wrote). The States-General, as expected, argued that their campaign in Friesland effectively held down Spanish forces that might be used against the French king and refused to allow the English to leave. Vere, pleading lack of instructions from Bodley, made no move. The siege of Steenwyck faltered when an assault failed, but at last on 24 June the town capitulated.[27]

It was at this point that English strategy shifted importantly. The Queen wrote to congratulate the Dutch on their success but in the same letter announced her decision to send 2,000 men from the Low Countries to Brittany. With Parma's retreat from France (in early June) the threat to the King's main forces had diminished and England could now concentrate on the worrying menace to their own security posed by the Spanish foothold at Blavet. Elizabeth hoped the Dutch would contribute forces to this enterprise. (The Dutch had just recalled Philip of Nassau's contingent with the King.)[28]

Maurice had now determined to open the siege of Coeverden, the second goal in the summer's campaign, although initially he sent only a part of his army. In the meantime Bodley and Vere wrestled with the Council of State, the States-General, and Maurice in an effort to secure consent to the royal demands. The count proved more amenable than the civil power and offered to send the English forces with him into garrison as replacements. The States-General formally replied to the Queen in late July. While applauding her prudence, they stood on the terms of the contract—that the companies serving in the field army should be released only on the

[27] SP 84/44/297, 318, 326, 337; 45/2–6, 9–10, 27, 39.
[28] SP 84/45/59–60, 66.

fall of Steenwyck and the dissolution of the army. The latter condition was of course unfulfilled; the fall of Steenwyck was a mere
incident in their larger strategy in the north. Therefore, they hoped
the Queen would not withdraw her forces. As a sweetener, they
offered continued naval aid (nine ships) on the Breton coast and
spoke hopefully of more support when possible.[29]

This led to a series of exchanges between Elizabeth and the
States in which both stubbornly held their ground. Events intervened when the enemy threatened Zutphen and the Dutch begged
that Vere's forces be sent to check the Spanish advance; Bodley
went so far as to allow them to move to Duisburg, where they
threatened the enemy but remained close to a port of embarkation.
But the advance of a Spanish relieving force towards Coeverden
made English help a necessity; Bodley shunted the decision onto
Vere's shoulders. The latter, taking matters into his own hands,
assented to the States' request, believing the action would be short
and that Coeverden would fall within eight days. His intervention
was timely; he gave vital assistance in repelling the Spaniard, and
by 8 September Vere could write of the fall of Coeverden and the
withdrawal of his forces.[30]

This event proved decisive in resolving the deadlock over the
dispatch of troops to Brittany. Tension relaxed, and, after some further exchanges, the States-General, while formally refusing its consent, turned a blind eye to the departure of the English forces, both
those of Vere and those of the Bergen garrison. (It took a suspension
of pay to coerce the States of Zealand into replacing the latter.)
Maurice had now finished his campaign and begun the process of
dispersing his forces. (The Dutch now even prepared to assent to a
new demand by Henry for a loan to his mercenaries.) The English
forces were moved to the ports, but a long spell of contrary winds
and problems about pilots delayed their sailing until the very end
of the year.[31]

The year 1592 had been as triumphant for the Dutch as 1591.
Their firm refusal to be distracted from the Friesland campaign
had been justified by events and these very successes had reinforced

[29] SP 84/45/68–69, 77, 89, 91, 100–1, 106–7, 121.

[30] SP 84/45/130, 132–33, 134–35, 138, 148–49, 158, 162–63, 179, 189, 191, 215;
Archives ou correspondance inedité de la Maison d'Orange-Nassau, ser. 2, ed. G. Groen
van Prinsterer (6 vols., Utrecht, 1857–62) 1: 207, letter 93.

[31] SP 84/45/217, 219–22, 227–28, 230–31, 233, 275–76, 294–95, 315; 46/29–31.

Dutch self-assurance. For the English it had been much less satisfactory: in Normandy their hopes for a decisive campaign had been
disappointed; in Brittany their forces were pinned down in fruitless
inactivity. Only in the Low Countries had English soldiers shared
in the joys of victory. Both English and Dutch could rejoice in the
final disappearance of their great foe, the Duke of Parma, who died
in December of that year.

In the Low Countries the new year's prospect for 1593 was measurably brighter, thanks to Maurice's summer victories, but at the
same time Anglo-Dutch relations were undergoing a significant
shift. It was signalled by the Queen's decisions in the Rouen campaign. In 1589, when Henry urgently needed help, Elizabeth had
dispatched Willoughby with a force of raw recruits hastily drawn
from the fields and pastures of Kent and Sussex. But in 1591, to
mount the more considered assault on Rouen, the Queen had
drawn on her veteran Low Countries companies. Seasoned, both
physically and professionally, they would provide the core of a force
that faced the very professional challenge of the sustained siege of a
well-fortified city. For the first time in the century England had
something resembling a trained army. Captains whose experience
in many cases ran well back into the 1570s and a soldiery number-
ing in its ranks veterans of three or four years' service formed a
reservoir of experienced fighters such as the country had not had
for some generations. Henceforward, to the end of the war and far
into the next century, the English government would have a pool
of professional soldiers to draw upon whenever it faced major military challenges. Convenient as this system was for the English, it
naturally aroused the anger and the fear of the Dutch, the former
because it diminished their limited military resources at moments
of great need, and the latter because they suspected the departing
companies would neither return nor be replaced.[32]

The corollary of this reorientation of policy was the almost contemptuous disregard for the strategic aims of the States. The goals
of the 1592 campaign were dismissed by the English as merely parochial—the conquest of a few towns. Any appreciation of the immediate strategic needs of the Dutch or of their longer-term aspirations was quite lacking. Even more than in the French case, the
English were slow to grasp the emergence of a specifically Dutch

[32] SP 84/45/166.

policy, self-consciously aiming at the realization of national purposes. The Dutch in fact resented the peremptory and high-handed demands of the Queen, which trampled on their growing sense of equality with the English and on their firm conviction of their own sovereign status.

Bodley's reactions are of particular interest. At the beginning of 1592 he had been contemptuous of Dutch military proposals, dismissing the previous year's successes as a mere fluke. But in September he admitted that the position was astonishingly better than anyone could have expected. A month later, surveying the Dutch domestic scene, he noted that the sense of dependence on England was rapidly dissipating. Some among the leaders believed that the States could stand on their own; others, more reserved in their judgments, would have substituted English money for men. He recognized the Dutch bitterness over English depredations on their ships carrying cargoes to Spain and their conviction that they could get no justice in the Queen's courts. At a more immediate level Bodley had now come to admit that the Council of State, the only venue where the English had political purchase, was powerless. Only the States-General counted. Slowly but realistically the English were being brought to realize that they were dealing with an ally, not a dependent, and one whose goals would not necessarily at every point coincide with theirs. It was a portent of a new era when, in December 1592, the States, after a dignified complaint about the withdrawal of English troops, briskly demanded what they could expect in the way of English military support in the coming year.[33]

The year 1593 was to be a quiet one militarily, a perceptible pause after the efforts of the past two seasons. The Queen expressed a hope that the Dutch efforts at home would be defensive and that means might be found to aid the French. This was the crucial year, in which Henry's fate hung in the balance and in which he swung events in his favor by his conversion. Maurice, after failing to surprise Gertruydenberg, settled down to a siege that lasted some months. (There was some discussion with the English of an attempt to surprise Dunkirk, but it came to nothing.) During the Gertruydenberg siege Maurice was attended by Vere with a force of some hundreds of English soldiers. After the capitulation of the town in mid-June the count paused uncertainly. The demoralization of the

[33] SP 84/45/244–46, 275, 299–302, 361–62.

southern provinces offered opportunities, but lack of transport hindered movement.[34]

Vere, writing in the aftermath of the victory, pushed for a reversal of English strategy, quite opposite to that pursued in 1592. In his view the vital front was in the Low Countries—Brabant particularly—the key to Flanders and Artois. With a much smaller force than in Normandy or Brittany the Queen could strike at the very root of Spanish power (of which the French front was merely the topmost branch). He threw out the bait of a proposal from "some principal men here." If the Queen would send over 3,000 men with one month's pay, they would undertake to provide continuing financial support. In fact, the siege of Gertruydenberg had been so costly (£30,000) that nothing more could be done this year. And the Queen after her disappointments in France was unlikely to patronize any more continental adventures.[35]

During this slackening of the military momentum another alteration in Anglo-Dutch military relations took place with the appointment of Vere to a colonelship in the States' service, this with the Queen's cordial approval. With his new dual allegiance he was commander of the residue of the English field army plus the English contingent in Dutch pay. This consolidated the already harmonious cooperation with Maurice, but it also pointed up the relegation of the English contingents to a purely auxiliary role within the States' military establishment, foreshadowing the peacetime arrangements of the next century.[36]

The garrison forces in the Queen's pay in April 1593 amounted to some 3,400 troops, of whom a third were in the isolated post of Ostend, a place of special concern to the English; the remainder were concentrated in the cautionary towns of Flushing and Brill. Bergen had now become entirely a Dutch responsibility. Even before the departure of the English for France the previous August, the English financial officers were congratulating themselves on the reduction in costs they had achieved since the war began. From an initial high of £134,271 they had lowered the Queen's charges by stages to £106,162. Reducing the number of horse and pruning back the officer corps had been the most notable economies. By the open-

[34] SP 84/46/62, 96, 98, 103–5, 108–9, 110–11, 149, 170, 177.

[35] SP 84/46/177, 190, 196–97.

[36] SP 84/46/103–5, 210, 221, 229; Tex 1: 159.

ing of 1594, the total expenditure had been brought below £100,000, down to £90,400.[37]

Whereas in the Low Countries the year 1593 was marked by a lull in the fighting, in France there was a sharp and dramatic turn in the fortunes of Henry IV when he announced his conversion to Catholicism. This depressed sentiment in the Low Countries. Although publicly the States expressed their continued confidence in the French king and faith in his promise not to make peace without their consent, privately they were anxious as to France's future interest in continuing the war. Their worries—and those of the English—were heightened by changes in the southern provinces, where the arrival of Archduke Ernest as governor-general heralded both restored confidence among his subjects and also the possibility of peace offers. Both Vere and Gilpin (the English representative during Bodley's home leave) were fearful of dovish opinion in the North. War weariness and Catholic hopes for toleration were factors, but what worried the English envoys even more was the volatility of a populace "given to changes and novelties and of the humor that if they once take a head it is hard to stay and much less revoke them." A pluralistic regime, resting on popular foundations, seemed to traditionalist Englishmen a recipe for disaster.[38]

On the military front the Dutch remained anxious to complete their conquest of the northern provinces, but a shortage of men and the flagging will of the States-General hindered a definitive move on Groeningen, the last major Spanish fortress in the area. The Queen's authority was invoked to pressure the States into backing the forward party, and, when Spanish efforts at relief became dangerously threatening in September, Vere was sent with eleven companies, including some 500 of the Queen's troops, to check the advance. The shortage of men revived hopes that the English forces might return from France, although, with true Dutch thriftiness, the States wished to delay their return to the spring of 1594 in order to save money; for the present the Council of State borrowed from the cautionary towns for supplementing their numbers. In fact, by November 1593 some 1,250 men had returned from Normandy, and by January 1594 there were some 5,550 foot and 300 to 400 horse (in list strength) available for field service (plus 1,400 in the

[37] SP 84/46/91; 45/102–3; 48/8.   [38] SP 84/47/11–12, 13, 15, 57.

cautionary towns). Presumably ten percent of these were dead pays, leaving an effective strength of 6,525.[39]

Vere and Gilpin, more cheerful now about domestic morale, wrote to reassure their government as to Dutch determination to fight and their conviction that there was no prospect of peace with Spain. Vere also wrote of plans for an assault on Groningen in March 1594. All this was meant to pave the way for the next Dutch move—a request to the Queen for 3,000 to 4,000 men to serve for four to six months. The States-General were pressing the provinces for a special tax levy, but they were short of men. During the fall and winter of 1593–1594 the Queen was besieged with urgent letters from Maurice, the States-General, Vere and Gilpin, pressing this request. Maurice asked in addition that Vere be allowed to recruit another English regiment for the States' service.[40]

The Queen responded with fair promptitude, in early January 1594. She consented to the request, granting the 3,000 men, but in such a way as to minimize her expenses. Acknowledging the dangers arising from the new archduke's arrival and his offers of peace and regretful that another threat from Spain straitened her own means, she was willing to spare the Dutch 1,500 out of her troops recently returned to the Low Countries from Normandy; the other 1,500 were to be recruited for States' service, as Maurice had requested. There were allusions in her letter to the unpaid accrued debt, but repayment was not made a condition for help. The recruits to be raised by Vere were, as he succinctly put it, "such as have no abode nor mind to labor, a kind of people most troublesome . . . and dangerous" to the realm.[41]

The enemy made the first move; Coeverden was put under siege by them and desperately needed relief. Forces were assembled and the Spanish forced to abandon the siege. Maurice then closed in on Groningen, opening the siege on 18 May 1594, but even as he mounted his batteries a sudden shift of scene altered the entire aspect of affairs. In a kind of replay of the siege of Coeverden two years before, Elizabeth suddenly and imperiously demanded the return of her troops. Bodley was sent with peremptory instructions to summon all English-born soldiers (i.e., Vere's recruits as well as the

[39] SP 84/47/28–29, 32–33, 39, 48–49, 51, 53, 59, 64–65, 68–69; 48/8, 27.
[40] SP 84/47/97–98, 113, 115–16, 121, 139–40, 179, 185; 48/16–17.
[41] SP 84/48/23–24, 55–56, 80–81, 91, 104–5.

Queen's own forces) for immediate transport to Brittany. He was also to demand Dutch naval support. The French threat to the haven of Brest rivetted English attention and roused English fears to a pitch of anxiety. Brest, in the Queen's view, was far more important than Groningen; if the Dutch were recalcitrant, the Queen would withdraw her forces from Ostend. So urgent was the matter that, if it took too long to move men from Friesland, Bodley could take 1,100 men out of the cautionary garrisons.[42]

The Dutch response, not unnaturally, was to insist that they could not forgo the services of the 1,500 they had raised on their own; the whole campaign, long planned and expensively financed, would collapse. But they showed a willingness to compromise. They offered to replace the English companies at Ostend and Flushing with Dutch and promised to send ships. In the course of June some 1,100 English troops from the garrisons of Flushing, Brill, and Ostend sailed for France. The Queen, disposed on her part to be helpful, offered to write to the discontented party within Groningen on whose help the besiegers counted. Through June hopes rose high, only to be dashed; then heavy rains fell, but the expectation of a short siege was not disappointed, and, when the town fell in mid-July, Vere was still on hand with his English contingent.[43]

[42] SP 84/48/93, 133–34, 151, 164–65, 168, 172, 175, 185–88, 210.
[43] SP 84/48/230–32, 247, 251, 255, 272, 281–82; 49/30, 224.

CHAPTER 14

FROM ALLIANCE TO

COLLABORATION, 1595-1603

ENGLISH ATTENTION was now centered on Brest. The Dutch had already promised naval aid, but Burghley had upped the English demands in new instructions to Bodley. The urgency of affairs at Brest was now such that the Queen moved to take up a Dutch offer, made earlier by the States, to provide military as well as naval aid. There followed a tangle of crossed letters, misunderstandings, and eventually a flaring quarrel between Bodley and Burghley. What the Queen wanted was ships, victuals, and powder, all of which the States were willing to supply if they were given specific quantities. Bodley's complaint was that he got no detailed instructions; Burghley angrily retorted that he had other things to do than supervise such minutiae and suggested that the Dutch were merely dragging their feet. Finally in September a contingent of six ships did sail and later joined the English at Brest. In the meantime some 1,100 English soldiers did in fact sail for Brittany, under Baskerville's command, leaving some 4,760 in the Low Countries, of which all but 1,500 were in the three garrisons of Ostend, Flushing, and Brill. In October news arrived of the fall of Crozon.[1]

The year that was drawing to a close was another one of Dutch successes, but in the anticlimax months following the fall of Groningen there were signs of flagging energy. The burden of military and fiscal exertion over several years had left the provinces weary

[1] SP 84/48/281–82, 289–90; 49/6–8, 16–17, 55, 56, 58, 64, 79, 83, 98–99, 110–11, 171–73, 181–82, 222.

and worn down. The exhaustion of the southern provinces, though it offered an opportunity for Dutch initiative, also relieved them of any pressing necessity for further action. Nor was it clear what military objective could next be pursued. Military activity in the Low Countries was entering an interval of doldrums triggered by the mutual weariness of both sides.[2]

The recent campaign shed interesting light on the continuing subtle alterations in Anglo-Dutch relationships. The Dutch had proved their effective self-reliance in the last two years, although there were still moments of strain, such as the manpower shortage on the eve of the Groningen campaign, when they had to turn to the English for support. But the accommodations made were more nearly those between equals. There was now a growing reciprocal relationship between the two allies. When the States needed to augment their forces, the new scheme for recruitment in England shifted the financial burden from the Queen to the Dutch while giving the latter access to a useful pool of manpower. When England in its turn needed military and naval reinforcements for the Brest enterprise, the States acceded to the withdrawal of English forces from the Low Countries and dispatched a naval squadron to Brittany. It was another important stage in the transformation from dependence to alliance. It meant also that the English tacitly abandoned their efforts to have a strong voice in Dutch affairs; the supple Gilpin, long-time resident and a Dutch speaker, replaced the more rigid Bodley and imperceptibly subsided into the role of an ordinary ambassador.

How far the relationship had been altered in English eyes by Maurice's successes was made clear when at the end of 1594 the Queen made a formal demand that the States begin repayment of their accrued debt to her. The subject had been bruited in the negotiations for the Groningen reinforcements but not pressed. Elizabeth now unlimbered all her diplomatic artillery. Taking a high line, she recounted her magnanimity in declining the proffered sovereignty of the provinces, her generosity in men and money, and the sacrifices her people had made. Spain, provoked by these actions, had attacked England directly, yet English aid to the provinces had not faltered. The ten years' war was, she asserted, the longest in history and England's sustained support unequalled.

[2] SP 84/49/43, 85, 87, 90–91, 100–1, 106.

Now, with a string of victories to their credit, with the interior provinces liberated, and in the enjoyment of a thriving trade—with the enemy—the time had come for an accounting. Even though there was no such clause in the 1585 treaty, there was, she claimed, a tacit understanding that once success ensued the States would recompense the Queen. She did not ask for a final balancing of the books but she did require installments of repayment on a regular basis to begin now. She asked that a States delegation come to London explicitly for this purpose.[3]

This demand fitted logically into a larger and more general reorientation of English policy. With the fall of the Spanish fort at Crozon, Elizabeth speedily liquidated her French commitments. Henry, solemnly crowned at St. Denis, was fast acquiring mastery of his kingdom; Spain's intervention had proved to be a disastrous folly. The Dutch had established a strong defensive position from which it would be very difficult—and probably impossible—for the Spanish to dislodge them. And by now the disarray of the southern provinces, wracked by mutinies and by civil discontent and lacking effective leadership, was evident to all. More important still from the English point of view was the growing menace of revolt in Ireland. Significantly, much of the force evacuated from Brittany was sent directly to Ireland. Given all these considerations, the Queen and her ministers saw this as the moment to begin a partial disengagement from the commitments made in 1585.

In Bodley's instructions on the debt issue, the Queen had referred to Spanish overtures to the States. In fact, over the roar of Maurice's cannon there had been a steady obbligato of diplomatic activity. From the first news of the appointment of Archduke Ernest as the new governor-general there had been rumors of peace overtures (even that would propose a restoration of the Pacification of Ghent), and at the end of 1593, after Ernest's arrival in Brussels, an emissary from the south had appeared at The Hague. This was followed up, after some delays, by a more formal proposal addressed to the various provincial states.[4]

Coming at a moment of ebbing energy in the aftermath of Maurice's victories, these overtures required careful handling. Olden-

[3] SP 84/49/277–82.
[4] SP 84/47/15, 57 195–96; 48/118–19, 133–34, 162, 191, 227; see also BL, Cotton Mss., Vespasian cviii, 234–40; Tex 1: 199–200.

barnevelt carefully tailored his response, first for domestic consumption in the northern provinces and second to thwart without openly rejecting the archduke's advances. Ernest's death in February 1595 put an end to such moves for the time being. The English, well informed by the Dutch, followed these negotiations with equanimity. Bodley was convinced that the States' continued resistance to Spain was a certainty. Indeed he suggested that in some ways they preferred the *status quo*, since linkage with the southern provinces would be possible only in the unlikely event that the Spanish vanished altogether.[5]

Ernest had also made overtures to Elizabeth through a private emissary, and she had proposed to send Sir Thomas Wilkes to Brussels (see Chapter 10). A passport was obtained for him, and rumors flew thick and fast in Brussels of a coming peace with England, but pressure from the States and from Henry IV, as well as the complications of the Lopez affair, halted the mission. Abortive though the effort was, for the first time since 1589 Elizabeth had made an overture towards the enemy. Both Ernest's efforts and the Wilkes episode mark the first faint foreshadowing of the renewed diplomatic maneuvers of the next half-dozen years.[6]

The Dutch, at the same time, were reaching out to extend their relations with France. Henry's conversion and the ensuing pacification of his kingdom raised worries about the future of Franco-Spanish hostilities. (There was as yet no actual declared war between the two powers.) The Dutch, anxious to secure France's continuing role in the struggle, now began to offer active cooperation on condition that Henry provide matching forces. In the fall of 1594 this scheme took on reality with the dispatch of Philip of Nassau with a force to join the Duke of Bouillon, convoyed by a cavalry force under Vere, who had a perilous trip but returned unharmed. The Queen was indignant over this use of her men but Vere was unrepentant. The results were negligible but the gesture had been made. Initiatives of this kind pointed the way to a possible tripartite alliance, aimed directly at frontal war with Spain.[7]

Bodley was now ordered to resume the diplomatic campaign for a start on debt repayment and a reduction in current costs. He

[5] SP 84/49/140–41.

[6] Tex 1: 200; 2: 154; HMC, *Hatfield* 5: 11–12, 19, 20, 34, 252; SP 49/110–11, 140–41, 159–60, 212; *DNB*, "Sir Thomas Wilkes."

[7] SP 84/49/62, 126, 149–41, and 9/29/94–12/10/94; Tex 1: 180.

asked for a lump sum immediately, to be followed by annual installments in the future and an abatement on the Queen's annual
expenditure in the Low Countries. The States-General predictably
procrastinated, alleging that the matter must go to the provincial
states. This, they argued, would generate deplorable publicity. The
populace would interpret the matter as an English withdrawal of
support. They recounted the burdens of the last few years and the
new ones they were assuming by offering aid to France, an action
that helped the common cause. Their people were weary and hoped
for a reduction, not an increase, of taxes, such as repayment would
entail.[8]

This response, equally predictably, irritated the Queen, who now
made her demands more specific. She calculated the debt at
£700,000 to £800,000; she wanted a first year's payment of £100,000
in two installments and the rest "to be annually according to that
value." The States remained unmoved and the deadlock persisted
through a series of repetitive and barren exchanges. The Queen had
little effective leverage by which she might force them to accept her
terms other than the loss of Vere's regiment. The men recruited for
the States' service had been kept on, at least for another season.[9]

The summer campaign of 1595 did not go well; the enemy's unexpected advance across the Rhine forced first a suspension and
then an abandonment of the siege of Grolle. The result was another
stalemate. The hope was that the Dutch army would be enough of
a menace to keep Spanish forces away from the French frontier,
but in fact the latter were strong enough to continue the siege
of Cambrai while maintaining an army east of the Rhine. These
frustrations and the French clamor for active support fortified the
States-General's arguments in resisting the Queen's demands for
repayments.[10]

These demands were thrust forward again in July with a new
instruction to Bodley. Along with all the familiar arguments used
in the past, he was now to include a threatened withdrawal of the
Queen's forces; he was given a little flexibility to dicker on the
£100,000 lump sum, but the Queen would not tolerate any conditions as to the number of troops to be maintained in the Low Coun-

[8] SP 84/50/29–30, 59–64.
[9] SP 84/49/90–91, 154–56, 247; 50/108–10, 127–28, 161, 167; 51/11–12, 17, 39–40, 215–16.
[10] SP 84/51/44, 49, 77, 91.

tries; that was to remain at her discretion. Bodley persuaded her to soften this threat by pointing out that, if it were carried out, the States would see this as removing any need for repayment. He suggested—and Elizabeth accepted—a vaguer form of threat. The exchange highlighted once again the limited options open to the Queen in this bargaining.[11]

This new bout of exchanges did move Oldenbarnevelt to shift away from the obstinate refusal the Queen had met so far. In a private and anonymous communication (from "a principal person of state") he offered a possible set of terms. For the present the States would pay £20,000 a year and give naval assistance as required, on the understanding that there be no separately negotiated peace and that an English establishment of 4,000 troops be guaranteed. For the future he offered annual repayments of £100,000 after the conclusion of peace and—a tentative feeler—an agreement that the States should assume all costs for the English soldiers if the Queen handed over the cautionary towns. This was, of course, no formal offer, but it was an important pointer to the thinking of the most powerful Dutch politician and to the possible shape of a workable compromise.[12]

At the official level the tussle between Bodley and the States-General continued with wearying repetitions of the same arguments—the Queen's outraged cries of ingratitude and reproach, the States' litany of their current woes: floods, dearth, French demands, war weariness. The unfortunate Bodley, caught in the middle, was the object of the Queen's frustrated fury. When he arrived with a set of Dutch proposals in May 1595 the Queen said she wished he had been hanged. To which Bodley responded, "And if with that I might have leave that I should be discharged I would say *benedetto il giorno, il mese e l'anno*." French demands on the Dutch were in fact being rapidly upped when the French town of Cambrai fell to the Spanish and a threat to Calais developed. The Dutch forces in France were concentrated around the Channel ports.[13]

It was not until November 1595 that the diplomatic jam began to ease. Early in the month Elizabeth wrote to Bodley with new instructions. While still insisting on the reasonableness of her demands and emphasizing the new strains created by the Irish prob-

---

[11] SP 84/51/46–47, 61–62. [12] Tex 1: 192; SP 84/51/59–60, 167.
[13] SP 84/51/122, 151, 157, 194, 242–45, 261–62; Birch 1: 244–45.

lem and the expectation of another armada, she agreed, for the time being, not to press for repayment, on condition the States provided naval assistance. This latter clause referred, of course, to the plans being made for a major naval enterprise in 1596.[14]

As the horizons of the English government shifted away from France to Spain itself, the importance of the Dutch alliance took on new dimensions. The services of their ships were now urgently requested for the Cadiz expedition. And that expedition itself would require the services of 12,000 to 15,000 men. Hence the Queen was prepared to set aside the annual installments of repayment if the States would assume the cost of paying the English auxiliaries (roughly £70,000 as against the annual sum of £20,000 suggested by Oldenbarnevelt). This compromise seems to have been the result of Privy Council intercessions with the Queen. These concessions were greeted with relief in the Low Countries; an embassy of thanks was proposed while the provinces were asked to fit out the necessary ships for Essex's fleet. On the main issue, the payment of the English troops by the States, there was a firm refusal. Such a step, the Dutch asserted, would effectively end the Treaty of Nonsuch. Bodley's advice was to let the matter rest, to accept a States mission to London, and then to continue to bargain face-to-face.[15]

The Queen grumblingly accepted the delays because of the impending Spanish threat, but Burghley warned that her temper might explode again at any moment; Oldenbarnevelt should prepare his embassy with great care and offer at least as much as in his first overture. The Dutch leader took this advice to heart and during the next few weeks labored mightily to persuade his fellows to a set of proposals that would be acceptable in London. This was uphill work, for the general disposition of the States-General was apathetic; they preferred watchful inaction at a moment when the arrival at Brussels of a new governor, the Cardinal-Archduke Albert, bringing men and money and possible new overtures of peace, made them apprehensive.[16]

At the end of January 1596 Bodley had a highly important and highly private conversation with Oldenbarnevelt in which the latter, largely repeating his suggestion of the previous year, sketched out the possible terms of a revised treaty. The Dutch statesman was

[14] SP 84/51/215–16, 219, 221.   [15] SP 84/51/221, 249–51, 255–57.
[16] SP 84/51/279; 52/18–19, 20, 33, 50, 59.

prepared to accept the burden of supporting the English field force; he proposed that 4,000 men be maintained at the States' charge. There would be annual repayments of £20,000 on the debt, no separate negotiations for peace, Dutch naval aid when the English required it. This was a highly secret overture; Oldenbarnevelt warned that much hard spadework remained to be done before the States-General and the provincial states could be brought around to such an arrangement.[17]

The advocate set to work among his colleagues in the Holland states as well as the States-General, and by the end of February Bodley could give a hopeful report that a conclusion would be reached shortly. At this moment, however, the pot was set boiling again by the arrival of Vere with a new commission from his government. He was to ask for the temporary withdrawal of an unstated number of English troops from the cautionary towns, from Ostend and from the field forces. The men were to be at Plymouth by March. He was to avoid discussion of the purposes or destination of the expedition for obvious security reasons. Since the States had already committed their ships to the enterprise, the object of this secrecy was presumably to keep the Spaniards guessing as to the actual destination. Guided by Oldenbarnevelt, the States readily agreed to the English proposition. In spite of their fears as to the cardinal-archduke's intention, they were willing to agree to heavy drafts on the garrisons plus five companies of Vere's English regiment. Dutch willingness to cooperate was all the more notable since Henry IV was now clamoring for assistance, a claim that the States would be hard-pressed to deny, given their anxiety to retain the French alliance. Bodley was deeply impressed—and particularly at Oldenbarnevelt's personal achievement—since the costs to the Dutch of the naval contingent plus those of replacing 2,500 English soldiers would come to some £100,000. But they were prepared to bear this burden in order to display the continuance of Elizabeth's protection. "So much it doth import to use her countenance and name and that these people and the enemy should not alter their conceit of the continuance of the succor."[18]

Necessarily Vere's mission intertwined itself with Bodley's treaty revision, and the colonel feared the new demands would sour will-

---

[17] SP 84/52/38–41.
[18] SP 84/51/255–57; 52/15, 35, 69–71, 82–83, 84, 96–97, 107–8, 113, 117–20.

ingness to assume the burdens of repayment. Oldenbarnevelt had brought his colleagues around to accepting the main points in his scheme: full release of the Queen from all charges for the English auxiliaries, £20,000 per annum, and at the end of the war £100,000 a year for five years. However, the revised treaty was to run only until the death of the Queen (unlike Nonsuch, which had included her successor). Moreover, the Dutch insisted on advance acceptance of all main points before they would send their delegation to England. Allegedly this was to avoid the need for reference to the States, but pretty clearly the intention was to force a commitment from the Queen. Elizabeth as usual reacted with a burst of anger that her financial terms had not been fully met. Unluckily Burghley was ill and Essex absent from court—men, whose views, Robert Cecil wryly commented, carried more weight than a person of his small judgment, and instead of counsel he could only yield obedience without argument. The result was a long, pessimistic, and somewhat incoherent letter from the Queen, upbraiding the States for their selfishness and greed and instructing Bodley to demand larger payments. Cecil's apologetic letter, which accompanied the Queen's, noted that in spite of all the rhetoric the Queen "would not have anything marred if more cannot be conveniently procured." It was more than a hint that Bodley should not allow the treaty to be shipwrecked on the Queen's tantrum. Through April the States apprehensively awaited Bodley's return with the Queen's final answer, while Oldenbarnevelt, apprised of her new demands, strongly argued against their being made at a time when provincial assent still had to be obtained. He stood firm in refusing to send a mission unless the Queen accepted in advance the substance of their proposals. By early June there was sufficient meeting of minds to justify the appointment of a mission.[19]

While the diplomats struggled with the tangle of opposed interests, Essex and Howard, with their Dutch colleagues, had gone to Cadiz and returned. On their arrival home the borrowed English forces were promptly returned to the Low Countries and permission given to recruit replacements for the regiment in Dutch pay. (Out of some 2,200 who went, almost 1,800 came back.)[20]

The mission finally set out at the beginning of the fall. Its instruc-

[19] SP 84/52/98, 111, 117–20, 123–24, 131, 132, 161, 163–64, 202–3, 210–11.
[20] SP 84/53/35, 41, 74.

tions were unaltered, so that it had virtually no power to bargain; Gilpin and Bodley's plea that they be given flexibility as to the financial terms (both annual payment and the final settlement) went unheard. Worse still, they spoke only for the States-General, although it was the provincial states that would have to find the money. The mission went badly from the start; early on, the envoys even talked of returning home. The States-General, writing directly to the Queen, lamented the lack of success but insisted that it was impossible to vary the terms they offered. Barely six weeks after their arrival at Greenwich the deputies were on their way home, empty-handed, fulfilling the pessimistic predictions of Bodley and Gilpin. Nevertheless, their failure had not soured Anglo-Dutch relations. The Queen, in a surprisingly moderate tone, wrote to the States-General expressing her regret, insisting that they would have to yield more, but ending on the hopeful note that there would be further discussion.[21]

This negotiation had overlapped yet another. As early as March, when Oldenbarnevelt had put forward his first proposals, the Dutch had intimated their hope for a tripartite league with England and France. This would effectively be recognition of their sovereign status. In the following May Elizabeth and Henry had in fact formalized the loose collaboration of seven years in a treaty of alliance, offensive and defensive (see Chapter 10). In the discussion leading up to it, Elizabeth had objected to recognizing the States as a sovereign power, clinging still to the notion that they were somehow under her protection, but she yielded on this. The treaty had made general provision for a wider membership. In August, when the Duke of Bouillon came to complete the ratification in London, he was charged with a further mission to The Hague, to draw the States into the larger league. He carried formal letters of recommendation from the Queen, reciting the common enmity to Spain that drew the signatories together and urging that the Dutch listen favorably to the French proposals. This dispelled the feeling in Holland that England was opposed to Dutch entry. The French envoy arrived in late September and appeared before the States-General. By mid-October basic agreement had been reached, although the States hesitated in granting the 4,000 troops he sought for his master's service. At the formal ceremonies of signing in November Gil-

---

[21] SP 84/53/25, 29, 70, 78, 88, 129, 131–32, 139, 184–85.

pin signed for England; the troops were promised but only if matched by a French force of 7,000 to 8,000 foot and 2,500 horse.[22]

The year 1597 was one of uncertainties and disappointments. The Dutch, rejoicing in the recently ratified alliance, saw it as a guarantee of continued Franco-Spanish hostility and looked expectantly towards proposals for a joint Franco-Dutch military venture. And indeed the Dutch found themselves in the flattering position of being wooed by each of their royal allies. The English were already laying plans for another great naval enterprise as early as February. The Queen asked for twenty ships to be at Plymouth by 20 April. (Gilpin was anxious to get in the English bid before the French made theirs). The Dutch would join an expedition to sail to the coast of Spain; Elizabeth expected prompt compliance as a *quid pro quo* for forbearing further demands for repayment of the debt and declared she would regard refusal as a scorn. Holland was favorable to the request, as was Maurice, who favored this as against the French proposal because it would not require soldiers. But there was also concern about the Queen's intentions and fears that she would demand troops for the enterprise. There was also worry about the command, especially that it might go to the highly unpopular Cumberland, who had roughly handled Dutch shipping. By late March the ships were preparing, but questions were still being raised as to English intentions. In April the commanders were told of the postponement of the enterprise—to their annoyance, since the cost of keeping the ships in readiness was high; in May they were still waiting. Then suddenly signals were changed; the Dutch were now asked to release 1,000 musketeers from the garrisons and to provide fifteen flyboats (in lieu of ten warships) to transport these troops, plus another 1,000 from England. Dutch acceptance was prompt, although it was unclear whether the goal of this enterprise was Spanish-held Calais or Spain itself. In the end, fear of a vast Spanish invasion preparation tipped the balance in favor of an attack on Spain itself. By 23 June the fleet was ready to set off under Essex's command on its star-crossed enterprise. But wind, weather, and too much wishful thinking frustrated all their

[22] SP 84/52/117–20; 53/19–20, 31, 57, 105–6, 123–24; Edward P. Cheyney, *A History of England from the Defeat of the Armada to the Death of Elizabeth* (2 vols., New York, 1914, 1926) 2: 145; Tex 2: 176.

hopes. The Dutch were glad to see their ships home again in November.[23]

Through much of this troubled year, as both English and Dutch nervously assessed the probable direction of French policy, military activity marked time. In the earlier months much energy was consumed in a squabble between Holland and Zealand that became so acrimonious that the Queen felt compelled to intervene as a mediator. Eventually the quarrel subsided and, under French pressure, Maurice took the field in August and besieged and took Berck and later some other towns. In November, in a self-congratulatory letter, he boasted to the Queen of having cleared all the land between the Rhine and the Ems.[24]

The English had once again pushed their view that there was a cheap and effective way to halt Spanish naval preparations. If only the supply of grain from the Eastland, much of it carried in Dutch ships, could be halted, the Spanish fleet would be starved into inaction. The issue, always seething just below the surface, now bubbled up again when the English government took the initiative in pressing for a prohibition on all grain shipments from the Baltic to Iberia. The States took the demands seriously, and there were extended debates on the issue. Oldenbarnevelt seemed genuinely anxious to accommodate the Queen, but the difficulties were obvious. Some half-measures were taken; there was a prohibition on export of locally grown corn, even consideration of a tax to cover the shortfall in revenue that would ensue if the trade were cut off, but the basic response was one of procrastination. No doubt Oldenbarnevelt hoped—and his hopes were realized—that, given time, the issue would die down and relations would not be permanently damaged. An underlying pragmatism on both sides allowed them to muddle along.[25]

However, before the year 1597 was over, English and Dutch diplomats and their respective governments had to face a more ominous prospect. Throughout the year the French had periodically pressured the States for some kind of military action to distract the Spanish while Henry IV pursued the recovery of Amiens. In some measure Maurice's campaign was a response to that pressure, but

[23] SP 84/54/3, 9–10, 48, 66, 68, 74–75, 96–97, 111–12, 138–39, 186–87, 216, 233–34, 259, 309; 55/16, 24, 35, 55, 66, 235–36.
[24] SP 84/54/167, 186–87, 207; 55/16, 66, 147, 155, 231.
[25] SP 84/55/82, 83, 88, 95, 101, 129–30, 171–72, 179.

French military actions were matched with diplomatic movement. Rumors—and more than rumors—of contact between the French and the Spanish through clerical intermediaries had been rife for months. Thus it could hardly have been a surprise when in late November Buzenval, the French ambassador, presented the States-General with a letter from his master announcing a peace offer from the archduke. (There was a similiar embassy to the English; see Chapter 11). The terms were favorable: the restoration of all occupied towns, except Calais. What should he do? What were the States' plans for the coming year? How much could they do to relieve his frontiers? His own people were war-weary and his other ally, Elizabeth, had seen fit to use her forces at a distance for two years past.[26]

The States in reply dodged the question of further aid by emphasizing the common goals of the war effort. For them this meant expelling the Spanish from the Low Countries, an achievement that would be of equal benefit to the other allies since it would deny the Spaniards the bases for making war on them. The present Spanish overture was obviously an effort to split the alliance at a moment when their own affairs were in disarray. But once peace had given Spain a chance to recover, it would surely renew the war. The best solution was continued war. The States managed to procrastinate on any final answer to the King and finally decided to send a mission to France and another to England, but they held up their departure while waiting to hear what Elizabeth's response to the French message would be. They were aware in general of its contents and applauded her rejection of peace, but they wished she had called Henry's bluff and matched the troops that he promised to field, if war were to continue.[27]

In fact, Elizabeth was once more shifting her strategy; the offensive efforts that had marked the past two seasons were now to be abandoned, and hence she no longer required Dutch naval aid. This in turn meant that she was free to revive her demand for a repayment schedule. The instructions given Robert Sidney, who replaced the ailing Bodley, were to cite the needs generated by the Irish rebellion and the threat of another Armada, and to press for a beginning of annual installments. The Dutch offer stood as it had been put forward earlier: small payments now, larger ones at the conclu-

[26] SP 84/55/1, 16, 181–82, 211, 215.   [27] SP 84/55/215–18, 277–78.

sion of peace, the maintenance of the English auxiliaries out of States' funds. Sidney was to counter with a general offer of continued protection if the annual payments were increased.[28]

However, this issue was soon to blend into the larger questions posed by the French dealings with Spain. By early 1598 peace between the two continental monarchs loomed as a real and immediate possibility. In January, much alarmed by the progress towards agreement, the States readied two delegations, one bound for Paris, the other for London. Henry had now advanced to the position of backing a Spanish proposal for English and Dutch participation in the peace conference. Relieved by the Queen's initial reaction that such a conference would be dangerous, the States reiterated their conviction that war was the only strategy to be followed with Spain. By late January both missions had departed, armed with the familiar argument that the Spanish aimed not at genuine peace but only at dividing the alliance. In fact, the archduke was now pursuing his goal not only through the agency of the French king but also through other channels. Gilpin reported a conversation between a Leyden merchant and the Brussels councillor, Richardot, offering toleration for the Protestants (and a military post for Maurice against the Turks) in an autonomous Netherlands ruled by the archduke and his Spanish bride. The Dutch, predictably negative, stressed that continuance of the war would probably bring revolt in the southern provinces once the peace effort failed.[29]

During April and May there was suspense pending the outcome of the two missions. Gilpin reported the gloomy expectation that Henry would make peace and the growing fears as to the effects on Dutch morale. War weariness and the discontents of the poorer provinces would provide an opening for the pro-peace party. The States-General were so nervous that they were concealing the dispatches they were receiving from England and France, and as the conviction deepened that a Franco-Spanish treaty was in the offing, worries about the reactions rose correspondingly. With the French alliance fast fading, the future of the English partnership became a matter of the greatest urgency.[30]

The mission to France, headed by Oldenbarnevelt, went to meet

[28] SP 84/55/285–88.
[29] SP 84/55/292–93; 56/3, 5, 13, 15, 19, 48, 61, 67, 71–73.
[30] SP 84/56/82–83, 87–88, 96.

not only the French King and his ministers but also an English delegation led by Robert Cecil, newly minted secretary of state and about to step into the shoes of his dying father as principal minister. Like Cecil, Oldenbarnevelt came armed with arguments to dissuade the King from peace and hopeful they might convince. And, like his English counterpart, he soon came to the conclusion that Henry, although perhaps against his own impulses, would opt for peace. At the same time Oldenbarnevelt made it clear to Cecil that the States would not accept the terms being held out by the Archduke Albert and would certainly continue the struggle. These realizations posed different problems for the two ministers. Peace between the two great continental powers would be at the best uneasy and troubled, and the possibility of resumed hostilities was high. In these circumstances Oldenbarnevelt still had bargaining counters. Even though she had concluded peace, France still had a substantial interest in seeing that the provinces remained a sharp and painful thorn in the Spaniards' side. So, when Oldenbarnevelt broached the question of continuing financial aid from Henry, he was gratified by the King's ready promise of money, a promise made concrete and specific before the Dutch mission left.[31]

Cecil for his part held no such cards. Continued war between the States and Spain was of the utmost importance to Henry; it would hold down a large part of the distrusted Philip's forces and exhaust his treasury, and it was likely to be an enmity of long duration. England's continued participation in the struggle was of course advantageous to Henry but not crucial; largely indifferent, he would not make any sacrifices or run any risks to insure either continuing war or an Anglo-Spanish peace.

This was the unpalatable message Cecil had to give his royal mistress. Her hopes that Henry would continue the war or, failing that, that the States would accede to some compromise agreement with Philip and thereby end the war, were dashed. Moreover, the Spanish, through the medium of the French king, were dangling an offer to treat for peace at any time within the next six months, in effect incorporating the English into the Peace of Vervins. Elizabeth was now forced to the wrenchingly painful choice between making peace without the States or continuing the war without French participation.[32]

[31] Tex 1: 264, 269, 270; 2: 296–318.   [32] HMC, *Hatfield* 8: 118–27, 154.

Obviously the first step, as Cecil saw it, was to sound out the Dutch leadership. At the very least this move would give an excuse for delaying an answer to the Spanish proposal; further, it offered a chance for probing Dutch intentions and, if the war were to be continued, of pressing the States for concessions to England at a moment of Dutch vulnerability. The Queen would "then have these two, which are of the best ministers the States have, humble petitioners to you in England." And the Queen could be assured "that they will do as much in it to ease you as can be found reasonable." Hence Cecil arranged that Oldenbarnevelt and his colleague, instead of returning home, should proceed to London for face-to-face talks with the Queen and her councillors.[33]

Oldenbarnevelt arrived with little hope, believing that England was prepared to make peace while retaining the cautionary towns, an act that would be in the highest degree prejudicial to the common cause. He had in fact decided to go on home without seeing the English leaders, but the joint urging of Cecil, Caron (the Dutch agent in London), and Essex persuaded him to go to London. The Queen's reception was indeed chilly at first meeting. She recounted the sacrifices of her people "now weary of these continued and endless vexations." The enemy offered peace and she was deeply disappointed in finding "they would not accord with Spain on any conditions and that they had no authority to offer us any other remedy for the wars, saving not to hearken to any peace." So she "fell from question of peace to what course they would propound for war, which might sufficiently fortify us upon our future refusal of any treaty (if so it shall be) for their sake." On these hints there followed discussion between Oldenbarnevelt and the English Council and a much more cordial parting with the Queen. The Dutch statesman left England with the understanding that England would be open to renegotiation of the treaty terms. Implicit in that understanding was the expectation of continued English support, in some form, for the provinces.[34]

---

[33] *Ibid.*, 123. They narrowly missed the returning mission, which had visited England while they were in France. It would seem, from undated documents, that very far-reaching concessions had been suggested by the Dutch mission and that they had had a hopeful response from Elizabeth. But nothing could be settled until the French decision was made. SP 84/56/106, 144, 145, 148.

[34] SP 84/56/115, 136–37, 141–42, 150–52, 155, 157–61; Tex 1: 272, 274; 2: 322; HMC, *Hatfield* 8: 198.

His task at home was not an easy one; war weariness and dismay at the French defection (and fear the Queen would follow suit) made many susceptible to the archduke's overtures, and although the leadership was determined to continue the fight, by no means all the provinces backed them. But Oldenbarnevelt was determined to use all his credit and skill to bring his countrymen to an acceptance of Elizabeth's terms. The hope of continued English assistance raised morale, and a correspondent of Essex's believed they would accede to anything the Queen asked. Nevertheless, fear that she would make peace persisted.[35]

In June 1598 Sir Francis Vere arrived, bearing the Queen's terms; his mission was merely to present them and to invite a States' mission with full powers to treat to go to London. There is no extant evidence of the discussions that preceded these instructions, but there is at least a hint of division within the Council. Essex, writing to Lord Henry Howard in May, painted a gloomy picture of England's plight, on every front. Among these evils not the least was that "our counsellors at home persuade what they can that we should abandon the States of the Low Countries, our only constant and able friends."[36]

The instructions that Vere carried were designed to state the English case in its strongest form and to put maximum pressure on the Dutch. The Spanish offer to treat for peace had been held in abeyance so that she might deal with the States, but time pressed and a speedy answer was necessary. Reviewing the past, Elizabeth boasted of English generosity and of their provision of aid for an unheard-of length of time. The Dutch had benefitted hugely, settled their government, expanded their commerce, and enlarged their territories while Elizabeth had exhausted her means on their behalf. Now, faced with a Spanish-inspired rebellion in Ireland, she was offered a clear choice—"either harken to peace when the offer made on so honorable circumstances or follow war with probability of good success." What reasons could they give why she should not take the opportunity now offered to relieve her people of these burdens? If the war was to continue they must present sufficient matter

[35] SP 84/56/96, 100, 104, 109, 138, 150–52, 162, 165–66; Tex 1: 275; HMC, *Hatfield* 8: 193–94, 214, 222.
[36] *Ibid.*, 169.

whereon to base such continuance and abandonment of the opportunity of peace.[37]

As to particulars she demanded the repayment of some good portion of the debt, and relief from all charges for the auxiliary troops as well as the continuing garrisons. The Dutch must also be prepared to give aid to England when required and assistance in any attack on Spanish dominions in Europe or overseas. Finally, she wanted a supply of victuals for her forces in Ireland. After Vere made his presentation to the States-General, he reported a very favorable reception, while privately he was assured of their acceptance of virtually all the demands. But they remained fearful the Queen would make peace, an event that would much disturb their people and that would pose the awkward problem of the cautionary towns. As to the latter, they were apprehensive that Elizabeth would play the market, in effect putting them up to bid, a competition that would be prohibitively expensive for the States. Fully aware of the Queen's demand for a speedy answer, they were ready to send a delegation by mid-July. Maurice wrote to Essex, who had courted Oldenbarnevelt in the earlier mission (although the earl had in fact just fallen from favor). Vere added his voice in a letter to the earl, assuring him of Dutch determination to meet the Queen's wishes (provided she did not ask for a large sum but would accept annual installments). He warned in the most urgent tones of the risks of English refusal. There was a strong peace party and, although Oldenbarnevelt and his colleagues were in the ascendancy at the moment, a rejection by the Queen would cut the ground out from under them and might well bring about a disastrous peace.[38]

The negotiations moved briskly; they were complete in a bare month. The main point of disagreement was the actual amount of the annual payments. In the end the Queen accepted the Dutch calculation as to the total debt, but they yielded on the size of the annual installments. The treaty, approved on 26 August 1598, ended the Queen's financial commitments (except for the cautionary garrisons), reduced the English participation in Dutch government to a single representative on the Council of State, and provided for repayment of a total debt of £800,000 (against an English

[37] SP 84/56/157–61.
[38] SP 84/56/157–61, 173, 181, 182, 184; HMC, *Hatfield* 8: 222–23, 245, 249, 250, 256–57; Tex 2: 329.

demand for £1,000,000), half to be paid in £30,000 annual installments (rather than £20,000) and the other half to be reimbursed
after peace was concluded. There was cause for mutual satisfaction.
The English had shed most of the financial burden they had borne
since 1585, and all their demands for reciprocal naval support had
been accorded. There were critics, however, who thought the
Queen had thrown away the game. They doubted that the Dutch
promises would be honored when the time came to pay the annual
installments. The Dutch on their side were assured of a substantial
English contingent in their armies and the continuing countenance
of the Queen. How active she would be in future hostilities against
the enemy remained less certain.[39]

In fact, the Queen had dealt with the dilemma forced on her by
the Treaty of Vervins in a characteristically ambiguous way. She
had not opted for peace with Spain, as Henry had, but she had
made a major reduction in her military commitments. The treaty
of alliance with the States was not dissolved, but English participation henceforward was that of a sleeping partner. Nor had the
Queen closed the door to further approaches from the other side.
As her instructions for Neville, the new ambassador to France,
made clear, she was prepared to listen to Spanish overtures although she would make no move herself.

During the course of the fall the terms of the new treaty came
into force as the English soldiers were transferred to the pay of the
States. Ratifications were exchanged, not without predictable frictions on both sides. In December the Queen once again made a
draft on her reservoir of trained troops, this time requiring 2,000
for service with Essex in Ireland. Vere was to take these men from
her garrison at Flushing if the field forces were too far away for
embarkation by 10 January 1599. She promised replacement by new
levies from England as soon as possible. The States-General responded promptly with a strong protest, alleging their particular
danger in the cold season (when the enemy could cross the frozen
rivers) and begging Cecil to interpose for them with the Queen. But
determined pressure from Vere and Gilpin plus an opportune thaw
brought the Dutch around to agreeing to the royal demand. Essex

[39] Tex 1: 275–77; SP 84/57/36–37, 68, 76, 260–61.

complained later that the Low Country contingent was of poor quality, to which Vere stiffly demurred.[40]

In the new year 1599 the Dutch roused themselves to a major and novel enterprise, the dispatch of a fleet to the Iberian coasts. An unprecedented tax levy was made to finance it. Vere, obviously impressed by their actions, wrote that he now believed, as he had not in the past, that the Dutch could defend themselves unaided. The fleet was in due course dispatched, although not to any great purpose, while at home the Dutch maneuvered to oust the Spaniards from the Rhine provinces.[41]

The settlement of 1598 marked a term not only in Anglo-Dutch relations but also in the course of the war. With France's withdrawal there was an end to the episodic and usually futile English interventions in French affairs. The agreement with the States shifted that relationship into a lower gear in which England became little more than a supplier of manpower to the Dutch military effort. An essential part of this agreement would remain in place after England made peace with Spain and would indeed continue in one form or another until the era of the Glorious Revolution. At the same time England effectively withdrew from active hostilities against Spain since the abortive naval expedition of 1597 was the last of its kind.

In consequence, relations between England and the provinces subsided into something more like routine diplomatic intercourse. The English agent, the experienced Gilpin, was now effectively as much an ambassador as his counterpart at Paris. Vere acted as an efficient intermediary for military matters. These consisted largely of regulating the movement of soldiers between England and the Low Countries, since Elizabeth continued to use the English forces there as a pool on which to draw in times of special need. A typical episode occurred during the invasion scare of 1599, when she required the dispatch home of 2,000 troops. There was the usual haggling with the Dutch authorities, who pooh-poohed the very existence of the menace (a skepticism that even Sir Robert Sidney shared). The Queen persisted; the States agreed to the dispatch of

[40] SP 84/57/94-97, 98, 104, 105, 119, 123, 147, 149-50, 168-69, 171-75, 186, 188, 201; 58/1, 7, 10, 19-21, 56, 64, 66, 70.
[41] SP 84/58/1, 68-69, 108-9, 213, 241-42.

1,000 men, but then with the dissipation of the threat the request was cancelled.[42]

These humdrum transactions were transformed when Elizabeth began to respond to the feelers put out by the Brussels government. As early as January 1599 the Flemish agent Coomans passed secretly over the North Sea and began a series of visits that gradually flowered into preparations for a formal and public treaty in the summer of 1600. As early as February the Dutch became aware of the comings and going of the agent, but it was not until April that Gilpin wrote officially to the States-General to inform them of Coomans's overtures and of the Queen's coolly correct response. By July there were rumors that Richardot would go to England, and Gilpin was reporting a strong belief that the Queen was about to make peace, even that commissioners had been appointed. Cecil, admitting the contacts made with Brussels, wrote to soothe the States, but they, as in the past, characterized these overtures as fraudulent and deceptive. Spain's real intentions, they asserted, were revealed by the invasion plans of recent months, plans checked by the Dutch expedition into Spanish waters.[43]

The Queen was being increasingly drawn to a serious exploration of Spanish intentions. A few weeks later she formally broached the possibility of an Anglo-Spanish peace with the Dutch government. This, of course, created much disquiet at The Hague. In particular, the possibility of a separate peace roused the spectres that had haunted the Dutch in 1598. What was to become of the cautionary towns? What about the effects of a freeing of traffic with the southern provinces? And, of course, what of the English troops in States' service? Not surprisingly, these moves revived the prospects of the pro-peace party in the provinces just at the moment when the archduke and the Brussels States-General were putting out feelers to the northerners. The States, anxious to retain their trust in the Queen but apprehensively nervous as to her intentions, reiterated the theme of Spanish duplicity and resorted to their favorite stalling device—reference to the provinces. As the months passed without any resolution, rumors floated about that the archduke had proclaimed freedom of trade with England, a sure sign that peace was already agreed. Sidney, assuming the peace would

[42] SP 84/59/7, 9–10, 17–18, 35, 40–41, 61.
[43] SP 84/58/9, 93–94, 120, 134, 138, 212; 59/29, 74–75.

be made, pressed the case for keeping Flushing as a replacement for Calais, but he did not doubt the Dutch would continue to fight so long as Holland and Zealand willed it. At the close of the year 1599 the Queen once again restated her case for the provinces's interests and promised consultation when the negotiations came to particulars.[44]

Through the spring of 1600 nerves remained on edge as hopes rose and fell. The Dutch feared that the archduke was so desperate for peace that he would concede much to England (although a Belgian magnate shrewdly observed that the peace would be valueless to the archduke unless it brought Holland and Zealand to terms). The prospect of an Anglo-Spanish settlement naturally turned Dutch attention to France. Vere warned that such an event would push the Dutch and the French into one another's arms; just at this moment the French found the means to make a small but significant payment on their debt to the States.[45]

While England and Spain continued their diplomatic sparring, the States, taking advantage of Spanish disarray, took to the field with the bold hope of seizing the Flemish coast and freeing Dutch trade from the ravages of the Dunkirkers. Their hopes that such a campaign might set off a revolt in the deeply discontented south were encouraged when the Brussels States-General sent a trumpet asking for the reception of commissioners. Almost at the same moment Maurice, having assembled the largest army seen in years, moved off across Flanders towards his goal, Dunkirk. Taken by surprise, he was forced into battle at Nieuport. The resulting victory was a barren one. Gilpin and other observers invoked divine favor as the only explanation for what, given Maurice's blunders, should have been a defeat. The English contingent had 800 casualties out of the 1,600 present; there was no hope for further action that year. The cost of the victory had outweighed its profits; more important, it had altogether dashed Dutch hopes of a successful conquest of the Flanders coast. This was bound to affect the calculations of the English government just as its commissioners set out for the meeting with their Spanish counterparts at Boulogne.[46]

In the provinces, given the failure of the campaign, the States-

---

[44] SP 84/59/80–81, 94–95, 98–99, 122–23, 124, 129–30, 140–41, 177, 191, 200–2, 216; 60/9, 53–54; Tex 1: 284.

[45] SP 84/60/53–54, 60–61, 78–79, 98–99, 106.

[46] SP 84/60/125, 155–56, 157, 159–60, 189–90, 205–6, 194; Tex 1: 284–93.

General, pressed by their counterpart at Brussels, felt obliged to agree at least to a meeting, held at Bergen-op-Zoom, just as the Anglo-Spanish conference at Boulogne broke up. It was no more successful; in this case it was the harsh demands of the northerners that speedily terminated the meeting.[47]

In the wake of these events Dutch affairs were in considerable disarray. The Spanish position in Flanders, so seemingly weak, had proved dismayingly strong; Maurice had not gained a foot of ground; the Dunkirk galleys continued to prey on Dutch shipping; and recent Spanish edicts banning trade into the southern provinces were squeezing the Zealanders very hard indeed. The States' financial affairs were in disorder; the repayments due to England were in arrears (£30,000 out of £60,000 due), the fleet unpaid. Worse still were the quarrels among the States' leaders. These so alarmed the English that Cecil wrote in his mistress's name, rebuking them for conduct unbecoming "a power fit to deal with great princes," while the Queen wrote directly to Maurice and the States-General.[48]

A momentary panic shook English confidence. Cecil reflected their views in a letter querying whether the Dutch were as absolutely committed to war as they alleged and casting doubt on their ability to wage it. In a postscript he went on to assure Maurice that the Queen "doth more inwardly free him [from] any cross disposition who is a prince of good blood and quality than she doth those others who she knows are most subject to rude and vulgar affections." In these phrases there surfaces the underlying disdain with which Elizabeth had always regarded the Dutch leadership. Gradually these dissensions quieted down, and by September Vere could write of reconciliation among the disputants and of public morale strong enough, he believed, to sustain even a lost battle. Responding to Cecil's letter, he found no inclination to peace with enemies who sought "to subvert God's true religion and the liberty of this land." As to their capacity to wage war he cited their prosperity, their united hatred of Spain, the strength of their geographical situation, and the opening of the East India trade.[49]

The developments of this eventful year served to show the con-

[47] SP 84/60/215, 216; Tex 1: 295–96.
[48] SP 84/58/117; 60/58–59, 285, 278–80, 287, 297, 298; Tex 1: 297.
[49] SP 84/60/302–3, 310–11.

tinuing divergences between the two allies, as they drifted further apart. Mutual hankering for peace was not sufficient to effect a settlement between Philip III and Elizabeth, but it was clear that if the Queen could find the right formula she would not hesitate to withdraw from the war. The sticking point was now not the Low Countries, but Ireland. There were still moments, as in the late summer of 1600, when the English were shaken by doubts about the States' powers of endurance, but these were passing tremors. The experience of the past two years, since 1598, had shown that with continuing French backing and with their own resources they could stand on their own feet without direct English assistance. The continuance of English forces in States' service and the fate of the cautionary towns were problems that could be resolved when the time came to deal with them, but the inclusion of the States in any peace settlement with Spain, which had still seemed a *sine qua non* two years ago, now faded out of English perceptions.

There was to be, however, one last flareup of Anglo-Dutch military collaboration. For years the isolated garrison of Ostend, the only Flemish seaport still in States' hands, had been a preoccupation of the English, who had supplied a large part of the garrison and usually its governor. Its importance to England lay in its position on the "invasion coast." Its loss, as Vere pointed out, would deprive the Engish of a choice haven on the Narrow Seas. Militarily its loss would relieve the constant pressure on the Spanish flank in Flanders which it provided and would force the building of stronger defenses for Zealand. The town could not be directly relieved by land, but it could be used as a base for forcing a battle, which, if won, would give control of the Flemish coast. From the Dutch point of view their lingering hopes of reducing Flanders required Ostend for their fulfillment. So for both allies there was a stake worth an all-out effort to hold the town.

The Dutch, taking advantage of the rupture of Anglo-Spanish negotiations, proposed to renew the assault on Flanders, checked at Nieuport in the previous year. The strategy would be two-pronged: a feint towards the Rhine to draw off enemy forces, while English and Dutch forces proceeded by sea to Ostend and used the town as a bridgehead for a breakout into Flanders. The English were asked for 3,000 to 4,000 men, and as bait the Dutch offered to make up the arrears on their repayment schedule. They also proposed, as an additional enterprise, a naval expedition against the Spanish ports, to end the invasion threat.[50]

The Queen responded with cautious approval; she was ready to provide the 3,000 men but would pay only for the costs of levying, arming, and transporting them; once on shore they would be the States' responsibility and were to be used only on the Flanders front. By June Maurice made his feint, against Berck, but the scheme went awry as the siege dragged on and the enemy got wind of the plan. Vere foresaw that they would ignore the diversion (even if Berck fell) and maintain their forces in Flanders. He saw no alternative now but to force a battle on the archduke, and that would require not only the use of English soldiers but also more flexibility as to where they might fight. He sought to convert Cecil to this variant strategy. Behind Vere's letter was the disagreement between Maurice on the one hand and Vere and Oldenbarnevelt on the other. The latter two were pushing the bolder scheme for invading Flanders, while Maurice, more cautious, intended only to relieve pressure on Ostend and remained cool to the larger plan. In fact, to Vere's fury, Maurice had broken with the earlier plans by ringing Berck with forts that needed a larger force and was now demanding the dispatch of English companies to join him.[51]

By this time an ominous reversal was taking place in Flanders; the archduke was moving forces against Ostend, and hopes for an offensive were fast being replaced by fears for the town's safety. The 3,000 men the Queen had offered for the siege of Sluys or Dunkirk were now desperately needed to secure Ostend. Maurice, stubbornly pursuing the siege of Berck, refused to release more than eight of the twenty English companies he had with him. Caron, no doubt on instructions from The Hague, reinforced Vere's plea for their dispatch to Flanders.[52]

By early July Vere had arrived to take command in person at Ostend; his concern now was to relieve the threat to the town, although he still had lingering hopes of an offensive. The Queen had sent 1,000 men, but 2,000 more were needed. Caron, echoing the views of the London magistrates, pointed out that a levy of 2,000 would provide a desirable purge of unwanted men "sans moeurs

[50] SP 84/61/75, 77–78, 81–82.
[51] SP 84/61/94, 102–3, 104, 122–23; Tex 1: 313ff.
[52] SP 84/61/125, 127–28, 129–30, 131–32.

ou gouvernment." The clamor for more men mounted when the arrival of Italian reinforcements for the archduke's army nullified the effects of Berck's fall. These urgencies communicated themselves to the court, and the Queen conceded the reinforcement of 2,000 men. It was fast becoming an article of faith that Ostend must be held, whatever the cost.[53]

Although the Queen was willing to commit these forces, she was indignant at Maurice's failure to continue his campaign after the fall of Berck and the failure of the Dutch ships to reinforce the Channel squadron she had mobilized to meet another invasion threat. Maurice did in fact move to besiege 's-Hertogenbosch but his pressure was not sufficient to draw off the besiegers of Ostend. Worse still, Vere suffered serious injury and had to withdraw to Middleburgh.[54]

At Ostend hopes rose and fell through the fall months. When Vere returned in September he thought the situation worse than when he had left. Maurice and the States continued to wrangle over possible diversionary moves. A flurry of hope that the French might provide some aid proved short-lived. In late October there was discussion of Vere's retirement from the Ostend command, but he hung on, although he believed nothing less than a reinforcement of at least 6,000 men would be required to lift the siege. He had lost all faith in any diversionary action. And indeed Maurice abandoned the siege of 's-Hertogenbosch in November and went into winter quarters. Vere predicted accurately that the present policy of holding on with a garrison of 3,000 to 4,000 men would in the long run be ruinous as the men became exhausted and the forts were eroded by the elements. The last spurt of active Anglo-Dutch military cooperation dwindled away futilely amidst mutual recrimination, disunity in the Dutch leadership, and English disillusionment with their allies' intentions.[55]

The final campaigning season of Elizabeth's reign repeated in general pattern the events of 1601. Concern over Ostend dominated the thinking of both governments. The Dutch asserted that they could not continue to bear the cost of the siege and rather desperately proposed an army royal of some 25,000 made up of Swiss, Germans, and an English contingent. The Queen was willing to

[53] SP 84/61/131–32, 151–52, 155, 159–60, 178, 191, 193; Tex 1: 314.
[54] SP 84/61/211–12.   [55] SP 84/61/314–15, 338–39, 358–60, 388–89, 340.

provide 3,000 new troops and to allow the States to fill up their depleted ranks by recruiting 3,000 more. Preparations went forward for a campaign in Brabant, but Maurice was unhappy at the Spanish refusal to fight, and his return empty-handed was a heavy disappointment after such a great effort. There would be nothing to show but another siege, that of Grave, which was likely to last the whole summer.[56]

Behind these moves there still lay as first priority the determination to break the siege of Ostend. Cecil pessimistically wrote that Ostend would ultimately fall because of the sea damage while the States preoccupied themselves elsewhere. (This was a persuasion shared by Oldenbarnevelt.) A series of desultory exchanges followed in which Maurice defended his moves as the best possible under the circumstances, a defense that the Queen was disposed to accept. In January 1603 the States were still reiterating their determination to hold Ostend, but there was an underlying lethargy and a deepening sense of futility. In the closing weeks of the reign Vere admitted that an offensive seemed overruled by nature and by the power of the rulers of these provinces. These last fruitless struggles to hold onto Ostend reflected the exhaustion of Dutch initiative and the drift towards the stalemate that in time would lead to the truce of 1609.[57]

The history of the Anglo-Dutch partnership between 1585 and the end of the Queen's reign stands in sharp contrast to English experience with their French ally. That whole history had been one of frustration and futility from the English point of view. In each instance in which cooperation was attempted, what seemed to be common purpose soon dissolved into mutual recrimination. In the Norman campaign Henry went off to confront Parma, leaving the siege of Rouen to wither on the vine and the English soldiers to perish in inaction. In Brittany the English were left largely to wander aimlessly across the province, their numbers ever dwindling. Only at Crozon was anything accomplished, and there it was only English initiative that set the enterprise going. At the first opportunity when she could safely retire, Elizabeth withdrew her forces.

But in the Low Countries—where Anglo-Dutch relations had been at a nadir in the wake of Leicester's ill-managed tenure of

[56] SP 84/62/44–45, 54, 66, 72, 79, 80–81, 84–86, 130–31, 138–39, 152–53, 160–61.
[57] SP 84/62/154–55, 160, 194, 205–7, 232–33, 234–35, 290–91, 303–4.

office—there had been a steady improvement in the relationship as each side gradually accommodated to the other. The English, albeit reluctantly, came to recognize the fact of Dutch independence and then slowly worked out a pattern of cooperation that was mutually beneficial. The utter dependence of the provinces on their English protector altered with the coming of the Armada, when Dutch ships played a significant role in its repulse by blockading the harbor mouths through which Parma would have to issue for his planned invasion. The provinces' promotion from protectorate to ally was even more powerfully promoted by their successful exploitation of the breathing space that Spanish preoccupation first with the Armada and then with France gave to them. From that point on the English were progressively more willing to yield the initiative in military matters to the Dutch and allow the use of their troops for campaigns planned and executed by the Dutch commanders. The *quid pro quo* for this was the right to withdraw English soldiers for campaigns in France, Spain, or Ireland when the need arose and Dutch naval assistance in the campaigns against the Spanish.

The serendipitous creation of a trained English soldiery that served as a surrogate professional standing army was of immense benefit to the government, even though the risk that both Dutch and English would be competing at the same time for the same troops was obvious and the occasions recurrent. But each side developed a pragmatic acceptance of the other's necessities and a kind of rhythm emerged that served to ease the strains of competition into a pattern of reciprocity, the English yielding to Dutch necessity in the Friesland campaign and the Dutch to English needs in Brittany or for the Cadiz voyage. The treaty of 1598, made when the urgencies of war had diminished, was another testimony to the strength of common interest and the pragmatic recognition of changing circumstances that cemented this partnership.

Unlike the Anglo-French collaboration, this was a partnership that yielded immediate and tangible benefits to each party. It is arguable that the provinces would not have been able to withstand Spanish pressure without the men and the money that England supplied, and that the English could reasonably claim a decisive role in the establishment of Dutch independence. Moreover, the relatively passive role that the Dutch were willing to assume meant that they were free to deploy these resources to their own best advantage and able to exploit their ally's assistance without granting any liens on their future as an independent state.

For the English the long-term advantages were equally important. The experience of the years since 1572 had made the establishment of an independent regime in the provinces an axiom of English policy. As Hatton argued before Parliament in 1586, England would not be safe if Spain were to "bring the Low Countries into a monarchal seat." In the same speech he implied that no great power would be a welcome neighbor in those quarters.[58] It was that fear that led to the first hesitant aid to the rebels from 1572 onward and the same logic that stood behind the sponsorship of Anjou in the early 1580's. By 1585 it was painfully clear that only direct English intervention could prevent the restoration of full Spanish power in the Low Countries, wielded by a monarch whose well-founded suspicion of English intentions was fast hardening into relentless enmity. The events of 1588 confirmed the English conviction that the Queen could not risk the reestablishment of effective Spanish authority in the rebellious provinces and that she could not consider the making of peace until there was full assurance that the provinces could sustain their own freedom from Spanish rule. By 1598 it was beginning to become apparent that such a goal did not necessarily demand a general peace, that there was a half-way house in which England could withdraw from active participation in the Low Countries campaigns without breaking altogether the cords that bound her and the States-General in a common interest.

[58] D'Ewes, 409.

PART V

THE THREE KINGDOMS

FIGURE 2. *Sir Richard Bingham, Governor of Connaught* (National Portrait
Gallery, London)

FIGURE 3. *Sir George Carew, Earl of Totnes, President of Munster* (National Portrait Gallery, London)

CHAPTER 15

THE NORTHERN NEIGHBOR

1581-1603

SCOTLAND, like Ireland, emerged only gradually into English consciousness in the sixteenth century. With the end of English attempts at conquest in the fourteenth century, relations lapsed into a sullen wariness, punctuated by bouts of open warfare, usually during periods of hostility with France. Hopes of improvement in relations raised by Margaret Tudor's marriage were set back by Flodden Field. It was Henry VIII's ham-handed intervention in the 1540's that set in motion a twenty-year train of events that altered the basis of Anglo-Scottish relations. His attempts to bully the Scots led only to French intervention on an unprecedented scale. The threat that that offered to England was ultimately averted, less by English effort than by a happy combination of circumstances—the rise of Scottish Protestantism and French civil disorder.

From 1560 onwards the ancient hostility between the kingdoms was gradually displaced by a sense of common interest based on a common religion. The return of Mary Stuart in 1561 threatened renewed tension, but she could not undo the religious revolution and upon her fall Scotland was ruled for twenty years by a series of regents, all committed to the maintenance of a reformed regime and necessarily to collaboration with England. Their power was constantly threatened by the existence of a continuing Catholic party, lacking religious leadership but consisting of a considerable body of nobles who, at least nominally Catholic, favored a Marian restoration and intrigued on the Continent to that end.

During these years of the royal minority Scotland could hardly be said to have had a place in the European comity of nations. In the absence of a guiding royal will, domestic politics became almost entirely a matter of noble rivalries, of incessant factional struggle for control of the boy King. These preoccupations meant that the rulers of Scotland had neither inclination nor opportunity to pursue a coherent or considered relationship with the outside world. The Protestant nobles who controlled the government looked anxiously to England for backing, while their Catholic opponents were reduced to fruitless intrigues in which they solicited the support of the Guises or the Habsburgs. This impotence suited the English well enough, since it was their consistent aim to isolate the northern kingdom from Continental influences. Many of Elizabeth's advisors urged a considered patronage of the Protestant leaders, but the Queen preferred to remain aloof from the endless squabbles of the Scots politicians and to content herself with intervention only when there was direct threat of French influence, as in 1573 in the siege of Edinburgh castle or at the end of the 1570's in the d'Aubigny episode.

By the end of the 1580's the situation was rapidly changing. The regency was now at an end; the normal condition of monarchical politics began to reappear as the young King sought to assert his own will. There was now a new sense of purpose, of direction, in Scottish policy as the King's ambitions revealed themselves and became a focus for action. They were from the beginning necessarily shaped by his special position. To James, as to his mother, it was more important that he was the heir of England than that he was King of Scotland. It was on his accession to the greater throne that his eyes were fixed. Of course, for the time being he was solely a Scottish ruler, but unlike his predecessors, the first five Jameses, he saw England not as a threat but as an opportunity. In the short run he must use every occasion that offered itself as a means for securing the certainty of succession, but never at the cost of alienating either the English queen, her councillors, or her subjects. In the meantime, he had his hands full with the task of establishing his authority in his native kingdom.

The Queen saw Scottish affairs in quite another light. For the past twenty years she had treated her neighbor almost as a British governor-general of India might have dealt with a neighboring native state in the early nineteenth century: as something less than a sovereign power, little more than a colony. But now two things— the reappearance of a King and the coming of the Spanish war— gave to Scotland bargaining power it had not had before and demanded of the Queen a more considered attention to her cousin and his realm. She had no interest in bringing James in as an active ally in the war, but his benevolent neutrality was a matter of prime importance to her. Scotland could too easily become that postern gate by which the enemy might break into her own realm. Like Ireland it could become to England what the Low Countries were to Spain. Therefore, it was imperative to be assured of the active cooperation of the Scottish crown in quashing any threat to the island's security, either by invasion or by conspiracy. This meant having the assured goodwill of James.

From the Queen's point of view this was a relatively simple matter. She knew well enough what were James's hopes for the English succession, and she assumed that these alone were potent enough to bend him to her will. She knew she held a trump card; her favor could make or break his chances for the English succession, and she did not believe he would be so unwise as to jeopardize those chances. She would, of course, never play the card, but, held up her sleeve, it had a sovereign potency. Her assurance that she held the upper hand in their relationship echoed in her letters to James; patronizing, even hectoring, she was always the mistress of the royal trade, instructing a somewhat backward, although not hopeless, apprentice. These in bold outlines were the terms in which the two sovereigns stood at the beginning of the 1590's, and, although much would transpire in the remaining years of Elizabeth's life, basically nothing in that relationship would alter.

The coming of war in 1585 made urgent a clear understanding with Scotland, and the veteran Randolph went north in 1586 to negotiate a treaty of alliance, offensive and defensive, to protect religion and assist one another in case of invasion. An additional letter under the Privy Seal assured James of financial assistance, without specifying a sum. In practice this came to an amount somewhere between £2,000 and £5,000 annually, some twenty payments over the years 1586–1603, averaging a modest £2,600 each. The agreement remained a treaty in potency and not in act; no forces were mobilized under its terms, but it provided a framework, a reference point, to which both parties could turn in the conduct of their relations with one another.[1]

The first test of the treaty came with the execution of James's mother. National feeling, not to mention common decency, required a show of indignation, but after a few face-saving gestures James retreated and relations were restored. In 1588 an overzealous envoy made a series of sweeping promises of money, an English title, and a guard to be paid for by the Queen. These promises—and common prudence—led the King to take precautionary measures against the Spaniard, none of which needed to be put to the test. The Armada gone, Elizabeth promptly repudiated her agent's unauthorized promises.[2]

In the post-Armada year English attention was focused on Scotland when in February 1589 the government intercepted the correspondence of a group of Scottish Catholic lords with Parma and Philip II, soliciting an invasion and promising support of such an action. The English Council promptly wrote to their agent at Edinburgh to require the imprisonment of these nobles, the most important of whom was the Earl of Huntly. He was briefly restrained and then released, to the anger of the English. What in London seemed a black and white distinction between Papist and Protestant, between treason and loyalty, in Edinburgh was seen as a whole rainbow spectrum of hues. Party labels were not really applicable in a world in which personal antipathies, family alliance, or mere opportunism counted for as much as religious preference. More important still was the weakness of a crown that lacked independent (and reliable) instruments of enforcement against a nobility that did not hesitate to use force against the sovereign. As an English observer wrote, "The King is not able to command his subjects by force as others; they obey him—at least the most of them—in slight matters not touching life," and Burghley, although displeased at James's proceedings, recognized that "the nobility there are not acquainted with absolute government of their King but rather are themselves in a sort absolute."[3]

Finally, there was the personal factor, the affection that James

[1] H. G. Stafford, *James VI of Scotland and the Throne of England* (New York, 1940), 293.

[2] *Calendar of State Papers Relating to Scotland and Mary, Queen of Scots, 1547–1603*, ed. Joseph Bain et al. (13 vols., London, 1898–1969) 9: 599.

[3] *Ibid.*, 682–98; *CSPSc* 10: 1, 11, 14.

felt for Huntly. The upshot was that instead of the condign punishment of the conspirators that Elizabeth had requested, there followed a political farce. The King dismissed Huntly's behavior as a
mere peccadillo of youth, and the whole episode was treated in personal rather than political terms. But the affair took a more serious
turn when the Earl of Bothwell, nominally a Protestant but allied
with the Catholic nobles for this occasion, appeared in arms and
joined Huntly. This demonstration had less to do with confessional
differences than with court politics; it was an attack on a common
political foe of both Bothwell and the Catholic party, Chancellor
Maitland. Jolted into action, the King, accompanied by a force of
Protestant lords, marched north and brought Huntly to submission
at the Brig o' Dee. The Queen was sufficiently mollified to provide
£3,000 "to pay for horsemeat," but in fact no serious attempt was
made to disarm or neutralize the Catholic party.[4] James's somewhat
cavalier attitude towards the plot may have been closer to the realities of the situation than the vociferous alarm of London. Conspiracy was an occupational habit among the Scottish nobility, and
James knew his men well enough to assess the real dangers. Scottish
politics were more violent but also more casual than English.

For the next year or so, James was absorbed in the business of his
marriage, a matter in which the English government had no major
stake. But when an alarm, occasioned by a Spanish ship at Leith,
occurred, the Queen was roused to the writing of another monitory
letter, referring to "his broken country so much infected with the
malady of strangers' humors and to receive no medicine so well
compounded as if the owner make the mixture appropriated to the
quality of the sickness." She warned him "that the ulcers were too
much skinned with the doulceness of your application." Once
again, the exaggerated fears of the English court proved false.
When yet another English outcry was raised at the end of 1590,
however, again implicating Huntly in dealings with Spain, James
insisted that no great danger would arise from the earl. To Elizabeth's self-satisfied comment that she thanked God for councillors
who always advanced the public weal, James replied rather mildly
that the work to be done by a King of Scotland would require three

[4] *CSPSc* 10: 3, 6–7, 11–12, 17–19, 23ff., 58, 60–61; HMC, *Hatfield* 13: 409–10,
412–13; John Bruce, ed., *Letters of Queen Elizabeth and King James VI of Scotland*,
Camden Soc. 46 (1849), 110.

reigns to accomplish. In December 1590 Huntly received full pardon for the charges made in the preceding year.[5]

The volatile politics of the court of Edinburgh took an especially bizarre turn in 1591. For the next couple of years they were dominated by the antics of Francis Stuart, Earl of Bothwell, the rogue male among the Scottish nobility. Descended from a bastard of James V, nephew to Mary Stuart's third husband, he had played more than one role: as the champion of the Kirk in the mid-1580's, as enemy to Arran in 1585, and then, changing sides, as an ally of Huntly and the Catholic lords in the Brig o' Dee affair. His ambition was unlimited, his scruples nonexistent, and his behavior unpredictable. His one consistent passion was a hatred of Chancellor Maitland. From the time of the King's return from Denmark in 1590, friction between sovereign and subject grew. The King's antipathy towards him hardened into determined hostility, and there ensued a long drawn-out duel between the two men. Bothwell found it hard to make his peace with the King after the Brig o' Dee affair; he talked of going abroad. James sought to acquire control of Bothwell's border lordship of Liddesdale, his power base, but without success. The earl retained his position on the border and cultivated the goodwill of the English.

In April 1591 the king struck hard when Bothwell was accused, tried, and condemned on a charge of witchcraft, practiced in order to kill his sovereign. James offered to let the earl off with exile, but Bothwell escaped from prison. There followed a dizzying sequence of events that reveals in stark clarity the disorders of the Scottish political world. In spite of being proclaimed a traitor, Bothwell was able to move freely about the country, appearing at various times in the streets of Edinburgh, on the borders, in Caithness, and on the sands of Leith. During 1592 he launched two assaults on the King's palaces at Holyrood and Falkland and was still at large in January 1593. Nothing could more vividly illuminate the limits of royal power in this violence-ridden society.[6]

In early 1592 Bothwell's actions were for a time overshadowed by another bloody event, the murder of the Stewart Earl of Moray

---

[5] Stafford, 53; APC 1589–90: 250–51; Bruce, 57–58; CSPSc 10: 435, 439.
[6] For Bothwell's career, see DNB and Stafford, 59; CSPSc 10: 297–98, 307, 311–12, 325, 331–32, 350, 359, 432, 501–20, 550, 584–85, 609–10, 614, 708.

by his family's enemy, the Earl of Huntly. The English government hoped to use this episode to destroy the Catholic leader and backed the Kirk spokesmen in bringing pressure upon James, but to no avail. Even the revelation by the English of more intercepted correspondence and of a proposed Spanish attack made no impression.[7]

Through the summer of 1592 Scottish affairs remained in utmost confusion. Bothwell made another assault on the royal household at Falkland in July. Chancellor Maitland, the King's principal minister and the mainstay of orderly government, was driven from court by his enemies while the various factions in the court jostled for power in a bewildering tussle in which first one and then another momentarily rose to the surface, only to sink again. In this confusion the English agent, Bowes, struggled manfully to bring James to act against the Catholic lords, but without success. Try as he would, he could not find the right instrument to accomplish his government's ends. The king gave fair words but failed to turn them into deeds. In large part this failure arose from sheer lack of power, in part from the royal partiality to some of the main actors, such as Huntly. And, as earlier, the king inclined to a less alarmist view of the real dangers that the schemings of the Huntly faction aroused. He had first-hand knowledge of the instability of their alliances, the limitations of their resources, and the sheer fecklessness of much of their activity.[8]

Unable to move the King, the English began to turn to alternative tactics to achieve their end. In the past it had been easy to coerce the Scottish government of the day by backing its opponents with money and covert encouragement. But to coerce and humiliate a reigning monarch whose goodwill was essential to English interests was a risky businesss. Nevertheless, the English began to think about using Bothwell for just this purpose. He had sought English aid and received at least surreptitious encouragement, although officially London had frowned on his actions and may even have aided James with cannon from Carlisle against the earl and his confederates. But in the fall of 1592 the English border officials, under instructions from Westminster, opened communications with the

[7] Stafford, 63–66; *CSPSc* 10: 683–93, 697–99, 725–26.
[8] *Ibid.*, 707–10, 724, 773, 775.

earl. In January 1593 James was complaining of the countenance given the errant earl in England.[9]

By then, friction over Bothwell had been overshadowed by a new development. In December 1592 English attention was once again fastened on Scotland with the discovery of a series of letters seized from George Ker, an intermediary in the correspondence between the Scots Catholic lords and Continental confederates, including Cardinal Allen. Most important was a series of blank sheets, subscribed by the Earls of Angus, Huntly, and Errol. They were to be filled in with assurances to Philip II and the Pope of full support for a force of 30,000 men to be sent next spring. The plot envisaged the enforced cooperation of James but not his deposition.[10]

Initially the King responded with vigor, imprisoning Angus and summoning the other principals to enter into detention. The Queen made haste to dispatch an ambassador, Lord Burgh, to strengthen the King's resolution and to punish the conspirators. In his instructions Burgh was commanded to organize an association of Protestant lords sworn to serve the King against his enemies and those of the state religion. It was to be done with circumspection and secrecy so as to veil English intervention; the Kirk leaders were to be consulted in the enterprise. The instructions also ordered Burgh to make representations on behalf of Bothwell, to consider whether he might not be more useful living than dead. At the same time the Queen sent an agent to deal secretly with Bothwell, offering him protection and expressing her belief that he was the victim of his enemies.[11]

By the time Burgh arrived, James was already on his way north to pursue the rebel earls. (Angus had escaped from prison; the others were taking refuge in the wilds of Caithness.) Burgh remained in Edinburgh until the King returned a month later; a band of nobles against the Catholic lords had been subscribed in his absence. The earls had retreated to the hills and then ventured out again as soon as the King went south; hence the journey had accomplished little or nothing. James, as usual full of promises, excused his failure

---

[9] Ibid., 724; 11: 17, 19; 12: 467; The Border Papers, ed. J. Bain (2 vols., Edinburgh, 1894–96) 1: 402–4, 406–8.

[10] CSPSc 11: 1–15, 16, 23, 43; The Warrender Papers, ed. A. L. Cameron and R. S. Rait (2 vols., Edinburgh, 1931–32) 2: 188–89.

[11] CSPSc 11: 15, 25, 44, 45–48, 69–70; see also ibid., 61–64 and 76, for Bothwell's declaration of innocence and thanks to the Queen.

by lack of means to deal with the pro-Spanish faction. As the ambassador observed, the nobility "are so interallied that, notwithstanding the religion they profess, they tolerate the opposite courses of the adverse parties and excuse or cloak the faults committed." The King now showed himself more keen in the pursuit of Bothwell than of the Catholic confederates but intimated that, if Elizabeth would restrain the earl in England while giving James aid, he would move against the Papists. An ambassador was sent to England with promises of a parliament at which the Catholic lords would be condemned, coupled with a request for money to pay 600 soldiers for six months to carry out the condemnations. Bowes strongly feared that, unless the money was forthcoming, Huntly and his friends would recover favor. The Parliament, when it met, took no action, on the grounds of insufficient evidence. This move followed news from London that the Queen had refused the requested financial aid for a force of soldiers.[12]

At this point Bothwell made another surprise appearance, this time at Holyrood House, throwing himself at the startled King's feet with a plea for pardon. He was granted the royal grace and after a hasty trial acquitted of the witchcraft charges. This coup delivered the court into the hands of the Stewart faction, the longtime enemies of Huntly and the Catholic lords. Bowes was now instructed to get in touch with the latter, although he was also to keep Bothwell on a string. The latter, upon his pardon, had proposed to the Queen that she should back him and an associated band of aristocrats in an enterprise against the Catholic faction. They promised not to act without royal Scottish authority, although for the present their intentions would be kept secret from the King. Elizabeth gave a reserved approval to their enterprise, but without any promise of money. At the same time she also expressed a hope that the Catholic earls might be brought to submit through her intervention. What the Queen sought was a settlement brought about by English influence in which all parties would be made to feel their dependence on English goodwill.[13]

James himself was solemnly reproached by Elizabeth for having "so variously and uncertainly proceeded that no good thereof has followed," and for having allowed himself to be bullied by a faction.

[12] *Ibid.*, 60, 65, 70–71, 72–73, 75–76, 85–87, 96–97, 99, 101, 114, 124, 125, 127.
[13] *Ibid.*, 141, 144, 150, 153–55, 157–59.

She called on him to settle on his councillors so that she should not continue to be confused as to his intentions "by variety of bruits, by contrariety in his actions and his sudden changes of favor." It was a well-orchestrated program of pressure on several fronts, all intended to bend James to Elizabeth's will. Bothwell's reconciliation with the King was short-lived. Within a month the weather cocks of the court were reversing direction, and the King was offering a pardon to the earl only on condition he depart the kingdom. Bothwell balked at the terms and refused to leave unless his properties were fully restored and future possession assured. At court Huntly's cause was favorably looked on and the prospect of his pardon heightened. Bowes continued to play both sides of the street, keeping open his lines with Huntly and his friends while espousing the cause of Bothwell with the King, keeping contact with him and opposing the interests of the Catholic lords, whose cause was now to be tried in Parliament. The King was urged by Elizabeth to deal firmly with the rebel earls but to admit them to favor if they renounced the old faith. She made the same point to them, rejecting their general offers of submission and insisting on an unreserved acceptance of the official faith.

The King was now moving actively on the earls' behalf; a convention was summoned for their trial and strong measures taken to prevent effective opposition. Reproached by Bowes, James frankly admitted that, pressed as he was by both Bothwell and the Catholic earls, he had to make a choice; he could not suppress both parties. Hence he had opted to come to terms with the stronger, "those three earls being three of the most ancient and strong noblemen in this realm." The ensuing convention did in fact pass an act of oblivion for the earls' offenses in the Spanish blanks affair, but it also imposed exile on any who would not subscribe to the articles of religion by next 1 February (but without loss of property). Correspondingly the recent royal pardon to Bothwell was rescinded and his immediate exile ordered.[14]

This act moved Elizabeth to the dispatch of yet another ambassador, Lord Zouche, with instructions to protest vehemently against the treatment of the earls, implying bluntly that this meant that the King was willing to listen to Spanish overtures. The King was

[14] *Ibid.*, 170–71, 178–81, 183–84, 196, 197, 209, 210–11, 211–12, 213–14, 216–18, 218–20, 222.

warned that the Queen would take all necessary measures to meet any foreign invasion of the island. Zouche had a second instruction. He was to get in touch with "certain lords and gentlemen there to maintain the established religion." They were to be told that Elizabeth would place forces in readiness on the borders and to inquire as to their willingness to cooperate. A half-promise of money was to be dangled in front of them. The Queen had now moved to the old tactic of deliberately patronizing an opposition to the Scottish government, this time in opposition to the King himself.[15]

Zouche took with him another of the Queen's stinging letters to James, in which she referred to a "seduced king, abusing council and wry guided kingdom." She doubted whether "shame or sorrow have had the upper hand" when she read his letter to her. "Who could suppose that your answer should satisfy any one with her four senses let alone five?" She continued in a familiar vein, urging him to act the king against these obvious traitors, and expressing astonishment that he could bear such humiliation. Burghley, in a letter intended for Maitland, urged the case against the King's actions. Hinting that James was about to deal with Spain, changing religion to obtain support for his claim to the English crown, the lord treasurer argued that God had upheld the Queen against all kinds of enemies for thirty-five years and undoubtedly would continue His protection. He went on further to remind the Scots of the English statutes that disallowed the title of anyone who attempted to impeach the Queen's estate during her life. There were, he reminded the Scots, other competitors for the succession. Elizabeth rounded off this correspondence with another letter of measured rebuke, ending in a blunt warning that James could have no contacts with foreign rulers "but we shall one way or other understand it. Persuade yourself that what has been or is determined, be it much or little, contrived by many or few, we are not so ignorant of it as to be found hereafter either deluded or unprovided."[16]

James continued a "wonderful uncertain course . . . which maketh her [the Queen] not a little to seek what way to run with him." Elizabeth now began to encourage the Bothwell faction to move. In a letter from Burghley they were warned that the Queen could not be a "beginner or inciter" of any open opposition to James, but if

[15] *Ibid.*, 239–41, 241–42, 244.
[16] *Ibid.*, 248, 251–52, 258–59; Bruce, 98–100.

they were to remove the evil instruments who were the cause of danger, they could count on her support. Clearly, she would not be an actor; that would be fatal to their purposes, but once successful they could trust to her patronage. Burghley firmly denied rumors that the Queen was dealing with their opponents. Money was promised for this assistance. (Cecil's marginal comment on the draft was, "this argueth the Queen would have her ministers to do what she would not avow.") Elizabeth as usual was desperate to preserve appearances and the dignity of princes. As the Treasurer wrote, "Any prince may be an assistant as long as subjects' quarrels one against another are in question, and not private actions against monarchs." Their actions must "accord with reverent regard to their anointed prince."[17]

James eluded the Queen's threats by withdrawing the pardon to the earls but insisting he could not prosecute them with rigor unless the Queen shall "enable us to this action." The Queen dismissed this as more of the same empty words she had heard before, and the ambassador, Zouche, was told to push the conspirators to action, with the reiterated warning that it must be of their own initiative; hence she would not provide them with "start-up" funds. James was again told that the Queen would assist those Scots who opposed foreign conspiracy.[18]

Unfortunately her envoys at Edinburgh (Zouche and Bowes) overstepped themselves by accepting a jewel in pawn from Bothwell; they were told to squirm out of this as best they might. Elizabeth continued firmly to deny any dealings with Bothwell and his allies, but she noted that the Catholic earls and their supporters were formally received at the Scottish court. It would not be surprising, she intimated, that she should favor those patriots who opposed Papist and Spanish plots. The ambassadors were ordered to press the King unmercifully, extracting if possible a written promise of firm action. There followed a stormy audience with James, in which he burst out that they treated him not as a sole sovereign but as the Queen's lieutenant, who had to account to her for his actions. Angry words passed on both sides, but James would concede nothing beyond promises to take legal action. If that failed he would use force, but that would require English financial assistance.[19]

[17] CSPSc 11: 266–67, 269, 270, 283.　　　[18] Ibid., 273, 276, 279, 281.
[19] Ibid., 285–87, 288–94, 295–97, 303.

Bothwell now roused himself to action and marched on Edinburgh with a force of some 600 foot; they skirmished successfully outside the capital but, when reinforcements from Fife failed to turn up, retired to the borders. The English agent was in despair at this ill-prepared and ill-conducted attempt, which augured poorly for future performance. Zouche returned emptyhanded and Bowes, now *persona non grata* at court, begged for recall. The hope of bullying James into compliance by direct coercion, backed by English sponsorship, had failed.[20]

It was now James's turn to dispatch his ambassadors, laden with grievances, to the English court. Elizabeth's complaints about James's failure to make good his promises were now matched by the Scots King's anger at the public entertainment in which the English border officials had flaunted their support for Bothwell. This led to nothing but more parrying between the two sovereigns. The Queen dangled the possibility of money as bait to secure action by the King. The waters were troubled again by the discovery that Spanish gold had been dispatched to the earls.[21] At last the King, hard pressed by the Kirk, felt himself strong enough to make a move, and in the Parliament held in June 1594 the Catholic earls were condemned and their lands forfeited. In the topsy-turvy manner of Scottish politics, Bothwell now swung around to considering an alliance with the earls as a means of blackmailing the king into concession. Initially he met with them and concerted plans for joint action. This led to an abortive scheme to attack Holyrood House, kill Sir George Hume, and kidnap the Dutch ambassadors at the royal christening. Its discovery ruined Bothwell's position and badly upset the Catholics' plans.[22]

Events lurched in another direction with the secret arrival of a Jesuit and a company of strangers, English and Spanish, near Aberdeen; when some of them were detained by the city magistrates, Huntly descended on the town and forced their surrender. The English government saw in this event yet another move in the general Spanish strategy. Thwarted in her invasion plans, Spain was now turning to subversion in her neighbors' kingdoms, both France and Scotland, hoping in the latter case to gain entrance to England. The King and his council were alarmed enough to summon an

[20] *Ibid.*, 304–6.   [21] *Ibid.*, 313–14, 332–35.
[22] *Ibid.*, 356–62, 363, 369, 375, 431–33, 434, 445.

expedition against the rebel earls, now assembling in force. But James began immediately dragging his feet, alleging the needs of the harvest, autumnal storms, and so on. A force of 1,000 men, assembled under Lords Argyll, Athol, and Forbes, balked at action and Bowes heard that the Spanish were proposing to them, through Huntly, alliance, religious toleration, and Spanish aid in men and money. The proposal was coupled with a threat of a trade embargo and help for the Scottish Catholics.[23]

After more delays it was finally decided that Argyll should lead his own clan against Huntly and the Gordons in the north while the King made his way to Aberdeen with another force. In spite of Argyll's defeat by his opponent, the King moved northwards to Aberdeen and laid waste the Gordon country, destroying the earl's house and those of his partners. The Catholic lords, now bound to Bothwell in a pact to seize the King, remained at large, and expensive forces had to be maintained in the north. Hopes that Elizabeth would provide a subsidy were dashed, and much bitter resentment ensued on the King's part. Nevertheless, pressure was maintained on the rebel lords and, after repeated delays, they finally embarked for the Continent. Bothwell, too, was run to ground and forced to make his departure overseas.[24]

The long, drawn-out crisis of the Spanish blanks was finally over. English concern in Scottish affairs receded rapidly. As James rather bitterly observed, now that the Catholic lords were gone, England would deny him aid as a king needless. Bowes, who had been begging for relief for months, was allowed to go home in October 1594, and thereafter England was represented at Edinburgh by one of his servants, who acted as an intelligencer and a conveyer of messages from the English government. Bowes's departure marked the end of a phase in Anglo-Scottish relations; it also coincided with a new epoch in Scottish politics. The abortive sponsorship of Bothwell was to be the last in a long line of English interventions in their northern neighbor's affairs. This traditional tactic of deliberate interference had now to be abandoned, as Scotland for the first time in decades exhibited the unwonted spectacle of effective royal leadership. James had refused to be bullied into actions

[23] *Ibid.*, 383–84, 386, 389–400, 401, 407–10.
[24] *Ibid.*, 432, 443–44, 457–61, 468, 469–70, 482, 483, 490, 515, 522, 534, 545, 556, 559, 575, 580–81.

that he foresaw would be futile, and he skillfully fended off English pressure, biding his time until he could act effectively. It was a triumph for him both in domestic politics and in his relations with Elizabeth. Increased mastery at home gave him more leverage with his English cousin.

With the death of Chancellor Maitland in late 1595 the King moved to assert his administrative and political control of affairs. The chancellor's office remained unfilled and the group of administrators collectively known as the Octavians took over. Contemporaries noted a new tone in the court, "now His Majesty begins to be seen king and to reign." Bowes later wrote of the "present calm in this estate after the late blasts and expectation of storms" and of the King's "good course for the advancement of religion, justice, peace and the increase of his revenues." The experiment of the Octavians and their financial reforms was to last but a year, and Scottish politics would remain as bewilderingly fluid as ever, but there were to be no more armed uprisings against the King, no more Bothwells roaming the countryside and disturbing the peace. In the remaining years before his accession to the English throne James would turn much of his energies to the task of taming the Kirk, with notable success.[25]

This enterprise, although primarily a domestic matter, had its effect on English policy. Bowes had hardly returned to Edinburgh in the early spring of 1596 when the inflammatory sermons of David Black, a minister at St. Andrews (who among other things declared Queen Elizabeth to be no more than an atheist), led to a confrontation between King and Kirk. The attempt to punish Black reawakened the underlying controversy as to the relative powers of crown and Kirk and led to a tumult in Edinburgh. This was followed by a royal proclamation roundly asserting the King's final judicial authority over the clergy, including punishment for seditious words spoken in the pulpit. The royal power was given public demonstration when, on the return of Huntly from abroad, the ministers of Aberdeen and Elgin were ordered to receive the earl's submission to the Kirk. The earl entered Aberdeen in state, restored in favor but submissive to the royal will. To all this the English envoy was but a spectator, and in the aftermath, at Robert

[25] *CSPSc* 12: 102, 116, 160–62; Maurice Lee, *John Maitland of Thirlestane and the Foundation of the Stuart Despotism in Scotland* (Princeton, 1959), 18–19.

Cecil's command, he exhorted the moderates among the clergy to press for a quiet end to these disturbances. The Queen on the other hand still looked to the clergy as allies and wrote to James urging that, at a time when Papist plots were stirring and the banished lords returned, he ought not to be too severe on those who, whatever their rashness, were inexorably tied to his cause. The zealous supporters of the Reformed faith, alarmed at what they saw as Papist influences at court, looked to England for support. The English ambassador was seen to be too closely identified with the clerical cause, and it was thought that possibly he should withdraw, leaving only an intelligencer in Edinburgh.[26]

This move was not necessary, but English influence in Scottish affairs was necessarily reduced by the weakness of its traditional ally, the Kirk, now divided within itself between radicals and moderates. There was little reason, however, for English apprehensions. The Catholic lords were much reduced in power, and content now to sue for bare toleration. England had less to fear from outside intervention. The remaining elements of stress in Anglo-Scottish relations lay as much as anything in the King's anxieties over the English succession. If these could be allayed, he would no longer be tempted to dabble in underhand approaches to Continental princes. There had been "trafficking from Rome and Spain about something and nothing" by Scots exiles and an overture to Spain and the Papacy by an agent almost certainly not authorized by James. The King had hoped to enter on the European stage by alliance with France; he had hoped also to be included in the Anglo-French treaty of alliance, but his overtures had been snubbed by Elizabeth. A similar bid to the States-General had been checked by English intervention.

These moves by James mirrored a complex of motives. In part they were no doubt intended simply to secure recognition of his place in the society of European sovereigns. Second, recognition by the Continental powers might be used to bolster his position as heir to Elizabeth. And last the King, frustrated by his impotence *vis à vis* his southern neighbor, sought whatever small leverages he could muster—seldom amounting to more than nuisance value—to prod the English Queen into some measure of concession. Her obstinate refusal to grant any open recognition of his claims drove James to

[26] *CSPSc* 12: 404–7, 410–11, 418, 424, 426, 448, 466, 475, 487.

continuing explorations in international politics—all of them irritating, but none of them truly dangerous to English interests.[27]

During these last years of the Queen's reign the English government maintained a suspicious watchfulness towards its northern neighbor. Shifts and changes in the endlessly fluid political groupings of the Scottish court were carefully monitored with a wary eye for any combination that might threaten English interests. More particularly this meant the predominance of any faction thought to have Spanish connections or Papist leanings. In April 1599 the Queen, "seeing the state of the kingdom [Scotland] is so subject to faction and alteration," asked for a list of notables who were patriotic, sound in religion, and able to mount resistance to pro-Spanish influences in the court. Sir William Bowes wrote reassuringly that Protestants outnumbered Catholics by two to one in the country at large. The temporary importance of the latter in the court would not, he was certain, be long-lived.[28]

A typical agenda of Anglo-Scottish business comes from May 1599 in the record of an audience of the English ambassador with James. The recently rehabilitated earl (now marquis) of Huntly had just been promoted in the peerage. To the Queen's suspicious interrogation the King replied that this was a move to assure the nobleman's continued loyalty to church and crown. A rumor that he was to be keeper of the prince and of Edinburgh Castle was dismissed as "mere imagination." The activities of Scottish agents on the Continent, on which Elizabeth cast a suspicious eye, were explained away as merely commercial in one case, as entirely unauthorized in another (the case of Pury Ogilvy, the Scot who had turned up at Rome with an alleged commission from James to the Pope). Disputes with the Kirk (traditionally allies of the English) were now settled. A Scottish Jesuit (and a Gordon), recently returned from the Continent, had been expelled. Allegations that councillors were unsound in religion were rebutted; all received the sacrament. Recent shifts in offices had been at the incumbents' request. English exiles had been admitted to the kingdom solely out of "princely piety" and denied access to the court. A messenger had indeed come

---

[27] *Ibid.*, 237, 315, 317, 323–25, 419, 484, 493, 512, 557–59. For the intrigue with Rome and Spain, see *ibid.*, 225–366, and see Stafford, 151, for a bibliography on the subject; on his efforts to ally with the Dutch, see Stafford, 133–38. For continuing contacts with the Kirk, see *CSPSc* 12: 134, 413–14, 428, 463–64, 475.

[28] *CSPSc* 13, pt. 1: 436–37, 460–61, 487–88.

from Tyrone, and that approach had been promptly reported to the Queen. Scottish agents in Brussels and elsewhere were not such as could be harmful to "Your Majesty's person or state." And was not Elizabeth better acquainted in Brussels than he? (The exchanges leading up to the Boulogne meetings had already begun.) On the latest border incident Elizabeth was simply misinformed as to the true circumstances of the case.[29]

This catalogue reflects pretty faithfully English anxieties over Spanish conspiracy in the island, pro-Spanish influences on the susceptible King, contacts with the Ulster rebels, and Scottish diplomatic initiatives abroad. English policy now, as in Mary Stuart's time, reflected a determination to insulate Scotland as far as possible from Continental contacts. Embassies or agents sent to the Continent or received from overseas were carefully watched, lest they should reflect some hint of intrigue against Elizabeth. James's effort towards alliance with France had produced nothing more than an empty embassy of honor, thanks to English pressure, and it was Elizabeth who had denied him inclusion in the Anglo-French treaty.[30]

The major component of Anglo-Scottish diplomatic business was border matters. Although settlement of border disputes was supposed to be in the hands of the respective wardens of the marches, such disagreements were in fact a staple item in every diplomatic exchange between the sovereigns, year in and year out. Usually some adjustment was arrived at without too much friction, but occasionally one of these incidents became inflated into a major row.

Such an occasion had arisen when in the spring of 1596 a notorious border worthy, Willie Armstrong (Will of Kinmont), was seized (on a day of truce) by the English and imprisoned in Carlisle Castle. The Scots border officer, the laird of Buccleuch, reacted by mounting a raid on the castle, which freed the prisoner. Elizabeth was in a fury and demanded that Buccleuch be handed over to the English for condign punishment. She intimated that James had had a hand in authorizing the raid and warned him that any delay in meeting English demands would be seen as a breach of amity. This was followed by one of her letters of stately reproach. The issue aroused much agitation among the Scots councillors, and the Cath-

[29] *Ibid.*, 488–92.   [30] *Ibid.*, 237, 315, 317, 484, 493, 536.

olic faction rose to support Buccleuch; the whole matter was referred to an assembly of the Estates. That body proposed a joint commission to arbitrate the matter. The King, in appearance at least, pressed for accommodation with the English demands. James's annuity from Elizabeth was held up but he refused to hand over Buccleuch, a stance supported by his new councillors, whom Bowes thought pro-papist and anti-English. The ambassador proposed the well-worn ploy of using the Scottish clergy as a lever against the King. The Queen's displeasure did not abate, and the wrangle went on through the summer. Elizabeth, having taken a high line, was not disposed to compromise even though the issue was not a major policy matter. Indeed, outside this one problem, there was little cause for English concern. Scotland was better governed and more orderly than ever before.[31]

For a time, matters improved; Buccleuch was held in ward at St. Andrews, and commissioners from both countries were named to settle border disputes. The Queen wrote a conciliatory letter. Indeed she even stooped to flattery in praising James for the imprisonment of Buccleuch, while still urging that the offender be surrendered to English justice. A payment of £3,000 by the Queen to James failed to shake his resolve, while Elizabeth now demanded the surrender of another border laird, Kerr of Cessford. Disorder continued on the borders; the commission broke up in confusion. The Queen talked of sending foot and horse to the scene, and Bowes raised the bogey of Spanish conspiracy, conjuring up the ghosts of Dacre and Neville and hinting at the involvement of the Ulstermen.[32]

Better sense gradually prevailed: the King reiterated his desire to redress English grievances; a treaty was concluded between the English and Scottish commissioners, although without the surrender of Buccleuch or Cessford. After more weeks of bickering it was agreed to exchange pledges from both sides in lieu of actual surrender of the culprits. In the end Buccleuch, unable to provide his pledges, gave himself up. The Queen, her honor satisfied, agreed to release him, promising her favor if he behaved well. Cessford went

---

[31] *Warrender Papers* 2: 292–99; *CSPSc* 12: 123–24, 216–18, 220–21, 233–36, 238–41, 250, 262, 265–66, 299–300.

[32] *CSPSc* 12: 304, 311, 312–13, 314, 316, 319–20, 327, 328–34, 349–51, 491–93, 497–98, 512, 514, 515, 521, 530.

through the same purgation and, with his release in April 1598, two years after the initial events, the episode was played out.[33]

Its origins seem to lie in the Queen's indignation at the invasion of her territory and the violation of her castle, an insult to English dignity not to be borne. Consequently she was relentless in pressing her demands on the Scots and inflating the dispute out of proportion. James, as in the Spanish blanks affair, played his cards carefully, placating Elizabeth's wrath, promising redress, but refusing to compromise his own dignity by giving way to her imperious demands. Gradually the temperature fell, and in the end the token gesture of surrender and brief detention satisfied the Queen's *amour propre* without sacrificing James's own kingly self-respect.

James on his side had quite a different set of goals. His short-term purposes were to preserve civil relations with England, which meant enduring a permanent English surveillance of his affairs and a barrage of English demands that he take action within his own kingdom. But he was determined to preserve his own dignity and, so far as possible, his freedom of action. Above all, he sought to prevent the creation of a Scottish faction dependent upon English patronage. In the latter aspiration he was in fact, although not intentionally, helped by Elizabeth's unwillingness to give long-term support to what she saw as unstable and unreliable combinations among the Scots aristocrats.

More immediately James, endemically short of funds, was a constant beggar for English subsidies. The £3,000 (or as he argued £4,000) guaranteed him in 1585 became a counter in every diplomatic exchange. The Queen withheld the payments whenever she wanted to put pressure on him. The payment was a modest but significant addition to his income, but equally important it was, in James's eyes, a symbol of his special relation to the English crown and an oblique acknowledgment of his rights as heir. From time to time, as in the case of the Spanish blanks, he tried to extract additional payments; this proved futile and James had to content himself with the £3,000, which in most years was paid over by London.

In all these matters James displayed shrewdness, patience, and flexibility as well as a sense of timing, but on issues that touched his delicate position as heir presumptive he could be as prickly and as obstinate as the Queen. In the spring of 1598 the English border

[33] *Ibid.*, 523–24, 550, 555–57; *CSPSc* 13, pt. 1: 163, 201.

officials arrested a certain Valentine Thomas, an adventurer of dubious past and a suspected papist. In prison he told a story of a secret interview with James in which the king allegedly urged him to kill Queen Elizabeth. James, initially troubled that the matter should have been concealed, soon became almost hysterical in his anxiety over the affair, declaring that it "[cut] him off from all his hopes and possibilities to come," destroying his princely reputation and blemishing his posterity forever. From then on, the situation became almost an obsession with him. The Queen's reassurances were unavailing; James insisted that the man's trial be postponed and then demanded a solemn act of the Privy Council (or Star Chamber) and a public proclamation of Thomas's villainy and his own innocence. The Queen sent a confession signed by Thomas with a declaration, formally sealed as letters patent, repudiating absolutely everything Thomas had alleged. She also stayed the trial. And, as a sweetener, the £3,000 annual payment was included. However, all this failed to calm James's anxieties, and he determined to return the letters (but not the money).

The King now proposed nothing less than a public trial before both English and Scottish judges; indeed, he even suggested it be held at Edinburgh or Berwick. To this Elizabeth returned a reasoned and reassuring letter designed to reduce the royal hysteria but also warning "that he shall find us far from anything which may diminish our own absolute power and greatness over all our own actions as we have been ... careful to stop any course that might either blemish any of his pretensions or further any others." At the root of the King's fears was the apprehension that the trial might bring him within the scope of the statute disabling any claimant who conspired against the Queen's life or estate. He had to rest content with the Queen's measures, but the matter rankled and was still being chewed over nearly two years later. All James's hopes focused on the glittering prize that still lay just beyond his grasp. Nothing must endanger his chances, and when they seemed at risk his shrewd common sense deserted him.[34]

Another, somewhat different episode in which James felt his sovereign rights were trampled on, was the Ashfield affair of 1599. Ashfield was a Buckinghamshire gentleman with papist connec-

---

[34] *Border Papers* 2: 520–22; *CSPSc* 13, pt. 1: 208, 213–14, 225, 231–32, 232–34, 239–40, 311–14, 357–58, 366–68, 393, 409–10, 457–58, 538–39; 13, pt. 2: 816–17, 821.

tions who had a passport from Willoughby at Berwick to go to
Scotland. His behavior there aroused the ambassador's suspicions
to such a degree that a public kidnapping was arranged and Ashfield was spirited off to Berwick. James was indignant at this flouting of his sovereignty, as were his subjects, and the ambassador had
temporarily to retire to Berwick. A special ambassador was sent to
London to pursue the matter. Elizabeth stood her ground and the
matter died away.[35]

The English government had an understandable fear of Spanish
conspiracy in Scotland. Equally, they were concerned about Scottish
participation in Irish affairs. There was a long tradition of mercenary service in northern Ireland by Scots clansmen from the Islands
and the Western Highlands. They were, Scots and Irish alike, part
of a separate Gaelic world. Forces drawn from the Isles had participated frequently in Ulster and Connaught affairs in recent decades. The governor of Connaught had achieved a great victory
over one such contingent in 1586 at Ardnarea in Sligo. One clan,
the MacDonalds, straddled both kingdoms with lands in Antrim
and in the Hebrides. They had long been a thorn in the side of the
Dublin government, which alternately sought to destroy them or to
use them as pawns in Ulster politics.[36]

Royal Scottish authority in the Western Isles and the adjoining
mainland was feeble at best. From the 1560's onwards the English
government, in its efforts to check Scots activity in Ireland, had
frequently dealt directly with the Earl of Argyll and with other
Highland chiefs. As the crisis in Ireland mounted after 1594, the
role of the Scots became more and more crucial. The strength of
their numbers and the quality of their martial skills weighed
heavily in the balance. The English government and the Irish council came to think seriously of enlisting them in the Queen's service
since as mercenaries they were ready to listen to the highest bid-
der.[37]

Although their nominal master was the King or, more realistically, a great regional lord such as Argyll, applications to both these
personages in October 1594 bore no fruit. Elizabeth quite naturally
sought to bypass official circles and to deal with the local chieftains,

[35] Stafford, 195–96; *CSPSc* 13, pt. 1: 499, 501, 506–7, 536–38.

[36] Gerard A. Hayes-McCoy, *Scots Mercenary Forces in Ireland, 1565–1603* (Dublin
and London, 1937), 174.

[37] *Ibid.*, especially chaps. 7 and 8.

with whom real power resided. The key figure in these negotiations was Lachlan MacLean of Duart, a chieftain whose clan had large holdings in Mull and the neighboring mainland and a long-time enemy of the MacDonalds. There was a Highland force preparing for Ulster, but they could not depart without securing the neutrality of MacLean. This enterprising chieftain not only offered to prevent their going but also went on to offer his services (and those of his kinsman Argyll) to the Queen. MacLean was deadly enemy to Tyrone, who had hanged his kinsman, Hugh Gaveloch O'Neill.[38]

This opened an intrigue, conducted for the Queen by her agent at Edinburgh, Nicolson, which was to simmer on for a long time, never quite reaching the boil. Nicolson made clear from the beginning that it would be a straightforward commercial transaction. "Let not Her Majesty think that nothing will do anything here nor trust to friendship before she be in covenant for it." Nothing was in fact offered, and little came of continuing exchanges, although MacLean did waylay a part of a Scots contingent on its way to Ireland, for which he was promised 1,000 crowns reward. Luckily for the English, the expedition came to naught when the leaders, having offered to sell their services to the Queen as well as to Tyrone, eventually retired in disorder.[39]

When Bowes returned to Scotland in February 1596 he was instructed to contact MacLean to obtain the services of a force of 3,000 to 4,000 men. Typically, the Queen wanted it on the cheap and arranged in such a way as to push the initiative on the Scotsman's shoulders. For the next year negotiations dribbled on between the English envoys and MacLean under Cecil's direction. A modest gift of £150 was bestowed on MacLean, plus smaller gifts to his servants, but nothing conclusive was achieved. Separate negotiations were conducted with Argyll through other emissaries at the same time.[40] These desultory proceedings reflect the doubts of the English leadership. Some, such as Lord Deputy Russell, strongly favored the employment of Scottish mercenaries; Burghley (and probably the Queen) remained skeptical. What was to prevent the Scots, once employed, from changing sides? Nevertheless, it was important to

---

[38] *CSPSc* 11: 466–67, 528, 529, 530, 557–58; Hayes-McCoy, *Mercenary Forces*, 240ff.

[39] *CSPSc* 11: 620, 667–69; Hayes-McCoy, *Mercenary Forces*, 251–54.

[40] *CSPSc* 12: 137–42, 144–45, 205–11, 214; Hayes-McCoy, *Mercenary Forces*, 265–68.

check Scottish intervention, and to that negative end MacLean and Argyll were kept on the string.

The failure of the 1595 expedition from the Scottish Isles to Ulster had discouraged any attempt in 1596, while James's drive against his rebels in 1597 had aborted action in that year. In 1598 MacDonald of Sleat, traditionally an ally of Tyrone, offered his services to the Queen, but this roused little interest at London. In any case, Highland politics were thrown into disarray by the murder of Lachlan MacLean in June 1598 and the subsequent defeat of the MacDonalds. Not until 1600 was there another serious consideration of employing Scottish mercenaries, but again nothing came of these preparations. In the aftermath of Kinsale James proposed to raise 2,000 Highlanders for the Queen's service in Ireland. This offer was thankfully declined.[41]

Quite apart from the problems of Scottish mercenaries, the English government had reason to fear dealings between Tyrone and James. As early as January 1597 there were rumors of a letter from Tyrone to James asking the King to undertake the protection of Ireland. Later in the year there were other contacts; James admitted to receiving a letter from the earl asking for troops, to which he had replied that he would do nothing harmful to the Queen. In the following spring the Irish council heard that James had offered to prevent an English landing at Lough Foyle, and Secretary Fenton was convinced that James was a secret backer of the rebels, whatever assurances to the contrary he might give. There was in fact a steady flow of munitions from Glasgow to the Ulster rebels even though James issued repeated proclamations against this trade and ultimately specifically against aid to the rebel earl. There was at least one letter to Tyrone in which the King accepted the earl's service, but only after the death of Elizabeth. This was seen by the English.[42]

James's dealings with Tyrone were a fairly straightforward piece of diplomatic insurance. Up to 1599 it was far from clear that the

---

[41] *CSPSc* 13: 191–92, 208, 261; Hayes-McCoy, *Mercenary Forces*, 283, 293–94, 297, 321, 323, 340; *CSPI* 9 (1600): 403; 10 (1600–1): 16, 123, 156, 157, 167–68, 183, 184, 242, 255–57; *Calendar of the State Papers for Scotland*, ed. M. J. Thorpe (2 vols., London, 1858) 2: 789, 808–9 (henceforth cited as Thorpe).

[42] Hayes-McCoy, *Mercenary Forces*, 285–86; Stafford, 186–89, 188 citing BL, Cotton Mss., Caligula D ii, fols. 348–49; *CSPSc* 12: 421, and 13, pt. 1: 86, 159; *CSPI* 6 (1596–97): 435, 447; 7 (1598–99): 128, 140, 142, 190.

rebellion would end in Tyrone's capitulation. James needed to look ahead to a time when Tyrone would be his own subject. Nothing substantial was done for the earl, other than winking at the flow of supplies from Scotland to Ulster, and, when the earl's hopes began to dim, James took care to draw back and, as noted, to offer troops to the Queen—when they were no longer needed. There was little the English could do other than to reproach the King and rebut his profuse denials of ill intent.

Retrospectively viewed, the years between the treaty of 1585 and the death of the Queen saw a marked change in the character of Anglo-Scottish relations, but one that the English were slow to grasp. Their settled policy since 1560 had been to treat Scotland as a dependency—not quite a colony, like Ireland, but at least a protectorate. As long as there was a minor on the throne, this approach had worked more or less satisfactorily. But with the coming of a king, even one with limited power, Scotland gradually recovered some freedom of action. So long as James's continuing weakness allowed foreign conspiracy to have a foothold in the realm, English distrust was deep and a policy of active intervention never far below the surface. Only gradually, as royal authority strengthened and the real dangers of Spanish plotting dwindled, did English suspicion relax to a degree. Ancient sources of friction, above all the borders, continued to generate friction between the kingdoms. And the English never yielded in their determination to keep Scotland's foreign relations in leading strings. Yet more and more, after 1600, these issues faded into the background as English and Scottish politicians began to face the day when they would share one single master.

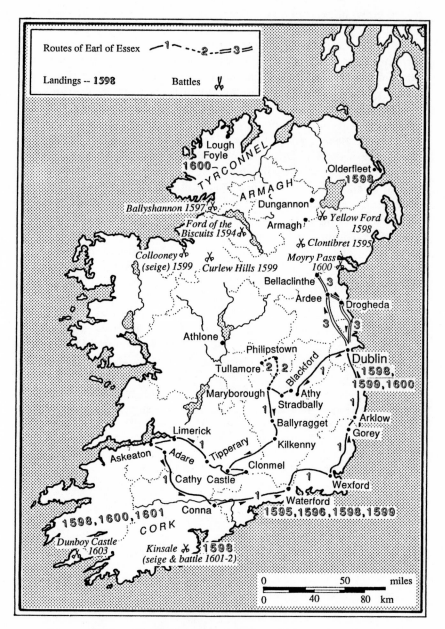

MAP 4. *Routes of the Earl of Essex in Ireland, April to September 1599.*
(Adapted from R. Edwards)

CHAPTER 16

IRELAND: THE BUILDING OF A

NEW ORDER, 1530-1593

QUEEN ELIZABETH wore two crowns and ruled over two kingdoms, separated by the waters of the Irish Sea. Such multiple sovereignties were common enough in the sixteenth century. Her successor would wear three crowns; Philip II could have worn a different one almost every day in the week. But Elizabeth's second kingdom, Ireland, was an anomaly. Philip's cluster of realms were all polities of the same genre. *Mutatis mutandis*, each exhibited much the same political institutions, which in each case rested on similar socioeconomic infrastructures. And in all of them the authority of the crown extended uniformly and effectively through the whole realm. In varying degrees they had shared in a common pattern of development from the feudal society of the early Middle Ages to the burgeoning monarchical states of the sixteenth century. To all this Ireland was a striking exception. Burghley, making the comparison with Spanish rule in Naples and Milan, pointed out that English rule over Ireland was "a strange example and such as is not found again in any place."[1] He further lamented that in other sovereigns' separated realms, local revenues covered expenditures, even providing surpluses. Elizabethan Ireland was a steady and increasing drain on the English exchequer.

English royal authority in Ireland rested *de jure* on a papal grant and *de facto* on conquest. In the early stages of the Anglo-Norman

[1] N. P. Canny, *The Elizabethan Conquest of Ireland, 1565–76* (Hassocks, England, 1976), 43, quoting SP 63/14/2.

invasion it might have seemed that the pattern of Irish experience would parallel that of lowland Scotland, as feudal structures of authority and landholding arrangements, which gradually penetrated and then displaced the older kinship society, were in turn utilized by the Crown to build its authority. The invaders' conquering impulse had been strong at the beginning, but it faded out before the process of transformation was complete. The result by 1500 was a bifurcated society. Although the lordship in some abstract sense embraced the whole island, in fact English or anglicized society and polity were limited to a portion of the country, principally the counties immediately around Dublin, parts of Leinster, and the port towns of Waterford, Cork, Galway, and Limerick. The rest of the island remained not only Gaelic-speaking but also Celtic in its social and political institutions, alien in virtually everything but its religion. In the course of the fourteenth century the English had given *de facto* recognition to this schism, and it had become an accepted fact of life in the island. Indeed, it may be argued that a kind of equilibrium had been established, which enabled the different communities to live together in rough harmony.[2]

This situation was made easier by the existence of a third grouping in this complex land. The English lordship was divided between the Pale, which in its politicolegal structure, and largely in its socioeconomic underpinnings, was a miniature England, and a surrounding penumbra of lands where the imprint of English ways was much fainter. These were the three great Old English[3] earldoms, of which Kildare lay largely within the Pale, while Ormond and Desmond stretched away to the south and west. In English eyes they represented a variant of familiar practice, the marcher lordship, in which substantial power was delegated to a palatine, a local lord, whose authority was then an amalgam of public and private elements. In the Irish setting they had taken on a special local col-

[2] For this general account of the years up to the late 1580's, I have relied particularly on Canny's work; Steven G. Ellis, *Tudor Ireland: Crown, Community, and the Conflict of Cultures, 1470–1603* (London and New York, 1985); Brendan Bradshaw, *The Irish Constitutional Revolution of the Sixteenth Century* (Cambridge and New York, 1979); Ciaran Brady, "The Government of Ireland, c. 1540–1583" (unpublished Ph.D. thesis, University of Dublin, 1980); and T. W. Moody et al., *A New History of Ireland*, Vol. 3 (Oxford, 1976).

[3] "Old English" is used henceforward to designate the English-speaking descendants of the original English settlers as distinguished from the members of the Gaelic-speaking community.

oring, for the Geraldines of Kildare and Desmond and the Butlers of Ormond ruled over a hybrid world in which Gaelic ways blended with English in a pragmatic combination, suited to a mixed society. The English monarchy had adapted these circumstances to its own use. The Kildare deputies of the late fifteenth and early sixteenth centuries upheld royal interests while securing their own local eminence and thereby providing a balance wheel for the politics of the whole island. The earl was at once the representative of royal power and the dominant local overlord. Regent for the king, palatine lord in his own liberty, he was in Gaelic eyes general overlord by the simple logic of his personal power. The tentacles of that power reached out to include the Pale, the other anglicized territories, and many of the Gaelic chieftaincies. It was an arrangement that gave substantial stability by bringing the diverse elements of the Irish world into a fragile but viable balance centered on the Kildare deputy. It was also a state of affairs in which, as in generations past, decisions about the life of Irish society were made in the island itself.

That balance and that autonomy were shattered once for all when English royal policy shifted in the 1530's. They had always rested on the willingness of the English crown to play a relatively passive role in Irish affairs. That era came abruptly to an end when Thomas Cromwell turned his attention to his master's second island. He was, of course, only minister to Henry's aspirations to greater power, but the concrete form that these took in Ireland was of the secretary's own shaping. For him Ireland was only one element in a larger whole. His aim was to consolidate royal authority in those outlying areas—Wales, the Scottish borders, Calais—where it had been dissipated into local hands. In Ireland, this meant initially the renovation of English legal and administrative machinery in the Pale and the abridgment (ultimately the extinction) of the palatine jurisdictions in the larger bounds of the lordship. Gaelic Ireland lay for the moment outside his calculations. Within these limits Cromwell's task was not qualitatively different from his efforts in other borderlands; quantitatively this was a much more formidable task.

He was not without allies in the community of the Pale, where a group of local leaders responded eagerly to his program of internal reform, based on a process of anglicization. But Cromwell was not content to rely on them alone, and the English agents who were

sent over to direct his policy proved to be the first of a new breed
who would multiply rapidly and whose presence would add a
whole new element to an already complex society. More immediately apparent was the shock that his policy administered to the
sensibilities of the Old English magnates. Although it was not
Cromwell's intention to destroy them, their reaction to the proposed changes was an extreme one. The open revolt of the Kildares
ended in the destruction of their power and of the balancing role
they had played in recent decades (an episode pregnant with meaning for the future). The incident left the other local dynasts suspicious and fearful. A policy that was viewed in London as the assertion—or rather the reassertion—of undoubted traditional royal
authority was seen in Ireland as an assault upon ancient and equally
undoubted right.

Cromwell's fall ended the first phase of renewed English intervention in Ireland, but the course was set. The next significant step
came in the early 1540's with the statutory transformation of the
medieval lordship of Ireland into the modern Kingdom of Ireland.
Interestingly, the impulse came from the reform party in Dublin
and was initially rejected by Henry, who was shrewd enough to see
the implied obligation of a royal authority that embraced the whole
island and would for its realization require an unprecedented and
intolerable financial outlay. Nevertheless, the King did in fact accept the new title and English policy over the next decades turned
haltingly but definitively to the greater task of bringing all Ireland
under effective English rule.

This was a task of the greatest magnitude. It was to prove to be
the most far-reaching undertaking of the Tudor monarchy other
than the making of the Reformation. The implementation of royal
authority within the lordship was formidable enough, but it could
at least proceed from existing institutions and past practice, however vestigial. Outside the lordship, however, what was required
was nothing less than the transformation of a whole society. The
Gaelic world lacked virtually every element that an Englishman
saw as necessary to right order. Fragmented, lacking any principle
or institution of central power, it was a society in which the center
of political gravity was very low, lodged in the local clan chief. He
derived his authority from hereditary claims of kinship that were
universally recognized but everywhere ill-defined. The exact nature
of his authority as ruler or as landlord was quite unclear; his own

legitimacy as rightful successor (to his predecessor) was often in debate, his relationship and that of his clan to other clans and clan leaders a subject of endless contention; and in the end it was brute force that settled most disputes and that made or unmade the career of the chief. The instruments of his power were the armed retainers, kinsmen, or mercenaries by which he enforced his will. The economy in which this order operated was by English standards a primitive one, lacking the institution of the manor or those of the town. In short, to the English mind Gaelic society represented not an alternative social order but mere anarchy. Surely anyone suffering under such miseries would eagerly grasp the blessings of English-imposed order.

For the Englishman there was a relatively simple recipe for ending what he regarded as social chaos. His own home society provided the model on which the Gaelic world must be reconstructed.[4] The greater clan chiefs must be transformed into noblemen—earls, viscounts, and barons—their kinsmen into landed gentry, and the cultivators into freeholders and copyholders. The rules of primogeniture for the descent of property and fixed contractual ties between lord and tenant must replace the fluctuating uncertainties of Gaelic practice. Above all, public and private authority must be clearly separated. The clan chiefs must become mere landowners while clansmen were to be subject to one lord only, the King. All alike must be subordinated to the rule of the common law, administered by royal justices and relying for its enforcement on the obedience of the population to the representatives of royal authority.

How was a program of such amplitude to be carried through? From as early as the 1520's thoughtful attention was given to the problem and a series of considered proposals put forward. They varied widely but they can perhaps best be viewed as the shading of a wide spectrum. All agreed on the need for "reformation," a shorthand term for the transformation of Irishmen into Englishmen—but what strategy would be used to accomplish it? Broadly speaking there were two extreme positions—conquest and assimilation. The former term did not imply a large-scale campaign, a foreshadowing of Oliver Cromwell or William III, but simply the use of force as occasion required, to coerce those who opposed the implementation of English rule. The important distinction for

[4] See David Quinn, *The Elizabethans and the Irish* (Ithaca, N.Y., 1966), 9–10.

those who held this view was what followed the use of force. The more radical position envisaged the plantation of English colonists in the conquered zones. Here again, what was proposed was not wholesale displacement but the creation of nodes of "civility," centers of English life that would by example and influence affect the surrounding Irish world. Those who were of less radical persuasion would use coercion as a preliminary, to be followed, if necessary, by more persuasive techniques, coaxing the Gaels into a voluntary acceptance of what Old English in Ireland and Englishmen at home alike regarded as a self-evidently superior social order. This view shaded naturally into an even more liberal disposition that would leave the whole process of anglicization to the gentler influences of persuasion, adaptation, and eventual assimilation. No one of these lines of action would carry the day singly in the next decades; elements of all would mingle in the policy of the English government towards Ireland later in the century.

In Ireland the shift in English intentions in the 1530's opened the way for the most far-reaching changes in Irish society since the twelfth century, which would alter the face of Ireland for good. The remainder of the sixteenth century would be an era of almost uninterrupted turmoil; by its close the institutions of the Gaelic world would be in ruin, the semiautonomous earldoms would have vanished, and the whole society of the island would be radically altered. In every part of the island there was a new presence in the contingent of English officials, clergy, landlords, and settlers—the "New English," the pioneers of the Ascendancy.

Ireland had become, for the first time, a focus of English attention. At Whitehall it stood high on the agenda of Council business (although often low in priority when it came to the making of decisions). In the realm of high politics Irish policy had become one of the major issues over which politicians wrangled and around which factions formed. And for a growing number of ambitious and land-hungry gentry Ireland was a mecca of tempting opportunity. Henceforth, Ireland, in one form or another, would be a staple item in the program of all English governments, and much of the course of Irish history would be shaped by decisions made in England.

Nevertheless, there was still a powerful dynamic powered by the actions of Irishmen in their own country. One impulse came from the Old English, especially those of the Pale, who had supported the initial Cromwellian moves towards reform and who hoped to play a large and constructive role in the anglicization of their island. Their heyday was during the deputyship of St. Leger in the 1540's, but their influence did not disappear even in the harsher years of the Elizabethan regime.

A countering impulse was to be found among those local lords, both Old English and Gaelic, whose traditional power was endangered by the new order. Beginning with the Kildare rebellion and the Geraldine League in the 1530's, resistance sputtered on through the risings of the Old English Desmonds and Butlers in the 1570's and 1580's down to the climactic duel with the Gaelic lord of Ulster, Tyrone, in the closing years of Elizabeth's reign. It would be easy to read this sequence of risings as a national struggle against a determined campaign of conquest. In the simplified contours of very-long-term historical perspective this interpretation may have some plausibility, but, viewed much more closely, within the immediate context of sixteenth-century events, it fades into an indeterminate blur. Both the actions of the English government and the Irish resistance to them were episodic, fitful, and confused.

While there certainly was a long-term intent to reduce Ireland to obedience to the English crown and to an acceptance of English ways, there was no timetable or strong sense of immediacy. Tudor policy towards Ireland, like much else in its activities, was shackled by the straitened resources of the English monarchy and neglected because of more pressing problems elsewhere. Elizabeth, cautiously husbanding her limited means, invariably opted for the defensive and cheaper option whenever she could. The advancement of English power in Ireland, whether by armed coercion or by the expansion of the bureaucratic apparatus, was appallingly expensive since the lesser island yielded pitifully small revenues of its own. Consequently successive deputies in Dublin found themselves under constant pressure to keep costs as low as possible. Only the urgencies of open resistance or widespread disorder were sufficient to pry open the royal purse strings. At the earliest possible moment, as soon as the immediate crisis was in hand, they snapped shut again. The underlying assumptions of the English government about Ireland remained unchanged and governed the course of action in any given crisis, but their implementation invariably faltered into half-hearted compromise. The result was likely to be a half-measure that pleased neither the advocates of force nor those of persuasion.

Nor was Irish resistance any more consistent or sustained. Far from being a considered and directed response to English aggression, it was fragmented, local, and tied to the particular interests of each chieftaincy, each frantic to protect its privileges. Each episode was distinct, a quarrel shaped by personal or familial animosities or ambitions. Only very slowly and very partially did Irish resistance rise to a sense of shared national or confessional grievance, and never to a considered alternative to English rule.

In the half-century following the fall of Thomas Cromwell a succession of English deputies struggled to realize in some form the goals he had first put forward. In the immediate wake of his fall the party of persuasion had its innings under the leadership of Deputy St. Leger.[5] A new strategy, aimed at drawing the Gaelic clan leaders into the English polity, was tried out. The scheme of surrender and regrant offered a legal formula by which the chieftain could submit to the English Crown, formally relinquishing his indeterminate powers over men and land, in order to be invested in return with a new legal persona as a landowner with defined and delimited landed estate, secure title, and fixed rights. The greater chiefs were offered the additional carrot of a peerage. Concomitant with the transformation of the warlord into a landed squire was the erection of English local government, the shiring of tribal territories, replacing the fluid uncertainties of the old order with the clear-cut contours of county organization—sheriffs, assizes, and juries. The old aristocracy could have a place in the new order, but they had to accept reduction to private status, shorn of their hereditary role and of the open-ended exercise of power.[6]

This policy of persuasion had but a short run; the death of Henry VIII and the resulting instability led to a swift succession of short-term deputies and a period of uncertain drift that lasted until the appointment of the Earl of Sussex late in Mary's reign; he would hold office (although only intermittently resident in Ireland) until 1564. One important step had already been taken before his arrival. The unruly O'More and O'Connor clans of Leix-Offaly, which earlier had been held in check by the Kildares, were now shackled by the establishment of two forts in their territories. More important was the ensuing scheme for settling a colony of "Englishmen born in England or Ireland" around the forts. Significantly the two new

---

[5] Bradshaw, 258–63.   [6] *Ibid.*, 261; Canny, 34–35; Ellis, 137–42.

posts would be named for the sovereigns, Philip and Mary, while Leix and Offaly would be transformed into King's and Queen's counties. The settlers would pay a rent to the Crown that, it was hoped, would pay garrison costs. The move was a response to an immediate problem: the disorders on the borders of the Pale, which in an earlier generation would have been dealt with by the authority of Kildare. But it proved to be a move pregnant with future consequences. In this first instance the policy of conciliation—of a slow, civilizing process—was set aside in favor of the direct use of coercion, the forcible removal of the native population and its replacement by Englishmen (or Old English). But the hope of converting Irishmen to English ways was not entirely lost to view. The presence of an English model would, it was hoped, lead to the anglicization of the Gaelic population, but the violent disruption of the old order was now seen as the necessary prelude to "reformation." Such a policy cast aside more liberal hopes of a peaceful and gradual transformation. Another token of changed attitude was the presence of the garrisons in the colonized counties, at Maryborough and Philipstown. There was now a small but permanent English army paid for largely from home and officered by Englishmen, a potent weapon of viceregal power.

The coming of Sussex as lieutenant also marked a deep and lasting alteration in the whole Irish political scene. He was a highranking nobleman of considerable standing at court. His appointment signalled a fundamental shift in the locus of power. It was the culmination of a change that had been in the making for several decades. Since 1534 virtually all the royal representatives in Dublin had been English. Now increasingly they would govern the island through an entourage of English officials and soldiers. The leaders of the Old English community would be crowded off the stage, reduced at best to mere coadjutors in the government of their country. In short, the question of personnel, of who would rule Ireland, was now a matter to be settled not in the island itself but by the jockeying of rival English politicians at the English court. Sussex owed his place to the influence of the Howard faction; his successor, Sidney, to the patronage of the Dudleys. Old English magnates, like Desmond and Ormond, as well as Gaelic lords like O'Neill, had to court the patronage of English councillors.

This, of course, meant that all decisions about the direction of Irish policy were made at Westminster. One must hedge that generalization carefully, however. All decisions, large or small, in the government of the Queen's dominions were made by the sovereign herself. Elizabeth's vision of Ireland was not a distinctive one; from her Irish as from her English or Welsh subjects she expected unquestioning obedience, and the open disorder that prevailed in the smaller island, the contemptuous flouting of constituted authority, led to outbursts of royal indignation. But here, as in other areas, the Queen cherished no ambitions for aggrandizement. She presumably shared the long-term, open-ended aim laid down in her father's time, of extending effective royal authority throughout the realm. But Ireland clearly did not engage the Queen's attention except when its affairs, by their sheer urgency, intruded on her consciousness. Her response at such moments was invariably conditioned by one overriding consideration—cost. From her accession onwards the Queen had struggled painfully to match outgo to income. Ireland was, at the best, a constant drain on the English treasury. Given its low priority on the Queen's agenda, she would inevitably choose the least-cost option. This royal predisposition vitally affected every aspect of English rule in Ireland. One initiative after another was crippled at birth or halted in midcareer by royal parsimony. The result was a jerky, stop-and-start course of action that disappointed the hopes of the New English activists while forfeiting the confidence of the Irish communities.

If royal interest in Ireland was minimal, that of the leading English councillors was much more active. Control of the deputyship and its patronage became a bone of contention between the Leicester faction and its opponents early in the reign. Secretary Smith risked his fortune—and sacrificed his son—in a vain attempt to establish a family satrapy in Ulster. This enterprise, that of the first Earl of Essex, and the Munster plantation were all heavily patronized by councillors and courtiers. Leicester's interest in Ireland was in large part that of a faction leader, seeking scope for his clientage, but the general expansionist outlook of the Dudley circle, on the Continent and overseas, squared with a similar policy in Ireland.

Burghley too developed a strong interest in Irish affairs and as early as 1565 had drawn up a comprehensive scheme for the settlement of Ulster. He would support the establishment of the provincial presidencies,[7] although he was not likely to forget the limita-

7 Canny, 62–63, citing SP 63/22/49 and SP 63/23/1.

tions of finance. But probably more than any other councillor he had a considered and consistent view of the Irish situation.

The intense interest of English politicians in Ireland gave a crucial new dynamic to the scene. Even though crown interest was essentially inertial in character, it was unthinkable that any sixteenth-century monarch would voluntarily abandon a part of his inheritance; the maintenance of royal reputation forbade it. And indeed the Tudor sovereigns were concerned to maintain and to extend their authority in their second kingdom, even though it was a languid impulse and, left to themselves, they gave it minimal attention. However, there were now powerful court interests eager to exploit the possibilities of Ireland, which pressed the Crown to more active measures. When such measures, underfinanced and overambitious, led to Irish resistance, the dignity of the Crown was impugned, and further initiatives followed of necessity. And so, step by step, impelled both by the growing ambitions of the New English and their sponsors at court and by the resistance of Irishmen to this new wave of conquest, the English government waded deeper and deeper into the morass of civil disorder.

The particular strategies of action in Ireland were shaped by the rulers on the scene. In Sussex, and more strikingly in his successors in the 1580's and 1590's, Sir Henry Sidney and Sir William Fitzwilliam, were found English politicians who made a career in Ireland, developing in the course of that career strong convictions as to how English rule should be exercised. Among the English the deputies were, of course, the most conspicuous but there were others hardly less important—the soldiers, Drury, Bingham, Bagenal, or the archbishop-chancellor, Loftus, for instance—who played almost as large a role.

All these men rejected any notion that Ireland was a coequal realm, sharing a sovereign with England, but governed by the leaders of the Irish community. This had been the tacit premise of Yorkist and early Tudor governments, and it was a thesis self-consciously maintained by the leaders of Old English society. For them the erection of an Irish monarchy had been the first step towards such a fulfillment of self-government. The New English—the distinction between Old and New English had become current in the 1570's[8]—were emphatic in viewing the scene in "colonial" terms.

[8] Ellis, 247.

For them the legal subordination of Ireland to England was absolute, and its pragmatic corollary was that the country must be ruled by a corps of English officials, responsible to London, making decisions without necessarily consulting with Irishmen. These decisions were to be determined by the interests of the larger country. The contrast with the most obvious precedent, that of Wales, was striking. The Welsh elite, having accepted English law and custom, were now allowed to participate in English political life, to sit in Parliament and to act as sheriffs and JP's at home. In Ireland, on the other hand, the natives, Old English or Gaelic, were increasingly to be crowded out of positions of responsiblity and power, to be replaced by an immigrant bureaucracy, military and civil.

The Elizabethan governors from Sussex onwards, taking counsel from their own kind and from their own experience on the spot, evolved a multipronged set of options as the basis for the advice that they gave the sovereign and the Privy Councillors in London. Both Sidney and Sussex had direct access to the highest circle of power and to the sovereign herself. Sidney is sometimes referred to as the first "programmatic" deputy, although at least some of his ideas had already been developed by Sussex.[9] Programmatic he was, in the sense that he had an overall scheme embracing the settlement, not only of the old lordship, but of the whole island. It drew in some part on the tradition of conciliation and assimilation but more heavily on that of coercion. The moderate tradition was represented by his plans for extending the operation of the common law, by the strengthening of existing institutions, and by their proliferation in the rest of the realm. This meant the shiring of the Gaelic areas, creating the machinery of county government, particularly the sheriff (a more important figure here than in lowland England) and regular assizes. The expansion of the common law would provide for effective criminal justice and for the application of common-law procedures and rules in property disputes. It would contribute to the destruction of the *de facto* politico-judicial role of the clan chiefs and thus become a strong solvent of the old order.

Another prong of Sidney's strategy derived from English practice (and his own experience as Lord President of the Council in the Marches of Wales). In the larger island the establishment of

[9] The term "programmatic" is one coined by Ciaran Brady in his "Government of Ireland."

provincial councils in the peripheral and most disturbed areas of the realm (the Welsh marches and the Scottish borders) had supplemented the normal machinery of the county. The judicial and administrative powers of the Councils provided an effective stiffening to the processes of the common law where they might be impeded by resistant local interests.

This was the model that Sidney proposed for Munster and Connaught (and more distantly for Ulster). Leinster was already for the most part assimilated to the English legal system, although there were pockets where the summary jurisdiction of a seneschal with martial law at his disposal was still necessary. In the two other provinces, however, a lord president with a council, composed of a law member or two and of local dignitaries, would have wide-ranging judicial and administrative authority. Local opinion in Ireland was initially favorable to such a scheme, but with a critical difference: the expectation that the presidencies would be filled by an Ormond, a Kildare, or a Desmond. The reformers in Dublin, as eager as Sidney for anglicization, envisaged a transformation of the system but a continuance of the old local leadership. This, of course, was not Sidney's vision. He added a clutch of English members to the council at Dublin and the presidencies went to other English nominees. As the new deputy saw it, the "reformation" of Ireland, its transmutation into a new "civility," could be achieved only if the driving force of change was lodged in the hands of his countrymen.

The first of the presidencies to come into being was that of Munster in 1566, but Ormond's influence at court and the Queen's parsimony combined to defeat Sidney's intention; it was not until 1571 that the office of president was filled, by the appointment of Sir John Perrot. After his departure in 1573 there was a vacancy for three years followed by the brief term of Sir William Drury, which ended with his departure for Dublin as Lord Justice in 1578. Between 1568 and 1583 the province was rent by two rebellions led by the Munster Geraldines, and the successive presidents spent their time in the bloody business of suppressing revolt rather than in the pacific tasks originally envisaged for their office. In both these uprisings Fitzmaurice, the leader of the insurrection, had raised the standard of religion, calling on Catholics to reject the heretic queen and her government.

In Connaught, where local opposition was more fragmented, the presidents (from 1569) had better success. They were able to shire the areas where English institutions did not exist and to establish the basic machinery of a new order. They also secured the collaboration of two powerful clan chiefs, the O'Brien (now Earl of Thomond) and the Burke (now Earl of Clanricard) by backing their authority. But the role of the English governors here, like that of their counterparts to the south, rested on force, and their authority on fear. The presidencies, intended as civil governments, became basically military regimes as the presidents were provided with a contingent of soldiers. The experiment succeeded in extending English authority into new areas but only at a very high cost in money and men and, in Munster, in fierce local hostility and the utter devastation of the countryside. The hope that the establishment of the provincial councils would be a prelude to the peaceful anglicization of the inhabitants had gone aglimmering.

Sidney was less than content with these two gradualist strategies, the aim of which was to provide a new matrix of politics and government with minimal disturbance of the countryside. In those unstable areas where tenacious and violent resistance obtained, more radical therapy was in order, surgical rather than medicinal. Following the model of Leix-Offaly Sidney looked to English colonization to solve the problem, by the physical displacement of the native population and their replacement, in part at least, by English settlers. They would establish a miniature English community with its full complement of gentry, husbandmen, and even townsmen. The local population would not be entirely displaced, but the Irish ruling class would be eliminated, and the powerful presence of an English colony plus the domination of an English elite would serve as strong magnets for ultimate anglicization. Not surprisingly Ulster, the most intractably Gaelic province, was envisaged as a site for such an enterprise.[10] Burghley had drawn up a full-fledged scheme for breaking up the O'Neill ascendancy, distributing some lands to the lesser Irish landowners, as Crown tenants, while turning Antrim over to English settlement. The whole province was to be ringed with English forts.

The scheme itself did not materialize but it gave rise to two private or semiprivate attempts at colonization in eastern Ulster. One was that of Elizabeth's secretary of state, Sir Thomas Smith, the other the somewhat grander effort of the first Devereux Earl of

[10] Canny, 62–63.

Essex. Both were privately financed, the first by a joint-stock sub-scription, the latter by a royal loan secured by a mortgage on the earl's estates. Both assumed the backing of royal garrisons to over-awe the countryside. Both aroused the bitterest hostility, led to sav-age fighting, and ended in failure. Many of the same sponsors (largely West Country gentry or Dudley clients) were prepared to invest in a scheme for large-scale settlement in Munster. This did not come to fruition, although a small-scale settlement near Cork under the auspices of Sir Warham St. Leger did survive to form a nucleus for the Munster plantation of the 1580's.

The strategy of colonization was the brainchild of Sidney and of the Dublin government; it was viewed somewhat differently by the English adventurers who were the actual participants and by the government in London. It had begun, as we have seen, as a reaction to peculiarly intractable pockets of Irish resistance to anglicization. Leix-Offaly and, on a much larger scale, Ulster were predomi-nantly Gaelic areas where there had been minimal penetration of English influence and hardly even a rudimentary structure on which to build an anglicized order. Here the logic of the coercive school seemed most plausible. But in fact it was not in these Gaelic areas where the most ambitious sixteenth-century colonization ef-forts were realized, but in Munster, a province of mixed English and Gaelic influence, where the infrastructure of English political order did in fact exist. It was in the wake of the Desmond rebel-lions, in which the resistance of an Anglo-Irish earl, backed by a cluster of Gaelic chiefs, was put down with utmost savagery, that a major distribution of lands to English undertakers was followed by a serious effort to import English settlers in large numbers.[11]

Here the interplay of official and private interests was at its clear-est. The government was anxious to find some formula of pacifi-cation for a physically wasted countryside where the old social order had been broken up. The native population, in the wake of savage guerrilla warfare, was seen not as suitable candidates for "civility" but rather as bands of dangerous enemies who must be kept under the strictest control. Only the radical solution of mass colonization and wholesale restructuring of the social order seemed to offer much hope.

[11] Michael MacCarthy-Morrogh, *The Munster Plantation: English Migration to Southern Ireland, 1583–1641* (Oxford, 1986).

For the English adventurers Ulster and, more promisingly, Munster opened up new horizons. They offered opportunities for which the doors were closed to them in England. Possession of the forfeited lands gave them the chance of establishing themselves and their descendants as landholding gentry in a new dominion of which they would be the masters. It was an opportunity such as had not offered itself to Englishmen since the days of Henry V—or, more appositely, of Richard Strongbow. What lay ahead, not yet visible in all its outlines, was the Ascendancy.

In this enterprise there was also a third party—the Queen and Privy Council in London—and their view of the matter differed from that of both Dublin Castle and the adventurers. For them, as always, the predominant consideration was expense. Sidney had promised that his program, after some initial costs, would be self-financing. In fact Irish charges on the English treasury had mounted year by year until they had become a major—and apparently permanent—item in the budget. A scheme that shifted part of the burden from the Crown to private enterprise was more than welcome, and Burghley and other ministers played an active role in promoting the Munster plantation. Walsingham and Hatton became investors.[12] The settlers, once established, would not only bring a reduced military budget but also provide income from crown rents that would cover the costs of local administration and help to make Ireland finally self-financing. Such a "privatization" of the Irish problem was of a piece with Elizabethan policy in other areas. Here, as in the naval assaults on Spain, the government had undertaken more than its resources could sustain and turned eagerly towards solutions that brought outgo nearer to income.

As things stood in the late 1580's no one of these parties—the English government, the Irish administration, or the undertakers (or the settlers)—had much cause for satisfaction. Worse still, the tangled events of these years had left a deadly legacy in the deterioration of relations between Englishmen and Irishmen. Prominent among the various factors that shaped this erosion of decent relations was the influx of newcomers from England. These men arrived conscious of themselves as rulers of a conquered people, contemptuous of the Anglo-Irish, and fiercely hostile towards the Gaelic community, which they regarded as barbarous, indeed sav-

[12] *Ibid.*, 21–22, 40.

age. With more than a tincture of ideas derived from Spanish attitudes in the New World, they compared the native population to the Scythians, Turks, or Vandals,[13] and treated them accordingly. Henry Sidney, commenting on the submission of a group of chiefs in 1576, wrote of them, "detesting and abhorring their degeneration and inveterate barbarity."[14] In the past the Gaels had been legally classified as the king's enemies and a strong sense of cultural difference existed. But it was not seen as unbridgeable; Gaelic Irish could become Anglo-Irish without great difficulty and in areas like the Desmond lordships the two cultures intermingled. But the New English attitude saw the native culture as inferior in kind to their own and indeed as antipathetic to all "civility." It must be snuffed out since its very existence was a threat to civilized order. Its utter destruction was a necessary preliminary to any scheme of reconstruction. And because the Irish were sociologically inferior, the rules that governed relations among enemies who were peers to one another no longer obtained.

The erosion of tolerance and decency in relations between the rival cultures was made infinitely worse by the endemic violence of these years. In a society where authority rested ultimately on force and where there was a class of permanent soldiery, the kerne and galloglass, who formed the armed bands of the chiefs, life was brutal enough at best. But the continual fighting between the English forces and the Gaelic armies—in Ulster against the O'Neills in the 1560's, in Munster against the Desmonds and their allies in the great rebellions, and everywhere in the country in the endemic explosion of violence—the constant practice of warfare brutalized both sides. Ruthless cruelty became a pattern as one brutality was avenged by another, as English contempt for their opponents deepened and Irish hatred of the alien grew. While the Old English were spared the worst of this, they nevertheless were treated with deepening distrust. This attitude was heightened by their lukewarm acceptance of the new faith and the suspicion that they still adhered to the old. The infection of antipopery, already so virulent in England, added to the measure of hostility towards all Irishmen.

Almost fifty years had passed since Thomas Cromwell had first

[13] Canny, 125–26, 133–34.
[14] Sir Henry Sidney, "Sir Henry Sidney's Memoir of His Government of Ireland, 1583," *Ulster Journal of Archaelogy*, ser. 1, 3 (1855): 312.

aroused active English interest in the subordinate realm. Since then Ireland had felt the steadily increasing pressure of strong government at Dublin backed by an English garrison. In the long perspective of four centuries the historian sees a definitive turning point in Irish history, the "Elizabethan conquest," the imposition of direct English rule throughout the island, the crushing of Gaelic culture, and—looking ahead—the beginning of the Ascendancy. From a contemporary point of view, however, the shape of things was not so clear. It was true that since the 1530's successive English rulers had made the implicit assumption that effective royal authority should be extended over the whole island. But the goal was an open-ended one and the impulse to achieve it had proved frequently inertial, at best spasmodic. Various strategies had been proposed, but they had been thwarted by Elizabeth's obsession with economy. Royal support of their schemes was never more than half-hearted. As a result, English actions in Ireland had largely been reactions to prior events in the island, shaped less by the preconceived intentions of the actors and more by circumstances. The presidencies, meant to be the harbingers of ordered civil government, became martial-law regimes struggling to suppress endemic threats of renewed rebellion. What had begun hopefully, as a plan for gradual transformation, had degenerated into a weary program of suppression. Two attempts at colonization had failed dismally and the third, in Munster, was a sickly infant in the late 1580's. Much destruction had been wrought in the fabric of Irish society, but the work of reconstruction was at best rough and ready, a hasty response to emergencies. The most hopeful structures were the composition of Connaught and the cess composition in the Pale, which seemed to promise a workable model acceptable to the various interests involved. How far reconstruction would proceed thereafter remained uncertain. From the mid-1580's the Queen, hard pressed by war on the Continent and on the high seas, was even more than usually reluctant to spare the large resources that further English advance in Ireland would require.

Posterity, with its fatal knowledge of the historical future, tends to see the state of Ireland in the 1580's as one of half-finished conquest, a process in midstream. Perhaps a better way to view it is as a society that had lost its equilibrium. Recovery might lead in various directions: the further and final extension of English power by force or, alternatively, some kind of rough balance among existing elements in the island. The Queen, it was clear, would be quite content with a formal acknowledgment of her authority from such Gaelic magnates as Hugh O'Neill, Earl of Tyrone. She balked at expensive proposals for new forts and additional garrisons, for all the apparatus that would be necessary to make nominal submission into real amalgamation. It was quite conceivable that the troubled coexistence that had obtained in the 1580's might continue for an indefinite time into the future. Whether that would happen now depended less on Westminster than in the recent past. Leicester, already preoccupied in the Low Countries, was dead before the end of 1588. The party at court most interested in an expansionist policy was now diverted from Ireland to the beckoning opportunities of war. Therefore, initiatives taken in Ireland, by the Gaelic leaders particularly, and even more importantly the probabilities of Spanish intervention, were to count for more in the shaping of events in the 1590's. In Ireland, as elsewhere, the control of events was in non-English hands.

What about the Irish reaction to the developments of the past thirty years? At the beginning of the Elizabethan era there had been considerable support in Old English circles, especially in the Pale, for a program of anglicization. This still prevailed; where difference now existed was regarding the strategies of implementation. In the Gaelic community there had been some willingness to embrace the advantages of surrender and regrant, but for the most part it was a very conservative and parochial world, resistant to change. Its concerns were more likely to be local, revolving around the internal politics of the clan or its relations with its immediate neighbors rather than the large-scale scene of the whole island.

The actions of successive English governors had gone far to erode the confidence, although not the loyalty, of the Old English community. Increasingly excluded from any definite role in the government of their own country, increasingly alienated in their religious opinions, they could only look on resentfully at the encroachments of the growing number of New English arrivistes. Some of them, such as the Desmond Geraldines or the cadet Butlers, viewed the program of Sidney and his collaborators as an assault on their very existence as aristocrats. They responded with violence, but it was the violence of protest rather than of rebellion, aimed at the lord president or the deputy but never at the sovereign. Gaelic resistance, on the other hand, began to show stirrings of another character. The possibility of invoking the aid of some Continental prince was now a thinkable alternative, while others, such as Fitzmaurice, were prepared to repudiate the authority of a heretic sovereign. Secretary Cecil had referred to Ireland as an anomaly in the European order. So it still was; the shape of the anomaly had altered substantially, but whether it would become recognizably like the other European realms remained to be seen.

CHAPTER 17

DEPUTY FITZWILLIAM AND THE

MacMAHON AFFAIR

THE ERA THAT OPENED with the arrival of Sir William Fitzwilliam
as deputy for his second term in the summer of 1588 was in retrospect to mark the last phase of the long, fumbling extension of English power through the whole of Ireland that had begun some
seventy years earlier. Looking back at the end of the century, Irish
observers saw in Fitzwilliam's deputyship a sharp turning point in
Irish affairs, the passing of a moment of relative calm and the be-
ginnings of new disorders that would reach their climax in his successors' terms.[1] It was also a moment when events outside the island
began to cast their shadows over its affairs. Fitzwilliam landed in
Ireland only a few weeks before the Armada appeared off Cornwall. The coming of full-scale war with Spain had far-reaching
consequences for Ireland, although of quite contradictory kinds. On
the one hand that event rivetted the attention of the English government on Continental and oceanic enterprises. They could only
hope that the quiet that reigned for the nonce in Ireland would
continue, since there were neither men nor money to spare for service across St. George's Channel. Nevertheless, Ireland could not be
neglected. Since the papally backed expeditions of 1579 and 1580
the English had feared that the Spanish would emulate their own
intervention in the Netherlands by a similar exploitation of Irish

[1] *CSPI* 8 (1599–1600): 221–24; 10 (1600–1): 118–26. See also Sir Henry Wallop's
narrative of events, beginning with Fitzwilliam's arrival, BL, Cotton Mss., Titus
C VII, 156–61.

discontents, either by backing rebellion or by landing forces there. By the end of Fitzwilliam's term these fears had become real. They would escalate in the late 1590's, and the last major engagement of the war between English and Spanish would be fought on Irish soil at Kinsale in 1601. Inevitably the international war was to spread to Ireland.

It was more important than ever that the Dublin rulers should not rock the boat; it was not a time for new initiatives, for experimentation, for "programs" for further change, or for increased expenditure. The great desideratum was to preserve the precarious balance of forces between the deputy's government and the restive Gaelic lords. But this hope was not to be realized. With the advent of Fitzwilliam the relatively stable relations between Dublin and the Gaelic lords of the north and west began to deteriorate. By the time of the deputy's departure in 1592, Tyrone, regarded in 1588 as a reliable supporter of royal authority, had become alienated from a regime that he regarded with deep distrust. Hugh O'Donnell, heir to the chieftaincy of the other great lordship in Ulster, having escaped from captivity in Dublin Castle, had become a focus of active disaffection and patron to the mutinous Gaelic lords of Fermanagh, Monaghan, and northern Connaught. From 1592 on, through the deputyship of William Russell, the situation worsened steadily as Tyrone and O'Donnell moved towards more and more open hostility to a regime that was drifting aimlessly, alternating threat with conciliation and quite unable to formulate any sustained line of action.

Fear-ridden suspicion on the one side and feeble, often divided, counsel on the other were a recipe for disaster, and from 1595 onwards both sides lurched towards open war. The challenge to English arms offered by the Gaelic princes in two battles, first at Clontibret and then even more crushingly at the Yellow Ford, forced the reluctant English government to act. After years of hesitation, inconsistency, and refusal to take any definite actions the Elizabethan government finally girded up its loins and dispatched an army royal to Ireland, resolved to destroy Gaelic power. The Essex fiasco delayed the enterprise, but under Mountjoy the last resistance of Tyrone and his allies was crushed. What had begun three quarters of a century earlier as a program for drawing the whole island under effective royal control by persuasion and assimilation had ended in a brutal war of conquest.

Deputy Fitzwilliam arrived at a moment of general quiet; it had not been the case for very long. The final departure of Sidney in 1578 had been immediately followed by the outbreak of the second Desmond rebellion. An interim regime under the veteran soldier Sir William Drury had struggled to suppress it until the appointment of another soldier, Arthur, Lord Grey, as deputy in 1580. He had gone far towards liquidating the Desmonds and their followers but at a fearsome cost to the population and land of Munster. It was a grim regime and even Grey's protégé, Spenser, called him "a bloody man who regarded not the life of Her Majesty's subjects no more than dogs, but had wasted and consumed all so as now she had nothing almost left but to reign in their ashes."[2] He had also alienated the community of the Pale by what they regarded as persecution.[3] After another interim regime under two justices (Loftus and Wallop), Sir John Perrot had succeeded as deputy in June 1584 to a wasted but, for the nonce, peaceful land.

His four-year tenure was a notable one. Not only a courtier of long standing (he had served Henry VIII) but also a personal favorite of the Queen and a protégé of Leicester, Perrot had held various commands in Ireland, including a term as president of Munster.[4] High-handed and short-tempered, he made enemies easily, especially among the New English establishment at Dublin. More than any deputy for thirty years past he listened to the voice of the Old English community, to the discomfiture and irritation of the immigrants. But his regime also marked a return to something of a "programmatic" approach.[5] Like Sidney he believed rebellion must be crushed (not pardoned) before reformation could proceed; no mercy should be shown until the sword had "meekened" all.[6] However, a yet unbridled people brought by force to yield to what is good would be good only while force constrained them. This would obtain "until their ignorance how far the good extends to their own

---

[2] Richard Bagwell, *Ireland under the Tudors* (3 vols., London, 1885–90) 3: 97–99, quoting Edmund Spenser.

[3] Bagwell 3: 99–102; Ellis, 282.

[4] Sir James Perrott, *History of . . . Sir John Perrot*, ed. Richard Rawlinson (London, 1728); ECS, *The Government of Ireland under . . . Sir John Perrot* (London, 1626), 123–24 [hereafter cited as ECS]; see also *Carew* 3 (1589–1600): 442–43, Perrot to Leicester 4/18/87.

[5] Brady, 415ff. [6] ECS, a4.

particular be taken away by their taste and feeling."[7] The cause of dissension once removed, the Irish would be "(as I suppose) easily made one with us and so as likely to be continued as any other generation whatsoever that in their place should be planted." The Queen "should govern Ireland equally, balancing her subjects according to their due deserts without respect of nation as having interest in God from them all alike."[8] No doubt "as all mankind besides, yea, even born in Middlesex," her Irish subjects were naturally "slippery, uncertain, and unruly" but they could be stayed by justice and force. Of these two he pithily observed, "justice may be executed with small boast but so cannot force."[9]

These liberal sentiments were embodied in a stern but just policy. Perrot's most considerable achievement was his readjustment of the Composition of Connaught, which had effectually reshaped the society of that province. His measures strengthened the vested interest of the two local magnates, the Earls of Thomond and Clanricard, in the new order.[10] He took the first steps towards a similar policy in Ulster with less success.[11] Initially he kept the turbulent rivalries of the northern province in hand by dividing authority in Ulster among the three contenders—the young Hugh O'Neill, grandson of the first Earl of Tyrone, Sir Turlough O'Neill, the present chieftain, and the English-born intruder, Sir Nicholas Bagenal. But with the failure of his composition scheme and lacking royal backing, he abandoned the attempt to establish a Crown presence in the province. He acceded to Hugh O'Neill's claim to the earldom of Tyrone although he opposed the further favor shown by the Queen in 1587.[12] His bold scheme for building towns, castles, and bridges—seven of each—at a cost of £50,000 naturally got short shrift at Westminster. In 1586 he had a specific command from the Queen to keep spending as low as possible now that she faced the costs of foreign war.[13]

[7] *Ibid.*, 36.   [8] *Ibid.*, 49–50.

[9] *Ibid.*, 52.

[10] See Bernadette Cunningham, "The Composition of Connacht in the Lordships of Clanricard and Thomond, 1577–1641," *Irish Historical Review* 24 (1984–85): 1–14.

[11] Hiram John Morgan, "The Outbreak of the Nine Years' War: Ulster in Irish Politics, 1583–96" (unpublished Ph.D. thesis, Cambridge University, 1987), 29; ECS, 28, 112.

[12] *Ibid.*, 38.

[13] ECS, 53–55, 116; Morgan, "Outbreak," 28, citing SP 63/122/94.

Perrot's tenure was a unique interval in which, for the last time in the reign, the Old English, within and without the Pale, and the Gaelic chiefs enjoyed a sympathetic hearing from an English governor. Sentiments such as those already quoted and a policy that sought to reconcile and to accommodate rather than to crush the Gaelic lords in the west and north did not endear him to the New English politicians at Dublin. He crossed swords with both Archbishop Loftus and the marshal Bagenal (with the latter there was a scuffle in the Council chamber) and he departed amidst their hearty curses while among the Old English and even among the Gaels there was reason for regret and apprehension.[14]

When Sir William Fitzwilliam arrived at Dublin to receive the sword of state on 30 June 1588, he faced a familiar scene; now in his late sixties he had first come nearly thirty years earlier, in the train of the Earl of Sussex with appointment as vice treasurer.[15] Since then he had served first as lord justice on several occasions and then from 1572 to 1575 as lord deputy. Although he was Sidney's brother-in-law his patron was Sussex, and his first term as deputy coincided with the temporary eclipse of Sir Henry. Fitzwilliam had pursued a minimalist policy, allowing initiative to pass into the hands of private adventurers in Smith's and Essex's ill-starred colonies in Ulster. His departure and the return of Sidney marked another spin in the wheel of court fortunes and a reversion to a more programmatic approach. But by 1588 Sidney was dead, and his patron, Leicester, already preoccupied with the Spanish war, died by the end of that year. With the passing of Walsingham in 1590 the old Dudley faction was decimated, and in any case the war with Spain took priority over other causes.

Fitzwilliam's first duty, once he was inaugurated, was to meet with his council. More than one face must have been familiar from his first term of office. The lord chancellor, Adam Loftus, Archbishop of Dublin, was a Yorkshireman who had also come over in Sussex's entourage, as his chaplain. His rise in the clerical hierarchy was hardly less swift than his climb to high civil office, as lord chancellor since 1581. Thoroughly integrated into the Pale society into which he had married, he had already wed a fair proportion of his

---

[14] Bagwell 3: 157–60.
[15] *APC* 1587–88: 406–7; he had been appointed 3 March 1588.

twenty children to the sons and daughters of leading Protestant gentry families of the Pale.

Loftus was the senior in years of service of a clutch of English officials who were the key figures in the government of Ireland. The chief fiscal officer, the vice-treasurer, was Sir Henry Wallop. A prominent Hampshire squire (MP for the county in 1569), he had come to the island in 1579 and had played a major role since then, as an initiator of the Munster plantation and an advocate of a stern policy towards the Irish. At one point, disgusted with Elizabeth's temporizing, he had contemplated a return home, but now he was a heavy investor in Munster land.[16]

Of longer standing even than Loftus were the Bagenals. The first of them, Sir Ralph, a veteran of Somerset's Scottish wars and a Staffordshire landowner, had commanded the Irish garrison in Edward VI's reign. His younger brother, Sir Nicholas, a client of the Dudleys, had begun his career in Ireland as a fugitive from justice after a murder at home. Employed first by Con Bacagh O'Neill, he had further experience in the French wars of the 1540's and then had been appointed marshal of the Irish army in 1547. From 1550 he was a member of council. Temporarily in eclipse under Mary, he regained his Irish post in the mid-1560's and had been one of Sidney's closest associates.[17] Having obtained a lordship in Ulster, around Newry, he built a base of family power as landowner and as local garrison commander and had ambitions to become president of the province. He was to die full of years in 1590, having already secured the reversion of the marshal's office for his son, Sir Henry. The latter, born in 1556, educated at Oxford, married a Welsh heiress and sat in the English Parliament, but concentrated his efforts on building a family empire in Ireland. The Bagenals had become assimilated into the Irish scene by intermarriage with almost every important Protestant gentry family in the Pale: Plunkets, Loftuses, Barnewalls.[18]

A third figure of major consequence was Sir Richard Bingham, governor of Connaught since 1584, another protégé of Leicester

---

[16] *DNB*, "Loftus" and "Wallop"; for Wallop, see also *The House of Commons, 1558–1603*, History of Parliament series, ed. P. W. Hasler (3 vols., London, 1981) [henceforth cited as *House of Commons*].

[17] Philip H. Bagenal, *Vicissitudes of an Anglo-Irish Family, 1530–1800* (London, 1925): for Sir Nicholas, see chap. 4; for Sir Henry, chaps. 6 and 9.

[18] *DNB*, "Bagenal"; *House of Commons*, "Bagenal."

(and later of Essex).[19] A veteran of Somerset's wars, he too had had a long military career, under Don John against the Turk, later under the Dutch, and then as a combatant in the Desmond rebellion. Iron-handed and self-assured, he had been markedly successful in controlling the turbulent gentry of Connaught although he had imperilled the Composition of 1585, an achievement of Perrot, which turned the local landowners into rent-paying crown tenants who provided sufficient revenue to pay for the costs of the presidency. This high-handed and hot-tempered soldier was to prove a major problem for the new deputy, as he had for Perrot.

Among the councillors regularly resident in Dublin there was still an Old English element, represented most strongly by the Dillons, Sir Lucas (Chief Justice of Common Pleas) and Sir Robert (Chief Baron of the Exchequer), members of a Pale legal dynasty. An English newcomer to the legal contingent was Robert Gardiner, Chief Justice of Queen's Bench since 1586.[20] This immigrant element had been recently reinforced by Thomas Jones, Bishop of Meath since 1584, a relative by marriage of Loftus and former dean of St. Patrick's. Born in Lancashire and educated at Cambridge, he had made his ecclesiastical career in Ireland from the first. Last but by no means least in the Dublin administration was the secretary, Sir Geoffrey Fenton. Born in Nottinghamshire, brother to a well-known naval commander, he, like Spenser, had been in the service of Lord Grey, and he had also made a literary name for himself as the translator of Guicciardini and other Italian, French, and Latin writers before settling down to a political career as Secretary in 1580.[21]

The council was a body of pivotal importance in Irish affairs. Its members were nominated in London, and the proportion of English-born had risen steadily through the reign. Not all of these immigrants had stayed, but a substantial residue, the weightiest part of the council, had settled down, establishing themselves and their posterity as permanent residents. Deputies, on the other hand, were birds of passage, rarely serving more than three to four years.

These circumstances alone placed a deputy at a disadvantage *vis à vis* his council; these disadvantages were compounded by the deputy's anomalous constitutional position. He was, of course, the

---

[19] *CSPI* 5 (1592–96): 124. [20] *CSPI* 4 (1588–92): 53, 153.
[21] See *DNB*, "Fenton."

Crown's direct representative, head of the "state at Dublin" in local terminology; but he was bound by his instructions to seek consultation and advice from his council—advice that, given their local knowledge and connections, he would ignore at his peril. Moreover, since appointment to the higher echelons of Irish offices rested with the Queen and not with the deputy, the councillors looked to London, where they had direct personal ties with the English Privy Councillors.[22] In many instances these were ties of clientage, but in any case the individual councillors could bypass the deputy by direct correspondence with the English court. As one observer put it, referring to Fitzwilliam, "for that he knew if he should displease them [the Dublin council] they being men of great friends and ambitions" could frustrate his hopes.[23] Still, his control over most minor officers gave him some leverage against his councillors. Moreover, the council itself was not likely to be united against the deputy, as it was fissiparous to a fault, torn by continual acrimonious quarrels. Two of the legal dynasties of the Pale, Dillons and Nugents, carried their feuds literally to the block, intertwining these local enmities with the larger political questions of the day. Under the late deputy Perrot—a man of ungovernable temper and eccentric, not to say mad, behavior—factions had grown up. His adherents were to find themselves in grave difficulties when Perrot himself became the only Elizabethan councillor (other than the Duke of Norfolk) to be condemned to execution.

When Fitzwilliam set out from London for Dublin he carried a detailed set of instructions from the Privy Council. Preoccupied with the looming threat of Spanish invasion, they put Ireland low on their list.[24] The island seemed to be in a reasonably quiet state; no urgent crisis faced the incoming deputy. Most of their instructions dealt with details of administration, the vexing question of the annual composition for ale and the adjoining counties of Leinster, the perpetual problem of army costs, and the adjustment of the Connaught composition.[25] Much remained to be done in launching the Munster plantation, which was troubled by the claims of local

---

[22] *CSPI* 4 (1588–92): 220; see *APC* 1587–88: 58, for the appointment of the keeper of the storehouse and seneschal of Clandeboy in London.

[23] Thomas Lee, "A Brief Declaration of the Government of Ireland . . . from the Year 1588 to the Year 1594," in *Desiderata curiosa hibernica*, ed. [J. Lodge] (2 vols., Dublin, 1772) 1: 103–4; Brady, 66.

[24] *APC* 1588–89: 73–75.   [25] *CSPI* 3 (1586–88): 455–57, 460–62, 490–93.

Irish landowners and by the shortcomings of the undertakers. A weighty judicial commission was sent from England to deal with the former.[26] In the affairs of the Gaelic north the Council took a hopeful view of Tyrone "as a good instrument for the stay of those parts." The commission granted him by the lords justices had worked well and should be continued. The quarrels between him and Turlough O'Neill should be left to be settled by the parties themselves. Hugh Roe O'Donnell, heir and prospective leader of the other great Ulster dynasty, now a hostage in Dublin Castle, should be kept there. In short, the deputy was to pursue a *status quo* policy that, it was hoped, would prolong the era of quiet.

When Fitzwilliam actually arrived his first task was to deal with the detritus of the Armada, cast up on the west coast. For a time there was in London and in Dublin great fear of a landing in force; reinforcements were lined up to be sent from England, and the deputy himself marched to the west, making a sweep through Connaught and Ulster and meeting most of the principal Gaelic gentry, along with the magnates O'Donnell and Tyrone, by whom he was handsomely entertained. The arrest of two local chiefs, Sir Owen MacTooley and Sir John O'Dogherty, on suspicion of concealing Spanish treasure, and their consequent long imprisonment, soured the welcome that the Gaelic chieftains had given the new deputy. Nevertheless, he had established civil relations with the Gaelic leaders.[27]

Revealing glimpses of the English sense of insecurity persisted. At the height of the Armada scare a secret postscript was attached to a letter from the deputy and council "signed by us only of the English," i.e., the English-born members of council. Calling for 2,000 men from England, it avowed their fear that not only Gaelic Ulster but the Pale as well would rise. Several months later the deputy noted that at the general thanksgiving for deliverance from invasion none of the Irish judges in Dublin communicated. These suppressed suspicions of the whole Irish community were always lurking in the background of the English rulers' consciousness.[28]

The first challenge to Fitzwilliam's authority was to emerge, however, not from Gaelic resistance but from within the ranks of

[26] *CSPI* 4 (1588–92): 5, 7.

[27] *Ibid.*, 52, 66, 69, 92, 100; *APC* 1588: 319, 330, 331; Fynes Moryson, *An History of Ireland, from the Year 1599 to 1603* (2 vols., Dublin, 1735) 1: 18.

[28] *CSPI* 4 (1588–92): 53.

his own officials. The stormy petrel of the English official world
was Sir Richard Bingham, governor of Connaught. Installed there
by Perrot in 1584, he presided over an area where English law and
legal institutions were still novel. In 1585 Perrot, pressured by his
Old English officials, had negotiated the Composition of Connaught, an elaborate program for anglicization. It had the support
of the newly made Earls of Clanrickard (Burke) and Thomond
(O'Brien).[29] It was a tripartite arrangement. In the past arbitrary
exactions, levied by the state or by the chieftains, had made life a
misery for the population. Now, under the composition, the Crown
received fixed payments levied on each quarter of land, while the
chief in turn received a fixed rent from his tenants. All benefitted—
the Crown and the chiefs by certainty of income, the peasantry by
fixity of rent. Uncultivated lands were exempted from payment to
the Crown, a system that pleased the landlord class and encouraged
the settlement of unoccupied areas. And the system paid off in another way; it provided adequate income to finance all the costs of
the Connaught presidency locally.

However, not all the local Connaught elite were satisfied with
the new order. Perrot and Bingham had effectively destroyed the
Mayo Burke chieftaincy when that clan rose with Scottish mercenary support in 1586. Perrot and Bingham had fallen out at this
time, and the quarrel had been carried up to the Privy Council,
which resorted to the Solomonic solution of dispatching Bingham
to the Low Countries in 1587. His return reflected his influence
with the Dudley connection at court.[30]

His harsh rule soon proved the source of new disturbance. In
April 1589 trouble broke out in the province, first with the rising of
the Clanwilliam Burkes, which was only partially crushed by Bingham. It was followed by a second revolt, that of the O'Rourkes of
Leitrim. Sir Brian O'Rourke had made surrender and regrant of
his lands but he refused to accept the new order. In 1588 he har-
bored Spanish fugitives; later he was accused of dragging about and
publicly insulting a wooden image meant to represent Queen Elizabeth. His revolt was crushed; he fled first to Donegal and then to
Scotland, where he was arrested and turned over to the English,

[29] Ellis, 288; see Cunningham, 1–14; *CSPI* 4 (1588–92): 481–83.
[30] Morgan, "Outbreak," 33; ECS, 92–107; Bagwell 3: 167; *Annals of the Kingdom
of Ireland by the Four Masters*, ed. John O'Donovan (3 vols., Dublin, 1848) 3: 1885,
1905.

who executed him at Tyburn. The O'Rourke inheritance was dispersed and the chieftaincy destroyed.[31]

A commission of councillors was dispatched from Dublin to act with Bingham in pacifying the country. Their first attempt failed but they were sent off for a second try. They were now at odds with Bingham, who had not scrupled to mock them publicly. Writing to Burghley, Thomas Jones, Bishop of Meath, the senior councillor involved, laid the blame for the rising on Bingham's harsh treatment of the Connaught men, the hanging of "some gentlemen of good sort" by martial law, the seizure of land, and the abuses of his officers. In Bingham's version it was the attempts of the chiefs to regain their "old seignories," with the right to arbitrary levies on their followers, that had led to the revolt. But, as the bishop wrote, "the more earnestly we commissioners sought for pacification, the more busily did Sir Richard . . . bend all his endeavors to war."[32]

This was the beginning of a political storm less bloody but hardly less tempestuous than combat in the wilds of Connaught. A desperate tussle began between the deputy and a part of his council and Sir Richard Bingham. The former, quoting the Queen's recommendation for a "temperate course of government," sought reconciliation in Connaught. Bingham wrote immediately to his patron Walsingham to protest. Fitzwilliam proposed to go in person to Galway but wrote protestingly of a rumored Privy Council letter to the restive Irish leaders that "even if not true will put the Irishry on a high pin." The harried deputy was already seeking a promise of recall not later than July 1590. He was able to secure the submission of two of the Irish chieftains, but they were derided by Bingham as "a couple of old doting fools." This, he continued, was no way to achieve a lasting peace. He attacked the malice of the Bishop of Meath and Chief Justice Sir Robert Dillon and their sinister influence on the deputy and the other councillors.[33]

By now the locus of struggle had shifted from Ireland to the English court. The correspondence cited earlier was addressed to the Privy Council, defending the Irish administration's actions, for

[31] CSPI 4 (1588–92), 142–44, 148, 167, 176–77, 204–5, 464–65; Bagwell 3: 212–17. For a full discussion of the O'Rourke affair, see the unpublished paper, "The Case of Brian O'Rourke," by Hiram Morgan. I am grateful to Dr. Morgan for the opportunity to read this paper.

[32] CSPI 4 (1588–92): 172, 179, 231–32; APC 1588–89: 259–60.

[33] CSPI 4 (1588–92): 183–84, 188–89, 193–94, 206–7, 209, 212, 215.

Bingham had gone directly to his powerful patrons in London. Already the Bishop of Meath had had a thorough dressing-down by Secretary Walsingham for his ill-usage of Bingham. Walsingham had been told that the bishop was a hypocrite, and now he believed it. How could the bishop be so unwise as to suppose the Connaught rebels could be dealt with save by the sword? This was followed by a letter of the secretary to the lord deputy that roundly rebuked him for the injustice of listening to rebels without giving Bingham a chance to reply. Nor did the deputy's intervention at Galway "stand with the Queen's honor that [the rebels] should be dandled in so dishonorable a sort." He was warned that Bingham was "not weakly so friended nor hath deserved so ill both of this state, and of that too, as he shall be shaked out of his government" without good cause. There followed a sharp hint, "it may fall out, my lord Deputy, to be your own case," for accusations against deputies were not unknown. In a bitter complaint to Burghley, Fitzwilliam suggested that, given the secretary's dislike, perhaps the Queen should appoint another deputy.[34]

The angry exchanges continued to rage; Bingham listed the deputy, Loftus, Jones, Dillon and Secretary Fenton as his enemies. The Privy Council ordered that Bingham's case should be heard at Dublin by the whole council before the sessions at Sligo and Galway. (Chief Justice Gardiner and Vice-Treasurer Wallop were supporters of Bingham.) The deputy reacted to this by pointing out that the Burkes, in terror of Bingham, would not risk their lives by going to Dublin to press charges, as Bingham well knew. The latter was in fact now asking Walsingham to move the trial to England since the Dublin council were all mere weak creatures of the deputy. The council tenaciously stuck to their guns, insistently rehearsing their measures of pacification and recounting instances of Bingham's oppressive regime. Now, in late October, Bingham had reached Dublin, where the hard-pressed deputy (fortified by three days of physic) proposed to hear the cause, but others suspected he would leave the matter in suspense.[35]

By now the rebellion had flared up again; the Burkes were once more in arms, and the Queen directed Fitzwilliam to assist Bingham in suppressing them. Bingham in turn was told to reconcile

[34] *Ibid.*, 208–9, 216–17, 226.
[35] *Ibid.*, 206, 219, 224, 228, 230, 241, 255, 268.

himself with the deputy while the rebels were pursued. Though promised a general acquittal, he was still rumbling away about reparation for time and costs. The Bishop of Meath and Chief Justice Dillon had been driven off the stage under royal disapprobation, but the deputy was still fighting, defending the two disgraced councillors and declaring of Bingham that "if there be an atheist upon earth, he is one," without scruple as to what he said or did. The quarrel dragged on into the spring of 1590. By March Bingham could report the pacification of the whole province except for O'Rourke's country. In the course of the year O'Rourke fled too and the rising died down.[36]

This episode has been worth the telling because it highlights the manner in which the government of Ireland was conducted. What is immediately apparent is the direct dependence on London at every level of administration. The lines of force moved, not in ordered sequence from Queen and Privy Council to deputy and council, but directly from the English court to each provincial center of English government in Ireland. Hence the deputy was hardly more than *primus inter pares*, and sometimes less, for it was not one's official status that determined place in the hierarchy of power but connections with a powerful court patron. Fitzwilliam, without the backing that Sidney had had from a potent court faction, or the royal favor that Mountjoy was to enjoy a decade later, was no match for Bingham, with the forceful voice of Walsingham to back him up. The position of the Dublin councillors was particularly awkward. Nominally an executive body, they were continually overborne by the court influence of the English-born members. This in turn begot factionalism within the council as each member scuttled for protection to an English patron. The deputy was thus deprived of the assistance of a reasonably unified and responsible body of advisors and associates.

This system also meant that no decision could be finally determined in Ireland. Often, rather than run the risk of an appeal to London, it was simpler not to act but to pass the buck by appealing to the Privy Council for antecedent guidance or, if overtaken by events, by waiting for London before taking effective action. The Act Books of the Privy Council are replete with instances of Irish business, great and small, which appear on their docket rather than

[36] *Ibid.*, 263, 268–69, 270–73, 276–77, 278, 281, 299–300, 307, 323, 329.

on that of the Dublin council. Under these circumstances the implementation of any consistent policy became virtually impossible.

Another feature of the episode is the revelation of a clear difference in view as between Dublin and Athlone. The rough and resolute soldier on the "frontier," faced with the immediacy of violence, thought largely in terms of its suppression. For him the Gaelic leaders and their armed followers were not unruly subjects of the Queen but savage and untrustworthy enemies, mere bandits, who needed to be exterminated. He foreshadows attitudes of the English settlers in America a generation later. At Dublin, on the other hand, there was a wider and more humane view, some sense of the interests of a whole national community. The Gaelic elite were men with whom some *modus vivendi* must be established, who must ultimately be coaxed and bullied into "civility." Interestingly enough it was a New English councillor, Bishop Jones, and an Old English lawyer, Dillon, who took up the cudgels in favor of moderation on this occasion. But, given the fact of Bingham's highly placed patron and the relative fiscal independence that the rents from the Composition gave him, they had small chance of success. This whole episode is illustrative of the growing paralysis of Irish administration occasioned by the factional struggles in the English court. Any initiative in Dublin was all too likely to be checked by an appeal to Westminster.

Connaught nearly monopolized the deputy's attention in his first year of office, although Ulster's affairs were rapidly looming larger. Munster, however, bulked much less importantly on his agenda. There the process of colonization had been underway for several years. It was not moving rapidly; problems of legal title had become acute as the lesser Irish landowners sought to avert the consequences of the Desmond attainders. The fluid nature of tenure under the old system made for insoluble legal puzzles as the lawyers tried to separate out the rights of the attainted earl from those of his tenants. A special commission from England, headed by Chief Justice Anderson, arrived almost simultaneously with the new deputy and held hearings on the Irish claims in Munster.[37]

In fact, the whole operation had been closely controlled from England. It was the Privy Council who circularized the west country and Cheshire gentry to recruit undertakers, who received and

[37] *CSPI* 4 (1588–92): 26.

vetted the applications for grants and who allocated them. Burghley himself gave the closest attention to all details, and Walsingham played almost as important a role (and became an investor in Irish lands).[38] By 1589 it was time to take stock of progress in an enterprise that showed signs of faltering. The Irish solicitor-general, Wilbraham, reported to Burghley that "all things wax faint in the enterprise; undertakers seek nothing but money and Irish lands yield nothing but meat." He was doubtful that any of them would find their quota of bona fide English settlers. Writing much the same message to Walsingham, he urged the fears of undertakers and of prospective settlers "with sight of this rude and tottering uncertain state." One undertaker accused his fellows of extortion and greed, seeking to live "by pay and prey."[39]

Some thirty-five grants had been made by 1588. A survey made late in that year enumerated 528 English households, tenants of twenty-three undertakers. The number needs to be substantially increased since there is no clear distinction between individuals and families, but it suggests a colony of some 2,600 English. The number of Irish tenants on these same lands was several times larger. The process was clearly slow and painful, and there was a slackening of interest as undertakers and settlers alike came face-to-face with the difficulties encountered. The failure of the English authorities to establish the necessary condition for colonization, an orderly and secure countryside, was a great discouragement to any but the most hardy. However, from Fitzwilliam's point of view Munster could be left to the care of Sir Thomas Norris, deputy to his brother, Sir John, president of the province, but currently employed as commander of the Lisbon expedition.[40]

A province whose affairs were more exigent was Ulster. The two great magnates of the North were the O'Neill, seated in Tyrone and Armagh, overlord of central Ulster, and the O'Donnell, lord of Tyrconnell (the modern Donegal). The O'Neill interest was divided between the aging Sir Turlough Luineach O'Neill, the clan chief, and his younger rival, Hugh, Baron of Dungannon and since

---

[38] MacCarthy-Morrogh, 38–40; *APC* 1586–87: 327–28.
[39] *CSPI* 4 (1588–92): 51–52.
[40] See MacCarthy-Morrogh, 69, 113, and A. J. Sheehan, "The Population of the Plantation of Munster: Quinn Reconsidered," in *Journal of the Cork Historical and Archaeological Society*, 2nd ser. 87 (1982): 107–17; BL, Cotton Mss., Titus C VII, 156–61.

1585 Earl of Tyrone.[41] The latter, soon destined to play so great a role in Irish history, was now in his thirties. In his youth he had been a protégé of Sidney and ward of an English settler, Giles Hovenden. Returning to Ireland in 1568, he was set up by the English as a counterpoise to Sir Turlough. Here, as in so many other cases, the weakness of a social order that lacked certain rules of succession enabled the English government to play the ancient game of divide and rule. Tyrone proved a faithful servitor of the Crown and led a troop of horse in the Desmond rebellion. He also fought for the Earl of Essex in 1573–1575. He was rewarded by the title his grandfather had received in return for a surrender and regrant, Earl of Tyrone, and by English backing in his rivalry with Sir Turlough for lease of the O'Neill lands. The acquisition of that lease made him effective master of the lordship of Armagh and leader of his clan in all but name.[42] Within the leased lands the earl held sway under Irish law, treating the entire estate as demesne, reducing the occupiers to mere tenants at will, and in effect turning landlordship into chieftaincy. The new earl stood out among the Gaelic lords as virtually the only one who was fully conversant with English custom and culture.

One of the deputy's first tasks was to adjudicate a dispute arising out of the O'Neill lease. In his instructions Fitzwilliam had been advised to remain neutral, leaving the matter to the two parties, but as early as October 1588 he was besieged by the litigants for a judgment and was himself seeking to know the Queen's pleasure. Her reply was a characteristically equivocating command to sustain the claims of Sir Turlough but to compound the case if Tyrone would not give in. The earl apparently accepted this when Fitzwilliam was in Ulster, but then in March 1589 firmly refused to yield up the lands. He had lost his longtime patron with Leicester's death in September 1588 and was now seeking to replace him with Walsingham.[43]

Fitzwilliam now went north with his council to settle the matter. He decided in favor of the earl when he discovered Turlough's intention to give the disputed lands to the sons of the late Shane

---

[41] The title was granted by Deputy Perrot in 1585 and confirmed by letters patent from England in 1587 (*APC* 1587–88: 74–75).

[42] Sidney, "Memoir," 92–93, 94; ECS, 91–92; Morgan, "Outbreak," 76–77, citing SP 63/79/5 and SP 65/8, fol. 51; *APC* 1587–88: 74–75.

[43] *CSPI* 4 (1588–92): 66, 73–74, 95, 119, 139.

O'Neill, a move that would destabilize the lordship by renewing factional struggle among the various branches of the ruling family. In April the quarrel became a live one when the MacShanes, backed by Turlough, raided Tyrone's lands and cattle. Both sides began importing Scots mercenaries. This drew the deputy north again to impose a peace. Tyrone was called to account for having hired Scots, but given license to attend the Queen. At the last minute he suddenly decided not to go to London. His motive was no doubt the affair of Hugh Gaveloch O'Neill, one of Shane's sons. Taken by Maguire, sold to Tyrone, he was hanged by the earl's order. Called on by the deputy to explain, Tyrone airily replied that he thought well to execute Hugh, the son of a traitor and himself a traitor. The council placed him under a £2,000 bond for appearance but left him free. Tyrone had in fact made humble submission to the deputy who had recommended his case to Burghley and urged a pardon. Then without further permission Tyrone proceeded to London, where he was kept under house arrest. Tyrone's defense makes interesting reading. Admitting his legal guilt under English law, he asserted that in Ulster "where there is neither magistrate, judge, sheriff, or course of the laws of this [English] realm" he was the Queen's lieutenant, bound to do justice in accordance with Irish custom. He went on to declare that when the law used in the "reformed parts of the realm" was decreed, he would take the lead in implementing it.[44]

The deputy and council, in a general survey of Irish affairs in spring 1590, candidly admitted that they had no power in Ulster and that the best they could hope of the Ulster chiefs was that they would remain neutral in an emergency (such as a Spanish invasion) until they saw which way the cards would fall. But among them, if any in Ulster were dutiful to the Queen, they placed their hopes in Tyrone, the recipient of English patronage. In another letter of about the same date they assessed the state of Ulster more specifically. Tyrone and Sir Turlough kept one another in check, but once the aging chieftain died, the earl "may show himself to be the man which now in his wisdom he hath reason to dissemble." With this in mind they advocated a discreet patronage of Shane O'Neill's sons. Tyrone, having attended court, made his submission, was duly pardoned, and in the summer returned to Ireland, grateful to

[44] *Ibid.*, 183–84, 227, 228, 247, 252, 261, 276, 298, 312–13, 326–27, 328.

Burghley for his help. The quarrel with Turlough continued to simmer and occasionally boiled up into a raid or a skirmish. In part these disturbances arose from the increasing infirmity of Sir Turlough, who could no longer control his followers.[45]

In August 1591 the recently widowed Tyrone upset the Irish applecart once again by carrying off and marrying Mabel, daughter to Sir Nicholas Bagenal and sister to Sir Henry, to the fury of the two. The Bagenals had established an interest in eastern Ulster at Newry early in the reign, and Sir Nicholas had ambitions to become president of Ulster. Perrot had recognized Bagenal as a major figure in the province in his three-fold division of influence (with Hugh O'Neill and Sir Turlough), and there was constant friction on the borders between Tyrone's lands and those of the Bagenals. They now attempted to prove that the earl had not been divorced from his first wife, but Tyrone defeated that ploy. Bagenal, developing a larger theme, urged on Burghley that the Queen take the opportunity offered by the suit between Tyrone and Turlough O'Neill to diminish the power of both. If they established that Turlough had only a life estate they could ultimately insure the distribution of his lands among the lesser septs, breaking up O'Neill superiority and increasing the royal revenue while reducing the province to obedience. Although he had a favorable hearing from Burghley, nothing was done.[46]

In the meantime an unexpected event had radically altered the picture in Ulster. In the western half of the province lay the lordship of Tyrconnel, where the O'Donnells held sway. Remote in their northwestern fastness, linked with the Scots Islanders, many of whom served as mercenaries, they were regarded with suspicion in Dublin. They were among the few Gaelic lords who had not acknowledged English supremacy by the process of surrender and regrant. In 1587 the putative heir to the clan leadership, the fifteen-year-old Hugh Roe, was kidnapped on Dublin's orders and held hostage in Dublin Castle for his father's good behavior. In 1589 Tyrone had sued to Walsingham for the release of the young man, whom he betrothed to his own daughter. The Dublin council backed this proposal, but in vain. Now in January 1592 the young O'Donnell effected his escape from the castle on a second attempt;

[45] *Ibid.*, 337–38, 338–39, 352, 356, 366, 384, 398, 438, 441–42, 446, 521.
[46] *Ibid.*, 409, 415, 433–36, 459–60, 480, 552–53; Morgan, "Outbreak," 63.

he fled to Tyrone at Dungannon and the earl provided an escort to Maguire territory. The young chief's first act on arrival at home was to expel the English sheriff, Captain Willis, who had established a base in Donegal Friary. His father then retired as chief, and Hugh Roe became the O'Donnell. There followed strife with the Turlough faction of the O'Neills but this was brought to an end by Tyrone's intervention; peace was established between the O'Neills and the O'Donnells. An alliance of sorts followed with the marriage of Tyrone's daughter to the Tyrconnel chieftain. This was a worrying development for the Dublin rulers, who had always counted on the ancient rivalry between the two Ulster lords. The deputy had initially proposed an armed expedition to bring pressure on the escapee, but he then accepted Tyrone as intermediary and the latter brought his son-in-law to Dundalk to make his formal submission to the deputy.[47]

These various transactions give revealing evidence of the uneasy but not wholly unstable relations between the Irish government and the great Gaelic chieftains, particularly Tyrone. While regarding him with a wary suspicion, the government nevertheless cultivated his goodwill and relied on his services to keep the north in some kind of order. Officials like Bagenal and Wilbraham could preach the advantage of a thorough "reformation" of Ulster on the model of Connaught or Munster, but there was no serious disposition in either London or Dublin to press such a program. When Tyrone boldly asserted his judicial authority by hanging Hugh Gaveloch, the English authorities were more than willing to accept his justification, and after a ritual submission in London he returned in triumph to his homeland. Alone among the Gaelic lords he had status of his own at court and support from Burghley. O'Donnell was less well placed, but even he, having flouted English authority by his escape and by expelling the sheriff from Tyrconnel, was received into grace. His rise to power, assisted by Tyrone, with whom he now had a marital link, meant that there was an alliance between the two Ulster overlords whose clientages embraced virtually the whole province. This unwonted unity of leadership in the Gaelic north would endure to the end of the struggle. For the pres-

[47] Lughaidh O'Clery, *Life of Aodh Ruadh O Domhnaill* (2 vols., Dublin, 1948–57), 1:7, 37, 41, 45–47, 49, 51; *CSPI* 4 (1588–92): 119, 268, 457, 462–63, 518–19, 520–23, 568–70; *Annals* 3:1933.

ent at least there was no indication that the English proposed any active measures against the Ulster lords, and indeed they showed every disposition to continue the *status quo* for an indefinite future.

Fitzwilliam, as we have seen in his dispute with Bingham, was inclined to favor a policy of moderation (or rather of economy), but he was not backward in seizing a chance to advance royal authority when an opportunity offered. One of the great sources of instability in Gaelic society arose from disputed succession to clan leadership. Since no clear rule prevailed, the death of a chieftain all too frequently led to a competition among rival claimants. This offered the Dublin authorities an opening wedge. By taking advantage of such a situation they could effectively shatter the old order of clan leadership. Perrot had intervened in Connaught when MacWilliam Burke of Mayo died and divided the seignory among five competitors, effectively breaking up the ancient order. A similar course was recommended in Leitrim when the O'Rourke fled after the rising of 1590.[48]

A similar problem—and a similar opportunity—arose with the death of the MacMahon chief, Sir Hugh Ross, in 1589. He was one of the satellite chieftains in the clientage of Tyrone and son-in-law of the earl, who had stood surety for his debts. MacMahon had made a surrender and regrant of his lands in county Monaghan in 1587. Two brothers were entitled in remainder according to the royal letters patent, but there were other claimants, each of whom hoped to be made the MacMahon. The deputy attempted to divide the lands among four of the claimants, "as this would be best for Her Majesty." Failing to win their agreement, he settled on Hugh Roe MacMahon as sole heir of all the MacMahon lands and sent 400 foot to assist him against his rival (in Gaelic law), the tanaiste (successor) Brian McHugh Oge. The latter fled to the neighboring Maguires of Fermanagh and then returned in force to recover the lands he had enjoyed in the past.

What happened next is less clear. By the end of 1589 MacMahon was in prison, allegedly for march offenses, such as cattle raiding. In March 1590 a more serious accusation was brought by the deputy, who now regarded MacMahon's behavior as nothing less than

[48] *CSPI* 4 (1588–92): 498–500 (for a general description of the situation), 466, 467, 470; Morgan, unpublished paper, cited n. 31. See also Wallop's account in BL, Cotton Mss., Titus C VII, 156–61.

treason and proposed to London a prosecution on this charge. The Queen ordered that he should not be prosecuted but that no one should be substituted in his place as the MacMahon. Fitzwilliam now proposed to accept an offer from the MacMahon claimants and to break up the inheritance among them. But in June 1590 he still hesitated as to whether to pardon Hugh Roe or to divide the territory. He denied accusations of personal profit, although he admitted he had been made large offers of cattle.[49]

By September he had orders from the Privy Council to proceed with a trial, but clearly was uncertain about obtaining a conviction. Justice Gardiner and the Solicitor were dispatched to sound out the local situation. A few days later Fitzwilliam set off for Monaghan, accompanied by MacMahon, with 300 soldiers. There Hugh Roe was duly tried and executed on the charge of levying private war on a kinsman and of rescuing traitors from the sheriff. The example to the Irish chiefs, the deputy declared, would be worth the slaughter of a thousand rebels in action. Over the next year, following directions from the Privy Council and the Queen, he parcelled out the MacMahon lands among 8 chief lords and 280 freeholders holding directly of the Crown. A garrison of 100 men was established at Monaghan town. Such was the official version.[50]

Among the Irish there was a different story. In 1593 it was alleged that Hugh Roe had initially won the inheritance by promising a bribe of 800 head of cattle. His real offense was failure to pay up. It was also asserted that the jury had been bullied into a conviction. It was widely believed that MacMahon had been railroaded by the deputy, that they had ridden to Monaghan on friendly terms, MacMahon believing he would be put in possession of his lands; the trial took him entirely by surprise. In popular usage it was said of someone whom one wished to see hanged, "God send him the MacMahon lordship." It was also widely asserted that Bagenal was the beneficiary of the whole operation.[51]

Certainly there are mysteries in the whole affair, and suspicion

[49] *CSPI* 4 (1588–92): 22, 224–51, 263, 315, 316, 318, 353, 499; Morgan, "Outbreak," 45–46; Peadar Macduinnshleibhe, "The Legal Murder of Aodh Rua McMahon, 1590," *Clogher Record* (1955): 39–52.

[50] *CSPI* 4 (1588–92): 362, 365, 369, 394, 427, 428; *APC* 1591: 329–30.

[51] SP 63/169/3; Sir James Perrott, *Chronicle of Ireland by Sir James Perrot*, ed. H[erbert] Wood (Dublin, 1933), 68; Moryson, *Itinerary*, pt. 2: 10; Moryson, *History* 1: 20.

of ill-dealing, whether justified or not, hung around Fitzwilliam. His initial intention to follow approved precedent by liquidating the lordship was diverted; he was even willing to lend Hugh Roe 400 foot to establish his claim. After the latter's arrest and imprisonment there followed nearly a year of indecision with reference back and forth between London and Dublin. At one stage the Queen was willing to spare the chieftain's life although at the expense of his lordship. The change of mind in London came tardily; quarrels between Fitzwilliam and Perrot, now a Privy Councillor, may have been the cause of delay. When the time for the trial approached Fitzwilliam obviously had doubts about getting a conviction and reserved the possibility of not proceeding.

A probable scenario of this episode has been reconstructed by a modern historian. According to this version, Fitzwilliam, dissatisfied with MacMahon's failure to establish his authority (or pay his cattle rent), listened to proposals from the tanaiste Brian Oge and the other MacMahon claimants. They were willing to accept the division of the lordship (and the extinction of the chieftainship) in exchange for the security of a royal title to their lands. Such a change would suit the English very well, providing a more stable settlement in Monaghan and liquidating the Gaelic socioeconomic structure. But Hugh Roe, who had legal title to all these lands, had to be removed. This could be done only by a trumped-up charge of treason and collusion between the deputy and the MacMahon claimants, who provided a complacent jury. Certainly they were the beneficiaries of the confiscation.[52]

Although the deputy heralded the execution as a wholesome and powerful lesson to the Irish aristocracy, it was probably not intially a carefully calculated act of policy. In its earlier stages personal considerations apparently dominated, and the matter may have gone to London simply because Fitzwilliam had to defend himself against accusations of bribe-taking. Only very belatedly did the Queen and/ or the Privy Council decide to make an example of MacMahon. But, once action had been taken, the whole episode escalated into a major policy decision with wide-ranging consequences.

Sir George Carew (the future president of Munster), Solicitor Wilbraham, Bagenal, and the deputy would all later cite Monaghan

[52] Macduinnshleibhe, 44–49. The English grantees received church lands, which were not part of the MacMahon holdings.

as a prototype for future policy. Fitzwilliam's actions there went further than previous attempts to reach a settlement of property rights, such as the composition of Connaught, since they destroyed the chieftaincy and turned the occupants of the MacMahon lands into simple freeholders under the Crown. Widely employed, the tactic would be a powerful weapon in the English drive to replace the Gaelic social and legal order by an English polity. The immediate reaction of the Gaelic aristocracy was a more personal one. The lesson drawn by them was one of dismayed distrust in the English rulers. The fate of MacMahon was seen as a singularly shocking act of betrayal. Moreover, the legal charges against him were viewed by the Irish as out of all proportion to the harshness of the sentence. He had been killed for what Tyrone described as "distressing [distraining] for his right according to custom." The deliberate destruction of the chieftaincy was an even graver matter, the harbinger of an attack on their very existence as a social order. Russell, Fitzwilliam's successor, later cited the Monaghan settlement as the "very seed of all our troubles."[53]

More particularly, the fall of MacMahon bore heavily on Tyrone. The late chieftain had been his client; the disappearance of the lordship shrank the penumbra of the earl's influence, while the English now had a base in Monaghan that flanked the earl's own lands in Tyrone. Worst of all, the event seemed to foreshadow his own possible fate. Later, when Tyrone refused to go to Dublin or even to meet the deputy in person, he alleged the fate of MacMahon as justification of his fears for his life. Certainly the Irish—and the English too—would come within a short time to look back on the MacMahon affair as the sharpest turning point in their relations with one another.

[53] Morgan, "Outbreak," 56, citing Lambeth, *Carew* Ms. 618, fols. 46, 67, citing SP 63/189/46 12; *CSPI* 4 (1588–92): 441–42, 458; Ellis, 297.

CHAPTER 18

FITZWILLIAM AND THE FIRST

RUPTURE WITH TYRONE

TRUST BETWEEN the Dublin government and the Gaelic chiefs had been badly eroded by the MacMahon episode. The delicate balance on which relations between them rested had been badly jarred by the ill-considered actions of the deputy, but now it was the actions of the Gaelic leaders that precipitated a new crisis. The Dublin government was thrust into a defensive stance made all the more uncomfortable by its own internal divisions, which in turn led to a series of clumsy, inconsistent, and feeble responses to the challenges thrown up to it. From 1593 to the end of Russell's tenure in 1596, and well beyond, the dance in Ireland was led by the Gaelic princes; the Dublin government proved an inept and wrong-footed partner.

It was some nine months after the execution of MacMahon in April 1593 that the deputy and council were shocked by frightening intelligence from several sources of a major and widespread conspiracy for a rising in the north to be combined with an invasion from Spain. Tyrone and O'Donnell, with the lesser chieftains of the north, were alleged to have made a pact with the papal primate of Armagh to join with the Spaniards, who were expected in mid-May next. The council sent for Tyrone to repair to Dublin. He himself was already appealing to England, both to the Privy Council and to Essex, against the malice of his enemies, who, he claimed, unjustly accused him.[1]

---

[1] *CSPI* 5 (1592–96): 94–95, 109.

The roots of the matter were to be found a year or so earlier. In 1592 a council of Irish Catholic bishops, led by the Primate Mac-Gauran, had decided on an appeal for Spanish help on behalf of their religion. Needing assurance of secular support, they sought O'Donnell as a leader. He, Maguire, and their allies agreed to back a mission; Tyrone was aware of the project but held aloof. Mac-Gauran was killed in a skirmish in June 1593, but Archbishop O'Healy of Tuam had an audience with Philip II in the autumn of that year. The king's response was to dispatch a fact-finding mission, but the ship on which they sailed disappeared, presumably shipwrecked. The English and Irish governments did not know the principal facts of this enterprise until the end of 1594 or the beginning of 1595.[2]

In the spring of 1593 the Irish council, in spite of a shower of reports, came to the conclusion that there was not sufficient ground to proceed against the earl. Fears of a Spanish descent were for the time being crowded out by more pressing matters. Within a week there was news from Athlone that Maguire, the lord of Fermanagh, aided by O'Donnell, had repulsed the sheriff of Fermanagh and threatened the borders of Connaught with 1,500 men. Other tidings came crowding in of a raid by Tyrone's half-brother in Cavan. The same letter that retailed this news told of the murder of another O'Neill, Phelim McMurrough, by servants of Tyrone. Fitzwilliam prepared to take 1,200 men to Dundalk, where Maguire and Tyrone were summoned to appear before him and the council.[3]

Although the Maguire rising opened a new chapter in relations between the English and the Gaels, it was in itself only one link in a long chain of events, a complex history of strife, involving a large cast of actors—Bingham, O'Donnell, the lesser chieftains whose lands lay in the border zone where the influence of O'Donnell intersected that of the president of Connaught, and ultimately O'Neill. The clue that leads us through this maze of conflict is to be found in the conduct of Hugh Roe O'Donnell.

Since his escape from Dublin Castle O'Donnell had been very busy. The prestige of his house had fallen in the years of his father's feeble leadership, when the O'Donnells were rent by feuds over the

---

[2] John J. Silke, "The Irish Appeal of 1593 to Spain," *Irish Ecclesiastical Record*, 5th ser. 92 (1959): 279–90, 362–71; Wallop in BL, Cotton Mss., Titus C VII, 156–61.

[3] *CSPI* 5 (1592–96): 85, 92, 96, 99–100, 102, 103.

succession and the scope of O'Donnell influence over their clients had shrunk. The young O'Donnell, anxious to restore the tarnished glories of his family, had been "holding meetings, being generous, joyous, roaring, restless, quarrelsome, aggressive," in his biographer's words. Having re-established his authority in Tyrconnell he had intervened in the affairs of the O'Neills. The resulting alliance with Tyrone against Turlough had been mutually advantageous but more particularly to Tyrone, to whom Turlough surrendered land and the chieftainship in May 1593. The two overlords, each with enhanced power, now began to collaborate in an alliance that reshaped the whole of Irish politics.[4]

In that partnership O'Donnell, the junior in years and in political experience, was usually the more aggressive, impatiently pressing for action and more reckless of consequences, while Tyrone—cautious, wary, and wiser in the ways of politics, both at Westminster and at Dublin—was a restraining influence on his impetuous ally. In the early 1590's it was O'Donnell who publicly espoused the causes of their rebellious countrymen on the Connaught borders while Tyrone played the role of mediator. In fact the deputy, and at least some of the councillors, put little faith in Tyrone's fair words and saw him as the real, albeit secret, mover in these affairs. The historian, while sharing their skepticism, can hardly do more than suspend judgment. It was O'Donnell who responded to the bishops' appeal, and it was he to whom they looked as leader of a Catholic enterprise. In 1592 he had initially supported the Mac-William Burke rising against Bingham but he abandoned them when he submitted to the deputy at Dundalk, under Tyrone's tuition.[5]

It was not long, however, before a new occasion involved O'Donnell in controversy with the Dublin government. In many respects it was in Connaught that a policy of accommodation between the old and new orders had proved most successful. The Munster presidency had nearly foundered on the rock of the Desmond risings, and English rule had finally established a Tacitean peace. In Connaught, on the other hand, the firm guidance of Sir Nicholas Malby and Sir Richard Bingham had gone far towards achieving a degree

[4] Morgan, "Outbreak," 105–16; O'Clery 1: 45–47, 49, 57, 59; *CSPI* 5 (1592–96): 99, 116; *Carew* 3 (1589–1600): 73–74; for much information about the career of O'Donnell, see *Annals* for 1592 and years following.

[5] *CSPI* 4 (1588–92): 545, 570, 590–94.

of stability. Here the two leading chiefs, the Burke and the O'Brien, now respectively Earls of Clanricard and Thomond, had accepted an arrangement that protected their magnate status, albeit within an English framework. Most of the lesser clans had followed suit in the Composition of Connaught. The Mayo Burkes, however, had bitterly resented the extinction of their chieftainship and had vainly risen against the governor. They were crushed, but not without involving their neighbors, the O'Rourkes, one of the principal clans of Leitrim, in conflict with the English. As we have seen, this resulted in the destruction of the O'Rourke chieftaincy in 1592.[6]

That was not the end of the story, however. In the fall of that year O'Rourke's surviving son, Brian Oge, took refuge with his neighbor, Maguire of Fermanagh. Here was the rub. Bingham could maintain English rule within his province and crush opposition by force, but there was a price to be paid. A policy of force begot armed resistance. As long as the defeated, beaten on their home ground, could still find asylum and count on aid from the untamed lords of Gaelic Ulster, their struggle could continue. Hence the suppression of one uprising and the dispersal of tribal lands became the cause for new friction that in turn touched off yet another explosion. In this continuous chain of causes and effects, Bingham, having quelled one recalcitrant clan, found himself faced with another—and ultimately with the great northern overlords.[7]

If the English governor found himself caught in a chain of consequences that he could not break, so was the Gaelic lord similarly trapped. He could hardly afford to stand by, an indifferent neutral, while one of his neighbors suffered the fate of the MacMahon in Monaghan, the extinction not only of his power but of his place in the world. This was particularly the case with the great families with ancient claims to overlordship. The destruction of a client (or potential client) was dangerous to the self-esteem of the overlord and to the prestige of his name. This was the situation that now faced both O'Donnell and Tyrone.

Sir Hugh Maguire, lord of Fermanagh, was ruler of the country around Lough Erne and master of the lake islands, a position of strength. "This Maguire thinks himself to be one of the best to keep his country against any power in Ireland." Sir Hugh, the head of the house, knighted by Fitzwilliam, was a client of O'Neill, to

---

[6] *Ibid.*, 464–65; *Annals* 3: 1911–13.   [7] *CSPI* 5 (1592–96): 38.

whom he paid rent, but also a neighbor and ally of O'Donnell. The latter's name was linked with that of Maguire as protector of the rebellious O'Rourke. Both were parties to the agreement with Archbishop MacGauran, who was in fact killed fighting along with Maguire. This led to a confrontation with Bingham. In March 1593 Brian Oge O'Rourke, in the absence of Bingham in Dublin, aided by galloglass of O'Donnell, seized Beleek and Bandrowes on the southern shore of Lough Erne. O'Donnell and Maguire then appeared in arms with 1,500 men and, shortly thereafter, in a confrontation with Willis, the new English sheriff of Fermanagh, overpowered the latter's soldiers and held them prisoners for a week until they were delivered by Tyrone.[8] Bingham pointed out with some satisfaction that Maguire was now outside the law, a traitor for whom no excuse could be made. The council at Dublin, to his disgust, ordered Tyrone to make a pacification with Maguire, who was required to meet them at Dundalk. Bagenal insisted that Tyrone was in fact the instigator of Maguire's actions and was the moving force in pressing charges against his hated brother-in-law.[9]

These events—both the alleged Catholic conspiracy and the rising of Maguire—signalled a new and sinister turn of events both for the government and for Tyrone. For the latter there was now a painful dilemma. In his tussles with Dublin he had until now more than held his own, thanks to his connections at court. As long as the issues at stake were largely confined to the traditional areas of the O'Neill lordship, he was able to maintain a fragile balance that secured his dominance in central Ulster while retaining a civil relationship with Dublin. But now events in other regions forced him to look farther afield and to involve himself in the fate of the remaining Gaelic lords. To some extent, as Bagenal and others insisted, Tyrone could and probably did guide the actions of O'Donnell, but his control over events in the western counties was at the best only partial. He was as much the creature as the master of events.[10]

These same events were equally disturbing to the government at Dublin. Deep disagreements as to how to deal with them surfaced

[8] *CSPI* 4 (1588–92): 499; 5 (1592–96): 85, 92, 112–13, 199–200; *Carew* 3 (1589–1600): 73–74; BL, Cotton Mss., Titus C VII, 156–61; Moryson, *History* 1: 27–28.

[9] *CSPI* 5 (1592–96): 105, 110; *Annals* 3: 1937–41.

[10] Moryson dates Tyrone's alliance with O'Donnell from the aftermath of the Maguire affair (*History* 1: 28).

quickly, and all was soon at sixes and sevens. Deputy Fitzwilliam and Sir Richard Bingham were once again at feud, both appealing to London. The result was a virtual paralysis of governmental action. The deputy and council were relying on Tyrone to halt Maguire's activities and had prohibited Bingham from attacking the latter. The governor of Connaught in a fury had written directly to Essex to report the latest incursion of Maguire. This in turn alerted the Queen and Privy Council. Elizabeth in a letter to Bingham praised his resistance to Maguire and revoked the deputy's prohibition against an attack. But then, in a characteristic half-step forward, half-step backward, she ordered him to forbear action if the Irish chieftain submitted to the deputy and promised to live peaceably. The Queen had also written Fitzwilliam a stinging rebuke for his dalliance with Tyrone and his commission to the latter to bring in Maguire. She commended his plea for recall and promised to take order for it. The Privy Council ordered the examination of the earl by the Irish judges. The deputy had in the meantime offered Maguire two months' protection pending negotiations, but the latter haughtily declined because he was required to disperse his soldiers. He frankly told the deputy that the protection would be valueless unless Bingham put his hand to it.[11]

Fitzwilliam justified his restraint of Bingham by the combination of circumstances—the weakness of the scattered English forces, the rumors of an impending Spanish landing, and the need to get the harvest in. A campaign against Maguire would only have meant the ravaging of Monaghan, "that young infant" so newly weaned to English rule. In the meantime he pursued a truce with Maguire through the agency of Tyrone, to whom he gave full powers to promise a three-month protection with assurance that Bingham would not move. If Maguire turned this offer down, the deputy would take action jointly with Bingham and Tyrone to crush him. Through the muddle of criss-crossing letters and royal reprimands the deputy and council had stuck to their original policy.[12]

Maguire hesitated, provisionally accepted the terms offered, and then, reassembling his forces, reentered Monaghan. The English now decided, in September 1593, to move against the rebel; there followed a campaign that involved the forces of Marshal Bagenal, of Tyrone, and of Bingham. While they were maneuvering uncer-

[11] *CSPI* 5 (1592–96): 122, 123, 124, 127–28.   [12] *Ibid.*, 130–31, 138–39.

tainly on the borders of Fermanagh, uneasily eyeing one another, Bingham filled the ear of the deputy with a stream of insinuations against Tyrone's loyalty. "Though for my own part I cannot distrust the earl but do hope he will prove an honorable and true subject," he asserted that both Maguire and O'Donnell were at the earl's bidding and that the latter was about to join the former in the field. The deputy's marginal notations on these letters provide an obbligato of sarcastic comment on the conduct of the Connaught governor. Fitzwilliam remained convinced that it was Bingham's harshness that had provoked the Maguire uprising.[13]

Tyrone had in fact warned the deputy of O'Donnell's hesitations and urged firm pressure on him. He brought his own forces to Fermanagh and entered into uneasy cooperation with his hostile brother-in-law. The two forces proceeded side by side, each warily watching the other while the commanders bickered over military cooperation. In the end it was a joint assault that broke Maguire's power, in a battle in which Tyrone was wounded. (Bingham was some miles away and did not participate in the battle.)[14]

The earl now sought to take advantage of his exploits to recover the confidence of the English government. He was aware that the deputy and council had been unhappy about his inactivity at the beginning of the campaign, and they had sharply commanded him to action. Giving a full account of the action to the Privy Council "because I know not whether Mr. Marshal hath given to me my due of this service," he announced his intention of going to Dublin to answer before the judges "the malicious accusation of mine enemies." He further pressed his suits for payment of his wife's inheritance and for the amalgamation of the two counties of Armagh and Tyrone under one sheriff. This demand reflected the earl's determination to keep intact the lordship of Tyrone, which comprised both counties. By dividing it the English had hoped to diminish his authority. As a *quid pro quo* for the last request he offered to build a gaol house "and do all other things which may be a mean to bring my rude country into civility."[15]

The earl had appeared before the Dublin council at Dundalk during the previous summer to hear the detailed charges, pressed

[13] *Ibid.*, 146, 162–63.
[14] *Ibid.*, 164–65, 167–69; Moryson, *History* 1: 30; *Annals* 3: 1941.
[15] *CSPI* 5 (1592–96): 170–72, 178.

largely by Bagenal. He had later written directly to the Privy Council. They had received from Dublin only the charges, without his answers, which in Tyrone's view exculpated him from any guilt. Somewhat shamefacedly the Dublin council now reported these to London. On several counts they had accepted his protestations of innocence, notably on the murder of Phelim O'Neill, and they admitted he had absolutely denied a meeting with the Catholic primate and having coerced the sheriff of Fermanagh. Indeed, he had rescued the sheriff from Maguire's men. The failure to remit these answers to London was laid at Fitzwilliam's door by the council.[16] All these events led Tyrone to a strong sense of grievance that his best efforts in support of Dublin had been deliberately ignored.

Tyrone had good reason to doubt the goodwill of Bagenal. The latter had kept a journal of his expedition, sent first to Dublin but then to Burghley; for the latter's eyes only, the marshal included spies' accounts of secret meetings between Tyrone, O'Donnell, and Maguire and the accusation that the earl had in fact instigated Maguire's rising.[17]

In all this tangle of charge and countercharge, of distrust and recrimination, the role of Tyrone is hidden in murky ambiguity. On the one hand he came forward as the mediator, rescuing Willis's troop in Fermanagh, dealing between Maguire and the government, restraining the impatient O'Donnell. His enemies, not without justification, more than suspected him of being the hidden mover behind both Maguire and O'Donnell. His situation was an uncomfortable one. Maguire was a client and a fellow chief whose political existence was at risk. To abandon his cause would be an abdication of his very *raison d'être* as an overlord. He would forfeit for good the confidence of the lesser chiefs who looked to him for support. He could bid farewell to any ambition of maintaining his ancestral eminence and would have to subside into being a mere titled landowner. But to back a chief who was in arms against the state at Dublin was to risk his whole credit with the English at Dublin and at court. Fortunately for him the schism within the council ranks and the quarrel between the deputy and Bingham postponed direct confrontation, at least for a time.

Tyrone had now withdrawn from further action against Maguire; the latter's fastness of Enniskillen did not fall to the English

[16] *Ibid.*, 147–49; Moryson, *History* 1: 32.   [17] *CSPI* 5 (1592–96): 181–82.

until February 1594.[18] Early in the new year the council drew the earl into negotiations with O'Donnell, who now sheltered Maguire, and letters of thanks for his service at Beleek were ordered to be written. Tyrone undertook the task but at the same time continued to complain of accusations against him by both Fitzwilliam and Bagenal and absolutely refused to have any dealings with the marshal or to allow him to deal with O'Donnell. Now regarding the deputy as much his enemy as the marshal, he began levying 1,900 men "for defense of the country" and seized the sons of Shane O'Neill, whom he refused to turn over to the government.[19]

By March 1594 matters were drawing to a crisis. O'Neill raids on the Bagenal lands in Antrim signalled open violence between the rivals (although the raids were carried out by lesser members of the clan). Fermanagh too was ablaze as local opponents of the O'Neills came under attack. The council now commissioned the judges, Loftus, Gardiner, and St. Leger—all English, but trusted by the earl—to meet Tyrone and O'Donnell at Dundalk in order to come to some settlement. Even a meeting proved difficult, as the skittish earl refused to enter the town for fear of his life at the hands of the deputy and the marshal. With great difficulty the commissioners eventually obtained interviews in the open, first with Tyrone alone and later with him and O'Donnell. The earl was in a very excitable mood and talked of a general plot against him, manifest first in the proceedings against MacMahon and Maguire, which he took as the beginning of a campaign to destroy him little by little. He foresaw that some small offense would be alleged against him, the opening wedge in an attack on his estate and life. O'Donnell was recalcitrant, refusing to trust any safe conduct from the commissioners and relying wholly on the earl. In the end the commissioners, lacking any instructions with which to woo the earl, could do no more than receive a letter of grievances from him; then, urged on by his militant followers, he departed. The commissioners patched up a kind of truce until the response to his grievances could be ascertained.[20]

Many of these grievances dealt with what the earl saw as Bag-

---

[18] *Annals* 3: 1949. Maguire laid it under siege from May onwards.
[19] *CSPI* 5 (1592–96): 202, 203, 209, 210, 214–15, 216.
[20] *Ibid.*, 220, 226, 234–36; *Carew* 3 (1589–1600): 87–89.

enal's encroachments on his power in Monaghan and Clandeboy, and some were complaints about his shabby treatment during the Beleek campaign. But at the heart of the earl's complaints was his perception of a deeply laid plot against his life, engineered by the marshal, who had bribed the deputy into cooperation. Tyrone compared his friendless condition in England, now that Leicester, Walsingham, and Hatton were dead, with the powerful backing of Bagenal. On their return from Dundalk the commissioners took a very conciliatory line, recommending the pardon of Maguire and the removal of Hanshaw, the seneschal of Monaghan, the hated enemy of the Gaelic leaders. But the bulk of the Dublin council were illdisposed to negotiate; they saw the combination of Tyrone, O'Donnell, and Maguire as a threat to the whole island, a first step in general insurrection and foreign invasion. Their recipe for action was to augment their armed forces. They appealed to England for at least 1,000 men, citing the murder of a government supporter in Kildare as a sign of spreading disorder. Fitzwilliam on his own argued with Burghley against any pacification of Tyrone.[21]

The English government reacted warily to the panic at Dublin. The marshal was forbidden to meddle with Tyrone, and the deputy was recalled. (The latter move had been long in the making; Fitzwilliam had sent one piteous plea after another for release, as his health declined.) But now he was on increasingly bad terms with his councillors. In early May 1594 news had arrived of the appointment of Sir William Russell as his successor, though the usual delays meant that several weary months would pass before that gentleman's arrival. However, his instructions were issued in early May and reflect the English government's views of the Irish imbroglio in this troubled spring. Nervously cautious, the Privy Council and the Queen ordered that Tyrone should be pacified; they hoped the withdrawal of Fitzwilliam and the prohibition laid on Bagenal would be sufficient, but if this did not work, armed force was promised to back up Dublin. Apparently it was assumed that Fitzwilliam would return immediately, and in his absence two Englishborn Lord Justices would rule: Chief Baron Napper and the Master of the Rolls, St. Leger. Russell was to back their actions against the native-born councillors who might malign them. But since Fitzwil-

[21] CSPI 5 (1592–96): 228, 237.

liam stayed on through the summer, there was in effect a lame-duck regime at Dublin, an uneasy stalemate, and a virtual paralysis of government. This was particularly unfortunate at a moment when Tyrone teetered between accommodation and defiance. Both sides marked time pending the arrival of the new deputy, on whom the earl pinned his hopes of redress. In this hiatus of power, Tyrone's henchmen continued their raiding in the border counties of Ulster.

The Earl of Ormond, the one great Irish lord who was a familiar of the English court (and distant cousin to the Queen), now returned to Ireland after a long absence. Burghley enlisted him as a mediator who might bring Tyrone to submit himself and his cause to judicial judgment. The lord treasurer pointed out that, now that the deputy was recalled, Bagenal was suspended from meddling with him. A correspondence ensued over a period of some months, but Tyrone would do no more than submit his demands for redress of the grievances of the Gaelic chiefs. By April 1595 Ormond was excusing himself from further dealings with Tyrone. That earl had in fact put out a feeler to the Earl of Kildare, offering him 2,000 men if the latter would attempt to suppress his enemies. Fitzwilliam's quarrels with his council grew more acrimonious as he refused to yield power to the Lord Justices, and so the time wore away until August. Russell, detained by contrary winds at Chester, had finally arrived early in that month. He received the sword of state on 11 August 1594.[22]

In his final report the retiring deputy summed up the state of the island as he turned it over to Russell. Three of the provinces were at peace, troubled only by that inveterate troublemaker, the bandit Feagh McHugh O'Byrne, in his Wicklow fastness. In Ulster Maguire, up in arms, controlled all Fermanagh except Enniskillen, aided by the close relatives and dependents of both Tyrone and O'Donnell. Although the two chiefs remained officially aloof from the Fermanagh chief, Fitzwilliam saw the state of Ulster as far more dangerous than in the past, "long replenished with more treason than we have known it to be in former times; not only the estate of the province" but that of the whole realm was threatened. This

[22] *Carew* 3 (1589–1600): 90–92; *CSPI* 5 (1592–96): 109, 165, 167, 201, 209, 212, 230, 237–38, 241, 242, 244, 247, 255, 258, 261, 283, 309.

assessment bore the confirmatory signatures of twelve councillors, of whom ten were English-born.[23]

Fitzwilliam's term as deputy had seen an ominous deterioration in the hitherto cooperative relations between Dublin and the great chief of the north. It is not altogether easy to account for this change. There were personal factors; Fitzwilliam won an unenviable reputation for corruption. It was alleged that he had come to Ireland in order to make "his commodity" of the kingdom. He was accused of having bought up imprest bills and pocketed fines and rents. He was suspected, even accused, of taking bribes in the MacMahon affair, and part of the bitterness over that matter was linked to the deputy's venal reputation. Whether such allegations were just or unjust, they were certainly current in contemporary Ireland. An observer summed up the deputy as one whose "experience made him able to know but his years did disable him to execute that he knew and to do what was requisite for so stirring a state." It was in fact his official actions as deputy that blackened his name among the Irish.[24]

There is no evidence that Fitzwilliam was planning a deliberate assault on the earl's position, but his handling of the MacMahon affair aroused the lurking fears that haunted the Gaelic chief's attitudes towards the Dublin regime. Their relations were always an uneasy mixture of trust and suspicion, always a wary calculation as to the sincerity of the other's intentions. Although the deputy and council relied on Tyrone's loyalty to shore up their power, they could not quite banish from their minds lingering doubts about his long-term ambitions. Would he be content to settle for the spacious but carefully fenced dignities of an English earl in place of the open-ended opportunities of a near-royal Gaelic prince? Certainly, from the time of the Maguire episode on, their doubts outweighed their trust, and he was successively excluded from their confidence. He on his side watched narrowly every move the deputy and council made for signs of new encroachments on his traditional rights. Fitzwilliam's behavior had aroused all the earl's worst suspicions and he felt driven to support Maguire. Yet he was all too aware of

---

[23] *Carew* 3 (1589–1600): 92–95.
[24] Morgan, "Outbreak," 155–56, quoting SP 63/169/203 and 201; see also Thomas Lee, 103–4, 117; and cf. Moryson, *History* 1: 18; *CSPI* 4 (1588–92): 315; Perrott, *Chronicle*, 57.

the risks that a personal quarrel with Fitzwilliam might compromise his whole position *vis à vis* the English power, both in Ireland and at the English court. His effort to play both sides had failed to win the renewed confidence of the Dublin council and had increased the number of his enemies there.

CHAPTER 19

RUSSELL AND THE COMING

OF WAR

THE NEW DEPUTY, Russell, the youngest son of the second Earl of
Bedford, had had a soldierly career, beginning in Ireland in 1579
when he fought against O'Byrne in Wicklow and was knighted by
Lord Grey. In 1585 he accompanied Leicester to the Low Countries
and succeeded his friend, Philip Sidney, as governor of Flushing.
Closely identified with the pro-Leicester faction, he resigned from
Flushing after his patron's withdrawal and was unemployed until
his appointment to Ireland in 1594. There was little in his record to
suggest administrative competence, and he was on his appointment
the least qualified governor of Ireland during these decades. On
past performance he might be supposed to represent the aggressive
policy of the Leicester faction towards Ireland, but death had wiped
out its leadership and there was no obvious successor as far as Irish
matters went. Although his arrival once again placed a soldier at
the head of Irish affairs, he was in fact soon crowded out of a martial role by the presence of Sir John Norris, recalled to his presidency of Munster and appointed general of the Irish forces. Norris,
a protégé of the Cecils and the most experienced of English commanders, quickly emerged as a rival to the deputy's authority.

Russell's most urgent task on acceding to power was the relief of
Enniskillen Castle, the former Maguire stronghold, where the English garrison was closely besieged by the rebels and their Scottish
mercenary supporters, hired by O'Donnell and countenanced by
Tyrone. An earlier relief force had been beaten back. Even while

385

he was seeking to put together a force large enough for his task, the deputy was astonished by the appearance of the Earl of Tyrone, who arrived in the capital without notice "offering all service to Her Majesty as becometh a good subject and standing only upon his innocency." Blaming his past behavior on his fear of Fitzwilliam, who had threatened his life, the earl promised to withdraw aid from Maguire and to cause O'Donnell to do the same. He also agreed to march on the Scottish mercenaries recently arrived at Lecale in county Down. Bagenal continued to press his charges against the earl, not only on Russell but also on Burghley.[1]

After his brief appearance in the capital, Tyrone retired northwards while the deputy moved with speed to relieve Enniskillen, accomplishing the mission in a brief campaign of twelve days. But Tyrone now seemed to swerve from the course he had promised at Dublin, refused to meet the deputy at Cavan, and declared that his followers were sworn to support Maguire and the O'Rourkes. O'Donnell offered to submit but made it a condition that pardons be issued to Maguire and the other rebels. If Her Majesty's "bad officers" were suffered to hold Maguire's and O'Rourkes's lands, the next blow would fall on him.[2]

Matters remained in abeyance; the truce with the rebels was extended by six weeks in early November, but Russell was warning Burghley that Tyrone's influence (even in the Pale), the strength of his support, his plentiful stock of munitions, and the pressure from the Catholic clergy made him a danger to the whole state. He urged the dispatch of troops from England. The experienced and shrewd Irish secretary, Fenton, on the other hand, consistently backed compromise. Emphasizing just as urgently as the deputy the strength of Tyrone's position, he drew the different conclusion that the use of force would be impossibly expensive. He even suggested the abandonment of English rule in Fermanagh.[3]

The Queen's attention was now finally caught by the Irish crisis, and she fired off a furious volley denouncing the Dublin council for having let Tyrone go when he was in the capital. But, under the influence of Robert Cecil, she softened her instructions somewhat, favoring the economical policy of divide and rule. The lesser Ulster

[1] *CSPI* 5 (1592–96): 258–60, 262–63, 265; *Carew* 3 (1589–1600): 95–96, 97; *Annals* 3: 1951–53.

[2] *CSPI* 5 (1592–96): 260, 267–68, 270, 271, 275.

[3] *Ibid.*, 260, 271, 275, 280–82.

landowners were to be favored at the expense of the overlords. O'Donnell was to be pardoned if he would abandon the cause of Maguire. Thus prodded, the council at Dublin summoned Tyrone to the capital, but he refused to come. Conciliation was not a success, but, lacking the means, Russell could not move effectively against the rebels and despairingly prepared to abandon Enniskillen and Monaghan.[4]

Throughout the winter of 1594–1595 the Dublin authorities kept up a steady drumbeat of demands for substantial reinforcement from England; every letter reiterated the theme of their inability to act unless English men and money were forthcoming. Their anxiety reflected not only the immediate circumstances but also their dawning awareness that Tyrone's forces displayed a degree of professional competence quite unknown before. A generation earlier Shane O'Neill had surrounded himself with a band of men trained in the modern arts of war. His grandson set about a systematic reorganization of his soldiery. Faced with the prospect of continuous warfare, the earl could not rely on the shortterm services of the "rising out," the general levy. The galloglas's were increasingly a spent force, and attempts to enlist Scots mercenaries were not very successful. Tyrone continued to use these traditional elements in his army but augmented his forces by the regular recruitment of large numbers of bonnaghts. These were men drawn from the ranks of the unemployed and the displaced, and lured by the prospect of pay. (They represented the same stratum of the population as their English counterparts except that the latter were drafted.)

Once enlisted, they were trained in the use of firearms and of the pike. Supplies of weapons and gunpowder were imported from abroad (largely from Scotland) or acquired through leakage from the English garrisons. Grain, produced at home, was carefully stored; cattle moved with the troops. By the mid-1590's Tyrone had at his disposal a professional army—trained, equipped, and supplied, and quite capable of meeting the English troops on equal terms.[5] His methodical training of his men in modern military techniques and discipline was beginning to pay off and, as events would soon prove, he began to display a new boldness in the field. The

[4] *Ibid.*, 284–85, 286, 291.

[5] See Gerard A. Hayes-McCoy, "Strategy and Tactics in Irish Warfare, 1593–1601," *Irish Historical Studies* 2 (1940–41): 261–63, and "The Army of Ulster, 1593–1601," *The Irish Sword* 1 (1950–51): 105–27.

Dublin authorities were at last able to persuade London of the seriousness of the situation, and in late winter 1594–1595 were promised that the troops being evacuated from Brittany, 2,000 in number, would be sent to Ireland under their commander, Sir John Norris, the absentee president of Munster.[6]

It was none too soon; the isolated fort on the Blackwater River in county Armagh was the outpost of English power at the gateway to Tyrone's own lands. In February 1595 the earl's forces assailed and captured the fort. In open defiance of the English, Tyrone was now waging war upon them. Elizabeth rebuked the council for the crime of having lost the fort; its captors were to be severely punished. But the promised forces from Brittany were slow in coming and numbered initially only about 1,100 war-weary men. Another 1,000 were being drafted in England, but east winds held them back for weeks, and when they arrived they lacked money and victuals. The new commander of the Irish army, Norris, was slower still in coming, and even before his arrival controversy was swirling around him. A draft proclamation against Tyrone as a traitor was prepared but its promulgation was left to Norris. The Queen still hoped that secret diplomacy might separate O'Donnell from the earl.[7]

Worse was to follow in the course of the spring. In May Enniskillen castle, relieved and replenished by the deputy in late 1594, was lost to the rebels. This closed the western approach to Gaelic Ulster as the loss of the Blackwater fort had closed the eastern. Only a week later there was yet another disaster. Bagenal was sent with a force to relieve the garrison at Monaghan; on his way back he was intercepted by Tyrone and his troops badly mauled at Clontibret. The marshal's force, having exhausted its ammunition, found itself stranded at Newry, too feeble to march the eight miles to Dundalk; evacuation by sea was urged. This was the news that greeted Norris when he finally arrived at Dublin in June 1595.[8]

In the short interval of less than a year since Russell's arrival, the situation had worsened. Tyrone had moved from sullen but inactive watchfulness to an open offensive against the English garrison and, at Clontibret, to deliberate assault on an English army. For the

[6] *CSPI* 5 (1592–96): 299, 300.

[7] *Ibid.*, 298–99, 305, 309, 311, 312, 313, 314, 317.

[8] *Ibid.*, 317, 319–20; G. A. Hayes-McCoy, "The Tide of Victory and Defeat: the Battle of Clontibret, 1595," *Studies: An Irish Quarterly Review* 38 (1949): 158–68.

first time a trained Irish army had faced an English force on terms of equality—indeed of superiority—in open conflict. It was no longer a question of hit-and-run guerrilla warfare but of war on the Continental model. Tyrone's training of his men in the contemporary techniques of war was proving its worth. English conciliation had been contemptuously brushed aside by a leader who felt a new sense of power. The Irish chronicler wrote that it was in this year, 1595, that "the entire province of Ulster rose up in one alliance and one union against the English."[9] At home the government began to take the Irish problem very seriously indeed. The Breton venture was quickly liquidated and English soldiers shifted to Ulster. From this time forward the English government, albeit with shuffling hesitation, gradually came to see Ireland as its main preoccupation and at last to give Irish affairs first priority in its deliberations. The perceived threat of a Spanish attack on the island persuaded the Queen to agree to the dispatch of the Drake-Hawkins expedition in this year. That continuing threat would strongly influence her consent to the ensuing fleets of 1596 and 1597.

The strategy that the deputy proposed to Norris on the latter's arrival provided for three separate forces, two of 1,500 each to move on Tyrone and Fermanagh, the third 500 strong, under Bingham, to attack O'Donnell from Connaught. But this scheme was now confounded, first by the loss of Enniskillen and the Blackwater fort and then by Bagenal's repulse at Clontibret. It was clear that his force was in grave danger from the much larger Irish army mobilized by Tyrone in the neighborhood. Norris was obviously staggered by the enormity of the task that faced him and altogether doubtful that with present resources he could make an impression during the current year. Hence he proposed to Robert Cecil (without informing Russell) that the whole enterprise be abandoned and in its place a force sent directly from England to Lough Foyle on the northern coast. A fort would be built there and from this back-door entrance the English could ravage both O'Donnell's and O'Neill's lands. It was a repetition of the strategy used against Shane O'Neill in the 1560's.[10]

For the moment, however, the deputy proceeded with his plans, concentrating a force at Newry and officially proclaiming Tyrone a traitor, in English and in Gaelic. He had some 2,800 men to face an

---

[9] *Annals* 3: 1959. [10] *CSPI* 5 (1592–96): 323–26.

army of nearly 6,000 under his opponent. In the past Irish forces had often outnumbered the English, but this time more important than numbers was the fact that the Irish leaders had an army of trained soldiers. Tyrone now sought to reopen negotiations with the English; the deputy and Norris initially rejected these overtures but nevertheless wrote worriedly to England on how to respond.[11]

With inadequate forces for a planned two-pronged assault, the deputy had to content himself with the establishment of a garrison in Armagh cathedral, with forty days' victuals, and then with retiring to the coast, skirmishing with Tyrone as he went. Norris remained in Dublin, ill, suspicious of Russell, and pressing for his own revocation. The deputy responded in kind, throwing up his hands and declaring that he left the war in Ulster wholly to Norris. So great was his irritation that he fended off even the possibility of a reconciliation. Secretary Fenton painted the gloomiest of pictures: the army shrunken to 1,600 to 1,700 men, largely through wholesale desertion (much of it to Tyrone). The treasurer, Wallop, added to this picture: there were barely 40 English out of 100 in the conscript companies; the force brought from Brittany was melting away from desertion.[12]

All the Irish correspondents agreed as to the lamentable state of army administration. Money came in belatedly in too small amounts; the forces were obliged to live off the country. When there had been only half a dozen companies this had been bearable; now, with fifty or so companies, the country was laid waste by their demands. Unwisely, biscuits and beer were baked and brewed in England, and they arrived spoiled. It would be more efficient, even if costly, to build brewhouses, bakeries, and storehouses in Ireland. The consequence of all these shortages was an appalling rate of desertion, compounded by captains who sold their men passes to return home. This in turn revealed the faults of officers appointed in England who regarded their posts as mere opportunities for profit.

Reinforcements were ordered, but the English government still hankered after a cheaper solution than force. In the meantime summer 1595 faded into fall with little to show; the proposed fort on the Blackwater was as yet unbuilt. Norris had achieved an indeci-

[11] *Ibid.*, 331–33, 335.
[12] *Ibid.*, 340–41, 343–45, 346, 349–52, 354, 357–58.

sive victory over Tyrone, but at the cost of a serious wound. He and the deputy bickered endlessly, each ascribing to the other the failure of the campaign. Reinforcements had been ready at Chester for some time but were held up by contrary winds. No further offensive could be hoped for until the spring of 1596.[13]

The root of this ill-success, as the English commanders continued to insist, lay in the scantiness of supplies. Wallop reminded the Privy Council of his earlier advice that these troubles would prove "the longest, most chargeable and most dangerous war" in men's memory in Ireland. The Queen disliked such great charges but "in such great actions as this, the charge must be great," and the "best means ... to ease the same is not in present sparing" but by fully meeting the army's needs now. Any other policy would only prolong the Queen's charges, waste life, spoil the country, and open the opportunity for foreign invasion.[14] The Queen, however, unmoved by such representations and weary of ever-increasing costs, was prepared to hear what Tyrone had to offer. So she "may have it appear that his proud heart is so come down as to offer to stand absolutely to Her Majesty's mercy, it will not be denied him."[15]

Tyrone did in fact write to Norris in late August with an offer of submission and a petition for pardon for himself and his adherents. This led to successive secret instructions from the Queen, first to the deputy and then to him and Norris alone. Tyrone was to be promised the lands of the barony of Dungannon, but those of the earldom of Tyrone were to be held back pending his future good behavior. The MacShanes were to be restored to their lands east of Lough Neagh. O'Donnell, O'Rourke, and Maguire were to have their pardons but lose some of their lands.[16]

Norris concluded a truce with Tyrone for a short time so that the earl might make his submission. The deputy, forwarding Norris's letter to England, urged that Tyrone's submission be followed by pardon, this in spite of correspondence with Spain that Russell had recently intercepted. But Russell, the Dublin council, and the Irish judges declined to be involved in drawing up the submission of Tyrone, and the deputy asked the Privy Council to appoint special commissioners for this purpose. He remained altogether skep-

---

[13] APC 1595–96: 38; CSPI 5 (1592–96): 363, 396, 402–6; Annals 3: 1971.
[14] CSPI 5 (1592–96): 402.　　　　[15] Ibid., 364.
[16] Ibid., 374, 417–18; Carew 3 (1589–1600): 123–24.

tical of Tyrone's sincerity. Submissions came in from Tyrone (who renounced the title of O'Neill, assumed since the death of Turlough) and from O'Donnell, and a cessation of arms until the new year 1596 was arranged.[17]

It was a delicate moment in the troubled relationship between Tyrone and the English. The earl was now in a position of strength. As effective lord of all the hereditary lands of the O'Neills, and an ally of O'Donnell, he had achieved the mastery of Ulster that had always been his goal. Had the overtures that he made to the English at this time been met with an acceptance of that role by—for instance—an offer of the presidency of Ulster, there might have been the basis for peaceful coexistence that would have allowed both the assertion of English sovereignty and the powers that Tyrone held to be integral to his hereditary role in the Irish world.

Instead, at this juncture dealings with the Gaelic chiefs became inextricably entangled with quarrels within the English leadership in Ireland. Both Russell and Norris agreed in supporting some measure of pacification, although both were pessimistic about long-term prospects. They were even prepared to overlook the recently uncovered correspondence with Spain. But Russell bitterly resented the virtually coordinate authority (and pay) given to the general, and there was angry disagreement over who was to handle the negotiations. The deputy refused to be involved in drawing up the terms of the submission, urging that commissioners be appointed by London for the purpose. Norris accused his rival of undercutting his authority and, in an appeal to the Queen, intimated that Russell was incapable of handling the negotiations himself. Norris's own health was in serious decline and he continued to beg for relief.[18]

Control of the discussion now passed to the deputy. Tyrone offered to pay a fine of 20,000 cattle for himself and his supporters to renounce jurisdiction over the lesser chiefs, and to accept sheriffs (provided they were neutral between him and his enemies) and a fort on the Blackwater. But he refused to meet the deputy, still fearing for his life and citing the fate of Hugh Roe MacMahon.[19] The Queen, to whose ears the very name of Ireland now sounded harsh, grew impatient. She conceded that if the ringleaders (i.e.,

[17] *CSPI* 5 (1592–96): 415, 417–18, 421, 422; *Carew* 3 (1589–1600): 96–97, 123–24.
[18] *CSPI* 5 (1592–96): 409, 417–18, 421, 422, 427–28.
[19] *Ibid.*, 441–42, 463–64, 470–71.

Tyrone and O'Donnell) would not yield without pardon for their followers, that should be granted, but the disposal of lands and fortunes was left to the Dublin councillors. To speed up matters she gave carte blanche to them to settle terms without fuller reference to Westminster.[20]

Sir John Wallop and Sir John Gardiner were given the thankless task of carrying out the royal instructions. Tyrone and O'Donnell pitched their demands high, upping them to nothing less than freedom of religion, full control over lands and men in Ulster, and a return to the *status quo ante* of 1589 (i.e., at the time of Sir Ross MacMahon's death). Even while these discussions proceeded, open violence was spreading through Connaught, and in December the Irish had surprised and taken Monaghan.[21]

It was not easy to persuade the Gaelic princes even to meet Wallop and Gardiner, and they absolutely refused to meet the deputy. The commissioners "spent a stormy and windy day" on horseback in a futile effort to bring their interlocutors to deal with them. The deputy saw the far-reaching demands of Tyrone and O'Donnell as the beginning of a general uprising. "I protest I think all the Irishry in general are either in action or conspiracy of rebellion." He asked for 300 horse, besides the 1,000 men preparing at Chester. In a thoughtful but pessimistic appraisal, Secretary Fenton, while despairing of a settlement with the Gaelic lords, urged a continuation of the truce so as to give time to strengthen the government's forces. He acknowledged that the Queen's "princely custom to take offenders by mercy, thinking thereby to bind them faster in duty and obedience" had failed. Yet he was urgent that the Queen should eschew war or at least postpone it. War, if it came, would have to be waged entirely with English men and money. Ireland itself was exhausted, and the prospect of war and its burdens threatened to turn discontent into disobedience. "These matters are sour, I know they cannot be acceptable to Your Lordship to read them," but they had to be faced. Gardiner was dispatched to London to confer with the Privy Council and the Queen on the proposed treaty with the rebels.[22]

Certainly in the short run Fenton's advice was being followed.

[20] *Ibid.*, 443, 446, 467; *Carew* 3 (1589–1600): 131.

[21] *Ibid.*, 132–35, 141–43; *APC* 1595–96: 267–70; *CSPI* 5 (1592–96): 440, 447–50.

[22] *Ibid.*, 437, 452–57, 457–59, 468; *Carew* 3 (1589–1600): 138; *APC* 1595–96: 267–70, 280–87.

The two commissioners were instructed to draw out the discussion and thus prolong negotiations by referring the more extreme demands to the Queen. The cessation of arms was extended to May 1596. Norris pointed out that the price of the truce would be high since the rebels would not abate their forces. More foot and horse, at least 200 of the latter, must be sent over. These requests reached London just as preparations for the Cadiz expedition were getting under way. The large commitments of men and material that it required made it more urgent than ever that demands from Ireland for soldiers be discouraged.[23]

Hence the Queen and Burghley hung on to the hope of pacifying the rebels by a free pardon, and once again Elizabeth ordered the offer to be made, conditional on their coming in to submit. The council dutifully followed instructions without the slightest hope of their efficacy. Wallop warned Burghley of the dangerous novelties of the war—the unity of the Ulster and Connaught chiefs under Tyrone and O'Donnell, the startling quality of the Irish forces. "They seem to be other enemies" than they were in times past. Indeed, he saw in the Gaelic leaders "a full resolution to set up again the Mack's and the O's and their lands to recover from the English" and to hold them as before the conquest. They now met the English in open field, no longer relying on guerrilla tactics. The extremity was such that there was no way but the sword; a great army under a noble personage must be sent. He pressed once again for the grand strategy of an assault on three fronts: against Tyrone from the Pale, on Tyrconnel from Connaught, and, by a landing on Lough Foyle, an assault from the rear.[24]

None of this was having much effect on the one person who really counted—the Queen. In early March 1596 she wrote to the deputy and council, expressing her deep displeasure with their proceedings. She condemned them for not having accepted the rebels' initial submission and wasting time in squabbling over details. The result was full-scale revolt in both Ulster and Connaught. Their remedies required men and money without offering reformation in government. She went on, "We conceived misgovernment there of late years has given cause and scope to these rebels to revolt." She

---

[23] *Carew* 3 (1589–1600): 145, 146, 148, 149, 166–67; *CSPI* 5 (1592–96): 462, 465.
[24] *Ibid.*, 467, 468–69, 470, 482; *Carew* 3 (1589–1600): 166–67; Wallop in BL Cotton Mss., Titus C VII, 156–61.

had a collection made of "errors and defaults" and of possible remedies.[25] Responding more particularly to the rebels' specific grievances, she refused to allow formally liberty of conscience, but she pointed out that there had been no prosecution for religion in the past, and by inference there was not to be any in the future. She conceded that there were to be no garrisons in Armagh or Tyrconnel and that sheriffs were to be local men. The latter was a major concession since it would return to a practice abandoned since 1547. Pardons were to be liberally distributed to the lesser fry.[26]

The burden of treating with Tyrone this time was by royal command laid on Norris, assisted by Fenton. Norris, in acknowledging the mission, once more rehearsed his differences with Russell, whose earlier intervention had awakened the deep distrust of Tyrone. The latter now refused to deal at all with the deputy and insisted that he trusted only Norris. Norris's letters were heavily colored with overt and covert criticism of the deputy and his associates. He emphasized that the quiet and safety of the realm depended not on the tenor of this treaty but "upon the wise and provident managing of the government hereafter." The continuing friction between the deputy and the general tangled the course of negotiations with Tyrone, but the latter finally agreed to meet Norris at Dundalk. There in late April, Norris and Fenton came to a tentative agreement. Maguire, MacMahon, and other chieftains made a formal submission, but in the Armagh garrison there was still a stumbling block. Tyrone made his other concessions dependent on its removal; the council at Dublin was ready to yield.[27]

This left unsettled the problem of Connaught. Norris and Fenton had already moved to obtain authority to act there. The deputy remained dissatisfied with these dealings, but Norris prepared to go to Connaught with some 2,000 men. Affairs in that province were reaching a new climax. Bingham had long been under attack by Secretary Fenton and by others of the Dublin establishment. Partly the antipathies were personal ones. The abrasive and arrogantly independent governor with powerful patrons at court was no favorite with his nominal superiors at Dublin. In part, also, there were real

[25] APC 1595–96: 267–70.   [26] Carew 3 (1589–1600): 168.
[27] CSPI 5 (1592–96): 493–95, 496–97, 497–99, 501–1, 504–5, 512–13; Carew 3 (1589–1600): 166–67, 172–74.

differences of principle. His opponents argued that his high-handed ways provoked more opposition than they suppressed.[28]

They now had the ear of the Queen, at a time when preparations for the Cadiz expedition hung in the balance. In stinging letters to the deputy and council she rebuked their disunity and their failure to find remedies for the present troubles. She would not turn her face from the accusations of misgovernment made by the Irish. "We have determined on a course of pacification and shall hold it a weakness in you [the deputy] if you require to be daily directed in all particulars, especially as your advices are bare and barren." She went on to order an investigation of Bingham's regime by a special commission composed of Dillon, Fenton, and Norris (enemies of Bingham). He was to repair to Athlone or Dublin so as to leave the investigation free from interference. The same letter ordered pardons for Tyrone and O'Donnell and lowered the rent of the latter. It finished with a general outburst against the vice-treasurer and other officers in Ireland. In this mood the Queen seemed disposed to believe the worst about them. At the same time Robert Cecil wrote that the treaty was not to be broken off except over matters of main importance.[29]

Bingham retired to Dublin, asking for removal of his case to the Privy Council, while Norris set out for Connaught. Even as he left, hopes for success were clouded by the landing of 1,000 Scots in the north. The deputy took advantage of his absence to press on Burghley the remote prospects of peace with either Tyrone or the other rebels and to urge reinforcements from England. Writing to Cecil at the same time, he asked to be revoked; he could no longer endure Norris's arrogance. By the end of June he was sure peace could not be made in Connaught and that war was coming. At the same time Tyrone's confidant and foster brother, Hovenden, warned his master that negotiations were about to break down and that war was near.[30]

In Connaught the peacemakers found their task a hard one. The local chiefs showed some disposition to accept the Queen's terms, but when Theobald McWilliam Burke of Mayo was about to sign he suddenly blotted out his name and in a *volte face* demanded a

---

[28] *CSPI* 5 (1592–96): 507, 509, 514, 515, 516, 525, 540.
[29] *Carew* 3 (1589–1600): 176–78; *CSPI* 5 (1592–96): 508, 520.
[30] *Ibid.*, 526, 528, 530, 534, 535–36, 537, 541; *Carew* 3 (1589–1600): 179–80.

whole series of concessions that together would have undone the work of the past fifteen years and restored his powers as a Gaelic prince. Worse still, he was backed by O'Donnell in these demands, and it soon became clear that he and Tyrone proposed to act as arbiters of the Connaught claims. Offered a fifteen-day truce on condition of giving pledges for peace, they refused, and in the end Norris had to make the humiliating concession of a truce without conditions. The army was dispersed into garrisons; Fenton returned to Dublin insisting that nothing could be hoped for in Connaught until Bingham was replaced. Tyrone remained at least outwardly cooperative; in July, after repeated delays, he finally accepted the royal pardon, loudly protesting his loyalty.[31]

In fact, during this early summer of 1596 Tyrone's position was powerfully strengthened by the intrusion onto the stage of a third party—the Spanish. Rumors of the arrival of arms and treasure from Spain had reached the government from time to time, and on several occasions there had been expectation of an actual landing. Fear of Spanish invasion dated back to the immediate post-Armada era in 1588 and to events in 1590. Troops were levied in England amidst rumors of a fleet sailing towards Ireland in the latter year. What is certain is that in the fall of 1595 O'Neill and O'Donnell had written to Spain asking for help in the name of their common religion. In the following spring, when Tyrone was parleying with the Dublin commissioners, a delegation from Spain landed in the north, led by Alonzo Cobos, an accredited agent of the Spanish king. He met a party of chiefs, including O'Neill and O'Donnell, and formally promised that if they continued their fight for the Catholic faith, they would lack no aid from his king. Tyrone made no secret of the visit, passed on Philip's letter to the Dublin council, and included his and O'Donnell's reply—that they were now in their princess's favor and could not satisfy his conditions.[32]

The earl's seeming frankness failed to convince many of his opponents. Bingham roundly asserted that Tyrone had signed an agreement with the Spanish. Norris, still hopeful of a settlement, had a somewhat different story—that O'Rourke, McWilliam Burke (Mayo), and others, promised a Spanish army by the emis-

---

[31] *CSPI* 6 (1596–97): 2–12, 33, 43–44.

[32] For the invasion fears, see *APC* 1589–90: 142–44, 218, 294–98; 1590: 78; *CSPI* 5 (1592–96): 325, 330, 371, 383, 390. For the Spanish mission, see *CSPI* 5 (1592–96): 406, 409, 518, 519, 526, 527; 6 (1596–97): 50.

sary, had themselves promised to make no composition with the English until August if they could have a supply of munitions in the meantime. O'Donnell and O'Neill had not signed but had certainly known of the agreement. However, an intercepted letter, dated in late August, contained an outright promise to obey Philip as their king and asked for the Cardinal Infante as a ruler. Other letters went to the Spanish commander in Brittany.[33]

Certainly the negotiations with Tyrone, which had been proceeding hopefully, now bogged down. Although Tyrone had accepted the royal pardon in July (after some delays on his part), a final agreement continued to elude the commissioners as summer 1596 turned to fall and fall to winter. What we may deduce is that Tyrone now felt he had two strings to his bow. A Spanish army was still only a distant possibility, but arms and money were coming in. The English knew all this—he had taken care they should. With this new and weighty counter in hand, Tyrone could raise his bargaining terms proportionately and bid ambitiously for even more favorable conditions in any long-term settlement.

In the meantime, among his opponents, the rift between the deputy and the general, which was becoming more and more open, gradually paralyzed the government of Ireland. Russell now condemned Norris and Fenton for the conclusion of the truce in Connaught. Tyrone, he held, was mainly killing time while he continued to gather strength. The rebels had doubled their numbers in the past years. The Leinster clans of O'Mores, O'Tooles, Cavanaghs, and O'Byrnes were stirring, part of a nationwide conspiracy. The deputy and council now asked for 3,000 foot and 300 horse. Russell in a self-pitying mood complained that he had little credit and asked for his revocation. Norris put his case in memoranda of late July. Beyond the deputy's distrust of Tyrone's intentions, Norris thought that the earl had been sincere in his pacific inclinations earlier in the year but that he was afterward alienated by Russell's actions. The earl would always stand warily on guard to protect his position, but he would not openly revolt, call in foreign aid, or allow the Pale to be spoiled. The dealings with the Spanish were the work of O'Rourke, McWilliam, and their supporters, not of the earl (although he knew of it). Citing Henry IV's dealings with the League as precedent, Norris urged a similar path of pacification and com-

[33] *CSPI* 5 (1592–96): 527; 6 (1596–97): 50, 110–12, 352–54.

promise. A small force would best serve in Ireland, provided it was mostly "mere English."[34]

It was the general's views that were most in accord with sentiment at court. In July Robert Cecil roundly told off the deputy. The latter had predicted war, but the secretary declared his preference for temporizing rather than being driven to the charge of new armies, particularly when the Queen wanted to see the result of her costly venture in Spain under Essex and Howard. Russell was reproached for predicting war, although he and the council had earlier recommended pacification on the grounds of English weakness. Cecil duly denied that he entertained "poor good will" toward the deputy, assuring him he would never raise another's reputation to diminish Russell's. In a letter from Burghley to his son, the former was blunt about his feelings towards Russell. In response to the deputy's plaint that Burghley sought out his faults, the treasurer commented, "I wish they did not need to be sought out."[35] But he pointed out the Queen's (somewhat unreasonable) complaint that the Irish council had become a mere "advertiser" instead of being an "advisor." Norris and Fenton were reassured by the Privy Council that their efforts to come to terms with Tyrone were approved; the Queen was still prepared to believe in his innocence if he would submit. But there must be a time limit. The Deputy's request for 3,000 men was met by a levy of 1,000.[36]

Fenton made one more effort in Connaught against the council's will, but by now Tyrone was distrustful of even Norris and sought private means to secure secret assurances from the Cecils. When O'Donnell attacked Boyle Abbey in Connaught, the deputy called for an end to negotiations, but Norris and Fenton struggled manfully on, securing pledges from O'Donnell and O'Rourke and a promise from Tyrone to meet them. A settlement seemed in sight if Bingham, whose mistakes had brought on the revolt, could be kept away.[37]

Bingham's views were set out in a letter to Chief Justice Gardiner. "He [Tyrone] findeth that his fair offers avail him often times much more than open wars, for whatsoever is promised, if it may be hurtful to him and beneficial to the state, it is never performed

[34] *CSPI* 6 (1596–97): 48–51, 54–59.   [35] Wright 2: 458.
[36] *Carew* 3 (1589–1600): 179–80; APC 1596–97: 39–42, 42–46, 128–33, 161–65.
[37] *CSPI* 6 (1596–97): 69–71, 86–88, 104, 106–08.

and he knoweth by experience how to deal with us, expecting still greater advantages and the foreign aid that is surely promised him."[38] The governor of Connaught had been kicking his heels in Dublin since May. Norris and Fenton had insisted that his case be heard in Connaught where all the witnesses would be available. Bingham, struggling for a hearing in Dublin where he had the backing of the deputy and most of the council, pressed his case on Burghley. In the end the Queen ordered that the trial should take place in Athlone before Norris, Fenton, and Chief Justice Gardiner. Bingham in desperation took French leave and set out for London without license, where he soon found himself in prison.[39]

The wrangle between the deputy and Norris went on, with Russell asserting that the general's policies would result in the loss not only of the north and west but also of the other provinces. Stung by Cecil's tart observation that the Dublin council were the cause of their own troubles, he gave vent to a *cri de coeur*. His advice had been ignored; others had been encouraged to follow a fatal policy of pacification. He concluded bitterly, "in the last Your Honor hath well concluded that this land is cursed to them that touch it."[40]

Morale in the army was at low ebb as disorder spread into Leinster and Munster. The mortality rate was high, as were desertions. An English officer noted with dismay the lack of courage of English soldiers in Ireland—and the superior training of their opponents. Annual costs to the Queen in Ireland now reached £130,000, roughly equivalent to annual costs in the Low Countries under the 1585 treaty. The deputy had virtually abdicated responsibility for Ulster (on instructions from England). Archbishop Loftus and Bishop Jones supported the deputy in his analysis, urging an end to conciliation and repeating the proposal for a threefold assault on Tyrone, Tyrconnel, and Lough Foyle. Even Fenton, Norris's loyal coadjutor, was wavering in his faith in lenience, but he still rather uncertainly recommended "to try and work from the Spaniard by time, rather than to run upon them with severity of force." Norris in turn blamed the deputy; if he (the general) had had absolute command, the present catastrophe would have been avoided.[41]

[38] Wright 2:471–75.
[39] *CSPI* 6 (1596–97): 37, 64–66, 88–91, 104–9, 112; *APC* 1596–97; 232.
[40] *CSPI* 6 (1596–97): 138–40, 159–60; *Carew* 3 (1589–1600): 184.
[41] *CSPI* 6 (1596–97): 142–43, 151, 154, 163, 164–65, 167–71, 175–76, 177–78.

The first sign of movement in this logjam came with the appearance of a new actor on the Irish stage. Sir Conyers Clifford was appointed chief commissioner in Connaught with the same powers as Bingham. A veteran of the Rouen campaign and Cadiz, a protégé of Essex, his appearance marked the first entry of the favorite into Irish affairs. Clifford was given no additional armed force and was expected to cover costs out of the provincial revenue; his appointment confirmed a continuing faith at Westminster in peaceful rather than war-like measures.[42]

The central schism in the Irish government, the conflict between deputy and general, still remained unaddressed. Fenton put it bluntly: these two principals, Menelaus and Scipio, must be dealt with; one must go, and for Fenton that meant Russell. Both in fact were begging for revocation. The council, at the end of its tether, dispatched Gardiner to London (without Fenton's knowledge).[43] This had its effect; at last the Privy Council reluctantly gave its full attention to Ireland. In a meeting before the Queen in the first days of 1597 they agreed on the recall of Russell and his replacement by Lord Burgh, while Norris was to return home temporarily; but the Dublin proposal for a three-pronged assault was rejected on grounds of victualling difficulties.[44]

These were very real. Both England and Ireland were suffering from the worst dearth of the century. Irish wheat was at 70s. a quarter; neither Wales nor Cheshire could provide butter or cheese. So desperate was the shortage of food in England that 2,000 men, waiting to sail for Ireland, were sent back home; the government could not find a way to provision them. They could not be sent over until supplies were acquired from the Baltic. A purely defensive policy was prescribed, an army to defend the Pale and Munster. No favor was to be shown Tyrone but in effect Ulster and Connaught were to be left to their own devices. The garrisons in the principal ports and on the Ulster frontier were to be strengthened by forces from England when victuals could be secured from the Continent. Negotiations with Tyrone were to continue, to hold him in play until he could be subdued by force. In short, the English government

[42] *Ibid.*, 178.　　　　　　　　[43] *Ibid.*, 182–83, 183–84, 186, 210.
[44] *Ibid.*, 189; *APC* 1596–97: 416, 421; Moryson, *History* 1: 47. Moryson says the Burgh appointment was engineered by Essex and directed against Norris, of whose military success at Brest he was jealous.

accepted the very unstable *status quo*, shoring it up as best it could and leaving the future uncertain.[45]

Throughout the winter of 1596–1597 violence flared in Connaught and on the Ulster borders; Tyrone, yielding to the relief of the Armagh garrison, asserted his loyalty in an interview with Fenton. Norris summed up the English dilemma. He was uncertain about Tyrone; some believed with good treatment he could be weaned from O'Donnell and the other chiefs; others, led by Russell, saw him wholly committed to Spain. The "most honorable and assuredest" course would be "a royal war," an all-out effort without regard to costs, but the state of Ireland would make it extremely difficult.[46]

This detailed narrative has had to be told because it makes apparent the aimless drift of Irish affairs. All parties—the Queen's government, the Dublin officials, the Gaelic leaders as well—had lost their compasses. At Dublin, as the two tired and aging adversaries squabbled with each other, there was not only a virtual paralysis of effective action but also a deep division of opinion as to what to do. Many were now convinced that they faced something far more dangerous than another episode of friction with a balky and recalcitrant chief. The quarrel with Tyrone had snowballed into large-scale violence that threatened the whole kingdom, offering all-too-tempting an opportunity for Spanish intervention and forcing upon the Queen the unpalatable prospect of a disastrously expensive and long drawn-out war. Others still clung to the hope of some kind of compromise with the earl and his allies, but successive rebuffs at his hand and the escalation of his demands had shaken their faith. In England the government, deeply involved in a direct assault on Spain and nervously watching the first signs of possible French disengagement, heard only what it wanted to hear from Ireland. Desperate to avoid being drawn into further drains on scant resources—resources now diminished by the visitation of dearth—it listened only to those voices from Dublin that counselled appeasement, and persistently urged the authorities to continue parleys with Tyrone.

Tyrone's game is harder to evaluate. His distrust of the Dublin leadership had now mounted stage by stage to absolute fear for his life at their hands and made him more susceptible to the intemper-

---

[45] *APC* 1597: 216, 343–44, 416–22.   [46] *CSPI* 6 (1596–97): 211, 218.

ate counsels of O'Donnell and his fellows. The English feebleness gave him ample opportunity to string out negotiations endlessly, but it is far from clear whether this was mere day-to-day opportunism or the pursuit of some larger goal. Certainly he was asserting and extending his leaderhip outside of Ulster, but this was a necessity hardly to be avoided. Violence was breaking out more and more widely in the absence of firm government in Connaught and in Munster. The earl, desperately seeking to protect himself from his enemies at Dublin, had no choice but to seek allies by patronizing rebels throughout the island. He had hopes too of eventual aid from Spain, which was sending intermittent but important supplies of arms and money. This meant that the earl could steadily raise his terms in successive parleys with the Dublin commissioners.

Yet his ultimate goal—if he had one—is still not visible. He was fighting a desperate battle to defend himself against what he saw as a threat to his inherited position. But he still envisaged himself as part of an Anglo-Irish world, as a subject of the Queen. Far more of a realist than O'Donnell or the lesser chiefs, he saw the necessity for compromise with the English. The Irish must obtain the best possible terms within the existing framework of circumstance. But such a compromise must be based on the best possible negotiating terms, exploiting to the fullest the hesitancy of the English government, nervously expectant of a Spanish invasion. Tyrone seems to have pitched his hopes high for what he might extract from his opponents. The terrible danger in these tactics was that in reaching too high he might convince the English that no basis for settlement existed.

CHAPTER 20

THE YELLOW

FORD

FROM LATE WINTER until May 1597 Irish affairs were largely marking time, pending the arrival of the new deputy, Lord Burgh, for
whom initial instructions were drawn up in early February. Tyrone
and Norris jockeyed warily on the Ulster borders. Russell held that
the truce was a trick by Tyrone to draw the English forces away
from Connaught, leaving the field open to O'Donnell, but Norris
concluded a cessation with Tyrone in February. The general was
slowly moving around to a recommendation of war. He wrote am-
bivalently to Cecil in February, agreeing with the Dublin authorities that a thoroughgoing war was the best course, but questioning
whether the consequences might be worse for the state than for the
rebels. In March he was grudgingly given authority by the deputy
to deal with the earl, but was soon complaining angrily of being
crossed in his negotiations by Russell. Tyrone openly declared he
would prefer Norris as deputy, and the latter hinted at his own
disappointment. The negotiations dragged on from week to week,
delayed by the arrival of a Spanish ship at Killybegs. By early April
even Fenton was in agreement with both Norris and Russell that
negotiations should cease. The commissioners returned from the
north without result.[1] In the intervening weeks, while Burgh was
wind-bound at Chester, Norris continued to advocate war. Russell
had a final triumph in the capture and death of Feagh McHugh

[1] *CSPI* 6 (1596–97): 21, 226, 227, 233–34, 239, 242, 246, 250, 254, 264.

O'Byrne, the Robin Hood of Wicklow, whose depredations had troubled whole generations of Palesmen.[2]

The rulers at Dublin can hardly have been cheered by the Queen's scathing valedictory on the Russell regime. Condemning their handling of Tyrone, she continued, "As it is but too apparent to the whole world there never any realm was worse governed by all our ministers from the highest to the lowest." A veteran officer on the scene summed up the past several years in equally scathing terms:

> They [the Irish] grew strong by the faction between the deputy and Sir John Norris and proud by Sir John Norris his temporizing and forbearance of wars. They were encouraged by the disgrace of the Governor of Connaught, by the overthrow at the Blackwater; proud for that no resistance was made by the President to withstand so small an incursion as was made into Munster and again proud for that so worthy a man undertook the wars and made so short an abode.[3]

Lord Burgh came with instructions to sweep clean the accumulated disorders when at last on 22 May 1597 he received the sword and took the oath. Burgh is perhaps the most obscure of the Elizabethan deputies (he lacks even a DNB entry). A man of about forty, he had for some years past served as governor of Brill, the least important of the cautionary towns, and seems not to have held major military responsibility. He had not been in favor at court for a time (although the cause is not clear). He probably owed his appointment to Essex's sponsorship. The office, however, was by now viewed by courtiers as the shipwreck of fortunes, and Robert Sidney's friends had been aghast when he was canvassed as a candidate. Moreover, Burgh, unlike his predecessors, had had no previous experience in Ireland. It is hard to see his appointment as marking a change of heart at court. The destiny of Ireland was again entrusted to a second-string figure.[4]

Burgh began his tenure with bold plans. Strengthened by the 2,500 troops who accompanied him from England, he could take a strong line. There would be no more dealings with Tyrone, whose overtures were given a haughty denial. Additionally bolstered by a

[2] *Ibid.*, 287–89; *Annals* 3: 2018–19.   [3] *Carew* 3 (1589–1600): 353.
[4] *CSPI* 6 (1596–97): 266, 291, 296–97, 316, 339–40; HMC, *Hatfield* 7: 175.

success of Clifford's in the west, the new deputy declared he would wage war. But such an enterprise required supplies, above all of food. The island was wracked by dearth, not only of grain but also of cattle. A request for more funds from England received the usual dusty answer; the Privy Council was appalled at charges of £12,000 a month, and the Queen much "distasted." She had unprecedently asked to look at the Irish accounts herself "and then do you guess what would follow." Burgh was warned to adapt himself to the royal attitude on expenses.[5]

The deputy had envisaged a major campaign that would revive the old plan for a threefold assault on the north, a scheme to which Cecil gave at least nominal approval. But after an initial success in revictualling the Blackwater fort, he had to abandon his larger hopes. By early August 1597 he was already in retreat to Newry, lacking sufficient victuals to remain on the Blackwater. He was soon back in Dublin, and Tyrone could think himself safe for this year. A few weeks later a sudden massing of Irish forces on the Ulster border drew the deputy into a hasty march north. Early in October, after a brief sickness, he was dead at Newry. His death followed by only a few days that of Sir John Norris.[6]

The affairs of Ireland were now at their lowest ebb. The dearth that gripped the whole island had crippled Burgh's plans for a campaign. Men sent over in May could not be used until July because of lack of victual. Desertion and deaths through malnutrition were at a peak. Although something like 10,300 men appeared on the muster list, Burgh had difficulty in fielding 1,700 in Tyrone, of whom only some 400 were English. Clifford in Connaught had some 1,500 men, of whom two-thirds were Irish. In December Ormond could find only 500 men out of eighteen companies (nominally 1,800 men), and of these 100 were unable to bear arms. The Queen's comment on this report was "a monstrous declaration . . . such a book never was methinks since the conquest of Ireland."[7]

Not surprisingly both Fenton and Chancellor Loftus were urging pacification at least for the time being, and the Privy Council in its instructions to the interim government necessarily prescribed a defensive stance. Ormond as general of the forces was to protect the

[5] *CSPI* 6 (1596–97): 301–3, 305, 306–7, 310, 315–16, 317–20; *APC* 1597: 24, 26–27, 240–45, 388.

[6] *CSPI* 6 (1596–97): 333–34, 341–42, 356–58, 366, 371–73, 398, 399–401.

[7] *Ibid.*, 367–68, 371–73, 418–19, 419–20, 436–37, 439, 467; *APC* 1597–98: 207–18.

Pale and hang on to existing positions. The Lord Justices, Loftus and Gardiner, warned of the spread of rebellion and, more important, of a new note in the rebels' demands. They now sought, not redress of grievances, but the recovery of their lands from English hands, the restoration of the old faith and of Irish law. But the Queen was still more concerned with the accounts of victuals consumed in the summer and the identity of the Londoners who had lent Dublin £3,000. She observed sardonically that the Dublin council could not account for its expenses but could be very precise as to its demands for money, down to the halfpenny. However, she promised a reinforcement of 900 veterans from France, each worth two of the raw recruits.[8]

By December 1597 the clock had turned back full circle when Ormond, now general of the army and responsible for all military matters, was instructed by the Privy Council to open negotiations with Tyrone. The earl allowed the provisioning of the Blackwater fort, but his demands had now expanded to wholly new dimensions. Besides pardon he asked liberty of conscience, a presidency of Ulster, withdrawal of English garrisons from all Ulster and from other Gaelic areas, and pardon for the Leinster rebels, the O'Mores and the O'Connors. In return he offered a two months' truce and the recall of his men from Leinster. He firmly refused to give his son as hostage. He might have asked even more had he known the Queen's instructions to Ormond and his colleagues, Fenton and Bishop Jones. In her anxiety to avoid further fighting she was prepared to offer a truce, even if Tyrone refused to provide a hostage. On due and humble submission she would pardon the earl and listen to his grievances.[9]

The reopening of dealings with Tyrone seemed to prefigure a weary repetition of past such negotiations. Initially Ormond held out the hope that, if a promise of peace for a two- to three-year period were offered, Tyrone would moderate his terms. This was echoed, not surprisingly, by Fenton: the patient was too sick for sharp medicine; two to three years' intermission of peace would reclaim the rebels and unknit the present conspiracy. For the present Ormond had secured a two-month cessation (from 22 Decem-

[8] Ibid., 400–1, 421–22, 423–24, 434, 436–37, 457–63.
[9] Ibid., 461, 463–64, 476, 481, 490–92, 493; APC 1597–98: 207–18.

ber 1597). Only thus could the Blackwater fort be revictualled, since the general could not put more than 700 men in the field.[10]

The Queen backed Ormond's policy of treating with Tyrone, insisting only that he must be rebuked for his tone of equality and forced to submit as a subject. But he was not to be put out of hope of royal favor and restitution of his former estate. Pressed as to a longer-term policy, whether peace or war, the Queen hedged; she would not commit herself to a term of years (as Fenton proposed) but would wait on the present dealings with Tyrone as a clue to future action. The Queen's hesitations at this juncture were determined by the problems of dearth, at home and in Ireland, and by the uncertainties of the international scene. French withdrawal from the war loomed just over the horizon. The Irish council was informed of the Spanish overtures for peace (made through Henry IV) and of Robert Cecil's intended mission to France. Clearly, the outcome of these larger prospects would govern the Queen's policy in Ireland.[11]

Ormond pressed Tyrone for a meeting in March 1598. When the Bishop of Meath met the earl later in that month the enlarged scope of the rebel's goals became all too clear. He would accept pardon himself only if it were also granted not only to the dependent chiefs of Ulster but also to the MacWilliams in Connaught and the O'Mores and O'Connors in Leinster. Their formal tribal titles were to be restored to MacWilliam and O'Reilly. The earl aimed at enlarging his circle of clientage and of achieving a leadership reaching well beyond the borders of his native province. In the end he refused to submit, and the best the bishop could extract was a continuation of the truce for six weeks. In a frank discussion among the three, Tyrone and O'Donnell admitted to the bishop that they sought to exclude the English altogether from their lands and those of their supporters.[12]

These parleys radically affected English opinion. Fenton, the most persistent and coherent peacemaker, now began to swing around to forthright advocacy of war as the only policy that would work. He had altogether lost confidence in Tyrone's peaceable in-

[10] *CSPI* 7 (1598–99): 1–6, 7, 8; *Annals* 3: 2051.
[11] *APC* 1597–98: 207–18; *CSPI* 7 (1598–99): 43–48.
[12] *Ibid.*, 69–70, 83–86, 110–20, 120–22.

clinations. And indeed, as soon as the truce ended, Tyrone surrounded the Blackwater fort and besieged Cavan Castle. Signs of disaffection appeared in Munster; open violence flared in Wexford. The Dublin council, reporting this spreading violence, declared it was not religion "nor old beggarly titles" that moved Tyrone. "It is the alteration of the government and the State that he aimeth at." The Irish too had a sense of impending crisis. This was, in the words of the chronicler, the summer that "rekindled the ancient flame of hatred."[13] London was at last beginning to respond to the changing mood in Dublin. In late May Burghley, taking notice of the scheme for a general campaign based on the old strategy of a three-pronged assault, drew up a memorandum asking for detailed estimates of men, money, and ships.[14]

The home government's response came only after a long and angry correspondence on corruption and inefficiency in Ireland, full of reproaches from London and embarrassed explanations from Dublin. The Queen could not understand why in spite of repeated remittances of funds to Ireland the troops there remained unpaid, and the government there in debt. She could get no clear report as to the size of her forces in Ireland. Secretary Fenton admitted he was mystified as to where the money went. The council blamed Ormond and past deputies. Information from serving officers confirmed the gross abuses in army administration. Failure to receive funds meant that the troops lived off the countryside as best they could while peasants and townsmen fled rather than face such exactions. Captains siphoned off funds before they reached the troops; inefficient and corrupt commissaries failed to give any accounting. Civil and military officials blamed one another. And now in the absence of a deputy there was not even the shadow of effective control from above.[15]

Amidst promises of amendment, and with strict supervision from London, the English government agreed to substantial reinforcements from home. In late spring 4,000 men were assembled and £24,000 sent over. Privy Council consent to a Lough Foyle ex-

[13] *Annals* 3: 2053–55.

[14] *CSPI* 7 (1598–99): 123–25, 142–43, 160–62, 169, 173–74, 178–83. For the Irish version of those exchanges, see *Annals* 3: 2053–55.

[15] *CSPI* 7 (1598–99): 23, 40–41, 43–48, 56–58, 126, 146–50, 205–10.

pedition was given in July, and a commission was given Sir Samuel Bagenal to command this enterprise. Embarkation of 2,000 men from England was planned for 20 August.[16]

In the meantime Bagenal's half-brother, the Marshal, prepared to relieve the Blackwater fort. As a bridgehead it was too isolated and too difficult to supply to be useful. Always of dubious value, it could all too easily be masked by Tyrone or taken, as had been the case in 1595. Nevertheless, the English determined to relieve it.[17] Setting out from Newry on 12 August, Bagenal was overwhelmed two days later at the Yellow Ford. Some 2,000 men were lost, including the Marshal himself. The Irish contemptuously allowed the evacuation of the Blackwater and Armagh garrisons (without their arms). The Lough Foyle force was diverted to Carlingford, and another 2,000 men were to be dispatched from England. The Queen, furious at the course of events, upbraided the Irish council and ordered a defensive stance on the Ulster frontier while pressing the war in Leinster.[18]

The Irish victory at Yellow Ford in effect signalled the transformation from sputtering skirmishes, punctuated by ineffectual truces, to open and continuing warfare. The consequences were quickly felt elsewhere in the island. In early October, Sir Thomas Norris reported the invasion of his province of Munster by 2,000 men under O'More and his allies. The undertakers and tenants fled in fear and the whole countryside erupted. "Among all other ill accidents of that state of Ireland there could come no worse news." Two thousand men were hastily embarked in Cornwall for direct dispatch to the threatened province. By the end of October the Lord Justices were writing of a general revolt aimed at shaking off all English government. A new revolt in Leinster was led by Lord Mountgarret, a Butler claimant to the Ormond title, while a self-styled Earl of Desmond revived the Geraldine cause in Munster. The Ulster leaders wrote to their allies in Leinster to raise that province and to stir Munster to action. Ormond demanded 4,000

[16] Ibid., 133, 149–53, 155–58, 172, 201–3, 227, 230–31; Carew 3 (1589–1600): 281; APC 1597–98: 567–68, 590–91; 1598–99: 55–60.

[17] See Hayes-McCoy, "Strategy and Tactics," 266, 268.

[18] CSPI 7 (1598–99): 217–19, 224–26, 229, 254–56, 257–59, 266; Carew 3 (1589–1600): 283; APC 1598–99: 73–74, 94–96; Annals 3: 2060–75.

more men while Bingham, recalled to Ireland as Marshal, reported that one-quarter of those recently sent over had deserted.[19]

A memorandum of early November outlined the requirements of a commander sent to recover Ireland. They included 12,000 foot and 1,000 horse, twelve pieces of great artillery, victuals and apparel for a year, and much else besides. Cecil wrote Ormond in November that some great person would be sent, probably but not certainly Essex. Some £36,000 was dispatched to pay arrears and satisfy the debts owed victuallers. This was to last until the great army passed over in February. The commanders in Ireland were to stand on the defensive in the interval. Munster was strengthened by 1,000 men before the old year was out and another 1,000 levied for Connaught.[20]

The misery that beset Ireland in the bleak winter of 1598–1599 was the final stage in a long process of destabilization that had begun many years earlier. The uncertain balance that had obtained between Tyrone and the State at Dublin had been shaken when Fitzwilliam's measures against the MacMahons in 1589–1590 awakened suspicion and fear in the breast of Tyrone. The escape of Hugh Roe O'Donnell provided him with an ally whose influence was always on the side of resistance to Dublin and who was ready to exploit the sullen resentment of those western chiefs who had suffered at the hands of Bingham. Against this flare-up of Gaelic defiance were the divisions within the ranks of the Dublin regime, first the rift between Bingham and his enemies in the council, and then the fatal division of authority between a resentful deputy and the strong-minded veteran Norris. Tyrone's suspicions were strengthened by the conflicting signals he received from Russell and Norris. Russell's replacement by an inexperienced and unknown deputy did nothing to resolve the crisis, and Burgh's death within a few months of his landing dissipated whatever credit the Dublin government still had. Tyrone now moved with increased boldness to widen his influence outside Ulster. When his hated enemy, Bagenal, was sent to relieve the Blackwater fort, the earl did not hesi-

---

[19] *CSPI* 7 (1598–99): 282, 300–2, 303, 304–9, 333–35, 339–40, 340–41; *APC* 1598–99: 237–38, 242; *Annals* 3: 2077.

[20] *CSPI* 7 (1598–99): 344–45, 350, 377–78, 381–83, 399–400; *APC* 1598–99: 312–15, 360–61.

tate to take to the open field. His crushing defeat of the marshal was a direct challenge to outright war.

Throughout these years, as the Irish situation steadily deteriorated, the English government, distracted by the approaching Franco-Spanish peace, by fear of another armada, and by its own offensives against Spain, gave less than half its attention to Ireland. Developments there were seen as vexatious distractions demanding men and money that could ill be spared. The instinctive reaction of the Queen was to take the line of least resistance (and least cost), to compromise, to appease, to pacify. The powerful voices of Leicester and Walsingham, once so vocal in Irish affairs, were stilled for good. An aging Burghley, although well informed and with firm convictions on Irish matters, was—like his mistress—distracted by greater problems. Essex, although the inheritor of a tradition of involvement, showed little interest in Ireland; the Irish lobby of earlier decades seemed hardly to exist. But now, with the gauntlet thrown down by Tyrone, it was no longer possible to avert English eyes from the Queen's other island. The army that they had to face was no longer a band of half-armed wood-kerne, as much bandits as soldiers, but a well-trained and disciplined corps of seasoned fighters, knowledgeable in the latest techniques of warfare and more than a match for the hastily recruited conscripts dragged from the ploughs or shops of the English shires.[21] There was no help for it but to fight a war more demanding and more costly than any with which the Elizabethan government had yet had to deal.

The Queen and her council now finally faced up to the far-reaching demands that Ireland made upon them. In sharp contrast to their response in past decades the most generous provision was made; nothing was to be denied that was necessary for winning a war. Gone were the old days, when a thousand or two men were reluctantly dribbled out, ill-furnished and unpaid. An infantry force of 16,000 men—backed by 1,300 horse and amply supplied with all the necessary supplies of food, munitions, clothing, and ships—was provided. As the Queen noted in her instructions to Essex, it was "a royal army paid, furnished in other sort than any king of this land hath done before." This force was some three times larger than the expeditionary army in the Netherlands and

[21] Hayes-McCoy, "Army of Ulster," 105–20, and "Strategy and Tactics," 255–79.

its projected annual cost of £290,000 was well over twice the annual charge allocated for Dutch service in the Treaty of Nonsuch. To the Irish chronicler it was the strongest force sent since Strongbow's invasion.[22]

Moreover, this was a campaign with a prearranged plan of action. Not only was it the largest land army the Elizabethan government had yet mounted, it was also the first for which large-scale strategy was devised in advance. The expeditions to the Continent had been largely open-ended, with considerable discretion given the commander, who in any case had ultimately to accommodate himself to decisions made by French or Dutch leaders. In the naval ventures the attempt to plan had been limited to little more than laying out general goals in an order of priority. By the very nature of the venture, the commanders, once they cleared port, had wide freedom of action. But here in Ireland the English government set itself not only to shape the strategy of campaign in advance but carefully to provide the means. Not only an immense army but also money, victuals, munitions, shipping—all were organized in advance with as much efficiency as the administrative structure was capable of mustering.

More important was the choice of supreme commander. In retrospect we know the appointment of Essex to have been an unhappy one, a failure from the government's point of view and a tragedy from the earl's. But in contemporaries' outlook it was a natural, indeed an inevitable, choice. The magnitude of the danger England faced, both from internal revolt in Ireland and from the prospect of Spanish intervention, was recognized by Queen and Council in the scope of their preparations. Such an enterprise required the services of one who could bring to it the luster of a great martial reputation, experience in high command, and the prestige of high rank. In the sparse ranks of England's soldiery there was clearly only one candidate available for the post—the hero of Cadiz, "Great England's glory and the world's wide wonder." He was the man who, as a contemporary wrote, "had full superintendency over all martial affairs and for his noble worth was generally loved and followed by the nobility and gentry."[23] In truth, the brilliance of his

[22] CSPI 7 (1598–99): 482–83; Carew 3 (1589–1600): 292–95; Moryson, History 1: 65–70; APC 1598–99: 360ff., for preparations; Annals 3: 2111.

[23] Moryson, History 1: 163.

reputation veiled the limitations of the earl's qualifications. At Rouen he had commanded barely a quarter of the force he took to Ireland, and at Cadiz land fighting had been limited to one sharp, short melee. He had never been the autonomous commander of a large army in a sustained campaign, and he knew little of the special tactics that Irish war required. Nor was he fortunate in having a staff of skilled lieutenants. John Norris was dead; Vere, no friend to the earl, away in the Low Countries. Of the local veterans Bagenal had of course died; Bingham had followed him to the grave just before Essex landed; Thomas Norris died of a wound in summer 1599. Nevertheless, it was as strong an appointment as could be made, given the expectations as to leadership in sixteenth-century societies, and the formal words of Elizabeth's instructions to Essex can be taken more or less at face value. "Having cast our eyes upon all our servants and compared them," she found Essex "before any other out of former experience of your faith, valor, wisdom, and extraordinary merit."[24]

We must give less credence, however, to the words that followed—that his "inwardness and counsel and favor with us" set him apart from his predecessors. In the previous summer, during a Council discussion of a successor to Burgh, Queen and favorite had quarrelled angrily. Elizabeth had boxed his ears; the earl had turned his back on her. This episode proved to be the end of a long relationship. The royal favor, once so warm, had cooled to a temperature less than tepid. There had been outward reconciliation, but the old intimacy was gone. Wary observers in the court doubted the sincerity of the Queen's forgiveness for Essex's behavior and regarded the reconciliation as very fragile. None of the parties concerned was happy with the prospects—neither the Queen, nor Essex, nor his entourage. Moryson goes so far as to aver that "his greatness was now judged to depend as much on Her Majesty's fear of him as her love of him."[25] This fatal distrust was to have far-reaching consequences.

As early as 10 December 1598 Cecil wrote to Conyers Clifford in Connaught that Essex would command the army royal; an official letter to the Irish council followed a month later. Reaction among

[24] *Carew* 3 (1589–1600): 292–95.
[25] John Harington, *Nugae Antiquae*, ed. Thomas Park (2 vols., London, 1804) 1: 239; Moryson, *History* 1: 63.

the soldiery in Ireland was cautiously favorable. However, the veteran captain Thomas Reade warned that Essex, a stranger to the country, must not expect to find "a gallant enemy which will meet him in the field and end his cause by the trial and fortune of a battle." It would be a very different kind of war than he had found in France or at Cadiz.[26]

Reade went on to outline a general strategy that echoed the thought of his predecessors for decades back and that had been implemented with success against Shane O'Neill in the 1560's. Ulster was to be ringed with garrisons, including posts at Ballyshannon, the key to the western land passage into the province, and Lough Foyle on the northern coast. The earl, arriving about the end of March, should limit himself to the relief of the Blackwater fort in May. He should then pause to allow time for forage to grow before making the crucial move through the other (eastern) land passage from Armagh to Dungannon in the heart of O'Neill country. Through the harvest season his force and those of the encircling garrisons should ravage the countryside to the utmost, retiring only in October. The ensuing famine would draw off many of Tyrone's followers and disintegrate his forces. Essex could concentrate on the reduction of Leinster in the winter months. In general outline this reflected faithfully the planning of the English government. All efforts were to be focused on the north; the destruction of the O'Neill/O'Donnell alliance having been accomplished, the uprising elsewhere could be easily dealt with.

Essex brought to his task a clear understanding of the strategy proposed and the tactics required for its exploitation, but the frame of mind in which he approached his task was one of extreme reluctance. In past enterprises he had assumed command brimming with self-assurance, confident of success and eager for the venture. But this time he set out on his journey to Ireland in a mood of such self-pitying pessimism as seemed to foredoom his enterprise. It was true that his task was onerous, and expectations high—"for many minds will attend the sequel of these proceedings and there will be much more expected of my lord's march than hitherto hath been performed by others in great authority." Yet the backing of the Privy Council was resolute and unstinting. They promised that reinforcements of 2,000 men would be sent every three months. Money for

[26] *CSPI* 7 (1598–99): 449–50, 452; *APC* 1598–99: 464–65.

a quarter's pay went with the earl; all the munitions required were to hand; victuals were provided for the present, replenishment contracted through July. The deaths of Bingham, Wallop, and Norris, coinciding with his arrival, had wiped out a corps of veterans but opened the way for younger blood in the key offices in the Irish establishment.[27]

Yet the earl's mood was resolutely gloomy. Even before sailing from England he was gravely doubtful as to the outcome of the enterprise. He warned that "Her Majesty must make account that all these great preparations will vanish into smoke and the charge thereof be utterly lost." He went on to say, "It is natural to my office to have cause to speak this language. I had a natural antipathy against this service because I foresaw the necessities and knew how unpleasing they would be not only to me, the propounder, but much more to Her Majesty, the hearer of them." He would do his best, "but neither can a rheumatic body promise itself that health in a moist, rotten country nor a sad mind vigor and quietness in a discomfortable voyage." The contrast with earlier service was no doubt vivid in his mind. Then he had been setting out on voyages of conquest with hopes of glorious victory and rich plunder. Now he was set to putting down a rebellion in a remote and poverty-stricken province; there could be little hope of glittering prizes here.[28]

Awareness of the difficulties of his task no doubt contributed to this gloom, but the deeper cause was the rift between him and the Queen. That relationship was now one of coldness on her side and a bitter sense of rejection on his. Although he had graduated from the status of mere favorite to the more difficult role of councillor some years before, he had never lost the sense of his special relationship with the Queen. Now that that relationship was ruptured he seemed to return to the attitudes of earlier years, seeing every issue in a highly personal light. In this mood the earl was prepared to take umbrage at every check to his desires. The royal refusal to make Sir Christopher Blount, the earl's stepfather, a councillor at Dublin, even while approving his appointment as marshal of the army, aroused a series of petulant responses from Essex, who saw in the rebuff evidence that the Queen had no confidence in him. In this "I sued to Her Majesty to grant it out of favor, but I spoke a

[27] *CSPI* 7 (1598–99): 477–80; 8 (1599–1600): 13. [28] *Ibid.*, 1, 10.

416

language which was not understood, or to a goddess not at leisure to hear prayers." He added, "I must save myself by protestation that it is not Tyrone and the Irish rebellion that amazeth me, but to see myself sent on such an errand at such a time, with so little comfort or ability from the court of England to effect that I go about."[29]

[29] *Ibid.*, 6; *APC* 1598–99: 692–93, 714–18.

CHAPTER 21

THE FAILURE

OF ESSEX

Essex arrived in Ireland in mid-April. After receiving an account of the present state of the kingdom from the council,[1] he proposed to launch an attack on Tyrone in his Ulster fastness. The Irish councillors strongly advised against this. Lack of forage until the summer was more advanced, shortage of beeves to feed the army, and the lack of carriage horses (to be brought from England) to draw the wagons—all militated against such a move.[2] The earl then proposed to move southward into Leinster and Munster. This would enable him to reassert English power in these disordered provinces, checkered with pockets of rebellion, and to provide for the security of the Munster coast against a Spanish threat. Finally, he planned to move westward for a consultation with Sir Conyers Clifford, the governor of Connaught, about a proposed assault on Ballyshannon. The Queen gave her specific assent to the Leinster expedition.[3]

Beyond these immediate moves lay the outlines of a larger strategy, a threefold assault against Ulster, outlined previously: two land forces, one from the Pale, the other from Connaught, and a sea-

[1] *CSPI* 8 (1599–1600): 14; *Carew* 3 (1589–1600): 298–300.

[2] *CSPI* 8 (1599–1600): 16–17.

[3] L. W. Henry, "The Earl of Essex in Ireland, 1599," *Bulletin of the Institute of Historical Research* 32 (1959): 12; *CSPI* 8 (1599–1600): 28. See also Henry's "Contemporary Sources for Essex's Lieutenancy in Ireland, 1599," *Irish Historical Studies* 11 (1958–59): 8–17.

borne invasion of the north coast. This strategy was not new; it had been used in 1566, repeatedly urged by the Irish council, and planned but diverted in 1597.[4] In 1598 an expedition to Lough Foyle was actually being organized but had to be diverted to Carlingford in the wake of the Yellow Ford disaster. The landing on the north coast was to be made in conjunction with the earl's invasion of Ulster through the Moyry Pass via Armagh.[5] A garrison based on Lough Foyle could strike at O'Neill's power in his own homeland. It would also serve as a magnet to detach dependent chieftains restless under his domination. Essex had asked the Privy Council for necessary ships and supply before he left England. Such a move had also been an assumption of the Irish government when Essex's appointment was first mooted and the Irish too had expected such an attack. In April Essex wrote from Ireland asking for ships to transport 4,000 foot and 100 horse for a landing in June. The Council responded by insisting he should first find as much shipping as possible in Ireland. Consequently nothing was done in England, while the earl was unable to find the ships in Ireland. In July, on his return from the south, Essex wrote that, after subtracting the garrison forces in the three southern provinces, there remained only 6,000 men to mount both an assault on Armagh and the Lough Foyle enterprise, a number far smaller than that of the enemy. Therefore, he ruled out any possibility of a Lough Foyle landing for that year.[6]

The failure to make any serious plans for the Lough Foyle expedition was fatal to the whole campaign; how it came about is something of a mystery. Essex made several requests for ships since he could not find the necessary supply in Ireland, but nothing was done at home. The Privy Council was distracted by fears of a Spanish invasion, which, of course, dominated its thinking about shipping. Not only was there unexplained lack of attention to the northern expedition, but the proposed assault on Ulster from the Pale was also denied necessary English support. To move the army's wagon train northwards Essex had to have strong English horses (the native Irish garron was too small a creature for this service). None were forthcoming from England. Whatever the causes of

---

[4] Henry, "Essex," 3, n. 4.   [5] *Ibid.*, 2–3.
[6] HMC, *Hatfield* 9: 93; *CSPI* 7 (1598–1599): 426, 451; 8 (1599–1600): 7, 19, 28, 92.

these deficiencies, Essex was clearly without the essential resources for carrying out the Queen's angry demands.[7]

The third prong of the planned assault, a move against the strategic ford at Ballyshannon, was still on the cards in July.[8] The key to this action was the castle of Sligo, held for the English by the local chieftain Donough O'Connor. It was to be used as a base for the onslaught on Ballyshannon. But O'Donnell moved first, besieged O'Connor straitly, and thus forced Clifford to attempt a relief.[9] That attempt ended in crushing defeat and the death of Clifford at the beginning of August.[10]

On his way back to the capital Essex had written the Queen with a considered assessment of the present Irish situation and his recommendations for future action. He took a gloomy view of Irish loyalty. All, he believed—nobles, townspeople, peasants, Old English, and Gaels—were disloyal to the Crown, whether they showed it openly or not. Their leaders' aims were to destroy obedience to the Queen and to root out all remembrance of English rule. Their armed forces were more numerous than the Crown's; indeed, the latter were hardly sufficient to provide a plaster to cover the wound, let alone cure the ailment. Repression of rebellion would be costly in money and time. Nevertheless, the English had strong advantages—control of all towns, castles, and ports; superior cavalry; better officers; and naval power that could blockade supplies of munition. Garrisons once established would be bases for wasting the land and reducing the people by starvation. This course of action echoed the received military wisdom and the declared policy of the Queen's government but offered no guide for the immediate future.

This sober diagnosis of Ireland's ills and his considered prescriptions for their cure then came to a sudden halt, and in the next paragraph the earl broke into a passionate torrent of accusation against his own enemies:

But why do I talk of victory or success? Is it not known that from England I received nothing but discomforts and soul's wounds? Is it not spoken in the army that Your Majesty's favor is diverted from

[7] Henry, "Essex," 20–22.
[8] *CSPI* 8 (1599–1600): 92; Henry, "Essex," 13.
[9] *Annals* 3: 2123.   [10] *CSPI* 8 (1599–1600): 113.

me and that already you do bode ill both to me and it? Is it not believed by the rebels that those whom you favor most do more hate me out of faction than them out of duty or conscience? Is it not lamented of Your Majesty's subjects both here and there that a Cobham or a Raleigh (I will forbear others for their place's sake) should have such credit and favor with Your Majesty?"[11]

The Privy Council was treated to a similar outburst, in which he asserted that his enemies at home were stabbing him in the back. "I provided for this service a plastron and not a curate [a breastplate not a backplate]. . . . And in professing myself unarmed on my back I meant that I lay open to the malice and practice of mine enemies in England, who first procured a cloud of disgrace to overshadow me and now in the dark give me wound upon wound." He predicted that the gentlemen volunteers would soon return home, abandoning a patron who could neither advance nor defend them.[12] Along with these outbursts there was a series of letters, dating back to his arrival, which insisted he must have more men and supplies if he were to accomplish his task. This letter included his decision to abandon the landing at Lough Foyle and an announcement that a move on Armagh would have to be postponed until after the harvest—too late to do much damage to the enemy.[13]

The disaster in Connaught only deepened the gloom with which the earl already viewed the whole Irish situation. In a series of letters in August he painted the blackest picture possible. The rebels were more numerous than supposed—20,000 to his 16,000—and better fighters to boot. Across the country the English effectively held only their garrisons, and when they stirred forth they were immediately attacked. Everywhere in the island, except in the immediate environs of Dublin, there was burning and spoiling. Neither Munster nor Connaught had a governor; his ranking commanders were few in number. Sickness was rife among the soldiery. And always there was the same refrain—the lack of royal backing. To win this war the Queen must have "ministers which must appear in more brightness than their own by the beams of her favor." For himself that season of royal favor had ended all at once. The

11 Devereux 2: 36–41; Birch 2: 415; Moryson, *History* 1: 80–85.
12 *CSPI* 8 (1599–1600): 76–77, 95–97.
13 *Ibid.*, 16–20, 27–29, 36–37, 91–95.

burden of his life was intolerable, and if it were not for the Queen's service he would quickly free himself from his office.[14]

In the meantime (7 and 30 July) Elizabeth herself had responded to the earl's earlier outburst in two long and forceful letters. She was now fully attentive to Irish matters and minced no words in making clear her orders and her expectation of obedience. In April the Queen had initially approved the Leinster-Munster expedition, but now in July, when no step had been taken towards engaging Tyrone, the royal patience snapped. (The Queen had not yet heard of the abandonment of the Lough Foyle scheme.) The ensuing letter from the sovereign was no mere display of royal displeasure but a measured and detailed indictment of the earl's actions. She began by discrediting the Leinster-Munster expedition. The capture of a castle or two from a "rabble of rogues" and the submission of a few rebel leaders could easily have been accomplished by the local president. To set forth a whole army against those "base rogues" who possessed no town or major stronghold and lacked any foreign assistance was not only wasteful of money, but made the Queen ridiculous in foreign eyes. Tyrone in the meantime "hath lived at his pleasure."[15]

Next she turned to the earl's choice of subordinates; commands were given to "young gentlemen who rather desire to do well than to perform it." Nor had Essex troubled to inform the government of the names of his appointees. The reference to "young gentlemen" no doubt aimed at such as the Earl of Rutland or the Earl of Southampton, the latter of whom Essex had made general of horse, an appointment that the Queen had promptly countermanded. She renewed her rebuke that he should employ one "whose counsel can be of little, and experience of none use" and ridiculed the argument that the volunteer gentlemen would now go home.

The Queen's dissatisfaction with Essex's conduct of the campaign was the first item in her measured rebuke of her commander, but she was even more concerned with a graver issue—the state of his mind. Here she was even harsher. Essex's conviction that he was being stabbed in the back was brusquely rejected as merely "exclaiming against the effects of your own causes." Was it not enough that he had had all he asked for in this service but that he should, contrary to the royal will, by particular acts promote men who dis-

---

[14] *Ibid.*, 121–23, 123–25, 125–26.   [15] *Ibid.*, 98–101, 105–6.

pleased the Queen? He must know "that whosoever it be that you do clad with any honors or places wherein the world may read the least suspicion of neglect or contempt of our commandments, we will never make dainty to set on such shadows as shall quickly eclipse any of these lustres."

Finally she came to the central defect of his service, the failure to move against Tyrone. Brushing aside his proposal for a sally into Offaly—that could be left to subordinates—she would tolerate no more delay or excuses. "We must now plainly charge you . . . with all speed to pass thither in such order as the axe may be put to the root of that tree which hath been the treasonable stock from whence so many poisoned plants and grafts have been derived." In the second letter (30 July) she made her commands even more explicit. "We do hereby let you know that the state of things standing as they do and all the circumstances weighed, both of our honor and the state of that kingdom, we must expect at your hands, without delay, the passing into the North" to accomplish what had been resolved at his departure and to show that six months' charges had not been wasted. This proceeding would assure that the Queen had no reason to repent of employing Essex and would secure her against the imputation of an ill-prepared enterprise. The royal letter was followed by others, even more emphatic, from the Privy Council, restating the same message. In the tones of a parent soothingly reassuring an anxious child, they rejected the imputation of any "indisposition" towards the earl as too trivial for serious consideration, "knowing you too wise to apply these descriptions to any of us."[16]

When the Queen heard of the decision to cancel the Lough Foyle attack, she rounded on Essex and the Irish Council with predictable anger. Carefully totting up the numbers of men available (including 2,000 more just authorized), she expressed her astonishment that Essex thought himself too weak to move effectively. She also hit out at his implication that he would obey her command to advance, but against his own better judgment. She curtly concluded "for Lough Foyle we doubt not but to hear by the next that it has begun and is not in question." The Privy Council again weighed in with similarly strong exhortations to action against Tyrone.[17]

This whole exchange was rendered more or less moot by the

[16] *CSPI* 8 (1599–1600): 105–7, 101–2, 111.   [17] *Ibid.*, 114–16, 117–18.

disaster in Connaught, where Clifford's death and the loss of 2,000 men spiked the last hope of implementing the planned grand strategy.[18]

Essex's pessimism had communicated itself to his officers. How low their morale had fallen is shown by a joint statement of sixteen ranking officers, from colonels to volunteers. With an army reduced by sickness and desertion, with the defeat in Connaught and the absence of a base on Lough Foyle, they asserted that no offensive at all was possible. Indeed they wanted to abandon Armagh and the Blackwater fort as mere useless consumers of victuals. The treasurer-at-war reported that not 10,000 out of the 17,000 to 18,000 in list were effectives.[19]

However, Essex, in receipt of Elizabeth's earlier command, had finally set out for Ulster in the last days of August, seeking an engagement with Tyrone.[20] The two armies eyed each other for a few days and then Tyrone made overtures to Essex, which after some dispute resulted in the famous meeting of the two and the agreement on 15 September to a truce for six weeks, renewable at six-week intervals until May Day next. After his return to England, Essex defended this action in a way that throws light on his highly personal view of his role in Ireland. He represented that Tyrone had no trust at all in the Dublin government and turned to Essex as the only intermediary who could obtain "secret and inward satisfaction" from the Queen. Armed with that assurance Essex could, he asserted, return to Ireland and conclude a viable settlement. Tyrone would admit garrisons to Ulster and generally accept a return to the *status quo ante* of the 1580's. For the time being his control of the lesser chieftains and his refusal to admit sheriffs would have to be tolerated. All this was to be a holding operation until the Queen's forces were stronger. Then secret preparations could be made for a deadly blow against the Gaelic lords. It was precisely the kind of patched-up stop gap arrangement that had been tried and had failed over and over again in the past.[21] What was new was Essex's intensely personal conception of his role. He believed his indispensable and unique position as favorite would loose the Gordian knot of Ireland's troubles and secure Tyrone's submission.

[18] *Ibid.*, 113; *Annals* 3: 2127–33.   [19] *CSPI* 8 (1599–1600): 126–27.
[20] *Ibid.*, 144–47, 154–55.
[21] *Ibid.*, 138–39, 144–47, 154–55; *Carew* 3 (1589–1600): 336–37.

During the interval between Essex's departure from Dublin and his agreement with Tyrone the Queen had written in weary disgust, accepting that there would be no campaign against the arch-rebel and inquiring what the earl proposed to do for the balance of the year.[22] But by now, within ten days of the interview with Tyrone, Essex was on his way to court to justify his actions and win the royal approval, leaving Ireland in the charge of Lord Justices.[23] By the end of the month he was at the court at Nonsuch. His brief and ill-starred career in Ireland was over. From an Irish point of view his tenure had been an anticlimactic episode. He had arrived with much fanfare and with such forces as no previous ruler had had at his disposal. The English government at last had shown every disposition to throw its whole weight behind a vigorous policy aimed at breaking Gaelic power altogether. The earl's failure meant not only a dismaying waste of resources, of men and of materiel, but also dealt a severe blow to the morale of the already dispirited forces in Ireland. It left everything to be done again; the whole enterprise would have to be remounted.

There necessarily followed an interval of uncertainty, compounded by Tyrone's wily diplomacy, but by the late winter of 1599–1600 the English government had recovered its balance, and resolute measures for subduing the rebel areas were well in hand. The first few months were a time of maximum confusion. Essex was still nominally Lord Lieutenant of Ireland and for some weeks after his departure it was more than half expected that he would return. Direction of the "State at Dublin" reverted to the veteran Loftus and Sir George Carey, treasurer-at-war since 1598; command of the army was vested in Ormond. In the provinces Essex had appointed his confidant, Sir Warham St. Leger, a local landowner, as military commander in Munster. Sir Henry Docwra, the president of Connaught, and his deputy were both absent in England, leaving the veteran soldier Sir Arthur Savage in charge.[24]

Essex, under house arrest since the evening following his arrival at court, obstinately defended his agreement with Tyrone. Indeed, he now asserted that the hope of peace in Ireland turned solely on their relationship. Tyrone was surrounded by pro-Spanish councillors, but there was a pro-English faction and "I made account as

[22] CSPI 8 (1599–1600): 144–47, 154–55.
[23] CSPI 8 (1599–1600): 156, 157–58.   [24] Ibid., 205–6.

long as I was favored and in any [way] enabled by Her Majesty" the latter would prevail. "I fear my disgrace and ruin may hinder Her Majesty's service." In fact the news of Essex's disgrace was concealed by the Dublin authorities in fear that its revelation would embolden the rebels. And when Tyrone ended the truce and refused to treat any further, he declared that if the Earl of Essex were here, "I should have reason and right due me." But by mid-October at the latest the Queen had determined Essex should not return.[25]

In the interim that followed, the authorities in Ireland had to pick up the pieces as best they could. The Lord Justices continued dealing with Tyrone through Essex's intermediary, Sir William Warren. The Queen, albeit reluctantly, acceded to the truce and to continuing negotiations with the rebel leader. She blamed Essex severely for his actions but was willing to accept the results of his agreement with Tyrone and to try once again for a pacification. In November Secretary Fenton was designated as her agent and given specific instructions on which he was to treat.[26]

The Queen in a series of letters to the Lord Justices laid out her proposed course of action. Once again she changed tack and ordered a serious effort to achieve a pacification. Essex's agreement with Tyrone was condemned, not for its substance but for its incompleteness. Mere truce, on terms of equality, could only advantage the Irish. Nothing had been concluded for future behavior (although Essex had specific powers to require this). The threads of negotiations were to be picked up and Tyrone assured that Essex's recall was not a repudiation of his agreement with the former. But his submission must be to the Queen, not to any lesser person. This done, he was promised the full protection of the law and full forgiveness of the past, even—the Queen piously added—as Almighty God forgives sinners. The other northern rebel leaders would be given similar treatment. But Tyrone must understand that the clock could not be turned back. There could be no restoration of the Desmond earldoms or any dismantling of the apparatus of government in the west or south. On religion he was to be reassured: "we leave to God Who knows best how to work His will in these things by means more fit than violence." The Irish authorities were

---

[25] *Ibid.*, 189–90, 190–91, also 201 (Pyne to Essex), 208–9; Sidney Papers 2: 134; Birch 2: 437.

[26] *CSPI* 8 (1599–1600): 157, 194, 215–17, 219–121, 227, 246–47.

informed of the negotiations now pending with the archduke; peace with Spain seemed highly probable, and the Irish could look for no assistance from abroad.[27]

All these hopeful preparations foundered before they were fairly launched. At the end of October Tyrone wrote to Ormond, denouncing the truce and refusing a parley with Fenton, alleging violations of the truce in Connaught. He insisted he was no traitor but that he fought for religion and the liberties of his country.[28] The Queen's instructions had allowed for just such a response by Tyrone. The strategy devised for Essex's expedition would be promptly put into action: all-out war would be waged against Tyrone; the first move would be a landing on Lough Foyle. But any immediate action was forestalled by another ploy of Tyrone, who in late November reopened parleys with Dublin and agreed to another truce until the New Year. Dublin opinion had now hardened to a conviction that no settlement was possible and that the only course was war. The time for temporizing was past, the sore "grown to another nature than to be cured by such kinds of medicine." Fenton, in a final repudiation of his past judgments, noted that the quarrel had shifted from popular grievances and complaints against over-heavy burdens. Now "he aspires to cantonize the kingdom or at least to prescribe limits and bounds to Her Majesty." A document in Cecil's possession listed Tyrone's demands, nothing less than the restoration of papal authority in Ireland, the return of the Desmond lands, a wholly Irish government and army, a Catholic university, and much else. The Secretary's marginal comment was "Ewtopia."[29]

Opinion in the Privy Council had now shifted to support for the judgment of the Irish council, and the Queen was moving in the same direction, albeit more slowly. Even in December she hoped for success in "that hopeless parley with the traitor"; at least she wanted to make one more try before sending more soldiers. The truce gave time for the threshing of grain in the Pale, but further discussions only confirmed the view that Tyrone was irreconcilable.[30]

At the end of the year the Queen began to move decisively. By

[27] *Ibid.*, 215–16, 218–19, 219–21, 229–33, 233–34; *Carew* 3 (1589–1600): 345–48.
[28] *CSPI* 8 (1599–1600): 204–5, 208–9, 240–41.
[29] *Ibid.*, 229–33, 245–52, 264–67, 273–74, 289–292, 305–7, 279–80.
[30] *Ibid.*, 275–76, 289–92, 300, 314.

Christmas Eve a levy of 4,000 foot had been decided on, with 3,000 to go to Lough Foyle. That force would be strengthened by a core of Low Countries veterans. It was also planned to plant a garrison at Ballyshannon on the border between Connaught and the O'Donnell lands. Within a week the levy had been increased to 5,000 foot and 200 horse. Already early in December Cecil could report the appointment of Lord Mountjoy as Essex's successor.[31]

The new deputy faced an even grimmer task than his predecessor. A survey of the Irish scene by a veteran Irish commander written at the beginning of 1600 gives all too vivid a picture of the problems Mountjoy would have to deal with. Irish morale had been immensely boosted by the failure of the greatest English captain in his encounter with them. The army the rebels faced had many shortcomings. As in the past, pay, victuals and clothing arrived long after they were needed. The natural consequence was that the soldier sold his arms and other equipment to keep body and soul together. The officers were a poor lot, more often chosen for favor than desert, dicers and wenchers, neglectful of their men. Those who were worthy were mostly veterans of France and the Low Countries, trained for a very different kind of warfare. Captains who looked after their men found themselves bankrupt, victims of dishonest victuallers. Nor were the men properly armed; their muskets were too heavy for guerrilla skirmishing and their other arms and armor more fit for the settled lands of the Continent than for the wilds of Ireland. And, of course, most of the soldiery were not English. As they deserted or died their ranks were filled up with native-born, whose loyalties were at best uncertain and who might well decamp with their equipment to the enemy.[32]

The weeks between Mountjoy's appointment and his arrival at the end of February 1600 were necessarily a ticklish time. The Irish government was fearful of disloyalty everywhere, even in the Pale and in the port towns. Tyrone had now broken out of Ulster and moved southwards through Westmeath towards Kilkenny. During his passage through the country not a word of his movements reached Dublin, a worrying sign of disaffection. By late February

[31] *Ibid.*, 314, 342, 346; *APC* 1599–1600: 24–25.
[32] *Carew* 3 (1589–1600): 353–55 (Sir John Dowdall); see also *CSPI* 8 (1599–1600): 475–77 (the bishop of Cork).

he was threatening Mallow, only a few miles north of Cork, and had passed the Blackwater River.[33]

Mountjoy had in the meantime received his instructions. He was given a reduced army of 12,000 foot and 1,200 horse with an annual budget of £208,000, over £50,000 less than that of his predecessor. The abuses of the past were to be remedied by strict surveillance and by a firm prohibition on recruitment of Irish. Advice on strategy showed that the English had learned from experience. Mountjoy was warned of Tyrone's oft-used tactic: when hard pressed by the English he made overtures of submission, bringing about a cessation long enough to waste the English army and break its effort, thereby winning new prestige in his countrymen's eyes. The new deputy was to avoid such a trap and on his side offer every bait to lure Tyrone's followers from their allegiance, playing upon the dissension and rivalries within the Gaelic ranks. Mountjoy was provided with a new provincial president in Munster, Sir George Carew, a Dublin councillor for some years and a favored client of Cecil. In one other, and very important, respect the *dramatis personae* in the Irish drama had changed. Burghley was dead, Essex in disgrace; Robert Cecil was now virtually sole minister and exercising close and continuous control over all Irish affairs. Nearly every officer of any importance in Ireland, civil or military, was corresponding directly with the Secretary since, as one of them put it, he is "now made choice of as the fittest and worthiest to direct and arrange the affairs of this kingdom and all men look to him for direction."[34]

The past career of the new deputy bore some striking resemblances to that of his discredited predecessor. The scion of an ancient but impoverished house (he had succeeded his brother in the title in 1594), he was eagerly ambitious to restore its reputation and fortunes. Almost an exact contemporary of Essex, he had like the latter caught the Queen's eye when he went to court in the 1580's. He too had served in the Low Countries in 1586 and had captained his own ship in the Armada year. Afterwards there was more service on the Continent, including a stint under Norris in Brittany. (Like Essex in 1589 he had slipped away with royal consent and was angrily summoned home.) In 1594 the Queen appointed him

[33] *CSPI* 8 (1599–1600): 384–85, 425–27, 455, 486; *Annals* 3: 2147–61.
[34] *CSPI* 8 (1599–1600): 402, 440–47; *Carew* 3 (1589–1600): 356–62.

captain of the major fortress of Portsmouth. In 1597 he commanded the land forces in the Islands voyage. Regarded as a rival by Essex, he had fought a duel with the earl, but afterwards they became firm friends and the young commander was numbered among the favorite's inner circle. According to Camden, it was Essex's opposition to Mountjoy's appointment to Dublin that led to the famous scene at the Council table in 1598, although court gossip rumored that Mountjoy would go to Ireland as deputy to Essex's lord lieutenancy. Certainly the friendship continued, for in 1599, when Essex returned home from Ireland, he entrusted his interests to Mountjoy and Southampton. Something more than mere suspicion connected the new deputy with his friend's designs in the autumn of 1599. Mountjoy's name certainly appeared in the evidence in the trials of 1601, and when he was setting out for Ireland, he wrote to Cecil, frankly recognizing his friendship for Essex but appealing now for the Secretary's strong backing in his new venture. It was this nobleman, modestly experienced on the battlefield, and enjoying a large measure of that royal favor that Essex had forfeited, who received the sword of state at Dublin on 28 February 1600. His record was a hopeful one, but he had yet to prove himself in a command of this magnitude. Unfamiliar with the Irish scene and equipped with an army barely two-thirds as large as Essex's, his task was to put down what was now full-fledged national rebellion.[35]

[35] HMC, *Hatfield* 7: 470; M. S. Rawson, *Penelope Rich* (London, 1911), 134–36; *The Letters of John Chamberlain*, ed. N. E. McClure (2 vols., Philadelphia, 1939) 1: 49, 151; Robert Naunton, *Fragmenta Regalia. Memoirs of Elizabeth, Her Court and Favorites* (London, 1824), 119–20, 132, 59; Birch 2: 184, 394; Camden, 580; Moryson, *History* 1: 124–25.

CHAPTER 22

THE TRIUMPH OF

MOUNTJOY

THE ARRIVAL of Mountjoy marked a major turning point in Irish affairs. Although many obstacles remained and setbacks had to be suffered, there was a sense of confidence and of decisiveness at the center. The contrast with his predecessor's regime was striking at every point. The captious fault-finding that greeted Essex's every move was replaced by cordial approval or even outright royal congratulation. Mountjoy's requests for support were speedily and efficiently met. The floundering uncertainties, the aimless drift of the past were replaced by a new purposefulness and consistency. Behind this transformation lay a changed outlook in the English court that was to affect Irish history for generations to come. Since the intervention of Thomas Cromwell in Irish matters seventy years earlier, there had been a settled intention to draw Gaelic Ireland under effective English rule and to transform it into an approximation of English society. The intention was there, but the drive to realize it had been spasmodic and uncertain. It had been shaped by a long debate about means. Was Ireland to be reduced by force or assimilated by example and persuasion? Over time the drift of policy had been towards the former alternative, but the dispute was by no means settled and, as we have seen, continuing hopes of a pacific accommodation had lingered on through the 1590's. The years the locusts ate, the years of royal indecision and of grasping New English ambition had ended them. Now a corner had been turned. With the coming of Mountjoy the whole energy of the English government was thrown into a campaign of brutal conquest. The war with Spain seemed at this moment to be winding down, as preparations were made for the conference at Boulogne. The crown could turn all its energies towards Ireland, bringing to bear its superiority in resources and crushing once and for all the remaining forces of resistance.

The effect on the local scene and on unfolding events was immediate. The history of Irish affairs in the latter half of the century had been largely a history of politics. Violence was, of course, endemic, but organized force was largely a threat, a ploy in the continuing political struggle. Politics had now been superseded by war, and armed force had replaced negotiation, intrigue, and the play of personalities as the sole arbiter of events. Necessarily, the historical account also changes; the history of Ireland from 1600 to 1603 is one of war. The military history has been ably recounted elsewhere, and there will be no attempt here to retell that story.[1]

The strategy that Mountjoy and Carew (who in February 1600 had been appointed his lieutenant in Munster) pursued was that which the advocates of force had urged for decades past—and used in the 1560's against Shane O'Neill and again in the Desmond wars in the 1580's. The role of the soldiers would involve neither the clash of arms on the battlefield nor the static enterprise of siege— the normal forms of Continental warfare—but something quite different. Garrisons established in strategically chosen strongpoints would provide bases for ravaging the countryside, particularly at harvest time. This policy was succinctly expressed by an English officer in Munster, who urged that all commanders be instructed to lay waste the lands and goods not only of traitors but also of "temporizing" subjects and those who could not defend themselves in towns and castles. Wherever a rebel took food by violence from a subject, that subject should abandon his land; if he did not, the lands would be wasted by the Queen's soldiers. Famine as much as the sword would be the weapon; when ploughing and breeding of cattle ceased, so would the rebellion.[2]

War on such terms was bound to be brutal in the extreme, but its horrors were exacerbated by English attitudes towards their enemies. This was not war, as on the Continent, between equals. The

[1] Cyril Falls, *Elizabeth's Irish Wars* (London, 1950).
[2] *APC* 1599–1600: 33; *Carew* 3 (1589–1600): 368–69; Moryson, *History* 1: 114–15.

Irish were rebels and had committed the cardinal secular sin of the age. As the English North had seen in 1569, rebellion was to be crushed with maximum severity and mercilessness. Sir John Dowdall, writing to Cecil from Ireland, had admitted that in famine the good would perish with the bad but then, he observed, "there are very few but have deserved at God's hand and Her Majesty's such a reward."[3]

Mountjoy's first task on his arrival was to deal with Tyrone's incursion into Munster, but his very presence solved that problem. As Fenton had pointed out earlier, Tyrone had not the strength to maintain an effective presence outside Ulster while adequately protecting his base. Now, with Mountjoy making vigorous preparations for a campaign in the north, the Irish leader hastened back to Ulster. The force for Lough Foyle, commanded by Sir Henry Docwra, was assembled at Chester. In May the deputy went to Newry just as Docwra sailed from Carrickfergus and by 21 May, while Mountjoy was distracting Tyrone's attention at Armagh, the landing was effected. The English authorities had learned from the previous year's experience, and this time ships and provisions were in ample supply. The success of these moves depended entirely on the provision of victuals from England; Ireland itself was suffering from the greatest famine known; human beings, horses, and cattle were alike starving. Yet this time, in sharp contrast with previous experience, the supply of food for the soldiers was adequate.[4]

In the south there had been a shock when in April Ormond was taken prisoner in a skirmish. There was considerable suspicion that his capture was no accident. Even so loyal a subject as the earl, longtime servant of the English state, was dubiously regarded now. In the end these suspicions were allayed when he was freed in June. It had already been hinted that he might wish to retire from his command. One of the few other Irish nobles fighting with the English, Lord Dunkellin, son of Clarickard, found himself under a similar cloud and sought to resign his command in Connaught since lack of confidence in him made his position intolerable.[5]

In general, however, English affairs prospered. The landing at Lough Foyle brought about the defection of Sir Art O'Neill, head

---

[3] *Carew* 3 (1589–1600): 355.

[4] *CSPI* 8 (1599–1600): 400, 498–99; 9 (1600): 22–24, 40, 61, 68–69, 81–83, 85–86, 121, 180–81, 188, 192–93, 194–98; *APC* 1599–1600: 108–11.

[5] *CSPI* 9 (1600): 8, 11, 87, 127–28, 137–39, 146–47, 167, 177–78, 237–38, 299.

of one of the rival branches of that family. In the fall the O'Donnell rival, Hugh Garve, followed suit. There was disappointment in the north, however, when lack of manpower prevented the establishment of a garrison at Ballyshannon. During the summer Mountjoy wasted Offaly and Leix, boasting of £10,000 worth of corn cut in the field. However, a plan to garrison Armagh was aborted, first by lack of victuals, then by Tyrone's forces and bad weather. But a fort was built halfway between Newry and Armagh.[6]

In the south the English fared better. There the pretended Desmond earl, the leader of the Munster revolt, was driven to cover, no better than a wood-kerne, as Carew boasted, and Florence MacCarthy, the other leading chief of the region, was ready to surrender. One other goal had been achieved. Carew could report great dearth in Munster, which he ascribed directly to the summer's campaign. No day had passed, he wrote, without report of killing and taking of prey. An infinite number of sheep and cattle had been taken "besides husbandmen, women, and children (which I do not reckon)." Some 1,200 "weaponed men" had been killed since the beginning of the year.[7]

There had been occasional rubs in the relations with the court. The Queen had ordered a reduction of Mountjoy's forces from 14,000 to 12,000. Immediately upon his arrival Mountjoy had begged for a revocation of this order. By June he was asking for an additional 2,000 infantry and 100 cavalry, a request granted by July. This army of 17,300 men was augmented by 1,000 to 2,000 Irish. By September the ban on Irish recruitment was being broken; each company was allowed a quota of 20 out of its strength of 100. In the fall, complaints began to come from England: why, with a force of this size, was so little being done? Mountjoy agreed to reduce his forces by 3,000, and a figure of 14,000 was finally agreed on. His budget was almost a third smaller than his predecessor's, but complaints about money were few and the late Burghley would surely have turned over in his grave if he had heard his successor Buckhurst's comment that it was better they should have too much than

---

[6] Ibid., 194–98, 221–22, 268–70, 279–83, 299–301, 335–36, 337–39, 392–94, 461–63, 469–70, 484, 520–22, 522–24; *CSPI* 10 (1600–1): 26–27.

[7] *Carew* 3 (1589–1600): 425–30, 442–43, 453–54; *APC* 1599–1600: 454.

too little, for if the expedition failed he and Cecil would have to bear the Queen's wrath.[8]

Mountjoy's military measures won the royal approval, but at the same time he was rebuked for being too soft with the insistent press of suitors for places in Ireland and too lenient in granting home leave to officers. In the summer his regime was charged with a whole budget of deficiencies—corruption, sale of justice, waste of money, neglect of religion.[9] Fenton, then in England, hinted that the deputy needed to be prodded into more activity. He had found both the captain of Carrickfergus and his deputy resident in England. The Irish secretary plainly said even more at court, as Mountjoy's anguished letter to Cecil reveals. He complained that he himself was believed in nothing while every discontented informer (i.e., Fenton) was given credit. His trust was in the Queen and her chief minister, but the latter had failed him. Although he had done better service than any other deputy, Cecil had now disabled him from further duty; he asked for recall. Descending to particulars, he asked how he could be expected to set out on an expedition without money and victuals.[10]

This outburst may have obliquely reflected another strand in the web of personal ties between the court and the Irish administration. Just as Fenton had a private correspondence with Cecil, Carew in Munster was even more intimate with the Secretary. Theirs was a correspondence of surprising warmth, in which the usually discreet Cecil was uncharacteristically frank. He was not only backing Carew to the hilt in Ireland but also pushing his cause at home. In the warmth of his friendship he assured his correspondent that Raleigh would never be a councillor without surrendering the captaincy of the guard to Carew. The favored position of the Munster president aroused the jealousy of the deputy, and a clash over the disposition of troops contributed to this friction. The very fact that Mountjoy had limited control over the forces in Munster highlighted the privileged position of Carew, who ruled over what was effectively an autonomous satrapy with links directly to London, bypassing Dub-

---

[8] *CSPI* 9 (1600): 1–5, 61, 66–67, 81, 217–18, 304, 314, 346–49, 445, 513–20; *Carew* 3 (1589–1600): 474–79, 484–85; Moryson, *History* 1: 119.

[9] *APC* 1599–1600: 454–56, 506–16; *CSPI* 10 (1600–1): 308–9, 324–27.

[10] *Ibid.*, 330–31, 397–98; *Carew* 3 (1589–1600): 440–41; 4 (1601–3): 99.

lin. In fact, similar direct ties between local officials in Ireland and the Secretary in London obtained throughout the island.[11]

Mountjoy's indignation cooled with time, although he was still defending himself through the autumn in letters that echoed some of the summer's wrath. His agitations were laid to rest by a personal letter from the Queen (addressed to Mistress Kitchen-maid) full of warm reassurances and praise. No man, she said, with so great a charge could avoid mistakes, "but I have never heard of any had fewer." Mountjoy's reputation as an effective soldier had been firmly staked out, and both the Queen and her ministers realized his value. Some rubs there might be between him and Carew, but the patent favor that the deputy enjoyed with the sovereign was an offset to the president's intimacy with the minister. Friction continued over the disposition of troops, as Carew urged the risks of Spanish invasion while the deputy insisted on the priority of the Ulster campaign, and there were still occasional hints of a certain unease between the deputy and the Secretary.[12]

In the campaign year of 1601 events moved slowly but purposefully. At the end of 1600 the submission of Donal Spanaigh Cavanagh broke the back of resistance in Leinster. The deputy took advantage of a disputed succession among the Maguires to back his candidate against Tyrone's. A similar case arose in Tyrconnel with the death of the O'Dogherty. Docwra and Tyrone backed the opposing claimants. The Lough Foyle garrisons pursued their bloody business in the Tyrone countryside while the deputy, operating from the Pale, went about the same work elsewhere. From Ferney he took no less than 3,000 cattle, and the submission of the Mac-Mahons and of their leader Ever McCooley followed.[13]

The establishment of the Lough Foyle force had accomplished the first stage in the overall strategy that aimed at strangling the Ulster Irish. Garrisons at Newry and Carrickfergus were bringing pressure to bear from the south and east, and a string of posts further west constricted Tyrone even more. The next big move would be the establishment of a post at Ballyshannon on the western bor-

[11] *Carew* 4 (1601–3): 48–57; *CSPI* 9 (1600): 360–64, 420, 446; 8 (1599–1600): 14–15 (note instructions in 1599 to the treasurer, master of the ordnance, and comptroller of victuals).

[12] *Carew* 3 (1589–1600): 481–82; *CSPI* 9 (1600): 187–88; BL, Cotton Mss., Titus C VII, 125.

[13] *CSPI* 10 (1600–01): 54–55, 57–58, 188–90, 244–46, 248–49; *Annals* 3: 2237.

der of O'Donnell's country. With these three pressure points oper-
ative, the final stages of suffocation could be carried out. The rav-
aged countryside of Ulster would no longer provide sustenance for
its inhabitants and the final collapse of resistance would ensue.

Preparations for the move on Ballyshannon went forward
slowly; Docwra was to be responsible but he could not move until
the requisite reinforcements and supplies arrived from England. By
June 1601 the deputy was ready for his part of the summer campaign in Ulster. Munster and Leinster were quiet, resistance almost
extinct. The pretended earl of Desmond had been smoked out and
captured, and in June Carew was proposing a general pardon for
the whole province, where the greater part of the population had
formally submitted. Connaught was the province most out of order;
Carew was asked by the deputy to send 1,000 foot and 50 horse
from his forces to Galway. Docwra, he hoped, would move to Ballyshannon. In the meantime, Mountjoy proposed to set up garrisons
in Lecale and at Armagh, a task that he accomplished with such
speed that both were in place by late June. The deputy was well
aware of the risks of a northern campaign that would leave the
south dangerously exposed in case of a Spanish landing, but he determined to take these risks rather than lose the campaigning season.[14]

Only one cloud darkened the deputy's horizon. In the investiga-
tions that followed Essex's rising, Mountjoy had been implicated in
the confessions of the conspirators. Rumor had it in Ireland that the
deputy would be spared only until he ended the war. Reassurance
from the Queen that her current displeasure arose solely from
Mountjoy's failure to answer a royal letter failed to convince him.
Some thought that he even contemplated flight to France. Certainly, contemporaries believed that his credit with the Queen was
damaged and that consequently he was now more than ever dependent on Cecil's goodwill. A letter from the deputy to Carew partly
confirms this. Declaring himself more beholden to the Secretary
than to any man, he adds, "the farewell my old friends gave me
makes his love more welcome unto me although my conscience is
clear that I was loyal to my old friendship to the last."[15]

[14] *CSPI* 10 (1600–1): 280–81, 299–300, 369–70, 372–73, 381–85, 394–96, 401–2;
Carew 3 (1601–3): 48–50, 87–92, 53–55, 85–86; *APC* 1600–1: 293, 306.
[15] Moryson, *History* 1: 204–5; *CSPI* 9 (1600): 308. Moryson writes of Mountjoy's
estrangement from two of his closest friends—unnamed.

Mountjoy's slumbering resentment of the more intimate confidence that obtained between Carew and Cecil flared up again in a letter to the president in August, full of hurt feelings because Carew had solicited power to nominate captains on his own, "the first example that ever any under another general desired or obtained like suit." Since it was the Queen's pleasure, he must endure, but he went on to complain angrily that Carew had held back some of the Munster companies, clean against the deputy's orders. "My lord, these are great disgraces unto me. . . . My allegiance and own honor are now engaged to go on with this work otherwise no fear should make me suffer this much." He added, "I know you are dear to one [Cecil] whom I am bound to respect with extraordinary affection." Carew evidently returned a soft answer to this outburst, for a few days later Mountjoy wrote accepting his explanation, "glad to take any satisfaction from one I have so worthily esteemed."[16]

Some kind of crisis had clearly arisen out of the revelations following Essex's uprising that had threatened Mountjoy's career, and he had reason to thank Cecil for support at this dangerous time. (This was more than hinted at by Cecil himself.) Whether through Cecil's intervention or not, the Queen had cast aside all aspersions on Mountjoy. In June the Privy Council conveyed the royal congratulations: she would not commend the success or endeavors of any governor more than Mountjoy's; he had restored the repute of English soldiers.[17] Whatever is to be made of the personal relationships, it is certain that the state benefitted from the collaboration of the three men. When the thunderbolt of Spanish invasion finally struck, control of Irish affairs was in far better shape than ever before. Two able commanders on the scene working in reasonably harmonious cooperation and mutual confidence were firmly backed by a chief minister at home who was thoroughly acquainted with every detail of their business and able to provide ample and speedy support from England. The contrast with the past condition of Irish administration could not have been more striking.

The Spanish threat—so long a bugbear of English imagining— now began to assume an ominous reality. In April the Privy Council thought chances of Spanish intervention slight, but by the end of June Cecil wrote of 4,000 to 5,000 men concentrated at Lisbon. "I

[16] *Carew* 3 (1601–3): 134, 151; see also *CSPI* 11 (1601–3): 241, 278–79, 353–54.
[17] *APC* 1600–1: 411.

cannot deny but make great prescription that you should have them in Ireland." The Queen acted by levying 2,000 men for Munster and holding 4,000 more in readiness. It was now (in August) taken for granted that a Spanish landing impended at any moment, and there was a false alarm of a fleet early in that month. Vigorous preparations were made by the Privy Council to meet the expected invasion. By the beginning of September the promised 2,000 had arrived and more were being levied.[18] It was none too soon, for on 22 September there was news from Cork of the arrival of twenty-eight sail of Spaniards at Kinsale.[19]

Ever since the late 1580's, the possibility of Spanish intervention in Ireland had hung in the air. Tyrone's dealings with Spain were well known; a fair amount of his correspondence had been intercepted. Supplies of arms and money had periodically reached him. Opinion among English leaders and officials had varied across a wide spectrum. Many held that the Spanish would never do more than send the odd consignment of arms, keeping revolt alive but eschewing direct intervention. Others, particularly in Ireland, were less optimistic, pointing to the possibility of a general insurrection that would turn Ireland into a British counterpart of the Low Countries. In 1596 and 1597 the naval expeditions of those years had been directed against the threat of Spanish attack on Ireland.

The arrival of the Spanish army at Kinsale thus made real a specter that had haunted the English for years past. In the earlier years of the war Spanish policy had concentrated on attacking England itself. Not until 1596, after Cadiz, did Philip consent to an expedition to Ireland. This was the fleet that was shipwrecked in October of that year. The king authorized another one in the next year; it suffered the same fate. By the time Tyrone's victory at the Yellow Ford had altered the character of the Irish wars, Philip II was already dying. Tyrone's emissaries, sent to secure an expeditionary force, had to deal with a new king and a new court, dominated by the Duke of Lerma, whose general policy was one of disengagement. Peace had already been concluded with France, and for the next two years the English and Spanish governments warily circled one another, finally agreeing to the abortive conference at Boulogne

[18] *Carew* 3 (1601–3): 58, 66–67, 95, 97–98, 100–1, 104, 110, 122, 140, 142; *CSPI* 11 (1601–3): 49, 58–59; *APC* 1600–1: 306–9; 1601–4: 70–71, 222–24; SP 78/46/109–12.
[19] *CSPI* 11 (1601–3): 81, 82.

in 1600. Cecil had hoped that the English could negotiate with victory in Ireland in hand. That hope was denied him, but he was still optimistic and trusted that successful negotiations would end the prospect of any Spanish aid to the Irish. The failure at Boulogne made the Spanish court more ready to listen to the pleas of the Irish chiefs. Already in summer 1599 a Spanish envoy, sent with a cargo of arms, had persuaded the Irish leaders to promise not to enter any agreement with Essex before November of that year, in return for a promise of a Spanish force. Spanish failure to fulfill that promise strained Irish patience, but in spring 1600 they agreed to hold out for another five months.[20]

In Spain the king and his councillors, tempted by the possibilities of an English succession crisis, hung fire on an Irish venture. Not until 1600 was there commitment to a sizable expedition, but little was done to prepare it, so the enterprise had to be postponed to the next year and the Irish persuaded to yet another extension of time to 25 July 1601. Peace between France and Savoy in January 1601 removed the threat of Franco-Spanish conflict and released the necessary resources for action in Ireland. At last, preparations began for fielding a force of 6,000 men.[21]

By summer 1601 the army was assembling but there was still great uncertainty as to its specific destination in Ireland. The Irish leaders had counselled that if the force were 6,000 or more it should land in Munster, where it would be joined by a local uprising. Any smaller army should go northwards to land at Limerick, where O'Neill and O'Donnell could readily join them with the principal Irish forces. The Spanish commanders who had to make the actual decision fell into bitter disagreement. The general, Aguila, wanted to go north, lacking all confidence in a rising in the south. His opponents, voicing Tyrone's views, insisted on Munster. The dispute was to last until the very moment of disembarkation.[22]

The complement of effectives who actually sailed was well below list, 4,400 instead of 6,000, plus some 1,400 auxiliaries. In the event only about 3,300 to 3,400 were set on shore. This, of course, reduced the Spanish force far below the limits—6,000—that Tyrone saw as a minimum for a self-subsistent army. His fears were justified by events. Apprehensive of an ambush on the way south and fearful of

---

[20] John J. Silke, *Kinsale* (Liverpool, 1970), 31, 74; *CSPSp* 4 (1587–1603): 656.
[21] Silke, *Kinsale*, 82, 84, 87, 90.   [22] *Ibid.*, 98–99.

leaving Ulster unprotected, Tyrone hesitated. The Munster chiefs, cowed by Carew's recent campaign, dared not stir in support of such a small force. Worse still, the local Catholic clergy, largely Old English, suspicious of Tyrone and obstinately attached to the Queen's sovereignty, preached against support for the alien invader.[23]

Mountjoy moved rapidly and decisively to lock up the Spanish in Kinsale by seizing the harbor forts and sealing off the haven. He had prompt and large-scale backing from England. Quite deliberately (and with Privy Council approval) he drew his forces south, leaving the Pale to fend for itself and forcing a reluctant Tyrone to march southwards. The Ulster chieftain would have preferred to stay on the defensive in the north, hoping the English would exhaust themselves in a winter siege in a bare countryside.[24]

The campaign that followed need not be recounted here. O'Neill and O'Donnell successfully brought their armies south. Mountjoy had penned up the Spanish in Kinsale, but he was in turn invested by the force of O'Neill and O'Donnell. In bitter winter weather and a wasted countryside his army was dying off from illness and exposure. Altogether, some 6,000 died. Had the Irish used a Fabian strategy they might have left the forces of nature to defeat the English, but the insistence of O'Donnell and the exigencies of the Spanish commanders forced the reluctant Irish earl to take the risks of a field engagement, precisely the kind of action for which his troops were least prepared. The result was a shattering defeat for the forces of the Ulster lords and the surrender of Kinsale a few days later. With this defeat there vanished any hope the Irish had of forcing England to come to terms with them.[25]

The Spanish effort, when it came, had been too little and too late. A poorly prepared and undermanned force was landed at an ill-chosen site, leaving them immobile and forcing Tyrone to abandon his position of strength in the north for a futile engagement against better-trained field forces.[26] In the end it was a close thing since the English were wasting away in their unsheltered winter camp. But

[23] *Ibid.*, 104, 108–11, 118; *CSPI* 11 (1601–3): 161–62.

[24] *APC* 1601–4: 292–94.

[25] *CSPI* 11 (1601–3): 216, 234–36; Silke, *Kinsale*, 136, 141–46; *Carew* 4 (1601–3): 199–200; *Annals* 3: 2267–89, 2299.

[26] *Carew* 4 (1601–3): 232. An immediate consequence of the journey southward was the establishment of an English foothold at Ballyshannon.

the pressure of the Spanish commander and of his own advisors forced Tyrone into an unequal and, inevitably, fatal struggle.

The damage to the Irish cause was immediately manifest. O'Donnell departed for Spain to seek help, only to die in that country before the end of 1602. Carew, writing in the wake of the Spanish surrender, argued that the remaining traitors should be pardoned. It would cost less than a campaign of extermination, and there was now no risk of a general uprising. "I cannot say they will be good subjects, but I think we shall not in our age see any dangerous or general revolt." Mountjoy took a similar line. The cost of prolonging the war would be immense, and he strongly urged a policy of pardon. The Privy Council had proposed that the Irish be disarmed; the deputy saw this as altogether impractical, indeed unrealizable, except gradually over a long period of time.[27]

In January 1602 Tyrone had already made overtures to the English, a move to which they were ready to respond since Cecil and the Lord Admiral Nottingham had previously given instructions about finding a suitable intermediary. The deputy's initial response was cold; he insisted on a written submission as a first step and outlined a series of stringent demands that would completely dismantle the structure of Tyrone's power. He had already returned to Dublin, leaving Carew to deal with the Kerry rebels. This area, west of Cork, was the one district where there was a general rising in support of the Spanish. The task was completed by June. In the north Docwra wrested the castle of Ballyshannon from Irish grasp in April and finally closed the last gap in the stockade fence that now surrounded Ulster.[28]

Mountjoy had hoped the summer's work would complete the ruin of Tyrone, but with negotiations continuing, the earl remained free through the winter of 1602–1603, albeit a hunted fugitive, hiding in the woods, moving from day to day and accompanied by only 50 to 60 kerne. Mountjoy was obviously nervous about reaching any agreement with Tyrone on his own (remembering his predecessor's experience). The Queen offered nothing but his life to the Irishman, although Mountjoy hinted to the sovereign that more generous terms might prevent his slipping off to Spain. In the end Tyrone

[27] *CSPI* 11 (1601–3): 275–78, 377–81; *Carew* 4 (1601–3): 200–2, 216–18.
[28] *Ibid.*, 212–14; *CSPI* 11 (1601–3): 391–92, 413–14.

made his unconditional surrender at almost the moment that the Queen's reign ended.[29]

The terms Mountjoy granted Tyrone (and the newly promoted O'Donnel Earl of Tyrconnel) were generous. On paper, at least, they were still the principal lords of Ulster, albeit shorn of their chieftaincies. Such a role of leadership within an English Ulster might have proved viable a decade earlier; in the wake of the intervening events, it proved too fragile to last.[30] The flight of the two Irish earls to Spain in 1607 ended large-scale resistance to English rule for nearly half a century. Not until English affairs fell into disarray in 1641 did Ireland stir once again.

The record of English involvement in these tangled transactions is reasonably full and the lineaments of action quite visible. Ever since the 1530's, when Thomas Cromwell had first stirred the torpid waters of Irish politics, the English government had entertained the intention of expanding royal authority in the sovereign's second realm. Slowly and spasmodically advances were made and by the 1580's some measure of English authority prevailed in all the provinces except Ulster. The goal had been not mere political hegemony but cultural transformation. Everywhere the English had sought to transmute Gaels into Englishmen. The policies employed in this process wavered uncertainly between the carrot of persuasion and the club of coercion. In Connaught a rough and ready policy of persuasion and conciliation had successfully wooed the local lords to some measure of acceptance of English rule and English ways. In Munster the Desmond lords had been ruthlessly crushed and the province wasted in the achievement of English supremacy. The experiment of provincial presidencies on the English model had alternated with attempts to plant English colonies on the lands of displaced Irish. The results were decidedly uneven and the inner contradictions of such an uneven development had gone far to destroy all Irish trust in English intentions and all English faith in Irish loyalty.

In the course of these events the nature of Irish politics had been transformed. First of all they had been subordinated to the politics of the English court. The Deputies at Dublin, their councillors, the provincial presidents, and many other officers looked to Westminster for patrons who would protect and promote them. The even

---

[29] *CSPI* 11 (1601–3): 412–13, 446–47, 514–15, 583–84.   [30] Ellis, 311–12.

more important corollary of that was the growing influx of English immigrants into Ireland, where they not only monopolized office but also set about acquiring estates and thereby laying the foundations of a new alien landed ruling class.

These changes, which were destroying the Gaelic world altogether and sadly eroding the position of the Old English, were the more keenly felt because of the absence of any guiding hand at the center of power. For the Queen Ireland stood at the very bottom of her list of priorities. Her normal reaction to Irish problems was one of exasperation and her decisions were always shaped by her rigorous parsimony in all Irish expenditure. Expediency and short-run considerations governed every action of the Irish authorities, with the worst possible results. Successive deputies were forced into a dreary alternation of confrontation, negotiation, and compromise that shattered their credibility. The weakness of the regime at Dublin and the indifference of the Queen left the field open to the influence of the New English. The latter were unflatteringly described by Mountjoy as being "like the men who followed David when he fled from Saul, men that were in trouble, vexed in mind and such as were in debt."[31] Scrambling for place, power, and possessions, they saw the Irish, Old English and Gaels alike, as their enemies. Native-born leadership dwindled; some of the old lords, like the Ormonds and the Kildares, were absorbed into the new order; others, like the Desmonds, suffered shipwreck and vanished from the scene. Only the two northern Gaelic lords, O'Neill and O'Donnell, retained their ancient autonomy outside the bounds of English rule. The Gaelic world and to some considerable extent the Old English came to regard the English regime with distrust and with fear.

When in the 1590's this distrust escalated into resistance, these tendencies were duly exaggerated. Not only the local New English but also the governors sent over from England, like Essex, Mountjoy, or Carew, viewed the whole Irish population with a mixture of contempt and fear. With the emergence of open conflict there was not only enmity between the contending parties but also a deeper ethnic hostility that poisoned attitudes on both sides and left little hope for future reconciliation.

The role of the English, as we have seen, is laid out for us in a reasonably full record that more or less speaks for itself. We can at

---

[31] *CSPI* 10 (1600–1), 251–55.

least follow that record through all its meandering, zigzag paths and obtain some reasonable sense of men's thinking and their intentions, as events unfolded. What is much less easy to follow—what indeed baffled contemporaries—is the motives and conduct of the key Irish figure, the Earl of Tyrone. It is a bafflement that the historian shares, since our sources are little better than theirs. We can see Tyrone solely or almost solely through his opponents' correspondence and through such fragments of his own writing as fell into their hands. Of his inner intentions it is very difficult to know anything.

What then can we say? First, that the earl had worked hard for close on a decade to maximize his power among his own ancestral clients and among the larger Gaelic community of the north. We know that he systematically built an army larger and more skilled than any before. And we know too that he deliberately sought the assistance of the King of Spain, with whom Elizabeth was at war. What are we to infer? The easiest inference, and one made readily by Tyrone's enemies, was that of simple treason—of a deliberate, deep-laid plot to end English rule and destroy the Protestant faith in Ireland. But many of the English leaders, including the Queen herself, while adopting an extreme rhetoric of political abuse, did not in fact look to Tyrone's utter destruction. No doubt, had he been killed in battle (or assassinated), they would have rejoiced. In fact, what they envisaged—and events in 1603 would bear this out—was not his utter destruction but his continued future as a submissive and rehabilitated member of the Irish community. In short, they saw him in the familiar guise of a troublesome vassal of the Crown, a discontented marcher lord, but not as the patriot leader of a national rebellion. The terms of the Peace of Mellifont, negotiated with the Irish leaders under the new king—although reflecting Elizabeth's views—bear out this interpretation of English views.

Posterity has cast Tyrone in a larger role. In his lifetime, among his countrymen, he began to be seen as more than a regional leader, as the spokesmen of a national and Catholic cause. In due time he was to become one of the early members of a line of heroes, of those Irish patriots who had summoned their countrymen to throw off the English yoke. Historians, perhaps more skeptical but not wholly cynical, have emphasized his political sophistication, his grasp of the brute realities of Renaissance politics in a larger context than his own dominions, and assessed him as something more than the traditional Irish warlord, but something less than an early-day national leader.

In the end, the historian can go only so far as the evidence points. What it reveals is a protean figure, responsive to the forces that shaped and reshaped him, but not a chameleon-like opportunist. Certain themes persist; certain goals are tenaciously pursued although the strategies change and, in changing, give new form to the goals.

From the time the young baron of Dungannon returned from England in 1568, he set his sights on recovering what he saw as his rightful heritage, the chieftaincy of the O'Neills and the lands that went with it. With equal determination he sought the role that the English Crown had given to his grandfather in the Anglo-Irish hierarchy as Earl of Tyrone. He won his earldom in 1585 and the chieftaincy ten years later. He was now able to draw on both the traditional aura of his ancestry and the formal status accorded him by the Crown. In the earlier years he sought and won the approval and confidence of the state at Dublin by service in the Desmond rebellions and by assistance in putting down the Nugent uprising in 1582.

What changed this ambitious but cooperative supporter of English authority, wise in the ways of English politics and willing to accommodate himself to the new order, into its boldest and most tenacious adversary? Retrospectively it was the MacMahon succession affair of 1589 that first aroused the new earl's suspicions and fears. The *volte face* of the Deputy and the apparent double-dealing with MacMahon aroused the deepest suspicions of English good faith and revealed the fragility of an Irish aristocrat's position at the mercy of an unscrupulous government.

The fate of MacMahon was a shock, but not a cause of immediate friction. The initiative in that action had been the deputy's; what followed next was of Tyrone's own doing. His abduction of Mabel Bagenal and the ensuing marriage raised up in the New English ranks a powerful enemy, a family whose landed ambitions in eastern Ulster already clashed with those of the O'Neill. What might have been a useful link with a rising New English family interest was turned into a deadly feud. Bagenal would take advantage of every possible occasion to level accusations of disloyalty at Tyrone and to stimulate the suspicions of the Dublin rulers. The quarrel with the marshal soon escalated into one with the Deputy as well. These frictions are indicators of a change in Tyrone's own position. Once he had obtained his earldom and recognized control over the O'Neill lands, he was no longer a supplicant for favor. With place and power of his own, he had a more difficult role to play. Dublin was both patron and enemy; he needed its support against his rivals within the Irish world, but he had also to be constantly vigilant against any encroachments by the government on what he considered to be his inalienable rights as lord of his people. He was committed to a dangerously difficult task, to be at once an earl in the kingdom of Ireland and a prince of Cenel Eoghain.

His attainment of power coincided with a period of instability at Dublin. Frequent changes in the deputyship and longish intervals of vacancy created a volatile uncertainty in a world where personal relationships among the magnates counted for much. In England the disappearance of the Dudley leadership left Tyrone without a patron at court. His laments about the death of Leicester and his efforts to secure Walsingham's backing are tokens of this situation. Tyrone, as much as any English nobleman, was dependent on a network of patronage ties and alliances, and his links with the English world were now much looser, in spite of a visit to London in 1590. At Dublin his quarrels with two successive deputies in the early 1590's brought home to him how fragile was his position, dependent as it was on the goodwill of shifting, short-term, and unpredictable leadership. What security he could obtain in one regime was likely to be dissipated in the next.

Conversely, the weakness of the regime and the vulnerability of these makeshift governors gave him more ground for maneuver. They led indeed to a sustained pattern of tactics in which obstinacy alternated with pliability, confrontation with compromise. As a short-term tactic it was quite successful; the insecure deputies, aware that the home government always wanted the cheapest option, would back down, anxious for peace and quiet at any price. But in the long run it made for increasing instability as each side came less and less to trust the other, and in the end it led to a complete breakdown of any mutuality.

At the same time Tyrone, increasingly nervous of English intentions, looked for allies among his own kind, above all in the other great Ulster lineages. He was too intelligent not to see that the defense of O'Neill rights was bound up with the defense of those of the other clan chiefs. It is a tribute to his talents that he was able to bring into being a confederacy of the Gaelic nobles, quite unusual in its strength and purposefulness. The advantages of a common front against the English were apparent, but the price to be paid was a high one. Tyrone found himself tied to men far less sophisticated in the politics of the larger world, parochial to a degree, impetuous and much more ready to spring to arms than to parley. This was particularly the case with the hotheaded lord of Tyrconnel. Tyrone had no choice but to associate himself with men in open revolt against English authority, and the image of the loyal and faithful coadjutor of the state at Dublin was soon tarnished, indeed replaced, by that of the crafty dabbler in treason: untrustworthy and in all his actions constantly suspect.

Thus, by a process that neither side willed, the protagonists drifted towards war. Neither consciously willed the destruction of the other, yet each came to see the other as a threat to its own existence. The English with their encroaching forts pressing on his boundaries seemed to the earl about to strike at the very base of his power. Both at Westminster and at Dublin Tyrone was perceived as a man who sought at the very least to hedge the royal (and English) dominion to the narrowest limits. A more radical view, systematically purveyed by the New English magnate Bagenal, portrayed him as a traitor who aimed at nothing less than the destruction of English rule. Tyrone's assault on Bagenal's army and his solicitation of Spain confirmed such a judgment, destroyed the last shreds of mutual trust, and left the fate of Ireland to the arbitrament of war.

Once the English government had finally nerved itself to sustained assault on the Gaelic lords, it could only be a matter of time until the superior weight and strategic advantage of English power told. Thenceforward Tyrone was fighting a rearguard action. His only hope lay in the Spanish intervention, which, when it came, proved a broken reed. The Essex interlude had delayed the process, but with the arrival of an able and determined deputy, backed by royal favor and the determined support of the Privy Council, the destruction of the Gaelic order proceeded apace. Ineffective intervention by Spain again delayed the final English triumph, but by the spring of 1603 the noose was finally tightened and the vitality of the Irish resistance extinguished.

PART VI
THE COURT:
THE REVIVAL OF
FACTION

FIGURE 4. *Robert Devereux, second Earl of Essex* (National Portrait
Gallery, London)

SERO SED SERIO

FIGURE 5. *Robert Cecil, first Earl of Salisbury* (National Portrait Gallery, London)

CHAPTER 23

THE RISE OF ESSEX

1584-1591

FROM 1585 ON, the attention of the Queen and her councillors was rivetted on the problems of waging war, and their actions were shaped in large measure by the contingencies of warfare on land and sea. But domestic politics did not stand still; here the agent of change was the hurrying chariot of time, which between 1588 and 1591 carried away all but one of the trusted ministers whose collaboration with the Queen had assured twenty years of stability in the political life of the English court. Of the four leading councillors of the pre-war years, Walsingham, Leicester, and Hatton had already disappeared by 1591; Burghley alone lingered on until 1598. In the final decades of her reign the Queen was virtually the sole survivor of her political generation. The necessary realignments that followed these events were made even more difficult by the certain knowledge that the close of her natural life was approaching. What was equally certain was that no human being could predict the timing of that event. While James of Scotland loomed as the most probable successor, Elizabeth's refusal to face the succession problem added to her subjects' sense of insecurity. Along with all the contingencies of war, they had to learn to live with this uncertain certainty.

The vacancies created by the death of the three great councillors and by those of their lesser colleagues, such as Hunsdon, Knollys, and Cobham, reopened the competition for high place that had been dulled since the beginning of the 1570's. What were the rules of the game within which this contest took place? The official image of sixteenth-century monarchy was one of majestic authority beneficently exercised and of humbly unquestioning obedience. It was a world where each individual accepted his assigned place within a hierarchical pyramid. Such a structure presumably left no room for thrusting self-advancement or jostling competition. In fact this unflawed façade masked a political world of seething rivalries, as troubled and restless as those of any populist regime.

The rules that governed this contest bore some resemblance to the more pacific game of chess. The royals here, as on the chessboard, had special and unassailable privileges. The seat of supreme power in this political order was outside the arena of contest. The protagonists had to concentrate instead on influencing, persuading, if possible manipulating, the monarch for their own advantage. Access to the life-giving waters flowing from the fountain of grace must be secured, perhaps even monopolized. Competitors must be shouldered aside. Those who won a privileged position in the inner circle sought in turn to exploit that advantage by acting as patronage brokers, mediating royal favor to their own clientages in the concentric circles of dependence that emanated from the Crown. So much, in general, would hold for all the Western European monarchies, but in particulars England parted company from the continental realms.

Perhaps the most striking difference between the insular and the Continental scenes was the relative absence in England of the great aristocratic alliances that formed the matrix of political activity in the courts of Spain and France. In the latter country they would provide the sinews of civil war and would not be finally brought to heel until the majority of Louis XIV. In Spain a less bloody but not less intense competition would rage around the throne of the seventeenth-century Habsburgs.

In England the last epoch of magnate domination of politics had ended in the bloody civil wars of the fifteenth century. Martial prowess came to be tested more often in the joust than on the battlefield, and the contests of politics were contained within the precincts of the court; they could occasionally be bloody but they no longer threatened civil war. The struggle was necessarily a muted one, subdued to a level of sobriety appropriate to the conventions of a rigidly hierarchical and totally deferential society.

At the same time royal control of the political process was firmly established as the noble dynasts dwindled into mere courtiers. Even the suspicion of illicit aspirations to power was sufficient to cut down both the Staffords and the Howards. The last halfhearted effort of Percy and Neville in 1569 served only to display their impotence. Moreover, the Crown, now endowed with greater freedom of action, was at liberty to widen the pool from which it recruited its servants, both its ministers of state and its subordinate officers. This process, which much enlarged the number of participants, was an important stage in the "nationalization" of politics, as the court superseded all lesser foci of power to become the sole magnet to which the aspiring careerist was drawn. Its attractive force now drew in members of the gentry and to some extent townsmen from every part of the country. There were, of course, as in France and Spain, noble councillors—Howards, Fitzalans, or Stanleys—but none of these aspired to the role of a Guise, a Montmorency, or a Guzman. The dynamic force in the Council came from ministers of humbler origin chosen for their political and administrative abilities, men who had won their spurs through proven competence. The list is a long one—headed by the great ministers Wolsey, Cromwell, and the two Cecils, but also including such names as Russell, Wriothesley, Sadler, Walsingham, and Smith, to name but a few. Some were men of professional qualifications, like Nicholas Bacon or Walter Mildmay; others were essentially courtiers, like the successive generations of Dudleys, Sidneys, or Knollys. But all had worked their passage, even a Leicester or a Hatton.

The men who filled the highest office around the Crown were at once clients of the sovereign and themselves patrons to those lesser men who sought advancement in the royal service. The formation of this network of patronage and clientage took on special characteristics in the years roughly from the late 1520's down to the reign of Edward VI. These decades saw the emergence of a new pool of higher royal servants. Many of them were university trained; all of them had, in one way or other, worked their way up the ladder of success by service in one or many capacities. They were professionals but not specialists—some as soldiers in the wars of the midcentury, others in the new financial bureaus, or others still in the diplomatic service of the Crown had won a permanent place in the highest political echelon. All were recipients of royal patronage; a few received peerages. But in all cases it was a patronage of service rather than of personal favor. Mostly politiques rather than devots, the majority of them contrived to serve Henry, Edward, Mary, and Elizabeth in turn. Court-based, without strong regional ties, they were servants of the Crown, not creatures of a faction, regional dynasts or favorites of one particular sovereign.

By the 1550's they were a factor to be reckoned with, forming a corps of talent that no monarch could ignore, as Mary was reluctantly compelled to admit. Connected by the circumstances of their careers, wary survivors of dizzying fluctuations on the political scene, and possessed of incomparable experience in administration and politics, they had become indispensable. There was continuity not only of association but also across time. Dudleys, Knollys, Sidneys, Cecils, Russells, and Howards represented at least the second and in some cases the third generation of courtier families, some of whose forebears had served the first Tudor. Many of them had sat at the same council table for as many as twenty years, and all would end their lives in the same service.

They both resembled and differed from their Continental confreres. There was the same demand for professional or semiprofessional services, but in England these did not lead to the appearance of a *noblesse de robe* nor to any clear sense of a distinction between soldier and civil servant. In England there remained an air of the gentlemen amateur, the cricket pitch rather than the soccer field. Moreover, there were no longer clerical competitors for office; the ecclesiastic in the service of the English Crown, so long a fixture of both politics and administration, vanished after 1558.

Elizabeth paid due tribute to this corps in forming her council and court. The men who had served her three predecessors mingled with some who had temporarily fallen out of the race under Mary. The new men who entered the council, like Bacon and Sackville, were out of the same drawer, products of the new bureaucracy of Henry's reign. Later additions, such as Mildmay, Smith, and Walsingham, were more of the same. These choices gave to the Elizabethan council a strongly professional tone, in which, whatever the personal and family ambitions of the members, the ruling ethos was one of public rather than private interest. It was no doubt fortified by a sense that they had now staked their fortunes in the service of a regime under constant threat of attack, even of extinction. Their own hopes were bound up with its survival.

Yet, for all her sensitivity to the contemporary political scene, Elizabeth was determined to assert the prerogative of the Crown to a free choice of councillors, whoever they might be or whatever their qualifications. Her actions were a vivid reminder that the highly personal character of late medieval monarchy had by no means been entirely displaced by recent changes. Leicester and Hatton were advanced to high office and a share in the royal confidence solely because of their personal attraction for the Queen, creatures entirely of her private preference rather than her political judgment. To promote them from personal intimacy to public eminence was a risky business for any ruler, all the more so for a woman. Dudley, as a candidate for the royal hand, excited the bitterest resentment. He aroused the antipathy, indeed the hostility, of both the meritocrat, Cecil, and the representative of the older nobility, Norfolk.

The result, not surprisingly, was the rise of faction within court and council that threatened to explode into open violence. But the wide-based conspiracy to marry Norfolk to Mary Stuart and to displace Cecil foundered on the rock of royal disapproval. The duke destroyed himself by his involvement with the conspirator Ridolfi. Thereafter Burghley and Leicester, the man of business and the personal favorite, found themselves yoked together in the service of their inexorable mistress, a partnership that led to workable cooperation. They were joined by another such pair, the professional Walsingham and a second favorite, Hatton, in an inner circle of confidence around the Queen.

For two decades after 1572 the system worked well. They paired off, one amateur and one professional to a side—Leicester and Walsingham, Burghley and Hatton. The former pair were resolute spokesmen for the evangelical thrust of the reformed faith at home and the interests of international Protestantism abroad. The latter, more secular-minded, stood for a more cautious and less ideological policy. This combination of divergent personalities and policies gave both coherence and diversity to the central government. The variety of views within the Council assured that no major body of public opinion went unrepresented. The arrangement made for a healthy tension; each side was assured of a voice, and the bottled-up resentments such as those that had triggered the attack on Henry VIII's policies in the 1530's were averted.

In domestic matters the decades between 1570 and 1590 were an optimal era for the smooth functioning of the patronage system. The Queen's sturdy loyalty to her chosen servants provided continuity and stability, in striking contrast to the hag-ridden later years of her father's reign. Aspirants seeking entrance to the political arena knew who the power brokers were and knew that there was more than one channel open. The necessary calculations of risk that any such aspirant had to make were simplified in a political climate in which the weather was so predictable.

The close of this relatively tranquil era coincided with the coming of war. Leicester died only a few weeks after the Armada left the English coast; Walsingham, after a period of illness, followed him in April 1590; and Lord Chancellor Hatton succumbed in the following year. Of the four inner councillors only Burghley survived, and he was increasingly troubled by the ills of old age as he moved into his eighth decade.

Their continuing presence had given not only personal continuity to political life but color and shape to policy. Necessarily the disappearance of three of them opened up a Pandora's box of new problems. Not least was the personal readjustment that their disappearance forced on the Queen. Her relationship with her servants was a two-sided one. Her steady and enduring favor won their loyalty and gave them a sense of security; the Queen on her side depended heavily on the comforting reassurance of familiar faces and long association, a major ingredient in her own psychological stability. At the age of sixty she found it difficult, very nearly impossible, to give her countenance to the new faces of a younger generation whom she regarded as mere boys, fit for court entertainments but hardly to be regarded as grave councillors of state.

The Archbishop of York, commenting on the choice of a new Lord President of the North, percipiently wrote that "the race of nobles the Queen found at her accession has passed away." She knew all the defects and infirmities of the nobility growing up under her but, he warned, "he who watches the wind shall not sow and he who considers the clouds shall not reap."[1] The Queen must allow the new generation to learn by experience and responsibility even as their seniors did. It was sound advice, but such as the Queen did not wish to hear. The introduction of new blood into the Council at a time when a whole generation of courtiers was passing from the scene was to prove hard indeed.

How hard it was for the Queen to break out of the accustomed

[1] *CSPD* 5 (1598–1601): cclxii, 64.

circle of familiarity is made evident by the pattern of replacements as the Council was depleted by death in the 1590's. At last a simulacrum of familiarity could be achieved by summoning the late incumbent's son to fill his father's seat at the Council table. In one instance after another this was the pattern. Already Buckhurst (Sackville) and Admiral Howard filled their fathers' seats; they were followed by the young Cecil, by another Knollys, by the second Lord Hunsdon; Fortescue was a veteran of the royal household, while other replacements like Stanhope or North were long-time courtiers and familiars of the royal circle.

But beyond the level of personalities was that of policy. With the passing of Leicester and Walsingham the forward party, which in peacetime had urged intervention and in wartime pressed for vigorous offensives against the enemy, was left without spokesmen at the high level. Who was to push their cause, who was to urge their case on the supreme decision-maker? Would the direction of the war, now in its most active phase, fall into the hands of those whose vision of strategy was solely defensive?

Most immediately vacant offices had to be filled. An undistinguished lawyer, Puckering, was given the lord keepership. For the moment Burghley assumed control of the secretary's work[2] but his duties as treasurer and the infirmities of old age made it impossible for him to carry on alone. Hence in August 1591, some sixteen months after Walsingham's death, the Queen admitted the 28-year-old Robert Cecil to the Council. (He had been knighted in May.) But the secretary's office remained vacant. The young Cecil was to be his father's coadjutor; within a year or two he became secretary in all but name. Nevertheless, he was in the Queen's eyes a probationer and would in fact serve almost a full apprentice's term of indenture before he actually received the secretary's office in 1596.

For the treasurer it was a moment for self-congratulation. Not only had he placed his favorite son on the ladder of promotion, but he had secured a foothold for the future advancement of his house beyond his own lifetime. For Burghley the politician was cast in a mold different from his predecessors as first minister. Up until the reign of the Queen's father the principal administrative officer of the Crown had nearly always been an ecclesiastic. Thomas Cromwell was the first to break this rule. His obscure origins, the wall of envious hate that surrounded him, and the fickleness of his royal master conspired to cut short his career. Burghley was more fortunate. The product of a more conventional background, the son of a second-generation court family, with university training and sponsorship, he was confident in the assured trust of his mistress. He moved in a political ambience in which her pluralistic policy of sharing favor lessened the tensions and blunted the potential violence of competition within the highest level of the court. Although Burghley lacked the range of vision of Cromwell and set himself more modest political goals, he nevertheless had a keen sense of statecraft and a set of political goals to which he adhered with consistency over a long career.

But along with these public aims, he set about with equal industry to advance the fortunes of his family. Like his seventeenth- and eighteenth-century successors he sought to build for his family's future, to secure the landed wealth, the titles, and the social connections that would assure his descendants a place among the elite dynasties of the English ruling classes. The great houses he built; the establishment of a strong local base in Hertfordshire, Northamptonshire, and Lincolnshire; and the carefully engineered marital alliances are all tokens of this political style. At the same time he necessarily sought to build an effective clientage, one that reached out beyond the court and beyond his regional connections to become truly national in scope. It bore more resemblance to the Robinocracy of Walpole than to the affinity of a Yorkist magnate or the household of Cardinal Wolsey.

For such ambitions the moment of Robert's promotion was of first importance. The death of Leicester had removed his long-term rival and left the Dudley interest in disarray. There was no voice in court or Council that could speak with the authority of the treasurer. There was now a golden opportunity. If Robert proved his worth as a councillor and if his father lived long enough to bridge the transition, it would be possible to transfer to the next generation not only the houses and lands acquired by the treasurer but also the intangible political assets accumulated in forty years of service. There was, of course, another consideration, one unspoken and unspeakable. The Queen was nearing the Biblical span; the time could not be far off when a new incumbent would occupy the throne. If all went well, Robert Cecil would be as indispensable to the next sovereign as his father had been to Elizabeth.

But these fair prospects were to be dimmed by the willful affections of the same ruler whose favor had steadily buoyed the Cecils' fortunes for nearly forty years. Elizabeth's eye fell upon a new favorite, who in a very short time made his debut on the stage of high politics. Earlier in the reign it had been mere royal caprice that singled out and promoted to major roles two leading councillors; so now again royal caprice took precedence over interests of state and transformed the political world with the Queen's patronage of a new and unpredictable personality. Elizabeth, by choosing Robert Devereux as a new favorite *en titre*, was about to release a wild bird among the thoroughly domesticated fowl of the English court.

For the Cecils the arrival of the new favorite did not endanger a position resting on the accumulated assets of the father's lifetime of faithful service. But his son had yet to work his passage before a successful transfer of the account could be made. This transaction was necessarily complicated by the appearance of Essex as a colleague and a rival. The Cecils' easy domination of a council in which the treasurer's voice commanded unchallengeable authority would now be contested by a restlessly ambitious man who held a special place in the Queen's estimation and who would contend with them as a patronage broker in a market in which they had enjoyed something like a monopoly. More important still, he would seek to advance his own career by pressing for a general strategy of all-out offense against the enemy with a concomitant commitment of resources, a policy that Burghley had consistently and vigorously opposed. Finally there was the looming question of the succession. Hidden within the struggle for power within Elizabeth's council was another much more dangerous contest, as English politicians uneasily jostled for advantage in the court of her putative successor.

Essex's entrance upon the court stage was very different from that of his two predecessors as favorites—Leicester and Hatton. First of all was the fact of his status. Leicester's ancestry had been a matter for reproach, even derision. Hatton was a nobody when he arrived at court. Essex, on the other hand, was a member of the ranking elite among the English nobility, the small band of some dozen or so earls. Although his father was the first earl of this creation, his ancestry was impeccable, and generations of noble, even royal, blood flowed in his veins. His father had won the favor of the Queen (he was one of the few peers promoted to an earldom); his mother, Lettice Knollys, was cousin to Elizabeth (albeit hardly a favorite at court), his stepfather, the Queen's "dear Robin." (Leicester had married Lady Essex in 1578, the year after the death of her first husband.)

A boy of nine on his father's death, the orphaned earl spent a short time in the household of Burghley before being sent in May 1577 to Cambridge, where he remained until 1580. In 1582, after a short stay in the house of Sir Francis Knollys, his grandfather, he went to live with the Earl of Huntingdon, Lord President of the North.[3] By 1584 he was in residence at his house of Lanfey in Pembrokeshire. As early as Christmas 1577 he had paid a visit to court and was received with marked favor by the Queen. Regular attendance at court seems to have begun about 1584.[4]

Essex's introduction to the world of affairs came under his stepfather's auspices when the latter sailed to the Low Countries in 1585. According to one story, Leicester brought forward his stepson as a counter to Walter Raleigh, then rising fast in royal favor.[5] Although barely twenty, he was made general of the horse to Leicester and, after the famous engagement at Zutphen in September 1586, was knighted for valor in the field. He spent some £4,000 on this expedition.[6]

By 1587, upon his stepfather's promotion to lord steward, Essex was so in favor with the Queen that she promoted him to master of horse, a post Leicester had held since the first days of the reign. It was worth £1,500 a year plus ample perquisites.[7] It meant, of course, regular attendance at court. This same year gives us a glimpse of the young favorite's touchiness and his willingness to confront his royal patroness without flinching. Visiting at the Earl of Warwick's seat in Essex, he was present when the Queen arrived and immediately commanded that Penelope Devereux, Essex's sister, be confined to her chamber. Essex did not hesitate to reproach the Queen as a mere tool of Walter Raleigh. The Queen retorted sharply and spoke ill of Essex's mother. Essex took himself and his sister away from the house. In the same letter that recounts this episode, he struck what was to become a familiar note of melodramatic desper-

[3] HMC, *Calendar of Bath Manuscripts at Longleat* (5 vols., London, 1980) 5: 249–50, 251 [hereafter cited as HMC, Bath Mss.].

[4] Devereux 1: 170, 172; 2: app., 487.

[5] William Winstanley, *England's Worthies* (London, 1660), 222.

[6] Tenison 8: 48.

[7] Devereux 1: 185; PRO C.66/1321 m[embrane] 35 (12/23/87).

ation. He announced that he would leave for Sluys (then under siege by the Spaniards). "If I return I will be welcomed home; if not *une belle mourire* is better than a disquiet life." This response might seem strange to some, but the Queen's extremely unkind dealing with him had driven him to it. He was stopped at Sandwich by royal orders.[8] Nevertheless, master of horse by the end of 1587, he was also an intimate of the Queen, her partner at cards nightly, returning to his lodging only when the birds began to sing.

During the Armada year he was again storming at the Queen because she had given the generalship of the horse in the army about her person to someone else. He told her he would rather serve privately in the field than take an office under such conditions. He did in fact serve at Tilbury but of course saw no action. In this same year he was given the Garter.[9]

When the English armada under Norris and Drake made ready to sail in 1589 Essex invested £7,000 of his scant estate in the venture, gambling on a rich return in booty. His debts were now £22,000 to £23,000, and as he saw it this was his best hope to escape from his poverty. He was frantic to accompany the expedition, but the Queen forbade it absolutely. Nevertheless, in open defiance of the royal will, the earl slipped out of court, rode to Plymouth in the company of Roger Williams, and, catching a pinnace, preceded the fleet, meeting it off the Iberian coast.[10] His relative Knollys was sent after him posthaste by the Queen, but too late to stop him. The Queen's wrath was truly royal in its explosive fury. Drake and Norris, rebuked for their carelessness, were ordered to arrest Williams and deprive him of his command, "for as we have authority to rule we look to be obeyed." She would tolerate no evasions, "for these be no childish actions nor matters wherein you are to deal by conning of devices, to seek evasions as the custom of lawyers is." The earl reached Lisbon and stuck his pike in one of its gates before the royal commands caught up with him and forced his return.[11] This episode brought Essex into close contact with Drake, Norris, and Williams, the most eager adherents of a vigorous offensive against

---

[8] Devereux 1: 186–89; Robert Cary, *The Memoirs of Robert Cary*, ed. F. H. Mares (Oxford, 1972), 11–12. Essex had apparently organized a following to go with him, but his precipitate departure left Cary high and dry.

[9] Devereux 1: 192–93.

[10] Tenison 8: 47; Devereux 1: 196–97; PRO, SP 12/223/68, 95; 224/85.

[11] Devereux 1: 204–5.

Spain. He provided them with an advocate in the highest circles; soon he would be the grand patron of their cause.

The opening of a French theater of war offered new and glittering prospects. His first effort to exploit them failed when he contested the command of the Norman expedition of fall 1589 with Willoughby.[12] But in the next year a grander opportunity offered itself. Already in April 1590 Henry IV had written to thank the earl for his affection and in May sent a messenger with an account of his recent military feats. Essex, he hinted, would surely regret his absence from these fields of glory. The earl and he were soon regular correspondents. Essex was also essaying the role of patron to Sir Henry Unton, soon to be ambassador to France.[13]

Essex's ambitions were entangled with his financial plight. His melodramatic declaration when he left for Portugal, that poverty forced him to the venture, had a ring of truth about it. "If I should speed well, I will adventure to be rich; if not I will never live to see the end of my poverty." His grandfather Knollys had warned him as far back as 1585 that he was the poorest earl in England. His father had recklessly squandered a substantial estate by his venture in Ireland and by the imprudent contract he had made with the Crown to finance that enterprise. He had left his son with a debt of some £18,000. The estate was, of course, burdened by the dowager's jointure, and the available income in the 1580's was probably not above £1,400, of which payments on the debt ate about half. His trustees had managed to reduce the debt substantially by the time the second earl launched his career. By 1593 his position was much improved. His net landed income (after subtracting his mother's jointure and other charges of like nature) was about £2,500 a year. The mastership of the horse was worth £1,500; he had an annuity charged on the customs of £1,000; from 1590 he enjoyed the lease of the sweet wines farm, which he sublet for £2,000. In 1593 his household steward took in £5,189. This was in fact a handsome income, but it hardly matched his extravagances. His service in the Low Countries cost £4,000, his Armada activities £3,500, and the Lisbon caper £7,000, and in these same years he spent £5,000 over and above his ordinary revenue for court expenditures. Entertainment for the French envoy Turenne in 1590 added up to £2,200, and the Rouen campaign overshadowed all earlier outlays with a

---

[12] Bertie, 406–7.   [13] HMC, *Hatfield* 4: 30, 32, 68.

mountainous £14,000. In 1590 he borrowed £3,000 from the Queen; he was also selling land from 1588 on. By 1590 his debts, on his own admission, amounted to £22,000 to £23,000. In the mid-1590's they had climbed to nearly £30,000. It was proposed to pay off this debt by selling land to that value, leaving the earl with a yearly rental of £1,787.[14]

Up to this point Essex's career was that of a singularly indulged favorite. The Queen, usually so parsimonious, had been abundantly generous. When in 1590 he married Frances Walsingham, the widow of his great friend and model, Sir Philip Sidney, there was the expected burst of royal disapproval, but it soon quieted and the Queen accepted the marriage without further ado (in sharp contrast to her later treatment of Raleigh). She had forgiven the Lisbon episode; he was undoubtedly favorite *en titre*, but he was not yet admitted to the inner circle of great politicians and he seemed no nearer to realizing his goal of military glory.[15]

The great turning point in his career came with his appointment to command the Norman expeditionary force in 1591. Some kind of English intervention had been in the making for some months; both governments favored it but differed as to the form it might take. When Turenne was dispatched by the French king in October 1590 his instructions ordered him to seek Essex's help, and Henry himself wrote to solicit the earl's support. Throughout the year there had been frequent messages back and forth, and Essex had even sought Henry's intervention with Elizabeth to secure leave to join the King for a few months. Turenne declared that the earl's affection for the King was so great that he had to be restrained rather than pushed.[16]

The Queen was slow in making up her mind as to the Nor-

---

[14] Devereux 1: 178, 206–9; 2: 486; Howell A. Lloyd, "The Essex Inheritance," *Welsh History Review* 7 (1974): 13–38; HMC, Bath Mss. 5: 252–53, 257, 275; Tenison 8: 48, 308–9; 10: 205; Dietz, 316, citing Harleian Ms. 167, fol. 139; PRO, C.66/ 1309 mm. 2–3, 1327 m. 8, 1336 mm. 34–35, 1350 m. 40, mm. 43–44, 1367 mm. 32–34, m. 27. His mother's jointure was £1,300 per annum.

[15] Devereux 1: 178; Tenison 6: 39–40; 7: 319; Sidney Papers 1: 312–13; HMC, *De L'Isle and Dudley*, 113; Lodge 2: 10–12, 15–18.

[16] Francis H. Egerton, Earl of Bridgewater, *The Life of Thomas Egerton* (Paris, ca. 1800), 317, 331, 332, 349–51; HMC, *Report on the Manuscripts of the Earl of Ancaster Preserved at Grimsthorpe* (London, 1907), 307; Devereux 1: 213–14; Tenison 8: 306. Turenne was entertained at Wanstead (HMC, Bath Mss. 5: 254); Lodge 2: 11–14.

mandy expedition, and for a time priority was given to the Breton campaign; Norris was dispatched thither in early May, and the force of 600 men under Williams at Dieppe ordered to join him. Essex had desperately wanted this command (with Norris as his lieutenant) and was furious when in fact the Queen gave it to Sir John. She refused him even though the earl remained on his knees for two hours.[17] He left the court to sulk and was only drawn back by a royal promise of something better.[18] It was not until late June that Elizabeth swung around to a decision to send a force to join Henry in besieging Rouen. Who was to command? Williams, one of the most experienced of English captains, was already there and he clearly hoped for the larger command.[19] But once it had been decided to send a sizable force to collaborate with the King in the siege, protocol as well as purely military considerations had to be taken into account. If the English commander was to have much leverage with the King he needed to be someone of rank and status, at least a nobleman and preferably a familiar of the Queen. For these qualifications Essex had no rival. The noble commander of the 1589 expedition, Willoughby, was now in retirement, suffering from ill health; none of the leading captains was of noble rank. Moreover, Henry had empowered his emissaries to suggest to the Queen the choice of Essex as commander.[20] Court gossip held that Essex's friends tried to dissuade him, urging him to imitate his step-father in a more "domestical greatness." But the writer added that he already had the support of the soldiers and the Puritans for his appointment. Essex was clearly prepared for a gamble; if he returned with honor he would be a great man in the state, his career fully launched.[21]

Certainly the contrast with 1589 was striking. Then he had been in the Queen's eyes a wayward youth, irresponsibly flying off to Portugal and requiring a peremptory royal command to behave himself. Now he was given command of a force of 4,000 men, committed to the first deliberately planned joint action with the King of France. The success of the venture as well as the reputation of English arms was in his keeping. Essex had grown not only in the royal estimation but also in his own ambitions. In 1589 the hopes of

---

[17] Francis Egerton, 385–86.
[18] SP 78/24/96; Lloyd, *Rouen*, 96; Francis Egerton, 385–86, 388.
[19] *L&A* 1590–91: 572.   [20] *L&A* 1591–92: 317 (519.xxxi)
[21] *CSPD* 3 (1591–94): ccxxxix, 70, 93; Lodge 3: 29–32.

personal glory and of recouping his fortunes had been his dominant motives. In 1591 it was a larger aspiration—to succeed as a commander of men and to take his place among the captains of Europe.

The Queen, however, intended to keep him on a short tether. Unlike Norris, sent off to Brittany on a mission of indeterminate length under uncertain and unpredictable conditions, Essex was charged with very specific instructions. He was to be limited solely to one action, the siege of Rouen. The Queen had, so she thought, a clearcut agreement with Henry for the accomplishment of this goal. Proximity to England seemed to allow an effective royal check on the earl's movements. To clinch the matter the Queen had appointed three tutorial guardians with whom Essex was to take constant counsel: the veteran diplomat Killigrew, Leighton, his uncle and governor of Jersey, and Unton, the new English ambassador.

However irksome these leading strings might be, they did not obscure the great leap forward that the earl's career had taken. What had moved the Queen to this promotion is of course veiled from us. The need for a commander of rank no doubt played a role, but more important was the success of the favorite in bending the royal will to his. His importunities had won the day. At the age of twenty-four he had fulfilled an ambition for a major command, a position for which Leicester had had to wait for almost thirty years. He had already been forgiven escapades that the older earl would never have dared attempt.

The royal decision to entrust Essex with this great command and thereby advance him to the first rank of politics revealed the antique underpinnings on which the Elizabethan political stage rested. Three generations of Tudor government had seemed to confirm the shift away from the personal monarchy of the late Middle Ages to a regime oriented to the needs of a more impersonal state—from household to bureaucracy. It is in just these years that official correspondents begin to use the old word "state" in a new way. Those dealing with Irish affairs frequently referred to the "state at Dublin," to the apparatus of power headed by short-term surrogates for royal majesty. And the practice soon spread to general correspondence—"the Queen and the state." Unconsciously these men were adapting to the notion of an abstract entity, a *res publica* that was separate from the person of the monarch. It was not a self-conscious assertion of a new political theory but simply an instinctive adaptation to the facts of political experience, especially those of a great European war. Now, suddenly, they were given a chilling reminder that the "state" was still embodied in a single person whose personal preferences and wayward affections could override all cool considerations of state. The charms of a handsome young man for an aging spinster could reshape the direction of the war.

Moreover, the favorite himself was odd man out in the sedate atmosphere of an elderly court. Essex in 1591 was twenty-four years old. In the Privy Council of that year no member, other than the newly inducted Robert Cecil (four years Essex's senior), had been born later than 1540. More important than the age gap were the differences in their whole political outlook. Essex was the embodiment of Shakespeare's third age, in pursuit of the bubble of reputation, the Privy Councillors more nearly representative of the fifth age. Virtually none of them, save the lord admiral, had ever seen action in the field or on the seas. Hunsdon alone had undergone baptism of fire in the far-off days of 1569. For the rest, they were creatures of the court and council, practiced administrators, skillful politicians, and adept courtiers. Essex, on the other hand, was consumed with a longing for the excitements of combat. That a sixteenth-century nobleman should entertain such an ambition was, of course, hardly surprising. For generations war had been the most honorable calling of an aristocrat. On the Continent the almost unbroken wars of the Habsburgs and Valois had created a military profession, the pursuit of which dominated the lives of many noblemen. But in England, since the end of the Hundred Years' War, there had been little scope for the profession of arms inasmuch as the military ventures of the monarchs had been short-lived and fitful episodes. There had been nothing equivalent to the buccaneering exploits that had bred a new race of warlike seamen. But now, with the coming of a war of overwhelming magnitude, when large-scale military operations were forced on the state leadership, there was at last a vent for the pent-up ambitions of a generation longing for the excitements of action. In Essex they had a powerful spokesman and, if he succeeded in France, a striking model.

Essex's first venture into the great wars lasted about six months. The episode was marked by histrionics, escalating to melodrama, in the relations between the Queen and the earl. Both participants behaved with equal extravagance. While much must be ascribed to the two personalities, Essex was, like Leicester in the Netherlands, the victim of conflicting and irreconcilable pressures. Elizabeth, having made a large commitment of money and men, expected a fair return on her investment. She was persuaded that the risks were not large and the gains certain. The fall of Rouen (and of the Seine valley) to Henry would secure the channel coasts and reopen trade with the Norman capital, while the pledged tax revenues of the port would pay off the French debt. Elizabeth envisaged a tidy, short-term operation with clearcut advantages to the English. She consistently failed to grasp the situation of her fellow monarch, distracted by war on many fronts and haunted by fear of Parma's return. Constrained to be as flexible as possible, nimbly dashing from one point of danger to another, Henry saw Rouen as one of several options that he might or might not be able to choose. The English forces were among the chessmen on his board, to be moved where they would serve to best advantage. Caught between the Queen's inflexible determination to carry through her scheme—in which she took for granted Henry's performance of his assigned role— and the latter's opportunistic maneuvers as he darted from one theater of action to another, it is no wonder that Essex found himself frustrated to the point of desperation.

The course of the campaign has been recounted elsewhere. The first crisis between ruler and commander arose when Essex travelled, at Henry's request, to meet the King. This risky episode, combined with the death of Essex's brother in what seemed a pointless skirmish, led to unmeasured rebuke by the Queen, who accused her general of irresponsibility to his army and negligence of her commands. Equally angry with Henry's failure to move on Rouen, she ordered withdrawal. But pressed by Burghley and other councillors, mollified by the successful capture of Gournay, and finally convinced by Essex himself in a hurried return, she extended the stay of her forces and even conceded a reinforcement of 1,000 foot and 450 sappers. But the operation quickly faltered; two assaults failed, the king departed, and by early January 1592 Essex was ready to give up the game and return home. The siege would drag on for several more months before its final abandonment.

The exchanges between Essex and Elizabeth during the Rouen campaign are a record not only of a military venture that went awry, but also of the tense and stormy relations between two high-tempered individuals. The earl's letter at his first arrival in France struck a familiar note of high flattery.[22] He conjured the Queen to be faithful to him. Even if he won the greatest honor "and yet another in mine absence should rob me of your gracious and dearest favor I were in his case qui mundum lucratus perdidit animam." But when he received her letters of rebuke in September, in which he was blamed as "negligent, undutiful, rash in going, slow in returning ... faulty in all things because I was not fortunate to please," he took a different, more manly tone. "Judge uprightly between the Queen and me whether she be not an unkind lady and I an unfortunate servant." This was followed by an eloquent and reasoned account of the real difficulties he faced. Again he told the Queen that "unkindness and sorrow have broken both my heart and my wits," but he stubbornly insisted he would end his life complaining of her ingratitude and approving his own constancy.[23]

Another letter of the same period was a *cri de coeur* that lay bare the mainsprings of his personality. To go home without doing anything would overthrow his reputation. Let him stay on with only his own horse for a month or six weeks. "This place while these great armies are unbroken will be the only school of our age and to go out of action when all other men come into action were to wear a note of perpetual infamy." After his return from England in October (when reconciliation had been achieved) he could write again in conventional vein that once he returned "no cause but a great action of your own shall draw me out of your sight for the two poles of your privy chamber shall be the poles of my sphere." After this the Queen's temper abated; she listened more calmly to the earl's exposition of the situation in Normandy and reluctantly conceded a reinforcement of 1,400 men.[24]

It is interesting to compare these exchanges with the whining self-pity of Leicester under similar circumstance in the Low Countries. Essex stands up, defends himself, and, while acknowledging royal privilege, refuses to accept what he sees as unwarranted and unreasonable rebuke. Even while he obeys, he stubbornly continues to insist that it is the Queen and not he whose judgment is at fault. But Essex could not restrain himself from a chivalric gesture and added color to the drab story of the siege by a personal challenge to the French governor, Villars, a challenge not only in behalf of his

[22] Devereux 1: 222–23.   [23] *Ibid.*, 233–35, 235–37, 240–41.
[24] *Ibid.*, 241–44, 249–50, 260–63.

more just cause but also because his Queen was more beautiful than the Frenchman's. This drew a letter of rebuke from the Council.[25]

After a winter in the muddy trenches of Rouen Essex came home, his bellicose passions sated for the moment, as the possibilities of success faded away. He had not won a battle or taken Rouen, but, despite this disappointment, there was a net gain to show from the venture. The Queen's anger at its failure was directed against the French king, not against the earl. He had demonstrated his ability to command an army. He had won grudging acknowledgment of his achievements from the Queen and had taken his place among the small band of English captains of reputation. Experience, rank, and the magnetism of his personality made him the lodestar of all those who for personal or public reasons hoped for a wholehearted offensive against the enemy. But for the present Essex returned to the court scene. His recent defeat in the competition for the Oxford chancellorship had been a reminder of the risks of long absence from court.[26]

[25] *Ibid.*, 273.   [26] Wernham, 372.

CHAPTER 24

ESSEX THE

COUNCILLOR

A FULL YEAR would elapse between Essex's return from France and his formal appointment to the Privy Council on 25 February 1593. Membership in this select circle of the Queen's most trusted advisors marked his full transformation from mere favorite to councillor of state. His own demeanor reflected this change of status. "His Lordship is become a new man, clean forsaking all his former youthful tricks, carrying himself with honorable gravity and singularly liked of, both in Parliament and at Council-table, for his speeches and judgment."[1] In the late 1580's he had been little more than a court pet, showered with royal attentions, petted and scolded. But now the command in Normandy had transmuted the courtier-favorite into a captain of international repute, a role that no English nobleman had filled for generations past. His military experience and his achievements were modest compared with those of such veterans as Norris, Vere, or Williams, but his rank and, more important still, his intimacy with the sovereign elevated him to a unique although somewhat spurious superiority to these mere colonels. In the midst of a great war this anomalous eminence gave him claims and expectations quite different from those not only of the Queen's captains but also of the magnates of the court. Yet, so long as he was not a Privy Councillor, he was not quite a full-fledged member of that establishment. The Queen's decision to ap-

[1] Devereux 1: 282.

point him was a signal mark of her confidence, for it demonstrated her acceptance of him not only within the inner circle of favor (where he was firmly established) but also within the inner circle of power.

The promotion cannot have come as a surprise. It had been rumored at least since his return from France, and was, in the light of past experience, a logical expectation. Both Leicester and Hatton, mere favorites at first, had been advanced to a public status when the Queen judged them capable of assuming it. Immediate circumstances favored it. In a wartime Council that lacked members with military experience he could be a useful addition. The royal disposition to advance him converged with the needs of the state; his rank and newly won reputation made him the obvious candidate.

Although the promotion was an honor, it was also a challenge to the earl, since it propelled him into a world of fierce and ruthless competition from which he had hitherto been aloof. As favorite he had enjoyed a privileged and protected status, sought after as much as seeking, a happy recipient of freely bestowed royal benefactions, whose cue was to respond with appropriate gratitude and devotion. In fact, so powerful were his attractions to the Queen that he was able to pit his will against hers and reverse the role of sovereign and subject by compelling her to accept his refusal to obey her commands—as in the Portugal expedition. Even more, he could, as in the Norman campaign, persuade her to entrust him, a youthful and inexperienced soldier, with a major military command.

Once he entered the Council, however, he had to leave behind his sole and privileged place, for the goals he now pursued were public ones, requiring the royal assent to decisions of policy and of strategy—the business of the whole state and not mere private transactions between royal mistress and pampered courtier. The Rouen command had obviously been the first stage in this ascent, but entry into the Council brought him onto a stage with many actors—and much action. He had now to face the competition of rivals, above all the established interest of the Cecils, father and son, an interest rooted not in the personal predilections of the woman but in the hard-won confidence of the sovereign in a councillor of near forty years' standing. This was a contest not for mere personal favors but for the mind and will of the sovereign, a debate over the most urgent and dangerous decisions of state at the peak of a great war and over the balance of power within the inner circle of domestic politics. It remained to be seen how effectively Essex could perform in the new and demanding role in which he was now cast.

Essex's entry into the Council brought him into a body in which the most powerful member was the veteran lord treasurer Burghley, the inmost confidant of the Queen since the first day of her reign. The death of Leicester and Hatton had given Burghley a scope such as he had not enjoyed since the first years of her reign. In effect he re-annexed his old office of secretary and added it to his treasurership. There was no voice in Council or court that could speak with the authority of the treasurer. More than ever all the strings of public business were in his hands. A shrewd observer writing in the fall of 1591 noted that "old Saturnus is a melancholy and wayward planet but yet predominant here and if you have thus to do it must be done that way and whatsoever hope you have of any other believe it not." In the same letter Sir Edward Norris is reported in disfavor with the lord treasurer "for nourishing and depending upon other besides His Lordship which will hardly be put up."[2]

While Essex was in Normandy the Cecil interest at court was measurably increased by the appointment of Robert Cecil as a Privy Councillor. The double burdens of the treasurership and the secretaryship were too much for the aging statesman, so the Queen was persuaded to the appointment of a coadjutor who would perform the duties of the latter office but without title or stipend. The young man settled quietly and inconspicuously into his new duties. Under his father's guiding hand he was initiated into the multifarious business of the state, acting sometimes as Burghley's deputy, sometimes as intermediary. More and more often, during the treasurer's increasingly frequent bouts of illness, he served as sole minister attendant, whose hand was to be seen in every department of public affairs. We have from February 1594 a slightly malicious and certainly envious picture from the pen of Essex's servant, Standen: "Sir Robert goeth and cometh very often between London and the court so that he come out with his hands full of papers and head full of matter so occupied passeth through the presence like a blind man not looking upon any."[3] No doubt father and son both hoped the

---

[2] Sidney Papers 1: 231 [331]–332; HMC, *De L'Isle and Dudley*, 122–23.
[3] Birch 1: 152–53.

Queen would give the latter formal appointment to the job he was effectively doing. Such an appointment was from time to time rumored, but Thomas Wilkes predicted there would be no secretary appointed in Burghley's lifetime.[4] The prediction would prove not far wrong; Robert Cecil was to serve nearly the full term of an apprenticeship before he was rewarded by formal appointment.

The Cecils could only view with distaste the intrusion of a volatile, restless, and ambitious newcomer, in their eyes another political buccaneer on the model of his late stepfather, who would compete with them as a patronage broker and would be an ardent advocate of the strategy of all-out offensive that Burghley had tenaciously opposed. They reacted with bland discretion. Far too shrewd to attempt to dislodge him from the royal affections, they played a careful hand, accepting him as a colleague in council and establishing outwardly cordial social relations.

There were moments of friction. There may have been a preliminary skirmish in 1590 when, after the death of Walsingham, Essex pressed for the restoration of Davison, the second secretary who had been the scapegoat for the execution of the Queen of Scots. His restoration would have countered the Cecils' ambitions for young Robert.[5] Again in the interval between the earl's return from the Continent and his entry into the Council, signs of friction between him and the younger Cecil showed themselves. The documents are elliptical, but it is at least clear that Essex was seeking to lessen the burden of his debts by a suit to the Queen in which Cecil had become a third party.[6] Apparently the Queen blew alternately hot and cold, promising and then reneging, and using Cecil as the intermediary to make known her pleasure. Essex became irritably suspicious of the other's role and intimated double-dealing. Even an apology failed to mollify him, and in an ill-tempered response the earl declared that since Cecil's dealing in the suit everything had gone badly. The details are unclear but the suit seemingly failed. The earl's letter reveals the petulant surprise of a spoiled favorite whose will had been crossed. Cecil's one surviving letter (if it does refer to this suit) suggests his resentment of a suitor who counts on

[4] Lodge 2: 245; Sidney Papers 1: 325–26, 329.
[5] Devereux 1: 209; N. H. Nicholas, *Life of William Davison* (London, 1823), 169, 171, 173–75.
[6] HMC, *Hatfield* 4: 199; Cecil Papers 2: 655–57.

his privileged relations with the Queen and brushes aside any inter-mediary—"for of other's breath he is careless."[7]

The Queen was fully aware of the tensions that her actions were creating in her court, but she was fully confident of her ability to keep them under control. Twenty years before she had faced a sim-ilar situation in the rivalry of Robert Dudley and William Cecil. She had had her own way, hitching them together in the same team and, with her firm hand on the reins, enforcing their cooperation. Elizabeth was determined on a repeat performance with new ac-tors, and in the early 1590's the expectation seemed not unreason-able.

What she failed to grasp was how unfitted Essex was to fill the role she planned for him. The odd man out in the Elizabethan po-litical world, his ambitions were in every important way very dif-ferent from those of his colleagues, particularly the Cecils. For them the public goals of politics were irenic, the preservation of peace at home and abroad; the private ones were the accumulation of office, titles, and land for the present and future advantage of themselves and their descendants.

For Essex his seat at the Council board was a springboard for quite other ambitions. What Essex hoped to leave his son was not great houses and broad lands but the intangible inheritance of his father's fame. His contemporaries might be content with the mock battles of the tiltyard on Accession Day. What the earl hungered for was the excitements of the great wars, the thunder of cannon, the clash of men and arms—and the European-wide renown of a great captain.

His private ambitions marched with public. He stood with those who insisted that Spain could be beaten only by a direct assault on the homeland and the colonies and by severing the artery through which flowed the American silver. But Essex dreamed not only of bringing Spain to the bargaining table but also of reducing her power so that Philip would be—in Raleigh's words—no more than

[7] Cecil's letter (HMC, *Hatfield* 4: 199–200), written to Heneage, refers to "him whom you call my friend which he must be if he do not wrong me." He goes on to write of the "wonders" found in the matter, but nothing had yet been heard from the Queen, "in whom I take it the stroke will lie." This letter is dated about a month earlier than Essex's letters (Cecil Papers 2: 655–57). It is worth noting that Essex sold £5,000 worth of land to Burghley in 1592 (Tenison 9: 33).

a king of figs and oranges, while Elizabeth would be the arbitress of Europe and mistress of the seas.

The disagreement with the Cecils could not have been more profound. For the treasurer the war, a regrettable necessity, was inevitably a defensive one, in which the possibilities of English action were straitly limited by the paucity of her resources. Victory would be attained if the *status quo ante* could be re-established. This meant the re-establishment of a French counterbalance to Spain and the existence of an autonomous Low Countries state. England could then return to the relative isolation of the past and the peaceful cultivation of her own garden.

Thus on both private and public grounds the Cecils and Essex occupied opposing positions. Nevertheless, it would be a misreading of events to see the politics of the 1590's as shaped by a straightforward rivalry between two sharply defined factions. It would be sounder to view them as moving on parallel tracks, most often collaborating in the conduct of the Queen's business, although at times veering into one another's path and striking off a shower of sparks. Social relations were civil, even cordial, with the usual exchanges of dinners and other courtesies. At times the two young men seem to have been on even warmer terms. Writing to Cecil of his disappointment in the Queen's refusal of the Brest command, Essex could write that "your offers of kindness and profession of affection is of me most willingly embraced and shall be justly requited."[8] Clashes did occur from time to time but the tenor of their relations was at least as even and affable as that of dealings between Burghley and Leicester.

Essex was intelligent enough to understand that, if either his private or his public goals were to be realized, he must establish his credentials as a councillor of state whose knowledge and judgment would bear weight with the Queen. A golden opportunity lay to hand in building up a system of foreign intelligence. The intelligence network that the late Secretary Walsingham had created had fallen into some disarray with his death. If Essex could provide a steady flow of reliable information from abroad he would acquire the kind of political ballast that would weigh with the Queen and incline her to listen to his persuasions.

The official sources of foreign intelligence that the English gov-

[8] Wright 2: 414; HMC, *Hatfield* 4: 524.

ernment possessed were to be found in the Low Countries and in France. Essex moved rapidly to key himself into this network. In the Netherlands there was, of course, the official English agent, Bodley, who sat on the Council of State and moved freely in Dutch circles. He and his assistant, the Dutch-speaking Gilpin, as well as the commanders of the English garrisons at Flushing, Brill, and Ostend, had many sources of information, not only in the United Provinces but also in the southern provinces, since intercourse with Antwerp and other southern cities was frequent and regular.[9] Essex opened up a regular correspondence with virtually all these English officials as well as with Sir Francis Vere, the English military commander in the Netherlands.

In France there was always an agent attendant on the peripatetic court of Henry IV: sometimes a formally accredited ambassador, more often an agent of lower status, but in any case these men provided a steady flow of information. Essex corresponded with the English agents and also maintained contact with the leading Huguenot lords, such as the Duke of Bouillon (Turenne). He also established a direct and personal link with the King himself, dating back to their meeting in 1591. He plainly regarded Essex as his advocate within the English Council and each successive French envoy was briefed to seek him and to enlist his aid in his mission.

Besides these public and official contacts the English government had built up under the direction of Walsingham a network of spies, costing some £2,000 a year.[10] This had been largely dissipated on his death. Horatio Palavicino, the emigré financier and occasional diplomatic agent, played a modest role as spymaster in the following years and supervised payments to various informers. Chasteaumartin, a French merchant at Bayonne, was perhaps the most regular.[11] By 1596 the Cecils had at their disposal little more than the digest of information that Palavicino put together for their benefit.[12]

Essex resolved both to exploit the existing intelligence network

[9] See HMC, *Hatfield* 5: 473, where Robert Sidney refers to one of the messengers who ordinarily went between Middleburgh and Antwerp.

[10] Conyers Read, *Mr. Secretary Walsingham and the Policy of Queen Elizabeth* (3 vols., Cambridge, Mass., and Oxford, 1925) 2: 371. In 1603 Robert Cecil had only £800 a year for this purpose (HMC, *Hatfield* 15: 151).

[11] His letters to Burghley are scattered through the Hatfield papers and the State Papers, Domestic.

[12] Stone, 252.

and to build one of his own, reporting directly to him. As his co-adjutor in this enterprise he enlisted Anthony Bacon, the younger son of the late lord keeper, who in 1592 had joined a secretarial staff that would number at least five or six principals within a few years.[13] Bacon had just returned from France after a stay of thirteen years. He had gone abroad with the backing of Walsingham and in due time had become an intelligencer for the secretary. Cast adrift by the death of his patron and facing personal difficulties, he had returned home.[14] He retained not only French contacts but also correspondents in Spain and he had had some personal dealings with Henry IV when the latter was King of Navarre. It was his brother Francis, since 1591 one of the earl's legal advisors and increasingly a confidant, who introduced him. The ambitious fledgling lawyer, rebuffed in pursuit of his career by his Cecil kin, now fastened his hopes for advancement on the favorite.

Anthony Bacon was able to provide another recruit later in the same year. Sir Anthony Standen (knight by courtesy of Mary Stuart) had had a long and colorful career that had begun in the service of Mary and Henry Darnley. Sent abroad to represent them, he had eventually entered the service of Philip II (1571), served his master in Flanders, travelled as far as Constantinople, and resided for some years in Florence. Sometime in the 1570's he became a spy for Walsingham, and it was the latter who ordered him to Madrid in 1588. There he received appointment and pension from the Spanish crown. His services to Walsingham were highly valued; they commanded a pension of £100 annually. An unfortunate turn of events led to his imprisonment by the French, a plight from which he was rescued by Bacon, who intervened with Burghley to obtain his release. He continued to send information to England until Philip reassigned him to Flanders. He took this opportunity to leave his Spanish master to return to England after a twenty-eight-year absence.[15] Burghley was of course aware of his return but suspicious of his loyalties. Standen, rejected by the treasurer, turned to An-

---

[13] Birch 2: 243.

[14] Daphne DuMaurier, *Golden Lads: A Story of Anthony Bacon, Francis and Their Friends* (London, 1975).

[15] For details of Standen's career, see L. Hicks, "The Embassy of Sir Anthony Standen in 1603," *Recusant History* 5 (1959–60); 91–127, 184–232; 6 (1961–62), 163–94; 7 (1963–64), 50–81.

thony Bacon and through him became a protégé of the earl and a member of the inner circle of confidants.

The next recruit to the earl's intelligence staff was an even more exotic figure: Antonio Perez, the fallen minister of Philip II, whose dramatic escape from imprisonment and flight to France had excited the widest interest. He arrived in England in the spring of 1593 in the suite of the French envoy, Beauvoir de Nocle the elder.[16] After February 1594 he was resident at Essex House until his return to France in July 1595. Perez was not only a resident in the earl's house but also his pensioner to the tune of £20 per month.[17] The Spaniard was received by the Queen and Burghley and moved freely in the highest English social and political circles during his stay. He was allowed to publish a Spanish account of his actions. (The printing of an English translation by one of Essex's secretaries was prohibited.)

With his many contacts Perez was especially useful in recruiting agents to serve Essex's network. The Spaniard chose Venice as a central listening post and even urged on the Queen the appointment of a resident ambassador.[18] She did in fact give her unofficial approval to the dispatch first of Peter Wroth in 1595 and then, on his death, of Dr. Henry Hawkins that November. A doctor of both the laws and a veteran of five years on the Continent, he was for some three years an informative intelligencer whose weekly dispatches were read to the Queen and used by Burghley as well as Essex.[19] Perez was also able to make available the services of a former servant of his, a Genoese named Giacomo Marenco, whose dispatches from Genoa were arriving by late 1594 or early 1595. He sent them through the hands of Hawkins. Later in 1597, Marenco was briefly in England, entertained by Essex.[20]

In Spain there was Anthony Rolleston, an emigré and double agent who with Anthony Bacon had served Walsingham and was now brought to Essex's employ by the former. He also took pay

[16] Gustav Ungerer, *A Spaniard in Elizabethan England: The Correspondence of Antonio Perez's Exile* (2 vols., London, 1974–76) 1: 184–90.

[17] The Queen helped Essex to bear the expense by a grant of lands in January 1595 (*ibid.*, 223 and n.)

[18] Ungerer 2: 170.   [19] *Ibid.*, 173 and Birch 2: 14, 23, 31, 38, 39, 132, 182.

[20] Ungerer 2: 178–83; see Birch 1: 311, 443–44, for instructions by Essex for agents abroad.

from Philip.[21] Later, when Rolleston sought to return, Edmund Palmer at St. Jean deLuz, another employee of Walsingham and a double agent, provided information.[22] In the 1590's two other agents of Essex resident in Spain, Marchant and LeBlanc, were in fact betrayed by Palmer.[23] In the less dangerous milieu of Italy Essex employed besides Hawkins a Florentine, a Signor Guicciardini, who not only sent news but also acted as intermediary with the Grand Duke Ferdinand, for whom he obtained a grain export license.[24] A more clandestine operation was that masterminded by Thomas Phelippes, cipherer extraordinary to Francis Walsingham and now, along with his mysterious associate, William Sterrill, employed by Essex for several operations abroad.[25]

It was perhaps characteristic of Essex's penchant for the odd man out that gathered around him in the inner circle of his intelligence operation three such figures as Anthony Bacon, Standen, and Perez, the first a psychotic invalid, the second a recusant and longtime double agent, the third the fugitive minister from the sinister court of the Escorial. Bacon, a recluse, could never nerve himself to an audience with the Queen and sank more and more into physical debility. Standen failed to win the confidence of either Elizabeth or the Cecils. Perez's personal indiscretions, both sexual and political, earned him the extreme distaste of the Queen. In these associations as well as others Essex showed both generosity and wide tolerance but also a lack of worldly wisdom.[26] Characteristically, when Perez left England in 1595 under royal disapproval he was accompanied by eight Englishmen, all of them servants of Essex.[27] One of them, Robert Naunton, was to remain in France until early 1598, an intermediary with Perez but also an independent informant. Perez himself, still under Essex's patronage, was cast in the role of a link

[21] Albert J. Loomie, *The Spanish Elizabethans: The English Exiles at the Court of Philip II* (New York, 1963), 109–10; Ungerer 1; Hicks.

[22] See HMC, *Hatfield* 4: 175–76; for details of Palmer's dealings, see *CSPD* 4 (1595–97): ccliii, 77, cclvii, 64, cclxix, 68; 5 (1598–1601): cclxxi, 219–20, 242; cclxxii, 27; cclxxv, 268; Birch 1: 94–95.

[23] Loomie, 65.

[24] HMC, *Hatfield* 5: 402, 437, 502, 506, 510; 6: 78, 154–56.

[25] *CSPD* 3 (1591–94): ccl, 62; ccxlii 5/30/92; ccxlv, 40; ccxlvi, 60; see also HMC, *Hatfield* 6: 511, 513, 516–17.

[26] Note the episode of Thomas Wright, S.J., whom he gave leave to visit friends in the North against the warning of Archbishop Hutton (Birch 1: 307).

[27] Ungerer 2: 1–14, 38; Lambeth Ms. 653/42.

between the French and English courts, and an extensive correspondence ensued until Perez's return to England with the French mission of 1596. Relations with the earl cooled somewhat after this, although correspondence continued for a time.

The Bacon connection led Essex into another foray into high politics, the appointment of Francis Bacon as attorney-general, an enterprise that seems to have preoccupied much of his first year on the Council. It was, of course, an effort to establish his credentials as a patronage broker, a favored intermediary with the Queen whose influence could secure promotion and place for aspiring suitors. Necessarily, this ambition brought him into rivalry with the Cecils, who, since the deaths of Leicester and Hatton, had had a virtual monopoly as patronage brokers.

Essex's effort to restore Davison to the secretaryship in 1590 had failed; he himself had been an unsuccessful candidate for the Oxford chancellorship in 1591. Now the earl determined to assert the strength of his influence by securing the patronage of a major governmental appointment. The attorney-generalship had fallen vacant by Sir Thomas Egerton's promotion to master of the rolls. When in July 1593 the earl gave his promise to back Bacon for this post,[28] there was already a candidate in the field, the experienced solicitor-general, Sir Edward Coke, backed by the Cecils. It was a rash promise, difficult of fulfillment, since Bacon had spoiled his chances with the Queen earlier in the year by a speech in Parliament obstructing the passage of the subsidy bill.[29] It was, however, not the first time Essex had sought to advance the cause of a lame duck, as instanced in his vain attempt to rehabilitate the unfortunate secretary Davison.[30]

The Bacon correspondence chronicles in some detail the earl's campaign to promote his protégé. In October in two interviews with the Queen Essex persuaded her to postpone the decision,[31] but when he became "more earnest than ever I did before in so much [the Queen] told me she would be advised by those that had more judgment in these things than myself." This did not discourage him from pressing this and other suits "according to his accustomed manner and forwardness to pleasure his friends" by engaging his

[28] Birch 1: 113.
[30] Devereux 1: 182–84, 209.
[29] D'Ewes, 483–84.
[31] Birch 1: 125–26.

reputation as a great courtier.[32] In December the earl departed from court suddenly, and rumor had it there was "great disgust between both parties" and "the other" was in great agitation. It was thought that the cause of this flurry was the Bacon appointment.[33] Yet by Twelfth Night there was full reconciliation, the Queen sitting next to the earl, "with whom she after devised in sweet and favorable manner." For the time being, the appointment was suspended, and Bacon promised another place if this went to Coke.[34] But the earl fretted at the royal inconstancy, caused, as he saw it, by his mighty enemies.

The issue simmered on; in February 1594 it boiled over in a conversation between Robert Cecil and the earl.[35] Essex intimated that Bacon was not the only young and inexperienced man seeking a promotion; Cecil defended himself by citing his apprenticeship under his father. He then advised Essex not to waste his time on the attorney-generalship but to push his protégé for the solicitor-generalship, a post of "easier digestion" for the Queen. To which he got the furious reply, "Digest me no digestions for the attorneyship for Francis is what I must have and in that will I spend all my power, might and authority and amity [sic] and with tooth and nail defend and procure the same for him against whensoever and whosoever gets this office out of my hands for any other; before he hath it shall cost him the coming by." But the worldly-wise Bacon took the hint and proposed to deal with Sir Robert.[36] By April 1594 Coke had his patent of office as attorney-general.

Essex then urged on the Queen Bacon's candidacy for the now-vacant solicitorship,[37] but Elizabeth, expressing her reservations, declined to continue the discussion and finally told him to depart if he had nothing else to talk of. Essex flounced off, saying that while he was with her he could but solicit the man and the cause. The solicitorship remained vacant for months. In January 1595 Burghley was pressing for a decision and the Cecil interest was at least nominally thrown behind Bacon's candidacy, but in the end the post went to Thomas Fleming.[38]

Essex had failed and he blamed the Cecils for his failure. No doubt they were anxious to maintain their influence as patronage

[32] *Ibid.*, 130–31.
[33] *Ibid.*, 138.
[34] *Ibid.*, 149–50.
[35] *Ibid.*, 152–53.
[36] *Ibid.*, 154.
[37] *Ibid.*, 166–67.
[38] *Ibid.*, 166–67, 195, 272 (11/6/95).

brokers, especially in the case of a major legal appointment. But their backing for Coke was probably also dictated by a shrewd perception that Sir Edward was likely to be the winning horse. They perceived, as Essex did not, that the Queen would make her own choice, on the merits of the candidate rather than the persuasions of his patrons. They realized also that the more pressure was applied on the Queen the more stubborn would be her refusal to seem to be manipulated. They had merely to stand by while Essex achieved his own self-defeat.

During these same months Essex sought to build his credit as a councillor of state by his energy and zeal in the Lopez affair. Rodrigo Lopez was a Portuguese Jewish physician long domiciled in England and eminent in his profession. From attendance on Leicester he had advanced to a higher place, taking the Queen herself as his patient.[39] At the beginning of 1594 he was arrested and charged with plotting to poison the Queen in return for 30,000 crowns to be paid by Count Fuentes, the Spanish commander in the Low Countries.[40] The alleged plot involved a clutch of Portuguese, servants of the impoverished pretender Don Antonio.[41]

At this distance of time it is difficult to untangle the many threads of this plot or to determine the probable guilt of Lopez. The prisoner was being held at Essex House (under Council orders). Essex was convinced of his guilt; Cecil doubted it and won the Queen to his view.[42] She roundly rebuked Essex as a "rash and temerarious youth" and accused him of malice, of accusing the innocent, and of besmirching her honor. The earl, in a rage, shut himself up for two days until the lord admiral mediated the matter. But in the end he had his way, since he headed the commission that tried and condemned Lopez.[43] The death warrant was held up for three months but finally Lopez went to the scaffold. An account, intended for publication, was written by Bacon.[44] Without mentioning names it gave prominence to the industry and zeal of the "noble personage" and to the "noble and steady hand [which] having once got one end of it was never left until every hold was undone." This triumph was a satisfactory set-off to Essex's defeat in the Bacon case.

[39] DNB, "Lopez." [40] See Cecil Papers 2: 669–75.
[41] See *CSPD* 3 (1591–94): 434–57.
[42] Devereux 1: 307–8; Birch 1: 149–50.
[43] *CSPD* 3 (1591–94); ccxlvii, 43. [44] Cecil Papers 2: 669–75.

In this year, filled with court intrigue and rivalry, one opportunity to escape to the simplicities of the battlefield offered itself when the government hastily assembled forces to deal with the fort the Spanish were erecting on the shores of Brest haven. The earl hoped for and sought the command; initially the Queen yielded: he and Lord Admiral Howard would share it; but after a few days she changed her mind and withdrew her consent. She consoled him with a gift of £4,000 and some gracious words. She loved him and the realm too much to hazard him in any lesser cause "than that which should impeach her crown and estate."[45]

These years of enforced inactivity, bound to the routines of Council and enmeshed in the intrigues of the court, cannot have been wholly happy ones for the restless earl. He had plunged into the melee of patronage politics with all his energies, making of the Bacon appointment "a thing as much bringing this great man's credit in question as any other hath managed all the time of his favor heretofore."[46] But the earl could not shed the ingenuousness of the favorite for the guile of the courtier. The first role was in many ways the easier: it involved only himself and the Queen; there was no third party on the stage. The goals that the favorite sought were personal favors for himself alone, and the means used to secure them the simple power of his own personal attractions over his susceptible mistress. Even when she denied him—as in the Breton command—the very denial was flattering in its expression of regard.

Now in his new role he had to realize first of all that he was seeking favors for others, not himself, and that his mere recommendation (based on friendships) was not enough. The candidates had to qualify in their own rights and to win royal approbation on their own merits. Essex could bring Bacon forward to the Queen's attention, but the royal judgment was swayed by a more objective assessment of past performance and of experience in a post demanding high professional skill. Moreover, the rejection of the earl's protégé was a public rejection, a public humbling of the earl; worse still, he had to endure not only the refusal of his candidate but also the acceptance of another's. It was painful and difficult to descend

---

[45] Birch 1: 181; Devereux 1: 311; see also HMC, *Hatfield* 4: 567; Wernham, 533–55. There exists an unsigned warrant appointing Essex and the lord admiral to command a force of 3,000 men for Brittany (Tenison 9: 317).

[46] Birch 1: 168–69.

from the spacious solitude where he alone basked in the royal sun's rays to the hurly-burly of politics, where royal favor or royal rejection fell indifferently on all, entailing the risks of loss in the endless competition of the political world.

The Queen, in the counsel she gave him when she denied him the Breton command, hinted at some of this. "Look to thyself, good Essex, and be wise to help thyself, without giving thy enemies advantage; and my hand shall be readier to help thee than any other."[47] The Queen intended that Essex should, like his predecessors Leicester and Hatton, work his passage as a councillor. The bestowal of her bounty would continue, but he could not expect the same special position as a councillor that he enjoyed as favorite. Appointments to office under the Crown, both high and low, were entirely at her disposal and determined by her judgment. Moreover, she would listen with equal attention and equal regard to the advice of other counsellors, and Essex could expect no more than equality as her servant. Just as Leicester had had to share with his rival, William Cecil, so Essex would have to share with Robert. Elizabeth continued to have perfect confidence that, as she had driven the team of those reluctant yoke-fellows Leicester and Burghley, so she could tame the younger generation to her bidding.

In his apprentice years on the Council Essex had stumbled badly in his first ill-conceived attempt to play the patronage broker. Nevertheless he had gradually made his mark in the Privy Council and in the general business of government. One obvious index of his conciliar role is the frequency of his attendance. Because of the lacunae in Council records from August 1593 to October 1595 and because of Essex's absences for the preparation and execution of his expeditions in 1596 and 1597, it is not easy to assemble exact statistics of the earl's attendances. In general it is fair to say that when he was not away on the high seas he was a regular but not assiduous attender. His absences were scattered and random, rarely for more than a single meeting. The months from late July 1598 to the end of March 1599 provide a fair sample. There were fifty-seven Council meetings when both Essex and Cecil were at court. Essex was present at thirty-five, Cecil at fifty-three.

With the fuller record from late 1595 on, it is easier to give some account of the earl's role in Council. He was now taking part in

47 *Ibid.*, 181.

routine affairs—serving on a committee on Portsmouth and one on subsidy evasion, or in conference with the lord treasurer and lord admiral; he was appointed to mediate a Brasenose College suit along with the Archbishop of Canterbury and Lord Buckhurst.[48] The extent to which Essex's reputation as a patron had grown is reflected in his correspondence. The letters on behalf of local gentry, clergy, lawyers, or those merely labelled as "suitors" fill much of two manuscript volumes.[49] His standing among the political elite is reflected obliquely in another way. On each county commission of the peace both lord chancellor and lord treasurer invariably appeared, *pro forma*. Other Privy Councillors appeared only in those counties where they had land or influence. But Essex significantly was a member of the commission in no less than seventeen counties.[50]

The earl was flexing his political muscle in other ways as well. In 1593 he began building an extensive parliamentary patronage. In the Parliament of that year thirteen members owed their seats to his backing, virtually doubling the number he could count in 1589. Six sat for the Welsh boroughs where Essex's local influence was strong, four for boroughs where he was high steward. Of these two were adjacent to clusters of his estates (Tamworth and Leominster); the others, Reading and Dunwich, were places where he had newly acquired influence. Two other members were dependents who were able to find seats for themselves. In background and occupation the members fall into two main groups. One, composed of men like Sir Francis Vere, Sir Thomas Baskerville, Sir Ferdinando Gorges, Sir Matthew Morgan, and the two Clifford cousins, Sir Nicholas and Sir Conyers, was a contingent of soldiers, veterans of the Low Countries and Rouen. (Baskerville was also a family connection and neighbor.) The other group, largely civilian, contained servants of the earl (like his secretary, Thomas Smith, or the family lawyer, Richard Broughton) or country neighbors of the Devereux.[51]

Four years later, in 1597, Essex's confidant, Sir Gilly Meyrick, was the organizer of electoral activity. His efforts found seats for ten members, again in the Welsh boroughs or in the towns of which

[48] HMC, *Hatfield* 5: 25, 108, 149, 535.   [49] BL, Harleian Ms. 6996, 6997.
[50] PRO C.66/1421.
[51] This paragraph and the succeeding one are drawn largely from information in *House of Commons*, particularly 1: 63–65.

Essex was high steward. He had now added Andover, Ipswich, Hereford, and Great Yarmouth to that list (although without any benefit from the last two). The object of this exercise was not of course to create a parliamentary bloc, a connection of the eighteenth-century type or even of the kind that appeared in the parliaments of the 1620's. It was rather an opportunity to display to the political world at large the extent of his influence as well as publicly to extend favor to men who were dependents within his sphere of patronage. (They do not seem to have been men who were otherwise likely to command attention in the House of Commons.)

The great patrons of the Elizabethan court attracted a clientage composed not only of ambitious laymen but also of aspirants to ecclesiastical promotion. Essex's stepfather, Leicester, had played a large role as the grand patron of the Puritan clergy. There was some expectation that the younger favorite would follow in his predecessor's footsteps. In 1591 he was accounted a friend of the Puritans[52] and for a time he met these expectations. He spoke up for the imprisoned cleric John Udall, and his support was solicited by another of the imprisoned radicals, John Penry. He was, however, also a friend and confidant of Archbishop Whitgift. The religious radicals continued to have lingering hopes of the earl's support, and some of them were loosely connected with the events of February 1601. Essex's links with the Scottish court may also have aroused hopes among those religious dissidents who looked for better things when a Presbyterian monarch ascended the throne.[53]

The recruitment of clients raises the larger question of Essex's purposes in building a patronage empire. The most obvious reason is that the presence of such a clientage was public and visible testimony to one's greatness, just as much as a great mansion or a splendid household. A more tangible payoff derived from a large clientage was what might be termed a multiplier effect. The favors bestowed by a patron created a counterbalance of debt owed him. This meant that the patron, besides his fund of credit with the Queen, could draw on the services of his clients, requesting them to utilize their official authority or local influence on his behalf or that of his other suitors.

[52] Lodge 2: 29–32.
[53] For this paragraph, see Patrick Collinson, *The Elizabethan Puritan Movement* (Berkeley and Los Angeles, 1967), 444–47.

But could a clientage be put to other uses? Obviously Elizabeth's court was not like that of the Valois, where dependents could become swordsmen when political life collapsed into violence. That is, not so long as the Queen lived. But Essex, like other English magnates, could never forget that the Queen was mortal and the succession unsettled. There were certainly circumstances under which the support of a clientage could be all-important. If there were open and violent disagreement about the succession, a following of courtiers, officials, and localities that could be mobilized would be critical. Soldiers would, obviously, be of particular importance, and Essex, like his stepfather, had a considerable military element among his dependents.

Indeed, Essex was becoming the Council specialist in martial affairs. This is apparent in the unofficial role that he was assuming in relation to the principal captains in the Low Countries. Vere in the field, and Burgh, Edward Norris, and Robert Sidney at Brill, Ostend, and Flushing were making routine and detailed reports to him. In these letters they reported on their own activities, purveyed intelligence gathered from their various listening posts, and pressed on him their own views on policy issues. Vere's letters from the camp form a regular series of detailed accounts of the army's movements and actions.[54] Clearly Vere saw these letters as more than a courtesy. On one occasion, lacking any news, he nevertheless reports, "I dare not but write for the discharge of my duty." In another letter of business about the transport of troops to Brittany, he writes to Essex as a superior who can give the necessary orders to facilitate supply and transport. In the same letter he awaits Essex's pleasure in the assignments of captains.[55]

Similarly, the commanders in the cautionary towns and Ostend regularly sought his support in their transactions with the home government while passing on intelligence from the Low Countries and farther afield. Burgh at Brill, a tearful correspondent always full of his own misfortunes (he was out of favor with the Queen) and a humble dependent on the earl's support, was nevertheless an intelligent observer and sometimes a shrewd commentator on Low Countries politics.[56] Robert Sidney at Flushing was on more equal

---

[54] HMC, *Hatfield* 5; see the index for a list of Vere's letters.
[55] *Ibid.*, 155–56, 404–5.
[56] *Ibid.*, 266–67. For Burgh's letters, see HMC, *Hatfield* 5, index.

terms, although he too, at this stage in his career, looked to Essex as a patron. A wordy correspondent, he never hesitated to push his pet schemes for action, but he too had good intelligence sources.[57] And Sir Edward Norris, governor at Ostend, although a committed Cecilian, was a regular and copious informant and on occasion a grateful recipient of the earl's support. These captains looked to Essex as the councillor most directly concerned with military matters, but also as a principal in foreign policy matters. So did the Dutch leaders; Count Maurice, Oldenbarnevelt, even the States-General itself, addressed themselves to Essex as a sure advocate of their causes.[58] Bodley, the English representative at The Hague, also wrote full and detailed reports, although his chief correspondent in the home government was supposed to be the lord treasurer. He drew down Burghley's wrath in 1594, accused of writing a letter to Essex before dispatching one to the treasurer. Gilpin, Bodley's assistant and successor, also reported regularly and fully to the earl, whom he regarded as his patron.[59]

Essex's correspondence by 1595 embraced a far-flung network of writers, great and small. To keep in touch with French affairs he heard regularly from Ottywell Smith, the English merchant at Dieppe, who not only provided information but also loaned money on Essex's security.[60] The governor of Dieppe, the minister of the French church in London, former French envoys to London, and paid intelligencers in Paris all contributed to his knowledge of French affairs.[61] Henry IV himself (as we have seen), besides exchanging courtesies with the earl, continued to recommend the successive French envoys, who were taught to regard the earl as their natural advocate at the English court.[62] When Sir Henry Unton, a longtime protégé of Essex, went as ambassador in 1595, Essex pressed on him a rather astonishing document,[63] which was intended to cue Henry in his negotiations with the English, instructing him what tactics to follow so as "to drive us to propound and

[57] For Sidney's letters, see HMC, *Hatfield* 5, index.

[58] *Ibid.*, 36, 197, 296.

[59] For Gilpin's correspondence, see HMC, *Hatfield* 5, index.

[60] For Smith's correspondence, see HMC, *Hatfield* 5, index.

[61] *Ibid.*, 303, 306, 322, 456 (Châtres at Dieppe); 254, 384, 427, 473, 481 (Fontaine); 400, 530 (Lomenie); 21 (Sancy); 47, 146, 178, 216 (Beauvoir la Nocle); 298, 308, 317, 377 (Wiseman); 385–86, 397, 403–4 (Edward Wilton).

[62] *Ibid.*, 306, 389–90, 500 for examples.   [63] Birch 1: 353–54.

to offer." Individual French commanders, such as Sourdeac, governor of Brest, or St. Luc, royalist captain in Brittany, naturally looked to Essex for assistance in their suits to the Queen.[64]

All these connections were of great value in the immediate context of affairs, but Essex looked beyond the present to the future. From the early 1590's onward, he assiduously wooed the King of Scotland, and by 1595 James VI, much like Henry IV, regarded him as a steady friend and reliable intermediary in his dealings with Elizabeth. Here he had a clear advantage over the Cecils. They, as active administrative officers of state, responsible for carrying out day-to-day relations with Scotland, had to do the Queen's bidding. It was they who had to bear the blame when the Queen held up James's annuity or dabbled in conspiracy with Bothwell. As things stood in the mid-1590's Essex's prospects under a Stuart successor were very bright indeed; those of the Cecils at the very least dim.

By 1595 Essex had achieved eminence as a councillor of weight in military and foreign affairs and as a personage of international stature to whom the kings of France and Scotland, the Stadtholder of the United Provinces, or the Grand Duke of Tuscany looked as an influential intermediary with the English queen. The real measure of Essex's power was, of course, his ability to persuade the Queen to the policies he advocated—to the shaping, above all, of war policy. By the beginning of 1596 there were plentiful signs that Elizabeth was once again, after an interval of almost five years, willing to countenance a direct attack on Spain. The way seemed to be opening for the realization of Essex's fondest ambitions.

By early 1595 the Queen had been brought to a renewal of naval war against Spain on a grand scale. Although Henry's successes had allowed the English to withdraw their forces from Brittany, they had also freed Spanish resources that could now be directed against England herself, and English counteraction was being urged by the advocates of the strategy of offense. In 1595 she consented to the Drake-Hawkins expedition against the West Indies. It is possible, although not certain, that Essex had hopes of commanding this voyage but met with royal disapproval.[65] Certainly the infantry who sailed with the fleet were commanded by Sir Thomas Baskerville, a protégé of the earl, and the company captains were also his cli-

---

[64] HMC, *Hatfield* 5: 321, 333; 6: 85.   [65] HMC, *Hatfield* 5: 127, 155–56.

ents.[66] But the preparations for the voyage were unaccountably delayed, and before the fleet was ready to sail fear of an invasion, planned for 1596, moved the Queen to an alteration of instructions. The admirals were first to linger off the Irish coast long enough to allow for the provision of a squadron for the protection of that island; then they were to sweep the Iberian coasts, doing as much damage as possible to invasion preparations; finally they were to strike for the plate fleet.[67]

Drake and Hawkins protested vigorously, and there followed a debate in the Council between those who favored a Spanish expedition and the backers of the island voyage. In the end the stalemate was broken by news of treasure unloaded in Puerto Rico from a crippled galleon, ripe for the taking.[68] Before the outcome of the Indies voyage could be known, other events distracted the earl's attention. The Queen was now moving towards disengagement on the Continent as Ireland bulked larger in English perceptions. Relations with the States were troubled by her insistence on debt repayment; those with France, by the Queen's resolution to withdraw all English forces. In October a new French envoy, Lomenie, sent to seek more English aid, infuriated the Queen first by insinuating that she was influenced by enemies of France in her court and second by hinting that, without further English aid, France would be forced to negotiate with Spain.[69] Like other French envoys he had been instructed to seek Essex's assistance[70] and had apparently followed—unsuccessfully—the earl's advice. Essex himself bewailed his failure to persuade the Queen to listen to Henry's plea.[71]

In other ways as well, it was an unhappy season for the earl. In November the solicitorship was finally awarded to Fleming, extinguishing Bacon's hopes. At the same time the English-Catholic exiles published the Doleman book, which laid claim to the English throne for the Spanish Infanta and which, dedicated to Essex, sang his praises. An opportune—perhaps psychosomatic—illness evoked

---

[66] See Chapter 6; Andrews, *Last Voyage.*

[67] For Essex's role in persuading the Queen, see Bodley to Cecil 8/17/95 (Cecil Papers 2: 689–90) and R. Sidney to Essex 11/6/95, on the need for the right men around the Queen (p. 697).

[68] Sidney Papers 1: 343–44.

[69] *Ibid.*, 354–55; Birch 1: 327; HMC, *De L'Isle and Dudley,* 178–80.

[70] HMC, *Hatfield* 5: 400, 530.   [71] Birch 1: 339.

a royal visit to his chamber and served to restore frayed relations with the Queen.[72]

By the end of the year the Queen's irritation with Henry IV had subsided sufficiently so that she could consider sending a new ambassador, Sir Henry Unton, to Paris.[73] There was conciliar division over this move; it was rumored that Burghley opposed a closer relationship with France,[74] but ultimately Unton set off. He was a longtime protégé of Essex, who had backed him during a long season of royal disfavor, and his appointment was a gratification to the earl.[75] The latter intended that Unton should go as much as his ambassador as the Queen's. His private instructions for the ambassador detailed a plan by which Unton would tutor the French king in the right tactics for bringing the Queen to heel, i.e., acceding to his demands.[76]

The royal instructions for the envoy were quite different in character, and their curt rejection of Henry's requests incited that sovereign to fury.[77] Unton himself was abashed by the royal displeasure, and "so much discomforted wishing I had spent twice as much as my journey will cost that I had not been employed therein." He begged Essex to secure his revocation.[78] By February relations with his patron had begun to sour. The confidences that Essex shared with Antonio Perez, his confidant in Paris, excluded the ambassador, "and therein the earl does not so kindly with me as I expected."[79] The unhappy ambassador fell ill shortly thereafter and died before the end of March.

Unton was in fact caught in a web of circumstance created by Essex's conflicting goals. Always a strong advocate of close relations with France, he had striven to bring about the formal treaty of alliance that was now on the stocks in the spring of this year. But the tone of Unton's mission had dimmed Henry's trust in the earl, and the new envoy, Sancy, sent over in January, was not a friend of Essex.[80] Indeed, the favorite's new scheme, to lead an expeditionary force against Spain, conflicted with French interests. Henry hoped

---

[72] Sidney Papers 1: 357–58, 359–60.   [73] *Ibid.*, 373–74, 376–77.

[74] Birch 1: 345.

[75] Unton had sought reconciliation with the Cecils in 1593, whether successfully or not cannot be certain (HMC, *Hatfield* 4: 362).

[76] Birch 1: 353–54.   [77] SP 78/37/25, 50; Birch 1: 374, 392–93, 395.

[78] Birch 1: 397; Cecil Papers 2: 701–6; see Unton 1–4, 18–19.

[79] Birch 1: 422–23.   [80] HMC, *Hatfield* 6: 42.

the formal alliance would bring England back to active military collaboration on the Continent, and he viewed the intended naval enterprise as a diversion of English resources from the real theater of war. When in April conclusion of the alliance was near, the Duke of Bouillon, accompanied by Perez, arrived at Dover with powers to sign but also with instructions to dissuade Essex from his new enterprise.[81] They were to find on arrival that they faced a *fait accompli*.

[81] Birch 1: 468.

CHAPTER 25

ENGLAND'S GLORY AND THE

WIDE WORLD'S WONDER

THE YEAR 1596, which was to be the most notable in Essex's career, dawned uncertainly for him. Well before the end of 1595 plans for a large-scale naval expedition, including a Dutch contingent, were under way, but its purposes were uncertain: roles as a channel squadron or as a fleet to meet Drake on his return were among the possibilities. Essex's role was equally uncertain: an army command in Brittany or a naval command off Ireland was mentioned.[1] The general commission to him and Admiral Howard did not issue until March, and it was about then that Burghley wrote definitively of a voyage to the Iberian coast.[2]

The voyage marked, of course, a sharp turn in Essex's fortunes. For the first time since 1591 he was to be allowed a command. Then, as a subordinate to Henry IV and held in tight leading strings by the Queen, he had lacked independence of action. Now, albeit in tandem with the lord admiral, he was in charge of an independent English enterprise, the very nature of which would free him from close royal supervision. Moreover, it would at last embody the strategy that the hawkish party had urged for at least a decade—an assault on the enemy on his home ground. More important still, it was a chance to transform the nature of the English war effort. From 1589 to 1595 it had aimed at nothing more than a merely defensive goal: fending off Spanish invasion, resisting Span-

[1] *CSPD* 4 (1595–97): cclvi, 77 (5 March 1596).
[2] *Ibid.*, cclvi, 95, 99. For the subsequent history of this venture, see Chapter 6.

495

ish domination of France, holding the Spanish forces at bay in the Low Countries. Now the activists saw an opening for a new and bold conception—bolder even than the current West Indian voyage—of a war that, they argued, would end not merely in the re-establishment of peace but in a resounding victory that would establish England's place among the great powers and the Queen's position as the arbitress of European politics.

The decision to launch this voyage coincided with—and was perhaps affected by—a crucial shift in Anglo-French relations that had its effect on Essex's own career. Henry's conversion and the consequent erosion of the Catholic League meant a shift from civil to international war. Elizabeth's ally was no longer a king without a crown, struggling desperately to hold his throne, but the head of a reconstituted French state. The re-establishment of a Continental balance of power was a cause for English rejoicing, but it also meant, as Burghley was quick to observe, that the old prewar relationships were now back in place.[3] The French government was no longer a clamorous client but an independent equal with whom normal power relationships obtained.

For Henry, English intentions were a vital factor in the decision that now loomed before him. Should he, as his Protestant advisors urged him, turn his energies to war with Spain, or should he follow the advice of Catholic counsellors and seek peace with Philip? The amount of English cooperation on which he could depend in case he chose war would weigh heavily in his decision. Essex was a passionate partisan in pressing for the formal alliance that the French were proposing in late 1595. After the ill-success of the Lomenie mission,[4] in which the earl's advocacy had gone for nought, he had, as we have seen, gone so far as to frame a set of private instructions for Ambassador Unton by which the latter was to coach the French response in such a way as to press the English to acceptance of the treaty.[5]

As the decision for the Spanish expedition took shape Essex shifted his views rapidly and radically, and his interests soon diverged from those of Henry IV. For him the coming expedition promised the fulfillment of his most deeply felt private ambitions and the realization of his public goals. It would not only lead to the

[3] Birch 1: 465–66.   [4] *Ibid.*, 296, 297, 327.
[5] *Ibid.*, 353–54.

defeat of the enemy but also to a great English triumph. For the French the whole enterprise was a wasteful diversion of resources from the central theater of war.[6] When Bouillon (accompanied by Antonio Perez) arrived with the mission of clinching the treaty, he did all he could to dissuade Essex from the enterprise and, failing that, joined his voice with others who were pressing the Queen to stop its sailing or at least withdraw the soldiers.[7] The French got their treaty, although the material aid they sought was pared down to a mere 2,000 men. A reconciliation with Essex was patched up, but he was by then drifting away from his close collaboration with the French King as he grasped the opportunity for achieving a personal, and solely English, triumph. These complexities could be left behind once the fleet cleared Plymouth and Essex could concentrate on the task he had set himself. "I know God hath a great work to work by me. I thank God I see my way both smooth and certain and I will make all the world see I understand myself," were his final words to Anthony Bacon.[8]

What that great work was he spelled out in a letter to the Queen written at his departure. A similar document of about the same date, dispatched to the Privy Council, outlined in brief form the same argument, linking his general strategy to his immediate tactics in this enterprise. The letter to the Queen set out his ideas on a grander scale.[9] He began by writing of the two opposing parties at court, "two sorts of persuaders." The first would have the Queen take a wholly defensive stand, reacting to the enemy's initiatives but taking none herself. This meant concentrating English efforts in the Low Countries. Against this strategy he argued the case for an offensive posture under the formal headings of honor, profit, safety, and "convenience of state." In former actions the English, fighting as mere coadjutors of the French, had played a role little different from that of the Swiss. In the present action the Queen was waging war like a mighty prince, and the glory would be solely hers, displaying strength of mind and royal constancy. To embrace another joint action with the French could be thought a sign of irresolution. The path of honor was clearly laid out.

As for profit, it was hardly necessary to point out the differences

---

[6] *Ibid.*, 450–52, 459–60; Sidney Papers 2: 36–37.

[7] Birch 1: 466, 483.   [8] *Ibid.*, 484.

[9] See Chapter 6; *CSPD* 4 (1595–97): cclix, 12; Devereux 2: 349–56; Birch 2: 19–20.

between Spain, a country rich in the treasures of both the Indies, and Flanders, one in which the enemy had nothing to lose but clothes, earth, and the stone of their forts. And as for safety—in Flanders the best troops in Christendom were entrenched in fortified towns; in Spain it was only the "besoygneyes," the local militia who would do no more than make a show of fighting. Above all, *raison d'état*, "conveniency of state," would be served. Spain would no longer be a menace to England or Ireland, and if the Queen would establish a base in Philip's dominions she could shift the war to his own soil. But let her adopt the alternative strategy—"spend your subjects and wealth to get fisher towns"—and there would follow the loss of Ireland and of command of the seas.

These were Essex's hopes as he set out; they were to be cruelly dashed by summer's end. First there were the bitter disappointments of the voyage itself: the refusal of his colleagues to accept his plan to hold Cadiz and then their unwillingness to pursue the plate fleet. We have already (Chapter 6) seen the coolness of the royal reception on his return. He was greeted at Plymouth by a letter in the Queen's best I-told-you-so vein. As she had expected, the voyage had been more "an action of honor and victory against the enemy and particular spoil to the army than any profitable to ourself."[10]

Essex had made plans for a published account of his exploits. In a secret instruction to his secretary Reynolds, written from Cadiz, he enclosed a text that the latter was to keep secret while he prepared a copy for the printers. The Archbishop of Canterbury was to be solicited to proclaim a public thanksgiving. The publication would appear anonymously under the initials of either Fulke Greville, his cousin and confidant, or Robert Beale, clerk to the Privy Council. But the sickness of Essex's messenger, Cuffe, and the treachery of his substitute, Ashley, aborted the whole scheme. Raleigh and Cecil had collaborated to promote another version; the printer had been forbidden to proceed with Essex's, the Primate inhibited from approving the text. Cuffe had been explicitly ordered by the Queen on threat of death not to print anything without her consent. Even before Essex's return Reynolds wrote to Bacon, "I fear the sea-faction do seek to disgrace my lord's noble action."[11]

Another initiative of Essex had also been checked. In a secret

---

[10] BL, Cotton Mss., Otho IX, fols. 363–34.   [11] Birch 2: 45, 80–82, 95.

instruction to Reynolds, written as the earl left the Spanish coast, the latter had been ordered to go to the French and Dutch agents (Fontaine and Caron) to prod them into persuading Elizabeth to send the whole returning army to besiege Calais or defend Boulogne. Second, they were to use Giles Fletcher (the Bishop of London's brother) as an intermediary to suggest to the Queen that the London citizens would make some offer to her to that end. Although Reynolds spoke to Fontaine, who in turn promised to reach Bouillon, there was little prospect of the Queen's agreeing to a French enterprise. In fact, she had already returned some soldiers to the Low Countries, and others were sent to Ireland. Fletcher did reach Burghley and stressed the citizens' interest in recovering Calais and their willingness to contribute. The treasurer merely agreed to remit the matter to his mistress. Essex's rather desperate plot to retain the army under his command for another fling had fallen flat.[12] The Queen, incensed at the failure to pursue the plate fleet, and informed that ample provisions were still on hand, attempted to relaunch the fleet for a renewed effort to intercept the silver, but by mid-August this scheme had to be abandoned, given the condition of the ships and the men.[13]

Essex had returned to court in haste, leaving Plymouth within four hours of landing. He found the Queen "possessed with discontented humors."[14] She complained of abuses in the handling of booty, deprecated the earl's role in the victory, and extolled that of the "sea-faction." Hitherto she had followed Essex's humor to her own damage; now she would please herself and serve her own. More shrilly she demanded an accounting of funds. There were no more beggars in her realm; all were rich from Cadiz—except the sovereign. Where was the £50,000 laid out in advance? Essex was warned by his friends at court that a plot had been laid to keep him away from the Queen by sending him to sea again.[15]

Gradually, however, the royal vapors cleared. News of the safe return of the plate fleet vindicated his judgment in urging pursuit.

---

[12] *Ibid.*, 77–78; Monson 2: 12 (remark about rowing one way, looking the other); Birch 2: 98–99, 93–94, 100–1; HMC, *Hatfield* 6: 321–22, 325–27, 328–31, 334, 336–37.

[13] *Ibid.*, 6: 328–29, 334; Birch 2: 94.   [14] *Ibid.*, 96.

[15] *Ibid.*, 101–2, dated 9 August; the friends were Worcester, Henry Howard, Dyer, and Greville. This report may have been linked to the Queen's effort to relaunch the fleet.

His opponents' refusal had lost the opportunity of intercepting it. At a banquet Essex gave to the French envoys in early September the Queen "used him most graciously" and praised the course of piety—attending prayers, hearing sermons, and waiting upon his wife—that the earl now affected.[16]

The earl had returned to a changed political world. During Essex's absence the Queen had approved the formal appointment of Cecil as Secretary and the promotion of his friend, Sir John Stanhope, to the treasurership of the Chamber and to the Privy Council. With characteristic evenhandedness the Queen, after Essex's return, advanced his uncle, Sir William Knollys, to be comptroller of the household and both Knollys and his friend, Lord North, to be Privy Councillors—appointments that Anthony Bacon saw as a counterbalance to the Cecilian promotions.[17]

Bacon's comment reflected a new and disturbing awareness of open factional division within the Council. It was apparent in the strained relations between earl and secretary. In an acrimonious dispute in the royal presence Essex protested the appointment of Cecil's ally, Sir George Carew, as a commissioner for prizes. "And this day I was more braved by your little cousin than ever I was by any man in my life," the earl told Bacon.[18] In a letter to Perez, Essex recounts his skirmishes with the Cecils. Having failed to condemn him for the military results of the expedition, they now accused him of allowing the booty to be embezzled. When he had successfully countered these charges, they made allegations about his personal life. Again he confounded them by his piety and by his renunciation of his earlier womanizing. He also asserted that after the appointment of Knollys and North there was a proposal to banish him to Ireland as deputy with an army and on his own terms, but he saw the trap and sidestepped it.[19] He would go to Ireland only if he had a considerable fleet and companies chosen by himself and on terms devised by him.

The events of the summer had in fact subtly altered power relationships within the Council and court. Cecil's appointment as secretary gave him no material accretion of power, but it significantly

[16] *Ibid.*, 122.

[17] *Ibid.*, 60–61, 119–121; HMC, *Hatfield* 6: 287–88; PRO C.66/1449 m. 32. Essex may have had a kind of equivalent in a substantial grant of land in fee simple at the same time (PRO C.66/1453 mm. 20–22).

[18] Birch 2: 131.   [19] *Ibid.*, 140–42.

elevated his status. He was no longer under the wings of his father; he stood on his own, the recipient of a signal affirmation of royal favor. He had now attained for the first time a position of equality with Essex. Moreover, his future was secured beyond the span of his father's life. He could now assert himself against the favorite in a way that would not have been possible earlier.

Essex's position had also changed. He returned from Cadiz endowd with a new political dimension. His victory had surrounded him with a blaze of glory such as no English captain had known for generations. As councillor and favorite he had shone in the reflected glory of the royal sun, but now he had an effulgence of his own. Francis Bacon was the first to warn his patron of the dangers inherent in this combination of popularity—a word of ominous meaning in Tudor ears—and military reputation. He urged him to shed these attributes and to essay the safer role of court politician.[20] Bacon no doubt reflected the unease of Essex's conciliar colleagues, heightened no doubt by his unsuccessful bid to retain control of the army he had taken to Spain. There was henceforth a sharp edge of distrust in the relations between the earl and his fellows at the Council board.

Essex may have taken his follower's advice, at least in part. There followed in the autumn months a reconciliation with the Cecils in which Raleigh—and possibly the Queen—played a role. Burghley complained pathetically that the Queen thought him too partial to the earl and that the latter thought him an enemy.[21] In Anthony Bacon's somewhat lurid prose, Essex "with bright beams of his valor and virtue has scattered the clouds and cleared the mists which a malicious enemy raised and stands well with the Queen, which has made the old fox to crouch and whine."[22]

All in all, Essex seemed to have swallowed the disappointments and frustrations of the Cadiz voyage and his cold reception at court. His public reputation was higher than ever; it was the successes of the raid rather than its failures that caught the public imagination—and stimulated Spenser's glowing tribute. And indeed, the safe arrival of the plate fleet seemed to vindicate the bolder course he had vainly urged on his timorous colleagues on the return voyage from Cadiz.

[20] *Ibid.*, 146–48; Devereux 1: 392.   [21] Birch 2: 159–60.
[22] Devereux 1: 394–401.

The final months of 1596 were disturbed by the appearance of the Spanish fleet off the coast, and it was not until December that the English were assured of its destruction in the autumnal storms. But the atmosphere at court remained charged; the Queen was in better humor, but tension between the factions continued. Even during the crisis of the invasion threat a court observer could write that opposing views as to appropriate defense moves were shaped by faction. The Queen was seen rather as using "her wisdom in balancing the weights than in drawing all to one assize; which shall be the wiser way *docebet dies*."[23]

In December Perez's correspondent in London wrote of Essex as subject to extraordinary melancholy and secluded in his chamber. In the New Year 1597 the earl, defending himself to Lady Bacon against the charge of adultery, was full of bitterness. "I live in a place where I am hourly conspired against and practiced upon what they cannot make probable to the Queen that they give out to the world. They have almost all the house to serve for instruments."[24]

When the Queen asked Essex for a paper on the proposed action against Spain, his worried servants feared he might be carried away by hopes of a great command. They urged him to "stand upon very honorable and profitable conditions and that this charge be rather offered by others than sought by him." There were echoes of Francis Bacon's advice of the previous fall; the earl should not present himself as an eager captain, but as a dutiful public servant. These preliminary plans included another joint command with Lord Admiral Howard.[25]

February found the earl more deeply depressed than ever. White, Sidney's agent in London, reported that Essex was keeping to his chamber and talking of a long visit to his estates in Wales, "and truly I believe he may do it for here there is little to be done." He followed with another letter of the same week; the earl was still sulking in retirement while Robert Cecil enjoyed great credit, spending most of the day in private conference with the Queen. Anthony Bacon wrote that the earl's indisposition had increased "with just cause of undeserved discontents of mind." White indulged himself in pious reflections about the ambitious hope and

---

[23] Sidney Papers 2: 7–8.   [24] Birch 2: 218–20.
[25] *Ibid.*, 266; *CSPD* 4 (1595–97): cclxii, 9, 16.

insatiable desire of those who set the height of their felicity in a prince's momentary favors.[26]

This episode resolved itself after a fortnight of melodramatics. "Full fourteen days His Lordship kept in; Her Majesty, as I heard, is resolved to break him of his will and to pull down his great heart, who found it a thing impossible and says he holds it from the mother's side, but all is well again and no doubt he will grow a mighty man in our state." Anthony Bacon wrote of the expectation of royal favor "correspondent to the expectation of the world and his most worthy merits."[27]

In the unstable climate of the court the weather changed with disconcerting suddenness. By March the earl was again contemplating a Welsh journey, and his secretary wringing his hands at the risks of absence from court, giving opportunity to "the cunning plotters and practicers" who worked on the discontented humors of the Queen. It was all the more exasperating as Reynolds admitted that the Queen "seeketh more to give him contentment than he her." It was now generally assumed that the earl would not command the coming expedition. Henry IV was quoted as saying that "S.M. ne laisseroit jamais son cousin d'Essex d'esloigner de son costillon."[28] Along with the question of command there was a family problem: the jointure of Dorothy Perrot, the earl's sister, in which the main actor was the lawyer Coke, and which involved not only family honor but the dignity of the aristocratic order. At the same time an effort was made to reconcile Cecil and the earl, but a visit from the secretary proved unavailing.[29]

In the first week in March Essex announced his intention of going to Wales by a circuitous route, which would keep him from court until Easter. Officially he was going for his health, but observers saw his absence simply in terms of the opportunity for his opponents "to effect their wills." The earl had already entered on another contest for royal favor. Lord Cobham, who, among his other offices, was warden of the Cinque Ports, was dying, and Essex was pressing the candidacy of Robert Sidney for this latter post against the Cecilian candidate, Cecil's brother-in-law, son and heir to the dying chamberlain.[30]

[26] Sidney Papers 2: 16, 17; Birch 2: 281–82.
[27] Sidney Papers 2: 19–20; Birch 2: 284–85.
[29] *Ibid.*, 290; Sidney Papers 2: 17–18, 22–23.

[28] *Ibid.*, 289–90, 305.
[30] *Ibid.*, 20–21, 23.

It was at this point that the impasse was resolved by the appearance—or rather re-entrance—of a third party on the court stage. Raleigh had shipwrecked his career by his marriage in 1592 and suffered a long banishment from the court. (In 1595 he had made his first voyage to Guiana.) But his service at Cadiz had refurbished his reputation and he now had hopes of restoration to the court. He visited both Cecil and Essex, urging upon the latter the demands of the public good, the quieting of the Queen's unease, and the advancement of a vigorous defense policy.[31] What followed was a tripartite treaty among these politicians to advance their individual and common interests. Some arrangement about the Perrot jointure seems to have been arrived at. But a larger bargain was also struck. The three would cooperate in promoting the naval expedition; they would press for Essex's promotion to office, i.e., the mastership of the ordnance; Cecil was to pursue the chancellorship of the duchy, and Raleigh was to be restored as captain of the guard. The death of the elder Lord Cobham made a convenient excuse for Essex's abandonment of his Welsh trip.[32]

All this was accomplished not without some ruffling of feathers. Essex's demands for the wardenship for Sidney were roundly denied by the Queen, and he again threatened to leave the court but was soothed by her offer of the ordnance office. There was yet another scene with the Queen about the signing of the patent, but the earl was given his appointment. He nevertheless still stormed against the junior Cobham, and the post remained vacant for the time being, the latter eventually receiving it in the autumn.[33]

The triple entente was sealed at a dinner in late April as Essex and Raleigh collaborated in assembling an army. Relations with the Cecils, father and son, became ceremoniously cordial. In May Burghley blessed the enterprise against Spain, praying that God would prosper it. Court news was full of the newly coined cooperation between the Cecils and Essex. Sidney wrote wistfully from Flushing, hoping that now that the earl and the adverse party were so "inward" he would not be forgotten by his patron. In June the alliance bore yet more fruit when Cecil brought Raleigh to court, where the latter was reinstated as captain of the guard. Essex was

---

[31] *Ibid.*, 24–25.　　　　　　　　[32] *Ibid.*, 24–25, 27; Birch 2: 295.
[33] Sidney Papers 2: 27, 29–31, 31–33; *CSPD* 4 (1595–97): cclxii, 105; Tenison 10: 183. The letters patent for the ordnance office were dated 19 March 1597.

absent but gave his blessing. The Queen gave her warm approval to the entente, especially praising Cecil for having taken the initiative towards Essex.[34]

Sir William Knollys, the earl's uncle, was more reserved. "If we live not in a cunning world, I should assure myself that Mr. Secretary were wholly yours, as seeming to rejoice at everything that may succeed well with you, and to be grieved at the contrary, and doth, as I hear, all good offices he may for you to the Queen. I pray God it may have a good foundation; and then is he very worthy to be embraced. I will hope the best, yet will I observe him as narrowly as I can." Another judgment, not on the alliance but on Essex's own goals in entering it, came from Francis Bacon: "My lord, when I first came to you I took you for a physician who desired to cure the diseases of the state. But now I doubt you will be like to those physicians who can be content to keep their patients long, because they would always be in request."[35]

Friendly relations survived the disappointments and frustrations of the summer. Cecil, relaying a report that the flota would arrive in September or October, wished "the Lord of Heaven will send it Your Lordship" and reassured him that if he came home with booty, he would be thanked, "but if you bring home yourself we will never chide you." He promised to do all he could to postpone Parliament until Essex's return. Raleigh, writing at the same time, was no less abundant in good will. On the return of the fleet after its first unsuccessful foray Burghley consoled Essex with pious reflections, recommending Psalm 107, particularly six verses, which he enclosed. He assured Essex that the Queen ascribed all these events to an act of God and absolved the earl of any fault in the matter. Cecil became almost playful; in one letter he related the Queen's pleasure in the earl's recent letter, "written more like angels than men, so much wisdom, so much caution, so much humility and such providence; nay, so great good-husbandry as I will keep it for a monument of your virtues. . . . I am a little saucy but I love to prattle with you while I may."[36]

While Essex was at sea a personal problem arose that led the earl's secretaries to seek Cecil's intervention with the Queen. The

[34] CSPD 4 (1595–97): cclxii, 124, 125 (4/20/97), 140; cclxiii, 66, 67, 74; Sidney Papers 2: 41–43, 48–51, 51–52, 53–54, 54–55.

[35] Birch 2: 350–51, 345.

[36] CSPD 4 (1595–97): cclxiv, 5, 9, 10, 49, 61; Tenison 10: 226–27.

sweet wines customs lease that the earl enjoyed would expire within a year. But to raise a loan on it now, to pay off a mortgage on their master's land, required a promise of renewal. Cecil rejected the secretaries' plea on the ground that he needed a written request from Essex himself in order to deal in the matter. They were left with no option but a direct petition to the Queen.[37]

In public matters, however, the secretary continued to be helpful, mediating to Essex's satisfaction an awkward dispute involving the lord admiral and Mountjoy. We know, of course, Cecil's privately expressed view that the second expedition would come to nought. When the storm-battered fleet returned, Burghley sent a rather condescending letter, assuring the earl that the Queen regarded the failure as an act of God for which he could not be blamed. Nevertheless, the treasurer regretted the escape of the "overplus," which would have been a "cordial to all our infirmities here."[38] Just before Essex returned, Cecil had reaped the reward he had promised himself since the pact of the last spring. Initially the Queen had balked at granting him the chancellorship of the duchy, but now in October she yielded. At about the same time his brother-in-law Cobham received the wardenship of the Cinque Ports, so fiercely contested the previous spring.[39]

What are we to make of this tangled narrative of clashing personalities, of fits of temper or sulks, and of court intrigue, which virtually paralyzed a wartime government wrestling with problems of the utmost urgency? While Essex kept to his chamber and the Queen fumed, the Council was struggling to calculate the prospects for another invasion attempt and to determine the appropriate response. At the same time, they were preoccupied with the clamorous demands for assistance from the French king, reeling from the loss of Amiens to the Spaniards.

It is not easy to assess the true state of affairs from the cryptic correspondence at our disposal, most of it from the pens of the Essex circle. In these quarters it was an article of faith that the Cecils and their adherents plotted relentlessly to poison the Queen's mind against the favorite. Essex himself certainly shared this view at

---

[37] *CSPD* 4 (1595–97): cclxix, 69; HMC, *Hatfield* 7: 283, 350, 376. The earl owed some £10,000 in mortgages. Cecil was helpful, however, in forwarding a personal suit by Reynolds, one of the secretaries (*ibid.*, 459).

[38] *CSPD* 4 (1595–97): cclxiv, 49, 50, 77, 160, 161; HMC, *Hatfield* 7: 361.

[39] Sidney Papers 2: 46–47, 63–64.

times, as his letter to Lady Bacon[40] reveals, although he was also capable of coming to an entente with his rival. What is not clear is just how far these suspicions were justified by the Cecils' own actions. How far was the conspiracy against Essex a product of his own overly sensitive and unbalanced psyche, powerfully influenced by his entourage, which made him all too prone to sense enmity and malice in every move?

Certainly Robert Cecil was in an increasingly powerful position. He was now replacing his ailing father as the Queen's chief minister, her confidant in all matters of business, and the channel of Crown patronage, high and low. But there is no evidence that he sought to destroy Essex's position as the Queen's leading advisor in military matters or as her most distinguished captain. It was to him that Burghley looked for advice as to how to deal with the Spanish threat. (It is just possible that the treasurer preferred Cumberland's cheaper scheme to Essex's and that he—or his son—was behind the Queen's hesitations about the whole enterprise in May, but the evidence all points the other way.)

All this suggests that the anguished self-pity of the earl and his sulky retirement into solitude in the early months of the year were a product of his own unstable and inwardly divided personality. During the years since he had become a Privy Councillor, Essex had worked hard to transform himself from the mere personal favorite, the pampered pet of a susceptible princess, into a weighty and responsible councillor of state. With a widespread intelligence network at his command, he could claim an expert and intimate knowledge of European affairs and familiarity with the rulers of France, the United Provinces, Scotland, and even Italy. Among these princes and potentates he was clearly accounted a leading minister of the English state. Within the Council he was the acknowledged master of all matters military, whose judgment was respected and whose policies won royal approval. Robert Sidney could write—with some degree of flattery but also much truth—that "the managing of all matters of war both by land and sea are almost in His Lordship's hands." A reflection of popular sentiment is mirrored in a letter from an English clergyman in Zealand. Rejoicing in Essex's fame abroad and favor with the Queen, he says, "All men's eyes are upon you now at home and abroad.... You are

[40] Birch 2: 18–20.

now expected to be as the steersman or master of the ship for counsel if God call my Lord Treasurer." However inaccurate as to the real situation at court, this remark does show the popular apprehension of the earl's position in the wake of Cadiz.[41]

The explosion of bitterness that followed immediately upon the return from Cadiz is easily attributable to the disappointments of the voyage and Essex's reception by the Queen. The timorousness or envy of his fellow commanders that had led to the abandonment of Cadiz and the failure to pursue the plate fleet had defeated his strategic goals and crushed all the high hopes with which he had set forth. The sour complaints of the Queen on his return and the sniping of his colleagues, who had deliberately sought to belittle his achievement, were crippling blows to his ego. There was a temporary rally as better relations with the Queen were established and a superficial reconciliation with the Cecils achieved. But when the crisis of the threatened invasion was past, reaction set in quickly. The following winter was one of depression and isolation, from which he was eventually drawn by the mediating skills of Raleigh and by the promise of new and exciting employment. As in the previous summer the exhilaration of action lifted his spirits and aroused his confidence, but when the 1597 season came to its dismal end after a long series of misfortunes and disappointments, the pattern of the preceding year repeated itself. This time the earl sank into a deeper and even more impenetrable gloom as his vision of the world around him darkened.

That world, as he now saw it, was a nest of vipers, of men and women whose sole object was to vilify and humiliate Robert Devereux, a world of venomous spite and undying malice. Not even majesty herself was exempt from blame. If her confidence in him was so slight as to be swayed by these patent falsehoods, he would not deign to plead his case with her. In a sense he had reverted to his old role of favorite, playing on his personal relationship with the sovereign and seeking to bend her to his will, to force her to acknowledge his true merit and the falsity of his opponents' allegations. It became a struggle of will as enraged majesty sought "to pull down his great heart." This was the situation at court in the late fall of 1597.

Having demobilized the fleet and made his proposals for future

[41] HMC, *Hatfield* 7: 156; 6: 478.

fleet arrangements, Essex pleaded sickness and in November retired to his house at Wanstead, without having attended at court. The Queen's displeasure was made known immediately. Hunsdon had excused him to the Queen on the grounds that he had gone to look after his estate. She tartly commented that as a councillor his first duty was to the estate of the realm, but in further conversation Hunsdon found nothing but kindness and comfort in her, if only "you will but turn about and take it." Burghley added his persuasions. In his first letter he urged the importance of business; in the second he decried the earl's absence, "whereby Her Majesty has want of her service and yourself subject to diversity of censures. . . . My good lord, overcome her with yielding, without disparagement of your honor, and plead your own cause with your presence, whereto I will be as serviceable as any friend you have."[42]

An even more urgent letter came from "thy true servant not daring to subscribe"—a short but cogent treatise on the nature of court politics.[43] The letter noted that the tactic of withdrawal would at best bring some small favor to coax him back (like the ordnance office in 1596). Indeed, feeding him with shadows while making his adversaries strong was already routine practice. But his absence left the field clear to his enemies to engross offices and honors. "The greatest subject that is or ever was greatest in the prince's favor in his absence is not missed, and a small discontinuance makes things that were as if they were not and breaks togetherness which gives way to wrath." He must sit in every council, let no thing be done without his privity. "Thou hast 100,000 true hearts in this small isle that daily expect and wish thy true contentment and the fall of them that love thee not." Echoing Bacon's advice, this partisan went on to urge a change of image. Essex wanted to be a general; that required no cultivation: all the famous soldiers loved him as friends, followers, or servants. The role he must play was that of courtier, dissembling his martial ambitions. There must be no more annual voyages, taking him away from court; Essex must, like Mordecai, be on hand to thwart the wicked purposes of proud Haman.

That fall the earl's discontents arose not only from the ill-success of the voyage itself but also from the Queen's expressed dissatisfaction with his performance. She alleged that Essex could have done more than he did. More important was a royal action that struck

---

[42] *Ibid.*, 479–80; *CSPD* 4 (1595–97): cclxv, 7, 6, 14, 23.   [43] *Ibid.*, cclxv, 10.

deep, wounding his prickly sense of his own honor and dignity and turning discontent into rage. Just before Essex returned from the Azores, Elizabeth promoted Lord Admiral Howard to be Earl of Nottingham, citing not only his Armada honors but also those of Cadiz, and according him first place in the latter victory. Furthermore, the new earl was created lord steward for the present Parliament. The earldom, combined with the great office of state Howard (as admiral) already held, would now give him precedence over Essex—a mere earl without a great office—in council, court, and parliament.[44]

Essex remained at Wanstead for some weeks, absenting himself from the Accession Day ceremonies, but he was not quiescent. He protested strongly the terms of Nottingham's patent that celebrated his victories, demanded they be altered, and then asked for a commission of inquiry. The Queen gave way on the alteration of the patent, but even then Essex was not satisfied, since it was implied the changes were made "because one man only stormed at it." In a passionate letter to the Queen he insisted that testimony to the injustice of the patent would be given by "5000 soldiers and more than that number of mariners," by the whole council of war, and by all the officers. "I persuade myself no Christian can be so wicked, subject so undutiful, or man so impudent as to deliver an untruth to Your Majesty of which a whole army by land and sea can convince him." Once again the favorite's tactic had worked; Queen and Council retreated before his fury. His dependent, Anthony Bacon, could write of the end of his master's eclipse "that the beams of his lordship's virtue and fame and merit can be no longer be shadowed by malice and envy."[45]

With the revival of the title of lord marshal, in abeyance since Shrewsbury's death in 1590, Essex was elevated to a pre-eminence over Nottingham. (Among the great officers of state the marshal preceded both the admiral and the steward.) At the beginning of this storm, court gossip had predicted that the peace between Essex and the Cecils would burst out to terms of unkindness and asserted that the Queen blamed the Cecils. But Burghley had been more than sympathetic when Essex returned with his broken fleet and had made a friendly plea to Essex to come to court. In the final

---

[44] Sidney Papers 2: 70, 74–75; Cheyney 2: 445–46.
[45] Sidney Papers 2: 77; HMC, *Hatfield* 7: 527; Birch 2: 364.

settlement of the matter Cecil seems to have played a helpful role, and the correspondence between the two is in warm terms. There is no surviving evidence that the Cecils pushed for Howard's promotion. He was after all the Queen's kinsman, one of her oldest friends, and almost the last survivor of her generation in the Council. At any rate the storm subsided; Essex returned to Council, and collaboration with Cecil became warmer than ever. Nevertheless, Essex had now alienated the admiral, who would, as future events revealed, become a steady partisan of the Cecils.[46]

In these two winters of storm and stress, with their recurrent bouts of sulky withdrawal and loud cries of persecution, Essex had responded to the disappointments of his two campaigns by a reversion to his old role as favorite, presuming on his personal relationship with the Queen and bullying her into an acceptance of his demands. It proved to be the last time that this gambit was effective.

The following months witnessed an interval of harmonious cooperation and unprecedented warmth between the secretary and the earl. The secretary was now ascending to the peak of his power; his father's faculties were fast failing; the Queen's confidence in the son was more manifest than ever. Henry IV now stood poised to make peace with Philip II; the English and the Dutch made one last convulsive effort to stave off this eventuality. Oldenbarnevelt, now incontestably the senior Dutch statesman, headed the States delegation to the French court; Cecil was the Queen's choice to lead her concomitant mission.

With Burghley virtually *hors de combat*, Essex found himself in an unprecedented position. In the past it had been he whose long absences gave free rein to the influences of his rival. Now the secretary was apprehensive about leaving the field free to Essex. Clearly, some kind of agreement was struck between them. In January Burghley issued a restraining order prohibiting the import of cochineal and indigo for two years, owing to the quantity captured by Essex in 1597 and now on hand in England. Essex was allowed to buy a portion of the stock at a very favorable price, well below market rates, and rumor had it he would receive £7,000 out of the deal. Cecil reputedly had engineered this concession from the

---

[46] HMC, *Hatfield* 7: 526–27; Sidney Papers 2: 74–75, 77; HMC, *De L'Isle and Dudley*, 302, 305. Howard received a profitable consolation prize in his appointment as chief justice of the forest courts (PRO C.66/1458 m. 39).

Queen. In return he had assurance from Essex that nothing unacceptable to his own interest should be done during his absence.[47]

Confirmation of the new entente and its nature comes from Robert Cecil's own pen. Writing on his arrival at Dieppe, the Secretary declared he was "not only inwardly contented with the knowledge of your care and affection but . . . apt to let it appear to my company how I am valued by you." The publicity of the agreement would put pressure on the earl to keep it.

> As the Queen's affairs must have a good portion of our minds I hope now God has disposed us to love and kindness we shall overcome all petty doubts about what the world may judge of our correspondency; our souls are witness that nothing is so dear to us as Her Majesty's service which prospered the worse through our pleasing our followers by contrariety in ourselves. I am rich in mind and body by this purchase of your noble favor and protection and next to God and my sovereign shall labor most to preserve and requite your friendship.

In a postscript he adds that "if some idle errand can send over Walter Raleigh let us have him."[48]

A few days later Burghley wrote urging his son to send a letter of thanks to Essex for the pains he was taking about matters that Cecil would normally handle. Other reports confirm the earl's diligence in attendance on the Queen and in the performance of the secretary's business. All foreign correspondence addressed to the Queen passed through Essex's hands. Moreover, Burghley's increasing debility virtually crippled his effectiveness.[49] Cecil appealed to Essex, "whose years are fit for sudden service and whose eyes are fixed more passionately though not more zealously" upon the Queen, to fill his father's place. When Burghley took a dangerous turn in his illness Essex hastened to write reassuringly to Cecil: "This is to tell you that when news of your father's illness came to my knowledge I had that sense of your interest every way as was fit for to answer the professions I have made unto you." And in a later letter he urged Cecil not to delay his return for Burghley's "bane of

[47] Sidney Papers 2: 83–84, 88–89; HMC, *Hatfield* 8: 36.

[48] *CSPD* 5 (1598–1601): cclxvi, 71.

[49] *Ibid.*, 73, 83, 115; SP 78/41/122, 141, 177; Sidney Papers 2: 91–92; HMC, *Hatfield* 8: 144.

body is greater than I have known him." Burghley himself, grimly clinging to life and to power, acknowledged Essex's active friendship for his son. The former had pressed the Queen that Cecil be given greater freedom of action in France, seeking to protect him against royal displeasure at disobeying her inflexible instructions.[50]

50 SP 78/41/141, 198, 229, 231, 253.

CHAPTER 26

THE FALL FROM

GRACE

For two months Essex took on the responsibilities of a first minister. He seems to have made little effort to exploit his unwonted monopoly of success. He did finally persuade the Queen to allow his mother, the Countess of Leicester, to kiss hands at court, and he did succeed in obtaining the appointment of his protégé, Willoughby, as governor of Berwick and warden of the East Marches. But Sidney's agent in London grumbled that Essex was not using his opportunity "to do good to his ancient friends." As Cecil's mission drew to its close and it became apparent that England and the States would be left alone to face the enemy, the focus of negotiations shifted to the Dutch delegation, headed by Oldenbarnevelt, which was now leaving France for England. Cecil enlisted Essex's help in the forthcoming encounter between the Queen and the Dutch envoy, so that when "Oldenbarnvelt comes you may fashion him as you will for I find he does respect you." In the same letter he asserted he had followed Essex's counsel, as well as he might.[1]

On the secretary's return to England on 1 May, his first act was to send off a confidential letter asking Essex secretly to send a coach to fetch him, declaring that he wrote as one "to whom I have professed entire love and service." He asked that his return be kept secret from everyone (except Burghley) until he was back at court.[2]

What are we to make of this episode of friendly cooperation be-

[1] SP 78/42/7.   [2] *CSPD* 5 (1598–1601): cclxvi, 117.

tween the rivals? Pretty certainly, their understanding was based
on a sober realization on both sides that a continuation of their
enmity could only damage the Queen's interests at a moment of
crisis. It required acts of good faith on both sides, although it was
Cecil who took the greater risk and Essex on whom the test of
sincerity fell most heavily. Proximity to the Queen was the talisman
of political success, and Cecil was loath to yield it to his rival; but
he had no other choice than to accept Essex's expressed goodwill at
face value. The earl, as Burghley bore witness, conducted himself
with the utmost correctness, displaying a sober responsibility much
in contrast to his recent behavior. He did all he could to secure
Cecil's reputation with the Queen and loyally backed the secretary
when the latter sought more freedom of action in dealing with
Henry. Essex for once played the role of the industrious, businesslike, and prudent councillor of state, which Bacon and others had
pressed on him in the past. He seems on the evidence also to have
acted as a man of honor towards his rival.

In the light of this episode what followed in the ensuing months
is all the sadder. With the Peace of Vervins an accomplished fact in
early May 1598, a new phase of action and of policy-making began
at the English court. The attention of the English Council was now
fastened on the proposals from the Spanish commissioners, passed
on by Henry IV, that England become a third party to the treaty of
peace. For months the pros and cons of the offer would be the subject of anxious debate within the government. Within a year there
would be an exchange of agents between London and Brussels.

All these events deeply affected the career of the Earl of Essex.
After his apprentice years on the Council he had finally been freed
in 1596 and 1597 to pursue his most clearly cherished goal, the career of a great commander. He had been able to transmute the arguments he had pressed at the Council board and in the presence
chamber into action on land and sea. He had not realized the goals
he had set himself, but hope of another chance had still existed.
Now all prospects of further action dwindled away. The pause,
which would lengthen into a virtual cessation of offensive action,
ended for the forseeable future the possibilities of another expedition. All the talk at Council was now of the likelihood of peace.
Obliquely and haltingly, the English government would grope its
way towards a settlement with Spain, although the war would continue. But it was a war with another enemy, fought not on the high

seas, the Iberian coasts, the Atlantic isles, or the West Indies, but in the bogs and woods of Ulster. For the earl all this meant that the high hopes of realizing his vocation had vanished.

The record of his activities is nearly a blank for the weeks following Cecil's return from France at the end of April. Naturally the secretary resumed control of his office and his central place in the royal counsels. One comment coming from these weeks suggested that though the earl "hath much countenance" at court, the new aspect of foreign affairs diminished his role and his influence. A clue to Essex's own feelings emerged in a letter of May (possibly intended for Henry Howard). Writing of the "general state of our affairs," he said "there is no one part of our sky clear." After a gloomy survey of the Irish rebellion, of Scottish intrigue, and of the growing hostility of the Hanse, Denmark, and Poland, he lamented the defection of France from the common cause. Worse still, at home councillors urged the abandonment of "our only constant and able friends," the States. Spain, weaker in arms than her foes, but shrewder in diplomacy, had already wooed France away and now hoped to complete her work by drawing off the English to peace, even though they knew (from intercepted letters) the Spanish resolve to extirpate religion and their faithlessness in any peace they may make. It was also about this time that he wrote his apology, defending his actions and his reputation over the past few years. Obviously he found himself very much on the defensive, his past under criticism and his future increasingly uncertain.[3]

Matters came to a head in Council discussion about the Spanish advances. The advantages and disadvantages of a treaty were argued at length, Burghley supporting peace, Essex insisting on continued war. The treasurer finally turned on the earl, saying he breathed nothing but war, slaughter, and blood. Taking out a psalm book he pointed to the verse, "Men of blood shall not live out half their days." At the same time Essex's old suspicions of the Cecils were rekindled. In a letter of late July to Cobham, Lord Grey (who had served under Essex in Ireland) complained hotly "that Essex has forced me to declare myself either his [friend] only or [else] friend to Mr. Secretary, protesting there could be no neutrality." On Grey's refusal, Essex cast him off utterly. The former

[3] Sidney Papers 2: 102–3; HMC, *Hatfield* 8: 169–70. Essex's apology became public by May 1599 (*CSPD* 5 [1598–1601]; cclxx, 203).

warned his correspondent that such behavior from this "great patron of the wars," if tolerated, would diminish the Queen's sovereignty and forfeit the respect of her nobles.[4]

The earl, set on a collision course, quarrelled not only with the
Cecils, but with the Queen herself. The date was presumably sometime in late June. (Essex attended no council meetings in July.) The
scene is described for us by Camden, who must have learned of it
from his patron, Robert Cecil. The episode occurred at a meeting
with the Queen, attended only by the earl, the lord admiral, Cecil,
and Windebank, the clerk of the signet. Under discussion was the
choice of a new Irish deputy. Burgh had died in the previous fall,
and the situation was worsening rapidly. The need for a strong
leader was apparent, but the appointment was still being regarded
from the point of view of English factional fighting. (Six months
later a cynical observer could write that the earl and the secretary
"play the table hard in the presence chamber and play so round a
game as though Ireland was to be recovered at [the game of] Irish.")
Ireland had become a graveyard of English political reputations,
and appointment as deputy was shunned as a sentence of Siberian
exile from which nominees fled in horror. Court gossip held that
Raleigh, Robert Sidney, and Christopher Blount had all refused it;
certainly Sidney's agent regarded the mere possibility "as a fair way
to thrust you to your own destruction."[5]

The Queen's choice for the job was Sir William Knollys, Essex's
uncle. His departure would deprive Essex of his principal supporter
in Council. The earl had backed Sir George Carew, a warm partisan of the Cecils and Essex's deputy in the ordnance office, in the
hope of ridding the court of him by banishment to Dublin. Failing
in his persuasions with the Queen, Essex lost his temper, turned his
back on the sovereign, and gave her a scornful look. Enraged, she
boxed his ear and bade him be gone and be hanged. The earl laid
hand on his sword and, when checked by the admiral, swore he
neither would nor could put up with such an indignity, even had it
come from Henry VIII. Flouncing off in a passion, he withdrew
from court.

How much the court world at large knew of these exact circum-

4 Camden, 555.

5 Ibid., 555–56; CSPD 4 (1595–97): cclxiv, 19; 5 (1598–1601): cclxvii, 5; Sidney
Papers 2: 96.

stances is unclear, but all, of course, observed his withdrawal from the court. Sir Edward Norris at Ostend wrote quite guilelessly that, while he was sorry for the earl's retirement from court, he knew "the end hath always been to Your Lordship's content with a greater assurance of Her Majesty's favor towards you." The earl was indeed pursuing the now familiar tactic of sulky seclusion at Wanstead. A veteran observer wrote, "He is still from court and vows not to come till sent for but none is overhasty to entreat him so it stands whose stomach comes down first." The same correspondent further reported the Queen as saying he had "played long enough upon her and she will play on him and stand on her greatness as he has done upon his stomach." This time it was the earl who yielded. News of the disaster to English arms at the Yellow Ford in Ulster gave him an excuse for offering his services: "duty was strong enough to rouse me out of my deadest melancholy." But he did not hesitate to reproach the Queen for her refusal to see him or his friends and her willingness to listen to his enemies. He justified his refusal to attend Council but offered his service to her if she would but command it.[6]

There had been earlier correspondence on the quarrel. Knollys had remonstrated with his nephew. Between the Queen's "running into her princely power" and the earl "persisting in your settled resolution," the peacemaker found his task hard. But he saw signs that the Queen wanted "to reduce you to a parley and if in substance you may have a good peace I beseech Your Lordship not to stand upon the form of treaty." (It is revealing that Knollys reverts to diplomatic terminology in describing the relations between the sovereign and her subject.) There were strong political reasons why the earl should return. Burghley had died in early August and, as Knollys emphasized, Essex's presence at the center of politics was essential when offices were to be disposed of and decisions made. The longer he stayed away, the harder the Queen's heart would grow. Essex was by now genuinely ill and the Queen "so variable and distracted in herself" that Knollys could give no advice.[7]

Another peacemaker, Lord Keeper Egerton, had also written Essex preaching a familiar homily. "The difficulty, my good lord, is to conquer yourself, which is the height of all true valor and forti-

[6] HMC *Hatfield* 8: 281, 318; *CSPD* 5 (1598–1601): cclxviii, 33, 78.
[7] Birch 2: 389, 390–91.

tude." Essex's reply was a passionate denial that the fault was his: "I can neither yield myself to be guilty, or this imputation laid upon me to be just." Subjects must abide by the laws of the natural order but princes were entitled to indulge in unreasonable and unjust behavior even towards those who had best served them. He saw his career as over; he still owed the Queen his duty; he would serve her as a clerk, but not as a villein or a slave. There was a final outburst: "What, cannot princes err? Cannot subjects receive wrong? I have received wrong and feel it." His friends "unadvisedly divulged" these effusions.[8] However, the storm finally subsided; the earl patched together an apology and the Queen accepted it. There may have been some reconciliation with Cecil. Essex was back in Council by mid-September after an absence of some twelve weeks and doing routine business with the secretary. Court gossip regarded their friendly relations as hollow.[9]

The death of Burghley had vacated the remunerative and much coveted mastership of the wards, an office "which in a credulous manner he [Essex] had promised to himself."[10] There were again rumors of new Privy Councillors, but it was thought that the impossibility of pleasing both sides ruled out any present decision. In appearance Essex had repeated his past successes. He had faced down the Queen and won re-admittance to favor, but in fact there were many differences in this episode. It had begun, not with a complaint of the earl about an alleged slight to his dignity, but with a direct insult to the Queen. If we are to believe Camden, Essex, despite all his protestations, was at fault and indeed guilty of gross bad behavior. Nor was it the Queen who had given way first; the earl had made the first advance. There had been no bauble to soothe his vanity, like the ordnance or the marshalship. Nor had there been any attempt to patch up a new entente with Robert Cecil, as there had been in previous instances.

With the proposed peace the first item on the agenda of government, the secretary had unquestioned mastery in the royal counsels. Essex's role as councillor was cast into discard. His career had come upon the shallows, but most important of all was the changed re-

---

[8] *Ibid.*, 384–85, dated 10/15/98, 386–88; see Lansdowne Ms. 87, fol. 52, for origin; also Devereux 1: 499–502; Camden, 555–56.

[9] HMC, *Hatfield* 8: 332, 338, 344, 390; Camden, 555–56; *CSPD* 5 (1598–1601); cclxviii, 56, 71, 75, 111; cclxx, 28.

[10] Camden, 570.

lationship with the Queen. The spell he had cast for so long had lost its potency and the favor he had always been able to count on, however wayward his course, was no longer a certainty.[11]

The sequence of events that culminated in the summer of 1598 went back to 1596, to the first of Essex's two great naval expeditions. He was now able to play the role for which he had so ardently longed. The experience was a disillusioning one. His influence with the Queen had secured him high command, but it was a command that had to be shared with others, who, in vital decisions, could and did gainsay him. Second, his royal patroness, far from appreciating his achievement, cast aspersions on it. Essex was brought reluctantly to realize that his conception of grand strategy and the Queen's were far apart. She was prepared to provide the means to cripple Spanish invasion preparations, or to make a grab for the treasure fleet, but she had no intention of backing his grander schemes of offense. At the very moment when his popular reputation at home and abroad was at its height, the Queen was coldly critical, full of nagging complaint, while he felt himself surrounded by a cloud of envy and slander.

Moreover, from the fall of 1596 onward he stood in open conflict with the Cecils and their allies on the Council. Reconciliations were patched together, but these were no more than truces in a continuing and open rivalry. The last of these, in the spring of 1598, endured as long as the English were seeking to keep the French from making peace with Spain. Once the Treaty of Vervins was signed, the rivals parted ways as the Cecils opted for negotiation with Spain while Essex inveighed against any dialogue with the enemy. Isolated in Council, he saw his leverage with the Queen dwindling and his hopes for a martial career extinguished. Very much the odd man out, he now fell prey to the underlying tensions of his own unstable character.

He had always shown a disposition to extravagant self-pity and susceptibility to a persecution complex. Only his repeated successes in facing down the Queen and bending her will to his had checked these tendencies. Now, when she turned on him in sharp disapproval of his actions, the underlying disposition of his personality reappeared. Initially his resentments were directed against those councillors who he believed were poisoning her mind against him.

[11] *CSPD* 5 (1598–1601): cclxviii, 33, 71, 87, 108; HMC, *Hatfield* 8: 318.

But the Queen came in for her share of blame simply by listening to them. Ultimately, in the famous scene of the summer of 1598, the dam of restraint broke and Essex loosed his fury on his sovereign.

The tensions of their relationship were of long standing. It had always rested on an uneasy basis. In the other closest relationships of the Queen's life—those with Burghley, Leicester, and Hatton—there had been an element of equality. That with Burghley had been a collegial one, resting on mutual trust and respect and, on his side, on a profound sense of deference for her royal office. Much the same was true of Hatton. Elizabeth and Leicester had once seemed about to be husband and wife, and, although that passion had cooled, their relations were those of two adults of the same age whose intimacy, begun in their youth, had matured with the years. However, the Queen's relationship with Essex—a man more than thirty years her junior—had begun late in her life and had always been one of inequality. Elizabeth's attitude had been at least half maternal while the earl's had been that of a petted child, confident that his charms would win whatever it was he desired. Essex had always strained at the tether by which this pseudo-filial status bound him. As he grew in ambition and in experience he chafed more and more at the royal indecision that hamstrung his best efforts. For him the royal mystique that enthralled Burghley had less power. Ultimately the strain was too great and the force of his pent-up frustration was discharged at the monarch herself.

But while the court was rent by these animosities, the problem that had precipitated Essex's original outburst grew in magnitude and intensity. In August the English had suffered a crushing defeat in Ireland; it was imperative that a new lord deputy be appointed and dispatched with powerful forces. As early as the beginning of November rumors that Essex would go to Ireland (as lieutenant and with Mountjoy as his deputy) had begun to circulate. They continued during the following weeks. Questions as to terms, the number of troops, support, and finance were all in debate. The first firm evidence of the appointment comes with a warrant of 23 December for £1,200 to raise 400 horse for Irish service. Lists of noblemen and gentlemen who would accompany Essex circulated, but matters remained in flux. Not until 1 March was a privy seal loan for the Irish service issued, by which time troops were already moving to the rendezvous for embarkation. Part of the problem was the personal debts of Essex and his father (as well as those of the crown to Earl Walter); this problem was finally settled and the small balance owed to the treasury cancelled. On 12 April the commission for the earl as lieutenant and general in Ireland was finally issued.[12]

Court gossip and a few official documents give us a bare outline of the process by which this appointment came about. Camden provides his version of the inside story, according to which the Council was disposed to name Mountjoy to the onerous Irish deputyship. But Essex obstinately opposed the proposal, arguing the scant military experience of the young lord (a mere company commander on the Continent), his mean estate, his lack of followers, and a bookish bent that ill consorted with the duties of the field. To other names he raised similar objections, insisting that only "some prime man of the nobility," with honor and state, respected by the soldiery and previously general of an army, would meet the requirements of the office. To the Council it was a clear case of self-nomination. His adversaries gave a very sinister interpretation to his motive. As they saw it, what he wanted was simply command of an army, "to engage the sword-men to him. Yea, so eager was he about the business that divers feared he was hatching some dangerous design."[13]

However, the same source avers that none were more eager for the appointment than the earl's enemies. Those in the court "who would rather have his room than his company cunningly aggravated and heightened and spurred him forward who was running before." Their insinuations that he had sinister plots afoot were given plausibility when his followers foolishly boasted of the earl's royal lineage, hinting that as a descendant of Edward III (through his ancestress Cicely Bourchier) he had a better claim to the succession than any other competitor. These "subtle and close" enemies under a show of friendship did further damage to the earl's reputation by raising too-high expectations in the popular mind, hoping his own ardor would be his undoing. There was no easier way to ruin a man than to thrust him to a task for which he was unfit. The earl, in Camden's view, either could not or would not perceive these arts.

What little we know from Essex's own words in this time tells a

---

[12] *CSPD* 5 (1598–1601): cclxviii, 108, 115; cclxix, 6, 19, 21 (p. 136), 49; cclxx, 52, 57, 168. Note the cryptic letter of Hunsdon to Cecil, 3/28/99 (*Ibid.*, 66). For the Irish debt, see PRO C.66/1497 mm. 1–3.

[13] Camden, 567–69.

somewhat different story. Our only evidence consists of two letters written at the turn of the new year 1599. To Fulke Greville he wrote almost despairingly. The Queen had laid upon him the heavy burden of Ireland but she withheld her confidence and favor, listening instead to his enemies' reports. He averred that it was not the love of the multitude or self-glorification that he sought, but "either to be valued by her above them that are of no value or to forget the world and be forgotten by it." In a longer letter to another confidant, Lord Willoughby, he began with the wry comment that Willoughby had a patron "that can procure nothing for himself or for any of his friends but once a year a breakneck employment." For himself he had no choice but to go to Ireland. "The Queen had irrevocably decreed it; the Council do passionately urge it; and I am tied by my own reputation to use no tergiversation." The last clause gets to the heart of the matter. If Ireland were lost and he, England's premier soldier, had refused his services at such a moment, not only would he be blamed but his reputation would be irreparably damaged. He was bound by his own past achievements.[14]

Essex went on in his letter to describe the political risks of absence and—a sideswipe at the Queen—the construction of princes who find *magna fama* more dangerous than *mala fama* and are contemptuous of subjects' successes. He was pessimistic about the chance of war: disease and famine were enemies enough without the rebels, whose successes emboldened them to more efforts. But he was determined to do his best even "when the state that set me out must conspire with the enemy against me." Failure would not be excused; success would only arouse envy. "The court is the center; but methinks it is the fairer choice to command armies than honor." Bacon, on the other hand, urged the appointment on Essex as a great opportunity for an act of statesmanship in ending the disorders in Ireland. Sir Francis urged the earl to a policy of conciliation towards Tyrone and intimated that he alone could woo the Irish chief.[15]

What emerges from these tortured epistles is first of all Essex's deep alienation from the Queen; the favorite has been transformed into an outcast who is treated with suspicion and dislike. At the same time he cannot refuse the proffered cup, however bitter the draft. The prisoner of his own reputation, he cannot desert in this

---

[14] HMC, *Hatfield* 9: 4, 9–11.   [15] BL, Harleian Ms. 4761, 156–71.

hour of need. The contrast between his mood now and that on the eve of his previous commands is striking. Then he set out full of confidence with a sense of high destiny; now he almost despairs before he even leaves England. In part it was no doubt a sober sense of the harsh realities of the Irish command—a record of English failure, guerrilla warfare in a forbidding countryside, dependence upon uncertain supplies from home. More daunting still was the sense that there was no glory to be won, no foreign conquest, no dazzling success against the greatest power in Europe, but merely the suppression by slow, tenacious attrition of a rebel Celtic chieftain. Finally there was the chilling realization that he had lost the silken clue that hitherto had always led back to the certain favor of his royal protectress.

What about the government that sent him out on this unpromising adventure? In Camden's view the appointment was a put-up job. The earl's opponents, playing on his own ambition, deliberately pushed him into a role that would only bring about his ruin. We can give due weight to Camden's report as to the motives of many at court. But the story is surely somewhat more complex. Essex was given a larger army by far than any of his predecessors and generous back-up support. It was clearly an all-out attempt to break the back of the rebellion, and he was the obvious choice as supreme commander. As in Leicester's case in 1585, the gravity of the crisis demanded the leadership of a great nobleman and, equally important, the best military talent available. From the official point of view, who but Essex could fill these requirements?

The Queen and the Council were caught between two equally unpalatable choices. Ireland's needs brooked no further delay, and Essex was the only plausible commander. He was, however, at the height of a popularity that no subject had enjoyed in Tudor times; he had a substantial following among the younger aristocracy, hankering for military careers, and was the patron of the officer corps throughout the armed forces. His hostility towards Cecil and his allies was patent. The Queen was now forced to realize that she had made a major political miscalculation, the gravest failure of judgment of the whole reign. Her belief that she could harness and drive Essex and Robert Cecil in a tractable team as she had harnessed Leicester and Burghley had over the long term been ill-founded. The consequences of this miscalculation now placed at risk her very government. She now had to take the gamble that the habits of loyalty and obedience to her would be stronger than Essex's hatred for the secretary.

The dangers were real. The drift of Essex's thinking well before he went to Ireland is revealed to us by his actions after he was appointed earl marshal. He set about a systematic search for the precedents relevant to the office and to the constableship, a second office to which it was suggested he was entitled by descent. This second great office had a tainted reputation, for it had been held that the constable could arrest the King. The steward and the constable together had led the baronial revolt against Edward II, and their opposition was justified in the medieval tract *Modus Tenendi Parliamentum*. More recently the Tudor pamphleteers Starkey and Ponet had emphasized the power of the constable to check royal misuse of power, even to the imprisonment of the ruler. The implications of all this for the contemporary scene hardly need explication.[16]

We know also, as contemporaries came to know in 1601, that the earl did seriously consider making use of the army to coerce the court. After he returned to Dublin from his southern expedition and a few days before he moved against Tyrone, he summoned Southampton, his protégé, and Sir Christopher Blount, his father-in-law, and announced that he must go to England; doubting the power of his enemies, he proposed to take part of the army with him to Wales. Once established there, he would send for more men and then march on London, confident that he could impose whatever conditions he wished. The two confidants urgently begged him to desist from this scheme. If he must go, he should take no more than an entourage large enough to guarantee his freedom from arrest.[17] In the end, as we know, he did nothing.

Whether any inkling of this reached the court, we cannot know. There was indeed a large-scale mobilization at sea and on land, commanded by Lord Admiral Nottingham, just at the time Essex was considering this scheme. It was occasioned by reports of major

---

[16] For this paragraph, I am indebted to Professor Richard McCoy, who permitted me to see his then-unpublished manuscript, "The Rites of Knighthood: The Literature and Politics of Elizabethan Chivalry." See *The Rites of Knighthood* (Berkeley and Los Angeles, 1989), chap. 4.

[17] *Correspondence of King James VI of Scotland with Sir Robert Cecil and Others in England*, ed. John Bruce, Camden Soc. 78 (1861), 91–100; HMC, *Hatfield* 11: 72–73.

Spanish naval concentrations (both ships and galleys) at the Groyne, which were expected to make for Brest and then land either in Kent or in the Thames valley. Popular opinion held that this was a mere pretense and that the mobilization was intended "to show some that are absent that others can be followed as well as they and military service directed as if they were present."

There was certainly a genuine invasion scare, based on extensive although conflicting reports from many sources. Nottingham's commission did give him power to resist threats and conspiracies against Her Majesty and her government as well as resist foreign invasion. There were to be two armies, one to repel invasion, the other to guard the Queen. The measures taken in London itself suggest a local rather than a foreign threat. Watch was kept every night; householders were ordered to burn candles in their windows; chains were stretched across the streets.[18] However, the mobilization almost certainly reflected the government's perception of a real external threat; a substantial naval force was sent to sea. (One by-product of this naval mobilization, intentional or not, was to deny Essex the ships he needed for Lough Foyle.) But it is also clear that there was widespread unease as to the intentions of the Earl of Essex. Camden quotes the Queen as saying that "he [Essex] had somewhat else in his mind than to do his prince service in Ireland (I know not on what jealousy and suspicion)."[19] There can be little doubt that the months when the earl had an army at his disposal were a time of grave anxieties for his opponents in the Council. During those weeks the civil peace of the realm hung in the balance, at the mercy of the uncertain impulses of the tormented nobleman at Dublin.

The course of events that followed his arrival in Ireland is recounted in Chapter 20. The unfolding acts of the drama were of a piece with the prologue acted out in England before Essex's departure. His almost paranoid conviction that he was being stabbed in the back by his enemies at home was matched by the Queen's sharp reprimands for his actions and sour rebukes for his state of mind. The fateful meeting with Tyrone and the earl's hasty return abruptly ended his last great essay in high politics.

[18] For the invasion scare, see *CSPD* 5 (1598–1601): cclxxii, 1–68; for the popular belief, see *ibid.*, 68 (Chamberlain to Carlton), and John Stow, *Annales of England* (London, 1605), 1309–10.

[19] Camden, 572.

From our perspective it is clear that Essex's political career ended with his detention the day of his arrival at court. From contemporaries' point of view, however, this was not so obvious. After all, the favorite had surmounted a whole series of earlier clashes with his royal patroness and, at least until the past year, had seemed impervious to the arrows shot by his opponents. For at least a year after his return, rumor and speculation hinted at the earl's recall to the court world, if not to his former eminence; it was not until the Queen's refusal to renew the sweet wines customs lease that his permanent exclusion from public life was evident to all.

Indeed, his position during the intervening months was anomalous, one for which there was uncertain precedent. Barring the unusual circumstances of Edward VI's reign, the last downfall of a major political figure had been in the Queen's father's time; but Wolsey and Cromwell had been great ministers, not favorites. Their downfall had in each case marked a revolution in court politics and sharp changes in policy. Wolsey's unwillingness to accept his fate and his persistent plotting to recover power had proved how dangerous the fallen minister could be and sealed his own fate. In Cromwell's case his enemies took no chances; he went from the council chamber to the Tower to the block at a headlong pace.

With Essex the case was different; it was his own miscalculated actions rather than his enemies' assault that brought him down. The accusations against him (and the ensuing condemnation) were not for treasonable actions, but for incompetence and for disobedience. He could hardly be brought to the block for such actions. Second, he was not an isolated court politician but a nobleman with great popular renown and a potential following, in the army, possibly in the City, and among many members of the nobility and gentry. Last, it might be supposed that in the Queen's heart there was still some residue of the affection with which she had regarded him for more than a decade. It might not be sufficient to restore him to his former eminence but (and this was the view of an observer as well placed as Mountjoy) it might serve to preserve his dignity.

The Queen's action in the months following his return from Ireland bore out some of these speculations. He was held in confinement "yet not in any prison, lest she might seem to cut off all hope of her former favor, but in the Lord Keeper's house."[20] Later he was allowed to return to his own residence, but still under house arrest. After some months of this genteel imprisonment the earl was brought, not to trial, but to a hearing before a body consisting of the Council, four earls, two barons, and four judges. The charges brought against him were a rather curious miscellany.[21] Alongside allegations of serious incompetence, such as the ill-advised expedition into Munster and the neglect of the Ulster front, he was accused of disobedience of royal orders in appointing Southampton general of the horse and of making too many knights. A graver charge arose from his conference with Tyrone, "which neither beseemed the Queen's Majesty nor the dignity of a Lord Deputy and which was the more suspicious, because it was in private." His accusers also cited letters written a year or two earlier using phrases uncomplimentary to the Queen: "Cannot princes err? Can they not wrong their subjects?" The earl's perseverance in defending his actions and in refusing unconditional submission led to a rebuke by the lord keeper and to a sentence that suspended him from all his offices (Privy Councillor, earl marshal, master of the ordnance) except the mastership of the horse, while placing him in custody during the royal pleasure.

In August 1600 Essex was released from custody and restored to liberty (albeit banned from the court). Prevailing court opinion continued to expect at least a partial restoration of his fortunes. The Queen's mildness of disposition, her steadfast loyalty to her servants, Devereux's nobility of descent, his abilities as a general, and his popularity at home were all adduced as reasons for such a view. Nor were his adversaries such deadly foes as to desire his utter ruin. To them it was sufficient that his greatness was humbled. Royal favor was after all an incalculable factor, and if in its rolling cycles Essex once again were to revolve towards the top, it was well not to risk irreparable rupture. Some thought that the honorable exile of a foreign embassy might serve until "fair weather should dispell these clouds and storms"; others held that retirement to a "private and contemplative life" might be the recipe "that his soul might seem to ascend by the same degrees by which his fortune had descended."[22]

[20] *Ibid.*, 574.   [21] *Ibid.*, 597–98.
[22] For this paragraph, see *ibid.*, 599–601.

These hopes and speculations, begotten of past experience, were belied by the present behavior of the Queen. Although she was willing to make small concessions to the earl's comfort and to give occasional halfhearted tokens of a softening attitude, her basic stance was one of relentless hostility to the late favorite. The distribution of libels in his behalf and the appearance in print of his *Apology* further exacerbated her bitterness.[23]

The earl remained in the country, appropriately submissive in his demeanor; he continued to solicit the Queen's renewed favor in letters of humble appeal. The real test of royal intentions came in the autumn of 1600, when the lease of the sweet wines, granted Essex in 1590, required renewal. By this time the accumulated long-term debt of the earl to his private creditors was at least £10,495 (and this omitted what he owed the moneylender Peter Van Lore) while his short-term debts, demanding immediate payment, totalled £5,635.[24] Continuance of the lease was essential to Essex's financial survival. More important, the royal decision would give a definitive signal as to his future fate. The Queen's answer to his appeal was brutally clear. In her words, "an unruly horse must be abated of his provender, that he may be the easilier and better managed." She commended the physicians' aphorism, "corrupt bodies, the more you feed them, the more hurt you do them."[25]

Her refusal ended an interval of what must have been for Essex sheer torment and for the whole court troubling uncertainty. Retrospectively we can see that Essex's career had been fatally ruptured as long ago as the scene in the summer of 1598. Elizabeth had advanced her young favorite initially in the expectation that he would play, allowing the difference in age, the same role as Leicester (or Hatton). In return for the favors that she heaped on him she expected absolute submission to the royal will. He was expected to dance attendance on her, spending most of his time at court and fitting into the routines of the court world. It was presumed that he would feed her vanity with the usual diet of flattery and the pleasing fiction of a pseudo-romance.

But, as we have seen, Essex was cast in a different mold from the older generation of courtiers; his ambitions were not so much political as martial. Reluctantly the Queen had given him his rein and

---

[23] HMC, *De L'Isle and Dudley*, 435, 459, 461.   [24] HMC, *Hatfield* 10: 348.
[25] Camden, 603.

allowed him to disport himself first in France and then, later in the decade, at sea. She had been surprisingly tolerant of his tantrums and sulks and given him far more freedom than she had conceded to his predecessors. But, however slack the rein, it was not to be loosed altogether; he had to acknowledge the ultimate inequality of their relationship. When he set his will against hers in the council chamber and in his continuing unrepentant assertion of his own dignity, he broke the fundamental rule of their relationship, and the bonds in which he had held her firm were severed forever, to be replaced by unremitting hostility. The inopportune crisis in Ireland had prolonged his political career, but it thrust upon him the kind of inglorious task for which his slender military talents were least suited. It is doubtful that under the best of conditions he could have sustained the slow, grinding drudgery of the kind of war that Mountjoy successfully fought. The poisoned relationship between sovereign and general almost guaranteed the failure of the enterprise.

The Queen's angry response to his failure left Essex in an impossible position. He was condemned not for any offense known to the law but for incompetence and failure to obey royal commands. His punishment was also anomalous banishment from the court, which meant not only political oblivion but also a degradation from the normal privileges of his order. The very irregularity of the proceedings emphasized that his punishment was an act of personal vindictiveness of the Queen rather than a formal condemnation by the state. It was meant to humiliate him in the most painful and public way. The best he could hope for was a grudging permission to retire into decent obscurity. With her refusal to renew the wine farm, even that was denied; the last glimmer of hope vanished, and he was inexorably cast into outer darkness, leaving him with little alternative but rebellion. Essex no doubt believed Elizabeth's decision was dictated by his rivals in the court. But Elizabeth, unlike her father, seldom yielded to presure from those around her, and the evidence before us suggests that it was the Queen's own bitter feelings that swayed her. Even a far less unstable personality than Essex's would have found the total humiliation of his position unendurable. Given the earl's paranoid sensibilities, the course of action that he followed was predictable. In February 1601—depressed and half-mad, obsessed with a persecution mania, fearing for his life— Essex led a tiny band of followers in a pathetic attempt to storm the court. Captured, tried, and condemned, he went swiftly to the block. No royal hesitation, such as had delayed the death of the Duke of Norfolk in 1572, gave him so much as an extra day of life.[26]

The drama that had begun a dozen or more years ago had played itself out. The Queen had made the most important misjudgment of her career. She had thought she had found in Robert Devereux a successor to the dead Leicester with whom she could pretend to renew her youth in another courtier's game of adored mistress and devoted suitor. But Essex was not to be tamed to his role and in the end the frustration of his martial ambitions led him to revolt against the restraints of his situation. This relationship was, by its very nature, fraught with danger to the polity. The problem was compounded when it became intertwined with the aspirations of the house of Cecil. Burghley's hopes of seeing his promising son step into his shoes, clouded by the rise of the new favorite, led to a rivalry that renewed the tensions of an earlier generation, when the elder Cecil had vied with Essex's stepfather for the royal confidence. Burghley and his son were quick to realize that an open challenge would only arouse royal displeasure to their own disadvantage. They played a waiting game, conciliating Essex whenever possible and exploiting the immense political credit that Burghley had built up with the Queen.

Their goal was to obtain for the son, on the death of his father, succession to the post of first councillor. The Cecils could not breathe easy until Robert Cecil's appointment as secretary made clear that he was no longer his father's mere shadow but now stood on his own footing with the Queen. The Cecil interest was secured beyond Burghley's lifetime and as long as Elizabeth lived. Robert Cecil now stood on terms of equality with the favorite. This relative stability was destroyed by Essex's own actions. When the earl, faced by the extinction of his hopes of martial glory, lost his self-control, he became a loose cannon that threatened the ship of state. His growing paranoia led him to view Cecil not only as a personal enemy but also as an evil counsellor who was leading the Queen dangerously astray. Under these circumstances Cecil was forced, in self-defense, into a head-on collision. However, it was not Cecil's

---

[26] See Lacey Baldwin Smith, *Treason in Tudor England* (London, 1986), and Mervyn James, "At a Crossroad of the Political Culture: the Essex Revolt, 1601," in his *Society, Politics and Culture* (Cambridge 1986), 416–65.

hostility that broke the earl's career, but the actions of Essex himself. The secretary owed his dominating position in the Council after 1598 less to his own skill in opposing Essex than to the latter's fatal blunders. Yet, even allowing for the role of Essex's own actions in all that happened, it was the Queen's decision that ultimately drove him to revolt.

To understand fully the puzzle that was the last fatal phase of Essex's career, we need to fit in one more piece. Since the late 1580's James VI had gradually emerged as that rising sun so dreaded by Elizabeth, and his rays had become increasingly visible in the English political landscape. Peter Wentworth, in his indiscreet attempt to press the succession issue in 1593, had openly named the Scottish king as most fit to succeed the Queen.[27] None would be so bold as to agree openly, but many must have privately shared his views. English politicians could hardly leave the Scottish king out of their calculations, but the Queen's ironclad refusal to broach the succession issue meant that they dared not make any public gesture towards him. Characteristically Essex, in his willful disregard of the common rules of politics, made overtures to the Scottish monarch as early as 1589.[28] They came to nothing at the time, but in the course of the 1590's Essex, alone among the great nobles, set out to woo James.

Once Essex set about building up a network of intelligence outside the realm, lines of communication were opened up with the Scottish court and with James himself. In 1593 Anthony Bacon, through the intermediation of David Foulis and later the Earl of Mar, had established contact with the Scottish monarch.[29] Fragments of the ensuing correspondence remain. At the same time Bacon made use of James Hudson, who also served the government as intelligencer in Edinburgh.[30] In a letter that the king wrote directly to Essex in 1594, he apologized for his long silence, excusing himself "because of the wrong you received there through."[31] Now he was sending two ambassadors whom he recommended to Essex, asking his support with the Queen to move her against those who preferred their own interests to hers. It may have been in response

[27] J. E. Neale, *Elizabeth I and Her Parliaments*, 1584–1601 (London, 1957), 262–63.

[28] HMC, *Hatfield* 3: 434–43.

[29] Birch 1: 162–63, 178.   [30] *Ibid.*, 128.

[31] *Ibid.*, 175.

to this letter that Essex replied with a fulsome declaration of loyalty to the King, in which he asserted that his countrymen "jointly united their hopes in Your Majesty's noble person as the only center wherein our rest or happiness consists."[32] The King, in another letter of 1594, says of Essex that he is glad to have in him another Sir Philip Sidney. He asks for continuance of the earl's affection and promises reward in proper time and place.[33] Essex's role as James's confidant was public. In 1598 the French ambassador could refer to the earl as the King's trusted intermediary at the English court.[34]

Against this harmonious strain of mutual admiration, there was an obbligato of complaint against the Cecils. Although James had once spoken of Burghley as the "fair and gravest" councillor in Europe, by the early 1590's he had come to regard the Cecils with little favor.[35] He blamed the lord treasurer for the delays in payment of his pension and ascribed to him and his son the English backing for Bothwell.[36] In 1593 James absolved Elizabeth of complicity with Bothwell, "but he could not acquit so clearly some of your councillors." In the following year a Scottish observer wrote, "I find a violent impression in His Majesty of the professed evil will of Burghley and Robert Cecil towards him," augmented by revelations of their dealings with Bothwell. Robert Cecil's interview with Bothwell at Rouen in 1598 only confirmed the royal dislike and distrust. The Cecils' patronage of John Colville, an erstwhile Scottish agent but now *persona non grata* at Edinburgh, also irritated James. These impressions of the King persisted into the late 1590's and, had the Queen died during these years, the position of the Cecils in the new court would have been very uncertain. When the lord treasurer died, it was said in Edinburgh that "nothing but their greatest unfriend is gone."[37]

When Essex's favor at court began to wane, it was towards Scotland that he turned his attention, possibly even before he went to Ireland.[38] During his stay there, as we have seen, he broached to

[32] *Ibid.*, 176, undated. [33] Ibid., 183.

[34] PRO 31/3/29: 12/12/98: 31/12/30: 2/19/99; Boissise, 480–83.

[35] Stafford, 49.

[36] Birch 1: 186–87, 229–30; *CSPSc* 11 (1593–95): 171–72, 369, 403, 492–93; 12 (1595–97): 349; 13 (1) (1597–1603): 259.

[37] *CSPSc* 11: 171–72, 369, 403, 492–93; 12: 307; 13, pt. 1: 188, 211, 259, 263, 272, 544–54, 555–56; Stafford, 201.

[38] See Blount's declaration in HMC, *Hatfield* 11: 47–49.

Southampton and Blount a scheme for taking part of his army to Milford Haven for a march on London. They both advised against it, and he abandoned the idea.[39] After Essex's return and during his confinement, however, Mountjoy and Southampton had conferred. The former, fearing Essex's utter ruin, had sent a messenger to the King of Scots, warning James that, unless the earl was saved, the government would be in the hands of the King's enemies, and offering his services. The royal reply was generally although rather vaguely encouraging, but asked for specifics. Mountjoy persisted and just before departing for Dublin offered to assist the King with the Irish army. James gave his general approval to some such scheme but in fact took no action. Apparently the conspirators hoped he would either enter England or at the least make a demonstration on the Borders. The Scottish reponse was favorable, but so dilatory that it reached Mountjoy in Ireland at a time when the troops he proposed to use (those destined for Lough Foyle) had already sailed for that destination. Essex himself, now drawn into the project, pressed Mountjoy to move on his own, bringing his forces to England. The latter resolutely rejected this scheme, refusing to act without the backing of "one who had interest in the succession." The earl's life, the deputy believed, was safe, and he was not prepared to take up arms merely to restore his fortunes. Essex then proposed that Mountjoy write "a letter of complaint of the misgovernment of the state," summoning the earl to redress it. This too the deputy rejected. His counsel to his erstwhile friend was to seek reconciliation with the Queen, resigning himself to a lesser role.[40]

Essex himself may have been in touch with the King during the two years before the uprising; so his secretary, Cuffe, averred. Certainly a more direct attempt to involve James was made on the eve of the uprising, when Essex wrote to the King asking him to send a special ambassador, fully in the royal confidence. For him Essex prepared a dossier. In this document he urged James to declare his right to the crown because "some very gracious with Her Majesty, being of extraordinary power and malice" would take advantage of the uncertainties of the succession to the ruin of the realm. He

[39] *A Complete Collection of State Trials*, comp. William Cobbett et al. (42 vols., London, 1816–98) 1: 1414; see also Camden, 575, 629; *Correspondence*, 107–8.

[40] *Correspondence*: confessions of Danvers (100–7), Southampton (96–100), Cuffe (86).

backed this assertion by pointing to the concentration of power in the hands of men hostile to the King's claims—Raleigh in the West Country, Cobham in Kent, the second Lord Burghley as lord president of the North, Carew in Ireland. All were closely tied to Cecil, who also dominated the lord treasurer (Buckhurst) and the lord admiral (Nottingham). These men, Essex asserted, were pressing the cause of the Spanish infanta; indeed one (Cecil) had declared her title better than any other competitor's. They sought peace with Spain, not for its own sake, but to advance their own interests, and they consorted with papists.[41]

This document was never delivered since, by the time Mar, James's ambassador, reached London, Essex was dead. Mar did, however, carry a set of instructions from his royal master.[42] He was to depend on the advice of "friends." If they were opposed to making a move, the ambassador should follow their counsel; but if they thought Scots participation, "your 'kything' [involvement] in it," would do good, "stand not upon terms and I shall avow you bravely." If it was lack of a head to enter into open action, let them be assured he would supply that place. But the King foresaw that the things might be "past all redding" before Mar arrived. In that case the ambassador was to busy himself building a party of support.

In a later instruction written after the event, the King gave further directions for finding out the state of discontent, whether it be with the present minister or with the regime at large. He was to make contacts in the City, with the lieutenant of the Tower, with the fleet, and with nobles and gentry. Secretary Cecil, "who is king there in effect," was to be alternately wooed with promises or threatened with vengeance "when the chance shall turn."[43]

James had for half a decade looked on Essex as his best supporter in England; the latter's expulsion from the court after his return from Ireland left him with difficult options. Cecil now enjoyed a monopoly of Elizabeth's favor, but James, like the English politicians, could not tell which way the cards would fall if Essex put fortune to the test; hence he was willing to play with fire. Presumably if Mountjoy had turned words into deeds, James would at the least have been ready to take advantage of the crisis that would have

[41] *Ibid.*, 81–84.   [42] Birch 2: 510.
[43] *Ibid.*, 511–13.

ensued. Whether he would have taken the plunge of abetting a coup against Elizabeth, one can only speculate, but he could not have avoided involvement one way or the other. Essex's ultimate failure of nerve spared him the decision.

Clearly, the government had reason to fear the fallen earl. Well before his fall, while he was still in Ireland, he had toyed with the idea of a coup and had not hesitated to exploit his popularity at the Scottish court for assistance in such a move. Relying on past friendship, he had sought to suborn Mountjoy's allegiance and, in his last desperate ploy, he had tried to invoke Scottish invasion. Uncertain of himself, he had up to the very end looked to others to take the lead in action, depending on their willingness to take large risks for his sake. Their coolness to an attempt on the court without Scottish backing and James's wary hesitations had kept him back. When he finally moved, it was the act of an ill-counselled, ill-informed, and isolated figure. His only followers were his immediate entourage, men whose fortunes depended entirely on his, and a handful of callow noblemen, impatient for adventure and promotion. The anticipated dividends of Essex's popularity, particularly in the capital, proved the merest mirage. Still, the outcome was a close thing. Had Mountjoy been less loyal or King James less cautious, the closing phase of the Queen's reign might have been clouded by violence and bloodshed. Elizabeth was fortunate that the only man who had the potential to raise a serious threat to her regime lacked the will-power to draw together the elements of combustion, let alone to fan them into a blaze.

RETROSPECTIVE

ESSEX'S RETURN from Ireland proved a landmark in the history of the reign. He was now driven from the political stage, although he remained a haunting presence in the wings until the fateful explosion of February 1601, and contemporaries continued to speculate on his return to favor. It was not to be; he had ceased utterly to influence the course of events. In consequence the rage of faction that had agitated English politics since the beginning of the decade had finally died away. A sole minister, Robert Cecil, held the stage without a rival to contest his influence.

There was an even more profound alteration. For half a century, since the death of Henry VIII, the rulers of England had found themselves driven by events. This was a dramatic reversal of earlier experience. Henry had been the master of his world and by his "mere will and motion" had made war and peace at his pleasure. When he determined to wrench his realm from the body of Catholic Christendom, no one could gainsay him. His successors, caught up in the consequences of his willful acts, had lost that freedom of action. Now the initiative to act lay with others—Continental monarchs (or their rebellious subjects), Irish chieftains, and Scottish nobles. And at home it was reform-minded clergy and their aristocratic patrons who took the lead in pressing for change. The Queen had been able to do little but react defensively to these unremitting pressures. Elizabeth, from the beginning of her reign, had been constantly forced against her will into making risky and unpalatable decisions. French intervention in Scotland, the civil wars in France itself, the rising in the Low Countries, and finally an unwanted war had forced her into a long series of actions that she would willingly have avoided. Even more irksome were the inexorable pressures exerted by her troublesome second kingdom. For decades she had been urged by the French, the Dutch, her council at Dublin, or her ministers at home to some new and perilous enterprise.

Now, for the first time in her reign, she was free from the most pressing of these demands. Domestic politics, rent for a decade by the rivalry of the Cecils and Essex, had fallen quiet. Robert Cecil, accorded full royal confidence, was a commanding presence in the Council. On the Continent the existence of a resurgent France preoccupied Spanish policy-making. In the Low Countries the English had subsided into a partnership with the States-General, who were now assured, if not of further conquest, at least of survival. The war at sea was a draw; neither side was prepared to risk another maritime defeat. The negotiations for peace trailed on uncertainly but without any compelling urgency. The last great challenge of the war came with the Kinsale expedition, but the English government was prepared for this; their luck held and the threat was quickly liquidated. None of this required much decision-making from the Queen. She needed only to confirm the measures that Cecil set in motion and Mountjoy executed.

At the same time her councillors and her courtiers were shifting their attention, looking less to the favors Elizabeth could bestow, and more and more to a future when her successor would be the source of bounty. Cecil moved with speed to mend his fences north of the border. Through the medium of Lord Henry Howard he established regular communication with the King of Scotland.[1] This was all the easier because of the uncontested authority he now enjoyed in the English court, a fact that James fully appreciated, referring to him as "Mr. Secretary who is king there in effect.[2]

This does not, of course, suggest that the Queen was any less in command of affairs. But the urgency of earlier years was relaxed, and she could fall back on the inertial role she had always preferred. Squabbles with Henry IV over French or English privateering were matters that were irritating but could be dealt with in routine diplomatic exchanges. In Ireland she could scold Mountjoy for waste and corruption in his administration, but the campaign had its own impetus that required little input from the Queen. In the last months of her life a major decision as to Tyrone's future loomed, but Elizabeth did not live to make it. The needs of Ostend required some additional effort on the Continent but no new turn in policy. All in all, there was the sense of a regime that had achieved its major aims and was resting on its oars, even drifting a little, while the political world nervously awaited the great change that could not be long in coming.

That change did come, after Elizabeth's brief illness, in March

---

[1] *Correspondence.*

[2] *The Secret Correspondence of Sir Robert Cecil with James VI, King of Scotland,* ed. Sir David Dalrymple, Lord Hailes (Edinburgh, 1766), letter I, 1–12.

of 1603. It brought to an end a reign of forty-five years in which Elizabeth's decisions, large or small, had shaped the public life of the nation. How far she had affected the broader culture of her age must be a question for debate, but in a political sense it had indeed been the age of Elizabeth. What now, in retrospect, can be said about the character and the quality of her rulership? The answer is necessarily long and complex, but as a beginning one first may ask what was the legacy she received from her predecessors, more particularly from the princes of her own house.

Elizabeth inherited from her medieval forebears a monarchy with a tradition of strongly centralized leadership, backed by a long-established and well-organized bureaucracy and hallowed by a myth of semidivine kingship. That monarchy had been damaged by the storms of the mid-fifteenth century, but in the process of restoration the Yorkists and the first two Tudors had substantially increased the effective authority of the Crown and added correspondingly to the machinery of government. Her father had augmented the financial resources of the Crown and established a highly effective executive instrument in the reformed Privy Council. Slimmed down, carefully defined, and equipped with the necessary bureaucratic apparatus, it provided an admirable institution for focusing both administration and politics in a single body at the service of the sovereign. Properly staffed, it could be a valuable instrument for the enforcement of the royal will.

The institutional structure that she inherited was strong and effective, but the uses that her two predecessors had made of it were very different. Her cautious grandfather had successfully sought to establish the monarchy as the conserving force that his subjects looked to as the guarantor of the order and stability of the social structure. Her father, on the other hand, had proved to be a royal revolutionary who, in his break with Rome, pulled apart a fabric centuries old. His coadjutor Cromwell did a skillful job in damage control and minimized the immediate consequences of the break. But the ensuing religious changes under Henry's two successors, in which the pendulum swung first to one extreme and then to the other, left to Elizabeth a dangerously unstable situation. The adherents of the old and the new faiths now stood in uncompromising opposition. Less visible at the moment of the Queen's accession was another problem that would soon emerge—the growing disagreements among the ranks of the reformers as to the shape of the new religious order.

If the domestic scene was clouded, the international prospect was a stormy one. Abroad as at home the Queen had lost the initiative that her father had enjoyed. Until the very last years of his reign Henry had been able to indulge himself in insouciant bouts of aggression against his neighbors, which, in an attenuated sense, continued the long tradition of English aggression against France and Scotland. But his bumbling intervention in Scotland in the 1540's quite suddenly brought about a reversal of fields, with England now cast in the unaccustomed role of victim, and France in that of aggressor. Almost at the same time the transformation of the loose confederation of the Low Countries into a province within a centralized Spanish empire altered the nature of the ancient "Burgundian" connection on which English political and economic strategy had been built. Hence the independence of action that England had hitherto enjoyed in dealing with her neighbors was now much restricted. These looming difficulties were compounded by the religious decision of 1559, which placed England, willy-nilly, in the reformed camp, just as the new religious alignments began to take on a political dimension that threatened the peace of Europe.

In short, Elizabeth acceded to a throne that rested on firm institutional structures, providing a firm base for a monarch who knew how to utilize them. But the immediate problems were vexing, even threatening. Unpalatable choices had to be made, at home and abroad. Over time the problems that faced her at her accession would change their shape in response both to the Queen's own actions and to external events, but in one form or another they would remain on her agenda through the whole of her reign. And the power to initiate action would remain in the hands of others—foreign rulers, Irish princelings, Puritan preachers. The Queen's power to control events was limited to defensive reactions to others' decisions.

Given these limiting conditions, what were the personal qualities she brought to bear on these formidable problems? What were the assets and the liabilities that appeared on her balance sheet? The question is not an easy one to answer, in no small part because Elizabeth, well before her death, was already enshrined in a myth that heavily veiled the historical personage. Posterity has made liberal additions to it, from the seventeenth century down to our own times. These embellishments have so encrusted the actual person as to create a kind of historical doll as richly and stiffly artificial as the figure shown to us in her portraits. One purpose of this book and of its two predecessors has been to penetrate the veils of legend by close observation of the Queen at work in her exercise of power, month by month, year by year. It is a technique with limitations; it will not necessarily tell us much about the private person of Elizabeth Tudor, but it will enable us to make some judgment about Elizabeth I in her public role as a sovereign. It has the advantage of focusing upon the Queen in the immediate context of her vocation, that of statecraft, and allowing us to make a judgment of her as a practitioner of her art, uncolored by the rich hues of the Elizabethan myth. This approach is a limited one since these judgments are confined within the same horizons that bounded the Queen's own view. It seeks to understand the Queen's career by narrowing our vision to approximate hers, seeking to grasp the assumptions on which she acted, and employing no more information than she had at her disposal in making her decisions.

Where to begin in such a quest? The Queen herself offers an important clue to one route of inquiry. The Renaissance conceit of the personal motto provided Elizabeth with the opportunity of advertising to the world her own self-conception, the face that she wished to present for public inspection, the role that she proposed to assume on the public stage. Her revealing choice of a motto was *semper eadem*—always the same. It was one to which she remained faithful for a lifetime; its significance would be patent in every dimension of her life. She was engaged in an unending battle to halt or at least to evade the processes of change. Take, for instance, the matter of her portraiture. Efforts were made (unsuccessfully) to provide a single pattern portrait of which all other paintings would be close copies.[3] The effort failed, but the intention is clear enough—to display to her subjects one unchanging, ageless countenance. Had the intention succeeded, art would have reflected nature. The living queen, like her portraits, defied time. The old woman of seventy, decked out in red wig, rouged and painted, persisted in presenting to her court the same visage as the young woman of twenty-five had displayed almost half a century ago.

[3] See Roy Strong, *Gloriana: The Portraits of Queen Elizabeth I* (London, 1987), 12–13.

These outward manifestations are faithful reflections of a fundamental inward reality.

This deep-rooted resistance to change took many forms, nowhere more apparent than in her circle of intimates. The attachments she formed at the beginning of the reign endured as long as the lives of these favored men and women. Cecil stood at her right hand for forty years, Leicester was her "Dear Robin" for thirty. Blanche Parry and the Countess of Nottingham attended her chamber for as many decades. Councillors left the Council board only when death removed them, and the Queen found solace for their absence by filling the vacancies with their sons. A circle of familiar faces, a known and unchanging social environment, was essential to the Queen's own inner well-being, and time alone was powerful enough to alter it.

The Queen's fundamental, almost inertial, conservatism was no doubt in large part a temperamental matter, but it chimed with the harmonies of the cultural cosmos that she inhabited. She believed as firmly (although not so argumentatively) as her successor in her divinely ordained commission. Like her Stuart successors, her vision of kingship was a static one; she saw the throne as a still center, the very presence of which insured the stability of the whole social and moral order. In any movement of change she scented danger, a menacing rupture in the social structure that threatened at the very least general disorder, at the worst, treason and rebellion. The restlessness of religious dissenters of the left or of the right, the stirring of Irish chieftains, or the risings in Holland, France, or Scotland were all of a piece, equally to be deplored. This deep unease with the perturbations of the unstable world around her profoundly affected her conduct of statecraft, as we shall see.

Nevertheless, the Queen's psychological immobility was only one side of her character. Such a characteristic might seem to imply some degree of lassitude, a lack of energy. But Elizabeth was very much her father's daughter and inherited in full the fierce energy of will that sought to bend everyone who came within its ambit to her commands and to bring under her control all events that might touch her. Elizabeth's singular role as the royal actress cast in a part written for a man was of first consequence. She was well aware that imperious mastery over all around her and the exercise of irresistible will were not attributes commonly attributed to her sex. If she was to be truly queen, she must assert these qualities in unmistakable ways. From the moment of her accession she did her utmost to demonstrate that, whatever her natural sex, as ruler she was as kingly as any of her predecessors.

This characteristic was visible at every level. In the immediate circle of her entourage Elizabeth ruled the personal lives of her intimates, as Walter Raleigh found to his cost. She resented even the ripple of change that was implied by the marriages of her entourage—and the implicit diminution of attachment to her person. In the central political task of the monarch, the distribution of patronage—that network that bound together the whole political community and insured the smooth functioning of the state machinery—Elizabeth took care to keep every string in her hand. This meant not only that the Queen made the appointments, but even that the routine details of service remained a matter for her decision. The record of Robert Sidney's endless maneuvering to obtain home leave from his governorship at Flushing is the kind of detail that makes evident the all-pervasive influence of the royal will. Councillors might plead in his behalf, but when the desired permission came it was not a response to such appeals but the Queen's own unconditioned act. So it went, in all appointments, high or low, in court, the church, the universities, the law courts, Ireland, or the overseas forces. Ministers might recommend, but the wiser ones, like Burghley, knew better than to press their case too far; any sense that they were trying to force the Queen's hand was a sure recipe for failure. In her own time and for her own reasons the Queen would make her choice.

In public business the same conditions obtained. Ambassadors abroad, the deputy and council in Ireland, commanders in the field, and ministers at court made no move without royal knowledge and royal approval. The Commons speaker made his daily report, and the royal interference in the business of the House is richly documented. This was no mere general supervision, a setting of goals or of programs that were left to the executant. At each stage the official must refer back to secure royal approbation. Norris in Brittany had to shape his campaign, phase by phase, in accordance with royal command; Essex in Ireland had to secure the Queen's approval for his every move. Only the naval commanders, incommunicado by the nature of their enterprise, were free from continuous royal intervention.

When money was in question, the Queen was even more exigent.

Muster lists were inspected, accounts called for, and angry letters of reproach dispatched to a delinquent officer. Each expenditure required royal consent. Fleet commanders, wind-bound at Plymouth, had to beg for another month's rations. Commanders in the field could not count on a steady flow of funds; each allocation had to be pleaded for anew. Short of funds and uncertain of future supply, they were puppets, jerked on a string in the royal hand.

Though the royal will was all-pervasive, the Queen's deep-rooted resistance to change meant that there was still a vital element missing in the equation of decision-making. The dynamo of her father's willful energy had been harnessed to specific purposes, to power the machinery that drove his many enterprises—war with France or Scotland, the divorce, and finally the realization of the supremacy. The contrast with his daughter's case was sharp. Elizabeth entertained neither personal ambitions nor larger policy goals. In large part this was an aspect of her sex. Elizabeth not only lacked the martial ambitions of other monarchs or of her own nobles but also positively despised the pursuit of the bubble reputation. Her contemptuous comments on Essex's exploits at Cadiz are a fair sample of her feelings. Neither did she share the religious enthusiasms of her brother and sister. Characteristically her approach to the religious problem at the outset of her reign was pragmatic and businesslike. The settlement, as far as we can see, was premised not on the realization of a religious ideal but on the achievement of merely utilitarian ends, not a positive approach but a negative one, an expedient measure designed to settle an urgent problem that inexorably required some kind of solution.

What was hard for her subjects to accept was her resolute determination not to marry. How far this was an entirely personal matter, how far a politic resolve to avoid the pitfalls into which Mary Stuart had stumbled, we cannot say. The only time she came close to taking a husband (the Anjou match), her intentions were again largely pragmatic. The marriage, if it came off, was intended to provide solutions to a cluster of urgent problems, not to gratify the personal preference of Elizabeth Tudor.

Elizabeth's indifference to the ordinary aspirations of her kind inevitably skewed English politics into unaccustomed shape. Eschewing marriage and lacking a certain heir, she was indifferent to a future in which she had no stake. The ordinary urge to maintain the dynastic succession had no place in her concerns. For some years her councillors strove as hard as they could to change her mind, but to no avail, and in the end they had to live unhappily with the troubling uncertainty of an unsettled succession. The existence of Mary Stuart, feared and hated yet possessed of an undoubted claim, worsened the situation. Her death not only removed an immediate threat to Elizabeth's safety but also in some measure eased the prospects for an untroubled succession, but it was the initiatives of her ministers that had cut the Gordian knot. Elizabeth, however, remained unyielding in her refusal to allow consideration of the succession, so vital to the future of the kingdom, to rise to the surface of public discussion. Here, as elsewhere, sheer luck played a disproportionate role in resolving a dangerous question.

A royal personality blending a willful determination to be sole commander and an equal indisposition to act made for a perverse situation in which the captain of the English ship of state, while keeping a firm hand on the tiller, gave no directions as to the intended destination of the voyage. The lack of focused royal ambitions or goals meant that the Queen's own initiatives were few and that, faced with intruding events, she hesitated uncertainly and preferred to wait upon developments rather than to shape them.

This royal passivity in the initiation of action had varying effects. Too often in concrete cases, when circumstances compelled action, she could command but she could not decide. The royal disposition to inaction, coupled with the determination to control men and events, became an unstable mixture, the consequences of which were manifest in one instance after another. Repeatedly she brought herself to the brink of decision, only to hover, to blow warm and cold, giving command only to revoke, and revoking the revocation. It was a pattern that characterized every major episode in the history of the reign. The commander of every expedition that set out on land or sea suffered from the royal indecision. In Ireland it led to the gravest consequences.

The paradoxical blend of willfulness and indecisiveness also posed problems for the Queen's councillors. On the one hand she required obedience to her commands as given, and they all suffered from her furious tongue-lashings when she disapproved of their actions. On the other hand the very lack of decisiveness left Elizabeth open to advice and gave her ministers the opportunity to press their own opinions. This made for a give-and-take atmosphere within the Council in which her advisors had the opportunity to say their piece freely. They had often to accept the rough side of her tongue, but at least she listened to them. The result was a public façade of royal resoluteness that masked a fluid process of decision-making. What remains hidden from us, for the most part, is the degree to which royal will was deflected by individual or collective conciliar persuasion. Among individuals, Essex had some spectacular successes in bending her will to his, although, as we know, he suffered as many defeats as victories. His triumphs were highly public; but they were doubtless far less numerous than the untrumpeted occasions when Elizabeth listened to the counsel of her oldest servant, Burghley. He enjoyed the immense advantage of sharing in most instances the same instinctive response to events. His wary discretion in setting pen to paper and the very fact of his constant attendance on the Queen mask from our view the true extent of what must have been the immense weight of his influence in shaping the royal decisions. Conciliar success in swaying the ruler was less visible, probably most often effective in tempering the wrath of her initial impulses. In the end we are left with the picture of a sovereign whose public stance of untrammeled royal independence veiled a reluctant flexibility born of her own inner uncertainties.

What has been said is relevant to the central issues of policy and of patronage that most engaged the royal attention. However, there were many areas of public policy in which the Queen manifested little visible interest. Here the members of Council seem to have had wide latitude in promoting measures of domestic legislation, in which the statute books abound. It is fair to suppose that their ambitious attempts at social engineering, such as the long line of Parliamentary acts culminating in the poor law, reflect little more than the tolerant good will of the Queen.

A perspective that contrasts the Queen with both her immediate predecessors, the princes of her own house, and her Continental contemporaries may add some additional sharpness to the portrait. Elizabeth and her grandfather, had they known each other, might each have found much to sympathize with in the other. Both, placed by circumstance in a defensive posture, reacted with the same wary caution. Both displayed something of the same skeptical detachment from the conventional aims of their royal contemporaries. And grandfather and granddaughter were alike in the careful choice of their servants and in the same steady loyalty, once trust was given. But Henry's opportunism was shaped by his larger goal, the defense and the perpetuation of the dynasty. Elizabeth's vision was much more a day-to-day one; she resisted any attempt to project a future that extended beyond her own lifetime.

As for her father, there were obviously both resemblances and differences. Both sovereigns filled the regal role in which they were cast with assured confidence. Each exploited the awesome authority of the office by an overpowering regal presence, and father and daughter alike mixed this characteristic with a persuasive affability. Henry's charm was perhaps a bit heavy-handed; Elizabeth's, a blend of wit and femininity, more winning. There, however, resemblances ended. Henry's reckless use of the power that he wielded, his lurching shifts of direction as he flung his country into war or dragged his subjects into the maelstrom of religious upheaval, stand in sharpest contrast to the steadiness and consistency of Elizabeth's policy. That contrast was clearly in the historian Camden's mind in writing the account of Henry that appears in the prologue to his annals of the daughter's reign. Respect for the sovereign struggles with indignation at the behavior of the man. The most he can grudgingly bring himself to say is, "a magnanimous Prince he was, in whose great mind were confusedly mixed many eminent virtues with no less notorious vices."[4]

The angularities of Elizabeth's character as measured against the characters of her two great contemporaries, Henry IV and Philip II, are implicit in much of what has been written earlier. With her brother of France the English Queen had much in common. His coolness to the religious passions of the age as well as his calculated pragmatism engaged her sympathies; she could understand, even if she could not approve of, his change of religion. Philip, on the other hand, stood at the polar opposite to the Queen's lukewarm Erastianism. She remained more than a little puzzled by the religious zeal that motivated so many of the Spanish king's actions. But in one outstanding respect she stood wholly apart from her royal contemporaries. She not only did not share but deeply abhorred their masculine obsession with the aggressive pursuit of power. Her dedication to the irenic defense of her realm and its people leaves her solitary among the princes of the sixteenth-century world.

With this catalogue of Elizabeth's personal traits in hand, what are we to say of her performance as a practitioner of the royal art

[4] Camden, 1–5.

547

of statecraft? What case can we make from the record of achievement—and failure—as set against her own measures of intention?

Foreign affairs would occupy much of the Queen's time and attention in the four and a half decades of her reign, but it was domestic politics that made the first claim on her attention when she came to the throne. That pressure would never cease so long as she reigned. Any effective stance on the European scene was posited on effective control of her own realm. This meant in the large sense maintenance of public order, prevention or suppression of open discontent, and provision for the reasonably smooth operation of the ordinary machinery of justice. The fulfillment of these goals depended on the exercise of royal skill in a second task, that of securing the cooperation of the ruling elites.

This task had several dimensions. In its broadest aspect it meant arousing a sense of conscious loyalty to her own person and securing the confidence of the governing classes in her ability to lead. To this end she bent all her considerable gifts of personality. Within the political core—court and Council—her blend of royal willfulness and princely graciousness assured unquestioned mastery of the inner elite. There could be no question of the Queen's independence of faction or favorite. And on her annual progresses she wooed the county elites with such skill that their response became almost adulatory in its enthusiasm.

She was supremely successful in winning the confidence and the loyalty of the political nation, but that task involved more than the assertion of the royal personality. Loyalty had to be cemented by the distribution of patronage, by appointments to offices in the gift of the Crown. This exercise had two sides to it. On the one hand the ruler had to choose servants, above all Privy Councillors, who had the requisite skills to assure effective leadership, both at the center and in the counties, and to carry out the multiple tasks of a busy government. At the same time she had to meet the expectations of the governing classes: first, of those who sought a career within the court or the administrative and legal bureaucracies, and second of the gentry of the shires who looked for one or more of those Crown appointments that would shore up their local pre-eminence. There were always more suitors than posts; striking a balance that would give satisfaction to the largest number and disappointment to the fewest made all the difference in the functioning of a political system that relied on the services of men who, in the case of the JP's or deputy lieutenants, were unpaid or who, like the courtiers and bureaucrats, were paid a retainer rather than a salary.

The Queen proved a skilled practitioner. In filling the ranks of the Privy Council she achieved a blending of meritocrats like Cecil or Nicholas Bacon, professional courtiers such as Lincoln or Howard, skilled civil servants like Mildmay and a few sleepers, and regional magnates, represented by a Derby or a Shrewsbury. The same mix continued *mutatis mutandis* throughout the reign, but the weight clearly lay with William Cecil and his allies, a contingent that carried forward the tradition of a Cardinal Morton, a Wolsey, or a Thomas Cromwell. Men of this genre lent a seriousness of tone, a continuing program of sustained and responsible concern for the public interest that distinguished Elizabethan government from its Jacobean successor. For this generation at least, English government made a significant turn away from the dynastic past towards the still-distant future of the early modern bureaucratic state.

Elizabeth not only chose well in staffing her Council but also made fully effective use of the newly reformed institution. The establishment of a compact political center on which all routine administrative business, policy consultation, and most of the political life of the court pivoted proved immensely successful in providing a strong, efficient, and unified leadership at the center, which in turn inspired trust and confidence in the counties. Even more important was the Queen's skill in suppressing factional quarrels within the Council—this in spite of the bitter rivalry between Cecil and Leicester. It was a very different body from the strife-torn council of Henry VIII, which the older members could remember, or the disorderly scramble for favor that the younger ones would see in James's time.

It is more difficult to render judgment on the functioning of the system away from the center. The local studies that have been made seem to confirm confidence in the center, reasonably ready obedience to its orders, and a high degree of efficient local autonomy. One crude but not insignificant index lies in the absence of any large-scale popular revolt (save for the abortive and tiny Oxfordshire stir in 1597). A second measure of achievement is the test of war. We have noted the success of the local magistracies in mustering forces for service abroad and the willingness of the country to pay the heavy costs of a prolonged war, marked by few victories. Third, there is the witness of Parliament. Not until the very last meetings of the reign was there a spurt of angry criticism of government actions, which struck for the first time the note of widespread grievance so familiar in the next reign. The record of the Elizabethan administration in meeting the needs of its subjects appears on the whole to deserve high marks.

How much credit can be given to the Queen? There is little evidence that she herself was involved or interested in the everyday routines of domestic administration. (Her spasmodic interventions in religious affairs are a partial exception.) Nevertheless, without the support as well as the freedom of action that she gave to the men who, carrying the burdens of this great task, assured its effective operation, the system would not have worked. No less important was the larger sense that the Queen, unlike her predecessors or her contemporaries abroad, would not sacrifice their lives and fortunes for her own aggrandizement or squander their wealth to gratify her own pleasures. The flowery rhetoric that celebrated Elizabeth as a goddess of peace and plenty rested on a record of demonstrable practice.

The second great domestic task that faced the Queen at her accession was the settlement of religion, of which something has already been said. Her approach was both pragmatic and principled: pragmatic in that it took what lay at hand—the half-finished structure of the Edwardian reform—and made it serve without further ado. Her further actions were principled, in that she laid down the firm and unshakable axiom that there was to be no more change. The revolution was over. In her view further tinkering with the structure of public worship would only arouse disagreements that would endanger the unity of the realm in the face of external menace. All efforts to press the Queen to continuing change were, as the definitive study of Elizabethan Puritans demonstrates, totally in vain.[5]

In her religious policy the Queen must be faulted on several counts. First was her refusal at the outset of her reign to give the bishops of the new order the kind of royal backing they desperately needed if the fragile authority of the new regime was to be solidified. Left to carry out the royal orders without visible royal support, they soon drew the fire of the critics, the more radical of whom now assailed the very institution of episcopacy, thereby imperiling

---

[5] See Collinson for the classical account of Elizabeth's relations with the Church.

the legitimacy of the settlement. There followed twenty years when the church drifted uncertainly. Its bishops were saddled with a set of royal instructions that they could not successfully enforce while faced with a slashing attack on their own legitimacy. Belatedly Elizabeth threw her authority behind Whitgift with sufficient strength to enable him to crush the radicals and mute the moderate reformers.

It is hard not to conclude that, had Elizabeth been willing to go halfway in meeting the demands of the moderate reformers, much of their criticism would have been stilled. Royal acceptance of the more moderate reforms, such as changes in the liturgy and a serious attempt to improve the quality of the clergy, would have remedied most of their grievances. Given the fissiparous tendencies inherent in a Bible-centered religion, it is not likely that the Queen could ever have realized the goal of national unity (and uniformity) that she believed in. Probably an unappeasable extreme left would have existed in any case, but a less intransigent royal attitude might have allayed the uneasy doubts about the truly reformed nature of the Church of England that troubled the consciences of many more moderate Protestants.

From the royal point of view, however, her adamantine determination not to alter the terms set in 1559 paid off handsomely, for it allowed the newly reorganized church to solidify, to harden and mature its institutional muscles. The new rites of the reformed church came, by their very endurance through nearly half a century, to displace the old in the popular consciousness; the church established by law became rooted in custom and habit. As the mold of the new order hardened, the Book of Common Prayer ousted the mass as the accepted norm of public worship. Moreover, the extended polemic between the critics and the defenders of the 1559 settlement led—first in the writings of Whitgift and then, more magisterially, in those of Hooker—to a sophisticated formulation of an ecclesiology for the establishment that would serve it well in the next century.

At the close of her reign the Queen could look with some satisfaction on the religious scene. The dissidents within the Protestant ranks had been tamed; the uniformity that she so highly valued was now in large part achieved. The presence of separatist groups was too small a cloud to dim the horizon. Only the adherents of the old faith stood out in stubborn refusal to conform.

The Queen's attitude towards her Catholic subjects assumed, as in the case of Puritan dissent, that removal of the leaders would suffice to destroy the movement. In the early years of the reign uncertainty as to the real strength of the adherents of the old faith led the government to tread softly. Such a policy was fortified by the conviction that what remained was merely the residue of a habitual piety that time would soon extinguish. Later, when the power of the missionary priests to revive the old religion became apparent, the Queen gave her assent to harsh measures against the priesthood and their lay patrons, although, significantly, she regularly intervened to soften the proposed rigor of the recusancy statutes. Here, as in the case of Protestant dissent, the object was not to root out belief but to destroy the articulate leadership, to snuff out defiance of the royal authority. Catholic priests, perceived as agents of an external power that aimed at destroying the whole regime, were singled out as more dangerous; nothing less than death or at least exile would suffice. The Puritan divines could be silenced by depriving them of their pulpits. However, when they seemed to pose real danger to authority the Queen was ready to send them to their deaths, as the fate of Penry and Greenwood proved. Deprived of their leaders, the mass of their followers could be left alone (as long as they made no attempts to act). Their communities would either die of inanition or survive at such a low level of vitality as to pose no threat to public order.

The importance of this royal pragmatism for the whole character of English Protestantism cannot be overestimated. Elizabeth's determination to stifle further debate about religious issues within the established church, and her insistence that the aims of the Catholic priests were political and not religious, shifted the whole base on which the national religious life now stood. From the official point of view the church came to be seen as a national and secular institution, no longer a mystical body but an aspect of the body politic within which adherence to its worship was a legal duty. State and church were partners, not in the ancient sense of *sacerdotium* and *imperium*, but as associates in a common enterprise, both subordinate to a lay authority. The role of Queen Elizabeth in promoting and establishing this new and radical order surely entitles her to the name of nursing mother to the Church of England. The settlement of 1559 would not have achieved such permanence had it not been for the resolute insistence of the sovereign in impressing her will on church and nation. It was an impress that, for better or worse, would last for generations to come.

The question of the national religion was closely tied to all matters touching England's relations with her neighbors. It was a factor, albeit not the sole one, in the first foreign crisis the Queen had to face—the revolt of the Scottish Lords of the Congregation against French hegemony. The pattern that unfolded in this instance was one that repeated itself several times in the next decade. Elizabeth was still an apprentice at the royal trade and in these years proved much more amenable to persuasion from below than she would be later. The record makes it clear that in 1559–1560 it was William Cecil who finally induced his reluctant mistress, step by step, to undertake all-out intervention in Scotland. The result was a stunning success: the eviction of the French from the island and the establishment of a Scottish regime dependent on backing from the south. Nevertheless, Cecil's boldness paid off less because of successful statecraft than out of sheer good fortune. Storms held back French reinforcements; the Queen Regent died opportunely; the first spasm of civil war shook the French court; finally, there was the backing of Spain, anxious to see the French ejected from their British foothold.

In 1562–1563 it was almost certainly Robert Dudley who persuaded the Queen to intervene in the French civil war, allying herself with the Huguenots and occupying Newhaven (Le Havre). This time she burned her fingers badly, and the royal distaste for dealing with rebels, aroused in Scotland, was now confirmed. It was the last time she listened to Dudley's schemes for foreign adventure. Her involvement in French affairs would of course continue, but her line of conduct would shift to a far more cautious stance.

The third foray into her neighbors' affairs came in 1569 with the seizure of the Spanish treasure. Once again it was Cecil who was the moving force in drawing his mistress into a nakedly aggressive action, openly provoking the Spanish king. It was a calculated gamble; Cecil counted heavily on Spanish preoccupation in the Mediterranean and Alva's unwillingness to risk war in the north when the provinces were so unsettled. The result was a diplomatic coup gratifying to English pride, although the longer-term advantages to England were not so evident. A gesture, but little more, had been made in detaching England from total dependence on the Flemish staple at Antwerp. Whatever credit there was belonged to the secretary rather than the Queen. It was the last time he would appear in so adventurous a role.

This was the final one of the three experimental essays in foreign policy. There would be no more aggressive initiatives (at least in Europe). Each had, so to speak, tested the waters; each had explored relations with one of England's three closest neighbors. From each the Queen had learned lessons that she would apply to future decisions. The debacle in France had ended the first English intervention in the burgeoning French civil wars; it shaped definitively future English policy towards the Huguenots. The Queen, badly stung by the experience, drew back from any more direct involvement. The French Protestants would continue to be patronized, but much more cautiously, always at arm's length, and in such a way as not to imperil relations with the French court. The clash with Spain had been less determinative: relations had been ruffled; English independence had been asserted; the limits of Spanish power had been revealed, but after an interval of glaring at one another, civil relations were coolly re-established.

The intervention in Scotland was a different matter: there were long-term consequences; it marked the first stage in a new English relationship with its northern neighbor. England had backed the formation of a new Protestant regime at Edinburgh, fragile in the extreme and looking to London for support. Many of the English councillors would have created a permanent dependency, based on regular pensions to the Scottish leaders. As in the French case Elizabeth rejected any such direct relationship. It would have cost money and it would have tied English policy to entangling engagements with unreliable allies. She preferred a looser policy, a waiting brief. England would leave the Scots to their own turbulent politics, reserving the right to intervene when anti-English influences seemed to prevail at Edinburgh. Intervention could take different forms: troops and artillery as in 1573, subsidies to malcontent factions, or conspiratorial patronage. The Scots were left on a loose rein, one that tightened whenever the English became worried. Royal policy here as elsewhere was minimalist, no long-term commitments to any one leader or faction; each act was to be an improvisation. It was not an easy policy to operate. It required careful timing and a knowledge of the Byzantine intricacies of Scottish politics which the English did not always assess accurately. But it was consistent and proved adequate to its purposes, which were to checkmate any further French influence in the northern realm. Many of her councillors felt uneasy at a policy that tolerated endemic chaos in the northern kingdom; they would have preferred assured and stable allies, but this countered the Queen's fundamental policy of maintaining maximum freedom of action.

The era 1558–1572 had been (except for Scotland) a time of discrete episodes, each self-contained. From the beginning of the 1570's England was drawn into a sequence of events that, linked in causal chains, led on to war. The repeated bouts of civil war in France and the Dutch revolt created a long-term situation that demanded continuing English responses. Even before that, at the beginning of the decade, English perceptions of their international relations were changing. Heralded by Burghley's paper of 1569, the English government was shifting its attention from France, whose ambitions had since the 1540's been the focus of English fears, to Spain. The transformation of the Burgundian lands into a province within a Spanish empire, and the confessional differences that now separated England and Spain, had aroused a deep unease among the English leaders. Their response was to seek an understanding with France, achieved in the Treaty of Blois. This move, in which the Queen proved an agile performer in the political ballet of a mock courtship, proved to be the last in which the English could move with the relative freedom they had enjoyed in the 1560's. Then commitments, like that at Newhaven, could be closed out at will.

Henceforward, events were the masters of men—and of the Queen. In April 1572 there was the revolt at Brill, and in August the newly coined French alliance was battered by the events of St. Bartholomew. These were the first two acts in a continuing drama in which Elizabeth found herself constrained to be an actor.

The new shape of Continental affairs led to division within the royal circle of advisors. From the beginning of the reign Cecil had stood for an activist approach, first in Scotland and more recently in the Spanish treasure ships affair. Dudley had been the promoter of the Newhaven venture but in the latter years of the decade had been absorbed by the court intrigues that swirled around the person of Mary Stuart. In the new decade, roles were transformed. Cecil (Burghley since 1571 and lord treasurer since 1572), so articulate and so forthright in his views in the early years of the reign, now became enigmatic, reserved, opaque in his prose, given to carefully balanced but unresolved assessments of England's options. Moreover, he was no longer the activist urging the Queen to risky ventures. When the developments of the 1570's raised the specter of open war, he became more and more the embodiment of caution, chary of risk-taking, the first to point out England's poverty of resources, the most insistent opponent of foreign entanglements. As far as one can see, his preference would have been an isolationist stance, a "fortress England," relying on a strong navy, coastal fortifications, and a resolute neutrality. When war came, he sought to limit the war effort to the narrowest limits consonant with state security.

Against this minimalist position stood the advocates of intervention, led by Leicester and Walsingham until their deaths, and then by Essex. In the prewar years they pressed for active support of the Dutch and the Huguenots; when war came their confessional orientation was more and more colored by nationalist aspirations— English paramountcy in the Low Countries, a challenge to Spanish oceanic and colonial dominance. In the 1590's the Queen would be under pressure from these contending advocates of two differing strategies.

The Queen's sympathies lay with her treasurer. Like him, she had striven desperately to avoid war and, when it came, to limit its scope, but they had not arrived at that conclusion by the same road. Elizabeth's position was almost instinctive, determined largely by temperament and by her position as a woman ruler. Burghley's was the outcome of observation, calculation, and coolly distanced judgment. Hence, although in broad agreement as to ends, they often differed in their reaction to individual events. The Queen's highly personal response echoed the Red Queen's in *Alice*. Like that sovereign she was given to snap judgments. Displeased with Henry IV, she ordered the immediate withdrawal of all her forces; furious at the failure to intercept the plate fleet, she ordered Essex and Howard to sea immediately on their return from Cadiz. Burghley, more deliberate in his response and less personal in his reactions, would then urge the Queen to reconsider, often but not always with success. He once wrote of the difference between him and his opponents in Council: "for though they were quick as most martial men are commonly and I slow, as men of years are, yet I used no delay for the purpose to understand the cause of the peril and so to provide remedy. In this I find ... that Her Majesty misliked not my slowness whereby I am the better confirmed in my opinion."[6] Ultimate decisions would thus reflect the complementary interaction of these two contrasting personalities. Instructions, letters of command, were couched formally in the royal voice, but more often than not, their words were in fact a blend of the Queen's and the minister's intentions. This was especially true in the 1590's, when Burghley was unchecked by any rival of equal seniority.

Nevertheless, the opposition party in the Council, the advocates of a forward strategy, did not go unheard. Repeatedly they were able to secure royal approval for large-scale action against the Spaniard. Burghley was enough of a pragmatist to yield consent and cooperation in these enterprises. But the hawks never won more than temporary backing for their ventures, for they failed utterly in converting the Queen to their expansionist vision.

All these circumstances worked together to transform the character of English policy-making. Accidents of personality combined with objective conditions to replace the traditional pursuit of royal ambition or dynastic advantage by a new political economy of interests. The needs of the state chimed with the conservative disposition of the sovereign and her minister. Threats from without not only endangered the monarch's throne (and her life) but also imperilled the new regime founded in the wake of the Reformation. Burghley by choice, and the Queen by necessity, were forced to govern their actions by giving first priority to the safety of the regime and of the state that it embodied. These were aims that the activists in the Council shared; the difference lay in their desire not merely to preserve but to expand English power and to raise their country to a new eminence in European politics. Yet all shared the larger vision that differentiated Elizabethan foreign policy from that of the Queen's predecessors. It was now the interests of the Queen and the state—the new concept that, as their correspondence reveals, had crept into their consciousness. These circumstances gave to English policy a rationalization that not only distanced it from its own past but also differentiated it from those of its monarchical neighbors, where the passions of the rulers and above all the overpowering consideration of reputation governed behavior.[7]

[6] Wright 2: 424–25.

[7] See the illuminating discussion of the driving forces in French and Spanish policy in Eliot.

The Queen's response to these contradicting counsels was characteristically opportunistic, taking each turn of events as it came. Tactics had to be formulated on the spot; in the years of peace the long-term strategy was consistent and clear—the maximum disruption of her neighbors' dominions, with minimal cost or risk to England. Such a strategy assumed that the rebel forces, while given encouragement, would sustain themselves without any direct English assistance. Ports would be kept open, refuge offered, goods supplied (on payment), and English volunteers winked at, but no direct aid in men, money, or supplies would be forthcoming. Elizabeth played this game with elan; she had all the lesser diplomatic talents—the techniques of half-promises and of carefully orchestrated delay, the feigned fits of anger—all the devices that prolonged negotiation and postponed action. With the Spanish this involved public disapproval of the rebels, an ostentatious neutrality. With France relations were more complex, since Elizabeth sought at different times the quite contradictory goals of furthering disruption within the French king's domains or of obtaining his commitment to a common anti-Spanish understanding. There was a basic confusion of aims here, which was to cost dearly. The longer the religious wars raged, the weaker the French monarchy became and the less able effectively to counter Spanish power.

The first real test of the Queen's conduct of foreign relations came when the limits of diplomacy were reached—with the collapse of Spanish authority in the Low Countries after the mutiny and the sack of Antwerp. The provisional government at Brussels, the States-General, was pleading for money, possibly men, in any case outright and public support. To grant their demand would be to challenge Spain directly. At the moment, Spanish power in the Low Countries was at its lowest ebb, and the weight of English support might be enough to persuade Philip to agree to some kind of compromise that would give the provinces the substance of autonomy while leaving him the shadow of sovereignty. Such a solution would have secured the basic English interest—a Low Countries regime autonomous in its own affairs but shielded by a power sufficient to fend off French aggression.

The Queen's decision not to intervene directly was one of the most crucial of her reign. She came very close to sending an army, and she did provide a loan (heavily secured). It was a decision that was swayed by her estimate of the state of affairs at Brussels, where

the cracks in the ramshackle alliance of towns and nobles, of Protestants and Catholics, were already showing. Elizabeth might well
doubt the wisdom of alliance with so shaky a partner. It was im-
probable that an English presence would have been sufficient to
stifle the deep disagreements within the unstable confederation.
Her judgment was borne out by events. The experience of the
1590's, when Anglo-Dutch cooperation proved fruitful, demonstrated that the necessary precondition of success was the establishment of a Dutch state. It was Dutch leaderhip, not the English presence, that achieved it. One can perhaps leave it to Netherlands
historians to judge whether such an outcome would have been possible in the 1570's.

Another weighty factor in the Queen's decision was her fierce
determination to retain as much freedom of action as possible. As
in Scotland or in France, she struggled to avoid the binding ties that
military alliance would entail. Elizabeth turned instead to the most
notable initiative of her career, the complex diplomatic web in
which she hoped to snare Philip. By her marriage with Anjou she
would bind France to a joint initiative in the Low Countries under
the leadership of her husband. Philip, she felt certain, would draw
back before this combination and come to terms with his Low
Countries subjects. On the French scene her marriage with the
duke would provide patrons for the Huguenots, protectors of their
privileges, and guarantors of their peaceful behavior. The financial
costs of supporting Anjou would be shared between the two
crowns. The French king would pay all the more gladly, freed of
his troublesome brother.

In her appreciation of the goals to be realized and the grand
diplomatic strategy that she devised, Elizabeth displayed intelligent
imagination. As a package the scheme offered something for everyone, even Philip, who would at least retain his sovereignty and be
spared the cost of further war. In the means to realize its goals,
however, the scheme was woefully deficient. Elizabeth failed to
gauge the decay of French power, eroded by civil war. She did not
see that Henry III's monarchy was no longer able to provide an
effective counterbalance to Habsburg power. By her support of the
Huguenots she herself had contributed to the dissolution of effective royal control. Second, there was her lack of sensitivity to the
more intangible dimensions of the scene. Blinded by her own
swelled egotism, she failed to realize that her own reputation as a

skillful dissembler made the French deeply suspicious of her intentions and quite unwilling to entrust their future to this duplicitous ally.

Similarly, she failed to grasp the alarm of many of her own subjects at the prospect of an alien and Catholic king. Leicester and his faction were obviously defending a privileged position, but they and many others genuinely feared the accession of a royal consort who was a member of a great Continental dynasty and the prospective king of France. They recalled the unhappy precedent of Mary Tudor's marriage. All ardent Protestants were appalled by the very notion of a Catholic consort. National feeling and religious sentiment were united in deploring the match. Last, there was the choice of Anjou as the principal actor in this drama. Elizabeth seemed ready to trust a man notorious for his bad faith, his untamed ambition, and the utter fecklessness of his behavior. On each and on all of these scores the Queen's scheme was fatally flawed.

Having catalogued the weaknesses in the scheme, one must then ask what alternatives were open to Elizabeth if a resurrection of Spanish power in the Low Countries was to be prevented. One option, direct support of the provinces by the English acting alone, has already been discussed. The fragility of the Brussels regime and Philip's determination to restore his power and secure Catholic orthodoxy made it altogether probable that this path would lead to a war that England would have to fight alone. The other obvious alternative would have been withdrawal to neutrality, strengthening the navy and fortifying the coasts, a policy that probably would have been Burghley's preferred course. This choice would have given many hostages to fortune for it would have left England without any leverage in Continental affairs, thereby allowing her potential adversaries a free hand to achieve the destruction of her most useful allies. There were also risks. First, Spain might calculate that its ultimate security could not be secured without breaking English power. Second, these fears might be reinforced by Philip's hopes of extinguishing heresy in the island. The Queen's choice had at least the advantage of postponing immediate confrontation. Above all—and this was of prime importance to Elizabeth—she might hope to remain in charge of events. As long as the action remained in the council chamber and not on the battlefield, she might be able to bend events to her will.

Such hopes were soon seen to be in vain. Any royal choice was necessarily a *pis aller*, and it was doubtful that any one of them would offer a realistic chance of attaining Elizabeth's goals. England had imperceptibly—and against the royal will—drifted into a position in which it was impossible either to opt out or to see a path that was not strewn with mines. To switch metaphors—Elizabeth was in the unhappy position of the lady on the tiger's back: to remain on or to get off was equally perilous.

The age of diplomacy had ended; the age of war had begun. At the beginning of her reign Elizabeth had set the maintenance of peace as her premier goal. For the first decade the task had been a manageable one, but from 1570 onward the Queen had to balance the continuance of peace against growing external threats to English security. Peace had remained the top priority, and she had believed that she could secure English interests by diplomatic means. The strategy was a mischievous and a dangerous one. On the Continent it was based on the patronage of domestic opponents of the French and Spanish crowns; in Scotland, on the practice of meddling in domestic politics when English interests were threatened. It was posited on the highly risky tactic of providing just enough assistance to keep opposition alive, but not enough to provoke retaliation by the established rulers.

In two areas, in Scotland and in France, Elizabeth had had reasonable success in realizing her purposes. Scotland had been kept free of alien influences; the postern door was safely guarded. Circumstances had abetted her efforts: disorder in their own country had closed out further French intervention, and the blunders of Mary Stuart had removed the most dangerous adversary without Elizabeth lifting a finger. The feeble Scottish regencies had obviously been wholly preoccupied with their own survival. The pro-English party had been able to stand on its own feet with little English aid. The crisis that might have demanded major English interference had never occurred.

In France the resolve to hold the Huguenots at arm's length had worked well enough. A safe refuge in England after the disaster of St. Bartholomew had helped them to regroup, and they continued strong enough to hold their own without the need to seek active English support. Yet their very survival entailed the paralysis of France in the international power struggle. It was in the Low Countries where the formula had totally failed. The royal reaction to the dramatic turnaround of rebel fortunes in 1576–1577 had paradoxically worsened England's problems. The restoration of the *status quo ante* of Charles V had always been the English hope and aim, and now it seemed within grasp. English support could insure its reality. But, as we have seen, faced with the abandonment of the sheathed exchanges of the fencing match for the bare blades of the duel, in which blood might be drawn, the Queen had flinched.

Elizabeth now faced the worst of all possible worlds. Not only had the chosen instrument broken in her hands, but, lacking any possible alternative policy, the Queen had to look on helplessly while reinvigorated Spanish power overwhelmed the Belgian provinces one by one. At the same time the possibility of effective alliance with France was fast fading as the Valois monarchy slipped into terminal decline. Worse still, Spanish power, particularly sea power, was formidably augmented by the acquisition of Portugal. Walsingham's mission to Paris—armed with unassailable arguments for an alliance, which painted the grim picture of a Spain more powerful than any combination that could be raised against her—came home empty-handed. The Queen understood well enough the dangers of her plight but could do nothing to alleviate them. Her diplomacy was bankrupt. Power to rule events lay in the hands of Philip and his great general. When the King became convinced that he must strike at England first if he wished to complete the reconquest of his provinces, there was no way of averting the blow.

It was the obstacle that England's intervention in Flanders presented to Philip's plans of reconquest that moved him to action against Elizabeth, but there was a secondary quarrel between the two monarchs caused by the depredations of her freebooters in his New World possessions. Her role in those enterprises had initially been discreet. Hawkins on his last voyage had the use of a royal ship, and in Drake's famous circumnavigation the Queen was a sleeping partner. On his return, however, she went out of her way to bestow the honor of knighthood on him. The English buccaneers who swarmed in the Spanish Indies were private adventurers, but among their backers were highly placed courtiers. The royal encouragement—indeed participation—seemed to contradict the cautious circumspection with which she conducted relations with Spain in Europe. The English sailors had given up all pretense of trade since Hawkins's final disastrous voyage in 1569 and were engaged in straightforward plundering of whatever Spanish wealth they could lay hands on. The boldest of them were outlining schemes, which they pressed on the Crown, for intercepting the plate fleets themselves and striking at the very heart of Spanish power.

How can one explain Elizabeth's willingness to put aside caution and more than half-openly encourage her subjects to prey upon her neighbor's wealth? In part the explanation lies with the oft-cited distinction between the European and the New World theaters. In the latter the sparse and scattered nature of European settlement and the vast ignorance of the still-uncharted wilderness left rights vague and undefined. It could be argued that the normal rules of international intercourse did not yet fully obtain where recognized boundaries had not been agreed upon. This provided a diplomatic and legal cover but hardly an explanation for royal English activity. The most probable answer to the question lies in simple royal greed. The prospect of a cash haul was an irresistible inducement to abandon caution and run risks. So it was in 1569 when the Spanish treasure ships took refuge in the West Country ports. It was this hope, so richly rewarded, that led to royal backing for Drake in 1577.

Once war began, an assault on the enemy's commerce and on his treasure fleets became an obvious strategy. A fleet of privateers was loosed on the Spanish. Their activities not only damaged the enemy but also brought revenue into the customs collections of the Crown. Every one of the royal fleets sent out was given the charge of assailing the plate fleets or the East Indian caravels; the capture of the *Madre di Dios* in 1592 whetted their appetites for more such riches. In 1595 the Queen hesitated in allowing Drake and Hawkins to sail, in the face of threatened invasion. But news of a stranded galleon in Puerto Rico soon swept aside the royal caution and triggered permission to sail. Hopes of a dazzling prize haunted the royal correspondence with the commanders, and bitter reproach followed on their failure. Elizabeth's obsessive worries about her poverty overrode her customary prudence when the glitter of gold was visible.

The eventual outbreak of war was a bitter pill for the Queen to swallow, and she struggled to deny the harsh reality until the appearance of the Armada left her no alternative. Even after signing the Treaty of Nonsuch and dispatching Leicester and his army to Holland, she sought first to limit the role of his army, and second to go behind Philip's back by negotiating a settlement with Parma.

She was quite prepared to ignore the role of the States-General in such an agreement and to sacrifice their interests to her own. So passionate was her own hatred of war that she could not conceive that her erstwhile brother-in-law would be so foolish as to wage it; surely he would draw back from the brink. There was in the Queen a singular failure of imagination. Cocooned in her own vast egotism, she was quite unable to rise to a conception of other rulers' needs and aims. She seemed unable to grasp the fact that her expeditionary force in the Low Countries was to Philip sure confirmation of his conviction that England was the prior enemy that must first be disposed of before the rebel provinces could be brought to heel.

Once the scope of Philip's initiative had been made obvious in the summer of 1588, the Queen's indignation at what she regarded as double-dealing and bad faith knew no bounds. Her perception of an insult to her as an individual rather than an act of state was a highly personal reaction. When the possibility of negotiations opened up in 1598, the Queen found it very hard to put any faith in the Spanish offers.

After the fall of 1588 the Queen had to assume, however reluctantly, the role of war leader. It was a painfully difficult one for her. Banned by her sex from taking the field as her father had, she was keenly aware of the loss of her valued independence of action. She had now to depend on the judgments of her soldiers in the planning of strategy and to entrust to them the carrying out of her orders in distant lands or on the high seas, well beyond the reach of effective royal control. These soldiers were themselves few in number and limited in experience. A handful of leaders, like Norris or Williams, had learned their trade on the job, as volunteers in the States army, but they had no experience in high command or grand strategy. Her seamen too had been teaching themselves the new art of naval warfare by trial and error. Her councillors, men reared up in a generation of peace, knew little about the making of war.

If the leaders were a collection of amateurs and semi-professionals, the men who had to execute their orders in mobilizing the conscript armies had even less tincture of professional skill or experience. We have seen how the peacetime machinery of local government was adapted to these new tasks, of supplying the men and materiel demanded by the field commanders. However clumsy the machinery, however great the waste, the armies did arrive in

Holland, France, and Ireland; the navies did sail for Spain, the Azores, and the West Indies. In all this the Queen played but a minor role; the task of supervising the operation, of prodding the local magistracies into action, and of handling central supply functions fell to her Privy Councillors.

On the Queen lay the heavy burden of making the large decisions of strategy, how to concentrate England's scarce military and naval power to best advantage. What line of action would be most effective in countering the enemy's intentions and ultimately bringing him to the negotiating table? Circumstance made such choices doubly difficult; already, from 1585 on, her government was heavily committed in the Netherlands by formal treaty. After 1588 the need to guard against another naval assault preoccupied the English government at all times and took priority over any offensive action. From 1589 the Queen had to provide for the urgent needs of her new ally, France. Finally, particularly after 1595, Ireland was the theater of a new and growing menace to English security.

The Queen's options were still further constricted by enemy initiatives, such as Normandy in 1589 or Brittany a year later. Nevertheless, in 1588–1589, again in 1591–1592, and after 1594 there were breathing spaces in which considered choices could be made as to how best to deploy England's arms. We have seen the alternative strategies that were urged on the Queen by the hawks and the doves, the contending factions of her advisors. There can be little doubt that her own inclination leaned heavily toward the minimalist position. Forced into the war against her will, she was determined to preserve as much as possible her own freedom of action and to commit the minimal resources that would realize the minimum conditions for a satisfactory peace. She was enough of a realist to listen to the activists when the threat of renewed invasion attempts made a descent on the enemy's coasts and fleets a sensible countermove. Nevertheless, she would make as few concessions as possible to the necessities of war.

Nothing illustrates more vividly or more significantly Elizabeth's approach to war-making than a comparison of her wartime fiscal practice with that of her neighbors, the kings of France and Spain. For them the winning of the war took first priority; their financial ministers were expected to find whatever money their masters asked for. Heavier and heavier taxation in forms old and new— large-scale borrowing, long-term debt, sale of offices, debasement of the currency, and even repudiation—was all used ruthlessly. Elizabeth, most unorthodoxly, reversed these priorities; it was fiscal policy that took precedence over war strategy. It was the financial resources of the realm that were to set limits on its military effort. This was to be a pay-as-you-go war.

Elizabethan war finance was based on peacetime practice. To keep clear of debt and, if possible, to lay away a nest egg were the essence of Elizabethan fiscal policy. These goals were achieved by the 1570's, when both inherited and current debt had been paid off, and over the next decade a modest surplus was accumulated. This was accomplished largely by a steady infusion of Parliamentary taxation—one subsidy per Parliament. The *quid pro quo* that elicited Parliamentary support was a stringent economy in Crown expenditures and abstention from aggression abroad. War, when it came, was to be financed from the same source; the subsidy was first doubled, then tripled, and finally, at the tense moment of the Kinsale landing, quadrupled. But the Queen was anxiously aware that the subjects' willingness to pay was finite. When even quadrupled parliamentary taxation failed to cover costs, the Queen showed her willingness to share the burden of war; the shortfall was met by sale of Crown lands. Cash flow was covered by short-term Privy Seal loans, promptly repaid. In other words, the same assumptions of fiscal responsibility that had ruled before the war still obtained. The nation was to provide the funds for fighting the war, but there was to be value for money. Funds were to be laid out only for strictly national purposes. These were interpreted by the Queen as purely defensive: the repulse of the enemy and cautiously limited alliance with those other powers who shared a common enmity against Spain.

Such a policy obviously imposed limits on strategy, both in planning and in execution. These financial limitations were felt throughout the war effort, but most apparently in the enterprises that the English launched by themselves. In 1589 private assistance had to be called in to fill out the fleet to its requisite size. London merchant shipping was enlisted; the carrot that was dangled before the owners was the prospect of prizes. The consequent instructions to the commanders muddled the strategic goals—destruction of the remnants of the Armada—with schemes for a princely booty, at Lisbon or in the Azores, that would cover the investors' outlay and, if possible, yield a handsome profit. This pattern repeated itself with some variations in the later naval expeditions. Their failures were due to a myriad of factors, but one constant was the necessities of royal financial policy, which invariably led to a confusion of strategic with profit-making aims. It was never clear to what extent these fleets were seriously intended to cut the Spanish lifeline from America and to what extent they were simply privateering enterprise on a grand scale.

On the Continent the financial bind was felt in different ways. Elizabeth could expect to recover her costs here, once the war was won. The Dutch were bound by the treaty provisions, the French by specific obligations solemnly sealed at each grant of a loan. The limits of English commitment are obliquely revealed by the size of the forces that were dispatched overseas. A conventional upper limit of about 6,000 seems to have pervaded English thinking on the matter. This was the force provided under the Treaty of Nonsuch. That limit was exceeded in France only during the relatively brief interval when there were English arms in both Normandy and Brittany. For an individual expedition 4,000 seems to have been the norm. Presumably the English government had a rule of thumb that set these figures as the maximum expenditure it could afford to lay out.

Financial considerations played a less direct role where they intersected with a different set of strategic aims. The contrasts between the French and Dutch experiences are instructive. The same underlying attitudes obtained in both cases: least expenditure of money and a resolute insistence on the primacy of English interests. In France there was a large general interest in the re-establishment of French power on the international scene. In 1590–1591, with the immediate survival of Henry IV assured, circumstance gave the Queen a breathing space in which to make a considered choice of general strategy. There were three options of action—in Flanders, in Normandy, and in Brittany. In the third case the Spanish pre-empted the decision by their landing at Blavet, which forced her to send a force there. In the other two, where she had a freer hand, money played a decisive role. Flanders was abandoned when it became clear that additional forces would be required; Normandy was the favored choice because it offered among other advantages the chance to recoup the French loans by control of the Rouen customs.

Rouen was a bitter lesson for the Queen. She had hoped, by pinning Henry down to the siege of the city where her troops would play a major role, to control the operation to her advantage, removing the threat of enemy presence so close to England, preventing a junction with the Spanish in Brittany, and acquiring the fiscal revenues of Rouen. Henry was to be bent to serve the purposes of his English sister. It was a wholly unreal reading of the French situation and failed accordingly. The Queen's pursuit of the special English interests in France clashed with Henry's perception of his English sister as an ancillary provider of men and money. Brittany was another example where again the Queen failed to see that what was for England a prime consideration was to Henry only a peripheral irritation. The result was a campaign that wasted English men and money to no purpose at all. The only way in which Elizabeth could have relieved her frustration was to follow Norris's advice and provide a force large enough to act independently, even perhaps seizing control of a port to hold in gage for the debt. But such a move would have run up against the royal determination to limit her commitments. Unable to abandon the province while the Spanish remained, she could only sputter in impotent rage. Except for the expulsion of the Spanish from their fort on the shores of Brest haven, the English had little to show in direct returns on their expensive investment in France.

The Low Countries tell a different story. Here the English had initially appeared as a protector who would provide not only the succor of men and money but also leadership in the struggle against Spain. Dutch disillusionment set in rapidly, and they moved to secure independence in the management of the war. The Queen made little effort to resist the States' determination to make their own decisions. Indeed, the ministers and commanders who advocated such resistance were disowned. The rise of the Oldenbarnevelt-Nassau coalition and their declaration of independence was accepted with relative ease. The reasons are not far to seek. Elizabeth fiercely opposed any move towards an English protectorship in the Low Countries and was happy enough to see them rowing their own boat. English intervention was intended to be short-term, the aim being to foster an ally, not a dependent: a sturdy, self-sustaining regime free from both Spanish and French domination. Second, there was the disguised economy arising from the fact that the Dutch were providing a training program from which the English could draw numbers of seasoned officers (and enlisted men) for their other campaigns. These circumstances led the Queen cheerfully to accept Dutch leadership in the crucial military operations of the decade.

In the end, of course, events on the Continent were beyond the control of the English. If the Dutch had lacked the military genius of a Maurice or the administrative and political talents of an Oldenbarnevelt, the English contribution would have gone for nought. The presence of the English forces in the Low Countries, those paid for by both the Queen and the States, was an important, perhaps determinative, augmentation of the slender manpower of the provinces, but the ability to exploit this resource was wholly Dutch.

Similarly, in France it was the leadership of Henry that restored his kingdom as a great power. Moreover, it was his political skills, as much as or more than his military talents, that brought victory over his enemies. In this, England could play at best only a subsidiary role. Her contribution to Henry's armies in their major offensives was marginal except in the fall of 1589, although even then the victory that saved the King was fought before the English landed.

On the sea the picture was, of course, wholly different. Here the effort was very largely English. At sea the Dutch played the same subsidiary role that the English played on land. On the face of it, these assaults on the Spanish coasts or their fleets went against the grain of the Queen's usual disposition to stick solely to defensive action. Certainly, three of the four great naval expeditions—that of 1589, and those of 1596 and 1597—were viewed by the hawkish party among the councillors as attempts at conquest, actions with long-term consequence. In 1589 it was Portugal, in 1596 Cadiz, and in 1597 Terceira, each of which was to serve as a foothold within Philip's domains for further offensive action. The Queen did not share their conception. Her consent was given in each case with quite different ends in view. In each instance the aim was essentially defensive—in 1589, the liquidation of the remaining Armada warships; in 1596 and 1597 (and in 1595 as well), counterthrusts against threatened invasion. She hoped to scotch the snake before it sprang. Second, although not less importantly, there was the prospect of booty. The Queen's peevish disappointment in 1596 is an instance of her hopes in this regard. Even with such a hope, each decision was for her a difficult one. Apart from the costs (which might be offset) there was the very reasonable fear that while her own ships were away on their mission the Spanish invaders would arrive to assail her unprotected coasts. The nightmare became real in 1601, although fortunately the invasion was on a small scale and in the remote reaches of southern Ireland.

These expeditions were marked by another characteristic of the Queen's war leadership: her hesitations, delays, and—worst of all—changes of mind. The naval commanders, schooled by experience, lived in constant fear of countermanding orders, up to the moment of sailing. The instances are legion. Field commanders overseas suffered in a slightly different mode, by her reluctance to replace the heavy losses of men that were an inevitable concomitant of sixteenth-century warfare. But they suffered even more from her constant changes of mind. Norris and Essex were both to endure the agonizing uncertainties that arose from angry orders to withdraw altogether, followed by a revocation of the order and then often by a reversal of the revocation. Worse still was the plight of Norris when, having been harassed by a succession of contradictory orders, he was told by the Queen to make the decision himself. It was a supreme case of buck-passing by the ruler and one in which the unlucky commander knew that he would in any case be the loser. There was a certain pattern to the bouts of indecision. Often they originated in a burst of fury after some setback or, more frequently, yet another failure of French support. There would follow Privy Council expostulations, a cooling of the royal temper, and a more considered view of the problem. Contemporaries were driven to desperation by these shifts and changes; some historians have censured the Queen severely.

Undoubtedly, royal hesitation added measurably to the burdens of her commanders and disrupted the timetables of operational plans. It is further evidence of the constitutional unwillingness of the Queen to act decisively in military as in civil matters. But the royal indecisivenesss has to be seen in context. There was little abiding trust between Elizabeth and her commanders. They feared her inconstancy and sensed her ultimate distrust. She saw them as dogs straining at the leash, likely to bound away in pursuit of that martial fame that she so heartily contemned. Their departure overseas heightened these tensions to the highest pitch.

Furthermore, she felt acutely the meagerness of her means, and the fear that any one of these ventures might end in complete disaster often weighed more heavily than the prospect of gain. These calculations were not unreasonable. Every large venture of the 1590's, with the partial exception of Cadiz, failed to achieve its goal. Promises and prophecies by the commanders and their supporters were consistently unrealized.

It is hard to strike a balanced judgment in assessing this unwarlike war leader. Her own strategic sense was not unsound. Her anxiety to protect her coasts against another Armada was justified by the renewed Spanish efforts later in the 1590's. She miscalculated the possibilities of English intervention in France and possibly missed an important opportunity to act against Parma in conjunction with Henry and the States in 1590. But the limits of English influence in France were at best small. It was probably a sound instinct not to make a heavy investment of resources in Brittany at the expense of other theaters of war.

Her overseas commanders had more cause for reproach. She had never understood or sympathized with their bold strategy of assault on Spain in her own dominions, on the Continent, or in the islands. She seemed to see them as replays of Drake's assaults in 1585 and 1587, mere raids aimed at crippling invasion preparations rather than part of a long-term strategy aimed at breaking Spanish power. She skimped on the means she gave these commanders and showed her displeasure at the absence of short-term gains in booty. Yet, as has been argued, adoption of the hawkish strategy would have required a massive increase in expenditure in pursuit of a scheme that, however intelligent in conception, was highly problematical in its chances of success. The Queen calculated that the odds of the gamble were too great.

The last years of the reign were filled with one great overriding problem: Ireland. The English record in Ireland during these years has been spelled out earlier: the muddled combination of firmness and weakness, of force brutally applied, and of easily bought compromise. From 1590 on, such fragile stability as existed was steadily eroded. The great Ulster lords came utterly to distrust and to despise English leadership, flirted with Spain, and defied successive deputies. The English bristled, threatened, and then backed down until the Irish leaders broke the uncertain rules of this game and won a victory too overwhelming to be ignored.

For all this the Queen had to bear full responsibility. It was she who had vetoed every initiative her ministers in Ireland had proposed, and it was by her orders that successive compromises were patched up with the Irish malcontents. She was as painfully slow to accept the grim realities of the problem as she had been to recognize Philip's unremitting hostility. Up to the last she urged renewed approaches to Tyrone. When she did commit herself to all-out war, she took advice, agreed to a well-planned overall strategy, and for once made ample provision for the necessities of an army of conquest. But her first choice of a commander, one whom she did not trust, temporarily paralyzed the English effort. Her final choice of Mountjoy seems to have rested on her personal preference for him as much as on any particular qualifications. Nevertheless, having made the appointment, she stood by him and gave him the backing necessary to accomplish his task.

Great damage was done by the Queen's neglect and by her refusal to pay serious attention to Ireland's problems. Her attitude here was of a piece with her general disposition to let sleeping dogs lie. Even if the Irish hound roused itself to bark and strain at the leash occasionally, in her view there were no grounds for a real effort to tame it. With so many other urgent items on her agenda, she pushed Ireland into lowest priority. In this she did no more than her predecessors. Like them, she believed her writs should run as easily in county Clare as in Middlesex; like them, she was not ready to provide the means to turn this vision into reality. Elizabethan policy in Ireland had disastrous consequences both for contemporary Irishmen and for their descendants, but, given the assumptions of the Tudors' leadership, the traditional laxness of their Irish policy was the least bad of the options before them—until Tyrone's power and the Spanish threat galvanized them to action. By then the only solution they could conceive was the use of brute force and final conquest, and for the Irish there was nothing left but desperate resistance. A combination of neglect and spasmodic violence produced a brew that poisoned permanently the relations of the two peoples who now lived in the island. The conquest was the one great success of Elizabethan arms and the most disastrous failure of Elizabethan policy-making.

Now, having completed this *tour d'horizon* of Elizabethan successess and failures, how are we to respond to the question posed earlier? To what extent had the Queen—within the framework of her own assumptions and her own aims—achieved what she sought? As far as her personal life went, she had successfully avoided marriage and had happy and stable relationships with two of the three men closest to her (Leicester and Hatton), while suffering utter shipwreck in the infatuation of her old age. She had established and maintained her mastery over the political scene, an achievement that laid the basis for sustained domestic peace and good order. Yet in the last decade of her reign she came near to losing this control. Her infatuation with Essex's charms led her into a serious miscalculation; she thought she could tame the new favorite as she had tamed Leicester. Her failure led to a crisis in which the possibility of violence flared up dangerously. It was Essex's failure of nerve, not the Queen's political skill, that dissolved the crisis.

With her mastery of the political scene went full responsibility for all the great decisions of state. On the central question of religion she had successfully halted any further change in the official structure of the church; by the end of her reign the reformers had been silenced or driven underground. Catholicism, against her expectations, survived, a fact that she tacitly recognized. On the international scene she had failed in her dearest aspiration, the maintenance of peace. Her greatest essay in foreign policy had collapsed of its internal weaknesses. Forced into war, she had mounted a successful defense but failed in the offensives to which she had only reluctantly consented. It was Dutch and French successes, to which England made only a marginal contribution, that halted Spanish power. In Ireland, in a war largely a product of her own ineptitude, after immense suffering and much loss of both English and Irish lives, she bequeathed to her successors an unwanted burden, which would weigh heavily on their shoulders for generations to come.

In spite of this catalogue of failure, one would have to say that from her own perspective the Queen could rest content as she surveyed the scene around her. At home the threat of internal strife, which had loomed threateningly at the beginning of her reign, had receded into the remote distance; the Catholics were a persecuted remnant, seeking nothing more than bare survival, the church established by law firmly seated. For these developments the Queen herself could claim much credit; she had imposed her will upon events. Abroad, the war, which she had failed to avert, was over; England had survived unscathed. The Continental balance, the perpetual rivalry between Spain and France, which had been the best guarantor of English safety in the past, was re-established. The old Burgundian polity, decked out in new garb, protected England's flank.

In all this the Queen could rejoice, but she could hardly assert that it was all her own doing. Indeed, in all her actions the Queen had had more than her share of good fortune. Her rival, the Scottish queen, had destroyed herself; so had the only subject who might have challenged her power. When her own policy failed to avert the war that she had so feared, the gods fought on her side. Wind, weather, and the enemy's misconceived strategy saved her kingdom from invasion. The two ugly ducklings whom she was forced to accept as allies turned into swans. In Ireland, after a long catalogue of muddle and confusion, she found the general who could win the war with the rebels. Some of her modern admirers would honor her with the style Elizabeth the Great; more aptly she might be entitled Elizabeth the Fortunate.

BIBLIOGRAPHY

MANUSCRIPTS

British Library
  Cotton Mss.
  Egerton Ms.
  Harleian Mss.
  Lambeth Ms.
  Lansdowne Ms.
  Sloane Ms.
Public Record Office
  Baschet Transcripts
  Patent Rolls
  State Papers, Foreign, 1592–1603
  State Papers, particularly 77, 78, 84

PRINTED SOURCES

Actes des Etats Généraux de 1600. Edited by M. L. Gachard. Brussels, 1849.

Acts of the Privy Council of England. New series, London, 1890.

Advertisements from Brittany and from the Low Countries in September and October. London, 1591. STC 3802.5.

Annals of the Kingdom of Ireland by the Four Masters. Edited by John O'Donovan. 3 vols. Dublin, 1848.

An Apologie of the Earle of Essex . . . Anno 1598. London, 1603.

Archives ou correspondance inedité de la Maison d'Orange-Nassau, ser. 2. Edited by G. Groen van Prinsterer. 6 vols. Utrecht, 1857–1862.

Birch, Thomas. *Memoirs of the Reign of Queen Elizabeth, from the Year 1581 till her Death,* etc. 2 vols. London, 1754.

Boissise, *see* Laffleur de Kergmaingant.

The Border Papers. Edited by J. Bain. 2 vols. Edinburgh, 1894–1896.

Bruce, John, ed. *Letters of Queen Elizabeth and King James VI of Scotland.* Camden Soc. 46 (1849).

Cabala sive Scrinia Sacra. Edited by Dudley Digges. London, 1654.

Calendar of Letters and State Papers Relating to English Affairs, Preserved Principally in the Archives of Simancas: Elizabeth. Edited by Martin A. S. Hume. 4 vols. London, 1892–1899.

Calendar of State Papers, Foreign Series, of the Reign of Elizabeth, etc. Edited by Joseph Stevenson et al. London, 1863–1950.

Calendar of State Papers Relating to Ireland, of the Reign of Elizabeth. 11 vols. London, 1860–1912.

Calendar of State Papers Relating to Scotland and Mary, Queen of Scots, 1547–1603. Edited by Joseph Bain et al. 13 vols. London, 1898–1969.

Calendar of the Carew Manuscripts Preserved in the Archiepiscopal Library at Lambeth, 1515–1624. Edited by J. S. Brewer and William Bullen. 6 vols. London, 1867–1873.

Calendar of the State Papers and Manuscripts, Relating to English Affairs, Existing in the Archives and Collections of Venice, and in Other Libraries of Northern Italy. Vols. 7–9 (1558–1603). Edited by Rawdon Brown et al. London, 1890–1897.

Calendar of the State Papers, Domestic Series, of the Reign of Elizabeth. Edited by Robert Lemon and Mary Anne Everett Green. Vols. 1, 2 (1547–1590); 3–6 (1591–1603); and 12 (addenda 1566–1625). London, 1856–1872.

Calendar of the State Papers for Scotland. Edited by M. J. Thorpe. 2 vols. London, 1858.

Camden, William. *Annals of Queen Elizabeth.* London, 1675.

Cary, Robert. *The Memoirs of Robert Cary.* Edited by F. H. Mares. Oxford, 1972.

Cecil, William, Lord Burghley. *A Collection of State Papers . . . Left by William Cecil, Lord Burghley.* Edited by Samuel Haynes and William Murdin. 2 vols. London, 1740–1759.

Chamberlain, John. *The Letters of John Chamberlain.* Edited by N. E. McClure. 2 vols. Philadelphia, 1939.

A Complete Collection of State Trials. Compiled by William Cobbett et al. 42 vols. London, 1816–1898.

Corbett, Julian S., ed. *Papers Relating to the Navy during the Spanish War, 1585–1587.* Navy Record Society 11. 2 vols. London, 1898.

Correspondence of King James VI of Scotland with Sir Robert Cecil and Others in England. Edited by John Bruce. Camden Soc. 78 (1861).

Desiderata curiosa hibernica. Edited by [J. Lodge]. 2 vols. Dublin, 1772.

Devereux, Robert, *see* Essex, Robert Devereux, second Earl of.

Devereux, Walter. *Lives and Letters of the Devereux, Earls of Essex, 1540–1646.* 2 vols. London, 1853.

D'Ewes, Simonds, coll. *A Compleat Journal of the Votes, Speeches and Debates, Both of the House of Lords and House of Commons throughout the Whole Reign of Queen Elizabeth*, etc. London, 1693; reprint, Wilmington, Del., and London, 1974.

ECS. *The Government of Ireland under . . . Sir John Perrot*. London, 1626.

The Edmondes Papers. Edited by C. G. Butler. London, 1913.

Egerton, Thomas, Baron Ellesmere. *A Compilation . . . Evidence . . . to Illustrate the Life and Character of Thomas Egerton, Lord Ellesmere*. Paris, 1812.

The Egerton Papers. Edited by J. P. Collier. Camden Soc. 12 (1840).

Essex, Robert Devereux, Second Earl of. "Omissions of the Cales Voyage." In Lediard, Thomas. *The Naval History of England*, 1: 337–42. London, 1735.

————. "The Voyage to the Iles of Azores, under the Conduct of the Right Honorable Robert Earle of Essex, 1597." In Purchas, Samuel. *Hakluytus Posthumus or Purchas His Pilgrimes*, 20: 24–33. Glasgow, 1907.

Gorges, Sir Arthur. "A Larger Relation of the said Iland Voyage, Written by Sir Arthur Gorges Knight, Collected in the Queenes Ship Called the Wast Spite." In Purchas, Samuel. *Hakluytus Posthumus or Purchas His Pilgrimes*, 20: 34–129. Glasgow, 1907.

Hakluyt, Richard. *The Principal Navigations, Voyages, Traffiques & Discoveries of the English Nation*, etc. Edited by Walter Raleigh. 10 vols. London and New York, 1927.

Harington, John. *Nugae Antiquae*. Edited by Thomas Park. 2 vols. London, 1804.

Hartley, T. E., ed. *Proceedings of the Parliaments of Elizabeth I*. Vol. 1: *1558–81*. Leicester, 1981.

Historical Manuscripts Commission. *Calendar of Bath Manuscripts at Longleat*. 5 vols. London, 1980.

————. *Calendar of the Manuscripts of the . . . Marquis of Salisbury . . . Preserved at Hatfield House, Hertfordshire*. 24 vols. London, 1883–1976.

————. *The Manuscripts of the Right Honourable F. J. Savile Foljambe, of Osberton*. 15th rpt., app., pt. 5. London, 1897.

————. *Report on the Manuscripts of the Earl of Ancaster Preserved at Grimsthorpe*. London, 1907.

————. *Report on the Manuscripts of Lord De L'Isle and Dudley Preserved at Penshurst Place*. Vol. 2. London, 1934.

The House of Commons, 1558–1603. History of Parliament series. Edited by P. W. Hasler. 3 vols., London, 1981.

A Journal or Brief Report of the Late Service in Brittany by the Prince de Dombes Assisted with Her Majesty's Forces under Sir John Norris, etc. London, 1591. STC 1315.6.

Laffleur de Kermaingant, P. *L'ambassade de France en Angleterre sous Henri IV: Mission de Jean de Thumery, sieur de Boissise (1598–1602)*. 2 vols. [Vol. 2 subtitle: *Pièces justificatives*.] Paris, 1886.

Lee, Thomas. "A Brief Declaration of the Government of Ireland ... from the Year 1588 to the Year 1594." In *Desiderata curiosa hibernica*, 1: 87–150. Edited by [J. Lodge]. Dublin, 1772.

The Letters of John Chamberlain. Edited by N. E. McClure. 2 vols. Philadelphia, 1939.

List and Analysis of State Papers, Foreign Series: Elizabeth I. Edited by Richard Bruce Wernham. 5 vols. to date. London, 1964–1989.

Lodge, Edmund. *Illustrations of British History*, etc. 2nd ed. 3 vols. London, 1838.

Monson, Sir William. *The Naval Tracts of Sir William Monson*. Edited by M. Oppenheim. 5 vols., Navy Record Society 22, 23, 43, 45, 47. London, 1902–1914.

Moryson, Fynes. *An History of Ireland, from the Year 1599 to 1603*. 2 vols. Dublin, 1735.

———. *Itinerary Written by Fynes Moryson*. 4 vols. Glasgow, 1907–1908.

Naunton, Robert. *Fragmenta Regalia. Memoirs of Elizabeth, Her Court and Favorites*. London, 1824.

O'Clery, Lughaidh. *Life of Aodh Ruadh O Domhnaill*. 2 vols. Dublin, 1948–1957.

Perrott, Sir James. *Chronicle of Ireland by Sir James Perrott*. Edited by H[erbert] Wood. Dublin, 1933.

———. *History of ... Sir John Perrot*. Edited by Richard Rawlinson. London, 1728.

Purchas, Samuel. *Hakluytus Posthumus or Purchas His Pilgrimes*. London, 1625; reprint, 20 vols., Glasgow, 1905–1907.

Raleigh, Sir Walter. *Works*. 8 vols. Oxford, 1829.

The Secret Correspondence of Sir Robert Cecil with James VI, King of Scotland. Edited by Sir David Dalrymple, Lord Hailes. Edinburgh, 1766.

Sidney, Sir Henry. *Letters and Memorials of State ... Written and*

Collected by Sir Henry Sydney, etc. Edited by Arthur Collins. 2 vols. London, 1746.

————."Sir Henry Sidney's Memoir of His Government of Ireland, 1583." *Ulster Journal of Archaelogy*, ser. 1, 3 (1855): 33–52, 85–109, 336–57.

Slingsby, William. "Relation of the Voyage to Cadiz, 1596." Edited by J. S. Corbett. Navy Record Society, *Miscellany* 1 (1902): 23–92.

State Papers Relating to the Defeat of the Spanish Armada, Anno 1588. Edited by J. K. Laughton. 2 vols. Navy Record Society 1, 2. London, 1894.

State Trials. See *A Complete Collection of State Trials.*

Statutes of the Realm. Edited by A. Luders et al. 11 vols. London, 1810–1828.

Stow, John. *Annales of England.* London, 1605.

Strype, John. *Annals of the Reformation.* 4 vols. Oxford, 1822–1824.

Tenison, E. M. *Elizabethan England.* 10 vols. Leamington, England, 1932–1951.

Unton, Sir Henry. *The Correspondence of Sir Henry Unton . . . in the Years 1591 and 1592.* Edited by J. Stevenson. London, 1847.

Vere, Francis. *The Commentaries of Sir Francis Vere.* London, 1657.

The Warrender Papers. Edited by A. L. Cameron and R. S. Rait. 2 vols. Edinburgh, 1931–1932.

Williams, Roger. *The Works of Roger Williams.* Edited by J. X. Evans. Oxford, 1972.

Wingfield, Anthony. "A True Discourse (as is Thought) by Colonel Antonie Winkfield Employed in the Voiage to Spain and Portugal, 1589," etc. In Hakluyt, Richard. *The Principal Navigations, Voyages, Traffiques of Discoveries of the English Nation*, etc., 4: 306–354. Edited by Walter Raleigh. 10 vols. London and New York, 1927.

Winstanley, William. *England's Worthies.* London, 1660.

Winwood, Ralph. *Memorials of State in the Reigns of Queen Elizabeth and King James I.* Edited by Edmund Sawyer. 3 vols. London, 1725.

Wright, Edward. "The Voiage of the Right Honorable George Erle of Cumberland to the Azores." In Hakluyt, Richard. *The Principal Navigations, Voyages, Traffiques of Discoveries of the English Nation*, etc., 4: 355–380. Edited by Walter Raleigh. London and New York, 1927.

SECONDARY WORKS

Adams, Simon L. "The Protestant Cause: Religious Alliance with the West European Calvinist Community as a Political Issue in England, 1585–1603." Unpublished D. Phil. dissertation, Oxford, 1973.

Andrews, Kenneth R. *Elizabethan Privateering*. Cambridge, 1964.

————. *English Privateering Voyages to the West Indies*. Hakluyt Soc., 2nd ser. 111 (1959).

————, ed. *The Last Voyage of Drake and Hawkins*. Hakluyt Soc., 2nd ser. 142 (1972).

Bagenal, Philip H. *Vicissitudes of an Anglo-Irish Family, 1530–1800*. London, 1925.

Bagwell, Richard. *Ireland under the Tudors*. 3 vols. London, 1885–1890.

Bertie, Georgina. *Five Generations of a Loyal Family*. London, 1845.

Boynton, Lindsay. *The Elizabethan Militia*. London, 1967.

Bradshaw, Brendan. *The Irish Constitutional Revolution of the Sixteenth Century*. Cambridge and New York, 1979.

Brady, Ciaran. "The Government of Ireland, c. 1540–1583." Unpublished Ph.D. thesis, University of Dublin, 1980.

Canny, N. P. *The Elizabethan Conquest of Ireland, 1565–1576*. Hassocks, England, 1976.

Cheyney, Edward P. *A History of England from the Defeat of the Armada to the Death of Elizabeth*. 2 vols. New York, 1914, 1926.

Coleman, C., et al., eds. *Revolution Reassessed*. Oxford, 1986.

Collinson, Patrick. *The Elizabethan Puritan Movement*. Berkeley and Los Angeles, 1967.

Corbett, Julian S. *Drake and the Tudor Navy*, etc. 2 vols. London, 1898.

Cruickshank, C. G. *Elizabeth's Army*. 2nd ed, Oxford, 1966.

Cunningham, Bernadette. "The Composition of Connacht in the Lordships of Clanricard and Thomond, 1577–1641." *Irish Historical Review* 24 (1984–1985): 1–14.

Dietz, F. C. *English Public Finance, 1558–1641*. New York, 1932.

DuMaurier, Daphne. *Golden Lads: A Story of Anthony Bacon, Francis and Their Friends*. London, 1975.

Edwards, Edward. *The Life of Sir Walter Raleigh*, etc. 2 vols. London, 1868.

Edwards, Ruth Dudley. *An Atlas of Irish History*. 2nd ed. London, 1973.

Egerton, Francis H., Earl of Bridgewater. *The Life of Thomas Egerton*. Paris, ca. 1800.

Eliot, J. H. *Richelieu and Olivarez*. Cambridge, 1984.

Ellis, Steven G. *Tudor Ireland: Crown, Community, and the Conflict of Cultures, 1470–1603*. London and New York, 1985.

Elton, G. R. *Reform and Reformation: England, 1509–1558*. Cambridge, Mass., 1978.

———. *Reform and Renewal*. Cambridge, 1963.

———. *Studies in Tudor and Stuart Politics and Government*. 3 vols., Cambridge, 1938.

———. *The Tudor Revolution in Government*. Cambridge, 1953.

Essen, Leon van der. *Alexandre Farnese*. 5 vols. Brussels, 1937.

Falls, Cyril. *Elizabeth's Irish Wars*. London, 1950.

Gregoire, L. *La ligue en Bretagne*. Paris and Nantes, 1856.

Hall, Hubert. *Society in the Elizabethan Age*. London, 1888.

Hayes-McCoy, Gerard A. "The Army of Ulster, 1593–1601." *The Irish Sword* 1 (1950–1951): 105–127.

———. *Scots Mercenary Forces in Ireland, 1565–1603*. Dublin and London, 1937.

———. "Strategy and Tactics in Irish Warfare, 1593–1601." *Irish Historical Studies* 2 (1940–1941): 261–263.

———. "The Tide of Victory and Defeat: The Battle of Clontibret, 1595." *Studies: An Irish Quarterly Review* 38 (1949): 158–168.

Henry, L. W. "Contemporary Sources for Essex's Lieutenancy in Ireland, 1599." *Irish Historical Studies* 11 (1958–1959): 8–17.

———. "The Earl of Essex in Ireland, 1599." *Bulletin of the Institute of Historical Research* 32 (1959): 1–23.

Hicks, L. "The Embassy of Sir Anthony Standen in 1603." *Recusant History* 5 (1959–1960): 91–127, 184–232; 6 (1961–1962), 163–194; 7 (1963–1964), 50–81.

James, Mervyn. "At a Crossroad of the Political Culture: The Essex Revolt, 1601." In his *Society, Politics and Culture*. Cambridge, 1986.

Jones, Frank F. *The Life of Martin Frobisher*, etc. London, 1878.

Lee, Maurice. *John Maitland of Thirlestane and the Foundation of the Stuart Despotism in Scotland*. Princeton, 1959.

Lloyd, Howell A. "The Essex Inheritance." *Welsh History Review* 7 (1974): 13–38.

Lloyd, Howell A. *The Rouen Campaign, 1590–1592: Politics, Warfare and the Early-Modern State.* Oxford, 1973.

Loomie, Albert J. *The Spanish Elizabethans: The English Exiles at the Court of Philip II.* New York, 1963.

MacCaffrey, W. T. *Queen Elizabeth and the Making of Policy, 1572–1588.* Princeton, 1981.

MacCarthy-Morrogh, Michael. *The Munster Plantation: English Migration to Southern Ireland, 1583–1641.* Oxford, 1986.

McCoy, Richard. *The Rites of Knighthood.* Berkeley and Los Angeles, 1989.

Macduinnshleibhe, Peadar. "The Legal Murder of Aodh Ruadh McMahon, 1590." *Clogher Record* (1955): 39–52.

McGurk, John. "The Recruitment and Transportation of Elizabethan Troops and Their Service in Ireland, 1594–1603." Unpublished Ph.D. dissertation, University of Liverpool, 1983.

Markham, Clements R. *"The Fighting Veres." Lives of Sir Francis Vere,* etc. Boston and New York, 1888.

Moody, T. W., et al. *A New History of Ireland,* Vol. 3. Oxford, 1976.

Morgan, Hiram. "The End of Gaelic Ulster: A Thematic Interpretation of Events between 1534 and 1610." *Irish Historical Studies* 26, no. 101 (May 1988): 8–32.

———. "The Outbreak of the Nine Years' War: Ulster in Irish Politics, 1583–1596." Unpublished Ph.D. thesis, Cambridge University, 1987.

Neale, J. E. *Elizabeth I and Her Parliaments, 1584–1601.* London, 1957.

Nicholas, N. H. *Life of William Davison.* London, 1823.

O'Mearain, L. "The English Army of Clontibret." *Irish Sword* 2 (1954–1956): 368–371.

Oppenheim, Michael. *History of the Administration of the Royal Navy.* London, 1896.

Outhwaite, R. B. "Studies in Elizabethan Government and Finance: Royal Borrowing and the Sale of Crown Lands, 1572–1603." Unpublished Ph.D. dissertation, University of Nottingham, 1964.

———. "The Trials of Foreign Borrowing: The English Crown and the Antwerp Money Market in the Mid-Sixteenth Century." *Economic History Review,* 2nd ser. 19 (1966): 288–305.

Owen, L. "The Population of Wales in the Sixteenth and Seventeenth Centuries." *Transactions of the Honourable Society of Cymmrodorion* (London) (1959): 99–113.

Parker, Geoffrey. *The Dutch Revolt*. London, 1977.

Pulman, Michael B. *The Elizabethan Privy Council in the Fifteen-Seventies*. Berkeley and Los Angeles, 1971.

Quinn, David. *The Elizabethans and the Irish*. Ithaca, N.Y., 1966.

Rabb, Theodore K. *Enterprise and Empire*. Cambridge, Mass., 1967.

Rawson, M. S. *Penelope Rich*. London, 1911.

Read, Conyers. *Lord Burghley and Queen Elizabeth*. London, 1960.

———. *Mr. Secretary Walsingham and the Policy of Queen Elizabeth*. 3 vols. Cambridge, Mass., and Oxford, 1925.

Schofield, R. "Taxation and the Political Limits of the Tudor State." In *Law and Government under the Tudors*, 227–55. Edited by C. Cross et al. Cambridge, 1988.

Scott, William R. *The Constitution and Finance of English, Scottish, and Irish Joint Stock Companies to 1720*. 3 vols. London, 1912.

Sheehan, A. J. "The Population of the Plantation of Munster: Quinn Reconsidered." *Journal of the Cork Historical and Archaeological Society*, 2nd ser. 87 (1982): 107–117.

Silke, John J. "The Irish Appeal of 1593 to Spain." *Irish Ecclesiastical Record*, 5th ser. 92 (1959): 279–290, 362–371.

———. *Kinsale*. Liverpool, 1970.

Smith, A. Hassell. *County and Court: Government and Politics in Norfolk, 1558–1603*. Oxford, 1974.

Smith, Lacey Baldwin. *Treason in Tudor England*. London, 1986.

Stafford, H. G. *James VI of Scotland and the Throne of England*. New York, 1940.

Stone, Lawrence. *An Elizabethan: Sir Horatio Palavicino*. London, 1956.

Strong, Roy. *Gloriana: The Portraits of Queen Elizabeth I*. London, 1987.

Tex, Jan den. *Oldenbarnevelt*. Translation by R. B. Powell. 2 vols. Cambridge, 1973. [Original edition in Dutch. 5 vols. Haarlem, 1960–1972.]

Thomson, G. Scott. *Lord Lieutenants in the Sixteenth Century*. London, 1923.

Ungerer, Gustav. *A Spaniard in Elizabethan England: The Correspondence of Antonio Perez's Exile*. 2 vols. London, 1974–1976.

Usherwood, Stephen and Elizabeth. *The Counter-Armada, 1596: The Journall of the "Mary Rose."* London, 1983.

Wernham, R. B. *After the Armada: Elizabethan England and the Struggle for Western Europe, 1588–1595.* Oxford, 1984.

――――. "Elizabethan War Aims and Strategy," In *Elizabethan Government and Society*, 340–368. Edited by S. T. Bindoff et al. London, 1961.

――――. "Queen Elizabeth I, the Emperor Rudolph, and Archduke Ernest, 1593–1594." In *Politics and Society in Reformation Europe*, 437–429. Edited by E. I. Kouri and Tom Scott. London, 1987.

Williams, Penry H. *The Tudor Regime.* Oxford, 1979.

Williamson, G. C. *The Third Earl of Cumberland.* London, 1920.

Williamson, James A. *Sir John Hawkins, the Man and His Times.* London, 1969.

Wright, Thomas. *Queen Elizabeth and Her Times.* 2 vols. London, 1838.

Wrigley, E. A., and R. S. Schofield. *The Population History of England, 1541–1871: A Reconstruction.* Cambridge, Mass., 1981.

INDEX

Printed in the United States
44155LVS00007B/100

9 780691 036519